CORRECTIONS IN THE 21ST CENTURY

Corrections: From Research, to Policy, to Practice is written by two authors with field experience in corrections as well as over 50 years of combined teaching experience.

Mary K. Stohr worked as a correctional officer and then as a counselor in an adult male prison in Washington State, and Anthony Walsh has experience in both law enforcement and corrections as a police officer, probation officer, and correctional officer at a juvenile detention center.

UNIQUE COVERAGE OF IMPORTANT TOPICS

- **Chapter 4: Ethics and Corrections:** A dedicated chapter on ethics prepares students to see the world of corrections through an ethical lens.

- **Chapter 7: Special Problem-Solving Courts in Corrections:** Includes coverage of ground-breaking approaches to sentencing through drug, mental health, veterans, and domestic violence courts and the community court process.

- **Chapter 10: Classification and Assessment of Offenders:** Important coverage of classification and needs assessment lays the foundation for understanding rehabilitation and helps students comprehend why it is imperative to our correctional systems.

- **Chapter 20: Comparative Corrections:** Provides a look into how corrections is approached in the United Kingdom, France, China, and Saudi Arabia to broaden students' understanding of correctional frameworks.

A NOVICE BOWS TO SUBCULTURAL PRESSURE
Mary K. Stohr

When I first started as a correctional officer at an adult male prison in Washington State, I was the second woman hired (and the first was hired a month before me). I was relatively well educated (two bachelor's degrees) and had worked at all kinds of jobs since age 10 but never in corrections. I was young (25), scared, and naïve. My first reports were rejected by my sergeant as too wordy, and I was thought to be too soft on the inmates. (I called the inmates Mr. this and Mr. that and treated them with courtesy.) After about four weeks on the job and in an effort to help me, a well-meaning sergeant took me aside and said, "Stohr, I'm worried about you. I'm not sure you can do this job. You've got to learn to write better [meaning less and in a more spare fashion—he might as well have said, 'Just the facts, ma'am'], and you've got to treat the inmates with less respect, or you aren't going to make it on this job."

We were in a back area of the control room, and he pointed to an inmate at the control room window—we'll call him Mr. Smith. He said, "That man Smith, he's a dirty baby raper [which I took to mean that Smith was a child molester]. He's been hanging around the window when you're here because you are too nice to him. You've got to treat him differently, or he'll take advantage of you." Essentially, he said you don't have to be mean (he wasn't that kind of man), but you shouldn't be friendly either.

Well, I took this sergeant's advice to heart, as I knew he was trying to help me, and there were a few of the staff at the prison who wanted to see me and the

SAGE PREMIUM VIDEO: BOOST COMPREHENSION. BOLSTER ANALYSIS.

SAGE premium video helps your students do both.

Corrections: From Research, to Policy, to Practice offers premium video, curated specifically for the text, to make learning more effective for all types of students. Accessed through an Interactive eBook, students go beyond highlighting and note-taking. Videos include:

- Premium video with assessment questions

- Videos of interviews with exonerated individuals from the Witness to Innocence national organization

- Interviews with correctional practitioners

- Former inmates talking about life on the inside

FROM RESEARCH TO POLICY

A FOCUS ON WHAT WORKS IN CORRECTIONS

POLICY & RESEARCH boxes cover how research has informed current practices and can improve future policies and procedures in correctional institutions.

IN FOCUS features offer students a deeper look at intriguing, real-world issues relating to chapter concepts and provide guiding questions for consideration and discussion.

ETHICAL ISSUE boxes ask students what they would do in a situation that presents common ethical dilemmas relating to corrections.

POLICY & RESEARCH — Mentally Ill Inmate Dies at Rikers

In a series of articles appearing in the *New York Times*, reporter Michael Schwirtz (2014a; 2014b) documents the abuse and neglect suffered by mentally ill inmates incarcerated in the Rikers Island jails. Rikers Island jails are a complex of 10 jails on an island in the East River of New York City. Twenty officers from Rikers have been prosecuted for assaults on inmates in the last five years. In mid-March 2014, a mentally ill inmate died from being left in an overheated cell at Rikers. But the particular subject of these articles is a 25-year-old inmate named Jason Echevarria, who was diagnosed with bipolar disorder. He was placed in a special mental-health unit at Rikers because of his diagnosed mental illness and because he had behavioral problems when in the general population of the jail. He had a record of attempted suicides while incarcerated at Rikers (Schwirtz, 2014a; 2014b).

Because there were problems with raw sewage coming out of toilets, on August 18, 2012, inmates were given a packet of powdered detergent that they were to use to clean up their cells (Schwirtz, 2014a, 2014b). By policy, inmates were supposed to be given detergent that was diluted by several gallons of water, but an inexperienced officer instead gave the full packets to inmates. Echevarria swallowed the toxic detergent, and as a result, his tongue and mouth skin were severely damaged as he vomited; he experienced extreme pain and expelled blood from his mouth over the course of sev... claimed that ...cries for help ...o his captain, ...not to talk to ...inmate was ...correctional ...o the captain ...distress and ...tance at least

once but was prevented from doing so by the captain. Both the captain and the officer came off their shifts without getting any medical assistance for the inmate. Mr. Echevarria was dead the next morning. The captain was demoted to an officer position, was arrested by the FBI, and is being prosecuted for violating the civil rights of Mr. Echevarria. The officer was fired and has filed a wrongful-termination suit, disputing the captain's claim that he was never told about Mr. Echevarria's health crisis.

DISCUSSION QUESTIONS

1. Why aren't correctional facilities well suited to handle the mentally ill?

2. Instead of incarcerating the mentally ill, what should public policy be instead?

United States Geological Survey

PHOTO 4.2: An aerial view of the Rikers Island jail complex.

IN FOCUS 5.2

Extension of the Due Process Model to Sentencing

A number of ethical and legal issues associated with plea bargaining led the U.S. Supreme Court to rule that defendants have the right to effective legal counsel during plea negotiations (*Lafler v. Cooper*, 2012). In this case, Anthony Cooper was charged with attempted murder for shooting a woman several times in the buttocks and thighs. Cooper turned down an offer to plead guilty in exchange for a sentence of 5 to 7 years in prison. Cooper's lawyer advised him against taking the plea, maintaining that he would not be convicted of attempted murder at trial because he did not shoot the woman above the waist. On his attorney's advice, Cooper went to trial and was convicted and sentenced to between 15 and 30 years in prison. The Supreme Court agreed with the argument that Cooper had been denied the right to a competent attorney and remanded the case back to court for resentencing.

In his dissent from the Court's 5–4 *Lafler* decision, Justice Scalia gave an excellent, succinct explanation of some of the problems associated with plea bargaining and why it is regarded as a "necessary evil."

In the United States, we have plea bargaining a-plenty, but until today it has been regarded as a necessary evil. It presents great risks of prosecutorial overcharging that effectively compels an innocent defendant to avoid massive risk by pleading guilty to a lesser offense; and for guilty defendants it often—perhaps usually—results in a sentence well below what the law prescribes for the actual crime. But even so, we accept plea bargaining because many believe that without it our long and expensive process of criminal trial could not sustain the burden imposed on it, and our system of criminal justice would grind to a halt. (p. 12)

DISCUSSION QUESTIONS

1. Why is plea bargaining regarded as a necessary evil?

2. What are some of the problems with plea bargaining?

ETHICAL ISSUE 4.2 ?

What Would You Do?

You are a probation officer with a large caseload of low-level drug offenders (mostly pot smokers). Some may be addicted to marijuana, and others may not, but you need to monitor them and ensure that they attend programming and provide clean urinalysis (UA) samples. The department of corrections you work for is in transition, however, moving from a more law enforcement focus to a greater treatment orientation. They have given you and other officers more leeway in decisions about whether to violate (write up) offenders who commit minor offenses. One of the UAs you take comes up dirty for marijuana, and you are faced with "violating" a client on your caseload who was convicted of felony drug possession. (There was enough to sell.) In all other ways, this client has done well, in that she has made all the meetings, been employed, and attended drug programming. Would you write a violation on this offender? (Doing so may result in jail time or a trip to prison.) Would it make any difference in your decision making if your client has two dependent children who will be placed in foster care should she be incarcerated? Why, or why not? Which ethical framework do you think best fits the decision you made?

TO PRACTICE

EQUIP STUDENTS WITH THE TOOLS THEY NEED TO UNDERSTAND AND IMPROVE THE SYSTEM

A final chapter on **CORRECTIONS IN THE 21st CENTURY** discusses the move from a penal harm to a penal help perspective to help students explore the paradigmatic shift and how it will affect their future work in the correctional system.

VINDICTIVE VERSUS **SENSIBLE SENTENCING**

"Jane" is a 30-year-old mother of three children, ages 8, 6, and 4. Her husband recently suffered a heart attack and died, leaving Jane with no money. Jane has only a 10th-grade education and cannot afford childcare costs, so she was forced onto the welfare rolls. When Christmas came around, she had no money to buy her children any presents, so she took a temporary Christmas job at the local megastore, where she earned $1,200 over a 2-month period. Jane did not report this income to the welfare authorities, as required by law, and a welfare audit uncovered her crime. The terrified

and deeply ashamed Jane pled guilty to grand theft, which carries a possible sentence of 2 years in prison, and was referred to the probation department for a presentence investigation report (PSI).

"Jim" is a 32-year-old male with a lengthy record of thefts and other crimes committed since he was 10 years old. Jim also pled guilty before the same judge on the same day and was likewise referred for a PSI. Jim had stolen money and parts totaling $1,200 from an auto parts store during one of his brief periods of employment.

CHAPTER OPENING VIGNETTES provide perspectives from correctional practitioners, inmates, and other individuals that show how research, policy, and practice play out in the real world.

PERSPECTIVES FROM A PRACTITIONER boxes profile a real correctional practitioner and address questions such as, What are the primary responsibilities in this job? Which qualities or characteristics are most helpful for this career? and What does a typical day look like?

PERSPECTIVE FROM A **PRACTITIONER**

Skyler Brouwer, Juvenile Probation Officer

Position: Juvenile probation officer

Location: Omaha, Nebraska

Education: Degree in criminal justice from the University of Nebraska at Omaha

How long have you been in your current position, and what, if any, previous criminal justice experience do you have?

Three years.

What are your primary duties and responsibilities?

My responsibilities are to effectuate positive behavior change in an effort to reduce the likelihood of offenders recidivating; to confirm that offenders are in compliance with their court orders through face-to-face contact and from collateral information from treatment and mental-health providers, drug testing, and school information; to assist offenders and their families with finding resources in the community that they can benefit from while on probation and to motivate the offenders to lead law-abiding and successful lives by building and maintaining positive rapport with the offenders, their family members, and the community support systems; and to update the court on progress or lack of progress through court reports, memos, emails, petitions, and face-to-face contact.

What are the characteristics and traits most useful in your line of work?

- Honesty
- Confidence
- Being able to think outside the box
- Empathetic
- Innovative
- Excellent writing and communication skills
- Consistent
- Motivating
- Fair
- Resilience

Please describe a typical workday.

A typical day includes conducting office and field visits with offenders, treatment providers, school administrators, counselors, and teachers to monitor compliance or noncompliance with court orders. Writing predispositional (presentence) and other reports occupies a considerable portion of a juvenile probation officer's time. Our department uses assessment instruments such as the Youth Level of Service/Case Management Inventory and the Adolescent Chemical Dependency Inventory. These instruments assist the probation officer with assessing the offenders' major needs, strengths, and barriers. The assessment breaks down into the following categories: prior and current offenses, education, substance abuse, family, personality/behavior, leisure and recreation, and attitudes/orientation. The Adolescent Chemical Dependency Inventory is an assessment that is a self-report test. This assessment obtains a lot of information in a short amount of time. The assessment screens the following: substance abuse and use, overall adjustment, and troubled-youth concerns. Other duties include attending court hearings; communicating with formal and informal supports of the offender through voice mails, phone calls, e-mails, and memos; and ensuring the safety of the community and of the offenders through the officer's efforts to assist them in their rehabilitation.

What is your advice to someone who wants to enter your field?

Be able to use your passion to think outside the box and assist people in becoming role models in their communities.

SAGE was founded in 1965 by Sara Miller McCune to support the dissemination of usable knowledge by publishing innovative and high-quality research and teaching content. Today, we publish over 900 journals, including those of more than 400 learned societies, more than 800 new books per year, and a growing range of library products including archives, data, case studies, reports, and video. SAGE remains majority-owned by our founder, and after Sara's lifetime will become owned by a charitable trust that secures our continued independence.

Los Angeles | London | New Delhi | Singapore | Washington DC | Melbourne

CORRECTIONS

CORRECTIONS

From Research, to Policy, to Practice

Mary K. Stohr
Washington State University

Anthony Walsh
Boise State University

Los Angeles | London | New Delhi
Singapore | Washington DC | Melbourne

$SAGE

FOR INFORMATION:

SAGE Publications, Inc.
2455 Teller Road
Thousand Oaks, California 91320
E-mail: order@sagepub.com

SAGE Publications Ltd.
1 Oliver's Yard
55 City Road
London EC1Y 1SP
United Kingdom

SAGE Publications India Pvt. Ltd.
B 1/I 1 Mohan Cooperative Industrial Area
Mathura Road, New Delhi 110 044
India

SAGE Publications Asia-Pacific Pte. Ltd.
3 Church Street
#10-04 Samsung Hub
Singapore 049483

Printed in Canada

ISBN 978-1-4833-7337-9

Acquisitions Editor: Jessica Miller
eLearning Editor: Laura Kirkhuff
Editorial Assistant: Jennifer Rubio
Production Editor: Jane Haenel
Copy Editor: Jared Leighton
Typesetter: C&M Digitals (P) Ltd.
Proofreader: Jeff Bryant
Indexer: Karen Wiley
Cover and Interior Designer: Scott Van Atta
Marketing Manager: Amy Lammers

This book is printed on acid-free paper.

17 18 19 20 21 10 9 8 7 6 5 4 3 2 1

BRIEF CONTENTS

DETAILED CONTENTS

© istockphoto.com/stocknroll

PART I: FOUNDATIONS OF CORRECTIONS

© istockphoto.com/Tomasz Wyszolmirskir

PART II: THE CORRECTIONAL SYSTEM

© AP Photo/Nati Harnik

PART III: CORRECTIONAL ADMINISTRATION

AP Photo/Eric Gay

PART IV: CORRECTIONAL CLIENTS

Part V: Special Topics in Corrections

PREFACE

Much has changed about corrections since Tony and I began our careers as practitioners and then academics many years ago. We witnessed the shift from the bare-bones harsh warehousing of inmates to the full flowering of treatment- and rehabilitative-focused environments for correctional clients. This is not to say that all correctional facilities and community corrections departments were simply warehouses or intentionally cruel to their inhabitants in the 1980s and early 1990s or that they have been solely focused on beneficial programming since then. (The first priority for correctional institutions and community supervision remains security and safety, and deterrence and retribution have not gone out of fashion.) But official missions have changed, staff have been retrained, and money has shifted to more programming, particularly when it is evidence based and results in a change in practices, and as a consequence, corrections today is different, and that is, for the most part, a good thing, in our estimation.

This book is focused on corrections as it is in the 21st century and the treatment and rehabilitative themes that drive it, rather than the warehousing and penal-harm sentiments of the 1980s and 1990s. We present the material in a lively and student friendly format and cover the typical topics in corrections and the research on corrections, but we also include five chapters on subjects not always (or never) covered in corrections texts: a chapter on "Special Problem-Solving Courts in Corrections," a chapter on "Correctional Programming and Treatment," a chapter on "Correctional Organizations and Their Management," a chapter on "The Death Penalty," and a chapter on "Comparative Corrections." The inclusion of these chapters makes this book both comparable to and distinct from other corrections textbooks. The organization and management and death penalty chapters are somewhat common to larger corrections textbooks, and that is one of the reasons why our book is similar to others. The inclusion of programming and treatment, special problem-solving courts, and comparative corrections, however, all reflect the changing policies and practices occurring in this newly made, evidence-focused world of corrections. These chapters provide a forum for the discussion of the freshest ideas emanating from and in use in the field. Finally, in the concluding chapter, we contextualize our age of corrections as one which is moving from a penal-harm to a penal-help perspective and explore how this paradigmatic shift will affect correctional organizations, their clients, and their workers well into the future (Stohr, Jonson, & Cullen, 2014).

STRUCTURE OF THE BOOK

The structure of the book is much like that found in other textbooks on corrections, with the notable additions just mentioned. We begin with an overview of corrections and some key concepts. We include two chapters on history, though many textbooks have only one. We include a chapter on ethics in corrections, as the fourth chapter, as it prepares students to review operations and institutional and individual actions through that kind of lens. We then follow the flow of the corrections system in the next eight chapters, ranging from sentencing to parole and prisoner reentry. The organization and management of correctional institutions and how staff experience the correctional world are the focus of the next two chapters. In the three chapters that follow, we address the reality for women, minorities, and juveniles in corrections. We then focus attention on legal issues, capital punishment, and comparative corrections. We end with a look to the future of corrections and what developments we might expect in the coming years, including a discussion of privatization in corrections, green prisons and jails, and the shift from penal harm to penal help in corrections.

DIGITAL RESOURCES

edge.sagepub.com/stohrcorrections

SAGE edge offers a robust online environment featuring an impressive array of tools and resources for review, study, and further exploration, keeping both instructors and students on the cutting edge of teaching and learning. SAGE edge content is open access and available on demand. Learning and teaching has never been easier!

SAGE edge for students provides a personalized approach to help students accomplish their coursework goals in an easy-to-use learning environment.

- Mobile-friendly eFlashcards strengthen understanding of key terms and concepts.

- Mobile-friendly practice quizzes allow for independent assessment by students of their mastery of course material.

- A customized online action plan includes tips and feedback on progress through the course and materials, which allows students to individualize their learning experience.

- Learning objectives reinforce the most important material.

- Video and multimedia links which appeal to students with different leaning styles.

- EXCLUSIVE! Access to full-text SAGE journal articles that have been carefully selected to support and expand on the concepts presented in each chapter.

SAGE edge for instructors supports teaching by making it easy to integrate quality content and create a rich learning environment for students.

- Test banks provide a diverse range of pre-written options as well as the opportunity to edit any question and/or insert personalized questions to effectively assess students' progress and understanding.

- Editable, chapter-specific PowerPoint® slides offer complete flexibility for creating a multimedia presentation for the course.

- EXCLUSIVE! Access to full-text SAGE journal articles that have been carefully selected to support and expand on the concepts presented in

each chapter to encourage students to think critically.

- Video and multimedia links include original SAGE videos and Researcher Interview videos.

- Lecture notes summarize key concepts by chapter to ease preparation for lectures and class discussions.

- Chapter-specific discussion questions to help launch classroom interaction by prompting students to engage with the material and by reinforcing important content.

ACKNOWLEDGMENTS

We would like to thank executive editor Jerry Westby. Jerry's faith, hard work, and incredible patience made this book both possible and fun to write. We also would like to thank our development editor, Jessica Miller, who helped shepherd the book through the writing process and whose gentle prodding ensured the deadlines would be met. With Jerry's retirement toward the end of this process, Jessica assumed responsibility and carried us through to the finish line. Our copy editor, Jared Leighton, ensured that the sentences were clean, the spelling correct, and every missing reference was found.

We would also like to acknowledge each other. We were colleagues at Boise State University for many years, the last several (before Mary moved to Missouri State in 2011 and then Washington State in 2013) with offices right next door to each other. We have come to appreciate the work and perspectives of the other. This work was a true collaboration between us and reflects our shared belief in the possibilities for decency and justice as that is elaborated on by social institutions and their workers and by individuals willing to change.

We are also grateful to the reviewers who took the time to review early drafts of our work and who provided us with helpful suggestions for improving the chapters and the book as a whole. There is no doubt that their comments made the book much better than it would have otherwise been. Heartfelt thanks to the following experts consulted on this text:

Francisco J. Alatorre, *New Mexico State University*

Jack Atherton, *Northwestern State University*

Amanda K. Cox, *The Pennsylvania State University*

Martha Earwood, *University of Alabama at Birmingham*

Allison J. Foley, *Augusta University*

Natalie W. Goulette, *University of West Florida*

Elizabeth Hagensen, *Bemidji State University*

Lashunda M. Horton, *Virginia State University*

Nerissa James, *Miami Dade College*

Korni Swaroop Kumar, *The College at Brockport*

Etta F. Morgan, *Jackson State University*

Breanne Pleggenkuhle, *Southern Illinois University Carbondale*

Erica M. Ross, *Cleveland Community College*

John Sieminski, *Manchester Community College*

Lenard Wells, *The University of Memphis*

Lorri Williamson, *University of Mississippi*

1

The Philosophical and Ideological Underpinnings of Corrections

TEST YOUR KNOWLEDGE

Test your present knowledge of corrections by answering the following questions as true or false. Check your answers on page 533 after reading the chapter.

1. Whatever we choose to call it, corrections is about punishment, and punishment requires philosophical justification.

2. The strongest deterrent against crime is the severity of punishment.

3. The fundamental principle of American justice is that the punishment should fit the crime; all other factors are irrelevant.

4. As bad as it may sound, people feel pleasure when wrongdoers are punished.

5. The law assumes that people are rational and possess freedom of choice.

6. Philosophies of punishment depend quite a bit on concepts of human nature. (Are we naturally good, bad, or just selfish?)

7. Studies find that when criminals are severely punished, they tend to be deterred from crime.

8. The U.S. criminal justice system operates primarily with a model that believes it more necessary to control crime than to preserve due process rights.

LEARNING OBJECTIVES

- Describe the function of corrections and its philosophical underpinnings

- Differentiate between the classical and positivist schools in terms of their respective stances on punishment

- Explain the function and justification of punishment

- Define and describe the major punishment justifications

- Explain the distinction between the crime control and due process models

WHAT IS **PUNISHMENT?**

Nathaniel Hawthorne's book The Scarlet Letter, first published in 1850 and read in high school by generations of Americans thereafter, opened with the words: "The founders of a new colony, whatever Utopia of human virtue and happiness they might originally project, have invariably recognized it among their earliest practical necessities to allot a portion of the virgin soil as a cemetery, and another portion as the site of a prison" (1850/2003, p. 1). Hawthorne is reminding us of two things we cannot avoid—death and human moral fallibility—and that we must make provisions for both. Of course, punishment is not all about prisons since other forms are available. In Hawthorne's novel, Hester Prynne had been found guilty of adultery and of bearing a child out of wedlock. While all too common today, in the 17th-century Massachusetts Bay Colony, it was a major crime against "God and man." The colony was a very close-knit and homogeneous community, meaning that there was strong and widespread agreement about the norms of acceptable behavior. Hester's behavior was viewed as so outrageous that among the various penalties discussed by women viewing her trial were branding with hot irons and death "for the shame she has brought on us all." However, she was sentenced to what we might call community corrections today. She was to forever endure the scorn of her community and to forever wear the badge of shame on her dress—an elaborately embroidered letter A, branding her as an adulteress.

Such a reaction to Hester's behavior was aimed just as much at onlookers as on Hester herself—"This could happen to me too!" That is, the authorities not only wished to deter Hester from such behavior in the future but also to dissuade all others from similar behavior. Few people give much serious thought to why we need correctional systems, what state punishment is, why we do it, and why the urge to punish wrongdoers is universal and strong. How did such an urge get into us? What are the origins of punishment? What would society be like without it? How do we justify imposing harm on others, and what do our justifications assume about human nature? These are the issues we explore in this chapter.

••• INTRODUCTION: WHAT IS CORRECTIONS?

As Hawthorne intimates in the opening vignette, the primary responsibility of any government is to protect its citizens from those who would harm them. The military protects us from foreign threats, and the criminal justice system protects us from domestic threats posed by criminals. The criminal justice system is divided into three major subsystems: the police, the courts, and corrections—which we may call the catch 'em, convict 'em, and correct 'em trinity. Corrections is thus a system embedded in a broader collection of protection agencies, one that comes into play after the accused has been caught by law enforcement and prosecuted and convicted by the courts.

Corrections is a generic term covering a variety of functions carried out by government (and increasingly private) agencies having to do with the punishment, treatment, supervision, and management of individuals who have been convicted or accused of criminal offenses. These functions are implemented in prisons, jails, and other secure institutions, as well as in community-based correctional agencies, such as probation and parole departments. Corrections is also the name we give to the field of academic study of the theories, missions, policies, systems, programs, and personnel that implement those functions, as well as the behaviors and experiences of offenders. As the term implies, the correctional enterprise exists to "correct," "amend," or "put right" the attitudes and behavior of its "clientele." This is a difficult task because many offenders have a psychological, emotional, or financial investment in their current lifestyles and have no intention of being "corrected" (Andrews & Bonta, 2007; Walsh & Stohr, 2010).

Cynics believe the correctional process should be called the "punishment process" (Logan & Gaes, 1993) because the correctional enterprise is primarily about punishment—which, as Hawthorne reminds us, is an unfortunate but necessary part of life. Earlier scholars called corrections what we now call **penology**, which means the study of the processes adopted for the punishment and prevention of crime. No matter what we call our prisons, jails, and other systems of formal social control, we are compelling people to do what they do not want to do, and such arm-twisting is experienced by them as punitive regardless of what name we use.

When the grandparents of today's college students were in their youth, few thought of corrections as an issue of much importance. They certainly knew about prisons and jails, but few had any inkling of what probation or parole was. This blissful ignorance was a function of many things. The crime rate was much lower in the 1950s and early 1960s; thus, the correctional budget was a minor burden on their taxes, and fewer people probably knew anyone who had been in "the joint." Today, the story is much different. The violent crime rate in 1963, for instance, was 168 per 100,000, and in 2012, it was 387, an increase of over 130% (Federal Bureau of Investigation [FBI], 2013a). In 1963, there were just under 300,000 people in prison in the United States; in 2012, there were just under 1,700,000, an increase of 466% (Sentencing Project, 2013). Much of this increase has been driven by the War on Drugs. Because illicit drug use was extremely rare prior to the late 1960s, there was no War on Drugs. Indeed, the only drugs familiar to folks in

Corrections: Functions carried out by government and private agencies having to do with the punishment, treatment, supervision, and management of individuals who have been accused and convicted of criminal offenses.

Penology: The study of the processes and institutions involved in the punishment and prevention of crime.

their prime during the 1950s and 1960s were those obtained at the drug store by prescription.

Because of the increase in crime and imprisonment, most people in the United States probably know someone who is or has been in prison or in jail. In 2012, about 1 in every 35 adults in the United States was incarcerated or on probation or parole, and many more have been in the past (Glaze & Herberman, 2013). In some neighborhoods, it is not uncommon for almost everyone to know many people under correctional supervision. For instance, almost one in three African American males in their 20s

PHOTO 1.1: Prison cells.

are under some form of correctional control, and one in six has been to prison (Western, 2006). The expenditures for corrections in 2011 for all 50 states was approximately $52 billion, with 88% going for prisons and 12% for probation and parole (Laudano, 2013).

FROM ARREST TO PUNISHMENT

Not everyone who commits a crime is punished. Many crimes are not reported, and even if they are, relatively few are solved. Figure 1.1 is based on data from the nation's 75 largest counties and indicates the typical outcomes of 100 felony arrestees (Cohen & Kyckelhahn, 2010). Only about two thirds of arrestees are prosecuted (sometimes because of lack of evidence). Of those prosecuted, some are found not guilty, and some

FIGURE 1.1   Typical Outcome of 100 Felony Defendants in the 75 Largest Counties in the United States

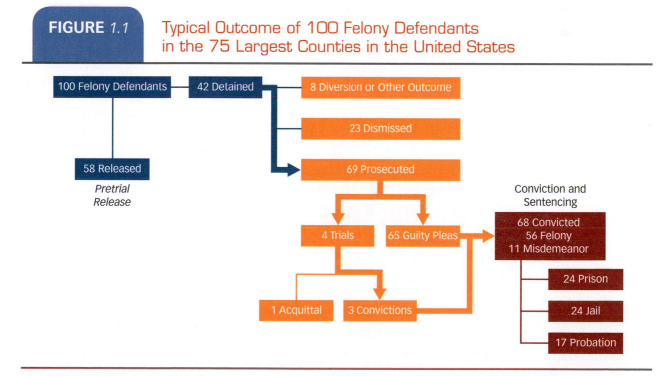

Source: Cohen and Kyckelhahn (2010).

are convicted of lesser (misdemeanor) offenses due to plea bargaining. This trip through the crime funnel typically results in less than 50% of arrests resulting in a jail or prison term. The impact of the War on Drugs is evident in that just over 37% of these arrests were for drug-related crimes (Cohen & Kyckelhahn, 2010). Note that only 4 out of the 69 arrests resulted in an actual trial, meaning that 94% of all felony prosecutions in the nation's 75 most populous counties resulted in a plea bargain in which a lighter sentence is imposed in exchange for a guilty plea.

THE THEORETICAL UNDERPINNINGS OF CORRECTIONS

Just as all theories of crime contain a view of human nature, so do all models of corrections. Some thinkers (mostly influenced by sociology) assume that the human mind is basically a "blank slate" at birth and subsequently formed by cultural experiences. These individuals tend to see human nature as essentially good and believe that people learn to be antisocial. If people are essentially good, then the blame for criminal behavior must be located in the bad influences surrounding them.

Others (mostly influenced by evolutionary biology and the brain sciences) argue that there is an innate human nature that evolved, driven by the overwhelming concerns of all living things: to survive and reproduce. These theorists do not deny that specific behaviors are learned, but they maintain that certain traits evolved in response to survival and reproductive challenges faced by our ancestors that bias our learning in certain directions. Some of these traits, such as aggressiveness and low empathy, are useful in pursuing criminal goals (Quinsey, 2002; Walsh, 2006). This viewpoint also sees human nature as essentially selfish (not "bad," just self-centered) and maintains that people must learn to be prosocial rather than antisocial via a socialization process that teaches us to value and respect the rights and property of others and to develop an orientation toward wanting to do good. Gwynn Nettler (1984) said it most colorfully on behalf of this position: "If we grow up 'naturally,' without cultivation, like weeds, we grow up like weeds—rank" (p. 313). In other words, we learn to be good, not to be bad; we will default to behaving badly in the absence of prosocial socialization (cultivation). The point we are making is that the assumptions about human nature we hold influence our ideas about how we should treat the accused or convicted once they enter the correctional system.

Before we get into the history of punishment, we want to present the first of many Perspective From a Practitioner sections. These sections are provided in each chapter for you to get a better sense of what the chapter is saying from the perspective of someone working in the field and perhaps also to provide the spark to make you want to go into that field. Our first perspective is from a long-serving prison warder, college professor, and prison consultant—who better to start our journey into the fascinating world of corrections?

●●● THE FOUNDATION OF CORRECTIONAL PUNISHMENT

Punishment: The act of imposing some unwanted burden, such as a fine, probation, imprisonment, or death, on convicted persons in response to their crimes.

Legal **punishment** may be defined as the state-authorized imposition of some form of deprivation—of liberty, resources, or life—upon a person justly convicted of a violation of the criminal law. The earliest existing written code of punishment was the Code of Ur-Nammu from Mesopotamia, although the Babylonian (also in Mesopotamia) Code of Hammurabi, created about 1780 B.C., is more complete and better known. These laws recognized the natural inclination of individuals harmed by another to seek revenge, but they also acknowledged that personal revenge must be restrained if society is not to be fractured by a cycle of tit-for-tat blood feuds. The law seeks to contain uncontrolled vengeance by substituting controlled vengeance in the form of third-party (state) punishment.

PERSPECTIVE FROM A PRACTITIONER

Robert Bayer, Prison Warden

Position: Former director of corrections and prison warden; currently an adjunct professor and prison consultant

Location: Reno, Nevada

Education: BA and MA, English literature, State University of New York at Oswego; Master of Public Administration and PhD, English and public administration, University of Nevada, Reno

What are the primary duties and responsibilities of a prison warden?

First, the warden is responsible for one facility in a much larger network of facilities. To some degree, a warden can be considered the mayor of a city and the director/commissioner is the governor of the state in which the city resides, ensuring that facility policies, procedures, and general orders are fine-tuned for that specific facility within the guidelines of the department. Additionally, the warden is usually responsible for the human resources, safety and security operations, budget development and implementation, and the institution's physical plant. He or she must manage critical incidents that arise and has the overall responsibility to ensure a positive work and living culture exists within that facility. To accomplish all of these tasks, the warden typically will bring extensive experience to the job. A warden is one of the highest-level management positions in a prison system and represents the "boots on the ground" administrator for the entire system.

What are the most helpful qualities or characteristics for one in this career?

The ability to be both an administrator and a leader, with a very thorough knowledge of how a prison functions and the laws, policies, and procedures promulgated by the system; the ability to see the overall big picture of corrections and how the facility functions within that picture; a comprehension of the budget process and calendar; and the ability to be politically sensitive, personable, approachable, intelligent, hardworking, and decisive yet thoughtful. As a leader, the

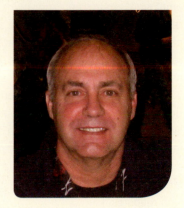

warden's actions must reflect the best traditions of the agency and be completely ethical in his or her decisions and actions. The warden should reflect all of the attributes prized in the frontline employee—loyalty, dedication, honesty, and reliability—and should instill confidence in all levels of staff and inmates. Staff wants a warden who is steady under pressure and not prone to swings in mood or behavior. Ultimately, though staff members may perform an infinite variety of jobs in the facility itself, they look to the warden to ensure they have the proper orders and resources needed to keep them safe, day in and day out. Finally, the warden must be a skilled communicator at all levels, with good writing and verbal skills, as well as effective listening skills.

In general, what does a typical day for a practitioner in this career include?

Various functions, but the day should cover all three shifts to foster good communication. One should be at the facility during each shift change to ensure access to staff as they leave and enter the next shift, personally greeting or chatting with the support staff before the workday begins. An early morning staff meeting with the associate wardens and the maintenance supervisor is essential to review the last 24 hours of shift activities and develop a priority list of operational issues that need resolution. Next, items on the in-basket are reviewed, delegated, or responded to, and it is important to physically "walk the yard" (for about 2 hours) on a daily basis to make upper management accessible to staff and inmates and to provide the opportunity for personal observation of any issues. This is also a time to obtain firsthand feedback as to the morale, conditions, and security of the yard. Next are formally scheduled meetings with inmate families,

(Continued)

(Continued)

employee group representatives, other agency representatives, and so on. Time is also spent reviewing new policies, reading inmate appeals and requests, responding to correspondence, and conducting any necessary interviews of staff. Work continues after 5:00 p.m., to complete paperwork, prepare court testimony, work on difficult personnel issues, and budget execution and construction. Once a week, do a facility inspection, looking at sanitation and security compliance while focusing on a different aspect of facility operations each week (such as fire suppression readiness).

What is your advice to someone either wishing to study or now studying criminal justice to become a practitioner in this career field?

Become a "triple threat" in the field, which includes having a solid understanding of operations, programs, and budget; knowing where you are going; and studying leadership and becoming a leader. Try to find a competent mentor in the field who will take an interest in your career and guide you on a path of experience and education that will facilitate achieving your goals. The best administrators become leaders in our field, and to succeed, one needs experience, training, and education.

Controlled vengeance means that the state takes away the responsibility for punishing wrongdoers from the individuals who were wronged and assumes it for itself. Early state-controlled punishment, however, was typically as uncontrolled and vengeful as any grieving parent might inflict on the murderer of his or her child. In many parts of the world, prior to the 18th century, human beings were considered born sinners because of the Christian legacy of original sin. Cruel tortures used on criminals to literally "beat the devil out of them" were justified by the need to save sinners' souls. Earthly pain was temporary and certainly preferable to an eternity of torment if sinners died unrepentant. Punishment was often barbaric, regardless of whether those ordering it bothered to justify it with such arguments or even believed those arguments themselves.

The practice of brutal punishment and arbitrary legal codes began to wane with the beginning of a period historians call the Enlightenment, or age of reason. The **Enlightenment** encompassed the period roughly between the late 17th century and the late 18th century and was essentially a major shift in the way people began to view the world and their place in it. It was also marked by the narrowing of the mental distance between people and the expanding of circles of individuals considered "just like us."

THE EMERGENCE OF THE CLASSICAL SCHOOL

Enlightenment:
Period in history in which a major shift in the way people viewed the world and their place in it occurred, moving from a supernaturalistic to a naturalistic and rational worldview.

Classical school:
The classical school of penology/criminology was a nonempirical mode of inquiry similar to the philosophy practiced by the classical Greek philosophers—one based on logic and reason.

Enlightenment ideas eventually led to a school of penology that has come to be known as the **classical school**. The leader of this school, Italian nobleman and professor of law *Cesare Bonesana, Marchese di Beccaria* (1738–1794), published what was to become the manifesto for the reform of judicial and penal systems throughout Europe, *Dei Delitti e delle Pene* (On Crimes and Punishments) (1764/1963). The book was a passionate plea to humanize and rationalize the law and to make punishment just and reasonable. Beccaria (as he is usually referred to) did not question the need for punishment, but he believed that laws should be designed to preserve public safety and order, not to avenge crime. He also took issue with the common practice of secret accusations, arguing that such practices led to general deceit and alienation in society. He argued that accused persons should be able to confront their accusers, to know the charges brought against them, and to be granted a public trial before an impartial judge as soon as possible after arrest and indictment.

Beccaria argued that punishments should be proportionate to the harm done, should be identical for identical crimes, and should be applied without reference to the social status of either offender or victim. Beccaria (1963) made no effort to plumb the depths of criminal character or motivation, arguing that crime is simply the result of "the despotic spirit which is in every man" (p. 12). He also argued that the tendency of "man" to give in to the "despotic spirit" had to be countered by the threat of punishment, which had to be certain, swift, and severe enough to outweigh any benefits offenders get from crime if they are to be deterred from future crime. He elaborated on these three elements of punishment as follows:

> *Certainty:* "The certainty of punishment, even if it be moderate, will always make a stronger impression than the fear of another which is more terrible but combined with the hope of impunity" (p. 58).

> *Swiftness:* "The more promptly and the more closely punishment follows upon the commission of a crime, the more just and useful will it be" (p. 55).

> *Severity:* "For a punishment to attain its end, the evil which it inflicts has only to exceed the advantage derivable from the crime; in this excess of evil one should include the . . . loss of the good which the crime might have produced. All beyond this is superfluous and for that reason tyrannical" (p. 43).

Beccaria makes clear that punishments must outweigh any benefits offenders get from crime if they are to be deterred from future crime. But such punishment should be as certain and as swift as possible if it is to have a lasting impression on the criminal and to deter others.

Beccaria also asserted that to ensure a rational and fair penal structure, punishments for specific crimes must be decreed by written criminal codes, and the discretionary powers of judges must be severely limited. The judge's task was to determine guilt or innocence and then to impose the legislatively prescribed punishment if the accused was found guilty. Many of Beccaria's recommended reforms were implemented in a number of European countries within his lifetime (Durant & Durant, 1967). Such radical change over such a short period of time, across many different cultures, suggests that Beccaria's rational reform ideas tapped into and broadened the scope of emotions such as sympathy and empathy among the political and intellectual elite of Enlightenment Europe. We tend to feel empathy for those whom we view as "like us," and this leads to sympathy, which may lead to an active concern for their welfare. Thus, with cognition and emotion gelled into the Enlightenment ideal of the basic unity and worth of humanity, justice became both more refined and more diffuse (Walsh & Hemmens, 2014).

Principle of utility: Positing that human action should be judged moral or immoral by its effects on the happiness of the community and that the proper function of the legislature is to make laws aimed at maximizing the pleasure and minimizing the pains of the population.

Jeremy Bentham

Another prominent figure was British lawyer and philosopher *Jeremy Bentham* (1748–1832). His major work, *Principles of Morals and Legislation* (1789/1948), is essentially a philosophy of social control based on the **principle of utility**, which posits that human actions should be judged moral or immoral by their effect on the happiness of the community. The proper function of the legislature is thus to make laws aimed at maximizing the pleasure and minimizing the pain of the largest number in society—"the greatest good for the greatest number" (p. 151).

If legislators are to legislate according to the principle of utility, they must understand human motivation, which for Bentham (1789/1948) was easily summed up: "Nature has placed mankind under the governance of two sovereign masters, pain and pleasure. It is for them alone to point out what we ought to do, as well as to determine what we shall do" (p. 125). This was essentially the Enlightenment concept of human nature, which was seen as hedonistic, rational, and endowed with free will. The classical explanation of criminal behavior and how to prevent it can be derived from these three assumptions.

PHOTO 1.2: Italian nobleman and professor of law Cesare Bonesana, Marchese of Beccaria (1738–1794), published what was to become the manifesto for the reform of judicial and penal systems throughout Europe, *Dei Delitti e delle Pene* (On Crimes and Punishments) (1764/1963).

THE EMERGENCE OF POSITIVISM: SHOULD PUNISHMENT FIT THE OFFENDER OR THE OFFENSE?

Just as classicism arose from the 18th-century humanism of the Enlightenment, positivism arose from the 19th-century spirit of science. Classical thinkers were philosophers in the manner of the thinkers of classical Greece (hence the term *classical*), whereas **positivists** took upon themselves the methods of empirical science, from which more "positive" conclusions could be drawn (hence the term *positivism*). They were radical empiricists who insisted that only things that can be observed and measured should concern us. This being the case, they believed that concepts underlying classical thought, such as rationality, free will, motivation, conscience, and human nature, should be ignored as pure speculation about the unseen and immeasurable. An essential assumption of positivism is that human actions have causes and that these causes are to be found in the uniformities that typically precede those actions. The search for causes of human behavior led positivists to dismiss the classical notion that humans are free agents who alone are responsible for their actions.

Enrico Ferri, one of the early positivists, gives us perhaps the best short description of the differences between classical and positivist schools:

> For them [the classicists] the facts should give place to syllogisms [reasoning from a taken-for-granted premise to a logical conclusion]; for us [positivists] the facts govern and no reasoning can occur without starting from the facts. For them science only needs paper, pen, and ink and the rest comes from a brain stuffed with abundant reading of books. . . . For us science requires spending a long time in examining the facts one by one, evaluating them, reducing them to a common denominator, [and] extracting the central idea from them. For them a syllogism or an anecdote suffices to demolish a myriad of facts gathered by years of observation and analysis; for us, the reverse is true. (in Curran & Renzetti, 2001, p. 16)

Positivists: Those who believe that human actions have causes and that these causes are to be found in the thoughts and experiences that typically precede those actions.

Early positivism espoused a hard form of determinism, such as that implied in the assertion that there are "born criminals." Nevertheless, positivism slowly moved the criminal justice system away from a concentration on the criminal act as the sole determinant of the type of punishment to be meted out and toward an appraisal of the characteristics and circumstances of the offender as an additional determinant. Because human actions have causes that may be out of the actor's control, the concept of legal responsibility was called into question. For instance, Italian lawyer *Raffaele Garofalo* (1852–1934) believed that because human action is often evoked by circumstances beyond human control (temperament, extreme poverty, intelligence, and certain situations), the only thing to be considered at sentencing was the offender's "peculiarities," or risk factors for crime.

Garofalo's (1885/1968) only concern for individualizing sentencing was the danger offenders posed to society, and his proposed sentences ranged from execution for those he called the *extreme criminals* (whom we might call psychopaths today), to transportation to penal colonies for *impulsive criminals*, to simply changing the law to deal with what he called *endemic criminals* (those who commit what we today might call *victimless crimes*). German criminal lawyer Franz von Liszt, on the other hand, campaigned for customized sentencing according to the rehabilitative potential of offenders, which was to be based on what scientists find out

Stock Montage/Getty Images

PHOTO 1.3: Jeremy Bentham's (1748–1832) major work, *Principles of Morals and Legislation* (1789/1948), is essentially a philosophy of social control based on the principle of utility, which posits that human actions should be judged moral or immoral by their effect on the happiness of the community.

about the causes of crime (Sherman, 2005). Customized sentencing, based both on the seriousness of the crime and the history and characteristics of the criminal (thus satisfying both classicists and positivists), is routine in the United States today.

••• THE FUNCTION OF PUNISHMENT

Video 1.1:
Wells Fargo
Restitution

Although most corrections scholars agree that punishment functions as a form of social control, some view it as a barbaric throwback to precivilized times (Menninger, 1968). But can you imagine a society where punishment did not exist? What would such a society be like? Could it survive? If you cannot realistically imagine such a society, you are not alone, for the desire to punish those who have harmed us or otherwise cheated on the social contract is as old as the species itself. Punishment aimed at discouraging cheats is observed in every social species of animal, leading evolutionary biologists to conclude that punishment of cheats is a strategy designed by natural selection for the emergence and maintenance of cooperative behavior (Alcock, 1998; Walsh, 2014). Cooperative behavior is important for all social species and is built on mutual trust, which is why violating that trust evokes moral outrage and results in punitive sanctions. Brain-imaging studies show that when subjects punish cheats, they have significantly increased blood flow to areas of the brain that respond to reward, suggesting that punishing those who have wronged us provides both emotional relief and reward (de Quervain et al., 2004; Fehr & Gachter, 2002). These studies imply that we are hardwired to "get even," as suggested by the popular saying, "Vengeance is sweet."

Sociologist *Émile Durkheim* (1858–1917) contended that punishment is functional for society in that the rituals of punishment reaffirm the justness of the social norms and allow citizens to express their moral outrage when others transgress those moral norms. Durkheim also recognized that we can temper punishment with sympathy. He observed that over the course of social evolution, humankind has moved from *retributive* justice (characterized by cruel and vengeful punishments) to *restitutive* justice (characterized by reparation—"making amends"). **Retributive justice** is driven by the natural passion for punitive revenge that "ceases only when exhausted . . . only after it has destroyed" (Durkheim, 1893/1964, p. 86). **Restitutive justice** is driven by simple deterrence and is more humanistic and tolerant, although it is still "at least in part, a work of vengeance" (pp. 88–89). For Durkheim, restitutive responses to wrongdoers offer a balance between calming moral outrage on the one hand and exciting the emotions of empathy and sympathy on the other.

THE PHILOSOPHICAL ASSUMPTIONS
BEHIND JUSTIFICATIONS FOR PUNISHMENT

A philosophy of punishment involves defining the concept of punishment and the values, attitudes, and beliefs contained in that definition, as well as justifying the imposition of a painful burden on someone. When we speak of justifying something, we typically mean that we provide reasons for doing it both in terms of morality ("It's the right thing to do") and in terms of the goals we wish to achieve ("Do this, and we'll get that"). In other words, we expect that punishment will have favorable consequences that justify its application.

Legal scholars have traditionally identified four major objectives or justifications for the practice of punishing criminals: retribution, deterrence, rehabilitation, and incapacitation. Criminal justice scholars have recently added a fifth purpose to the list: reintegration. All theories and systems of punishment are based on conceptions of basic human nature and thus, to a great extent, on ideology. The view of human nature on which the law in every country relies today is the same view enunciated by classical thinkers Beccaria and Bentham—namely, that human beings are hedonistic, rational, and possessors of free will.

Retributive justice:
A philosophy of punishment driven by a passion for revenge.

Restitutive justice:
A philosophy of punishment driven by simple deterrence and a need to repair the wrongs done.

Hedonism is a doctrine that maintains that all life goals are desirable only as means to the end of achieving pleasure or avoiding pain. It goes without saying that pleasure is intrinsically desirable, pain is intrinsically undesirable, and we all seek to maximize the former and minimize the latter. We are assumed to pursue these goals in rational ways. **Rationality** is the state of having good sense and sound judgment. Rational sense and judgment is based (ideally) on the evidence before us at any given time, and the rational person revises his or her reasoning as new evidence arises. Rationality should not be confused with morality because its goal is self-interest, and self-interest is said to govern behavior whether in conforming or deviant directions. Crime is rational (at least in the short run) if criminals employ reason and act purposefully to gain desired ends. Rationality is thus the quality of thinking and behaving in accordance with logic and reason such that one's reality is an ordered and intelligible system for achieving goals and solving problems. For the classical scholar, the ultimate goal of any human activity is self-interest, and self-interest is assumed to govern our behavior whether it takes us in prosocial or antisocial directions.

Hedonism and rationality are combined in the concept of the **hedonistic calculus**, a concept introduced by Jeremy Bentham. The hedonistic calculus is a method by which individuals are assumed to logically weigh the anticipated benefits of a given course of action against its possible costs. If the balance of consequences of a contemplated action is thought to enhance pleasure and/or minimize pain, then individuals will pursue it; if not, they will not. If people miscalculate, as they frequently do, it is because they are ignorant of the full range of consequences of a given course of action, not because they are irrational or stupid.

The final assumption about human nature is that humans have free will that enables them to purposely and deliberately choose to follow a calculated course of action. This is not a radical free will position that views human will as unfettered by restraints but rather a free will in line with the concept of human agency. The concept of **human agency** maintains that humans have the capacity to make choices and the responsibility to make moral ones regardless of internal or external constraints on their ability to do so. This is a form of free will that is compatible with determinism because it recognizes both the internal and external constraints that limit our ability to do as we please. If we grant a criminal the dignity of possessing agency so he or she can purposely weigh options before deciding on a course of action, "he or she can be held responsible for that choice and can be legitimately punished" (Clarke & Cornish, 2001, p. 25). It is only with the concept of agency that we can justifiably assign praise and blame to individual actions.

••• THE MAJOR PUNISHMENT JUSTIFICATIONS

Even though we assume that most people agree society has a right and a duty to punish those who harm it, because punishment involves the state depriving individuals of life or liberty, it always has been assumed that it is in need of ethical justification. Punishment justifications rise and fall in popularity with the ideology of the times, but there are five that have been dominant in the United States over the last century: retribution, deterrence, incapacitation, rehabilitation, and reintegration. We start with the most ancient: retribution.

RETRIBUTION

Retribution is a "just deserts" model demanding that punishment matches as closely as possible the degree of harm criminals have inflicted on their victims—what they justly deserve. Those who commit minor crimes deserve minor punishments, and those who

---

Hedonism: A doctrine maintaining that all goals in life are means to the end of achieving pleasure and/or avoiding pain.

Rationality: The state of having good sense and sound judgment based on the evidence before us.

Hedonistic calculus: A method by which individuals are assumed to logically weigh the anticipated benefits of a given course of action against its possible costs.

Human agency: The capacity of humans to make choices and their responsibility to make moral ones regardless of internal or external constraints on their ability to do so.

Retribution: A philosophy of punishment demanding that criminals' punishments match the degree of harm they have inflicted on their victims—that is, what they justly deserve.

commit more serious crimes deserve more severe punishments. This is the most honestly stated justification for punishment because it both taps into our most primitive punitive urges and posits no secondary purpose for it, such as rehabilitation or deterrence. In other words, it does not require any favorable consequence to justify it except to maintain that justice has been served. Logan and Gaes (1993) go so far as to claim that only retributive punishment "is an affirmation of the autonomy, responsibility, and dignity of the individual" (p. 252). By holding offenders responsible and blameworthy for their actions, we are treating them as free moral agents, not as mindless rag dolls pushed here and there by negative environmental forces. California is among the states that have explicitly embraced this justification in their criminal code (California Penal Code Sec. 1170a): "The Legislature finds and declares that the purpose of imprisonment for a crime is punishment" (as cited in Barker, 2006, p. 12).

In his dissenting opinion in a famous death penalty case (*Furman v. Georgia*, 1972) in which the Supreme Court invalidated Georgia's death penalty statute, Justice Potter Stewart noted the "naturalness" of retribution and why the state rather than individuals must assume the retributive role:

> I cannot agree that retribution is a constitutionally impermissible ingredient in the imposition of punishment. The instinct for retribution is part of the nature of man, and channeling that instinct in the administration of criminal justice serves an important purpose in promoting the stability of a society governed by law. When people begin to believe that organized society is unwilling or unable to impose upon criminal offenders the punishment they "deserve," then there are sown the seeds of anarchy—of self-help, vigilante justice, and lynch law.

DETERRENCE

The principle behind **deterrence** is that people are deterred from crime by the threat of punishment. Deterrence may be either specific or general. **Specific deterrence** refers to the effect of punishment on the future behavior of persons who experience it. For specific deterrence to work, it is necessary that a previously punished person make a conscious connection between an intended criminal act and the punishment suffered as a result of similar acts committed in the past. Unfortunately, it is not always clear that such connections are made or, if they are, that they have the desired effect. This is either because memories of the previous consequences were insufficiently potent or because they were discounted. The trouble is that short-term rewards (such as the fruits of a crime) are easier to appreciate than long-term consequences (punishment that may never come), and there is a tendency to abandon consideration of the latter when confronted with temptation unless a person has a well-developed conscience and is future oriented. The weak of conscience and the present oriented tend to consistently discount long-term consequences in favor of short-term rewards.

Committing further crimes after being punished is called **recidivism**, which is a lot more common among ex-inmates than rehabilitation. Recidivism refers only to crimes committed after release from prison and does not apply to crimes committed while incarcerated. A study of 404,638 state prisoners released in 2005 in 30 states found that 68% were arrested within three years of release, and 77% were arrested within five years (Durose, Cooper, & Snyder, 2014), and these are just the ones who are caught. The average number of arrests per offender was 2.9, which means that those 404,638 offenders were responsible for over 1,173,000 arrests in the five years from 2005 to 2010. Among those who do desist, a number of them cite the fear of additional punishment as a big factor (R. Wright, 1999).

As Beccaria insisted, for punishment to positively affect future behavior, there must be a relatively high degree of certainty that punishment will follow a criminal act, the punishment must be administered very soon after the act, and it must be painful. The most

Journal Article 1.1: Do More Police Lead to More Crime Deterrence?

 Web 1.1: Deterrence

Deterrence: A philosophy of punishment aimed at the prevention of crime by the threat of punishment.

Specific deterrence: The supposed effect of punishment on the future behavior of persons who experience the punishment.

Recidivism: Occurs when an ex-offender commits further crimes.

important of these is certainty, but as we see from Figure 1.2, showing clearance rates for major crimes in 2014, the probability of being arrested is very low, especially for property crimes—so much for certainty. Factoring out the immorality of the enterprise, burglary appears to be a rational career option for a capable criminal.

If a person is caught, the wheels of justice grind very slowly. Typically, many months pass between the act and the imposition of punishment—so much for swiftness. This leaves the law with severity as the only element it can realistically manipulate (it can increase or decrease statutory penalties almost at will), but it is unfortunately the least effective element (M. O. Reynolds, 1998). Studies from the United States and the United Kingdom find substantial negative correlations (as one factor goes up, the other goes down) between the likelihood of conviction (a measure of certainty) and crime rates but much weaker correlations in the same direction for the severity of punishment; that is, increased severity leads to lower offending rates (Langan & Farrington, 1998).

The effect of punishment on future behavior also depends on the **contrast effect**, defined as the contrast or comparison between the possible punishment for a given crime and the usual life experience of the person who may be punished. For people with little to lose, arrest and punishment may be perceived as merely an inconvenient occupational hazard. But for those who enjoy a loving family and the security of a valued career, the prospect of incarceration is a nightmarish contrast. Like so many other things in life, deterrence works least for those who need it the most (Austin & Irwin, 2001).

General deterrence refers to the preventive effect of the threat of punishment on the general population; it is thus aimed at *potential* offenders. Punishing offenders serves as an example to the rest of us of what may happen if we violate the law, as we noted in the opening vignette. As Radzinowicz and King (1979) put it, "People are not sent to prison primarily for their own good, or even in the hope that they will be cured of crime. . . . It is used as a warning and deterrent to others" (p. 296). The threat of punishment for law violators deters a large but unknown number of individuals who might commit crimes if no such system existed.

Contrast effect: The effect of punishment on future behavior depends on how much the punishment and the usual life experience of the person being punished differ or contrast.

General deterrence: The presumed preventive effect of the threat of punishment on the general population.

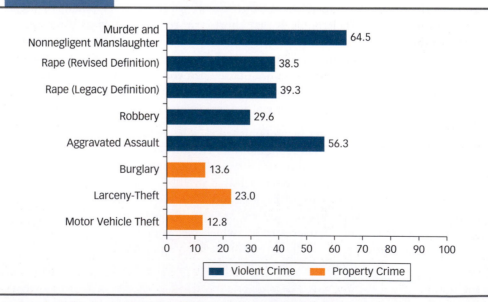

FIGURE *1.2*   Percentage of Crimes Cleared by Arrest or Exceptional Means* in 2014

Crime	Percentage
Murder and Nonnegligent Manslaughter	64.5
Rape (Revised Definition)	38.5
Rape (Legacy Definition)	39.3
Robbery	29.6
Aggravated Assault	56.3
Burglary	13.6
Larceny-Theft	23.0
Motor Vehicle Theft	12.8

■ Violent Crime   ■ Property Crime

*A crime cleared by "exceptional means" occurs when the police have a strong suspect but something beyond their control precludes a physical arrest (e.g., death of suspect).

Source: FBI (2015). Courtesy of U.S. Government Printing Office.

Are we putting too much faith in the ability of criminals and would-be criminals to calculate the costs and benefits of engaging in crime? Although many violent crimes are committed in the heat of passion or under the influence of mind-altering substances, there is evidence underscoring the classical idea that individuals do (subconsciously at least) calculate the ratio of expected pleasures to possible pains when contemplating their actions. Gary Becker (1997) dismisses the idea that criminals lack the knowledge and the foresight to take punitive probabilities into consideration when deciding whether or not to continue committing crimes. He says, "Interviews of young people in high crime areas who do engage in crime show an amazing understanding of what punishments are, what young people can get away with, [and] how to behave when going before a judge" (p. 20). Of course, incentives and disincentives to law-abiding or criminal behavior are perceived differently because of the contrast effect and ingrained habits. As Ernest van den Haag put it, "Law abiding people habitually ignore criminal opportunities. Law breakers habitually discount the risk of punishment. Neither calculates" (cited in Walsh, 2015, p. 93). This does not mean that criminals are impervious to realistic threats of punishment.

Deterrence theorists do not view people as calculating machines doing their mental math before engaging in any activity. They are simply saying that behavior is governed by its consequences. Our rational calculations are both subjective and bounded; all of us do not make the same calculations or arrive at the same game plan when pursuing the same goals. Think how the contrast effect would influence the calculations of a zero-income, 19-year-old high school dropout with a drug problem, as opposed to a 45-year-old married man with two children and a $90,000 annual income. We all make calculations with less-than-perfect knowledge and with different mind-sets, temperaments, and cognitive abilities, but to say that criminals do not make such calculations is to strip them of their humanity and to make them pawns of fate.

More general reviews of deterrence research indicate that legal sanctions do have "substantial deterrent effect" (Nagin, 1998, p. 16; see also R. Wright, 1999), and some researchers have claimed that increased incarceration rates account for about 25% of the variance in the decline in violent crime over the last decade or so (Rosenfeld, 2000; Spelman, 2000). Paternoster (2010) cites other studies demonstrating that 20% to 30% of the crime drop from its peak in the early 1990s is attributable to the approximately 52% increase in the imprisonment rate. He states, "There is a general consensus that the decline in crime is, at least in part, due to more and longer prison sentences, with much of the controversy being over how much of an effect" (p. 801). Of course, this leaves 70% to 75% of the crime drop to be explained by other factors. Unfortunately, even for the 30% figure, we cannot determine if we are witnessing a *deterrent* effect (i.e., has crime declined because more would-be criminals have perceived a greater punitive threat?) or an *incapacitation* effect (i.e., has crime declined because more violent people are behind bars and thus not at liberty to commit violent crimes on the outside?). Of course, it does not have to be one or the other, since both effects may be operating. Society benefits from crime reduction regardless of why it occurs.

INCAPACITATION

Incapacitation refers to the inability of criminals to victimize people outside prison walls while they are locked up behind them. Its rationale is summarized in James Q. Wilson's (1975) remark: "Wicked people exist. Nothing avails except to set them apart from innocent people" (p. 391). The incapacitation justification probably originated with *Enrico Ferri*'s concept of social defense. For Ferri (1897/1917), in order to determine punishment, notions of culpability, moral responsibility, and intent were secondary to an assessment of offenders' strength of resistance to criminal impulses, with the express purpose of averting future danger to society. He believed that moral insensibility and lack of foresight, underscored by low intelligence, were criminals' most marked characteristics. For

Incapacitation: A philosophy of punishment that refers to the inability of criminals to victimize people outside prison walls while they are locked up.

Ferri, the purpose of punishment is not to deter or to rehabilitate but to defend society from criminal predation. The characteristics of criminals prevented them from basing their behavior on rational calculus principles, so how could their behavior be deterred?

Incapacitation obviously "works" while criminals are incarcerated. Elliot Currie (1999) stated that in 1995, there were 135,000 inmates in prison whose most serious crime was robbery and that each robber on average commits five robberies per year. Had these robbers been left on the streets, they would have been responsible for an additional 675,000 robberies (135,000 × 5) on top of the 580,000 actual robberies reported to the police in 1995. Additionally, Johnson and Raphael (2012) estimated that each additional year spent in prison in the United States prevented 2.5 violent crimes and 11.4 property crimes for the period between 1978 and 1990.

The incapacitation issue has produced some lively debates about the relative costs and benefits to society of incarceration. Attempts to estimate these have proven difficult and controversial. In 1987, economist Edwin Zedlewski (1987), using national crime data, calculated that the typical offender commits 187 crimes a year and that the typical crime costs $2,300 in property losses or in physical injuries and human suffering. Multiplying these figures, Zedlewski estimated that the typical imprisoned felon is responsible for $430,000 in monetary costs to society each year he remains free. He then divided that figure by the cost of incarceration in 1977 ($25,000) and concluded that the social benefits of imprisonment outweigh the costs by 17 to 1.

Zedlewski's findings have been severely criticized, including a critical article by supporters of incarceration who argued that the typical offender commits 15 crimes in a year rather than 187 (DiIulio & Piehl, 1991), which reduces the benefit–cost ratio to 1.38 to 1 rather than 17 to 1. The different estimates of criminal activity are the result of Zedlewski using the mean number (arithmetic average) of crimes per year and DiIulio and Piehl using the median number (a measure of the "typical" in which half of criminals commit fewer than 15 crimes, and half commit more). Using the mean inflates the typical by averaging in the crimes committed by the most highly criminally involved offenders. Using only the dollar costs to estimate the social costs of crime, of course, ignores the tremendous physical and emotional costs to victims, as well as other important considerations (S. Walker, 2001).

Selective incapacitation: Refers to a punishment strategy that largely reserves prison for a distinct group of offenders composed primarily of violent repeat offenders.

© iStockphoto.com/LOUOATES

PHOTO 1.4: While this person is locked up, he cannot victimize those outside the prison—incapacitation.

SELECTIVE INCAPACITATION

The difference between the "typical" offender and the heavily crime-involved career criminal brings up the idea of **selective incapacitation**, which is a punishment strategy that largely reserves prison for a select group of offenders composed primarily of violent repeat offenders, but it also may include other types of incorrigible offenders. Birth cohort studies (a *cohort* is a group composed of subjects having something in common, such as being born within a given time frame and/or in a particular place) from a number of different locations find that about 6% to 10% of offenders commit the majority of all crimes. For instance, two large Philadelphia cohort studies of almost 10,000 boys each, born in 1945 (Wolfgang, Figlio, & Sellin, 1972) and 1958 (Figlio, Tracy, & Wolfgang, 1990), found that while about one third of young boys got caught up in the jaws of the criminal justice system, a very small proportion of them committed a highly disproportionate number of offenses. In the 1945 study, 6% of the cohort

(18% of the offenders in the cohort) committed 71% of all of the homicides, 73% of the rapes, 82% of the robberies, and 69% of the aggravated assaults. In the 1958 study, 7.5% of the cohort (23% of the offenders) accounted for 61% of the homicides, 75% of the rapes, 73% of the robberies, and 65% of the aggravated assaults.

Saving prison space mostly for high-rate violent offenders better protects the community and saves it money. The problem with this strategy, however, involves identifying high-rate violent offenders *before* they become high-rate violent offenders; identifying them after the fact is easy. Generally speaking, individuals who begin committing predatory delinquent acts before they reach puberty are the ones who will continue to commit crimes across the life course (DeLisi, 2005; Moffitt & Walsh, 2003). The incapacitation effect is more starkly driven home by a study of the offenses of 39 convicted murderers committed *after* they had served their time for murder and were released from prison. Between 1996 and 2000, they had 122 arrests for serious violent crimes (including seven additional murders), 218 arrests for serious property crimes, and 863 other arrests among them (DeLisi, 2005, p. 165).

No one argues for an increase in the incarceration of low-rate, low-seriousness offenders. As we increase incarceration more and more, we quickly skim off the 5% to 10% of serious offenders and begin to incarcerate offenders who would best be dealt with within the community. In monetary (and other social cost) terms, we have a situation economists call the *law of diminishing returns*. In essence, this means that while we may get a big bang for our buck at first (incarcerating the most serious criminals), the bang quickly diminishes to a whimper and even turns to a net loss as we continue to reel in minor offenders, which is why it is imperative to develop methods of assessing and classifying offenders more effectively.

Video 1.2: Motivating Offender Change

Among other things, we have to consider relating to the incapacitation effect are the criminogenic and labeling effects of incarceration. Yes, imprisonment takes criminals off the street for a period, but imprisonment also exposes the convict to greater levels of criminal attitudes and values and leads to increased friendships with other criminals and perhaps recruitment into prison gangs with "franchises" on the outside, which may ensnare the convict in a lifetime of crime. Even if the convict is not induced to further crime by the prison experience, the *ex-con* label is a major impediment to gaining legitimate employment upon release. Thus, the value of the incapacitation effect may be neutralized by these countervailing effects. Of course, this is not to say that people who have committed horrible violent crimes or who continuously victimize their communities with less onerous ones should not be incarcerated. But it bears thinking about when it comes to nonviolent, relatively minor offenders whose problems (typically drug abuse) may be addressed by community corrections agencies.

The problem is predicting which offenders should be selectively incapacitated. Although there are a number of excellent prediction scales in use today to assist us in estimating who will and who will not become a high-rate offender, the risk of too many false positives (predicting someone will become a high-rate offender when, in fact, he or she will not) is always present (Piquero & Blumstein, 2007). However, incarceration decisions are not made on predictions about the future but rather on knowledge of past behavior—the past is prologue, as Shakespeare said.

AP Video 1.1 Lohan Rehab Court

REHABILITATION

The term **rehabilitation** means to restore or return to constructive or healthy activity. The approach of this book is rehabilitation oriented. Your authors are not naïve "bleeding heart" dreamers; we have both served in the criminal justice trenches as a correctional officer and prison counselor (Stohr) and as a police officer and probation officer (Walsh), and we are well aware of the values, attitudes, and behaviors of criminals. Nevertheless, we consider it sound fiscal and criminal justice policy to be forward looking by trying

Rehabilitation: A philosophy of punishment aimed at "curing" criminals of their antisocial behavior.

POLICY AND RESEARCH   Economists Look at Incapacitation

Research drives correctional policy, and correctional policy drives research, but what is occurring outside of the correctional context in the broader society drives both. Concerns about the effectiveness of rehabilitation programs, rising crime rates, and the public's outrage that resulted in the early 1970s sparked new interest in incapacitation as a crime prevention strategy. As a result of new incapacitation-based policies of the 1970s and 1980s, rates of imprisonment in the United States rose dramatically. This increase in imprisonment has generated its own set of policy concerns, such as what to do about overcrowding and budgetary concerns over the costs of imprisonment.

While correctional researchers tend to look at punishment policies with their eyes on constitutional issues and the effects treatment programs on recidivism, economists cast their eyes on cost–benefit analyses seen in terms of dollars—the cost of incarcerating more offenders versus the monetary loss from crimes committed by criminals in the community. Let's take an economist's view of the DeLisi (2005) study in the main body of this chapter. What would be the dollar cost saved had these 139 murderers not been released? The total social cost of a single murder has been estimated at $8,982,907, and the average cost of other "serious violent crimes" (rape, aggravated assault, and robbery) has been estimated at $130,035 (McCollister, French, & Fang, 2010). Seven murders ($62,880,349) and 115 other serious violent crimes ($14,954,063) yield a total of $77,834,412, or $15,566,882 per year over the five-year period, and that is without adding in the 218 arrests for serious property crimes and the 863 "other" arrests.

In 2006, the Italian government passed the Collective Clemency Bill (CCB), ordering the release of one third of Italy's prisoners (about 22,000) with three years or less left to serve on their sentences. This would be roughly equivalent to the United States releasing 756,000 inmates into the community. The CCB resulted from budgetary prison-overcrowding concerns, and it gave criminologists an excellent chance to gauge the effects of incapacitation by tracking released inmates. Buonanno and Raphael's (2013) analysis of released convicts found that the incapacitation effect was between 14 and 18 extra crimes committed per year per criminal. (They only included theft and robbery arrests in their analysis.)

Did the policy produce its stated goals? The answer depends on how you look at it. Prison overcrowding was eliminated, so that goal was realized. Prison authorities saved an estimated 245 million euros ($316 million), so the policy "worked" for them. But what about Italian society? Buonanno and Raphael (2013) estimated that crime costs were between 466 million and 2.2 billion euros, or between approximately $606 million and $2.9 billion. They state, "Overall, the pardon falls far short of passing cost–benefit analysis determining a 'social' cost between 10 and 60 thousand euros per prisoner per year" (p. 2463). Although this economic analysis shows a huge financial loss to society attributable to the CCB, it does not take into consideration other social costs of crimes committed by released prisoners, such as the emotional and physical costs of being victimized and the general feeling of the inadequacy of the state to protect its citizens.

An economic study of the effects of selective-incapacitation policy in Holland concluded that it reduced recidivism substantially and that "the social benefits of long-term incapacitation of prolific offenders outweighed the social costs" (Vollaard, 2013, p. 281). Surveys of these offenders showed that many of them "see the long-term prison sentence as an opportunity to break with a life dominated by drug use rather than as a severe punishment. . . . Some 60% of the convicted offenders state that they feel substantially better after the enhanced prison sentence" (p. 282). However, long term was defined as two years, which is less than most U.S. prison sentences for offenders, and these Dutch offenders were provided with intensive rehabilitation programs. Although the Dutch crime problem is less serious than that of the United States, there may be a lesson in the Dutch experiment with selective incapacitation of repeat nonviolent offenders with drug problems for the United States that may lead it to incarcerate more judiciously (selectively).

DISCUSSION QUESTIONS

1. If these studies show that the financial costs of the crimes committed by released prisoners are greater than the costs of continued incarceration, why do we see people arguing that releasing more prisoners would save money?

2. Discuss the economic and social implications of Matt DeLisi's study of the recidivism of 139 murderers. Should such people ever be released?

3. What lessons does the Dutch study have for the United States, and what are the barriers to implementing them?

Sources

Buonanno, P., & Raphael, S. (2013). Incarceration and incapacitation: Evidence from the 2006 Italian collective pardon. *American Economic Review, 103*, 2437–2465.

DeLisi, M. (2005). *Career criminals in society.* Thousand Oaks, CA: Sage.

McCollister, K., French, M., & Fang, H. (2010). The cost of crime to society: New crime-specific estimates for policy and program evaluation. *Drug and Alcohol Dependence, 108*, 98–109.

Vollaard, B. (2013). Preventing crime through selective incapacitation. *Economic Journal, 123*, 262–284.

to prevent crime from happening rather than simply punishing it when it does. Whereas deterrence and incapacitation are mainly justified on classical grounds, rehabilitation is primarily a positivist concept. The rehabilitative goal used to be based on a medical model that viewed criminal behavior as a moral sickness requiring treatment. Today, this model views criminality in terms of "faulty thinking" and criminals as in need of "programming" rather than "treatment." Figure 1.3 highlights the shifts in correctional policy throughout the 20th century to the present.

The present emphasis on rehabilitation is driven both by economics (it is cheaper) and by decades of research aimed at discovering "what works" in correctional assessment and treatment. The goal of rehabilitation is to change offenders' attitudes so that they come to accept that their behavior was wrong, not to deter them by the threat of further

Video 1.3:
Education Opportunities in Washington State Prisons

Audio 1.1:
Reintegration

FIGURE 1.3   Swings in Correctional Policy Emphases: 1900–Present

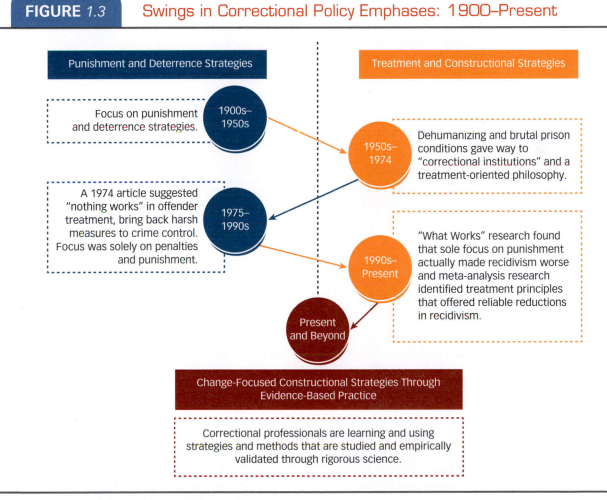

Punishment and Deterrence Strategies

Treatment and Constructional Strategies

Focus on punishment and deterrence strategies.

1900s–1950s

1950s–1974

Dehumanizing and brutal prison conditions gave way to "correctional institutions" and a treatment-oriented philosophy.

A 1974 article suggested "nothing works" in offender treatment, bring back harsh measures to crime control. Focus was solely on penalties and punishment.

1975–1990s

1990s–Present

"What Works" research found that sole focus on punishment actually made recidivism worse and meta-analysis research identified treatment principles that offered reliable reductions in recidivism.

Present and Beyond

Change-Focused Constructional Strategies Through Evidence-Based Practice

Correctional professionals are learning and using strategies and methods that are studied and empirically validated through rigorous science.

Source: Walters, Clark, Gingerich, & Meltzer (2007).

TABLE *1.1*   Summary of Key Elements of Different Correctional Perspectives

	RETRIBUTION	DETERRENCE	INCAPACITATION	REHABILITATION	REINTEGRATION
Justification	Moral Just deserts	Prevention of further crime	Risk control, community protection	Offenders have correctable deficiencies	Offenders have correctable deficiencies
Strategy	None: Offenders simply deserve to be punished	Make punishment more certain, swift, and severe	Offenders cannot offend while in prison	Treatment to reduce offenders' inclination to reoffend	Concrete programming to make for successful reentry into society
Focus of perspective	The offense and just deserts	Actual and potential offenders	Actual offenders	Needs of offenders	Needs of offenders
Image of offenders	Free agents whose humanity we affirm by holding them accountable	Rational beings who engage in cost–benefit calculations	Not to be trusted but to be constrained	Good people who have gone astray and will respond to treatment	Ordinary folk who require and will respond to concrete help

Video 1.4:
Malloy Rolls Out
Reintegration
Program to Help
Prisoners Find
and Keep Work

Reintegration: A philosophy of punishment that aims to use the time criminals are under correctional supervision to prepare them to reenter the free community as well equipped to do so as possible.

punishment. We defer further discussion of rehabilitation until Chapters 8 and 10, devoted to correctional assessment and classification, and treatment and rehabilitation.

REINTEGRATION

The goal of **reintegration** is to use the time criminals are under correctional supervision to prepare them to reenter (or reintegrate with) the free community as well equipped to do so as possible. In effect, reintegration is not much different from rehabilitation, but it is more pragmatic, focusing on concrete programs such as job training rather than attitude change. There are many challenges associated with this process, so much so that, like rehabilitation, it warrants a chapter to itself and will be discussed in detail in the context of parole.

ETHICAL ISSUE 1.1

What Would You Do?

You are the director of your state's department of corrections. The state governor trusts your judgment and gives you free rein to administer the state prisons as you see fit within the bounds of the state and U.S. constitutions. Your belief in human responsibility and autonomy has given you a philosophical and emotional attachment to the retribution justification for punishment. However, you have read the various studies on the successes of the Dutch experiment with the rehabilitation of carefully selected offenders whose primary problem is substance abuse. Would you ignore them and stick with your "gut-level" beliefs in just deserts, or would you do whatever you could to identify candidates for a similar program, target resources there, and do what you could to secure their parole as timely as possible after two years? Give reasons why or why not.

Table 1.1 is a summary of the key elements (justification, strategy, etc.) of the four punishment philosophies or perspectives discussed. The commonality that they all share to various extents is, of course, the prevention of crime.

••• THE DUE PROCESS AND CRIME CONTROL MODELS

A useful way of grounding discussions about the correctional system is to see how it stacks up in terms of Herbert Packer's (1964) crime control versus due process models. Packer (1964/1997) proposed two *ideal-type models* (based on pure types that exaggerate differences) reflecting different value choices undergirding the operation of the criminal justice system. The major tension between these two models is the emphasis on justice for an offended community and justice for those who offend against it. Equally moral individuals and cultures can hold very different conceptions of justice, with some placing an emphasis on justice for the offended community and others on justice for those who offend against it.

Audio 1.2: Due Process and the Trial of Terrorism Suspects

THE CRIME CONTROL MODEL

The first model is the **crime control model**. This model emphasizes community protection from criminals and stresses that civil liberties can only have real meaning in a safe, well-ordered society. To achieve such a society, it is necessary to suppress criminal activity swiftly, efficiently, and with finality, and this demands a well-oiled criminal justice system where cases are handled informally and uniformly in "assembly line" fashion. Police officers must arrest suspects, prosecutors must prosecute them, and judges must sentence them, "uncluttered with ceremonious rituals that do not advance the progress of the case" (Packer, 1997, p. 4). To achieve finality, the occasions for challenging the process (appeals) must be kept to a minimum. The assumption is that such a process will more efficiently screen out the innocent and that those who are not may be considered "probably guilty." Packer does not want us to think of a presumption of guilt as the conceptual opposite of the presumption of innocence, but rather, "reduced to its barest essentials and when operating at its most successful pitch [the crime control model consists of two elements]: (a) an administrative fact-finding process leading to the exoneration of the suspect, or to (b) the entry of a plea of guilty" (1997, p. 5).

AP Video 1.2: Snowden

Web 1.2: The Crime Control Model

THE DUE PROCESS MODEL

The **due process model** is the second model. Rather than a system run like an assembly line, the due process model is more like an obstacle course in which impediments to carrying the accused's case further are encountered at every stage of processing. Police officers must obtain warrants when possible and must not interrogate suspects without the suspect's consent, evidence may be suppressed, and various motions may be filed that may free a factually guilty person. These and other obstacles are placed in the way to prevent the efficient and speedy processing of cases. If the person is convicted, he or she may file numerous appeals, and it may take years to gain closure of the case. The due process model is more concerned with the integrity of the legal process than with its efficiency and with legal guilt rather than whether the accused is factually guilty. Factual guilt translates into legal guilt only if the evidence used to determine it was obtained in a procedurally correct fashion.

Crime control model: A model of law that emphasizes community protection from criminals and stresses that civil liberties can only have real meaning in a safe, well-ordered society.

Due process model: A model of law that stresses the accused's rights more than the rights of the community.

CHOOSING A MODEL

Which model do you prefer, and which model do you think best exemplifies the ideals of justice? It may be correct to say that under a crime control model, more innocent people may be convicted, but that depends on which country we are talking about and how far along the continuum it goes in its practices. It is also true that under a due process model, more (factually) guilty people will be set free, but again, that depends on the country and the extent to which the model is "pure." In the first instance, the individual has been unjustly victimized, and in the second, the

© iStockphoto.com/gerenme

PHOTO 1.5: The crime control model avers that criminal cases should be processed in assembly line fashion—efficiently and with finality.

© iStockphoto.com/Bluiz60

PHOTO 1.6: The due process model purposely puts obstacles in the way of processing criminal cases efficiently and with finality.

community has been unjustly victimized. It is clear that both models have their faults as well as their strengths. The danger of a runaway crime control model is a return to the days when due process was nonexistent, and the danger of a runaway due process model is that truth and justice may get lost in a maze of legal ritualism. But remember that these are ideal-type models that do not exist in their "pure" form anywhere in the world; rather, all criminal justice systems lie on a continuum between the crime control and due process extremes.

Packer's models are more about the processes followed in the police and prosecution legs of criminal justice (the catch 'em and convict 'em legs), but they also apply to the third leg—the correct 'em leg—of the criminal justice system. While it may be true that there is less public concern for the rights of convicted criminals than for the rights of accused criminals and while it is also true that convicted criminals have fewer rights than do law-abiding folks, the criminal justice model followed by the police and the courts is also the model followed by its correctional system. The due process model has led to the existence and expansion of community alternatives to punitive institutionalization, such as probation and parole, halfway houses, community treatment centers, diagnostic models that assess offenders for probation or parole eligibility, rehabilitative programs, work release programs, and an enhanced concern for the rights of offenders who are incarcerated or under community supervision. All of these models, institutions, systems, and rights are examined throughout this book.

SUMMARY

- Corrections is a social function designed to hold, punish, supervise, deter, and possibly rehabilitate the accused or convicted. Corrections is also the study of these functions.

- Although it is natural to want to exact revenge ourselves when people do us wrong, the state has taken over this responsibility for punishment to prevent endless tit-for-tat feuds. Through social evolution, the state has moved to more restitutive forms of punishment that, while serving to tone down the community's moral outrage, tempers it with sympathy.

- Much of the credit for the shift away from retributive punishment must go to the classical school of criminology, which was imbued with the humanistic spirit of the Enlightenment. The view of human nature (hedonistic, rational, and possessing free will) held by thinkers of the time was that punishment should primarily be used for deterrent purposes, that it should only just exceed the gains of crime, and that it should apply equally to all who have committed the same crime regardless of any individual differences.

- Opposing classical notions of punishment are those of the positivists, who rose to prominence during the 19th century and who were influenced by the spirit of science. Positivists rejected the philosophical underpinnings regarding human nature of the classicists and declared that punishment should fit the offender rather than the crime.

- The objectives of punishment are retribution, deterrence, incapacitation, rehabilitation, and reintegration, all of which have come in and out of favor over the years.

- Retribution is simply just deserts—getting the punishment one deserves—with no other justification needed.

- Deterrence is the assumption that the threat of punishment causes people not to commit crimes. We identified two kinds of deterrence: specific and general. The effects of deterrence on potential offenders depend to a great extent on the contrast between the conditions of punishment and the conditions of everyday life.

- Incapacitation means that the accused and convicted cannot commit further crimes (if they did so in the first place) against the innocent while incarcerated. Incapacitation works only while offenders are behind bars, but we should be more selective about whom we incarcerate.

- Rehabilitation centers on efforts to socialize offenders in prosocial directions while they are under correctional supervision, so they will not commit further crimes.

- Reintegration refers to efforts to provide offenders with concrete skills they can use that will give them a stake in conformity.

- Throughout this book, we will be offering comparative perspectives on corrections from other countries, focusing primarily on the United Kingdom, France, China, and Saudi Arabia. These countries best exemplify their respective legal traditions and are situated quite far apart on Packer's crime control–due process model of criminal justice.

- The United States leads the world in the proportion of its citizens that it has in prison. Whether this is indicative of hardness (more prison time for more people) or softness (imprisonment as an alternative to execution or mutilation) depends on how we view hardness versus softness and with which countries we compare the United States.

KEY TERMS

Classical school 6

Contrast effect 12

Corrections 2

Crime control model 19

Deterrence 11

Due process model 19

Enlightenment 6

General deterrence 12

Hedonism 10

Hedonistic calculus 10

Human agency 10

Incapacitation 13

Penology 2

Positivists 8

Principle of utility 7

Punishment 4

Rationality 10

Recidivism 11

Rehabilitation 15

Reintegration 18

Restitutive justice 9

Retribution 10

Retributive justice 9

Selective incapacitation 14

Specific deterrence 11

DISCUSSION QUESTIONS

1. Discuss the implications for a society that decides to eliminate all sorts of punishment in favor of forgiveness.

2. Why do we take pleasure in the punishment of wrongdoers? Is it a good or bad thing that we take pleasure in punishment? What evolutionary purpose does punishment serve?

3. Discuss the assumptions about human nature held by the classical thinkers. Are we rational, seekers of pleasure, and free moral agents? If so, does it make sense to try to rehabilitate criminals?

4. Discuss the assumptions underlying positivism in terms of the treatment of offenders. Do they support Garofalo's idea of individualized justice

based on the danger the offender posed to society or von Liszt's idea of individualized justice based on the rehabilitative potential of the offender?

5. Which justification for punishment do you favor? Is it the one that you think "works" best in terms of preventing crime, or do you favor it because it fits your ideology?

6. What is your position on the hardness/softness issue relating to the U.S. stance on crime? We are tougher than other democracies. Is that acceptable to you? We are also softer than more authoritarian countries. Is that also acceptable to you? Why, or why not?

USEFUL INTERNET SITES

Please note that the sites listed can be accessed at edge.sagepub.com/stohrcorrections.

The Corrections Connection: http://www.corrections.com

A great source for all kinds of correctional topics—updated weekly

Philosophy of Punishment: http://www.iep.utm.edu/punishme

A large and diverse number of sites devoted to the topic of punishment

$SAGE edge™

Sharpen your skills with SAGE edge at **edge.sagepub.com/stohrcorrections**. SAGE edge for Students provides a personalized approach to help you accomplish your coursework goals in an easy-to-use learning environment. You'll find action plans, mobile-friendly eFlashcards, and quizzes as well as video, web, and resources and links to SAGE journal articles to support and expand on the concepts presented in this chapter.

2

Early Corrections

*From Ancient Times
to Colonial Jails
and Prisons*

TEST YOUR KNOWLEDGE

Test your present knowledge of correctional history by answering the following questions (some as true or false). Check your answers on page 533 after reading the chapter.

1. Certain themes appear over and over in the history of corrections. (True or false?)

2. The kind of punishment one received for wronging others in ancient civilizations often depended on the wealth and status of the offended party and on the offender. (True or false?)

3. Which of the following was the first type of correctional facility: prisons, bridewells, debtors' prisons, or jails?

4. Galley slavery ended when the technological innovation of sails was employed to propel ships. (True or false?)

5. Transportation was a means of filling the colonies of Great Britain with wealthy merchants and business people. (True or false?)

6. What was John Howard of 18th-century England best known for?

7. The concept of the *panopticon*, devised by Jeremy Bentham, included the ingenious combination of labor and money to improve conditions of prisons. (True or false?)

8. William Penn's great law was based on Quaker principles and de-emphasized the use of corporal and capital punishment. (True or false?)

LEARNING OBJECTIVES

- Explain the origins of corrections

- Discuss how what we do now in corrections is often grounded in historical experience (or a repeat of it)

- Compare the different types of corrections used historically

- Identify some of the key Enlightenment thinkers, their ideas, and how they changed corrections

- Describe colonial jails and early prisons in America and how they operated

- Compare early American prisons with early European and British prisons

NARRATIVE OF THREE MEN PLACED IN THE MISSOURI STATE PRISON FOR HELPING SLAVES ESCAPE VIA THE UNDERGROUND RAILROAD (1847)

George Thompson

A multitude attended us to the prison; and the office was crowded while we were loosed from our chain, stripped, examined, recorded, one side of our hair cut close—arrayed in shining colors, and another chain put upon each of us. . . . We were treated very ungentlemanly (by the Warden and Overseer)—charged with lying when we told the simple truth, in the honesty of our souls; and then threatened with punishment—denounced as worse than highway robbers, cut-throats, or wholesale murderers, and as meaner than chicken thieves—threatened with having our tongues wired—and other things too vile and wicked to repeat.

THE RULES

1. *You must not speak to any prisoner, out of your cell, nor to each other in your cell.*

2. *You must not look at any visitor—if it is your own brother, if you do, I'll flog you.*

3. You must always take off your cap, when speaking to an officer, or when an officer speaks to you.

4. You must call no convict "Mr."

Frequently afterwards, we were checked for applying Mr. to a convict.

(This is the real-world narrative of what happened when three men were first placed in the Missouri State Prison for helping slaves escape via the Underground Railroad. This account of how they were treated that first night is by George Thompson [1847, pp. 132–133], from his book *Prison Life and Reflections*.)

Video 2.1: Secrets of the Tower of London

••• INTRODUCTION: THE EVOLVING PRACTICE OF CORRECTIONS

The history of corrections is riddled with the best of intentions and the worst of abuses. Correctional practices and facilities (e.g., galley slavery, transportation, jails and prisons, and community corrections) were created, in part, to remove the "riffraff"—both poor and criminal—from urban streets or at least to control and shape them. Prisons and community corrections were also created to avoid the use of more violent or coercive responses to such folk. In this chapter and the next, the focus is on exploring the history of the Western world's correctional operations and then American corrections specifically and the recurring themes that run through this history and define it.

It is somewhat ironic that one of the best early analyses of themes and practices in American prisons and jails was completed by two French visitors to the United States—*Gustave de Beaumont* and *Alexis de Tocqueville*—who experienced the virtual birthing of prisons themselves while the country was in its relative infancy, in 1831 (Beaumont & Tocqueville, 1833/1964). Tocqueville, as a 26-year-old French magistrate, brought along his friend Beaumont, supposedly to study America's newly minted prisons for nine months. They ended up also observing the workings of its law, its government and political system, and its race relations, among other things (Damrosch, 2010; Tocqueville, 1835/2004).

| **FIGURE** *2.1* | Key Events in Corrections: Ancient Times to 1789 A.D. |

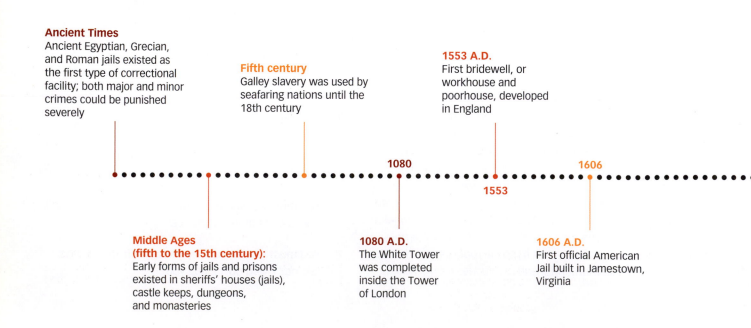

Ancient Times
Ancient Egyptian, Grecian, and Roman jails existed as the first type of correctional facility; both major and minor crimes could be punished severely

Fifth century
Galley slavery was used by seafaring nations until the 18th century

1553 A.D.
First bridewell, or workhouse and poorhouse, developed in England

1080

1606

1553

Middle Ages (fifth to the 15th century):
Early forms of jails and prisons existed in sheriffs' houses (jails), castle keeps, dungeons, and monasteries

1080 A.D.
The White Tower was completed inside the Tower of London

1606 A.D.
First official American Jail built in Jamestown, Virginia

The irony is that as outsiders and social critics, Beaumont and Tocqueville could so clearly see what others, namely Americans, who were thought to have "invented prisons" and who worked in them, were blind to. In this chapter, we will try to "see" what those early French visitors observed about Western—and specifically American—correctional operations.

Few visitors to the United States—or residents for that matter—explored or commented on the early correctional experience for women, *Dorothea Dix* being a notable exception. (There will be more about her and her observations about the state of corrections in 1845 in Chapter 3). Yet some of the themes that run through the practice of corrections apply to women and girls as well—but with a twist. Women have always represented only a small fraction of the correctional population in both prisons and jails, and the history of their experience with incarceration, as shaped by societal expectations of and for them, can be wholly different from that of men. As literal outsiders to what was the "norm" for inmates of prisons and jails and as a group whose rights and abilities were legally and socially controlled on the outside more than that of men and boys, women's experience in corrections history is worth studying and will be more fully explored in Chapter 11.

What is clear from the Western history of corrections is that what was *intended* when prisons, jails, and reformatories were conceived and *how they actually operated*, then and now, were and are often two very different things (Rothman, 1980). As social critics ourselves, we can use the history of corrections to identify a series of "themes" that run through correctional practice, even up to today. Such themes will reinforce the tried, yet true, maxim, "Those who cannot remember the past are condemned to repeat it" (Santayana, 1905, p. 284). Too often, we do not know or understand our history of corrections, and as a consequence, we are forever repeating it.

PHOTO 2.1: In 1831, Alexis de Tocqueville, as a 26-year-old French magistrate, brought along his friend Gustave de Beaumont to study America's newly minted prisons.

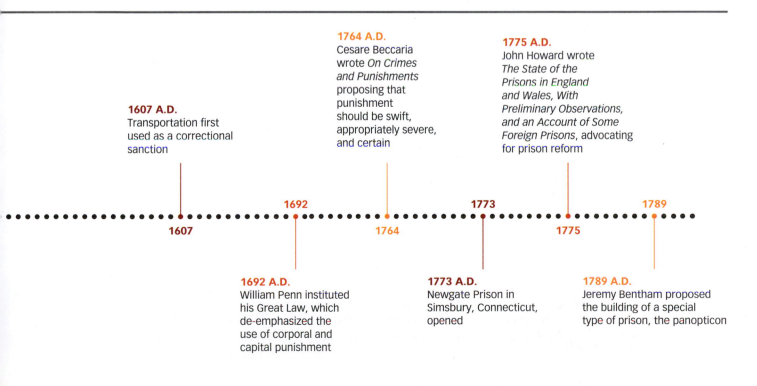

1607 A.D.
Transportation first used as a correctional sanction

1692 A.D.
William Penn instituted his Great Law, which de-emphasized the use of corporal and capital punishment

1764 A.D.
Cesare Beccaria wrote *On Crimes and Punishments* proposing that punishment should be swift, appropriately severe, and certain

1773 A.D.
Newgate Prison in Simsbury, Connecticut, opened

1775 A.D.
John Howard wrote *The State of the Prisons in England and Wales, With Preliminary Observations, and an Account of Some Foreign Prisons*, advocating for prison reform

1789 A.D.
Jeremy Bentham proposed the building of a special type of prison, the panopticon

1607   1692   1764   1773   1775   1789

THEMES: TRUTHS THAT UNDERLIE CORRECTIONAL PRACTICE

There are some themes that have been almost eerily constant, *vis-à-vis* corrections, over the decades and even centuries. Some such themes are obvious, such as the influence that money—or its lack—exerts over virtually all correctional-policy decisions. Political sentiments and the desire to make changes also have had tremendous influence over the shape of corrections in the past. Other themes are less apparent but no less potent in their effect on correctional operations. For instance, there appears to be an evolving sense of compassion or humanity that, though not always clear in the short term, in practice, or in policy or statute, has underpinned reform-based decisions about corrections and its operation, at least in theory, throughout its history in the United States. The creation of the prison, with a philosophy of penitence (hence the *penitentiary*), was a grand reform itself, and as such, it represented, in theory at least, a major improvement over the brutality of punishment that characterized early English and European law and practice (Orland, 1995).

Some social critics do note, however, that the prison and the expanded use of other such social institutions also served as a *social control* mechanism to remove punishment from public view while making the state appear more just (Foucault, 1979; M. Welch, 2004). This is not to argue that such grand reforms in their idealistic form, such as prisons, were not primarily constructed out of the need to control, but rather, there were philanthropic, religious, and other forces aligned that also influenced their creation and design, if not so much their eventual and practical operation (Hirsch, 1992). Also of note, the social control function becomes most apparent when less powerful populations, such as the poor, minorities, the young, or females, are involved, as will be discussed in the following chapters.

Other than the influence of money and politics and a sense of greater compassion and humanity in correctional operation, the following themes are also apparent in corrections history: the question of how to use labor and technology (which are hard to decouple from monetary considerations); a decided religious influence; the intersection of class, race, age, and gender in shaping one's experience in corrections; architecture as it is intermingled with supervision; methods of control; overcrowding; and finally, the fact that good intentions do not always translate into effective practice. Though far from exhaustive, this list contains some of the most salient issues that become apparent streams of influence as one reviews the history of corrections. As was discussed in Chapter 1, some of the larger philosophical (and political) issues, such as conceptions of right and wrong and whether it is best to engage in retribution or rehabilitation (or both, or neither, along with incapacitation, deterrence, and reintegration) using correctional sanctions, are also clearly associated with correctional change and operation.

EARLY PUNISHMENTS IN WESTERNIZED COUNTRIES

Human beings, throughout recorded history, have devised ingenious ways to punish their kind for real or perceived transgressions. Among tribal groups and in more developed civilizations, such punishment might include, among other tortures, whipping, branding, mutilation, drowning, suffocation, executions, and banishment (which, in remote areas, was tantamount to a death sentence). The extent of the punishment often depended on the wealth and status of the offended party and the offender. Those accused or found guilty who were richer were often allowed to make amends by recompensing the victim or his or her family, whereas those who were poorer and of lesser status were likely to suffer some sort of bodily punishment. Whatever the approach and for whatever the reason, some sort of punishment was often called for as a means of balancing the scales of justice, whether to appease a god or gods or later Lady Justice.

As David Garland (1990) recounts, "Ancient societies and 'primitive' social groups often invested the penal process with a wholly religious meaning, so that punishment was understood as a necessary sacrifice to an aggrieved deity" (p. 203). As urbanization took hold, however, and transgressions were less tolerated among an increasingly diverse people, the ancients and their governing bodies were more likely to designate a structure as appropriate for holding people. For the most part, such buildings or other means of confining people were often used to ensure that the accused was held over for trial or sometimes just for punishment (Orland, 1975, p. 13). Fines, mutilation, drawing and quartering, and capital punishment were popular ways to handle those accused or convicted of crimes (Harris, 1973; Orland, 1975).

> Although mutilation ultimately disappeared from English law, the brutality of Anglo-Saxon criminal punishment continued unabated into the eighteenth century. In the thirteenth century, offenders were commonly broken on the wheel for treason. A 1530 act authorized poisoners to be boiled alive. Burning was the penalty for high treason and heresy, as well as for murder of a husband by a wife or of a master by a servant. Unlike the punishment of boiling, that of burning remained lawful in England until 1790. In practice, and as a kindness, women were strangled before they were burned. The right hand was taken off for aggravated murder. Ordinary hangings were frequent, and drawing and quartering, where the hanged offender was publicly disemboweled and his still-beating heart held up to a cheering multitude, was not uncommon.
>
> In addition, until the mid-19th century, English law permitted a variety of "summary" punishments. Both men and women (the latter until 1817) were flagellated in public for minor offenses. For more serious misdemeanors, there was the pillory, which was not abolished in England until 1837. With his face protruding though its beams and his hands through the holes, the offender was helpless. Sometimes, he was nailed through the ears to the framework of the pillory with the hair of his head and beard shaved; occasionally, he was branded. Thereafter, some offenders were carried back to prison to endure additional tortures. (Orland, 1975, p. 15)

THE FIRST JAILS

Jails were the first type of correctional facility to develop, and in some form, they have existed for several thousand years. Whether pits, dungeons, or caves were used or the detainees were tied to a tree, ancient people all had ways of holding people until a judgment was made or implemented (Irwin, 1985; Mattick, 1974; Zupan, 1991).

According to Johnston (2009), punishment is referenced in a work written in 2000 B.C. and edited by Confucius. The Old Testament of the Bible refers to the use of imprisonment from 2040 to 164 B.C. in Egypt, as well as in ancient Assyria and Babylon. Ancient Greece and Rome reserved harsher physical punishments for slaves, whereas citizens might be subjected to fines, exile, imprisonment, death, or some combination of these (Harris, 1973).

> Ancient Roman society was a slave system. To punish wrongdoers, *capitis diminutio maxima*—the forfeiture of citizenship—was used. Criminals became penal slaves. Doomed men were sent to hard labor in the Carrara marble quarries, metal mines, and sulphur pits. The most common punishment was whipping— and in the case of free men, it was accompanied by the shaving of the head, for the shorn head was the mark of the slave. (Harris, 1973, p. 14)

Early versions of *gaols* (or jails) and prisons existed in English castle keeps and dungeons and Catholic monasteries. These prisons and jails (not always distinguishable in form or function) held political adversaries and common folk, either as a way to punish them or incapacitate them or to hold them over for judgment by a secular or religious authority. Sometimes, people might be held as a means of extorting a fine (Johnston, 2009). The

AP Video 2.1: Tom Mooney in Gaol

Audio 2.1: Reading Gaol, Where Oscar Wilde Was Imprisoned, Unlocks Its Gates for Art

use of these early forms of jail was reportedly widespread in England, even a thousand years ago. By the ninth century, Alfred the Great had legally mandated that imprisonment might be used to punish (Irwin, 1985). King Henry II, in 1166, required that where no gaol existed in English counties, one should be built (Zupan, 1991) "in walled towns and royal castles" (Orland, 1975, pp. 15–16) but only for the purpose of holding the accused for trial. In Elizabethan England, innkeepers made a profit by using their facility as a gaol.

Such imprisonment in these or other gaols was paid for by the prisoners or through their work. Those who were wealthy could pay for more comfortable accommodations while incarcerated. "When the Marquis de Sade was confined in the Bastille, he brought his own furnishings and paintings, his library, a live-in valet, and two dogs. His wife brought him gourmet food" (Johnston, 2009, p. 12S). The Catholic Church maintained its own jails and prison-like facilities across the European continent, administered by bishops or other church officials.

In fact, the Catholic Church's influence on the development of Westernized corrections was intense in the Middle Ages (medieval Europe from the fifth to the 15th centuries) and might be felt even today. As a means of shoring up its power base *vis-à-vis* feudal and medieval lords and kings, the Catholic Church maintained not only its own forms of prisons and jails but also its own ecclesiastical courts (Garland, 1990). Though proscribed from drawing blood, except during the Inquisition, the church often turned its charges over to secular authorities for physical punishment. But while in their care and in their monasteries for punishment, the Catholic Church required "solitude, reduced diet, and reflection, sometimes for extended periods of time" (Johnston, 2009, p. 14S). Centuries later, the first prisons in the United States and Europe, then heavily influenced by Quakers and Protestant denominations in the states, copied the Catholics' monastic emphasis on silence, placing prisoners in small, austere rooms where one's penitence might be reflected upon—practices and architecture that, to some extent, still resonate today.

GALLEY SLAVERY

Journal Article 2.1: Early Use of Imprisonment as Punishment

Another form of "corrections," **galley slavery**, was used sparingly by the ancient Greeks and Romans but more regularly in the late Middle Ages in Europe and England, and it stayed in use until roughly the 1700s. Under Elizabeth I, in 1602, a sentence to galley servitude was decreed as an alternative to the death sentence (Orland, 1975). Pope Pius VI (who was pope from 1775 to 1799) also reportedly employed it (Johnston, 2009, p. 12S). Galley slavery was used as a sentence for crimes as a means of removing the poor from the streets. It also served the purpose of providing the requisite labor—rowing—needed to propel ships for seafaring nations interested in engagement in trade and warfare. For instance, galley slaves were reportedly used by Columbus (Johnston, 2009). The "slaves" were required to row the boat until they collapsed from exhaustion, hunger, or disease; often, they sat in their own excrement (M. Welch, 2004). Under Pope Pius, galley slaves were entitled to bread each day, and their sentences ranged from three years to life (Johnston, 2009). Though we do not have detailed records of how such a sentence was carried out, and we can be sure that its implementation varied to some degree from vessel to vessel, the reports that do exist indicate that galley slavery was essentially a sentence to death. Galley slavery ended when the labor was no longer needed on ships because of the technological development of sails.

POVERTY AND BRIDEWELLS, DEBTORS' PRISONS, AND HOUSES OF CORRECTION

However, galley slavery could only absorb a small number of the poor who began to congregate in towns and cities in the Middle Ages. Feudalism—and the order it imposed—was disintegrating; wars (particularly the Crusades prosecuted by the Catholic Church) and intermittent plagues did claim thousands of lives, but populations were stabilizing and increasing, and there were not enough jobs, housing, or food for the poor. As the cities became more urbanized and as more and more poor people congregated in them,

Galley slavery: A sentence forcing the convict to work as a rower on a ship.

IN FOCUS 2.1

The Tower of London

PHOTO 2.2A: The infamous White Tower inside the Tower of London complex.

PHOTO 2.2B: Side view of the Tower of London as it appears today.

There are few international iconic prison images as prominent as that of the Tower of London, located on the River Thames in the center of London, England. Begun after 1066, when William the Conqueror captured the city of Saxon London in the Norman invasion, the centerpiece of this castle complex, the White Tower, was completed in roughly 1080 (Impey & Parnell, 2011). The Tower of London today has a number of buildings, including the White Tower, along with several towers and gates on its double walls. At one time, it included a moat, which has since been filled in. Sited in old London, today it is surrounded by modern buildings and near-ancient structures alike. Over the centuries, it has been added to by various kings and used to defend the city, as a royal palace and a symbol of power for royalty, as a mint for royal coinage, as an armory, as a treasury for the royal jewels, as a conservator of the King's Court's records, as a kind of zoo for exotic animals gifted to the royalty, as a tourist attraction for centuries, and, for our purposes, as a prison and a place of execution.

Its role as a prison began early in 1100, lasting until the 1820s, and then it was a prison again during World War II (Impey & Parnell, 2011). For the most part, there were no separate prison quarters for its mostly exalted prisoners, other than a shed constructed in 1687 for prison soldiers. Therefore, political and other prisoners were accommodated in whatever quarters were available. For instance, Anne Boleyn, who was Henry the VIII's second wife, was married at the tower; executed there three years later, in 1526; and buried there. The young Princess Elizabeth (Anne's daughter) was also held at the tower by her half-sister, Queen Mary I, until Elizabeth attained the throne as Elizabeth I. Sir Thomas More spent a year (1534) imprisoned in the tower before his execution, and Sir Walter Raleigh spent 13 years (1603–1616) imprisoned in the tower; both men were imprisoned for allegedly committing treason. Notably, William Penn, discussed in other parts of this book, was imprisoned at the tower for seven months in 1668–1669 for pamphleteering about his Quaker religion. Their incarceration in the tower, as well as many others of rank and wealth, was not as hard as it would have been if they had been sent to public prisons of the time—and even sometimes included luxurious accommodations and servants. Torture did happen at the tower (the use of the rack and manacles, etc.), but its use was relatively rare, as it had to be sanctioned by a special council. Executions occurred inside the walls of the Tower of London, but most occurred on nearby Tower Hill or elsewhere near the complex.

DISCUSSION QUESTIONS

1. Why do you think the Tower of London has survived so long?

2. If you were going to be held in a prison or jail, would you prefer the "tower" or more modern correctional institutions? Justify your answer.

governmental entities responded in an increasingly severe fashion to the poor's demands for resources (Irwin, 1985). These responses were manifested in the harsh repression of dissent, increased use of death sentences and other punishments as deterrence and spectacle, the increased use of jailing to guarantee the appearance of the accused at trial, the development of poorhouses or bridewells and debtors' prisons, and the use of "transportation," discussed later (Foucault, 1979; Irwin, 1985).

Eighteenth-century England saw the number of crimes subject to capital punishment increase to as many as 225, for such offenses as rioting over wages or food (the Riot Act) or for "blacking" one's face so as to be camouflaged when killing deer in the king's or a lord's forest (the Black Act) (Ignatieff, 1978, p. 16). New laws regarding forgery resulted in two thirds of those convicted of it being executed. Rather than impose the most serious sentence for many of these crimes, however, judges would often opt for the use of transportation, whipping, or branding. Juries would also balk at imposing the death sentence for a relatively minor offense and so would sometimes value property that was stolen at less than it was worth in order to ensure a lesser sentence for the defendant. In the latter part of the 1700s, a sentence of imprisonment might be used in lieu of or in addition to these other punishments.

Bridewells, or buildings constructed to hold and whip "beggars, prostitutes, and nightwalkers" (Orland, 1975, p. 16) and later to serve as places of detention, filled this need; their use began in London in 1553 (Kerle, 2003). The name came from the first such institution, which was developed at Bishop Ridley's place at St. Bridget's Well; all subsequent similar facilities were known as bridewells.

Bridewells were also workhouses, used as leverage to extract fines or repayment of debt or the labor to replace them. Such facilities did not separate people by gender or age or criminal and noncriminal status, nor were their inmates fed and clothed properly, and sanitary conditions were not maintained. As a consequence of these circumstances, bridewells were dangerous and diseased places where if one could not pay a "fee" for food, clothing, or release, the inmate—and possibly his or her family—might be doomed (Orland, 1975; Pugh, 1968). The use of bridewells spread throughout Europe and the British colonies, as it provided a means of removing the poor and displaced from the streets while also making a profit (Kerle, 2003). Such a profit was made by the wardens, keepers, and gaolers—the administrators of bridewells, houses of correction (each county in England was authorized to build one in 1609), and gaols—who, though unpaid, lobbied for the job, as it was so lucrative. They made money by extracting it from their inmates. If an inmate could not pay, he or she might be left to starve in filth or be tortured or murdered by the keeper for nonpayment (Orland, 1975, p. 17).

Notably, being sent to debtors' prison was something that still occurred even after the American Revolution. In fact, James Wilson, a signer of the Constitution (and reportedly one of its main architects) and a Supreme Court justice, was imprisoned in such a place twice while serving on the Court. He had speculated on land to the west and lost a fortune in the process (Davis, 2008).

TRANSPORTATION

Yet another means of "corrections" that was in use by Europeans for roughly 350 years, from the founding of the Virginia Colony in 1607, was **transportation** (Feeley, 1991). Also used to rid cities and towns of the chronically poor or the

Bridewells:
Workhouses constructed to hold and whip or otherwise punish "beggars, prostitutes, and nightwalkers" and later to serve as places of detention.

Transportation: A sentence exiling convicts and transporting them to a penal colony.

Public domain

PHOTO 2.3: Drawing of the inside of a Bridewell in London (1808–1811). Bridewells helped criminalize social problems, like poverty.

criminally inclined, transportation, as with bridewells and gaols, involved a form of privatized corrections, whereby those sentenced to transportation were sold to a ship's captain. He would, in turn, sell their labor as indentured servants, usually to do agricultural work, to colonials in America (Maryland, Virginia, and Georgia were partially populated through this method) and to white settlers in Australia. Transportation ended in the American colonies with the Revolutionary War but was practiced by France to populate Devil's Island in French Guiana until 1953 (M. Welch, 2004). M. Welch notes that transportation was a very popular sanction in Europe:

> Russia made use of Siberia; Spain deported prisoners to Hispaniola; Portugal exiled convicts to North Africa, Brazil and Cape Verde; Italy herded inmates to Sicily; Denmark relied on Greenland as a penal colony; Holland shipped convicts to the Dutch East Indies. (p. 29)

In America, transportation provided needed labor to colonies desperate for it. "Following a 1718 law in England, all felons with sentences of 3 years or more were eligible for transport to America. Some were given a choice between hanging or transport" (Johnston, 2009, p. 13S).

It is believed that about 50,000 convicts were deposited on American shores from English gaols. If they survived their servitude, which ranged from one to five years, they became free and might be given tools or even land to make their way in the New World (Orland, 1975, p. 18). Once the American Revolution started, such prisoners from England were transported to Australia, and when settlers there protested the number of entering offenders, the prisoners were sent to penal colonies in that country, as well as in New Zealand and Gibraltar (Johnston, 2009).

One of the most well-documented penal colonies was **Norfolk Island**, 1,000 miles off the Australian coast. Established in 1788 as a place designated for prisoners from England and Australia, it was regarded as a brutal and violent island prison where inmates were poorly fed, clothed, and housed and were mistreated by staff and their fellow inmates (Morris, 2002). Morris, in his semifictional account of efforts by *Alexander Maconochie* to reform Norfolk, notes that Machonochie, an ex–naval captain, asked to be transferred to Norfolk, usually an undesirable placement, so that he could put into practice some ideas he had about prison reform. He served as the warden there from 1840 to 1844. What was true in this story was that "in four years, Maconochie transformed what was one of the most brutal convict settlements in history into a controlled, stable, and productive environment that achieved such success that upon release his prisoners came to be called 'Maconochie's Gentlemen'" (Morris, 2002, book jacket). Maconochie's ideas included the belief that inmates should be rewarded for good behavior through a system of marks, which could lead to privileges and early release; that they should be treated with respect; and that they should be adequately fed and housed. Such revolutionary ideas, for their time, elicited alarm from Maconochie's superiors, and he was removed from his position after only four years. His ideas, however, were adopted decades later when the concepts of *good time* and *parole* were developed in Ireland and the United States. In addition, his ideas about adequately feeding and clothing inmates were held in common by reformers who came before him, such as John Howard and William Penn, and those who came after him, such as Dorothea Dix.

? ETHICAL ISSUE 2.1

What Would You Do?

You are the manager of a bridewell in 1600s England. Most of the people you house are desperately poor and displaced people (people from the countryside who have moved into the towns with few skills or connections to help them). Your income derives from charging the inmates of your bridewell for their keep, but many of them do not have the funds to pay you, so you have some difficulty paying your own bills and are in danger of defaulting on debts and ending up in debtors' prison yourself. Yet if you don't feed and clothe them, some of your charges are likely to die of starvation, exposure, or typhus (gaol fever). What do you do? What do you think John Howard would recommend that you do?

Norfolk Island: An English penal colony, 1,000 miles off the Australian coast, regarded as a brutal and violent island prison where inmates were poorly fed, clothed, and housed and were mistreated by staff and their fellow inmates.

••• ENLIGHTENMENT—PARADIGM SHIFT

SPOCK FALLS IN LOVE

As noted in Chapter 1, the Enlightenment period, lasting roughly from the 17th through the 18th century in England, Europe, and America, spelled major changes in thought about crime and corrections. But then, it was a time of paradigmatic shifts in many aspects of the Western experience, as societies became more secular and open. Becoming a more secular culture meant that there was more focus on humans on Earth, rather than in the afterlife, and as a consequence, the arts, sciences, and philosophy flourished. In such periods of human history, creativity manifests itself in innovations in all areas of experience; the orthodoxy in thought and practice is often challenged and sometimes overthrown in favor of new ideas and even radical ways of doing things (K. C. Davis, 2008). Whether in the sciences with Englishman Isaac Newton (1643–1727), philosophy and rationality with the Englishwoman Anne Viscountess Conway (1631–1679), feminist philosophy with the Englishwoman Damaris Cudworth Masham (1659–1708), philosophy and history with the Scotsman David Hume (1711–1776), literature and philosophy with the Frenchman Voltaire (1694–1778), literature and philosophy with the Briton Mary Wollstonecraft (1759–1797), or the Founding Fathers of the United States (e.g., Samuel Adams, James Madison, Benjamin Franklin, Thomas Paine, and Thomas Jefferson), new ideas and beliefs were proposed and explored in every sphere of the intellectual enterprise (J. Duran, 1996; Frankel, 1996). Certainly, the writings of *John Locke* (1632–1704) and his conception of liberty and human rights provided the philosophical underpinnings for the Declaration of Independence, as penned by Thomas Jefferson. As a result of the Enlightenment, the French Revolution, beginning in 1789, was also about rejecting one form of government—the absolute monarchy—for something that was to be more democratic and liberty based. (Notably, the French path to democracy was not straight and included a dalliance with other dictators, such as Napoleon Bonaparte, who came to power in 1799.)

Such changes in worldviews or paradigms—as Thomas Kuhn (1962) explained in his well-known work, *The Structure of Scientific Revolutions*, which discusses nonlinear shifts in scientific theory—usually come after evidence mounts, and the holes in old ways of perceiving become all too apparent. The old theory simply cannot accommodate the new evidence. Such an event was illustrated on a micro, or individual, level in an episode of the original *Star Trek* television show when Spock (the logical, unemotional, and unattached second officer) fell in love with a woman for the first time after breathing in the spores of a magical flower on a mysterious planet. Those who experienced the Enlightenment period, much like reformers and activists of the Progressive Era (1880s to the 1920s) and civil rights era (1950s and 1960s) in the United States that were to follow centuries later, experienced a paradigm shift regarding crime and justice. Suddenly, as if magic spores had fundamentally reshaped thought and suffused it with kind regard, if not love, for others, humans seemed to realize that change in crime policy and practice was called for, and they set about devising ways to accomplish it.

PHOTO 2.4: Philosopher John Locke's writings and his conception of liberty and human rights helped to provide the philosophical underpinnings for the Declaration of Independence.

JOHN HOWARD

John Howard (1726–1790) was one such person who acted as a change agent. As a sheriff of Bedford in England and as a man who had personally experienced incarceration as a prisoner of war himself (held captive by French privateers), he was *enlightened* enough to "see" that gaols in England and Europe should be different, and he spent the remainder of his life trying to reform them (J. Howard, 1775/2000; Johnston, 2009). Howard's genius was his main insight regarding corrections: that corrections should not be privatized in the sense that jailers were "paid" by inmates a fee for their food, clothing, and housing (an inhumane and often illogical practice, as most who were incarcerated were desperately poor, a circumstance that explained the incarceration of many in the first place). Howard believed that the state or government had a responsibility to provide sanitary and separate conditions and decent food and water for those they incarcerated. His message of reform included these central tenets:

1. The fee system for jails should be ended.

2. Inmates should be separated by gender and offense. (Single celling would be optimal.)

3. Inmates should be provided with sanitary conditions and clean and healthful food and water.

4. Staff should serve as a moral model for inmates.

5. Jails and prisons should have a set of standards and be independently inspected to ensure these standards are maintained.

? ETHICAL ISSUE 2.2

What Would You Do?

You are a Tory Loyalist (to the Crown of England, King George III) in the Connecticut colony in 1777. Because you are an outspoken critic of the American Revolution, you are imprisoned in the Newgate Prison in Simsbury, Connecticut, for the duration of the war. Provisions in the prison are horrid, with minimal food and dark, dank conditions in the mine shaft; however, the people guarding you are decent and do what they can to make you and the other prisoners comfortable. Because of the distraction of the war, however, security is not as tight as it might be, and you see an opportunity to escape. What do you think you would do? If you escaped, would you try to fight on the side of England? What will be the consequences for your family (you have a wife and four children at home) and your family business (you are tea manufacturer) should you do this? What do you think John Locke would recommend?

His humanity was apparent, in that he promoted these ideas in England and all over the European continent during his lifetime. He was able to do so because he inherited money from his father, his sister, and his grandmother and used those monies to improve the lives of the tenants on his land and the inmates in correctional facilities. His major written work, *The State of the Prisons in England and Wales, With Preliminary Observations, and an Account of Some Foreign Prisons* (1775/2000), detailed the horror that was experienced in the filthy and torturous gaols of England and Europe, noting that despite the fact that there were 200 crimes for which capital punishment might be prescribed, far more inmates died from diseases contracted while incarcerated. (Note to reader: The English used by Howard in the following quote sometimes substitutes the letter *f* for the letter *s*.):

> I traveled again into the counties where I had been; and, indeed, into all the reft; examining Houfes of Correction, City and Town-Gaols. I beheld in many of them, as well as in the County-Gaols, a complication of diftrefs: but my attention was principally fixed by the gaol-fever, and the fmall-pox, which I faw prevailing to the deftruction of multitudes, not only of felons in their dungeons, but of debtors alfo. (p. 2)

John Howard (1775/2000) found that gaol fever was widespread in all kinds of correctional institutions of the time: bridewells, gaols, debtors' prisons, and houses of correction. Notably, in larger cities, there were clear distinctions among these facilities and whom they held, but in smaller towns and counties, there were not. In the neglect of inmates and the underfunding of the facilities, Howard found them all to be quite similar.

He noted that in some bridewells, there was no provision at all made for feeding inmates. Though inmates of bridewells were to be sentenced to hard labor, he found that in many, there was little work to do and no tools provided to do it: "The prifoners have neither tools, nor materials of any kind; but fpend their time in floth, profanenefs and debauchery, to a degree which, in fome of thofe houfes that I have feen, is extremely fhocking" (p. 8). He found that the allotment for food in county jails was not much better, remarking that in some, there was none for debtors, the criminal, or the accused alike. He noted that these inmates, should they survive their suffering, would then enter communities or other facilities in rags and spread disease wherever they went.

In his census of correctional facilities (including debtors' prisons, jails, and houses of correction or bridewells) in England and Wales, John Howard (1775/2000) found that petty offenders composed about 16% of inmates, about 60% were debtors, and about 24% were felons (which included those awaiting trial, those convicted and awaiting their execution or transportation, and those serving a sentence of imprisonment) (Ignatieff, 1978, p. 25). Ironically, Howard eventually died from typhus, also known as gaol fever, after touring several jails and prisons in Eastern Europe, specifically the prisons of tsarist Russia.

BENTHAM AND BECCARIA

Audio 2.2: Burning Down the Panopticon

As mentioned in Chapter 1, the philosophers and reformers Jeremy Bentham (1748–1832) in England and Cesare Beccaria (1738–1794) in Italy, separately but both during the Enlightenment period, decried the harsh punishment meted out for relatively minor offenses in their respective countries and, as a consequence, emphasized *certainty* over the severity and celerity components of the deterrence theory they independently developed. Beccaria (1764/1963), in his classic work *On Crimes and Punishments*, wrote,

> In order that punishment should not be an act of violence perpetrated by one or many upon a private citizen, it is essential that it should be public, speedy, necessary, the minimum possible in the given circumstances, proportionate to the crime, and determined by the law. (p. 113)

He argued that knowledge, as that provided by the sciences and enlightenment, was the only effective antidote to "foul-mouthed ignorance" (p. 105).

IN FOCUS 2.2

Modern-Day John Howard—Dr. Ken Kerle

The Corrections Section of the Academy of Criminal Justice Sciences (ACJS) established the John Howard Award in 2009 and gave the first one to a modern-day John Howard, Ken Kerle (retired managing editor of *American Jails* magazine). Kerle has spent much of his adult life trying to improve jail standards, both here in the United States and abroad. As part of that effort, he has visited hundreds of jails in this country and around the world. He has advised countless jail managers about how they might improve their operations. He has increased the transmission of information and the level of discussion between academicians and practitioners by encouraging the publication of scholars' work in *American Jails* magazine and their presentations at the American Jails Association meetings and by urging practitioners to attend ACJS meetings. Kerle (2003) also published a book on jails titled *Exploring Jail Operations*.

DISCUSSION QUESTION

1. Knowing how much the old and the new John Howards of this world accomplish, what are the things that hold you back from becoming such a person yourself?

Bentham (1789/1969) also proposed, in his *Plan of Construction of a Panopticon Penitentiary House*—though the funding of it was not approved by King George III—the building of a special type of prison. As per Bentham, the building of a private prison-like structure—the **panopticon**, which he would operate—that ingeniously melded the ideas of improved supervision with architecture (because of its rounded, open, and unobstructed views) would greatly enhance supervision of inmates. Such a recognition of the benefits of some architectural styles as complementary to enhanced supervision was indeed prescient, as it presaged modern jail and prison architecture. His proposed panopticon would be circular, with two tiers of cells on the outside and a guard tower in its center, with the central area also topped by a large skylight. The skylight and the correct angling of the tower were to ensure that the guard was able to observe all inmate behavior in the cells, though owing to a difference of level and the use of blinds, the keeper would be invisible to the inmates. A chapel would also be located in the center of the rounded structure. The cells were to be airy and large enough to accommodate the whole life of the inmates in that the cells were to "serve all purposes: work, sleep, meals, punishment, devotion" (Bentham, 1811/2003, p. 194). Somehow, Bentham notes in his plan, without elaboration, that the sexes were to be invisible to each other. He does not call for complete separation of all inmates, however, which becomes important when discussing the Pennsylvania and New York prisons in Chapter 3, but he does assert that the groups of inmates allowed to interact should be small, including only two to four persons (Bentham, 1811/2003, p. 195).

As an avowed admirer of John Howard, Bentham proposed that his Panopticon Penitentiary would include all of the reforms proposed by Howard and much more. Bentham (1811/2003) promised that inmates would be well fed, fully clothed, supplied with beds, supplied with warmth and light, kept from "strong or spirituous liquors" (p. 199), have their spiritual and medical needs fulfilled, be provided with opportunities for labor and

Panopticon: A prison design in which multitiered cells are built around a hub so that correctional staff can view all inmates without being observed.

PHOTO 2.5: The Stateville prison in Illinois was built as a panopticon, with rounded architecture and a central tower for officers. Panopticons were devised to enhance the supervision of inmates but may have been more effective at enhancing the observation of officers by inmates.

education ("to convert the prison into a school" [p. 199]), "share in the produce" (p. 200) to incentivize the labor, be taught a trade so that they could survive once released, and be helped to save for old age (pp. 199–200). He would also personally pay a fine for every escape, insure inmates' lives to prevent their deaths, and submit regular reports to the Court of the King's Bench on the status of the prison's operation (pp. 199–200). More-over, he proposed that the prison would be open in many respects, not just to dignitaries but to regular citizens, and daily, as a means of preventing abuse that might occur in secret. Bentham also recommended the construction of his prisons on a large scale across England, such that one would be built every 30 miles, or a good day's walk by a man. He planned, as he wrote in his 1830 diatribe against King George III, wryly titled "History of the War Between Jeremy Bentham and George the Third—by One of the Belligerents," that "but for George the Third, all the prisoners in England would, years ago, have been under my management. But for George the Third, all the paupers in the country would, long ago, have been under my management" (Bentham, 1811/2003, p. 195).

Though his plan, in theory, was laudable and really visionary for his time and ours, he hoped to make much coin as recompense for being a private prison manager—to the tune of 60 pounds sterling per prisoner, which, when assigned to all inmates across England, was a considerable sum (Bentham, 1811/2003, p. 195). What stopped him—and the reason why he was so angry with his sovereign—was King George's unwilling-ness to sign the bill that would have authorized the funding and construction of the first panopticon. Bentham alleged that the king would not sign because the powerful Lord Spenser was concerned about the effect on the value of his property should a prison be located on or near it. Bentham's prison dream was dead, but eventually, he was awarded 23,000 pounds for his efforts (p. 207). It was left to others to build panopticon prisons in both Europe and the states in the coming years.

WILLIAM PENN

Video 2.2: Inside Eastern State Penitentiary

William Penn (1644–1718), a prominent Pennsylvania Colony governor and Quaker, was similarly influenced by Enlightenment thinking (though with the Quaker influence, his views were not so secular). Much like Bentham and Beccaria, Penn was not a fan of the harsh punishments, even executions, for relatively minor offenses that were meted out during his lifetime. While in England and as a result of his defense of religious free-dom and practice, he was incarcerated in the local jails on more than one occasion—and even in the Tower of London in 1669—for his promotion of the Quaker religion and defiance of the English Crown. He was freed only because of his wealth and connections (Penn, 1679/1981). As a consequence, when he had the power to change the law and its protections and reduce the severity of punishments, he did so. Many years later (in 1682), in Pennsylvania, he proposed and instituted his **Great Law**, which was based on Quaker principles and de-emphasized the use of corporal and capital punishment for all crimes but the most serious (Clear, Cole, & Reisig, 2011; Johnston, 2009; Zupan, 1991). His reforms substituted fines and jail time for corporal punishment. He promoted Pennsylvania as a haven for Quakers, who were persecuted in England and Europe gen-erally, and for a number of other religious minorities (Penn, 1679/1981). His ideas about juries, civil liberties, religious freedom, and the necessity of amending constitutions—so they are adaptable to changing times—influenced a number of American revolutionaries, including Benjamin Franklin and Thomas Paine.

Many of Penn's contemporaries were not of the same frame of mind, however, and after his death, the Great Law was repealed, and harsher punishments were again instituted in Pennsylvania, much as they existed in the rest of the colonies (Johnston, 2009; M. Welch, 2004). But the mark of his influence lived on in the development of some of America's first prisons, as you'll see in Chapter 3.

Much like Howard and Bentham, Penn was interested in reforming corrections, but he was particularly influenced by his Quaker sentiments regarding nonviolence and the

Great Law: William Penn's idea, based on Quaker principles, de-emphasized the use of corporal and capital punishment for all crimes but the most serious.

value of quiet contemplation. The early American prisons known as the Pennsylvania model prisons—the Walnut Street Jail (1790) in Philadelphia, Western Pennsylvania Prison (1826) in Pittsburgh, and Eastern Pennsylvania Prison (1829) in Philadelphia—incorporated these ideas (Johnston, 2009). Even the New York prison system (Auburn and Sing Sing), often juxtaposed with Pennsylvania prisons based on popular depiction by historians (see Beaumont and Tocqueville, 1833/1964), included contemplation time for inmates and a plan for single cells for inmates that reflected the same belief in the need for some solitude.

PHOTO 2.6: William Penn proposed and instituted his Great Law, which was based on Quaker principles and de-emphasized the use of corporal and capital punishment for all crimes but the most serious.

••• COLONIAL JAILS AND PRISONS

The first jail in America was built in Jamestown, Virginia, soon after the colony's founding in 1606 (Burns, 1975; Zupan, 1991). Massachusetts built a jail in Boston in 1635, and Maryland built a jail for the colony in 1662 (J. V. Roberts, 1997). The oldest standing jail in the United States was built in the late 1600s and is located in Barnstable, Massachusetts (Library of Congress, 2010). It was used by the sheriff to hold both males and females, along with his family, in upstairs, basement, and barn rooms. Men and women were held in this and other jails like it, mostly before they were tried for both serious and minor offenses, as punishment for offenses, or to ensure they were present for their own execution.

Such an arrangement as this—holding people in homes, inns, or other structures that were not originally designated or constructed as jails—was not uncommon in early colonial towns (Goldfarb, 1975; Irwin, 1985; Kerle, 2003). As in England, inmates of these early and colonial jails were required to pay a "fee" for their upkeep (the same fee system that John Howard opposed). Those who were wealthier could more easily buy their way out of incarceration, or if that was not possible because of the nature of the offense, they could at least ensure that they had more luxurious accommodations (Zupan, 1991). Even when jailers were paid a certain amount to feed and clothe inmates, they might be disinclined to do so, being that what they saved by not taking care of their charges they were able to keep (Zupan, 1991). As a result, inmates of early American jails were sometimes malnourished or starving. Moreover, in the larger facilities, they were crammed into unsanitary rooms, often without regard to separation by age, gender, or offense, conditions that also led to disease and early death. Nonetheless, Irwin (1985) does remark that generally, Americans fared better in colonial jails than their English and European cousins did in their own, as the arrangements were less formal and restrictive in the American jails and were more like rooming houses. Relatedly, Goldfarb (1975) remarks,

> Jails that did exist in the eighteenth century were run on a household model with the jailer and his family residing on the premises. The inmates were free to dress as they liked, to walk around freely and to provide their own food and other necessities. (p. 9)

As white people migrated across the continent of North America, the early western jails were much like their earlier eastern and colonial cousins, with makeshift structures and

Web 2.1: Newgate Prison

Web 2.2: Eastern State Penitentiary: A Prison With a Past

Old Nowgate Prison, near Hartford. Conn.

PHOTO 2.7: Newgate Prison, a working copper mine, served as an early colonial prison.

cobbled-together supervision serving as a means of holding the accused over for trial (Moynihan, 2002). In post–Civil War midwestern cities, disconnected outlaw gangs (such as the Jesse James Gang) were treated in a harsh manner. Some communities even built *rotary jails*, which were like human squirrel cages. Inside a secure building, these rotating steel cages, segmented into small "pie-shaped cells," were secured to the floor and could be spun at will by the sheriff (Goldfarb, 1975, p. 11).

Of course, without prisons in existence per se (we will discuss the versions of such institutions that did exist shortly), most punishments for crimes constituted relatively short terms in jails; public shaming (as in the stocks); physical punishments, such as flogging or the pillory; or banishment. Executions were also carried out, usually but not always for the most horrific of crimes, such as murder or rape, though in colonial America, many more crimes qualified for this punishment (Zupan, 1991). As in Europe and England at this time, those who were poorer or enslaved were more likely to experience the harshest punishments (Irwin, 1985; Zupan, 1991). Similar to Europe and England in this era, jails also held the mentally ill, along with debtors, drifters, transients, the inebriated, runaway slaves or servants, and the criminally involved (usually pretrial) (Cornelius, 2007).

Though the Walnut Street Jail, a portion of which was converted to a prison, is often cited as the first prison in the world, there were, as this recounting of history demonstrates, many precursors that were arguably "prisons" as well. One such facility, which also illustrates the makeshift nature of early prisons, was the **Newgate Prison in Simsbury, Connecticut** (named after the Newgate Prison in London). According to Phelps (1860/1996), this early colonial prison started as a copper mine, and during its 54 years of operation (from 1773 to 1827), some 800 inmates passed through its doors. The mine was originally worked in 1705, and one third of the taxes it paid to the town of Simsbury at that time was used to support Yale College (p. 15). "Burglary, robbery, and counterfeiting were punished for the first offense with imprisonment not exceeding ten years; second offence for life" (p. 26). Later, those loyal to the English Crown during the U.S. Revolutionary War—or Tories—were held at Newgate as well. Punishments by the "keeper of the prison" could range from shackles and fetters as restraints to "moderate whipping, not to exceed ten stripes" (p. 26). The inmates of Newgate prison were held—stored, really—in the bowels of the mine during the evening (by themselves and with no supervision) and during the day were forced to work the mine or were allowed to come to the surface to labor around the facility and in the community. Over the course of the history of this facility, there were several escapes, a number of riots, and the burning of the topside buildings by its inmates. Early versions of prisons also existed in other countries.

Newgate Prison in Simsbury, Connecticut: An early colonial prison (1773–1827) that started as a copper mine. Many of its inmates would work the mine during the day and sleep in it at night. During the Revolutionary War, some Loyalists to the English Crown were held here.

••• COMPARATIVE PERSPECTIVE

EARLY EUROPEAN AND BRITISH PRISONS

Some early European versions of prisons bucked the trend of harsh physical punishments even for minor offenses. Others—but only a few—even classified their inmates not just by economic and social status but by gender, age, and criminal offense. For instance, in the Le Stinche Prison, built in Florence, Italy, in the 1290s, the inmates were separated in this way (J. W. Roberts, 1997). Later, the Maison de Force Prison in Ghent, Belgium

PERSPECTIVE FROM A PRACTITIONER

Marianne Fisher-Giorlando, Board Member of Louisiana State Penitentiary Museum Foundation

Position: Board member of the Louisiana State Penitentiary Museum Foundation, commonly known as Angola Museum; chair of the Education Committee; and member of the Accession/Deaccession Committee

Location: Angola, Louisiana

What are your primary duties and responsibilities?

As chair of the Education Committee, I oversee the oral history project and the biannual symposium, in addition to the ongoing project of developing education programs. I also do the research and sometimes write the narratives for new and rotating exhibits.

The purpose of the Oral History Committee is to collect oral histories from present and former employees of the Louisiana Department of Public Safety and Corrections, past and present prisoners, and those who have lived at Angola as free people. The interviews will be used to complement exhibits and be available to researchers.

Symposiums are designed to educate the public about the history and contemporary policies, practices, and programs of Louisiana's correctional system. Symposium topics have included the history of Angola, prison music at Angola, and the recent one for 2014, "Farming on the Farm: Agricultural Operations at the Louisiana State Penitentiary at Angola."

In general, what does a typical day working in this position look like?

My day is never typical. It can start with a text, e-mail, or phone call requests, sometimes before 7 a.m. And I am involved in any one of the following activities or a bit of all of them in one day.

I work closely with the director of planning and development, Genny Nadler-Thomas, to schedule the exhibit calendar for the year. This plan is often revised, depending upon unanticipated events and opportunities. We just finished with a Smithsonian Museum on Main Street traveling exhibit, "The Way We Worked." From initial notice and

training for that exhibit, other museum employees and I worked on it off and on for more than two years.

The museum has a website where people can make inquiries about Angola. Requests that are sent to me can vary anywhere from, "Do you have a record of my ancestor who I just found out was incarcerated at Angola in the early 1900s," to "I was born at Angola," to a request from Warden Cain about how and why the present name of the convict cemetery is Point Lookout. The ancestor requests oftentimes include very sparse information, with only a name and a wide range of potential dates. I love digging out this information for people. They are always so happy to receive information about their long-lost relative.

Just recently, I interviewed the first female warden at Angola, who was appointed in the late 1970s. She is a legend at Angola for many reasons. She not only supervised *The Angolite*, the prison newsmagazine, but she went back to school to take journalism classes to "do the best job possible."

I also cowrote a $40,000 planning grant proposal to the National Endowment for the Humanities to digitize Angola's old Receiving Center's ID records and plan a research center for the museum's collections.

Finally, I coordinate the traveling exhibit, *Farming on the Farm*, which has been on display in 10 different libraries during 2013–2014.

What is the importance of corrections museums and the study of correctional history?

If we do not know our history, we are doomed to repeat it. In the United States, we cannot afford to repeat the dreadful practices and treatment of prisoners that were our embarrassing history, especially now in light of such serious budget cuts for so-called frivolous things, such as the arts and education in prisons.

(Continued)

(Continued)

Corrections museums can provide stimulating questions about why we did what we did historically and why we do what we do now in the field of corrections. If done well, corrections museums can portray both the "keeper" and the "kept" in more than the stereotypical representations of their roles as generally portrayed in the community.

What would be your advice to someone either wishing to study or now studying criminal justice to become a practitioner in this career field?

I think you would find this field infinitely intriguing and rewarding. I do. I believe people starting in the field would be vital to a corrections historical museum, as they bring new eyes to the same material. Because the nature of this work requires interactions with present and former employees of correctional institutions and current and former prisoners, the work is not limited to the museum space but requires almost daily visits to all corners of the prison. Therefore, the newcomer to this field would learn about the prison—keepers and kept—in a different manner than a typical new prison employee.

I am retired from teaching corrections in a criminal justice department for over 27 years, and I found this work makes use of the knowledge I have about the field but also expands my boundaries by asking me to use that knowledge in a distinctly different manner in planning exhibits and writing the narratives for the accompanying catalogs.

Web 2.3: British Prisons

(1773), placed serious offenders in a different section of the prison from the less serious. A juvenile reformatory was even built in a separate wing of the Hospice of San Michele in Rome (1704) (J. W. Roberts, 1997). An architectural depiction of the Ghent prison shows an octagonal shape, with a central court and then a partial view of separate living areas or courts for exercise for women, vagrant men, and other men. Much like the American colonies and England, however, the early European prisons and jails classified inmates by their social status and their ability to pay, with the concomitant amenities going to the wealthier.

> Incarcerated nobles who could pay the heftiest fees lived in comparative comfort with a modicum of privacy; less affluent prisoners were confined in large common rooms; the poorest inmates, and those who were considered the most dangerous, had to endure squalid dungeons. It was not unusual for men, women, and children, the sane and the mentally ill, felons and misdemeanants, all to be crowded indiscriminately in group cells. (J. W. Roberts, 1997, p. 5)

Another, less enlightened type of prison existed in England in the form of the **hulks**, derelict naval vessels transformed into prisons for the overflowing inmates in England. Used in tandem with transportation and other forms of incarceration in the mid-1700s and then increasing in use in the gap between the end of transportation to the American colonies with the Revolutionary War and the beginning of transportation of "criminals" to Australia, the last hulk was used on the coast of Gibraltar in 1875 (J. W. Roberts, 1997, p. 9). The English even confined some prisoners of war in a Hudson River hulk during the American Revolution. Inmates of these hulks were taken off to labor during the day for either public works or private contractors. The conditions of confinement were, predictably, horrible. "The hulks were filthy, crowded, unventilated, disease-ridden, and infested with vermin. The food was inadequate and the discipline was harsh" (J. W. Roberts, 1997, p. 11). Some inmates housed on the lower decks even drowned from water taken on by these broken-down ships.

A major proponent of reform of English prisons was *Elizabeth Gurney Fry*, a Quaker (1780–1845). She was an advocate for improved conditions, guidelines, training, and work skills for women inmates (J. W. Roberts, 1997). She provided the religious instruction herself to the women inmates.

Hulks: Derelict naval vessels transformed into prisons and jails.

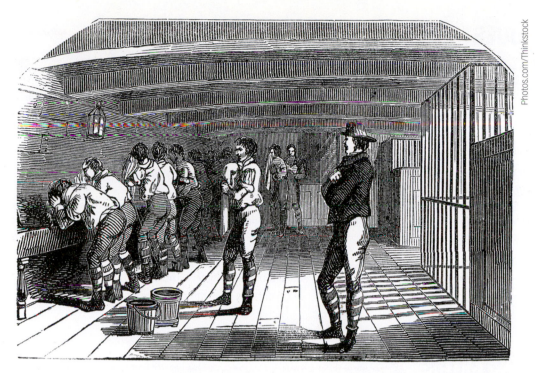

Photos.com/Thinkstock

PHOTO 2.8: Drawing of inmates in the hulk prison washroom. The living conditions on hulks were horrific, and disease was rampant.

SUMMARY

- Human beings have been inventive in their development of punishments and ways in which to hold and keep people.

- Correctional history is riddled with efforts to improve means of correction and reform.

- Those accused or convicted of crimes who had more means were less likely to be treated harshly or punished severely.

- Sometimes, the old worldviews (paradigms) are challenged by new evidence and ideas, and they are then discarded for new paradigms. The Enlightenment period in Europe was a time for rethinking old ideas and beliefs.

- Bentham, Beccaria, John Howard, and William Penn were all especially influential in changing our ideas about crime, punishment, and corrections.

- Correctional reforms, whether meant to increase the use of humane treatment of inmates or to increase their secure control, often led to unintended consequences.

- Some early European and English versions of prisons and juvenile facilities were very close in mission and operation to America's earliest prisons.

KEY TERMS

Bridewells 32

Galley slavery 30

Great Law 38

Hulks 42

Newgate Prison in Simsbury, Connecticut 40

Norfolk Island 33

Panopticon 37

Transportation 32

DISCUSSION QUESTIONS

1. Identify examples of some themes that run throughout the history of corrections. What types of punishments tend to be used and for what types of crimes? What sorts of issues influence the choice of actions taken against offenders?

2. How were people of different social classes treated in early jails and bridewells?

3. We know that transportation ended because of the development of sails, which was an improvement in technology. Can you think of other types of correctional practices that have been developed, improved upon, or stopped because of advances in technology?

4. What role has religion played in the development of corrections in the past?

5. What types of things have remained the same in corrections over the years, and what types of things have changed? Why do you think things have changed or remained the same?

6. Several historical figures mentioned in this chapter advanced ideas that were viewed as radical for their day. Why do you think such ideas were eventually adopted? Can you think of similar sorts of seemingly "radical" ideas for reforming corrections that might be adopted in the future?

USEFUL INTERNET SITES

Please note that the sites listed can be accessed at edge.sagepub.com/stohrcorrections.

American Correctional Association: www.aca.org

> The ACA is an organization that has, for 146 years, focused on professionalizing corrections in the United States. Their website and materials provide information on the latest training, research, and ideas in corrections.

American Jail Association: www.corrections.com/aja

> The AJA is an organization that also focuses on professionalization in corrections but as it involves jails. Their website provides information about the latest training, trends, and research in jails.

American Probation and Parole Association: www.appa-net.org

> The APPA is an organization that focuses on the professionalization of probation and parole or community corrections. From their website, you can learn about the best research and training and the newest ideas about practices in community corrections.

Bureau of Justice Statistics: www.bjs.gov

> The BJS provides an incredible wealth of information about all manner of criminal justice topics, including

corrections. It is one of our go-to websites when we are investigating a correctional topic (or police or courts, etc.).

John Howard Society of Canada: www.johnhoward.ca

> The John Howard Society, named after the jail and prison reformer of the same name, is an organization devoted to the reform of correctional institutions. From their website, you can learn about any progress being made on that front.

Pennsylvania Prison Society: www.prisonsociety.org

> As with the John Howard Society, the Pennsylvania Prison Society in the United States is devoted to the reform of prisons. They have a long and revered history in this area, and their website should be a go-to source for those interested in this area of study.

Vera Institute: www.vera.org

> The Vera Institute has been behind some of the biggest criminal justice reforms of the last 40 years. Check out their website to learn what important reforms and issues are on the correctional horizon.

$SAGE edge™

Sharpen your skills with SAGE edge at **edge.sagepub.com/stohrcorrections**. SAGE edge for Students provides a personalized approach to help you accomplish your coursework goals in an easy-to-use learning environment. You'll find action plans, mobile-friendly eFlashcards, and quizzes as well as video, web, and resources and links to SAGE journal articles to support and expand on the concepts presented in this chapter.

3

Correctional History

Early Prisons to Corrections Today

TEST YOUR KNOWLEDGE

Test your present knowledge of correctional history by answering the following questions. Check your answers on page 533 after reading the chapter.

1. What are the main differences between the Pennsylvania prison system and the New York prison system?

2. Most scholars believe that the Walnut Street Jail, as refurbished, became the first American prison in 1790. (True or false?)

3. The Auburn Prison featured complete separation from other inmates. (True or false?)

4. The complete separation of inmates was abandoned under the New York System of prisons. (True or false?)

5. After visiting the Eastern Pennsylvania Prison, Charles Dickens was an advocate for the "silent and separate" system of the Pennsylvania prisons. (True or false?)

6. In order to maintain control in the early years at the Auburn and Sing Sing prisons, the liberal use of "the lash," along with other methods, was required. (True or false?)

7. Dorothea Dix favored the New York prison system over the Pennsylvania system. (True or false?)

8. The 1870 American Prison Congress was held to celebrate the successes of prisons. (True or false?)

9. The Elmira Reformatory used the marks system to encourage good behavior. (True or false?)

10. To be termed a correctional institution, a prison should have some rehabilitation programming for inmates. (True or false?)

LEARNING OBJECTIVES

- Describe the origins of early modern prisons

- Evaluate the two predominate prison systems of the early 1800s and their strengths and weaknesses

- Summarize what the social critics (Beaumont, Tocqueville, and Dix) thought of the early prisons and why

- Explain why reform of prisons and jails was needed and how those reform efforts worked out

- Assess where we are today in America in terms of prison types and how we got there

- Describe the prevailing themes in correctional history

JIM CROW TREATMENT IN PRISONS

A black Folsom [prison] inmate named W. Mills complained about this [the racial segregation of prison jobs in the 1940s] in a letter to the Governor's Investigating Committee in 1943. "Our servitude here is limited to inferior work. The only work that is given to Negroes is such as porter work, digging in the ground and breaking rock or whatever else the white inmates don't want to do." Among the most powerful testimonies offered to racial segregation in the California Prison System came from Wesley Robert Wells, a black prisoner who contested the conditions of prison Jim Crow, and whose death sentence for throwing an ashtray at a guard became a rallying point for civil rights and radical labor advocates in the 1950s. Wells explained that racism abounded in the California Prison System when he arrived there in 1928. "There was a lot of jimcrow [sic] stuff in Quentin in those days—just like there is now, and if you objected you were a marked number. . . . I was young and I held my head up. I didn't take no stuff from prisoner, stoolie, or guard. As a result, I got it bad. I got the strap, the rubber hose, the club, the curses" (Blue, 2012, pp. 66–67).

••• INTRODUCTION: THE GRAND REFORMS

I. N. Phelps Stokes. Collection of American Historical Prints.

Correctional institutions:
Institutions that carefully classify inmates into treatment programs that address their needs and perceived deficiencies. They are also intended to be places where inmates can earn *good time* and eventual parole.

In this chapter, we review the attributes of the seminal prison models of the early 1800s, known as the Pennsylvania prison system (including the Walnut Street Jail and the Western and Eastern Pennsylvania prisons) and the New York prison system (including the Auburn and Sing Sing prisons). We include the eyewitness accounts of the operation of such systems in their early years, as these are provided by Beaumont, Tocqueville, and Dix.

Out of these two systems, the rampart for all American and many European prisons was constructed. As it became clear that neither prison model accomplished its multifaceted goals and that its operation was so distorted and horrific for inmates, changes were gradually made as new reform efforts ensued. The Elmira Prison in New York was perhaps the most ambitious of these efforts, in the latter part of the 1800s, which, in turn, set the stage for the later development of **correctional institutions**. Though the implementation of the reform ideals at Elmira is much critiqued, it certainly was much more humane than the convict-leasing system that operated at that time in the South. Folsom Prison in California in the 1940s, as described by inmate Wells, with its racial segregation, men laboring in rock quarries for lack of better work, and little programming, is representative of the Big Houses that preceded more concentrated efforts at rehabilitation that came with correctional institutions of the 1960s and 1970s. (More about these topics will be presented later in the chapter.)

PHOTO 3.1: Drawing of the Walnut Street Jail (circa 1799). This jail made early attempts at correctional reforms.

What does become crystal clear from this two-chapter review of the history of corrections in the United States is that there are several themes that run through it. One such theme, of course, is the cyclical need for reform itself—but to what purpose it is not always clear.

FIGURE *3.1*   Key Events in Corrections: 1790 to the Present Day

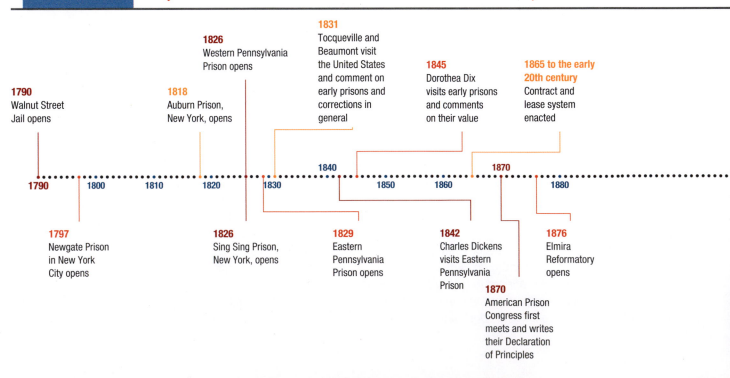

1790
Walnut Street Jail opens

1797
Newgate Prison in New York City opens

1818
Auburn Prison, New York, opens

1826
Western Pennsylvania Prison opens

1826
Sing Sing Prison, New York, opens

1829
Eastern Pennsylvania Prison opens

1831
Tocqueville and Beaumont visit the United States and comment on early prisons and corrections in general

1842
Charles Dickens visits Eastern Pennsylvania Prison

1845
Dorothea Dix visits early prisons and comments on their value

1870
American Prison Congress first meets and writes their Declaration of Principles

1865 to the early 20th century
Contract and lease system enacted

1876
Elmira Reformatory opens

••• EARLY MODERN PRISONS

THE WALNUT STREET JAIL

The **Walnut Street Jail** was originally constructed in 1773 in Philadelphia, Pennsylvania, and operated as a typical local jail of the time: holding pretrial detainees and minor offenders; failing to separate by gender, age, or offense; using the fee system, which penalized the poor and led to the near starvation of some; and offering better accommodations and even access to liquor and sex to those who could pay for it (Zupan, 1991). It was remodeled, however, in 1790 and reconceptualized so that many correctional scholars, though not all, regard it as the first prison.

The remodeled cell house was a frame construction and was built for the inmates of the "prison" section of the jail, with separate cells for each inmate. Based on the reforms that John Howard (and later Bentham and Fry) had envisioned for English and European jails, several reforms were instituted in this prison: The fee system was dropped, inmates were adequately clothed and fed regardless of their ability to pay, and they were separated by gender and offense. Children were not incarcerated in the prison, and debtors were separated from convicted felons. Though inmates were to live in isolated cells (to avoid "contaminating" each other), some work requirements brought them together. In addition, medical care was provided, and attendance at religious services was required. The availability of alcohol and access to members of the opposite sex and prostitutes was stopped.

The impetus for this philosophical change came from the reform efforts of the Philadelphia Society for Alleviating the Miseries of Public Prisons (or the Philadelphia Prison Society, currently known as the Pennsylvania Prison Society), led by *Dr. Benjamin Rush*, who was a physician, reformer, statesman, and a signatory of the Declaration of Independence. Rush agitated for laws to improve the jail's conditions of confinement and a different belief about correctional institutions—namely, that they could be used to reform their inmates (Nagel, 1973; J. W. Roberts, 1997). Ideally, the Walnut Street Jail (prison) was to operate based on the religious beliefs of the Quakers, with their emphasis on the reflective study of the Bible and abhorrence of violence, which was so prevalent in other

Walnut Street Jail: Originally constructed in 1773 in Philadelphia, Pennsylvania, and remodeled in 1790 into the first full-fledged prison. The fee system was dropped; inmates were adequately clothed and fed, regardless of their ability to pay; and they were separated by gender and offense. However, because of problems in implementation, by 1816, the prison was reportedly operating no better than before the reform and remodel.

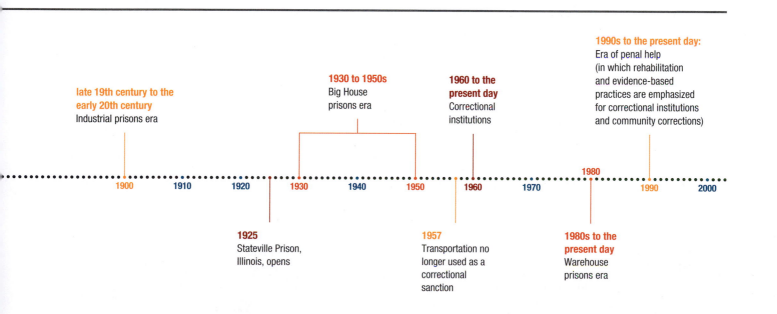

correctional entities. In 1789, the General Assembly of Pennsylvania enacted legislation based on these recommendations, and the Pennsylvania system was born (Nagel, 1973).

The Walnut Street Jail, as a prison, was also an entity with a philosophy of penitence, which, it was hoped, would lead to reform and redemption. This philosophy was combined with an architectural arrangement shaped to facilitate it by ensuring that inmates were mostly in solitary cells. As John W. Roberts (1997) aptly notes, the reason the Walnut Street Jail's new wing was the first real prison, as opposed to the other prisons such as Newgate of Connecticut that preceded it or some of the early European prisons, was "because it carried out incarceration as punishment, implemented a rudimentary classification system, featured individual cells, and was intended to provide a place for offenders to do penance—hence the term 'penitentiary'" (p. 26).

But in reality, the Walnut Street Jail soon became crowded, reportedly housing four times its capacity. As Johnston (2010) notes, "At one point 30 to 40 inmates were sleeping on blankets on the floor of rooms [which were] 18 feet square" (p. 13). Moreover, the institutional industry buildings that provided work for inmates burned down, leading to idleness, and by 1816, the Walnut Street Jail (prison) was little different from what it had been before the reforms (J. Harris, 1973; Zupan, 1991).

As Beaumont and Tocqueville (1833/1964) commented in 1831, after visiting and analyzing several prisons and jails in the United States, the implementation of the Walnut Street Jail had "two principal faults: it corrupted by contamination those who worked together. It corrupted by indolence, the individuals who were plunged into solitude" (p. 38).

NEWGATE PRISON, NEW YORK CITY

Yet another **Newgate Prison, in New York City** (1797), was modeled after the Walnut Street Jail prison (as were early prisons in Trenton, New Jersey [1798]; Richmond, Virginia [1800]; Charlestown, Massachusetts [1805]; and Baltimore, Maryland [1811]) and even improved upon that model in some respects (J. W. Roberts, 1997). Thomas Eddy, the warden of Newgate, was a Quaker.

The focus at the Newgate Prison in New York was on rehabilitation, religious redemption, and work programs to support prison upkeep; it did not use corporal punishment. The builders of Newgate even constructed a prison hospital and school for the inmates. Unfortunately, because of crowding, single celling for any but the most violent inmates was not possible, and a number of outbreaks of violence erupted (such as a riot in 1802).

●●● EMERGING PRISON MODELS

THE PENNSYLVANIA PRISON MODEL (SEPARATE SYSTEM)

Newgate Prison in New York City: Operated based on Quaker ideals, so it focused on rehabilitation, religious redemption, and work programs to support prison upkeep and did not use corporal punishment. Unfortunately, because of crowding, single celling for any but the most violent inmates was not possible, and a number of outbreaks of violence erupted.

The Western Pennsylvania Prison (1821) was built in Pittsburgh, followed by the Eastern Pennsylvania Prison (1829) in Philadelphia, which was to replace the Walnut Street Jail prison (Nagel, 1973). The Western Pennsylvania Prison, built eight years before Eastern, is little remarked upon or studied in comparison to Eastern. It was devised to operate in a solitary and separate fashion for inmates. Even labor was to be prohibited, as it was thought that this might interfere with the ability of the criminal to reflect and feel remorse for his or her crime (Hirsch, 1992). Despite the lessons learned from Auburn Prison (part of the New York system, which we will describe further on)—namely, that complete separation without labor can be injurious to the person and expensive for the state to maintain, a point made by Tocqueville and Beaumont—Western Pennsylvania Prison was built to hold inmates in complete solitary confinement (hence the use of the term *separate system*), with no labor, for the full span of their sentence. However, as Beaumont and Tocqueville (1833/1964) remark about Western Pennsylvania Prison, reducing all communication and thus contamination, in the authors' view, was almost impossible at this prison:

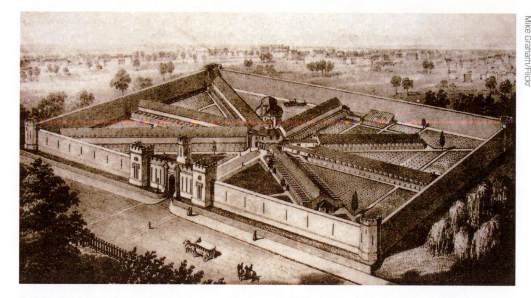

PHOTO 3.2: Eastern Pennsylvania Prison was the largest building in America in the 1820s. (Lithograph, circa 1855.)

Each one was shut up, day and night in a cell, in which no labor was allowed to him. This solitude, which in principle was to be absolute, was not such in fact. The construction of this penitentiary is so defective, that it is very easy to hear in one cell what is going on in another; so that each prisoner found in the communication with his neighbor a daily recreation, i.e. an opportunity of inevitable corruption. As these criminals did not work, we may say that their sole occupation consisted in mutual corruption. This prison, therefore, was worse than even that of Walnut Street, because, owing to the communication with each other, the prisoners at Pittsburgh (Western Pennsylvania Prison) were as little occupied with their reformation, as those at Walnut Street. And while the latter indemnified society in a degree by the produce of their labor, the others spent their whole time in idleness, injurious to themselves and burdensome to the public treasury. (p. 44)

As a consequence of these problems of architecture and operation, the Western Pennsylvania Prison was abandoned as a model, and the Eastern Pennsylvania Prison came to epitomize the **Pennsylvania prison system**, as opposed to the New York system of building and operating prisons. At Eastern Pennsylvania Prison, known as "Cherry Hill" for much of its 150 years of operation, the idea that inmates could be contaminated or corrupted by their fellow inmates was officially embraced.

Eastern Pennsylvania Prison was designed and built by the architect John Haviland, a relative newcomer from England. It cost three quarters of a million dollars to build, which was an incredible expenditure for the time. It was the largest building in America in the 1820s (Alosi, 2008; Orland, 1975). The prison itself was huge, with seven massive stone spokes of cells radiating off of a central rotunda, as on a wheel. A 30-foot wall was constructed around the outside perimeter of the prison, thus physically and symbolically reinforcing the separation of the prison and its inhabitants from their community (Nagel, 1973). The cells were built large (15 by 7.5 feet with 12-foot ceilings), and those on the lowest tier had their own small outside exercise yard attached, so that inmates could do virtually everything in their cells (J. Harris, 1973; Orland, 1975). The cells had both hot water and flush toilets, reportedly the first public building in the country to have such amenities. There were 400 solitary cells in this prison (Orland, 1975). At first, inmates were not to work, but that dictate was later changed, and they were allowed to work in their cells (J. Harris, 1973). As Johnston (2010) explains,

Video 3.1:
Eastern State
Penitentiary

Journal Article 3.1:
All the Women in
the Maryland State
Penitentiary:
1812–1869

Pennsylvania prison system (Walnut Street Jail, Western and Eastern Pennsylvania Prisons): Prisons that emphasized silence and isolated inmates in their cells, restricting their contact with others. They reinforced the need for penitence.

> The solution to the problem of criminal contamination for the reformers was to be a regimen of near-total isolation and absolute separation of prisoners from one another, the use of numbers rather than names, and a program of work, vocational training, and religious instruction, all taking place within the inmate's individual cell. (p. 13)

The only contact inmates were to have with the outside was with the clergy and some vocational teachers: "The reading of the Scriptures would furnish the offender with the moral guidance necessary for reform" (Nagel, 1973, p. 7). They had no access to visitors or letters or newspapers. Even their exercise yards were surrounded by a high stone fence. When they were brought into the prison and were taken for showers or to see the doctor, they had to wear a mask or a draped hood so as to maintain their anonymity and to prevent them from figuring out a way to escape (Alosi, 2008). As to how else they could occupy their time, "they made shoes, wove and dyed cloth products, caned chairs, and rolled cigars. Those products were sold to defray prison costs" (J. W. Roberts, 1997, p. 33).

The stated purpose of the solitary confinement was to achieve reform or rehabilitation. Quakers believed that God resides in everyone, and for a person to reach God, he or she must reflect. Silence is required for self-reflection, the Quakers thought. The Quakers also believed that as God was in everyone, all were equal and were deserving of respect (Alosi, 2008).

Solitary confinement, as a practical matter, remained in existence at Eastern Penitentiary until after the Civil War but was not formally ended until 1913 (Alosi, 2008). When it was rigorously applied, there are indications that it drove inmates insane. In fact—and tellingly—most of the European countries that copied the Eastern Pennsylvania model and its architecture did not isolate the inmates for this reason. Moreover, at a minimum, solitary confinement debilitated people by making them incapable of dealing with other people. For instance, the wardens' journals for Eastern in the early years indicate that it was not uncommon for an inmate to be released and then to ask to be reinstated at Eastern because he or she did not know how to live freely. Some inmates, once released, would actually sit on the curb outside the prison, as they said they no longer understood the outside world or how to function in it (Alosi, 2008).

Though the separation of inmates under the Pennsylvania system was to be complete, there are indications that it was not. In testimony before a special investigation by a joint committee of the houses of the Pennsylvania Legislature in 1834 (before the whole prison was even completed), it was noted that a number of male and female inmates (there were a small number of female inmates housed separately at Eastern) were used for maintenance, cleaning and for cooking at the facility and roamed freely around it, speaking and interacting with each other and staff (Johnston, 2010). Moreover, there were indications from this testimony that inmates were tortured to maintain discipline: One had died of blood loss from the iron gag put in his mouth, and another went insane after buckets of cold water were poured on his head repeatedly. It was alleged that food and supplies meant for inmates were given to guards or community members by the prison cook (who was a wife of one of the guards). There were also indications of the use and abuse of alcohol by staff and inmates and of sexual improprieties involving the warden and his clerk, some male inmates, and the female cook. Though ultimately charges against the warden and his clerk related to these improprieties were dropped, the cook was blamed, and the guards who testified about the scandal (the whistle-blowers) were fired.

In addition to these problems of implementation at Eastern, a debate raged among prison experts regarding the value of separation. As a result of the experiment with Western Pennsylvania Prison and its early use at Eastern Pennsylvania Prison and Auburn Prison, the idea of *total separation* was under siege. As mentioned, it was observed that for those truly subjected to it, solitary confinement and separation caused serious psychological problems for some inmates. Despite these problems, about 300 prisons worldwide copied the Eastern Pennsylvania model, and tens of thousands of men and women did time there, including the 1920s gangster Al Capone. It was a famous prison worldwide because of its philosophy, its architecture, and its huge size. It even became a tourist attraction in the 19th century, to the extent that famous English author Charles Dickens noted it as one of the two sights he wanted to see when visiting the United States (the other was Niagara Falls) (Alosi, 2008). It turns out, after a visit of a few hours and talking to inmates, keepers, and the warden, Dickens was far from impressed with its operation (see In Focus 3.1).

AUBURN, SING SING, AND THE NEW YORK (CONGREGATE) SYSTEM

The **New York prison system** was preferred over the Pennsylvania system and was copied extensively by American prison builders, in part because it disavowed the solitary confinement that Dickens and others lamented in the Pennsylvania prisons. Beaumont and Tocqueville (1833/1964) commented that the use of solitary confinement as normal practice for all inmates was ended at Auburn because it drove inmates insane. But it is not that the builders and planners for the Auburn Prison in New York learned from the Pennsylvania system; rather, they learned from their own dalliance with solitary confinement. At first, the inmates of Auburn were housed in solitary confinement in their cells, a practice that was abandoned by 1822 because it led to mental anguish

and insanity for inmates, and it hampered the efficient production of goods that can only be done in the congregate. By 1822, a total of 5 prisoners had died, 1 had gone insane, and the remaining 26 were pardoned by the governor of New York, as their mental faculties had deteriorated to such a great extent (Harris, 1973, p. 73). The governor ordered that inmates be allowed to leave their cells and work during the day, and in 1824, a legislative committee recommended the repeal of the solitary-confinement laws (Harris, 1973).

Beaumont and Tocqueville (1833/1964) supported the practice of maintaining the solitude of inmates at night and their silence during the day as they worked, as they believed, along with the Quakers of Pennsylvania, that solitude and silence led to reflection and reformation and also reduced cross-contamination of inmates. As to labor, they claimed, "It fatigues the body and relieves the soul" (p. 57), along with supplementing the income of the state to support the prison.

The Auburn (New York) Prison cornerstone was laid in 1816, received its first inmates in 1817, and officially opened in 1818, but it was not finished until 1819 (Harris, 1973). *Elam Lynds* (1784–1855), a strict disciplinarian and former army captain, was its first warden in 1821. Auburn has been in existence ever since (200 years at the time of this writing, in 2016), though its name changed to the Auburn Correctional Institution in 1970.

ETHICAL ISSUE 3.1

What Would You Do?

You are a new pastor in the Eastern State Penitentiary when Charles Dickens, the celebrated English author, visits the prison in 1842. Your position is tenuous at the prison, and you have been told it is dependent on your meticulous adherence to the rule of silence for inmates. Though you are not a proponent of this kind of control of inmates, the warden has made it clear to you that your livelihood and that of your family (you have eight children) depends on your complete compliance. For some reason, Mr. Dickens chooses to visit inmate cells and observe them while they work making shoes or weaving. You have been instructed to report whether inmates speak or even look at Mr. Dickens (as they have been instructed not to under penalty of confinement in a segregation cell for months, with only food and water). In the course of your rounds, you note that Dickens routinely and secretively—presumably so as to protect inmates from punishment—attempts to engage inmates in conversation. In a few instances, you have overheard inmates whisper responses to his queries. You cannot be sure that a guard has not also observed this behavior and has seen you in the vicinity when it occurred. What would you do? Would you report the offense? Would you ask Dickens to stop speaking to inmates (or would you just ask for his autograph)?

Video 3.2: The Electric Chair: An Experiment Born in Auburn

New York prison system (Auburn and Sing Sing): Prisons included congregate work and eating arrangements but silent and separate housing.

IN FOCUS 3.1

Charles Dickens's Impressions of Eastern Pennsylvania Prison and the Silent System in 1842

In its intention, I am well convinced that it is kind, humane, and meant for reformation; but I am persuaded that those who devised this system of Prison Discipline, and those benevolent gentlemen who carry it into execution, do not know what it is that they are doing. I believe that very few men are capable of estimating the immense amount of torture and agony which this dreadful punishment, prolonged for years, inflicts upon the sufferers; and in guessing at it myself, and in reasoning from what I have seen written upon their faces, and what to my certain knowledge they feel within, I am only the more convinced that there is a depth of terrible endurance in it which none but the sufferers themselves can fathom, and which no man has a right to inflict upon his fellow-creature. I hold this slow and daily tampering with the mysteries of the brain, to be immeasurably worse than any torture of the body: and because its ghastly signs and tokens are not so palpable to the eye and sense of touch as scars upon the flesh; because its wounds are not upon the surface, and it extorts few cries that human ears can hear; therefore I the more denounce it, as a secret punishment which slumbering humanity is not roused up to stay.

I was accompanied to this prison by two gentlemen officially connected with its management, and passed the day in going from cell to cell, and talking with the inmates. Every facility was afforded me, that the utmost courtesy could suggest. Nothing was concealed or hidden from my view, and every piece of information that I sought, was openly and frankly given. The perfect order of the building cannot be praised too highly, and of the excellent motives of all who are immediately concerned in the administration of the system, there can be no kind of question. . . .

Standing at the central point, and looking down these dreary passages, the dull repose and quiet that prevails, is awful. Occasionally, there is a drowsy sound from some lone weaver's shuttle, or shoemaker's last, but it is stifled by the thick walls and heavy dungeon-door, and only serves to make the general stillness more profound. Over the head and face of every prisoner who comes into this melancholy house, a black hood is drawn; and in this dark shroud, an emblem of the curtain dropped between him and the living world, he is led to the cell from which he

PHOTO 3.3: Charles Dickens

never again comes forth, until his whole term of imprisonment has expired. He never hears of wife and children; home or friends; the life or death of any single creature. He sees the prison-officers, but with that exception he never looks upon a human countenance, or hears a human voice. He is a man buried alive; to be dug out in the slow round of years; and in the mean time dead to everything but torturing anxieties and horrible despair. . . .

My firm conviction is that, independent of the mental anguish it occasions—an anguish so acute and so tremendous, that all imagination of it must fall far short of the reality—it wears the mind into a morbid state, which renders it unfit for the rough contact and busy action of the world. It is my fixed opinion that those who have undergone this punishment, MUST pass into society again morally unhealthy and diseased. (Dickens, 1842, n.p.)

DISCUSSION QUESTIONS

1. What did Dickens not like about the Pennsylvania prison, if anything?

2. What, if anything, did he like, and why?

PHOTO 3.4: Auburn Prison, officially opened in 1818, is still in operation today, though its name has changed to the Auburn Correctional Institution.

PHOTO 3.5: Sing Sing Prison, modeled after Auburn Prison, was built by inmates from Auburn Prison in 1825.

Auburn's cells were built back to back, with corridors on each side. The prison has always had a Gothic appearance, and its elaborate front and massive walls have been maintained up until today, with towers and a fortress facade. Auburn Prison has a storied history that spans from the virtual beginning of prisons in the United States to the present day. As was already noted, Beaumont and Tocqueville visited it and recommended it over the Pennsylvania prisons. Auburn opened with a solitary-confinement system, which was very quickly abandoned and replaced with the congregate but silent system, which formally lasted until the beginning of the 20th century. It was the progenitor of such widely adopted practices as the lockstep walk for inmates, the striped prison uniforms and the classification system that went hand in hand with it, and the well-known ball and chain. Warden Lynds believed in strict obedience on the part of inmates and the use of the whip by staff to ensure it (Clear, Cole, & Reisig, 2011). Under his regime, inmates were forbidden to talk or even to glance at each other during work or meals. Solitary confinement and flogging were used for punishing and controlling inmates. As noted in the foregoing, except for a few years at the beginning of Auburn's history, inmates were single celled at night, and the cells were quite small, even coffin-like (7 × 7 × 3.5). During the day, the inmates worked together, though silently, in factories and shops (J. W. Roberts, 1997).

The small cells, like those at Auburn, were cheaper to build, and prisons could house more inmates in the same amount of space than prisons with larger cells. Also, congregate work allowed for the more efficient production of more products, and thus, more profit could be made (J. W. Roberts, 1997). However, putting all of these inmates together in one place presented some difficulties in terms of control and management. This is why the control techniques represented by the use of the lash, solitary confinement, marching in lockstep, and the requirement of silence came into play. As John W. Roberts (1997) notes, "Ironically, whereas the penitentiary concept was developed as a humane alternative to corporal punishment, corporal punishment returned as a device to manage inmates in penitentiaries based on the Auburn System" (p. 44).

Sing Sing Prison was modeled after Auburn architecturally in that the cells were small, and there were congregate areas for group work by inmates, but its cellblocks were tiered and very long. Inmate management and operations exactly mirrored the Auburn protocols. In fact, Sing Sing was built by Auburn inmates under the supervision of Auburn's Warden Lynds.

The prison was built on the Hudson River, near the towns of Sing Sing and Mount Pleasant (and for many years, the prison was referred to as Mount Pleasant), from locally quarried stone. Products produced at the prison could be transported to local towns via the river. Inmates sent there would refer to it as being sent "up the river," as it is 30 miles north of New York City (Conover, 2001). Its name derives from the Indian phrase *Sint Sinks*, which came from the older term *Ossine Ossine* and ironically means "stone upon stone" (Lawes, 1932, p. 68).

Warden Lynds picked 100 men from Auburn Prison to build Sing Sing in 1825. The story of its construction, in silence, as relayed by Lewis Lawes (1932), a later warden of Sing Sing, goes like this:

> Captain Lynds, then the foremost penologist of the day, was insistent, to the point of hysteria, on silence as the backbone of prison administration. "It is the duty of convicts to preserve an unbroken silence," was the first rule he laid down. "They are not to exchange a word with each other under any pretense whatever; not to communicate any intelligence to each other in writing. They are not to exchange looks, wink, laugh, or motion to each other. They must not sing, whistle, dance, run, jump, or do anything which has a tendency in the least degree to disturb the harmony or contravene to disturb the rules and regulations of the prison." . . . The sea gulls in the broad river, darting in large flocks here and there on the water, chirped raucously at these strange creatures sweating at their tasks in silence. Stone upon stone. (pp. 72–73)

Once constructed, it was noticed that with some effort, inmates could communicate between the closely aligned cells, but nothing was done to rebuild the cells. Moreover, as the inmates from the old New York Newgate Prison were moved to Sing Sing right away and so were additional inmates from Auburn, the prison was full at 800 inmates by 1830 (Lawes, 1932).

Prison labor in the early years of prisons (before the Civil War) was contract labor and subject to abuse. Contractors would pay a set amount for inmates' labor and then would make sure they got the most work out of them, cutting costs where they could and bribing wardens and keepers when they needed to. Eventually, such contracts were ended, as the cheap labor made prison-produced goods too competitive with products made by free workers (Conover, 2001).

When one thinks about old prisons, those castle-like fortress prisons, the image of Auburn and Sing Sing inmates and prisons come to mind, even unknowingly. So many U.S. prisons copied the New York design and operation of these prisons that even if one is not thinking of Auburn or Sing Sing per se, one is likely imagining a copy of them. By the time Beaumont and Tocqueville (1833/1964) visited the United States in 1831, they reported that Auburn Prison had already been copied in prisons built in Massachusetts, Maryland, Tennessee, Kentucky, Maine, and Vermont.

It was not just the physical structure or the silent but congregate inmate management that was copied, however, from Auburn and Sing Sing, but the inmate discipline system as well. Orland (1975) summarized the Connecticut prison regulations of the 1830s, which were borrowed from the New York model:

> Inmates were exhorted to be "industrious, submissive, and obedient;" to "labor diligently in silence"; they were forbidden to "write or receive a letter" or to communicate in any manner "with or to persons" without the warden's permission; they were prohibited from engaging in conversation "with another prisoner" without permission or to "speak to, or look at, visitors." (p. 26)

IN FOCUS 3.2

The Pentonville Prison

Though most American prisons of the 19th century ended up copying the Auburn and Sing Sing (New York model) prisons in design and operation, Pentonville Prison, opened in London, England, in 1842, was modeled on the Pennsylvania prisons (Ignatieff, 1978). Inmates were confined in their rather large cells for most of the day, except for chapel (where they had their own solitary box) and recreation (where they had their own isolated yard). In their cells, inmates worked on crafts and at looms. As with the Pennsylvania prisons, at Pentonville, silence was enforced, and inmates were sent to solitary dungeon rooms for disobeying the rules. But also, as with the Pennsylvania prisons, inmates devised ways to communicate between cells by tapping messages to each other at night. At first, as with the Pennsylvania prisons and initially with Auburn Prison, inmates were confined completely to their cells for 18 months. However, as inmates experienced the predictable mental illnesses associated with this isolation, such periods were eventually reduced to nine months for new inmates (Ignatieff, 1978).

DISCUSSION QUESTION

1. Why do you think England adopted the Pennsylvania model for this prison rather than the New York model?

••• EARLY PRISONS AND JAILS NOT REFORMED

Lest one be left with the impression that all prisons and jails in the early 1800s in America were reformed, we should emphasize that this was not the case. Beaumont and Tocqueville (1833/1964) commented, for instance, on the fact that the New Jersey prisons, right across the river from the reformist New York system, were vice ridden and that Ohio prisons, though ruled by a humanitarian law, were "barbarous," with half of the inmates in irons and "the rest plunged into an infected dungeon" (p. 49). But in New Orleans, they found the worst, with inmates incarcerated with hogs. "In locking up criminals, nobody thinks of rendering them better, but only of taming their malice; they are put in chains like ferocious beasts; and instead of being corrected, they are rendered brutal" (p. 49).

As to jails, Beaumont and Tocqueville (1833/1964) noticed no reforms at all. Inmates who were presumed innocent or, if guilty, had generally committed a much less serious offense than those sent to prison were incarcerated in facilities far worse in construction and operation than prisons, even in states where prison reform had occurred. In colonial times, inmates in American jails were kept in house-like facilities and were allowed much more freedom, albeit with few amenities that they did not pay for themselves. Dix (1843/1967) described many jails, particularly those that did not separate inmates, as "free school[s] of vice." However, as the institutionalization movement began for prisons, jails copied their large, locked-up, and controlled atmosphere, without any philosophy of reform to guide their construction or operation (Goldfarb, 1975). By mid-century, some jails had employed the silent or separate systems popular in prisons, but most were merely congregate and poorly managed holding facilities (Dix, 1843/1967). Such facilities on the East Coast, by the latter quarter of the 1800s, were old, crowded, and full of the "corruptions" that the new prisons were trying to prevent (Goldfarb, 1975). In the end, Beaumont and Tocqueville (1833/1964) blamed the lack of reform of prisons in some states and the failure to reform jails hardly at all on the fact that there were independent state and local governments who handled crime and criminals differently: "These shocking contradictions proceed chiefly from the want of unison in the various parts of government in the United States (p. 49).

PRISONS: "THE SHAME OF ANOTHER GENERATION"

The creation of prisons was a grand reform, promoted by principled people who were appalled at the brutality of discipline wielded against those in their communities. Prisons were an exciting development supported by Enlightenment ideals of humanity and the promise of reformation. They were developed over centuries, in fits and starts, and had their genesis in other modes of depriving people of liberty (e.g., galley slavery, transportation, jails, bridewells, houses of corrections, and early versions of prisons), but they were meant to be much better—so much better—than these.

It is not clear whether the problems arose for prisons in their implementation or in their basic conceptualization. In societies where the poor and dispossessed exist among institutions in which law and practice serve to maintain their status, is it any wonder that prisons, as a social institution that reflects the values and beliefs of that

IN FOCUS 3.3

Lewis E. Lawes's Observations About Sing Sing History and Discipline

In 1920, Lawes began his tenure as Sing Sing warden and later commented on how the severity of prison discipline had waxed and waned at this prison over the years. At first, it was very severe, with the use of the cat-o'-nine-tails whip. "It was made of long strips of leather, attached to a stout wooden handle, and was not infrequently wired at the tips. The 'cat' preferred its victim barebacked" (Lawes, 1932, pp. 74–75). Under a warden, in 1840, however, the cat was retired, and inmates could have a few visits and letters. A Sunday school and library were constructed, and the warden walked among the men. Within a few years, though, a new warden was appointed with a new political party in power, and all of the reforms were abandoned, and the cat was resurrected. A few years later, when a reportedly insane inmate was literally whipped to death, the public was outraged, and the use of the lash declined for men and was prohibited for women. The prison discipline was consequently softened, and this cycle continued for the rest of the 1800s, from severe to soft discipline. Lawes maintained, after reviewing all of the wardens' reports since the opening of Sing Sing, that escapes were highest during times of severe punishment, despite the risks inmates took should they be caught.

He also observed that the prison had problems with management and control in other ways, noting that by 1845,

an outside accountant found that the prison held 20 fewer female and 33 fewer male inmates than it had officially on the books, that $32,000 was missing, and that there was no explanation as to where these people were or where the money had gone (Lawes, 1932, p. 82). The warden's and other official reports indicated that inmates were poorly fed and that diseases were rampant at Sing Sing. By 1859, some of Sing Sing's small cells became doubles to accommodate the overcrowding, and the punishments got worse. By 1904, the official report was that the prison was in a disgraceful condition. Lawes (1932) writes, "Such was the Sing Sing of the Nineteenth Century. A hopeless, oppressive, barren spot. Escapes were frequent, attempts at escape almost daily occurrences. Suicides were common" (p. 88).

DISCUSSION QUESTIONS

1. Why is total control in prisons almost impossible to achieve?

2. What does it take to achieve close to total control?

3. Do you think prisons of today should be operated in the way that Sing Sing was in its early days? Why, or why not?

society, would serve to reinforce this status? All indications are that most prisons, even those that were lauded as the most progressive in an earlier age of reform, were, by the mid-19th century, regarded as violent and degrading places for their inmates and staff.

DOROTHEA DIX'S EVALUATION OF PRISONS AND JAILS

Dorothea Dix was a humanitarian, a teacher, and a penal and insane asylum reformer who, after four years of studying prisons, jails, and almshouses in northeastern and midwestern states, wrote the book *Remarks on Prisons and Prison Discipline in the United States*, in 1843 (reprinted in 1845 and 1967). The data for her book were assembled from multiple observations at prisons; conversations and correspondence with staff, wardens, and inmates in prisons; and a review of prisons' annual reports.

Dix tended to prefer the Pennsylvania model over the New York model because she thought inmates benefited from separation from others. However, she forcefully argued that both prison models that had promised so much in terms of reform for inmates were, in fact, abject failures in that regard. She found these and most prisons to be understaffed, overcrowded, and run by inept leaders who changed much too often. She noted that at Sing Sing, about 1,200 lashes, using the cat-o'-nine-tails, were administered every month to about 200 men, an amount she thought too severe, though she believed the use of the lash, especially in understaffed and overcrowded prisons like Sing Sing and Auburn, was necessary to maintain order (Dix, 1843/1967). In contrast, at Eastern Penitentiary, she commented that punishments included mostly solitary confinement in darkened cells, which, to her, appeared to lead to changes in the behavior of recalcitrant inmates. Dix argued, as far as inmate discipline goes, "Man is not made better by being degraded; he is seldom restrained from crime by harsh measures" (p. 4).

Thus, Dix argued against the long sentences for minor offenses that she found in prisons of the day (e.g., Richmond, Virginia; Columbus, Ohio; Concord, Massachusetts; and Providence, Rhode Island) and the disparity in sentencing from place to place. She thought such sentences were not only unjust but that they led to insubordination by inmates and staff who recognized the arbitrary nature of the justice system. On the other hand, in her study of prisons, she found that the pardoning power was used too often, and this again led, she thought, to less trust in the just and fair nature of the system and to insubordination among its inmates.

Dix also remarked on the quality and availability of food and water for inmates in early correctional facilities. She found the food to be adequate in most places, except Sing Sing, where there was no place to dine at the time of the second edition of her book (1845), and the water inadequate in most places, except the Pennsylvania prisons, where it was piped into all of the cells. Her comments on the health, heating, clothing, cleanliness, and sanity of inmates also were detailed, by institution, and indicated that though there were recurrent problems with these issues in prisons of the time, some prisons (e.g., Eastern Penitentiary) did more than others to alleviate miseries by changing the diet, providing adequate clothing, and making warm water for washing available to inmates.

Library of Congress

PHOTO 3.6: Dorothea Dix was a humanitarian, a teacher, and a penal and insane asylum reformer who, after four years of study of prisons, jails, and almshouses in northeastern and Midwestern states, wrote the book *Remarks on Prisons and Prison Discipline in the United States*, in 1843.

She did not find that more inmates were deemed "insane" in Pennsylvania-modeled prisons based on her data—or at least not more than one might expect, even in the Pennsylvania prisons. Given the history of the separate system being linked to insanity, she was sensitive to this topic. However, by 1845, when she published the second edition of her book, inmates at Eastern were not as "separate" from others as they had been, both formally and informally, and this might explain the relative paucity of insanity cases in her data. By this time, inmates were allowed to speak to their keepers (guards) and attend church and school.

Dix also explored the moral and religious instruction provided at the several state prisons and county prisons (jails) that she visited. Except for Eastern Penitentiary, she found them all deficient in this respect and that the provisions of such services were severely lacking in the jails.

Dix studied a peculiar practice of the early prisons: allowing visitors to pay to be spectators at the prisons. Adults were generally charged 25 cents, and children were half price in some facilities. In Auburn, in 1842, the prison made $1,692.75 from visitors; in Columbus, Ohio, in 1844, the prison made $1,038.78; and Dix documented five other prisons that allowed the same practice, a practice she thought should be "dispensed with" as it "would not aid the moral and reforming influences of the prisons" (p. 43). Of course, this fascination with watching inmates continues today, with reality-based television shows filmed in prisons and jails.

Finally, Dix tried to explore the idea of recidivism, or, as she termed it, reform. She wanted to know how many inmates leave their prison and are reformed or "betake themselves to industrious habits, and an honest calling; who, in place of vices, practice virtues; who, instead of being addicted to crime, are observed to govern their passions, and abstain from all injury to others" (p. 66). When she asked about how many inmates were reformed, she found that none of the prisons had records in that regard but that wardens tended to think most inmates were reformed because they did not return to that particular prison. She was doubtful that this failure to return to that prison should be regarded as an indication of low recidivism, as she suspected that inmates got out, changed their names, and dispersed across the countryside, where they could return to crime undetected. In most respects and in all of these areas, she concluded from her study of several prisons that Eastern Penitentiary was far superior to most prisons and that Sing Sing Prison was far inferior, but she thought even Eastern Penitentiary was far from perfect. Rather, she called for more focus on the morals and education of the young and on preventing crime as a means of improving prisons and reducing their use—a call that sounds very familiar today.

THE FAILURE OF REFORM IS NOTED

Dix's writings foretold the difficulties of implementing real change, even if the proposal is well intentioned. Simply put, prisons in the latter half of the 19th century were no longer regarded as places of reform. As Rothman (1980) states,

> Every observer of American prisons and asylums in the closing decades of the nineteenth century recognized that the pride of one generation had become the shame of another. The institutions that had been intended to exemplify the humanitarian advances of republican government were not merely inadequate to the ideal, but were actually an embarrassment and a rebuke. Failure to do good was one thing; a proclivity to do harm quite another—and yet the evidence was incontrovertible that brutality and corruption were endemic to the institutions. (p. 17)

Newspapers and state investigatory commissions, by the mid-19th century, were documenting the deficiencies of state prisons. Instead of the relatively controlled atmosphere of the Pennsylvania or Auburn prisons of the 1830s, there was a great deal of laxity and brutality (Rothman, 1980). Prisons were overcrowded and under-staffed, and the presence of prison contractors led to corruption, such as paying off wardens to look the other way as inmate labor was exploited or, alternatively, the wardens and staff using inmates and their labor for their own illegal ends. At Sing Sing, an 1870 investigation found that inmates were largely unsupervised, had access to contraband, and were unoccupied for most of their sentence (Rothman, 1980). A lack of space and staff were likely to lead to more severe punishments to deter misbehavior. Therefore, when their keepers did pay attention to inmates, it may have been to administer brutal medieval-style punishments, which included the "pulley," where inmates were hung by their wrists or by their thumbs; the iron cap or cage, which inmates were forced to wear on their heads and which weighed 6 to 8 pounds; being tied up with their hands so high behind them that they had to "stand" on their toes; or the "lash and paddle" (Rothman, 1980, p. 19). Solitary confinement in a dark, dungeon-like cell was popular, too, especially with little sustenance (water and bread) and a bucket. A Kansas prison employed the "water crib":

> The inmate was placed in a coffin-like box, six and one-half feet long, thirty inches wide, and three feet deep, his face down and his hands handcuffed behind his back. A water hose was then turned on, slowly filling the crib. The resulting effect of this procedure was the sensation of slowly drowning, with the inmate struggling to keep his head up above the rising water line. (Rothman, 1980, p. 20)

? ETHICAL ISSUE 3.2

What Would You Do?

You are Dorothea Dix, the American humanitarian and penal and insane asylum reformer, and you are visiting prisons and jails in the United States in the 1840s. The task you have set for yourself is to document what appears to be working and what does not in the facilities you visit. You pride yourself on maintaining high moral standards. You are not opposed to the use of the lash in some circumstances, but its overuse, you think, is counterproductive in that it turns men into "brutes" rather than reforming them. In the course of your visit to Sing Sing, where the lash is used for the smallest offense, you notice that an emaciated inmate steals a piece of bread off a tray. The warden, though known for his harsh treatment of inmates, has treated you with every courtesy, and you know that he would expect you to report this offense. What would you do, and why? Do you think that your decision is colored by the time period you live in? Why, or why not?

••• THE RENEWED PROMISE OF REFORM

THE 1870 AMERICAN PRISON CONGRESS

The first major prison reform came approximately 50 years after the first New York and Pennsylvania prisons were built, doubtless as a result of all of those calls for change. The 1870 American Prison Congress was held in Cincinnati, Ohio, with the express purpose of trying to recapture some of the idealism promised with the creation of prisons (Rothman, 1980). Despite their promises of reform and attempts at preventing "contamination," the early prisons had become, by the 1860s, warehouses without hope or resources. All of the themes mentioned at the beginning of Chapter 2—save the desire for reform, and that was remedied with the next round of reforms to follow the Congress—applied to the operation of the 19th-century prisons: They were overcrowded, underfunded, brutal facilities where too many inmates would spend time doing little that was productive or likely to prepare them to reintegrate into the larger community.

Appropriately enough, then, the Declaration of Principles that emerged from the Prison Congress of 1870 was nothing short of revolutionary at the time and provided a blueprint for prisons we see today (Rothman, 1980). Some of those principles were concerned with the grand purpose of prisons—to achieve reform—while others were related to their day-to-day operation (e.g., training of staff, eliminating contract labor, and the treatment of the insane) (American Correctional Association, 1983).

ELMIRA

As a result of these principles, a spirit of reform in corrections again spurred action, and the **Elmira Reformatory** was founded in 1876 in New York (Rothman, 1980). The reformatory would encompass all of the rehabilitation focus and graduated reward system (termed the **marks system**, as in, if one behaves, it is possible to earn marks that, in turn, entitle one to privileges). The marks system, as mentioned in Chapter 2, was practiced by Maconochie and later by Crofton in Irish prisons and was promoted by reformers. Elmira was supposed to hire an educated and trained staff and to maintain uncrowded facilities (Orland, 1975).

Zebulon Brockway was appointed to head the reformatory, and he was intent on using the ideas of Maconochie and Crofton to create a "model" prison (Harris, 1973, p. 85). He persuaded the New York legislature to pass a bill creating the indeterminate sentence, which would be administered by a board rather than the courts. He planned on the reformatory handling only younger men (ages 16 to 30), as he expected that they might be more amenable to change. He planned to create a college at Elmira that would educate inmates from elementary school through college. He also sought to create an industrial training school that would equip inmates with technical abilities. In addition, he focused on the physical training of inmates, including much marching but also the use of massages and steam baths (Harris, 1973). The marks system had a three-pronged purpose: to discipline, to encourage reform, and to justify good time, in order to reduce the sentence of the offender. Brockway did not want to resort to the use of the lash.

Much lauded around the world and visited by dignitaries, the Elmira Reformatory and Brockway's management of it led to the creation of good time, the indeterminate sentence (defined in Chapter 5), a focus on programming to address inmate deficiencies, and the promotion of probation and parole. "After Brockway, specialized treatment, classification of prisoners, social rehabilitation and self-government of one sort or another were introduced into every level of the corrections system" (Harris, 1973, pp. 86–87).

Unfortunately and as before, this attempt at reform was thwarted when the funding was not always forthcoming, and the inmates did not conform as they were expected to. The staff, who were not the educated and trained professionals that Brockway had envisioned, soon resorted to violence to keep control. In fact, Brockway administered the lash himself on many occasions (Rothman, 1980). It should not be forgotten, however, that even on its worst day, the Elmira prison was likely no worse—and probably much more humane—than were the old Auburn or Sing Sing prisons.

THE CREATION OF PROBATION AND PAROLE

Probation and parole, which we will cover in Chapters 8 and 12, were developed in the first half of the 19th century, and their use spread widely across the United States in the early 20th century. The idea behind both was that programming and assistance in the community while supervising the offender could reduce the use of incarceration and help the offender to transition more smoothly back into the community. Doubtless, the intent was good, but the execution of this reform was less than satisfactory; however, it did represent an improvement over the correctional practices that preceded it (Rothman, 1980).

Elmira Reformatory: Founded in 1876 in New York as a model prison in response to calls for the reform of prisons from an earlier era, it aimed to encompass all of the rehabilitation focus and graduated reward system that reformers were agitating for.

Marks system: A graduated reward system for prisons in which, if one behaves, it is possible to earn "marks" that, in turn, entitle one to privileges.

••• AMERICAN CORRECTIONS IN THE 20TH AND 21ST CENTURIES

SOUTHERN AND NORTHERN PRISONS AND THE CONTRACT AND LEASE SYSTEMS

Southern prisons, because of the institution of slavery, developed on a different trajectory from that of other prisons. As indicated by Young's (2001) research, prisons in the South were little used before the Civil War. In agriculturally based societies, labor is prized and needed in the fields, particularly slave labor, and that served as a basis for the Southern economy. Once slavery was abolished with the 13th Amendment to the Constitution, Southern states, in the Reconstruction period following the Civil War, began incarcerating more people, particularly ex-slaves, and recreating a slave society in the corrections system. As Oshinsky (1996) documents for Mississippi prisons, blacks were picked up and imprisoned for relatively minor offenses and forced to work like slaves on prison plantations or on plantations of Southern farmers.

In the North, Midwest, and, later, the West, prisons were built somewhat on the Auburn model, but for the most part, corrections officials abandoned the attempt to completely silence inmates. It was no longer emphasized, as maintaining such silence required a large staff and constant vigilance, and these were usually not available in the understaffed and overcrowded facilities (J. B. Jacobs, 1977). Inmates in such prisons worked in larger groups under private or public employers, and order was maintained with the lash or other innovations in discipline, as discussed in Chapter 2 (see also Lawes [1932], regarding the management of Sing Sing). Though there was no pretense of high-minded reform going on in these prisons, their conditions and the accommodations of inmates were thought to be far superior to those provided in Southern prisons of the time. Conditions under both the **contract and lease systems** could be horrible but were likely worse under the Southern lease system, where contractors were often responsible for both housing and feeding inmates. Such contractors had little incentive for feeding or taking care of inmates, as the supply of labor from the prison was almost inexhaustible.

Industrial Prisons

The contract system morphed into industrial prisons in the latter part of the 19th and first few decades of the 20th century in several states. Inmates were employed either by outside contractors or by the state to engage in the large-scale production of goods for sale in the open market or to produce goods for the state itself. Eventually, as the strength of unions increased and particularly as the Depression struck in 1930, the sale of cheap, prison-made goods was restricted by several state and federal laws, limiting the production of goods in prisons to just products that the state or nonprofits might be able to use.

CORRECTIONAL INSTITUTIONS OR WAREHOUSE PRISONS?

In James Jacobs's (1977) classic book, *Stateville: The Penitentiary in Mass Society*, the author describes the operation of and environmental influences on **Stateville Prison** in Illinois. It was built as a panopticon in 1925 in reaction to the deplorable conditions of the old Joliet, Illinois, prison, built in 1860. Joliet was overcrowded, and Stateville Prison was built to relieve that overcrowding, but by 1935, Stateville itself was full, at 4,000 inmates, and the population at Joliet had not been reduced at all.

In a reformist state such as Illinois at the time (juvenile court reform began here, and it was one of the first states to initiate civil service reforms), Stateville was conceived

Audio 3.1: Former Inmate Becomes Advocate for Prisoner Reform

Web 3.1: Center for Prison Reform

Contract and lease systems: Systems devised by prisons to hire out inmates' labor to farmers or other contractors.

Stateville Prison: Built in Illinois as a panopticon in 1925 in reaction to the deplorable conditions of the old Joliet, Illinois, prison, built in 1860.

PHOTO 3.7: Texas State Penitentiary at Huntsville prison yard in the 1870s. Huntsville is another example of a Big House prison.

as a place where inmates would be carefully classified into treatment programs that would address their needs and perceived deficiencies and where inmates could earn good time and eventual parole. Inmates were believed to be "sick," and a treatment regimen provided by the prison would address that sickness and hopefully "cure" them so that they might become productive members of society. Thus, correctional institutions would use the **medical model** to treat inmates. Even though it was built as a maximum-security prison, Stateville's conception fit the definition of a correctional institution, where inmates were not to be merely warehoused but corrected and treated. However, though inmates in the Illinois system were classified, and good time was available for those who adhered to the rules, there was little programming available, the prison was crowded, it was understaffed, and the staff who were employed were ill trained (J. B. Jacobs, 1977). Moreover, the first 10 years of operation were filled with disorganized management and violent attacks on staff and inmates in a prison controlled by Irish and Italian gangs.

In essence and despite the intent to create a correctional institution, Stateville became what is termed a **Big House prison**. These, according to Irwin (2005), are fortress stone or concrete prisons, usually maximum security, whose attributes include "isolation, routine, and monotony" (p. 32). Strict security and rule enforcement, at least formally, and a regimentation in schedule are other hallmarks of such facilities. The **convict code**, or the rules that inmates live by vis-à-vis the institution and staff, is clear-cut: "1. Do not inform; 2. Do not openly interact or cooperate with the guards or the administration; 3. Do your own time" (p. 33).

The next 25 years of Stateville Prison (1936–1961) were marked by the authoritarian control of one warden (Ragen), the isolation of staff and inmates from the larger world, strict formal rule enforcement, and informal corruption of those rules. Some of the trappings of a correctional institution were present (i.e., good time for good behavior and parole), but inmates, for the most part, were merely warehoused, double and triple celled. Those inmates who were favored by staff and the warden were given better housing and a whole array of privileges. Corruption seethed under the surface, with the relaxation of rules for tougher inmates, black-market trade by both staff and inmates, and the warden turning his head when beatings of inmates by staff occurred. By the mid-1950s, Ragen, who had been appointed director of corrections for the state in 1941, was redefining its purpose as one of rehabilitation (J. B. Jacobs, 1977). So that his prisons would appear to be at the forefront of the move to a rehabilitative focus, the numbers of inmates in school and in vocational programming did increase, though staff, under the guise of providing vocational training, were able to use the inmate labor to repair their appliances and cars for free.

By the 1960s, Stateville and other Illinois prisons, much like the rest of the country, were under pressure internally by more career-oriented professionals interested in management of prisons and externally by greater racial consciousness and an emerging inmates' rights movement. Eventually, such prisons had to open their doors to other ideas and perspectives and sometimes the press, as well as court-mandated legal review of their practices (J. B. Jacobs, 1977).

The 1960s through the 1990s saw a boom in prison building across the country, most of the medium- and minimum-security variety, which were more likely to classify inmates according to both security and treatment needs, institute rehabilitative programming

Audio 3.2: Obama Visits Federal Prison in Oklahoma to Tout Criminal Justice Reform

Medical model: Rehabilitation model that assumes criminals are sick and need treatment.

Big House prisons: Fortress stone or concrete prisons, usually maximum security, whose attributes include "isolation, routine, and monotony." Strict security and rule enforcement, at least formally, and a regimented schedule are other hallmarks of such facilities.

Convict code: Informal rules that inmates live by vis-à-vis the institution and staff.

(although the amount and value of this have varied from state to state and by time period), and employ the use of good time and parole (except in those states ... ... abolished it as part of a determinate-sentencing schema; see Chapter 5). Thus, by the 1960s and 1970s, the ideal of a correctional institution had been more fully realized in many parts of the country and in some prisons. However, the extent to which it truly was realized is in doubt. Staff hired to work in these prisons, other than the few treatment staff, tended to have only a GED or high school diploma and were not paid a professional wage. The prisons were understaffed. Also, they often were crowded, and educational and other treatment programs, even work programs, were limited. Good time was usually given, though inmates could lose it. They did not, in fact, earn it; rather, they did time and got it. Parole was typically poorly supervised, and by the 1970s and through the 1980s and early 1990s, several states and the federal government eliminated it as they moved to determinate sentencing (see Chapter 5).

By the mid-1970s, a conservative mood regarding crime had gripped the country, and skepticism had developed about the value of rehabilitative programming. The media and politicians played on the fear of crime, and despite the fact that overall street crime has been decreasing since the early 1980s in the United States, and violent crime has been decreasing since the mid-1990s, a prison-building boom ensued (Irwin, 2005). Prisons of the 1980s, 1990s, and into the 2000s reflect all of these earlier trends and influences. The maximum- and supermaximum-security prisons of today (and possibly some medium- and minimum-security prisons) are merely **warehouse prisons**, where inmates' lives and movement are severely restricted and rule bound. There is no pretense of rehabilitation in warehouse prisons; punishment and incapacitation are the only justifications for such places. The more hardened and dangerous prisoners are supposed to be sent there, and their severe punishment is to serve as a deterrent to others in lesser security prisons.

These lesser security prisons, the medium- and minimum-security prisons, which compose roughly two thirds of all prisons, do still have the trappings of rehabilitation programming, though it is limited in scope and funding, and they usually afford good time and even parole. (Most states still have a version of these.) They, too, are often crowded and understaffed, and their staff are not as educated or well paid as one might wish. However, such prisons do approximate the original ideal of a correctional institution.

The rest of this book will be focused primarily on the correctional-institution model as it is often imperfectly implemented in the United States. There are some who argue (e.g., Irwin, 2005) that the rehabilitative ideal is not realized in prisons and, instead, that programming is too often used to control inmates rather than to help locate another life path for them that does not involve crime. Correctional institutions intended to rehabilitate instead end up warehousing the "dangerous classes" (Irwin, 2005) or the poor and minorities. Of course, our history of corrections would lead us to be skeptical of any easy claims to rehabilitative change. (For a fuller discussion of rehabilitative programming, see Chapters 10, 11, and 12.) As will be explored in this book, too often a plan, though well intentioned, is inadequately conceived and executed, and as a result, nothing changes, or worse, we achieve precisely the opposite results.

AP Video 3.1: Texas Prison Reform

●●● THEMES THAT PREVAIL IN CORRECTIONAL HISTORY

There are several themes that are interwoven throughout the history and current operation of corrections in the United States. The overriding one, of course, has been money. Operating a correctional institution or a program is a costly undertaking, and from the first, those engaged in this business have had to concern themselves with how to fund it. Of course, the availability of funding for correctional initiatives is shaped by the political

Warehouse prison: Large prisons, of any security level, where inmates' lives and movement are severely restricted and rule bound. There is no pretense of rehabilitation; punishment, incapacitation, and deterrence are the only justifications.

PERSPECTIVE FROM A PRACTITIONER

Pat Mahoney, Alcatraz Corrections Officer

Position: Corrections Officer and Boat Captain

Location: Alcatraz Federal Penitentiary

How long were you a corrections officer on Alcatraz?

From 1956 to 1963, so seven years—the best seven years of my career. Alcatraz was a special place, from the guards to the convicts.

What were the primary duties and responsibilities of a corrections officer on Alcatraz?

There were about 15 positions, from tower, to kitchen, to garbage truck, to prison industries, supporting food and water deliveries, and supervising convict efforts for clean up and all the other daily requirements. It was surprisingly busy. Corrections officers also manned the gun gallery in the cell house. Roles were changed about every three months. I was originally a corrections officer; then, I was promoted to boat captain. I was also always on call if any work had to be done. I also supervised a crew that did maintenance for the actual prison.

In general, what did a typical day for a corrections officer on Alcatraz include?

In the cell house, there were several in charge of convict teams that cleaned the cell house continuously. They supervised or conducted inmate counts. They also had to get convicts from their cells to visiting attorneys, the barbershop, showers, meals, and work locations. The hours were always busy. Boredom was not ever a factor. Everyone had things to do at all times. The tower guards were the least active but had regular duties and communication with

others. Tower guards also watched the bay and occasionally saw a boat in distress, so they became a primary communicator to the Coast Guard for boats around Alcatraz.

Life on the Rock was fun when not on duty. We had a social hall, two bowling lanes, commissary for food, a playground for the kids, a handball court, and regular family dinners. About every three weeks, we had an island-wide dinner for all guards and families at the social hall. The view from the island was always tremendous. We looked right on downtown San Francisco.

What would your advice to someone either wishing to study or now studying criminal justice to become a corrections officer be?

The key is to be honest. If convicts think for a second that you are not honest, they will try to work you until you get fired or hurt. They can sense if someone is not honest. It was an exciting role, meeting some of the best and worst of society at Alcatraz. In prison, there are no weapons for the guards on the floor. All know this, so there is a common respect. You need good people skills to work with some who may have issues.

Note: Words written by Steve Mahoney (born on Alcatraz), as given by Pat Mahoney (corrections officer and boat captain, Alcatraz).

AP Video 3.2:
US Senate
Criminal Justice

sentiments of the time. Not surprisingly, schemes to fund correctional operations often have included ways to utilize inmate labor. Complementary themes that have shaped how money might be made and spent and how inmates or clients might be treated have included a move to greater compassion and humanity in correctional operations; the influence that the demographics of inmates themselves have played (e.g., race, class, and gender); religious sentiments about punishment and justice; architecture, as it aligns with supervision; the pressure that crowding places on correctional programs and institutions; and the fact that though reforms might be well intentioned, they do not always lead to effective or just practice. Again, this list of themes is not exhaustive, but it does include some of the prevailing influences that span correctional history in the United States and that require the attention of each successive generation.

SUMMARY

- Howard, Beaumont and Tocqueville, and Dix all conducted studies of corrections in their day and judged the relative benefits of some practices and institutions over others, based on their data.

- The Pennsylvania and the New York early prisons were the models for most American prisons of the 19th century.

- The ideal conception of prisons was rarely achieved in reality.

- Elmira Prison arose out of a prison reform movement that occurred roughly 50 years after Auburn Prison was built.

- The Southern and Northern versions of prisons that followed the Civil War were not like Elmira and instead were focused on utilizing inmate labor for the production of goods for private contractors.

- Stateville Prison, though conceived as a correctional institution and all that that implies, for the most part became a Big House prison.

- Correctional institutions, as a type of prison, do exist in a less-than-perfect form in the United States.

- Correctional institutions, as that term has been expanded to apply generically to jails, prisons, and some forms of community corrections, have been shaped by several themes throughout their history. These themes, though apparently constant, are a product of the times. For instance, Eastern Penitentiary would not be built today as a *general-use prison* because it would be considered cruel to isolate inmates from other human contact. Yet this kind of isolation, sometimes even with the tiny cells, is seen as beneficial by those who today build and operate supermaximum-security prisons for "special uses" to control "incorrigible" inmates (Kluger, 2007).

- In the following chapters, we will see such themes and the history of corrections, as detailed here, dealt with again and again. However, although we continue to repeat both the mistakes and successes of the past, that does not mean we cannot and have not made any progress in corrections. There is no question that, on the whole, the vast majority of jails and prisons in this country are much better than were those for much of the last 200 years, though the unprecedented use of correctional sanctions in the United States would be regarded by some as overly harsh and thus a regressive trend. These themes presented here represent ongoing questions (e.g., how much money or compassion or religious influence is the "right" amount), and as such, we are constantly called upon to address them.

KEY TERMS

Big House prisons 64

Contract and lease systems 63

Convict code 64

Correctional institutions 48

Elmira Reformatory 62

Marks system 62

Medical model 64

New York prison system 53

Newgate Prison in New York City 50

Pennsylvania prison system 51

Stateville Prison 63

Walnut Street Jail 49

Warehouse prison 65

DISCUSSION QUESTIONS

1. Discuss the relative benefits and drawbacks of the Pennsylvania versus the New York model of early prisons. What did Beaumont and Tocqueville and Dix think of them, and why? Which type of prison would you rather work in or be incarcerated in, and why?

2. What role did Penn, Bentham, Beccaria, and Howard play in reforming the prisons and jails of their time? Are the concerns they raised still valid today?

3. How has the question of inmate labor shaped the development of prisons over time?

4. Note why there is often a disconnect between the intentions of reformers and the ultimate operation of their reforms. Why is it difficult for theory to be put into practice? How might we ensure that there is a truer implementation of reforms?

5. How are the themes that run through the history of corrections represented in current practices today? Why do these themes continue to have relevance for correctional operations over the centuries?

USEFUL INTERNET SITES

Please note that the sites listed can be accessed at edge.sagepub.com/stohrcorrections.

American Correctional Association: www.aca.org

The ACA is an organization that has, for 146 years, focused on professionalizing corrections in the United States. Their website and materials provide information on the latest training, research, and ideas in corrections.

American Jail Association: www.corrections.com/aja

The AJA is an organization that also focuses on professionalization in corrections but as it involves jails. Their website provides information about the latest training, trends, and research in jails.

American Probation and Parole Association: www.appa-net.org

The APPA is an organization that focuses on the professionalization of probation and parole or community corrections. From their website, you can learn about the best research and training and the newest ideas about practices in community corrections.

Bureau of Justice Statistics: www.bjs.gov

The BJS provides an incredible wealth of information about all manner of criminal justice topics, including corrections. It is one of our go-to websites when we are investigating a correctional topic (or police or courts, etc.).

John Howard Society (Canada): www.johnhoward.ca

The John Howard Society, named after the jail and prison reformer of the same name, is an organization devoted to the reform of correctional institutions. From their website, you can learn about any progress being made on that front.

New York Correction History Society: www.correctionhistory.org

If you are interested in the history of corrections in New York State (and of course, we are because the New York model was so important in the history of American corrections), then you should check out this website.

Office of Justice Research: nij.gov

As with the Bureau of Justice Statistics, the OJR, under the National Institute of Justice, website highlights some of the best research out there on corrections (particularly probation and parole) and other criminal justice topics.

Pennsylvania Prison Society: www.prisonsociety.org

As with the John Howard Society, the Pennsylvania Prison Society in the United States is devoted to the reform of prisons. They have a long and revered history in this area, and their website should be a go-to source for those interested in this area of study.

Vera Institute: www.vera.org

The Vera Institute has been behind some of the biggest criminal justice reforms of the last 40 years. Check out their website to learn what important reforms and issues are on the correctional horizon.

$SAGE edge™

Sharpen your skills with SAGE edge at **edge.sagepub.com/stohrcorrections**. SAGE edge for Students provides a personalized approach to help you accomplish your coursework goals in an easy-to-use learning environment. You'll find action plans, mobile-friendly eFlashcards, and quizzes as well as video, web, and resources and links to SAGE journal articles to support and expand on the concepts presented in this chapter.

4 Ethics and Corrections

TEST YOUR KNOWLEDGE

Test your knowledge about ethics in corrections by answering the following questions. Check your answers on page 534 after reading the chapter.

1. Ethics and morality are the same thing. (True or false?)

2. What is the difference between deontological and teleological approaches to ethics?

3. The ethical-formalism framework includes the belief that there is a universal law that includes clear rights and wrongs. (True or false?)

4. Utilitarianism follows the principle that what is good is that which results in the greatest utility for the greatest number. (True or false?)

5. Most religions include a universal set of rights and wrongs. (True or false?)

6. Noble-cause corruption is the idea that it is okay to do the wrong thing if it is for the right reasons. (True or false?)

7. A correctional officer who engages in unethical behavior for personal gain is practicing official deviance. (True or false?)

8. There are characteristics of correctional work that make it more susceptible to ethical violations. (True or false?)

Check your answers on page 534 after reading the chapter.

LEARNING OBJECTIVES

- Explain the differences between ethics and morality

- Describe the different ethical frameworks

- Analyze why people are motivated to commit ethical violations

- Identify why corrections workers might be prone to ethics violations and how they might be prevented

A NOVICE BOWS TO SUBCULTURAL PRESSURE

Mary K. Stohr

When I first started as a correctional officer at an adult male prison in Washington State, I was the second woman hired (and the first was hired a month before me). I was relatively well educated (two bachelor's degrees) and had worked at all kinds of jobs since age 10 but never in corrections. I was young (25), scared, and naïve. My first reports were rejected by my sergeant as too wordy, and I was thought to be too soft on the inmates. (I called the inmates Mr. this and Mr. that and treated them with courtesy.) After about four weeks on the job and in an effort to help me, a well-meaning sergeant took me aside and said, "Stohr, I'm worried about you. I'm not sure you can do this job. You've got to learn to write better [meaning less and in a more spare fashion—he might as well have said, 'Just the facts, ma'am'], and you've got to treat the inmates

with less respect, or you aren't going to make it on this job."

We were in a back area of the control room, and he pointed to an inmate at the control room window—we'll call him Mr. Smith. He said, "That man Smith, he's a dirty baby raper [which I took to mean that Smith was a child molester]. He's been hanging around the window when you're here because you are too nice to him. You've got to treat him differently, or he'll take advantage of you." Essentially, he said you don't have to be mean (he wasn't that kind of man), but you shouldn't be friendly either.

Well, I took this sergeant's advice to heart, as I knew he was trying to help me, and there were a few of the staff at the prison who wanted to see me and the other woman fail. I also paid attention to his advice, as he was well respected and had welcomed me to the job. (He was an uncle to the first woman hired.) I diligently studied the reports of other officers and tried to imitate them. As a result, my reports were suddenly accepted. But the thing I did that was small and that I regret was that I treated Mr. Smith with less respect than he probably deserved; not that he wasn't a child molester (I read his file when I became a counselor and had access to it), but he was still a human being, he was in my care, and how I acted was not professional. The next time Mr. Smith came to the window for his meds, I did not meet his eyes; he became Smith without the Mr., and I was quite abrupt with him. This kind of behavior characterized most of our interactions from then on. The sympathetic sergeant witnessed this and literally patted my back and said, "Stohr, you'll be alright," and that was it; I was accepted into the subculture, at least by him, but I wasn't entirely happy about it or proud of myself.

••• INTRODUCTION: TO DO THE RIGHT THING!

Video 4.1: Surveillance Video Shows Guards Let Teen Prisoners Fight

As you likely gathered from Chapters 2 and 3 on the history of corrections, ethical abuses have always been a problem for corrections workers. Their jobs are largely hidden from public view, somewhat cloaked in secrecy, with enormous amounts of discretion, and they deal with people in their care who have few rights and protections. Moreover, as we will discuss throughout this book, these are jobs (e.g., correctional officers, sergeants, lieutenants, and captains; probation and parole officers; correctional counselors; and numerous other positions) that do not always have professional status in terms of pay, training, experience, or educational requirements (these problems are all particularly true for correctional officers, less so for the other positions listed here) that would ensure the best people are always hired and that they use their discretion wisely. Therefore, unqualified people are sometimes in these demanding correctional jobs, and because of this, they are more likely to make bad and sometimes unethical choices.

It cannot be overemphasized, however, that the vast majority of correctional staff, whether a correctional officer working in an adult facility or a probation officer working with youth in the community, are *ethical* in their work practices, meaning that they do the right thing. It is those few bad apples who leave a negative impression of corrections work and workers. Luckily, there are things an organization and its managers and workers can do to minimize abuse of power and resources by staff and to correct the misbehavior of some staff. The development of codes of ethics, the professionalization of staff, and the routinization of policies and procedures are all key to preventing ethical abuses. In this chapter, we will review those efforts to reduce corruption and abuses in corrections, which might be both unethical and illegal (see In Focus 4.1), but first, we will discuss what ethics are and are not and the source of ethical and unethical behavior.

DEFINING ETHICS: WHAT IS RIGHT (AND WRONG)?

Web 4.1: ACA Code of Ethics

As mentioned in the foregoing, **ethics** is the study of what is right and wrong, and to be ethical is to practice in your work what is "right" behavior. But you might ask (rightly!), What is right behavior? In a larger sense, it is what is legal (what the law is), and in an organizational sense, it is what is legal, too, but also what is allowed and not allowed according to codes of ethics and policies and procedures of that workplace. So a person could sexually harass others in the workplace (for example, make negative comments about them or undermine their work because of their gender), but this behavior, though unethical and perhaps prohibited by the workplace code of ethics and policies and procedures, may not rise to the level of illegal behavior.

Ethics: The study of right and wrong professional conduct.

Morality, we should note, is not the same as ethics, as it concerns what is right or wrong in the personal sphere, whereas ethics is concerned with the professional sphere. People

IN FOCUS 4.1

A Lack of Ethics: Florida's YSI Private Prisons for Youth

In Florida, all of the juvenile prisons in the state are operated by private companies, and Youth Services International (YSI), a for-profit company owned by former hotelier James F. Slattery, operates about 9% of them (Kirkham, 2013, p. 1). YSI also operates detention centers and boot camps. Slattery's company has been able to secure these contracts and many others in other states such as Georgia, Maryland, Nevada, New York, and Texas, worth over $100 million in the Florida contracts alone, despite the fact that the Justice Department has investigated complaints about them in several of these states. Auditors in Maryland found that YSI workers have encouraged fighting between inmates, and staff reportedly routinely fail to report "riots, assaults and claims of sexual abuse" (Kirkham, 2013, p. 2). A Bureau of Justice Statistics report indicated that a YSI facility in Palm Beach, Florida, had the "highest rate of reported sexual assaults out of 36 facilities reviewed in Florida" (Kirkham, 2013, p. 2). YSI had only 9% of the state contracts for youth beds in the state of Florida, but it had 15% of the cases of excessive force and injured youth (Kirkham, 2013, p. 8). Local public defender's offices and the Southern Poverty Law Center have complained about the handling of youth and conditions at YSI facilities with little response by the state. In an investigation by a *Huffington Post* reporter, where official records were reviewed and former employees were interviewed, Kirkham (2013) found the following:

- Staff underreported fights and assaults to avoid scrutiny and the possible loss of contracts.
- Staff abused youth in the facilities by hitting and choking them, sometimes to the point of fracturing bones.
- Turnover of staff was high.
- Food was restricted and prepared incorrectly or in an unsanitary manner, and youth were encouraged to gamble with others to win their food portions.

When the reporter asked why, with this dismal record of care, YSI was continually offered contracts, the answer he received from those concerned about the treatment of juveniles both inside and outside of the state of Florida was that YSI supported the political campaigns of Florida's and other states' politicians with hefty donations. The company has donated more in Florida to politicians than two of the largest companies in the state,

> donating more than $400,000 to state candidates and committees over the last 15 years, according to the HuffPost's review. The recipient of the largest share of those dollars was the Florida Republican Party, which took in more than $276,000 in that time. Former Florida Senate President Mike Haridopolos, an avid supporter of prison privatization, received more than $15,000 from company executives during state and federal races. (Kirkham, 2013, p. 6)

According to sources cited in the article, margins are narrow in the operation of correctional facilities (in other words, there is not a lot of fat in publicly operated prisons or jails), so if private-prison companies want to make money for their owners and investors, it means that they have to cut staff pay or benefits, slash programming, or feed people less, and it appears that all three of these things are happening at YSI facilities, indicating unethical (if not illegal) behavior by politicians, company managers, and correctional officers on the line.

DISCUSSION QUESTIONS

1. Based on the above narrative, what factors led to the abuses reported in the YSI facilities?

2. What steps can be taken to reduce the incidence of such abuses in like facilities?

3. How is staffing tied up in the nature and amount of the abuse?

tend to base their beliefs about what is right or wrong, ethical or unethical, and moral or immoral on what they have learned from any number of sources. For instance, it is not difficult to figure out what the right thing is to do in the case of the death of Mr. Echevarria (as showcased in the Policy and Research box) because what we have learned from our family, schools, religious teachings, workplace policies, or other sources have helped us determine our own sense of right and wrong in such instances.

PHOTO 4.1: A correctional officer opens a gate for an inmate. The security of an institution relies on the vigilance of officers' closing and locking gates.

••• ETHICAL FOUNDATION FOR PROFESSIONAL PRACTICE

It is not clear how much of an ethical foundation most humans are born with, though it is clear that several institutions try to instill one in their members. The family is likely the most influential social institution to inculcate ethics and morality. Educational institutions, both K–12 schools and colleges, all in some way or another and usually in many ways, discuss what is right and wrong in many different situations. Diverse religions all convey a sense of right and wrong, and a key concept emanating from many of them is the *golden rule*, or "do unto others as you would have done unto you." Other institutions—such as the military, social and professional clubs, even kids' sports teams, and, of course, the work environment itself— all strive to instill a moral or ethical framework in their members. The larger culture and life experiences doubtless also contribute to one's sense of right and wrong.

Much of the research on ethics also reviews the theoretical bases for decisions involving ethics (Braswell, McCarthy, & McCarthy, 1991; Pollock, 1994, 1998, 2010; Rohr, 1989; R. C. Solomon, 1996). The philosophical touchstones that are referenced as guides to human decision making are ethical formalism, utilitarianism, religion, natural law, the ethics of virtue, the ethics of care, and egoism.

Moral behavior is shaped by both deontological and teleological ethical systems, and these touchstones are subsets of them. **Deontological ethical systems** are concerned with whether the act itself is good, and **teleological ethical systems** are focused on the consequences of the act. If the act itself is moral or ethical, then someone who is guided by a deontological framework is not concerned about the consequences of the act. It is enough to just act in a moral fashion. Someone who is guided by a teleological ethical system does not care so much about the rightness or the wrongness of the act but about whether the consequences of the act are good. Pollock (1998; 2010) defines the ethical frameworks that derive from these ethical systems in her book, *Ethics in Crime and Justice: Dilemmas and Decisions.*

ETHICAL FORMALISM

She defines **ethical formalism** as "what is good is that which conforms to the categorical imperative" (Pollock, 1998, p. 48). Under this system, there is the belief that there is a universal law that includes clear rights and wrongs. The philosopher Immanuel Kant (1774–1804) noted that there is a categorical imperative that requires that each person act as he or she would like all others to act (very much like the golden rule mentioned in the foregoing). Kant also believed that people must seek to be guided by reason in their decision making. Ethical formalism falls under a deontological system, as the focus is on the act and its rightness (or wrongness), rather than on the consequences of the act and their goodness (or badness). It is a position that does not account for gray areas: An act is either right, or it is wrong. So some acts, such as murder, lying, and stealing, are always wrong, even when the end of these acts is good.

Deontological ethical systems: Systems concerned with whether the act itself is good.

Teleological ethical systems: Systems focused on whether the consequences of the act are good.

Ethical formalism: Determines morality based on a universal law that includes clear rights and wrongs.

POLICY AND RESEARCH   Mentally Ill Inmate Dies at Rikers

In a series of articles appearing in the *New York Times*, reporter Michael Schwirtz (2014a; 2014b) documents the abuse and neglect suffered by mentally ill inmates incarcerated in the Rikers Island jails. Rikers Island jails are a complex of 10 jails on an island in the East River of New York City. Twenty officers from Rikers have been prosecuted for assaults on inmates in the last five years. In mid-March 2014, a mentally ill inmate died from being left in an overheated cell at Rikers. But the particular subject of these articles is a 25-year-old inmate named Jason Echevarria, who was diagnosed with bipolar disorder. He was placed in a special mental-health unit at Rikers because of his diagnosed mental illness and because he had behavioral problems when in the general population of the jail. He had a record of attempted suicides while incarcerated at Rikers (Schwirtz, 2014a; 2014b).

Because there were problems with raw sewage coming out of toilets, on August 18, 2012, inmates were given a packet of powdered detergent that they were to use to clean up their cells (Schwirtz, 2014a, 2014b). By policy, inmates were supposed to be given detergent that was diluted by several gallons of water, but an inexperienced officer instead gave the full packets to inmates. Echevarria swallowed the toxic detergent, and as a result, his tongue and mouth skin were severely damaged as he vomited; he experienced extreme pain and expelled blood from his mouth over the course of several hours. A correctional officer claimed that he responded to Mr. Echevarria's cries for help by reporting his health problems to his captain, who told the correctional officer not to talk to him about this again unless the inmate was dead. Despite this warning, the correctional officer claimed that he reported to the captain twice more about the inmate's distress and even tried to call for medical assistance at least

once but was prevented from doing so by the captain. Both the captain and the officer came off their shifts without getting any medical assistance for the inmate. Mr. Echevarria was dead the next morning. The captain was demoted to an officer position, was arrested by the FBI, and is being prosecuted for violating the civil rights of Mr. Echevarria. The officer was fired and has filed a wrongful-termination suit, disputing the captain's claim that he was never told about Mr. Echevarria's health crisis.

DISCUSSION QUESTIONS

1. Why aren't correctional facilities well suited to handle the mentally ill?

2. Instead of incarcerating the mentally ill, what should public policy be instead?

United States Geological Survey

PHOTO 4.2: An aerial view of the Rikers Island jail complex.

UTILITARIANISM

Utilitarianism is defined as "what is good is that which results in the greatest utility for the greatest number" (Pollock, 1998, p. 48). So morality is determined by how many people were helped by the act. The philosopher Jeremy Bentham (1748–1832) believed

> **Utilitarianism:**
> Determines morality based on how many people were helped by the act.

AP Video 4.1:
Rikers

that people will do a "utilitarian calculus" as regards how much pleasure or pain a given act will garner, and they will act on that to maximize pleasure. But when one's pleasure conflicts with the greater good for society, then one must bow to the greater good, under a utilitarian perspective. As utilitarianism is focused on the end—whether it is moral or immoral or ethical or unethical—achieved by an act, it falls under the teleological system.

RELIGIOUS PERSPECTIVE

People who employ a **religious perspective** to guide their decisions believe that "what is good is that which conforms to God's will" (Pollock, 1998, p. 48). This is a perspective that weighs what is right or wrong based on one's religion and covers all facets of living and relationships with others. How one treats others, how one lives his or her life, and one's understanding of the meaning of life itself are all influenced by this religious perspective. Under this perspective, both the means and the ends are foci of interest and are perceived through the lens of what one believes his or her god or gods would want. Most religions include a universal set of rights and wrongs, much like ethical formalism, and they have, as mentioned already, a form of the categorical imperative or the golden rule. Although there is widespread agreement across religions on some matters, there is much disagreement about social practices, such as drinking alcohol, dancing, certain kinds of foods, behavior on holy days, how appropriate clothing is, and the political and social status of women and other minorities, such as members of LGBTI (lesbian, gay, bisexual, transgender, and intersex) communities.

Religious perspective: A perspective that weighs what is right or wrong based on one's religion.

PHOTO 4.3: An elaborate cathedral front, symbolic of the wealth and artistry devoted to religious practice over the centuries.

NATURAL LAW

Adherents of an ethical framework based on **natural law** believe that "what is good is that which is natural" (Pollock, 1998, p. 48). Behavior is or should be motivated by what is universally understood to be right and wrong. Using reason, all humans can figure these rights and wrongs out. The major difference between a natural-law believer and someone who is guided by a religious perspective is that, in the latter case, the supreme being or beings are the ones who determine what is right and wrong, whereas under a natural-law perspective, these rights and wrongs are just clear and knowable through reason. Under this perspective, we know what truth and decency are, and so we just need to act on our natural inclination in that direction. These natural laws about what is right and wrong are believed to be cross-cultural and true over time; they are not relative to time or place. Moreover, out of these natural laws flow natural rights, such as those accorded to citizens under the Constitution of the United States.

ETHICS OF VIRTUE

Believers in the **ethics of virtue** think that "what is good is that which conforms to the golden mean [the middle ground between positions]" (Pollock, 1998, p. 48). Instead of focusing on the nature of an action, the question here is whether the person is virtuous or good. The end to be achieved is to live a good and moral life by performing virtuous acts. Such virtues include "thriftiness, temperance, humility, industriousness, and honesty" (Pollock, 1998, p. 43). Models of virtue provide examples for those interested in living with integrity and according to a code of ethics.

ETHICS OF CARE

Relatedly, an **ethics of care** is centered on good acts. It is a deontological perspective. Those who subscribe to this framework believe that "what is good is that which meets the needs of those concerned" (Pollock, 1998, p. 48). Under this perspective, the care and concern for others is paramount. This is a perspective that is regarded as more "feminine," as it is believed that women, as a group, are more attuned to the needs of others. Carol Gilligan (1982) found in her research on moral development that women's perspective differs from men's in this area. Women are more likely to be concerned about the care of others as guiding how they behave. Peacemaking and restorative justice are thought to derive from the ethics-of-care framework.

EGOISM

The last ethical framework that Pollock (1998) mentions is one based on the individual—namely, **egoism**. Under this framework, the needs of self are most important, so acting to satisfy one's own wants and needs under this framework is acting ethically. As the act is the focus here, egoism falls under the deontological perspective. Even when acting on behalf of others, it is believed that one is acting out of *enlightened egoism*, or helping and caring for others so they will do the same for you when you are in need of assistance.

●●● WHY PEOPLE BEHAVE UNETHICALLY

Despite the influence of these ethical frameworks, there are several reasons why people behave unethically. The most obvious and perhaps the most common reason is for *personal gain* or *out of selfishness*. For instance, the owner of YSI, which manages private prisons for juveniles in Florida, clearly benefits financially from cutting staff salaries and inmate food (this has to be unethical, right?), and not surprisingly, the result is poorly

Natural law: Adherents of this framework believe what is good is what is known to be so.

Ethics of virtue: A framework that emphasizes the virtue of one's character over actions.

Ethics of care: A framework centered on good acts in which the care of and concern for others is paramount.

Egoism: Under this framework, the needs of self are most important, so acting to satisfy one's own wants and needs is acting ethically.

ETHICAL ISSUE 4.1

What Would You Do?

You are a new manager (two weeks on the job) of a public correctional institution (jail) that has experienced several ethical crises in the last year. Your jail has been sued twice successfully in the last year for overcrowding and neglect of the mental-health needs of inmates. You were hired to "clean up" the ethical environment of the facility, though you already recognize that the staff subculture in the jail is intransigent and resistant to change. What steps would you take to transform this jail to accomplish the desired change? What resistance do you expect to encounter, and how do you think it can be overcome?

operated and, at times, dangerous facilities (see In Focus 4.1). The captain supervising the Rikers jail mental-health unit when Mr. Echevarria died, if he did what he is accused of—ignoring the desperate health needs of an inmate—behaved both criminally and unethically for selfish reasons: He did not want to be bothered (see Research and Policy box). The remedy for such a motivation is multifaceted and will be discussed momentarily.

OFFICIAL DEVIANCE

Another reason people in corrections might behave unethically is official deviance. **Official deviance** is defined by Lee and Visano (1994) as

> actions taken by officials which violate the law and/or the formal rules of the organization, but which are clearly oriented toward the needs and goals of the organization, as perceived by the official, and thus fulfill certain informal rules of the organization. (p. 203)

Audio 4.1: Investigation Into Private Prisons Reveals Crowding, Under-Staffing and Inmate Deaths

Lee and Visano (1994) studied officials' behavior in both the United States and Canada, and they found that many deviant acts by criminal justice actors are not committed for personal gain but are committed to help the organization or to be in compliance with subcultural goals. If the subculture values secrecy and protection of fellow officers, as is true for subcultures in corrections, then one might be called upon to lie, even on the witness stand and under oath, to protect that officer when he or she is charged with wrongdoing (Stohr & Collins, 2014). The important point here is that the organizational member who lies or engages in other acts of official deviance gains nothing from engaging in the deviance; it is the organization or other organizational members who benefit. The penalty for organizational members who refuse to engage in official deviance might be shunning, harassment, or even firing for unsubstantiated reasons. The remedies to reduce official deviance are noted in the following (after the discussion of noble-cause corruption).

Journal Article 4.1: Noble Cause Corruption

NOBLE-CAUSE CORRUPTION

A third reason why criminal justice workers and corrections workers, in particular, might engage in unethical behavior might be that they are motivated by noble-cause corruption. Crank and Caldero (2000) define the **noble cause** for police officers as a

> profound moral commitment to make the world a safer place to live. Put simply, it is getting bad guys off the street. Police believe they're on the side of angels and their purpose in life is getting rid of bad guys. (p. 35)

Official deviance: When officials act in a way that benefits their organization but violates laws or formal rules.

Crank and Caldero (2000) identify two noble-cause themes that explain police officer behavior: "The smell of the victim's blood" and "the tower" (p. 35). What they mean by the smell of the victim's blood is that police officers are motivated to act to protect and save victims. But in the course of trying to protect victims, they may step over an ethical line and lie, plant evidence, or abuse force so as to catch the "bad guy" by whatever means. And it is always the ends (e.g., catching the "bad guy") that are more important than the means (e.g., acting professionally and ethically) with noble-cause corruption.

Noble cause: A profound moral commitment to make the world a safer place to live.

What Crank and Caldero (2000) mean by "the tower" is that police officers, when confronted with a shooter in a tower, will run to the tower (they will act in the face of danger) when everyone else is running from it. Because they are inclined to run to the tower—metaphorically, at least—and also because their job requires that they *act* in dangerous situations, they may cross the ethical and legal line by overreacting or making rash decisions. They will "run to the tower" because they want to make things right. Crank and Caldero (2011) and others (e.g., Bartollas & Hahn, 1999; O'Connor, 2001) think that the police are motivated by their desire to make the world right. They tend to see the world in black and white, and when a suspect interferes with this perception, the police might engage in unethical behavior because it is inspired by acting in the cause of "rightness." The problem is that the police are not always right, and they cannot always see what is right (as with all of us).

Noble-cause corruption, as an explanation for unethical behavior by corrections workers, makes a great deal of sense. One of the authors, when working in a male prison as an officer many years ago, was told right away which inmates were in for "child molesting," though this information was supposedly confidential between the counselors and their clients (see the related story that appears at the beginning of this chapter). It was boldly stated that such inmates were not to be treated with respect by staff and were to be regarded with an additional dose of suspicion. Interactions with other correctional professionals over the years, in all kinds of correctional settings, reinforced this experience that correctional staff are motivated in their actions by "the victim's blood," especially when that victim is a child.

© REUTERS/Robert Galbraith

PHOTO 4.4: Correctional staff confer in the yard next to a housing unit at the Corcoran State Prison in Corcoran, California. Effective and honest communication between officers is a key component of correctional institutions.

People who are attracted to work in corrections are also doers and people who want to make the world right. They will not hesitate to "run to the tower" to accomplish this feat either. The authors know of several stories of officers in federal prisons, state prisons, and jails who were thrilled to be called to engage in the quelling of altercations in corrections. These are stories of correctional staff who enthusiastically "ran to the tower" to "make the world right," but at least in a few of these cases, those officers admitted that more force by staff was used to stop fights and put down disturbances than was strictly necessary. Once the fists started flying, the adrenaline took over, and the sense that force was being used to do good made its use, even its excessive use, justified.

Noble-cause corruption, as with official deviance and deviance for selfish ends, is all the more likely to occur in environments where the behavior of actors is hidden and little supervised, and the clients are powerless. These factors all accurately describe correctional environments. Most correctional work is done in some isolation from the larger community, and this is particularly true of prisons and jails. Even community correctional officers operate in environments in which the interactions are personal, and their content is not documented. Supervisors' span of control is stretched, and they don't always have adequate time to review an individual actor's behavior. Correctional clients are some of the most powerless people in the United States. By law, they have very few rights and legal protections, and thus, they are subject to the behavior of both ethical and unethical correctional personnel. Top all of these organizational and individual characteristics off with the fact that correctional staff have a great deal of **discretion** (defined here as the ability to make choices and to act or not act on those choices), and there is only one more ingredient necessary to make the perfect admixture for unethical behavior: the influence of a negative subculture.

Audio 4.2: NYC Correction Officers' Union Head Charged in Corruption Probe

Discretion: The ability to make choices and to act or not act on them.

IN FOCUS 4.2

Subcultural Values of Probation and Parole Officers

In ethics training exercises in 1994 and 1995, probation and parole managers in a western state identified the subcultural values of the community corrections officers they supervised (Stohr & Collins, 2009). They were as follows:

1. Always aid your coworker.

2. Never rat on coworkers.

3. Always cover for a coworker in front of clients.

4. Always support the coworker over the client in a disagreement.

5. Always support the decision of a coworker regarding a client.

6. Don't be sympathetic toward clients. Instead be cynical about them (to be otherwise is to be naïve).

7. Probation/parole officers are the "us" and everyone else is the "them," including administration, the media, and the rest of the community.

8. Help your coworkers by completing your own work and by assisting them if they need it.

9. Since you aren't paid much or appreciated by the public or the administration, don't be a rate buster (i.e., don't do more than the minimal amount of work).

10. Handle your own work and don't allow interference. (p. 63)

DISCUSSION QUESTIONS

1. Which of these subcultural values do you think makes the workplace better for staff but can lead to unethical behavior?

2. How might correctional managers and workers concerned about unethical behavior in the workplace prevent some of the most destructive of these values from being embraced in the workplace?

Source: *Criminal justice management: Theory and practice in justice-centered organizations*, by Stohr and Collins (2009), p. 63. By permission of Oxford University Press, USA.

Video 4.2:
San Antonio Tourists Sue Austin Police Claiming Excessive Force

SUBCULTURE

In fact, a key feature of correctional environments that would make staff and management more prone to engage in unethical behavior is the presence of a strong negative subculture. **Subcultures** are subsets of larger cultures with their own norms, values, beliefs, traditions, and history. They can be positive in their promotion of prosocial values and support of their members, but they can also be negative when they promote antisocial values and, in correctional work (or police work, too), unethical behavior. In an ethics training course conducted by one of the authors and a colleague for probation and parole managers, the participants identified several barriers to ethical practice in their workplaces. Most of these barriers Kauffman (1988, pp. 85–112) identified in his study of correctional officers, and Pollock (1994, p. 195) did so in her text on ethics and the negative side of subcultures (see In Focus 4.2).

••• HOW TO PREVENT UNETHICAL BEHAVIOR AND PROMOTE ETHICAL WORK PRACTICES

Subculture: A subset of a larger culture, with its own norms, values, beliefs, traditions, and history.

As you can see, a few of these subcultural values are positive in that they provide support of coworkers, but the ones that support coworkers, even if they are wrong or engaged in wrongdoing vis-à-vis their clients or the work, are negative and promote an unethical work environment. Most of the managers at that ethics training session reported that unethical behavior was common on the job and ranged from the routine, like rudeness to clients and their families, to the rare, like lying on reports and verbal and physical abuse of clients. The subcultural values listed before, however, made it difficult for managers to address the unethical behaviors.

This is why the organizational and individual remedies to prevent unethical behavior, whatever its motivation and in spite of the subculture, are multifaceted and include at least these:

▶ AP Video 4.2:
Freddie Gray

1. Hire people who are less likely to be motivated by personal gain. To do this, correctional organizations need a well-developed selection process, with extensive background checks on potential hires (Stohr & Collins, 2014).

2. Pay people a professional wage, as then they will be less likely to be tempted to engage in unethical behavior for personal gain.

3. Encourage professional development of employees through further education, training, and engagement in professional organizations, as employees who are immersed in a professional and learning subculture are more likely to encourage positive change in others and improve the workplace, and they may be less likely to be tolerant of a workplace subculture that fosters unethical behavior.

4. Develop an ethics code with employee input, and review it regularly in the department. By involving a cross-section of staff in the development of an ethics code, more staff are likely to feel like they "own it" and therefore support it.

5. Require extensive training in ethics at the beginning of employment and throughout the employee's career. More and ongoing training will reinforce the need to behave ethically, and it will undercut negative subcultural influences.

6. Supervise people sufficiently, and check up on what they are doing and how they are doing it.

7. Provide support for positive changes in the workplace that will enhance the ability of workers to do the job right. Sometimes, staff will claim that they cannot act ethically because there are not enough resources (e.g., time or staff) to do so; by ensuring there are enough resources—and this is hard to do in the public sector these days—managers make it possible for employees to do the work the right and ethical way.

8. Discipline violators of ethics, and if the violation of the rules or law is serious enough, fire them. Doing this will reinforce a positive subculture that is supportive of ethical work practice.

9. Promote those who behave ethically, and include ethics-related measures in evaluations. By doing this, managers will motivate all to support ethical practice.

10. Encourage whistle-blowing (the reporting of wrongdoing or problems in the workplace), and

Mikael Karlsson/Alamy Stock Photo

PHOTO 4.5: Corrections officer interacting positively with inmates.

IN FOCUS 4.3

The Abuse of Solitary Confinement in Florida

In March 2016, the Florida American Civil Liberties Union sent a letter to the U.S. Department of Justice's Civil Rights Division requesting a federal investigation into the overuse of solitary confinement (also known as restricted housing and isolation) by the Florida Department of Corrections (Simon & Wetstein, 2016). They noted that fully one in eight inmates in Florida prisons were held in solitary confinement. They also found that the numbers revealed a potential racial bias for males and females and those diagnosed with a mental illness in Florida prisons, as African Americans were overrepresented among those in solitary when compared to the number of blacks in the general population. They also found that about 23% of those with a mental illness in Florida prisons were kept in solitary confinement. Notably, much of this information was obtained through Freedom of Information Act requests, not provided voluntarily by the FDOC. Finally, the ACLU detailed a number of cases, from several prisons, where mentally ill and other inmates placed in solitary died because of neglect or outright torture by correctional staff. Some of those cases from the ACLU letter (Simon & Wetstein, 2016) are summarized here:

Randall Jordan-Aparo died in 2010, "after being gassed three times while in a solitary confinement cell" (p. 4). He had been ill and was denied medical care despite the knowledge that he had a rare blood disorder.

Rommell Johnson died in 2010, after being gassed twice with chemical agents within a five-minute span of time. He was asthmatic, and the medical examiner ruled that he died as a result of the gassing, which brought on a fatal asthma attack.

Darren Rainey died in 2012, "when he was tortured in a locked shower rigged to be controlled by guards from the outside, with its water temperature at approximately 180 degrees" (p. 4). Though his skin was literally falling off of his bones when he was found in the shower, the medical examiner ruled the death "accidental," and no one has been disciplined or fired as of March 2016.

Latandra Ellington died in 2014, alone in a solitary-confinement cell, reportedly from heart disease. Her family claimed she had no heart problems. "She had been placed there after she filed a complaint alleging that Sgt. Patrick Quercioli had engaged in sex with another prisoner, and threatened to kill Ellington" (p. 5). The family-sponsored autopsy found no heart disease "but found excessive bruising, and a lethal level of Amlodipine, a blood pressure medication, in her system" (p. 5).

Yalex Tirado died in solitary confinement in 2014 in a prison for juveniles with no explanation for his death provided by the facility. "This is a prison where, as The Miami Herald has reported, the sodomizing of inmates with broomsticks by other inmates has been common, and where nine guards have been charged over the last two years with battery or facilitating the entry of contraband" (p. 5).

DISCUSSION QUESTIONS

1. How likely do you think it is that these deaths and the abuse of solitary are isolated incidents and not representative of regular practice in these Florida prisons? What evidence do you have to support your argument?

2. If you had witnessed abuses such as these, what action, if any, would you have taken to stop them?

3. If staff are found to be guilty in the deaths of these inmates, what punishments do you think they deserve? Do you think that the staff who witnessed these kinds of abuses but did not report them should also be disciplined in some way? Why, or why not?

make it possible for people to do so anonymously. Despite an ethical manager and workers' best efforts, there is sometimes illegal or unethical behavior going on in the workplace, and because of the power of subcultures, correctional workers need to be able to report this behavior without fear of reprisal.

11. Develop the means for all employees to provide input into the decisions that are made by and for the organization, as doing so is more likely to be a check on management, uses the knowledge workers have, instills ownership of the work by those who do it, and leads to greater job satisfaction, less turnover, and more commitment to the job (Stohr & Collins, 2014).

12. Encourage involvement of outsider review and professional engagement (have an oversight board, support involvement in professional organizations, and provide access to researchers, politicians, and the media), as more openness is more likely to reduce unethical behavior and defuse the power of negative subcultures.

By using these remedies, the correctional manager and, where applicable, the correctional worker are more likely to turn the subculture into a positive support system that promotes ethical behavior. The remedies are also likely to increase professionalism and reduce abuse of clients.

••• WAR ON DRUGS = ATTACK ON ETHICS?

Wars are a popular thing for politicians to wage. Wars on poverty, crime, and drugs were the brainchildren of several presidents and carried on by others since the 1960s. The terminology of war is powerful and connotes a level of serious attention to a topic that few other terms convey. Campaigns, assaults, and offensives are waged in wars with some urgency behind them. A war means that all available resources and attention will be devoted to that effort, and those who do not agree—well, they are like traitors to a righteous cause. Yet these political wars, somewhat like wars waged with weaponry made of steel, are problematic, as they are fighting social ills—poverty,

Career Video 4.1: Former Drug Investigator

Web 4.2: Drug Policy Alliance

| **FIGURE** *4.1* | Public Views on Drug Policy in the United States |

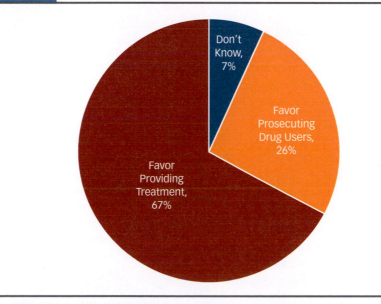

Don't Know, 7%

Favor Prosecuting Drug Users, 26%

Favor Providing Treatment, 67%

Note: Survey conducted February 14–23, 2014.

Source: "America's New Drug Policy Landscape," Pew Research Center, Washington, DC (April, 2014) http://www.people-press.org/2014/04/02/americas-new-drug-policy-landscape/4-2-14-1/

PHOTO 4.6: The war on drugs led to drug seizures like these.

ETHICAL ISSUE 4.2   ?

What Would You Do?

You are a probation officer with a large caseload of low-level drug offenders (mostly pot smokers). Some may be addicted to marijuana, and others may not, but you need to monitor them and ensure that they attend programming and provide clean urinalysis (UA) samples. The department of corrections you work for is in transition, however, moving from a more law enforcement focus to a greater treatment orientation. They have given you and other officers more leeway in decisions about whether to violate (write up) offenders who commit minor offenses. One of the UAs you take comes up dirty for marijuana, and you are faced with "violating" a client on your caseload who was convicted of felony drug possession. (There was enough to sell.) In all other ways, this client has done well, in that she has made all the meetings, been employed, and attended drug programming. Would you write a violation on this offender? (Doing so may result in jail time or a trip to prison.) Would it make any difference in your decision making if your client has two dependent children who will be placed in foster care should she be incarcerated? Why, or why not? Which ethical framework do you think best fits the decision you made?

crime, and substance abuse—which, though admittedly harmful, are somewhat intractable and very complex and therefore require sustained effort and multifaceted solutions. Because of the nature of the problems, wars on them never seem to end because the problems do not end. Though the Iraq War seemed to never end (lasting at least eight years), consider that the war on drugs was first mentioned by President Nixon in 1971 and has been waged by every president since. We currently spend at least $51 billion each year on the war on drugs in this country, and that does not account for the millions who have passed through correctional doors as enemy combatants in the war and the billions it has taken to pay for their arrest, prosecution, and incarceration; nor does it account for the lost tax revenue and disrupted families and lives the war has left in its wake (the collateral damage). Many scholars, commentators, and even politicians now consider the war on drugs to be an abject failure, in that it has not reduced the supply or use of illicit drugs, and instead, it has galvanized the illegal drug trade and corrupted government officials in this country and Mexico and Central and South America (Cullen, Jonson, & Stohr, 2014). According to the Drug Policy Alliance (2016) (an organization whose mission is to end the war on drugs), the following outcomes have resulted from the war on drugs:

- Amount spent annually in the United States on the war on drugs: **More than $51,000,000,000**

- Number of people arrested in 2014 in the United States on nonviolent drug charges: **1.56 million**

- Number of people arrested for a marijuana law violation in 2014: **700,993**

- Number of those charged with marijuana law violations who were arrested for possession only: **619,809 (88%)**

- Number of Americans incarcerated in 2014 in federal, state, and local prisons and jails: **2,224,400 or 1 in every 111 adults**, the highest incarceration rate in the world

- Proportion of people incarcerated for a drug offense in state prison that are black or Hispanic, although these groups use and sell drugs at similar rates as whites: **57%**

- Number of people killed in Mexico's drug war since 2006: **100,000+**

- Number of students who have lost federal financial aid eligibility because of a drug conviction: **200,000+**

- Number of people in the United States who died from a drug overdose in 2014: **47,055**

- The Centers for Disease Control and Prevention found that syringe access programs lower HIV incidence among people who inject drugs by **80%**. One-third of all AIDS cases in the United States have been caused by syringe sharing: **360,836 people**. U.S. federal government support for syringe access programs: **$0.00**, thanks to a federal ban reinstated by Congress in 2011 that prohibits any federal assistance for them. (p. 1)

So the point is that the war on drugs has been a huge resource suck, which has distracted our attention from drug treatment and real prevention, punished addicts, disproportionately incarcerated minority group members, and likely cost trillions of dollars over time. (It has been going on for 45 years at the time of this writing.) More to the point, it has challenged the ethical behavior of corrections officials by forcing them to overincarcerate some relatively minor offenders who got caught in its net. Correctional workers in prisons, jails, and detention centers or working in probation and parole and even their managers have little to no control over whom they are given to incarcerate or supervise in communities. But they are affected by the drug war because their facilities and caseloads have been crowded by such offenders, which has made carrying out their tasks very difficult and sometimes ethically challenging. They have been involved in drug monitoring and treatment to a much greater extent than if the war had not been waged. They have had to supervise people who—compared to robbers and rapists—do not really merit the use of incarceration and perhaps even community supervision. Therefore, we would add one more remedy to the list that will help organizations prevent unethical behavior, but this remedy must be understood by policy makers: Consider the likely outcomes of wars or other grand schemes on the ethics of the actors or soldiers tasked with carrying them out, and consider the larger social impact of waging war on your own citizens.

SUMMARY

- Ethical work practice is a messy business, sometimes clear-cut but often fraught with anxiety. The nature of corrections work and the organization's attendant subcultures often create situations where ethical dilemmas are common and their resolution difficult. Moreover, the kinds of people hired in corrections work, those with a noble-cause bent, are sometimes more susceptible to engaging in ethical abuses, though that is not their intent. Thankfully, there are things that organizations and individuals can do to prevent ethical abuses, but they require some resource commitment and resolve.

KEY TERMS

Deontological ethical systems 74

Discretion 79

Egoism 77

Ethical formalism 74

Ethics 72

Ethics of care 77

Ethics of virtue 77

Natural law 77

Noble cause 78

Official deviance 78

Religious perspective 76

Subculture 80

Teleological ethical systems 74

Utilitarianism 75

DISCUSSION QUESTIONS

1. Where do we learn our sense of right and wrong? Why do you think that some sources are more powerful in influencing people than others?

2. What makes the correctional workplace more susceptible to unethical behaviors than most workplaces? If you were to work in corrections, how would you make sure that you always made the "right decision"?

3. What can organizations do to prevent noble-cause corruption? Do you think you are a person who could be corrupted this way?

4. Which ethical framework best describes your feeling about ethics? Why do you think this is applicable to you?

5. Discuss how the drug war has affected corrections and how it has threatened the ethical practice of workers.

USEFUL INTERNET SITES

Please note that the sites listed can be accessed at edge.sagepub.com/stohrcorrections.

American Civil Liberties Union (ACLU): www.aclu.org

The ACLU has been at the forefront of the effort to protect inmates from abuses in corrections for many years. On their website, you will learn about their successes in this area and where they think more effort is warranted.

The Sentencing Project: www.sentencingproject.org

The Sentencing Project has been fighting for decades for the reduction of sentences for crimes in this country. On their website, they feature the areas in which they have achieved some successes and where more attention is still needed.

Southern Poverty Law Center: www.splcenter.org

The Southern Poverty Law Center is focused on identifying and ending hate crimes in this country. On their website, you'll learn about where hate-centered organizations are located and what they are up to.

Drug Policy Alliance: www.drugpolicy.org

The DPA has been involved in changing U.S. policy on drugs. On their website, they feature how much they have achieved and what still needs to be done.

$SAGE edge™

Sharpen your skills with SAGE edge at **edge.sagepub.com/stohrcorrections**. SAGE edge for Students provides a personalized approach to help you accomplish your coursework goals in an easy-to-use learning environment. You'll find action plans, mobile-friendly eFlashcards, and quizzes as well as video, web, and resources and links to SAGE journal articles to support and expand on the concepts presented in this chapter.

Sentencing

The Application of Punishment

TEST YOUR KNOWLEDGE

Test your present knowledge of the criminal sentencing process by answering the following questions as true or false. Check your answers on page 534 after reading the chapter.

1. Basic principles of justice mandate that the criminal justice system punish every person convicted of committing the same crime equally, regardless of other differences.

2. The only concern at sentencing is the severity of the crime the defendant has committed.

3. Three-strike laws are laws that allow states to possibly imprison for life a person who has been convicted of a third felony.

4. If a person is convicted of two different crimes committed on two different occasions, he or she must be sentenced to consecutive terms (one to be served after the other is completed) of probation or prison.

5. Because victims or their survivors can unfairly prejudice a judge against a defendant, with the exception of death penalty cases, victims or survivors cannot have any input into the sentencing decision.

6. Except for statutory limitations, judges basically must decide on an appropriate sentence for convicted felons without any guidance or advice.

7. Blacks and other minorities are frequently subjected to discriminatory sentencing.

8. Separate courts exist for criminals with special problems, such as drug addiction.

9. All states use guidelines to help judges make sentencing decisions.

LEARNING OBJECTIVES

- Explain how modern sentencing engages Aristotle's notion of justice

- Describe the different types of sentencing and their rationales

- Assess the benefits and criticisms of plea bargains

- Discuss the role of victim impact statements and the issues surrounding sentencing disparity

- Identify the purpose of presentence reports and sentencing guidelines, as well as the contentious issues surrounding them

VINDICTIVE VERSUS SENSIBLE SENTENCING

"Jane" is a 30-year-old mother of three children, ages 8, 6, and 4. Her husband recently suffered a heart attack and died, leaving Jane with no money. Jane has only a 10th-grade education and cannot afford childcare costs, so she was forced onto the welfare rolls. When Christmas came around, she had no money to buy her children any presents, so she took a temporary Christmas job at the local megastore, where she earned $1,200 over a 2-month period. Jane did not report this income to the welfare authorities, as required by law, and a welfare audit uncovered her crime. The terrified

and deeply ashamed Jane pled guilty to grand theft, which carries a possible sentence of 2 years in prison, and was referred to the probation department for a presentence investigation report (PSI).

"Jim" is a 32-year-old male with a lengthy record of thefts and other crimes committed since he was 10 years old. Jim also pled guilty before the same judge on the same day and was likewise referred for a PSI. Jim had stolen money and parts totaling $1,200 from an auto parts store during one of his brief periods of employment.

These two cases point to a perennial debate about the appropriate sentence for people who commit the same crime. Recall the classical and positivist schools of thought discussed in Chapter 1. Although both positions are ultimately about the role of punishment, the classical position maintains that punishment should fit the crime and nothing else. That is, all people convicted of identical crimes should receive identical sentences, regardless of any differences they may have. The classical position maintains that Jane and Jim freely chose to commit the crimes, and the fact that Jim has a record and Jane does not is irrelevant. The positivist position is that punishment should fit the offender and be appropriate to rehabilitation. Jane's crime and Jim's crime were motivated by very different considerations; they are very different people morally, and blindly applying similar punishments to similar crimes without considering the possible consequences is pure folly. Think about these two cases and your own position on them as you read about the purpose of sentencing, the way sentencing guidelines are structured, and the uses of the PSI.

••• WHAT IS SENTENCING?

Feature Video 5.1: "Witness to Innocence" Death Row Exonerees Share Their Stories

Sentencing refers to a postconviction stage of the criminal justice process. A **sentence** is the punitive penalty ordered by the court after a defendant has been convicted of a crime either by a jury, following a bench trial by a judge, or in a plea bargain. Sentencing typically occurs about 30 days after conviction. The goals of sentencing are to implement one or more of the punishment philosophies discussed in Chapter 1: retribution, deterrence, incapacitation, or rehabilitation. In some states, juries may be entitled to pronounce a sentence, but in most states and in federal court, sentencing is determined by a judge—except in death penalty cases, where it is the jury's responsibility. The penalties meted out at sentencing can range from various forms of probation, coupled with fines, restitution, and/or treatment orders; house arrest or electronic monitoring; work release; jail or prison time; or the death penalty, all of which are discussed elsewhere in this book. The severity of the penalty depends on the crime or crimes for which the defendant is convicted and the extent of his or her criminal history, although other factors, both legitimate and illegitimate, may also come into play.

Feature Video 5.2: Goal of Sentencing

It is a major concern of the American criminal justice system that punishments received by defendants at sentencing should be consistent with justice. **Justice** is a moral concept that is difficult to define, but in essence, it means to treat people in ways consistent with norms of fairness and in accordance with what they justly deserve by virtue of their behavior. Perhaps the best definition was provided by the Greek philosopher Aristotle many centuries ago: "Justice consists of treating equals equally and unequals unequally according to relevant differences" (Walsh & Stohr, 2010, p. 133). In sentencing terms, this means that those who have committed the same crime and have similar criminal histories are considered legal "equals" and should be treated equally. Those who have committed different crimes and have different criminal histories are considered legal "unequals" and therefore should be treated unequally; that is, one should be treated either more leniently or more harshly than the other.

Sentence: A punitive penalty ordered by the court after a defendant has been convicted of a crime either by a jury or judge or in a plea bargain.

Justice: A moral concept about just or fair treatment consisting of "treating equals equally and unequals unequally according to relevant differences."

You may ask what these "relevant differences" are and who defines them. Strictly speaking, the relevant differences in sentencing should be limited to legally relevant factors (crime seriousness and prior record), but extralegal factors are often also brought into play, such as gang affiliation, a history of substance abuse, employment status, and family status. Depending on what these factors are, justice is either served or not served by adding them. A judge who sentences a remorseful mother (such as Jane, in the vignette) whose children would become wards of the state if she were sent to prison to probation rather than to prison is probably acting justly. This may be so even if the judge sentences an unremorseful single male to prison who has committed the same crime and has a criminal record identical to the mother, and thus, the judge is treating legal equals unequally. On the other hand, if the judge sentences legal equals unequally only because one defendant is a woman and the other a man, he or she is not acting justly.

••• TYPES OF SENTENCES

INDETERMINATE SENTENCE

A prison sentence a person receives can be indeterminate or determinate. An **indeterminate sentence** is one in which the actual number of years a person may serve is not fixed but is rather a range of years—for example, the person "shall be imprisoned for not less than 2 or 3 years to 10 years." More serious crimes move both minimum and maximum time periods upward. Indeterminate sentences were previously much more common than they are today, but a number of states still retain this

PHOTO 5.1: Fairness in sentencing is often a difficult goal to attain, with many factors to consider, such as the type of crime committed, the criminal history of the offender, and the requirements of the judicial system.

system. Indeterminate sentences fit the positivist's rehabilitation philosophy of punishment because they allow for offenders to be released after they have served their minimum period if they demonstrate to the parole board's satisfaction that they have made efforts to turn their lives around. Such sentences are tailored to the offender and aimed at rehabilitation, rather than tailored to the crime and designed to be strictly punitive.

The indeterminate-sentencing model prevailed most strongly under the so-called medical model, whereby offenders were considered "sick" and in need of a cure. Because some criminals may be "sicker" than others, the time made available for the "cure" must be flexible. Offenders that behaved themselves in prison and could demonstrate that they were "reformed" could be rather quickly released; ill-behaved and stubborn offenders may have to serve the upper boundary (10 years in the previous example) and be released, "rehabilitated" or not. It has been precisely because of its flexibility that indeterminate sentencing has been accused of contributing to sentencing disparity. For instance, even if two offenders receive the same "2 to 10 years," one may serve only 2 years because he or she can keep out of trouble and knows how to play the rehabilitation/parole game while the other, who is more rowdy and does not play the game as well, may serve 2 or 3 more years. Supporters of the model, however, will reply that it is not the judiciary that is at fault (after all, both were sentenced identically by judges), but rather, it is the inmates themselves who caused the discrepancy by their different behaviors while incarcerated.

Prisoners released from state prisons in 1996 served an average of only 44% of their sentences under predominantly indeterminate-sentencing structures (Ditton & Wilson, 1999). Rising crime rates in the 1980s and early 1990s saw a groundswell of opposition to what many saw as "mollycoddling" criminals, and there were many calls for longer sentences. In response to public demands, most states enacted **truth-in-sentencing laws**. These laws require that there be a truthful, realistic connection between the custodial sentence imposed on offenders and the time they actually serve, and they mandate that inmates serve at least 85% of their sentences before becoming eligible for release. In addition, many states restrict good-time credit and/or parole eligibility. As a result, average time served rose sharply for all federal offense types in recent years (see Figure 5.1).

Indeterminate sentence: A prison sentence consisting of a range of years to be determined by the convict's behavior, rather than one of a fixed number of years.

Truth-in-sentencing laws: Laws that require there be a truthful, realistic connection between the sentences imposed on offenders and the time they actually serve.

DETERMINATE SENTENCE

Determinate sentences became more prevalent after the enactment of truth-in-sentencing laws. A **determinate sentence** means that convicted individuals are given a fixed number of years they must serve, rather than a range. Under a determinate-sentencing structure, the maximum prison time for a given crime is set by the state legislature in state statutes. This structure is more in tune with the classical notion that the purpose of punishment is to deter and that all who commit the same crime must receive a fixed sentence. This does not mean that everyone convicted of the same crime receives the same set penalty. For instance, the maximum time for burglary may be set at 15 years, and a repeat offender may be sentenced to the full 15. Another person who is a young first offender may receive only 5 years. Whatever the sentence, offenders know under this sentencing structure how much time they will have to serve. Longer and more determinate sentences satisfy the urge for greater punishment for offenders, and they serve an incapacitation function. However, time off for good behavior is still granted.

MANDATORY SENTENCE

Another type of sentencing is **mandatory sentencing**, sometimes known as mandatory-minimum sentencing. Mandatory sentencing can exist in the context of both determinate- and indeterminate-sentencing structures and simply means that probation is not an option for some crimes and that the minimum time to be served is set by law. It is set by law because legislative bodies in various states have decided that some crimes are just too serious for probation consideration (certain violent crimes), or they have decided that there is a particular problem, such as drug trafficking or the use of a gun during the commission of a crime, that requires mandatory imprisonment as a deterrent.

Audio 5.1: Judge Regrets Harsh Human Toll of Mandatory Minimum Sentences

Determinate sentence: A prison sentence of a fixed number of years that must be served, rather than a range.

Mandatory sentence: A prison sentence imposed for crimes for which probation is not an option, where the minimum time to be served is set by law.

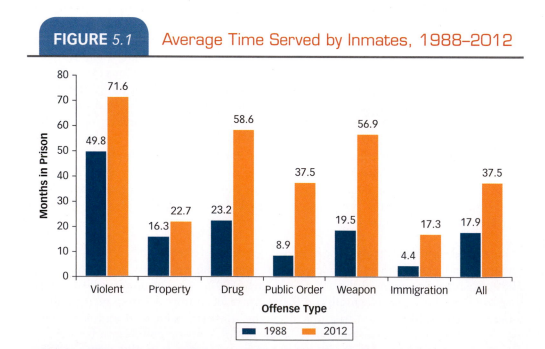

FIGURE *5.1*   Average Time Served by Inmates, 1988–2012

Note: Data show average time served by inmates released from prison in 1988 and 2012. Public order offenses include tax law violations, bribery, perjury, racketeering, extortion, and other crimes.

Source: © The Pew Charitable Trusts. Pew figure based on the following sources: Bureau of Justice Statistics, *Federal Criminal Case Processing 1982–1983*, Table 18 (1988 data); *Federal Justice Statistics 2012—Statistical Tables*, Table 7.11 (2012 data)

CONCURRENT AND CONSECUTIVE SENTENCES

Prison sentences imposed for two separate crimes, whether they occurred during the same incident (e.g., robbery and aggravated assault) or in different incidents (e.g., two separate burglaries), can be ordered to be served concurrently or consecutively. A **concurrent sentence** is one in which two separate sentences are served at the same time. If the robbery and aggravated-assault crimes both carry sentences of 10 years, for instance, the offender's release date would be calculated on the basis of 10 years rather than 20 years. A **consecutive sentence** is one in which two or more sentences must be served sequentially (one at a time). If our robber/aggravated assaulter received two 10-year sentences to be served consecutively, his or her release date would be based on 20 rather than 10 years. Consecutive sentences therefore increase the time a person spends in prison. The judge's decision to impose concurrent or consecutive sentences for persons convicted of two crimes may rest mainly on factors such as the seriousness of the crime, criminal history, and plea bargain arrangements.

HABITUAL-OFFENDER STATUTES

Habitual-offender (or "three-strikes-and-you're-out") **statutes** are derived from the same punitive atmosphere that led to truth-in-sentencing statutes. These statutes essentially mean that offenders with a third felony conviction may be sentenced to life imprisonment regardless of the nature of the third felony. This is a way of selectively incapacitating felons only after they have demonstrated the inability to live by society's rules. This all sounds fine until we factor in the financial costs of these sentences. Few of us would be against the lifetime incarceration of seriously violent offenders, but many states include relatively minor nonviolent crimes in their habitual-offender statutes. For instance, the U.S. Supreme Court upheld the life sentence of a felon under Texas's habitual-offender statute even though the underlying felonies involved nothing more serious than obtaining a total of less than $230 over a 15-year period by false pretenses (fraudulent use of a credit card and writing bad checks) in three separate incidents (*Rummel v. Estelle*, 1980). Very few of us would consider this a just sentence, and apart from the disproportionate nature of the sentence, the cost to the taxpayers

Career Video 5.1: Supreme Court Librarian

Journal Article 5.1: Prosecutors and Mandatory Minimum Sentencing

AP Video 5.1: Holmes

Concurrent sentence: Two separate sentences are served at the same time.

Consecutive sentence: Two or more sentences that must be served sequentially.

Habitual-offender statutes: Statutes mandating that offenders with a third felony conviction be sentenced to life imprisonment, regardless of the nature of the third felony.

PHOTO 5.2: The defendant receives his punishment after being found guilty or pleading guilty, and after undergoing a presentence investigation.

PHOTO 5.3: From left, Sequoia Earl, 11, Floyd Earl, 8, and Deonta Earl, 6, hold photos of their father, Floyd Earl, who is in jail for a term of 25 years to life, during a protest against California's "three strikes" law Saturday, March 9, 2002, at the federal building in the Westwood area of Los Angeles.

of Texas of keeping Rummel in custody is many thousand times greater than the $230 he fraudulently obtained.

Life without parole (LWOP): A life sentence with the additional condition that the person never be allowed parole.

A life sentence still carries with it the possibility of parole, but some life sentences are imposed as **life without parole (LWOP)**. Such sentences may seem popular with the public at large until they get the bill. According to Nellis (2010), in 2008, there were 140,095 prisoners serving LWOP sentences in the United States, a 400% increase from 1984. LWOP sentences are usually imposed on those convicted of murder, but habitual property offenders have also been given such sentences. Long-term incapacitation of violent and/or habitual offenders is sound policy, but how much time is enough? In one large-scale study, only one fifth of lifers who were released after long stays (15 to 30 years) in prison were rearrested within 3 years versus two thirds of nonlifers who were released (Mauer, King, & Young, 2004). Old age is the best "cure" for criminal behavior that we have, so perhaps releasing lifers after 20 to 30 years of imprisonment is both humane and fiscally responsible. Given the ever-increasing medical needs of people as they age, elderly inmates add a highly disproportionate financial burden on the taxpayer.

ETHICAL ISSUE 5.1 ?

What Would You Do?

You are a prosecutor in a state with a strict three-strikes law. You have been assigned the case of 46-year-old Billy Banks, who has been arrested and charged with burglary. Billy has two previous felony convictions—one for auto theft and a previous burglary conviction—although you know he has committed many other crimes. Billy shoplifted merchandise worth $145 from a local department store. This amount is low enough to charge Billy with a misdemeanor petty theft, but since he admitted entering the store with the express purpose of shoplifting, he was charged with a burglary, which is defined as "the unlawful entry of a structure to commit a felony or theft." What are the pros and cons of charging Billy under the three-strikes law? And what would you charge him with?

ALTERNATIVES TO INCARCERATION

Judges have many sentencing options open to them besides straight imprisonment. The fact is that over 90% of sentences imposed in our criminal courts do not involve imprisonment (Neubauer, 2008).

AP Photo/Damian Dovarganes

Shock Probation

One type of sentence that does include imprisonment is shock incarceration, also called **shock probation**. This type of sentence is used to literally shock offenders into going straight by exposing them to the reality of prison life for a short period, typically no more than 30 days, followed by probation. Shock probation is typically reserved for young, first-time offenders who have committed a relatively serious felony but who are considered redeemable.

Split Sentences

Split sentences are sentences that require felons to serve brief periods of confinement in a county jail prior to probation placement. Jail time may have to be served all at once or may be spread over a certain period, such as every weekend in jail for the first year of probation placement. This is designed to show offenders that jail is a place to stay away from and thus to convince them that it would be a good idea to abide by all of the conditions imposed by the court. Another form of split sentence is work release, whereby a person is consigned to a special portion of the jail on weekends and nights but released to go to work during the day. Thus, these mainly noncustodial sentences typically mean a probation sentence coupled with certain conditions that must be followed in order to remain in the community. The conditions may involve such things as paying fines,

Feature Video 5.3: Challenges with the Prosecutor

Video 5.1: Walgreens Robber Sentence Reduced to Shock Probation

Shock probation: A type of sentence aimed at shocking offenders into going straight by exposing them to the reality of prison life for a short period, followed by probation.

Split sentences: Sentences that require convicted persons to serve brief periods of confinement in a county jail prior to probation placement.

IN FOCUS 5.1

Sentencing by Civil Commitment for Sex Offenders

The animus that society has toward criminals is nowhere more obvious than in the case of sex offenders. In 1997, the U.S. Supreme Court upheld a Kansas statute (*Kansas v. Hendricks*, 1997) aimed at keeping sexual predators behind bars under civil-commitment laws *after* they have served their prison terms if they demonstrate "mental abnormality." The decision paved the way for other states and for the federal government to pass similar involuntary-commitment laws. Despite being placed in confinement against one's will, a civil commitment is not considered punishment in the eyes of the law because it is not a decision rendered in criminal court. Prior to 1990, civil commitments were limited to those said to suffer from mental illness, but to cover sex offenders, several states have loosened their criterion for commitment to "mental abnormality," as opposed to "mental illness."

The most notorious contemporary example is that of Nushawn Williams (aka Shyteek Johnson). Nushawn was convicted in 1997 of having unprotected sex with numerous girls and women, including a 13-year-old girl, in drugs-for-sex encounters, knowing that he was HIV positive. He was sentenced to 12 years in prison, but at the completion of his sentence, the state of New York refused to release him under its Mental Hygiene Law. In 2013, a jury determined that he was a dangerous sex offender with a mental abnormality and should be detained. In 2014, the New York State Supreme Court ordered that Williams be committed to a secure treatment facility as a sexual predator. According to Dennis Vacco, who was New York attorney general when the state legislature passed the Mental Hygiene Law,

> It was designed to keep the most vicious sexual predators from ever getting back out on the street, and in this instance, I couldn't think of anybody who is more eligible for the application of this statute than Nushawn Williams. (Ewing & Dudzik, 2014, n.p.)

Whatever your thoughts are about sex offenders in general, Williams had demonstrated his wanton disregard for others, knowingly infecting his victims with a deadly virus. Such laws have created a category of individuals defined as "abnormal" who may be punished indefinitely for what they *might* do if released.

DISCUSSION QUESTION

1. Some people believe these laws to be wrong and discriminatory. Others laud them as protecting the public from predatory and dangerous individuals who can almost be guaranteed to offend again if released. What do you think?

Video 5.2:
Man in Revenge
Porn Case Gets
"Split Sentence"

paying restitution, attending drug and/or alcohol treatment, doing community service, remaining gainfully employed or looking for work, and any number of other more specific conditions. These different noncustodial sentences and probation conditions will be discussed more fully in the chapters on probation, parole, and treatment.

Audio 5.2:
High Court
Expands
Defendants' Plea
Bargain Rights

••• PLEA BARGAINING

Before defendants are sentenced, a lot more activity has been going on in the courthouse corridors that in the courtroom as prosecutors and defense attorneys haggle over a defendant's fate independent of judge and jury. As you will note in Figure 5.2, at least 90% of all felony convictions come not from jury trials but from the kind of "negotiated justice" we call plea bargaining (Siegel, 2006). **Plea bargains** are agreements between defendants and prosecutors in which defendants agree to plead guilty in exchange for certain concessions. These concessions typically are a reduction in the charge or charges filed against the defendant. For example, a defendant may be initially charged with two counts of burglary, and the prosecutor will reduce it to one count if the defendant pleads guilty to it, or if it was initially one count, the prosecutor may reduce it to a lesser offense carrying a lighter punishment. Less typical are cases in which the prosecutor agrees to a lighter sentence in exchange for a guilty plea.

Feature Video 5.4:
Appeal Process

This type of bargain is less typical because whereas charge reduction is the prerogative of the prosecutor, sentencing is the prerogative of the judge, and the judge may not agree to the negotiated sentence. A judge is not even required to agree with a charge reduction. For instance, a defendant charged with rape may have reached an agreement with the prosecutor to plead to a lesser charge such as lewd and lascivious conduct. However, new information may come to the judge's attention in the presentence investigation report (to be discussed later) that the prosecutor was not aware of. In this case, the judge may instruct the prosecutor to investigate this new information further and come back with a new plea or proceed to trial. Judges thus retain final authority over sentencing decisions and are not bound to accept prosecutors' deals with defendants.

It is rare that judges refuse to accept a plea, however, because accepting plea agreements alleviates the necessity of more trials on their already overcrowded dockets. Like everyone else, judges like to make their work quickly and efficiently disposed of. Judges also view plea bargains as contracts between prosecutors and defendants. If a defendant breaks the plea bargain, the prosecutors are no longer bound to uphold their part of the deal. If, on the other hand, a prosecutor reneges on a plea bargain, the judge might allow a defendant to withdraw his or her guilty plea or require the prosecutor to honor it.

BENEFITS OF PLEA BARGAINS

For their part, the quick and easy disposal of cases lightens prosecutors' workloads, which they also find attractive. More importantly for them, plea bargaining assures a conviction, even if it is for a lesser charge and lesser sentence, and also avoids long and expensive trials, which they may lose. Prosecutors may plea bargain with one defendant to further their case against another defendant who they consider more culpable or a "bigger fish" to fry. Thus, they may accept a plea bargain in return for the damaging testimony of the less culpable defendant to be assured of at least one "big" conviction.

It would seem that plea bargaining offers something for everyone while leaving no one completely satisfied. Victims may be the least satisfied, but at least they have the satisfaction of certain conviction and some punishment for offenders. The police also enjoy a benefit from a plea bargain in that they are saved from numerous appearances in court, even though they may be dissatisfied with more lenient punishment. Judges and prosecutors, as we have seen, benefit from the speedy and efficient clearing of cases, and

Plea bargain:
Agreements between defendants and prosecutors in which defendants agree to plead guilty in exchange for certain concessions.

Web 5.1:
Victim Impact
Statement

FIGURE *5.2*   Percentage of Cases That Result in a Plea Bargain, 2012

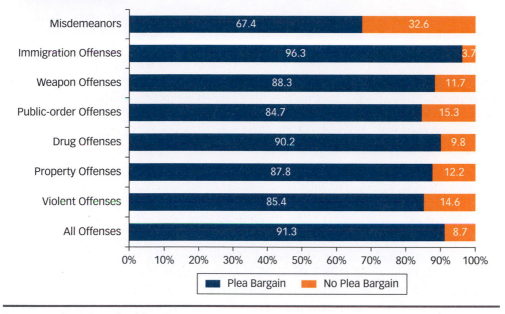

Source: Motivans (2015). Table 4.2.

the community as a whole saves the cost of a trial. Even criminals gain when their plea bargains result in more lenient treatment than they otherwise may have received. Thus, while the plea-bargaining process draws a lot of criticism, the principal parties in the legal drama appear quite comfortable with it.

CRITICISMS OF PLEA BARGAINS

Conservatives condemn plea bargaining as unwarranted leniency because criminals are punished for crimes that bear little resemblance to the ones actually committed. Liberals criticize plea bargaining because it coerces suspects to surrender their Sixth Amendment right to a trial, their Fifth Amendment privilege against self-incrimination, and their right to any subsequent appeal of their conviction. They give up these rights because they have admitted to their guilt on paper and verbally in open court at sentencing.

One of the major criticisms of plea bargaining is that because of prosecutors' desires to put more cases in their "win" column as quickly, quietly, and efficiently as possible, they often overcharge (that is, charge more serious crimes than the evidence warrants) in order to gain bargaining leverage (Caldwell, 2011). This results in risk-averse defendants often being coerced into pleading guilty on charges for which they are actually guilty and which could be proven "beyond a reasonable doubt" at trial, and thus, they are receiving no "bargain" at all (Wright & Miller, 2002). The pressure on prosecutors with huge caseloads is great, and this may sometimes lead them to threaten defendants with dire consequences if they refuse to bargain.

The U.S. Supreme Court upheld the constitutionality of such threats in *Bordenkircher v. Hayes* (1978). Hayes had been indicted for forgery, a crime for which the maximum penalty in Kentucky at the time was 10 years. The prosecutor offered to recommend 5 years if Hayes pled guilty, which he refused to do. The prosecutor then informed Hayes that he would seek a second indictment charging him as a habitual offender if he insisted on a trial. Hayes still refused and was indicted as a habitual offender, found guilty, and sentenced to life imprisonment rather than the 5 years he was offered. An appeals court overturned Hayes's conviction as a habitual offender, but the U.S. Supreme Court reaffirmed his conviction and declared that in the tit-for-tat world of plea bargaining, there was no element of punishment or injustice in what the prosecutor did since Hayes was free to accept or reject his offer.

It is not only prosecutors who may become vindictive about a defendant's refusal to accept a plea agreement. Judges have been accused of operating according to the "you take some of my time, I'll take some of yours" rule (Uhlman & Walker, 1980). This essentially means that if you insist on your right to a trial and waste my time, I will make you pay a price for it. No wonder that "experienced" defendants are anxious to bargain, but what about those who insist on their due process rights? "Such defendants may be viewed as disruptive, as lacking in any show of contrition and, therefore, deserving of more severe treatment. If convicted, they will receive sentences in excess of the norm" (Abadinsky, 2009, p. 229).

Although it is true that defendants who go to trial receive more severe sentences if convicted, this is to be expected because these defendants are being sentenced for a more serious crime than are those who plead guilty to a reduced charge or for a specific sentence. But there still appears to be an element of punishment attached to noncooperation. Adjusting for the effects of prior record, crime seriousness, and charge reduction, one study found that defendants found guilty at trial were 4.76 times more likely to be imprisoned than those who pled guilty, and among those who went to prison, trial defendants received an average of 13.5 more months than plea defendants (Walsh, 1990). We cannot say with certainty if these differences represent a penalty tacked on to the sentences of those defendants audacious enough to demand their constitutional rights or whether it represents a reward in the form of leniency for those kind enough not to "waste" the court's time.

IN FOCUS 5.2

Extension of the Due Process Model to Sentencing

A number of ethical and legal issues associated with plea bargaining led the U.S. Supreme Court to rule that defendants have the right to effective legal counsel during plea negotiations (*Lafler v. Cooper*, 2012). In this case, Anthony Cooper was charged with attempted murder for shooting a woman several times in the buttocks and thighs. Cooper turned down an offer to plead guilty in exchange for a sentence of 5 to 7 years in prison. Cooper's lawyer advised him against taking the plea, maintaining that he would not be convicted of attempted murder at trial because he did not shoot the woman above the waist. On his attorney's advice, Cooper went to trial and was convicted and sentenced to between 15 and 30 years in prison. The Supreme Court agreed with the argument that Cooper had been denied the right to a competent attorney and remanded the case back to court for resentencing.

In his dissent from the Court's 5–4 *Lafler* decision, Justice Scalia gave an excellent, succinct explanation of some of the problems associated with plea bargaining and why it is regarded as a "necessary evil."

In the United States, we have plea bargaining a-plenty, but until today it has been regarded as a necessary evil. It presents great risks of prosecutorial overcharging that effectively compels an innocent defendant to avoid massive risk by pleading guilty to a lesser offense; and for guilty defendants it often—perhaps usually—results in a sentence well below what the law prescribes for the actual crime. But even so, we accept plea bargaining because many believe that without it our long and expensive process of criminal trial could not sustain the burden imposed on it, and our system of criminal justice would grind to a halt. (p. 12)

DISCUSSION QUESTIONS

1. Why is plea bargaining regarded as a necessary evil?

2. What are some of the problems with plea bargaining?

••• IMPACT STATEMENTS AT SENTENCING

VICTIM IMPACT STATEMENTS

In 1982, President Ronald Reagan created the President's Task Force on Victims of Crime. One of the outcomes of this was the inclusion of victim impact statements at sentencing. A **victim impact statement** (VIS) allows persons directly affected by the crime (or victims' survivors in the case of murder) to inform the court of the personal and emotional harm they have suffered as a result of the defendant's actions and, in some states, to make a sentencing recommendation. VISs are typically incorporated into presentence reports written for the court by probation officers. The opportunity to provide input into the sentencing decision and the recognition that the harm is suffered by individuals, not the state, is considered a valuable aid in the emotional recovery of victims and may even aid the rehabilitation of some defendants by forcing them to confront the harm caused by their actions (Walsh, 1986).

VISs have been challenged as prejudicial and a return to a more conservative punitive stance toward punishment because such statements can lead to sympathy for the victim and hostility toward the defendant (Paternoster & Deise, 2011). However, in *Payne v. Tennessee* (1991), the U.S. Supreme Court upheld the constitutionality of VIS testimony in the sentencing phase of a trial, and all 50 states now include the use of VISs in the form of written or oral statements at sentencing. But how influential are they in terms of the actual sentence imposed? Overall, the evidence is ambiguous, although in capital cases, where juries rather than judges decide the sentence, they seem to be influential (Paternoster & Deise, 2011). Research in noncapital cases tends to show that VISs actually have little effect on sentencing decisions after the effects of legally relevant variables (seriousness of crime and prior record) have been accounted for (Walsh, 1986). This sometimes leads to resentment and dissatisfaction with the sentencing process among victims (or their survivors) who believed that their recommendations would carry more weight than they did (Meredith & Paquette, 2001).

Victim impact statement: A statement made by persons directly affected by a crime (or victims' survivors in the case of murder) to inform the court of the personal and emotional harm they have suffered as a result of the defendant's actions and, in some states, to make a sentencing recommendation.

© iStockphoto.com/Rich Legg

PHOTO 5.4: Victim impact statements give voice to victims and/or their families, but defense lawyers decry them as unfair to their clients.

SENTENCING DISPARITIES: LEGITIMATE AND ILLEGITIMATE

A **sentencing disparity** occurs when there is wide variation in sentences received by different offenders. This disparity is legitimate if it is based on considerations such as crime seriousness and/or prior record but discriminatory if it is not. We think of sentencing disparities as discriminatory if there are differences in punishment in cases in which no rational justification can be found for them. The biggest concern is racial discrimination. There is no doubt that the American criminal justice system has a dark history of racial discrimination, but does this indictment still apply?

African Americans receive harsher sentences on average than white or Asian American offenders, a fact often seen as racist. Sentencing variation is reasonable and just if the group being more harshly punished commits more crimes than other groups but discriminatory and unjust if they do not. All data sources show that African Americans commit more crime, especially violent crime, than whites or Asians (FBI, 2013b).

But the question is whether this racial disproportionality in offending is sufficient to account for the disparity in sentencing. One sentencing scholar concluded that it was not: "Racial bias continues to pervade the U.S. criminal justice sentencing system [although] the effects of this bias are somewhat hidden . . . or may even have less to do with the race of the defendant than with the race of the victim" (Kansal, 2005, p. 17). Another scholar concluded the opposite: "Although critics of American race relations may think otherwise, research on sentencing has failed to show a definitive pattern of racial discrimination" (Siegel, 2006, p. 578). Different researchers thus arrive at different conclusions, but there is widespread agreement on one point: The more stringent researchers are in controlling for the effects of legally relevant variables (crime seriousness and criminal record), the less likely they are to find racial discrimination (Siegel, 2006). One study of over 46,000 federal defendants in 23 states found no evidence of racial bias after controlling for legally relevant variables (Wang, Mears, Spohn, & Dario, 2013). Figure 5.3 shows the average length of sentences received for various types of crimes for black and white males and females.

Sentencing disparity: Wide variation in sentences received by different offenders that may be legitimate or discriminatory.

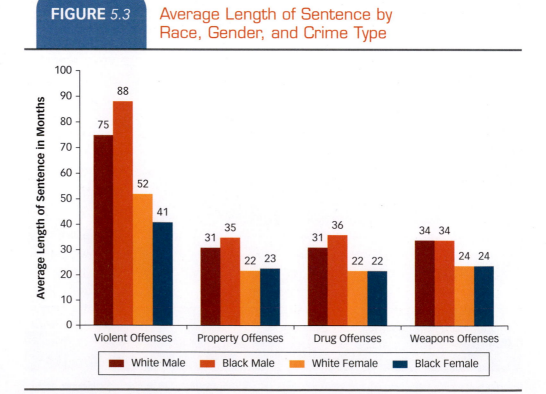

| FIGURE 5.3 | Average Length of Sentence by Race, Gender, and Crime Type |

Source: Durose, Farole, and Rosenmerkel (2010). *Felony sentences in state courts, 2006.* Washington, DC: Bureau of Justice Statistics.

POLICY AND RESEARCH

Sentencing for Crack Versus Powder Cocaine

One of the biggest concerns in the sentencing disparity literature is the disparity in sentencing for possession of crack versus possession of powder cocaine. Of particular concern is that those who use or sell crack cocaine tend to be African Americans, and those who use or sell powder cocaine tend to be white. In 1988, Congress passed the Anti–Drug Abuse Act, which established a 100-to-1 quantity ratio differential between powder and crack cocaine. According to a U.S. Sentencing Commission Report to Congress in 1995, in 1986, Congress was reacting to media hype about how addictive crack was, how crack babies are severely impaired, and how crime related to crack use was out of control. At the time of this 1995 report, the commission knew that "88.3 percent of the offenders convicted in federal court for crack cocaine distribution in 1993 were Black and 7.1 percent were Hispanic," and critics were concerned that instead of fair and evenhanded sentences for all, the effect of the Anti–Drug Abuse Act was to be unfair and harsh in sentencing of racial minorities (U.S. Sentencing Commission, 1995a, p. 1).

Although the Anti–Drug Abuse Act has been characterized as racist, according to African American law professor Randall Kennedy (1998), the Congressional Black Caucus strongly supported the legislation and pressed for even tougher penalties. Nobody would call black congresspersons racist; it is more sensible to conclude that they were deeply concerned with how crack was decimating black communities.

As opposed to the attention received by the crack/powder cocaine disparities, very little attention has been paid to the disparities in the federal methamphetamine sentences. According to Heather MacDonald (2008),

> The press almost never mentions the federal methamphetamine-trafficking penalties, which are identical to those for crack: five grams of meth net you a mandatory minimum five-year sentence. In 2006, the 5,391 sentenced federal meth defendants (nearly as many as the [5,619] crack defendants) were 54 percent white, 39 percent Hispanic, and 2 percent black. But no one calls the federal meth laws anti-Hispanic or anti-white. (n.p.)

Public domain

© iStockphoto.com/Photo_HamsterMan

PHOTOS 5.5 AND 5.6: Crack cocaine is made by combining cocaine, baking soda, and water, which is then cooked. The high from crack comes within seconds and lasts from 5 to 35 minutes. It is the most addictive substance known.

Of course, drug laws are not "anti" any race or ethnic group; they are simply antidrug. If they disproportionately impact a particular racial or ethnic group, it is a matter of the drug preferences of that group. The U.S. Sentencing Commission (1995b) informs us that

> Whites account for 30.8 percent of all convicted federal drug offenders, Blacks 33.9 percent, and Hispanics 33.8 percent. Sentencing patterns for some drugs show high concentrations of a particular racial or ethnic group. Most strikingly, crack cocaine offenders are 88.3 percent Black. Conversely, methamphetamine offenders are 84.2 percent White. (p. 152)

(Continued)

(Continued)

Nevertheless, criticisms of the act mounted, and in 2009, a congressional subcommittee was convened to discuss the matter. Subcommittee chair Robert C. Scott made the following remarks:

> One thing that I do believe with all my heart is that when these laws were passed, the proponents of these laws, like Chairman Rangel, believed it was the best thing. . . . He said we were told if you don't pass these tougher sentences on crack cocaine, then it is a racist move. You don't care about the communities in Black neighborhoods, because this is killing Black youth. (U.S. Congress, 2009, n.p.)

As a result of this hearing, the **Fair Sentencing Act** was introduced and passed by Congress in 2009. Under the act, the amount of crack cocaine subject to the 5-year minimum sentence was increased from 5 grams to 28 grams, thus reducing the 100-to-1 ratio to an 18-to-1 ratio (28 grams of crack gets as much time as 500 grams of powder cocaine). Thus, there is still a large sentencing differential between possessors of crack versus possessors of powder cocaine. This ratio probably reflects lawmakers' perceptions that crack is more intimately related to violence and to a higher probability of addiction than the powder variety.

DISCUSSION QUESTIONS

1. Do you agree that penalties for crack should be higher than for powder cocaine?

2. If the Congressional Black Caucus was the instigator of the Anti–Drug Abuse Act, why do you think so many people consider it a racist act?

3. If the penalties for methamphetamine trafficking are identical to the penalties for crack trafficking, why don't we hear complaints of racism since, just like crack offenses are overwhelmingly committed by blacks, meth offenses are overwhelmingly committed by whites?

Sources

Kennedy, R. (1998). *Race, crime, and the law*. New York: Vintage.

MacDonald, H. (2008). Is the criminal-justice system racist? *City Journal*. Retrieved from http://www.city-journal.org/2008/18_2_criminal_justice_system.html

U.S. Congress. (2009). *Unfairness in federal cocaine sentencing: Is it time to crack the 100 to 1 disparity?* Hearing before the Subcommittee on Crime, Terrorism, and Homeland Security, U.S. House of Representatives. Retrieved from http://www.gpo.gov/fdsys/pkg/CHRG-111hhrg49783/html/CHRG-111hhrg49783.htm

U.S. Sentencing Commission. (1995a). *Annual report*. Washington, DC: Author.

U.S. Sentencing Commission. (1995b). *Report on cocaine and federal sentencing policy*. Retrieved from http://www.ussc.gov/report-cocaine-and-federal-sentencing-policy-3

Sentencing research is complicated and typically reports average effects, among which are multiple interacting variables hiding specifics. Table 5.1 shows the average length, in months, of felony sentences in state courts in 2006 broken down by race and gender (Durose, Farole, & Rosenmerkel, 2010). You can see that black males have longer sentences than whites, and males have longer sentences than females. Also note that for violent offenses, white females receive longer sentences than black females. However, no conclusions about racial or gender bias can be drawn from the table because it tells us nothing about how serious each of the crimes was (some robberies, sexual assaults, and assaults are more vicious than others, for instance) or the criminal histories of the men and women represented in the table.

Fair Sentencing Act of 2010: The act mandated that the amount of crack cocaine subject to the 5-year minimum sentence be increased from 5 grams to 28 grams, thus reducing the 100-to-1 ratio to an 18-to-1 ratio (28 grams of crack gets as much time as 500 grams of powder cocaine).

••• STRUCTURING JUDICIAL SENTENCING CHOICES

At one time, the sentencing of convicted criminals was almost entirely within the discretion of the sentencing judge. The judge could craft a punishment that he believed to be an appropriate fit for the crime, according to his temperament or philosophy. This is the kind of unbridled discretion that so troubled Cesare Beccaria in the 18th century.

TABLE *5.1*   Average Length of Felony Sentences in 2006* by Offense, Race, and Gender

MOST SERIOUS CONVICTION OFFENSE	MEAN MAXIMUM SENTENCE LENGTH IN MONTHS FOR PERSONS WHO WERE			
	WHITE		BLACK	
	MALE	FEMALE	MALE	FEMALE
All offenses	40 months	25 months	45 months	25 months
Violent offenses	75	52	88	41
Murder/Nonnegligent manslaughter	265	225	266	175
Sexual assault	115	72	125	32
Robbery	89	61	101	54
Aggravated assault	42	30	48	29
Other violent	43	55	41	17
Property offenses	31	22	35	23
Burglary	41	29	50	34
Larceny	24	17	23	19
Fraud/Forgery	27	22	27	23
Drug offenses	31	22	36	22
Possession	21	17	25	15
Trafficking	39	26	40	27
Weapon offenses	34	24	34	24

*Most recent data available

Source: Durose, M. R., Farole, D. J., & Rosenmerkel, S. P. (2010). *Felony sentences in state courts, 2006*. Washington, DC: Bureau of Justice Statistics.

Thanks to the march of the due process model in criminal justice, judicial discretion has been seriously curtailed, and judges must now make sentencing choices within the limits of sentencing statutes determined by legislative bodies. They still have discretion within those limitations, however, and we need to know how they structure their choices. Suppose a defendant has gone to trial (thus, there is no plea bargain for the judge to entertain) and has been found guilty of, say, burglary, which carries a statutory sentence of anywhere from probation to 10 years in prison. The defense pleads for a probation order, and the prosecution demands 10 years. What is the judge to do? How will he or she respond to these conflicting demands? What is a fair and just outcome for both the offender and the offended community?

The seriousness of the crime and the offender's criminal history are, of course, always the primary considerations, but the offender's characteristics (other than race/ethnicity, gender, religion, sexual orientation, and social class) may, depending on jurisdiction, be deemed legitimate considerations. Some states (e.g., Illinois) allow for a wide range of mitigating (serving to lessen punishment) and aggravating (serving to increase it) circumstances to be considered, whereas others (e.g., Minnesota) explicitly forbid them (Spohn & Hemmens, 2012). In the opening vignette, Jane's status as a mother of three young children is a mitigating factor, and Jim's immersion in the criminal lifestyle and poor employment history are aggravating factors.

What about a characteristic such as psychopathy? Should it be considered an aggravating factor at sentencing? Judges seem to be especially influenced by expert testimony if it involves biological factors. For instance, 181 judges from 19 states were presented with a hypothetical case of a psychopathic defendant who had robbed a restaurant and pistol-whipped the manager (Aspinwall, Brown, & Tabery, 2012). Almost all judges in the study considered psychopathy to be an aggravating factor, but if they were also presented with explanations for the condition based on brain imaging, they tended to lessen the severity of their sentences. All 181 judges were informed that the defendant was a psychopath, but only a random half were provided with biological evidence relating to the causes of psychopathy, with half of them getting the evidence from the defense, arguing that it should be mitigating, and half from the prosecution, arguing that it should be aggravating. Averaged over all judges, the hypothetical psychopath received a longer sentence than typically given to nonpsychopaths for aggravated assault, but judges who were given biological explanations for psychopathy imposed an average of about one year less than judges who did not get that information (12.83 versus 13.93 years).

Figure 5.4 presents an "idealized" choice-structuring chart for judges involved in sentencing, illustrating the various factors they look at when making their decisions. The task looks formidable, but thankfully, judges have a lot of help to ease their task in the form of reports written by probation officers, sentencing guidelines, and risk and needs assessment instruments. We now discuss those reports (PSIs) and guidelines. Risk and needs instruments are discussed in the chapters on classification and assessment and on offender treatment.

THE PRESENTENCE INVESTIGATION REPORT

To assist judges in making a sentencing decision, **presentence investigation reports (PSI)** are used. There are few documents as important to the defendant as the PSI. It is used for many other purposes besides sentencing, such as treatment planning, classification to supervision levels in probation or parole departments and prisons, and parole decisions (Walsh & Stohr, 2010). A PSI is usually completed in 30 days or less so that the convicted individual can be sentenced in a timely manner. PSIs are usually written by probation officers informing the judge of various aspects of the offense for which the defendant is being sentenced, as well as information about the defendant's background (educational, family, and employment history), gang ties, substance abuse, character, and criminal history. Because of plea bargaining, judges typically know very little about the circumstances of the offense or the offender. On the basis of this information, officers make recommendations to the court regarding the sentence the offender should receive. Because probation officers enjoy considerable discretionary power relating to how their reports are crafted to be favorable or unfavorable to offenders, many scholars view them as the agents who really determine the sentences that offenders receive (Champion, 2005). Other researchers, however, suggest that the high rate of judicial agreement with officer recommendations reflect an anticipatory effect, whereby officers become adept at "second guessing" a judge's likely sentence for a given case and recommend accordingly (Durnescu, 2008).

In Focus 5.3 is an example of a (fictional) PSI containing the usual required information. PSIs come in a variety of sizes, the smallest being a one- or two-page short-form report used in misdemeanor cases or less serious run-of-the-mill felony cases. For serious or complicated cases, we may see 10- to 15-page reports, although the trend is toward smaller reports. The report given here is an example of a midrange report used

Presentence investigation report (PSI): Report written by the probation officer informing the judge of various aspects of the offense for which the defendant is being sentenced, as well as providing information about the defendant's background (educational, family, and employment history), character, and criminal history.

FIGURE *5.4*   The Process of Sentence Structuring

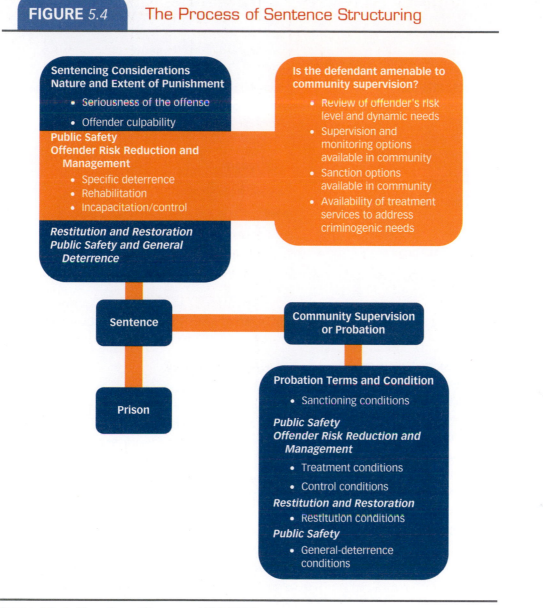

Source: Adapted from Casey, Warren, and Elek (2011).

for relatively serious crimes, although the trend is for shorter, more concise reports focusing primarily on legally relevant variables.

PSI Controversies

Although the PSI has generally been considered a positive aid to individualized justice, it is not without its problems. Because the future of a defendant depends to a great extent on the content of the report, the information contained therein should be reliable and objective. All pertinent information must be verified by cross-checking with more than one source, and that source should be reliable.

If you were the subject of a PSI, would you not like to see what was in it so that you could challenge any erroneous information harmful to you contained in it? There have been a number of arguments for and against allowing defendants and their attorneys access to the PSI. It is feared that if victims and other informants from whom the investigating officer has sought information know that the offender will see their comments,

IN FOCUS 5.3

Example of a PSI

GEM COUNTY ADULT PROBATION DEPARTMENT

Williamstown, Iowa 74812

Name: Joan Place	Judge: Franklin Riley
Indictment No.: CR 6742	Probation Officer: James Smith
Age: 28	Attorney: William Paley
Race: White	
Sex: Female	Offense: Forgery
Marital Status: Divorced	Conduct (IRC #2908) two counts

Circumstances of the offense

On 8/10/94, Mr. John Smith, security operative for the Omaha Trust Company (OTC), reported to the police that the defendant cashed forged checks in the amount of $917.00 at various OTC branch banks. These checks were drawn against the account of one Mrs. Patricia DeValera, 4561 Black St. The defendant stole Mrs. DeValera's checks while employed by her as a nurse's aide. Mr. Smith also indicated that the defendant cashed forged checks in the amount of $575.00 on the account of Mr. Richard Blane, a former boyfriend of the defendant. The total loss to the Omaha Trust bank is $1,492.00.

Defendant's version

The defendant's written statement is reproduced verbatim below: "Took checks filled it out in amount I needed for drugs and signed it, forged a name and cashed the checks in Aug. of 1994. No, I did not pay back the person. I was so drug dependent that I took my boyfriends checks, Mrs. Devaleras checks too. All I could live for at the time was heroin and alcohol (mainly beer). I'm sorry I did these things, normally I wouldn't of forged the checks if I wouldn't of needed drugs. All I could do was live for drugs. I've been threw the withdrawals of drugs when I put myself in the treatment center on Wilson St." It is noted that the defendant places the blame for her criminal activity on her craving for heroin and alcohol. Her statements of remorse ring rather hollow in light of her new forgery arrest while undergoing presentence investigation. She was arrested on this new charge on 2/22/95 and released on $1,000 bond (10% allowed). Upon learning of this new arrest, I rearrested her on 2/24/95 and placed her in the county jail, where she has been ever since.

Prior record

Juvenile: None known

Adult:

8/18/94: OPD Forgery, 5 counts, amended to one count (present offense)

11/6/94: OPD Forgery, 3 counts, pending under CR841234.

2/5/95: OPD Forgery, pending

Above record reflects juvenile, OPD, BCI, and FBI record checks.

Present family status

The defendant is the fourth of five children born to Ann and Frank Place. Her father passed away in January of 1991. On 6/17/85, the defendant married one James Fillpot. Mr. Fillpot was described as a heavy drug abuser and is now serving a life sentence on an aggravated murder charge. (He was convicted of murdering the defendant's alleged lover.) The defendant divorced Mr. Fillpot shortly after his 1989 conviction, and shortly thereafter (6/89), she married one Ralph Burke. Mr. Burke is an alcoholic with an extensive criminal record. After an extremely abusive two years of marriage, the defendant's second marriage ended in divorce on 5/12/92. No children were born during either of these marriages. At the time of her arrest, the defendant was living with her mother at the previously listed address.

Present employment or support

The defendant is unemployed at the present time and was existing on $76.00 in food stamps at the time of her arrest. She receives no general relief monies. Her last period of employment was as a nurse's aide for Mrs. DeValera, one of the victims of the present offense. This employment was for the period encompassing March through August 1993. The defendant's longest period of employment was with the Red Barron Restaurant, 3957 Laskar Rd., as a waitress from March 1988 through November 1991. This employer has not responded to our request for information as yet.

Health: physical

The defendant describes her current physical health as "O.K." She relates no significant hospitalizations, diseases, or current health problems, with the exception of her substance abuse. Her substance abuse is quite extensive. She claims that she has spent anywhere from $20 to $300 per day on heroin. Needle marks on her arms attest to her frequent usage. She also relates that she likes to consume six to 12 beers per night, which she claims that she receives free from boyfriends. Her substance abuse goes back to her first marriage 13 years ago, when Mr. Fillpot introduced her to heroin. Her second husband, Mr. Burke, got her heavily involved in alcohol. She admits that she has experimented with many other drugs but states that heroin and beer are her drugs of choice. This officer contacted the Wilson Street Drug Rehabilitation Facility regarding the defendant's claimed attendance there. It appears that she did voluntarily admit herself there but left after the first 15-day phase. I also made an effort to get her into the ROAD drug rehabilitation program. However, after two interviews with ROAD personnel, the defendant was denied admission because they thought that her only motive for seeking admission was her current legal difficulties.

Health: mental

The defendant is a 1981 graduate of Borah High School. She graduated 287th out of a class of 348. She attained a cumulative GPA of 1.64 on a 4.0 scale. Although no IQ information is available, the defendant impresses as functioning well within the average range of intelligence, as gauged by her written and verbal statements. She did indicate that she was easily led and that she does not think much of herself. Her choice of marriage partners (both very abusive to her) and her current boyfriends gives the impression that she is attracted to men who will verify her low opinion of herself.

Statutory penalty

N.R.C. 2913.31

Forgery "shall be imprisoned for a period of 6 months, 1 year, or 1 and one-half years and/or fined up to $2,500."

Evaluative Summary

Before the court is a 28-year-old woman facing her first felony conviction. However, she has numerous other forgery charges pending at this time. There would seem to be little doubt that the genesis of her criminal activity is her severe abuse of alcohol and drugs. She also appears to possess a low concept of herself, as indicated by her very poor choice of marriage partners, both of whom were serious substance abusers and both of whom were physically abusive to her. She appears to be intimately involved in the drug subculture. I initiated the procedure to get the defendant admitted to the ROAD residential drug treatment center. However, after conducting two interviews with the defendant, personnel from the ROAD decided that her motivation for seeking treatment was her current legal difficulties, and thus, her application was denied. They did indicate that they would reconsider her application after the disposition of the present offense. Therefore, I recommend that the defendant be placed on probation and ordered to pay complete restitution and to pursue entry into the ROAD. It is also recommended that she remain in the county jail after sentencing to reinitiate her application with ROAD.

Approved	Respectfully Submitted
_____	_____
James F. Collins	**Joyce Williams**
Unit Supervisor	**Probation Officer**

they will refuse to offer their information; thus, the judge will not have complete information on which to make the sentencing decision. However, 16 states currently require full disclosure; other states require disclosure but erase information that may lead to retaliation, such as the officer's recommendation or negative comments from informants. Despite objections and real concerns about confidentiality, the trend is to allow defendants access to their PSI reports. For instance, in the federal system, Section 3552 of the U.S. Code states,

The court shall assure that a report filed pursuant to this section is disclosed to the defendant, the counsel for the defendant, and the attorney for the Government at least ten days prior to the date set for sentencing, unless this minimum period is waived by the defendant. The court shall provide a copy of the presentence report to the attorney for the Government to use in collecting an assessment, criminal fine, forfeiture or restitution imposed.

ETHICAL ISSUE 5.2

What Would You Do?

You are a probation officer writing a presentence investigation report on 29-year-old Robert Jackson, who was arrested for carrying a concealed weapon (CCW). Robert is very concerned about his arrest and fears going to jail, losing his job, and not being able to support his wife and two children. At the conclusion of the PSI interview, he shakes hands with you and passes on a $100 bill. Would you report this attempted bribe and make matters worse for Robert, or would you return the money with a stern lecture and then forget about it?

 AP Video 5.2: Holder

 Video 5.3: Thousands Released Early From Prison Under New Sentencing Guidelines

United States Sentencing Commission: A commission charged with creating mandatory sentencing guidelines to control judicial discretion.

Sentencing guidelines: Scales for numerically computing sentences that offenders should receive based on the crime they committed and on their criminal records.

In the federal system and in some state systems, probation and parole officers no longer write PSI reports. Rather, they merely complete sentencing guidelines and certain other assessment tools and calculate the presumed sentence (Abadinsky, 2009). This and a number of other factors may be signaling a move away from individualized justice (the idea that punishment should be tailored to the individual and be consistent with rehabilitation) and back to the classical idea, discussed in Chapter 1, that the punishment should fit the crime and serve as a retributive or deterrent factor.

SENTENCING GUIDELINES

We saw in Chapter 1 that a major concern of the classical school of criminal justice was to make the law more fair and equal by removing a great deal of judicial discretion and providing standards set by the legislature for making punishment for equal crimes standard. Prior to 1984, federal judges enjoyed almost unlimited sentencing discretion, as long as they stayed within the statutory maximum penalties. This led to a lot of criticism regarding sentencing disparities and moved Congress to establish the **United States Sentencing Commission**. This commission was charged with the task of creating mandatory sentencing guidelines to rein in judicial discretion (Reynolds, 2009). **Sentencing guidelines** are forms containing scales with a set of rules for numerically computing sentences that offenders should receive based on the crime(s) they committed and on their criminal records.

Guidelines are devised by federal or state sentencing commissions and provide classifications of suggested punishments based on an offender's scores on those scales. Because guidelines are a set of rules and principles that are supposed to decide a defendant's sentence, they curtail the discretionary powers of judges, as was intended by Congress. Most people view this as a good thing since unbridled discretion can lead to wide sentencing disparities based only on a judge's subjective evaluations and whims. At one extreme, we might get "hanging" judges, and at the other extreme, we might get "bleeding-heart" judges. So a defendant's fate may depend largely on the temperament or ideology of the judge by whom he or she has the good luck or bad fortune to be sentenced.

Guidelines thus provide structured predictability to criminal sanctions by taking Aristotle's definition of justice ("treating equals equally and unequals unequally according to relevant differences") and assigning numbers to these relevant differences. The sample guideline in Figure 5.6 illustrates how numbers are assigned to various aspects of a case that are considered relevant to sentencing. The guidelines used by the federal government and some states limit themselves to crime seriousness and prior record, whereas others are more comprehensive and assign points not only for the statutory degree of seriousness of the offense and prior record but also on the amount of harm done; whether the offender was on bail, probation, or parole at the time; prior periods of incarceration; and a number of other factors. These numbers are then applied to a grid at the point at which they intersect, which contains the appropriate sentence.

PERSPECTIVE FROM A PRACTITIONER

Laura Kiehl, Presentence Investigator

Position: Presentence investigator

Location: Boise, Idaho

Education: BA in sociology, minor in English, Boise State University; master of arts in criminal justice (in progress) Five years

What are the primary duties and responsibilities of a presentence investigator?

The goal of the presentence investigator is to provide the court with a depiction of a criminal defendant once he or she has been found guilty of a felony offense. My goal is to not only document the defendant's version of the crime he or she committed but also to provide the court with an outline of who that person is as an individual. This information comes from a one-on-one interview with the defendant, as well as from collateral contacts made with friends, family, employers, educators, and medical professionals. With this information, I prepare a PSI for the sentencing judge that contains information pertaining to the instant offense, criminal history, family and social history, educational background, employment history, and medical and substance abuse history, and I document the defendant's goals for the future. I also provide the court with a recommendation for sentencing. The recommendation includes my perception of the criminal defendant based on my interactions with him or her, as well as my contacts with collateral sources. There are three main options for recommendations: probation, rider (retained jurisdiction—meaning that the offender will spend a short time, typically 90 days, in prison, followed by probation), and prison. Within the three recommendations, I add specific treatment and programming guidelines that might benefit the defendant. The recommendations I make are based on the defendant's risk factors and criminal history, combined with any additional concerning or protective factors I have determined through the investigative process.

One of the most important traits for someone to have as a presentence investigator is a desire to get to know people. The saying, "You catch more flies with honey than with vinegar," goes a long way in this line of work. The defendant has already been convicted, and therefore, it is not the job of the presentence investigator to interrogate. I find that my best interviews, which have gained the most

information valuable for the court, were interviews where I made the defendant feel comfortable and feel that he or she could trust me to tell his or her story in a fair and honest manner. An investigative mind is also beneficial, as learning to "dig" for information is part of what makes this job fun and interesting on a day-to-day basis.

In general, what does a typical day for a presentence investigator include?

My workdays vary a great deal. We work a flexible schedule and are only required to be in the office 20 hours per week. One reason for the flexible schedule is due to our need to be at the jails or prisons in order to conduct interviews with defendants who are in custody, awaiting sentencing. We are also able to type our reports from home or wherever we work best. Some days, I will start at the office, go to the jail for an interview, and spend the rest of my day typing from home with my dog sitting beside me. Other days, I will be in the office all day for out-of-custody interviews and making collateral contacts. Some days, I have writer's block and take the day off, knowing that I will be more productive on a different day. The flexibility has allowed me to be more productive on a day-to-day basis.

What is your advice to someone either wishing to study or now studying criminal justice to become a practitioner in this career field?

If you want to be a presentence investigator, hone your writing skills. Ultimately, while this job is investigative in nature, the report should be the main focus and needs to be well written and detailed. Reports can take between 10 and 12 hours (or more) to complete. Also, you cannot be afraid to ask questions. I have heard some of the craziest stories from criminal defendants, some of which were extremely uncomfortable to hear. Defendants willing to open up and provide details about their lives need an investigator who is not afraid to keep asking questions. Be ready to be surprised on a daily basis! This job is never boring and is different and challenging every day, with every different case.

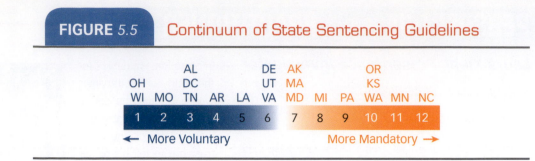

FIGURE 5.5   Continuum of State Sentencing Guidelines

Source: Kauder, N. B., & Ostrom, B. J. (2008). *State sentencing guidelines*. National Center for State Courts. http://www.vcsc.virginia.gov/PEW-Profiles-v12-online.pdf

Video 5.4: United States Sentencing Commission

Given the usefulness of guidelines, it is unfortunate that not all states use them and that among the states that do, they vary greatly in quality. In 2008, the National Center for State Courts (NCSC, 2008) evaluated the guidelines used in all 21 states and assigned them points based on a number of criteria. The most important of these criteria were whether or not they were voluntary or mandatory, whether or not compelling and substantial reasons were required for departures from guideline sentences, and whether or not written reasons must be provided for any such departures. The higher the score, the better the guideline is according to NCSC criteria. Figure 5.5 presents the NCSC's evaluation of the guidelines of the 21 states that had them in 2008. North Carolina's guidelines received maximum points.

Although they were mandatory in the federal system for many years after their creation, at present, they are only advisory. By mandatory, we mean that the sentence indicated by the guideline must be imposed unless there are compelling reasons for not following it. Advisory guidelines are used simply to guide the judges' decisions by providing a uniform set of standards for them to consult if they wish. According to Lubitz and Ross (2001), sentencing guidelines have achieved a number of outcomes consistent with this classical ideal and with Aristotle's definition of justice. These outcomes include the following:

1. A reduction in sentencing disparity.

2. More uniform and consistent sentencing.

3. A more open and understandable sentencing process.

4. Decreased punishment for certain categories of offenses and offenders and increased punishment for others.

5. Aid in prioritizing and allocating correctional resources.

6. Provision of a rational basis for sentencing and increased judicial accountability.

Figure 5.6 is a sentencing guideline that takes into consideration many more factors than the seriousness of the offense and prior record and leaves quite a bit of room for subjective judgment, especially in the culpability, mitigation, and credits section. How would you complete this guideline for the Joan Place case outlined in our sample PSI? What degree of culpability or mitigation would you assign her, and what credits would you give her?

THE FUTURE OF SENTENCING GUIDELINES

As useful as guidelines have proven to be for reducing sentencing disparities and curtailing judicial discretion, their future format and function is by no means assured. As

FIGURE 5.6   Example of a Comprehensive Sentencing Guideline

FELONY SENTENCING WORKSHEET:

DEFENDANT'S NAME: _____   **CASE NO.:** _____

OFFENSE RATING

1. Degree of Offense:

Assess points for the one most serious offense or its equivalent for which offender is being sentenced, as follows: 1st degree felony = 4 points; 2nd degree felony = 3 points; 3rd degree felony = 2 points; 4th degree felony = 1 point.   _____

2. Multiple Offenses:

Assess 2 points if one or more of the following applies: (A) Offender is being sentenced for two or more offenses committed in different incidents; (B) offender is currently under a misdemeanor or felony sentence imposed by any court; or (C) present offense was committed while offender on probation or parole.   _____

3. Actual or Potential Harm:

Assess 2 points if one or more of the following applies: (A) Serious physical harm to a person was caused; (B) property damage or loss of $300.00 or more was caused; (C) there was a high risk of any such harm, damage, or loss, though not caused; (D) the gain or potential gain from theft offense(s) was $300 or more; or (E) dangerous ordinance or a deadly weapon was actually used in the incident, or its use was attempted or threatened.   _____

4. Culpability:

Assess 2 points if one or more of the following applies: (A) Offender was engaging in continuing criminal activity as a source of income or livelihood; (B) offense was part of a continuing conspiracy to which offender was a party; or (C) offense included shocking and deliberate cruelty in which offender participated or acquiesced.   _____

5. Mitigation:

Deduct 1 point for **each** of the following, as applicable: (A) There was substantial provocation, justification, or excuse for offense; (B) victim induced or facilitated offense; (C) offense was committed in the heat of anger; and (D) the property damaged, lost, or stolen was restored or recovered without significant cost to the victim.   _____

NET TOTAL = OFFENSE RATING   _____

DEFENSE RATING

1. Prior Convictions:

Assess 2 points for each verified prior felony conviction, any jurisdiction. Count adjudications of delinquency for felony as convictions.   _____

Assess 1 point for each verified prior misdemeanor conviction and jurisdiction. Count adjudications of delinquency for misdemeanor as convictions. Do not count traffic or intoxication offenses or disorderly conduct, disturbing the peace, or equivalent offenses.

2. Repeat Offenses:

Assess 2 points if present offense is offense of violence, sex offense, theft offense, or drug abuse offense, and offender has one or more prior convictions for same type of offenses.   _____

3. Prison Commitments:

Assess 2 points if offender was committed on one or more occasions to a penitentiary, reformatory, or equivalent institution in any jurisdiction. Count commitments to state youth commission or similar commitments in other jurisdictions.   _____

4. Parole and Similar Violations:

Assess 2 points if one or more of the following applies: (A) Offender has previously had probation or parole for misdemeanor or felony revoked; (B) present offense committed while offender on probation or parole; (C) present offense committed while offender free on bail; or (D) present offense committed while offender in custody.   _____

5. Credits:

Deduct 1 point for each of the following as applicable: (A) Offender has voluntarily made bona fide, realistic arrangements for at least partial restitution; (B) offender was age 25 or older at time of first felony conviction; (C) offender has been substantially law abiding for at least 3 years; and (D) offender lives with his or her spouse or minor children or both and is either a breadwinner for the family or, if there are minor children, a housewife.   _____

NET TOTAL = OFFENDER RATING   _____

(Continued)

FELONY SENTENCING WORKSHEET: (continued)

Indicated Sentence:

Circle the box on the chart where the offense and the offender ratings determined on the previous page intersect. This indicates a normal sentencing package. If the indicated sentence appears too severe or too lenient for the particular case, do not hesitate to vary from the indicated sentence. In that event, however, list the reasons for the variance in the space provided on the next page.

OFFENSE RATING	OFFENDER RATING				
	0-2	3-5	6-8	9-11	12 OR MORE
6 OR MORE	Impose one of three lowest minimum terms **No probation**	Impose one of three highest minimum terms **No probation**	Impose one of three highest minimum terms **No probation**	Impose one of two highest minimum terms. Make at least part of multiple sentences consecutive. **No probation**	Impose highest minimum term. Make at least part of multiple sentences consecutive. **No probation**
5	Impose one of three lowest minimum terms — Some form of probation indicated only with special mitigation	Impose one of three lowest minimum terms **No probation**	Impose one of three highest minimum terms **No probation**	Impose one of three highest minimum terms **No probation**	Impose one of two highest minimum terms. Make at least part of multiple sentences consecutive. **No probation**
4	Impose one of two lowest minimum terms — Some form of probation indicated	Impose one of three lowest minimum terms — Some form of probation indicated only with special mitigation	Impose one of three lowest minimum terms **No probation**	Impose one of three highest minimum terms **No probation**	Impose one of three highest minimum terms **No probation**
3	Impose one of two lowest minimum terms — Some form of probation indicated	Impose one of two lowest minimum terms — Some form of probation indicated	Impose one of three lowest minimum terms — Some form of probation indicated only with special mitigation	Impose one of three lowest minimum terms **No probation**	Impose one of three highest minimum terms **No probation**
0 - 2	Impose lowest minimum term — Some form of probation indicated	Impose one of two lowest minimum terms — Some form of probation indicated	Impose one of two lowest minimum terms — Some form of probation indicated	Impose one of three lowest minimum terms — Some form of probation indicated only with special mitigation	Impose one of three lowest minimum terms **No probation**

Source: Ohio Bar Association.

mentioned above, the federal guidelines are now only "advisory," meaning that judges can consult them and follow them or not, which has opened the door, once again, to unwarranted sentencing discrepancies that guidelines were supposed to rein in. The turnabout began with the recognition of the separation of responsibilities of the trial judge and the trial jury. The role of judges is to be finders of law; the role of juries is to be finders of facts. A famous case based on that principle came before the U.S. Supreme Court in 2005 (*United States v. Booker*, 2005).

The circumstances of the case are that Freddie Booker was arrested in 2003 in possession of 92.5 grams of crack cocaine. He also admitted to police that he had sold an additional 566 grams. A jury found Booker guilty of possession with intent to sell at least 50 grams, for which the possible penalty ranged from 10 years to life. At sentencing, the judge used additional information (the additional 566 grams and the fact the Booker had obstructed justice) to sentence Booker to 30 years. Booker's sentence would have been 21 years and 10 months based on the facts presented to the jury and proved beyond a reasonable doubt.

Booker appealed his sentence, arguing that his Sixth Amendment rights had been violated by the judge "finding facts" when this is the proper role of the jury. An earlier federal appeals court had ruled that the facts of prior convictions are the only facts judges can "find" as justification for increasing sentencing. In other words, anything other than prior record that is used to increase a criminal penalty beyond what the guidelines call for must be submitted to a jury and proved beyond

PHOTO 5.7: In states with sentencing guidelines, the guidelines "advise" the judges about the appropriate sentence based on a number of factors in addition to crime seriousness and prior record.

a reasonable doubt. The Supreme Court agreed with Booker that his sentence violated the Sixth Amendment and sent the case back to district court with instructions either to sentence Booker within the sentencing range supported by the jury's findings or to hold a sentencing hearing before a jury (Bissonnette, 2006).

The remedial portion of the Court's opinion (what can be done to prevent this happening again?) is much more controversial. The Court held that the guidelines were to be advisory only and, therefore, no longer binding on judges. However, the Court did require them to "consult" the guidelines and take them into consideration, but there is no way of assuring that judges comply. John Ashcroft, the U.S. attorney general at the time, called the decision "a retreat from justice," and Representative Tom Feeney decried, "The extraordinary power to sentence" was now afforded federal judges who are accountable to no one and that the decision "flies in the face of the clear will of Congress" (Bissonnette, 2006, p. 1499). In fact, Booker was resentenced by the same judge to the same 30-year sentence that he originally received. Because the sentencing guidelines had then become merely advisory, the judge did not have to further justify his sentence since it was within the range of the statutorily defined penalty. The Court's ruling on guidelines only applies to the federal system at present.

IN FOCUS 5.4

Policy Statement of the American Correctional Association Regarding Sentencing

Because of changing sentencing policies (determinate, mandatory minimums, and particularly the policies driven by the war on drugs), there has been a huge increase in the prison population in the United States. According to the American Correctional Association (ACA), sentencing policies should be aimed at controlling crime at the lowest cost to taxpayers, and offenders should be placed in the least restrictive environment consistent with public safety. The ACA strongly promotes and supports any policies that render sentencing fair and rational and has issued its 2009 official statement on sentencing policy reproduced below.

The American Correctional Association actively promotes the development of sentencing policies that should

A. Be based on the principle of proportionality. The sentence imposed should be commensurate with the seriousness of the crime and the harm done;

B. Be impartial with regard to race, ethnicity, and economic status as to the discretion exercised in sentencing;

C. Include a broad range of options for custody, supervision, and rehabilitation of offenders;

D. Be purpose-driven. Policies must be based on clearly articulated purposes. They should be grounded in knowledge of the relative effectiveness of the various sanctions imposed in attempts to achieve these purposes;

E. Encourage the evaluation of sentencing policy on an ongoing basis. The various sanctions should be monitored to determine their relative effectiveness based on the purpose(s) they are intended to have. Likewise, monitoring should take place to ensure that the sanctions are not applied based on race, ethnicity, or economic status;

F. Recognize that the criminal sentence must be based on multiple criteria, including the harm done to the victim, past criminal history, the need to protect the public, and the opportunity to provide programs for offenders as a means of reducing the risk for future crime;

G. Provide the framework to guide and control discretion according to established criteria and within appropriate limits and allow for recognition of individual needs;

H. Have as a major purpose restorative justice—righting the harm done to the victim and the community. The restorative focus should be both process and substantively oriented. The victim or his or her representative should be included in the "justice" process. The sentencing procedure should address the needs of the victim, including his or her need to be heard and, as much as possible, to be and feel restored to whole again;

I. Promote the use of community-based programs whenever consistent with public safety; and

J. Be linked to the resources needed to implement the policy. The consequential cost of various sanctions should be assessed. Sentencing policy should not be enacted without the benefit of a fiscal-impact analysis. Resource allocations should be linked to sentencing policy so as to ensure adequate funding of all sanctions, including total confinement and the broad range of intermediate sanction and community-based programs needed to implement those policies. (Walsh & Stohr, 2010, pp. 135–137)

This public correctional policy was unanimously ratified by the ACA in 1994 and reviewed and amended in 1999, 2004, and 2009.

SUMMARY

- Sentencing is a postconviction process in which the courts implement one or more of the punitive philosophies: retribution, deterrence, incapacitation, or rehabilitation. Sentencing decisions should be in accordance with justice.

- There are three major sentencing models: indeterminate (a range of possible years), determinate (a specific number of years), and mandatory (can exist under either of the above models but means that the person must be sent to prison; probation is not an option).

- Truth-in-sentencing laws have led to longer sentences, a stronger move to determinate and mandatory sentencing, and statutes such as habitual-offender statutes.

- Sentencing disparities—sentences not accounted for by legally relevant variables—are a major concern in the criminal justice system. A big concern is whether African Americans' more severe sentences are accounted for by their greater involvement in crime or by racism. The sentences imposed for crack versus powder cocaine possession has been a contentious issue because of racial differentials in the possession and sale of crack versus cocaine.

- Efforts have been made to "individualize" justice by providing judges with presentence reports, written by probation officers, which contain many factors about the person the judge is to sentence. A big controversy involving these reports is whether the defense should be able to view them.

- Sentencing guidelines are designed to eliminate sentencing disparities by submitting the seriousness of a person's crime and his or her prior record (in some states, additional information is included) to a scoring system. The person is then supposed to be sentenced the same way as every other person who receives the same score.

- Certain legal problems with sentencing under guidelines moved the U.S. Supreme Court to rule that the federal guidelines, which were previously mandatory, were now to be merely advisory. This opens up the door, once again, for wide levels of judicial discretion and, thus, for sentencing disparity.

KEY TERMS

Concurrent sentence 93

Consecutive sentence 93

Determinate sentence 92

Fair Sentencing Act of 2010 102

Habitual-offender statutes 93

Indeterminate sentence 91

Justice 90

Life without parole (LWOP) 94

Mandatory sentence 92

Plea bargain 96

Presentence investigation report (PSI) 104

Sentence 90

Sentencing disparity 100

Sentencing guidelines 108

Shock probation 95

Split sentences 95

Truth-in-sentencing laws 91

United States Sentencing Commission 108

Victim impact statement 99

DISCUSSION QUESTIONS

1. Is it ever just, right, and moral to sentence equals in terms of legally relevant variables unequally? Give an example.

2. If you are being sentenced for a felony, would you prefer to know when your date for parole consideration is to come, or would you prefer an indeterminate sentence where you could possibly "work your way out" and get released earlier?

3. What is your opinion of habitual-offender statutes that lock people up for life if convicted of a third felony?

4. What research strategy is required to assess the racial sentencing disparity issue?

5. What are the pros and cons of allowing the defense access to the presentence investigation report? Where do you stand on the issue?

6. Sentencing guidelines were designed to rein in excessive judicial sentencing discretion, and most criminal justice personnel consider this a very good thing. Why did the U.S. Supreme Court throw a wrench into the works by making the federal guidelines advisory only?

USEFUL INTERNET SITES

Please note that the sites listed can be accessed at edge.sagepub.com/stohrcorrections.

The Corrections Connection: www.corrections.com

> *This site provides news, resources, and discussions about various corrections issues.*

Internet Encyclopedia of Philosophy: Punishment: www .iep.utm.edu/punishment

> *A nice (but deep) philosophical discussion of the many issues involved in punishment.*

Sentencing Guideline Manual: www.ussc.gov/guidelines-manual/guidelines-manual

> *As indicated, this site provides everything you always wanted (or didn't want) to know about sentencing guidelines.*

Sentencing Law and Policy: sentencing.typepad.com

> *Lots of interesting information about laws and policies related to sentencing.*

The Sentencing Project: www.sentencingproject.org/template/index.cfm

> *A partisan advocate of liberal sentencing policy, it supplies lots of information.*

$SAGE edge™

Sharpen your skills with SAGE edge at **edge.sagepub.com/stohrcorrections**. SAGE edge for Students provides a personalized approach to help you accomplish your coursework goals in an easy-to-use learning environment. You'll find action plans, mobile-friendly eFlashcards, and quizzes as well as video, web, and resources and links to SAGE journal articles to support and expand on the concepts presented in this chapter.

6 Jails and Detention Centers

TEST YOUR KNOWLEDGE

Test your present knowledge of jails by answering the following questions as true or false. Check your answers on page 534 after reading the chapter.

1. Most jails are operated by states.

2. Jails for juveniles are usually referred to as detention centers.

3. Most inmates of adult jails have been convicted of a crime.

4. The drug war has disproportionately affected the number of minorities and women incarcerated in jails.

5. Jails have become the most likely social institution to hold the mentally ill in the United States.

6. Incarcerated women tend to have fewer medical problems than incarcerated men.

7. Female staff in jails are more likely to be the perpetrators of sexual victimization of male inmates than are male staff.

LEARNING OBJECTIVES

- Describe the origins of jails

- Identify the types of jails in operation

- Explain how jails process individuals

- Assess how jails affect and are affected by overcrowding, race, gender, age, and special needs of their inmates

- Describe the various approaches jails take to address medical problems of inmates

- Discuss how jails manage sexual violence, gangs, and suicides

- Explain the kinds of innovations happening in jails and how they are working out

A MENTALLY ILL INMATE IN THE DONA ANA COUNTY JAIL, NEW MEXICO

Stephen Slevin, 59, was an inmate for 22 months in the Dona Ana County Jail in Las Cruces, New Mexico ("$15.5 Million Settlement," 2014, p. 20). He was first booked into the jail on charges of driving while intoxicated and receiving or transferring a stolen vehicle in August 2005 (a friend had let him borrow the car to drive across the country). He had a history of suicide attempts and mental illness, so the jail officers in booking placed him in an empty padded cell for two days before he was assessed by the mental-health unit. He was then eventually sent to solitary confinement, where he had no contact with a judge or medical personnel for the next 18 months. It was noted that upon entering the jail, he had been a well-nourished and healthy male with a mental illness. After the 18 months in solitary confinement and a psychiatric evaluation, however, he smelled; had overgrown nails and hair; was malnourished, at 133 pounds; and "complained of paranoia, hallucinations, bed sores and untreated dental problems" ("$15.5 Million Settlement," 2014, p. 21). Slevin had pulled out his own infected tooth while incarcerated, as no dental care was provided to him. A month after this evaluation, he was again placed in solitary confinement but was finally released in June 2007, when the charges were dismissed. He sued in federal court, alleging a violation of his civil rights and false imprisonment, and a federal jury agreed and awarded him $22 million dollars. When Dona Ana County appealed this decision, a federal judge affirmed the punitive and compensatory damages in the original award. To avoid further appeals by the county, however, Slevin settled with them and their insurer for $15 million dollars in 2013 ("$15.5 Million Settlement," 2014, p. 20).

••• INTRODUCTION: THE COMMUNITY INSTITUTION

The American jail is a derivative of various modes of holding people for trial that have existed in Western countries for centuries. Whether fashioned from caves, mines, or old houses or as separate buildings, **jails** were developed originally as a primary means of holding the accused for trial, for execution, or in lieu of a fine. As was noted in Chapter 2, jails were called gaols in the England of the Middle Ages and were operated by the *shire reeve*, or sheriff, and his minions.

Jails have been in existence much longer than prisons, and their mission is much more diverse, especially now. These days, jails are usually local and community institutions that hold people who are presumed innocent before trial; they hold convicted offenders before they are sentenced; they hold more minor offenders who are sentenced for terms that are usually less than a year; they hold juveniles (usually in their own jails or separated from adults or before transport to juvenile facilities); they hold women (usually separated from men and sometimes in their own jails); they hold people for the state or federal authorities (there are some exclusively federal jails); and depending on the particular jail population being served and the capacity of any given facility, they serve to incapacitate, deter, rehabilitate, punish, and reintegrate.

Though described as correctional afterthoughts by scholars and despite their multi-faceted and critical role in communities, jails have often received short shrift in terms of monetary support and professional regard (Kerle, 1991, 2003, 2011; Thompson & Mays, 1991; Zupan, 1991). The vast majority of jails are operated by county sheriffs, whose primary focus has been law enforcement rather than corrections. As a result, jail facilities have often been neglected, resulting in dilapidated structures, and jail staffs have had less training and pay than probation and parole officers in communities or correctional staffs working at the state or federal level in prisons. Jail staffs also often receive less pay and training than deputy sheriffs working in the same organization (sheriff's office) as the jail. Research indicates that many in the general public may even view jails as more punitive than prisons (see, e.g., May, Applegate, Ruddell, & Wood, 2014). The late comic Rodney Dangerfield's perennial lament, "[They] don't get no respect," surely applies to jails more than perhaps any other social institution.

In this chapter, we discuss how this forgotten social institution fulfills a vital community role, one that includes all of the functions described in the preceding paragraph, as well as serving as a repository for people who are only nominally criminal and have nowhere else to go (e.g., the homeless or the mentally ill). The role of jails also includes the holding of some state or federal inmates, as prisons are too full. In some larger counties, the holding of longer-term sentenced inmates or those who have numerous physical, mental, and substance abuse problems—not to mention educational deficits—has led to more programming and treatment in jails. Part and parcel of this interest in treatment is the emergence of community reentry programs, as will also be discussed in the chapter on parole (Chapter 12), as a means of preventing crime and addressing the multifaceted needs of ex–jail inmates. In this chapter, these emerging trends will be explored, as will the challenges jails face, but first, we will discuss the types of institutions that constitute jails.

JAIL TYPES

The typical jail is operated by the sheriff of a county. However, some cities, states, and the federal government operate jails, and sometimes, multiple jurisdictions combine resources

Jails: These are local community institutions that hold people who are presumed innocent before trial; convicted people before they are sentenced; convicted minor offenders, who are sentenced for terms that are usually less than a year; juveniles (usually in their own jails, separated from adults, or before transport to juvenile facilities); women (usually separated from men and sometimes in their own jails); and people for the state or federal authorities. Depending on the particular jail population being served and the capacity of the given facility, they serve to incapacitate, deter, rehabilitate, punish, and reintegrate.

to administer a jail that serves a region. Some counties have hired jail administrators to oversee the operation of the jail, taking it out of the hands of the local sheriff. Jails for adults are sometimes called detention centers, and jails for juveniles are almost always referred to as detention centers. Some American Indian tribes have their own jails, and many police departments have short-term lockup facilities to hold suspects or those accused of crimes. Currently, there are about 2,900 jails in the United States, and 68 jails are operated by American Indian tribes (Minton, 2014; Minton & Golinelli, 2014; Sabol & Minton, 2008). When a state or the federal government (or another governmental entity) has inmates for a jail but no facility of its own in a given vicinity, the entity will typically ask the county to hold that inmate. Counties are usually more than willing to do this,

PHOTO 6.1: Travis County Jail

as they are paid a fee that often exceeds the cost of holding inmates, which makes holding inmates for other jurisdictions a money-making enterprise.

Most jails are composed of one or two buildings in close proximity to each other. They are usually operated somewhat close to a city or town center, except when located on reservations or at military facilities. Larger jail jurisdictions (over 1,000 inmates) will often operate more than one jail.

Many jails have adopted technological changes that have greatly enhanced their ability to supervise and control inmates. The use of cameras, voice-operated and visual-check-operated doors by a control center, electronic fingerprint machines, and even video arraignments and visiting are revolutionizing the jail experience. Certainly, these changes are making the facility more secure, but also, in the case of video visiting, they may make it easier to maintain contact with the outside.

Career Video 6.1:
Jail Administrator

Web 6.1:
American Jail
Association

••• JAIL INMATES AND THEIR PROCESSING

Jails operate 7 days a week, 24 hours a day, as crime does not take a holiday. They hold all kinds of inmates, from the serious convicted offender awaiting transport to a state or federal prison, down to the accused misdemeanant who cannot make bail. About 60% of jail inmates have not been convicted of the crime for which they are being held; they are awaiting court action (Minton, 2010; Minton & Golinelli, 2014, p. 1). Jails receive inmates from local, state, federal, and tribal police officers. In 2013, they processed 11.7 million inmates (down from a peak of 13.6 million in 2008), with most inmates in and out within a few days or a week, some within hours, though others might be held for more than a year, particularly if they are sentenced state or federal inmates (Minton, 2010; Minton & Golinelli, 2014, p. 4). Because of their complicated and diverse role and as a means of keeping track of the inmates they are responsible for holding, jails will often follow a set procedure that is prescribed by both tradition and practice.

The first part of the typical processing of an inmate at a county or city jail is the delivery of the arrestee to the facility by a law enforcement officer. As is discussed in the following, many arrestees may be stressed, upset, mentally disturbed, or intoxicated. In the latter case, the officer may choose to administer a Breathalyzer test at the jail.

If the arrestee is injured, the jail's booking staff may require that the arrestee be taken by law enforcement to the hospital to be checked out before he or she is admitted to the jail.

If not injured, the law enforcement officer will fill out the paperwork for admittance of the arrestee to the facility. Usually, the arrestee is still with the officer when this is occurring and often still in handcuffs. Once the required paperwork and processing are completed, the jail will accept the arrestee, search him or her, and begin its own paperwork for admitting the arrestee. At this juncture and depending on the alleged offense, the arrestee may be allowed to contact family and friends and/or a bail bondsman. The arrestee might be released directly into the community if the alleged offense is minor. However, if the alleged offense is serious enough, the arrestee will need to await arraignment by a judge to determine bail and, in the interim, might be booked into the jail.

During the booking process, jails will often strip search arrestees (now inmates), take their property, and issue clothing and other essentials. If the new inmate is intoxicated or belligerent, booking staff may place him or her in a special holding cell. In the latter case, this might involve a padded room or a restraint chair. Once the inmate is sober and calm, he or she is then classified and moved to a more permanent housing area in the jail. Larger jails often keep new inmates in a separate area or cell before they place them in a general housing unit so that they can be observed and classified (based on the inmate's alleged offense, alleged criminal coconspirators, criminal history, gang involvements, health and other needs, etc.).

••• TRENDS IN JAIL POPULATIONS

OVERCROWDING

Overcrowding: A phenomenon that occurs when the number of inmates exceeds the physical capacity (the beds and space) available.

As indicated in other sections of this book, jails have to deal with the same kinds of overcrowding issues that have afflicted prisons. **Overcrowding** occurs when the number of inmates exceeds the physical capacity (i.e., the beds and space) available. Each year and over the last several decades, the number of jail beds needed by jurisdictions has increased, and they have been filled almost as soon as they have been built (see Figure 6.1; Minton, 2010). However, between 2008 and 2009, there was an unprecedented decrease in jail inmates of 1.1%. As of midyear 2014 (the latest data available at the time of this writing), on average, jails were operating at 84% of their capacity, and the highest capacity for the last decade (2000–2009) was achieved in 2006 and 2007 at 96% (Minton, 2010, p. 5; Minton & Golinelli, 2014, p. 3). Between 2013 and 2014, the amount of bed space increased (Minton & Zeng, 2015, p. 4). This percentage use of capacity is actually better than in past years, when jails of the 1980s and 1990s were operating at well over their rated capacity (Cox & Osterhoff, 1991; Gilliard & Beck, 1997; Klofas, 1991).

Getty Images/AFP PHOTO/Jeff Haynes

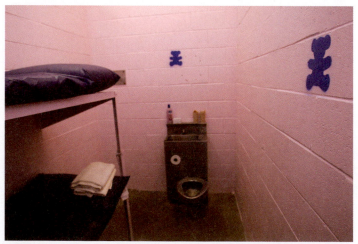

PHOTO 6.2: A double-bunk jail cell. The pink interior paint is meant to sooth detainees.

PERSPECTIVE FROM A PRACTITIONER

Brian Cole, County Corrections Director

Position: Director of the county department of corrections

Location: Shawnee County Department of Corrections, Kansas

Education: BA in criminal justice and BA in psychology, Washburn University, 1989

What are the primary duties and responsibilities of a director of a county department of corrections?

Under administrative direction of the Board of County Commissioners, this position administers the adult and juvenile detention programs of Shawnee County, Kansas; ensures offenders placed in custody are housed in a safe, secure manner and that offenders receive appropriately fair and humane treatment by staff; monitors the overall security of the centers and regularly tours the facilities to ensure the highest security standards are maintained; proactively seeks to improve offender processes to enhance the security and efficiency of the agency; creates and expects a staff culture of integrity in the reporting of misconduct by other staff and offenders; and visits offender living units and speaks with offenders to gain sense of morale of offenders and to monitor operations.

This position oversees programs to ensure compliance with federal, state, and local laws, regulations, and accrediting entity standards; plans and coordinates the annual budget, staffing, and program needs for the department; and ensures expenditures are within budget parameters and proactively seeks and implements methods by which the department can save funds.

This position also proactively recommends changes to the physical plant that will provide enhanced efficiency and security; creates future projections for physical plant expansion; develops and maintains positive working relationships with employees of other county agencies, other law enforcement agencies, colleges and universities, and other agencies and organizations as appropriate; delegates an appropriate amount of work to staff to encourage their professional growth and seeks opportunities for professional self-growth; and seeks and completes public speaking engagements to promote positive community relations. The person holding this position is expected to respond to media requests, as appropriate, and attend community functions as a representative of the department.

What characteristics make a good director of a county department of corrections?

- Integrity
- Leadership
- Flexibility
- Initiative
- Sense of humor
- Compassion for staff
- Proactive
- Confidence
- Public speaking skills
- Good written and verbal communication skills

What is a typical day like for a director of a county department of corrections?

A typical day for me would be one that starts with meeting with staff and determining the priorities of the day. In corrections, you never have a "clean desk." As one project ends, you always are starting a new one. On a daily basis, I speak with my executive team to get a brief update on projects, personnel, budget, special-needs inmates, and physical-plant issues. I also meet with our mental-health team leader daily to review high-risk inmate statuses. Each day, I spend time researching current events and legal trends, trying to stay as proactive as possible to avoid complacency and litigation. I speak with inmates on a daily basis and answer requests. I spend time meeting with the public to ensure our agency is meeting and

(Continued)

(Continued)

exceeding citizen expectations, and I provide feedback to our commissioners.

What is your advice to someone either wishing to study or now studying criminal justice to become a practitioner in this career field?

Working in the field of corrections takes committed people. On a daily basis, you work with incarcerated individuals who have made (in some cases) some very bad life decisions. You have to be one who can separate emotion from your job and understand that you are managing people and managing problems. You have to have an appreciation for the environment you are working within. This is a stressful but very rewarding job. Corrections can be a career, not just another job. You make decisions each day that could mean the life or death of inmates, staff, and the community. You cannot take short cuts. Learn as much as you can about your agency, the philosophy, and the culture that the leader of the organization has put in place. You have a great opportunity to help others, work as a team, and truly better your community.

What are the biggest challenges facing corrections?

Mentally Ill Inmates

Jails are becoming community mental-health facilities for the mentally ill. With this being a trend in some parts of the country, a citizen has a better chance of receiving treatment in a jail than in his or her community. As directors, we must educate our staff to meet this challenge. One way is through crisis intervention team (CIT) training.

It is a fact that some people with mental illness will end up in jail. In some instances, this may be the safest and best option for them. However, inmates in jail go into crisis, and correctional staff must be able to handle these emergency situations. Through CIT training, our staff has been able to identify crisis situations, defuse these situations, communicate with the inmates in crisis, and, most of the time, see the incidents to a positive resolution that does not result in harm to the inmate or staff. The end result is officer and inmate safety, and then, we will refer the inmate to mental-health services for treatment. We have CIT training available two times a year for all staff.

Transgender Inmates

Historically, correctional institutions have classified inmates by their genitalia, not by their gender identity. Often transgender women are placed in male housing units, and transgender men are placed in female housing units. Transgender inmates have the right to be treated with dignity and respect and be free from harm and harassment.

A key federal court opinion out of the First Circuit Court of Appeals shed light on an issue that all correctional managers must be aware of. Increasingly, correctional managers must take the proactive steps to create and implement policy that begins with the early identification of transgender inmates, completion of medical and mental-health evaluations and treatment (including gender reassignment surgery), proper housing, programs, and clear protocols for routine interactions, such as showering and pat downs. As with every category of individual liberties, it is incumbent upon correctional leadership to identify and address inmates' rights, as framed by legislative, executive, and judicial decisions.

Also and notably, even an average of 84% for 2014 means that half of the jails in the United States are operating at over that average.

Moreover, the percentages of capacity can be misleading when one considers overcrowding. Certain sections of jails are designated for specific types of inmates that cannot or do not mix well (e.g., males and females but also juveniles, arrestees, inmates with medical problems, gang members, etc.). The percentage capacity may indicate that the jail is not completely full, but any given section might be overwhelmed with inmates.

Such overcrowding limits the ability of the jail to fulfill its multifaceted mission: Less programming can be provided, health and maintenance systems are overtaxed, and staff are stressed by the increased demands on their time and the inability to meet all inmate needs. From the inmates' perspective, their health, security, and privacy are more likely to be threatened when the numbers of inmates in their living units increase, and the amount

FIGURE *6.1*   Inmates in Local Jails, 1980–2014

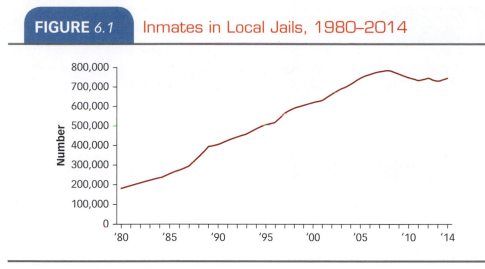

Note: Inmates confined at midyear.

Source: Minton and Zeng (2015, p. 3).

of space—and possibly, the number of staff—does not. The jail staff also lose their ability to effectively classify and sometimes control inmates; they may be unable to keep the offenders convicted of serious crimes away from the presumed-innocent unconvicted or more minor-offending inmates. Judges and jail managers will struggle over how to keep the jail population down to acceptable limits, and as a result, even serious offenders may be let loose into communities as a means of reducing the crowding. Therefore, though the "get-tough" laws in many states were passed with the explicit intent of incarcerating more people for longer, their actual unintended effect in some jails may be to incarcerate serious offenders less (as there is no room) and all offenders in less safe and less secure facilities.

Though suits by jail inmates are usually not successful, some are. Welsh (1995) found, in his study of lawsuits involving California jails, that the issue courts gave greatest credence to was overcrowding. Perhaps this is because overcrowding is clearly quantifiable (the rated capacity is clear, and the inmate count is obvious), but it is likely that it was regarded as so important by courts because it can lead to a number of other seemingly intractable problems, such as those just mentioned.

GENDER, JUVENILES, RACE, AND ETHNICITY

As indicated from the data supplied in Table 6.1, most jail inmates are adult minority males, though the number of whites represents the largest racial grouping of the men, and the number of whites as a proportion of the total men has increased markedly, particularly since 2010. Women comprised over 12.2% of jail inmates in 2009, but that increased to almost 15% by 2014, which is more than in 2000 (11.4%) (Minton & Zeng, 2015, p. 4). The reason often cited for the overall increases in incarceration in jails and prisons and the increases for women and minorities in jails

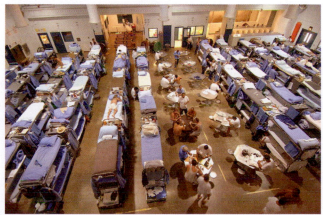

PHOTO 6.3: Inmates in the Reception Housing Area of a California State Prison. California, like many states, has suffered from severe overcrowding in recent decades.

California Department of Corrections and Rehabilitation

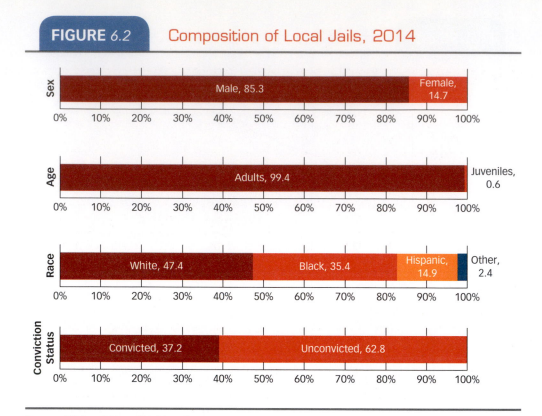

FIGURE *6.2*   Composition of Local Jails, 2014

Sex: Male, 85.3 | Female, 14.7

Age: Adults, 99.4 | Juveniles, 0.6

Race: White, 47.4 | Black, 35.4 | Hispanic, 14.9 | Other, 2.4

Conviction Status: Convicted, 37.2 | Unconvicted, 62.8

Source: Minton & Zeng (2015, p. 3).

and prisons, in particular, has been the prosecution of the drug war since the 1980s and 1990s. The "get-tough" policies, which have led to longer periods of incarceration in prisons, have also led to a greater propensity to catch and keep low-level drug offenders in jails (Irwin, 2005; Owen, 2005; Welch, 2005; Whitman, 2003). The focus of arrests in the drug war has often been on the low-level sellers, rather than the buyers or the drug kingpins, and that has netted more minorities and women into the system. Mandatory sentences, juvenile waivers, and sentence enhancements for certain offenses have collectively led to longer sentences for most offenders and backed up the numbers of offenders in some jails either awaiting transfer to state or federal prisons or doing their time in the jails, rather than in the overcrowded prisons.

It is not clear why there have been recent declines in the numbers of minorities (particularly African Americans and Hispanics), vis-à-vis whites and women, incarcerated in jails, a particularly notable phenomenon in large-city jails (Minton, 2010; Minton & Golinelli, 2014; Minton & Zeng, 2015). It could just be a minor shift that will not become a trend, or it could signal a longer-term change in the use of jails due to the recession of 2007 to 2010, a rethinking in the prosecution of the drug war, or some other variable not yet identified by

© REUTERS/Lucy Nicholson

PHOTO 6.4: A female jail inmate awaits her cell assignment. Women comprised over 12.2% of jail inmates in 2009 (Minton & Golinelli, 2014, p. 7).

TABLE 6.1 Percentage of Inmates in Local Jails, by Characteristics, Midyear 2000 and 2005–2014

CHARACTERISTIC	2000	2005	2006	2007	2008	2009	2010	2011	2012	2013	2014
Sex											
Male	88.6%	87.3%	87.1%	87.1%	87.3%	87.8%	87.7%	87.3%	86.8%	86.0%	85.3%
Female	11.4	12.7	12.9	12.9	12.7	12.2	12.3	12.7	13.2	14.0	14.7
Adults	98.8%	99.1%	99.2%	99.1%	99%	99.1%	99.0%	99.2%	99.3%	99.4%	99.4%
Male	87.4	86.5	86.3	86.3	86.4	86.9	86.7	86.6	86.1	85.4	84.8
Female	11.3	12.6	12.9	12.8	12.6	12.1	12.3	12.6	13.2	13.9	14.6
Juveniles[a]	1.2%	0.9%	0.8%	0.9%	1%	0.9%	1.0%	0.8%	0.7%	0.6%	0.6%
Held as adults[b]	1.0	0.8	0.6	0.7	0.8	0.8	0.8	0.6	0.6	0.5	0.5
Held as juveniles	0.2	0.1	0.2	0.2	0.2	0.2	0.3	0.2	0.1	0.1	0.1
Race/Hispanic origin[c]											
White[d]	41.9%	44.3%	43.9%	43.3%	42.5%	42.5%	44.3%	44.8%	45.8%	47.2%	47.4%
Black/African American[d]	41.3	38.9	38.6	38.7	39.2	39.2	37.8	37.6	36.9	35.8	35.4
Hispanic/Latino	15.2	15	15.6	16.1	16.4	16.2	15.8	15.5	15.1	14.8	14.9
Other[d,e]	1.6	1.7	1.8	1.8	1.8	1.9	2.0	2.0	1.9	2.1	2.3
Two or more races[d]	–	0.1	0.1	0.1	0.2	0.2	0.1	0.2	0.2	0.2	0.1
Conviction status[b]											
Convicted	44%	38%	37.9%	38%	37.1%	37.8%	38.9%	39.4%	39.4%	38.0%	37.2%
Male	39	33.2	32.8	32.9	32.3	33	–	–	–	–	–
Female	5	4.9	5	5.2	4.8	4.8	–	–	–	–	–
Unconvicted	56.0%	62.0%	62.1%	62.0%	62.9%	62.2%	61.1%	60.6%	60.6%	62.0%	62.8%
Male	50	54.2	54.3	54.3	55.2	54.8	–	–	–	–	–
Female	6	7.7	7.8	7.7	7.8	7.4	–	–	–	–	–

Note: May not sum to total due to rounding.

a. Persons under age 18 at midyear.

b. Includes juveniles who were tried or awaiting trial as adults.

c. Estimates based on reported data and adjusted for nonresponse.

d. Excludes persons of Hispanic or Latino origin.

e. Includes American Indians, Alaska Natives, Asians, Native Hawaiians, and other Pacific Islanders.

— = Data not collected.

Source: Minton & Zeng (2015, p. 3).

POLICY AND RESEARCH

High Schools in Jails

For many years, versions of high schools have existed in juvenile detention facilities. High school classes and the ability to earn high school credits and degrees have existed in America's prisons and larger jails. But the Five Keys Charter School in San Francisco, California, claims to be the first complete high school inside an adult jail (J. Tucker, 2014). Started in 2003, the Five Keys Charter School graduated 20 students in 2014, and 600 total have received a high school diploma or a certification of completion or equivalency diploma since its inception (J. Tucker, 2014, p. 1). "The school's philosophy is founded on the five keys to an inmate's success: connection to community; a focus on family; recovery from substance abuse; education; and employment" (J. Tucker, 2014, p. 1). Notably, these are the same areas that are a focus of other reentry programming. In a simple comparison of graduates' recidivism (44%), as compared with other inmates (68%), the high school graduates do much better (J. Tucker, 2014, p. 1). If subsequent research includes matching of graduates with those who didn't graduate on key characteristics (such as criminal history, age, gender, mental illness, etc.) and also finds reduced recidivism, this high school in an adult jail could save the public millions of dollars while creating safer communities.

DISCUSSION QUESTIONS

1. Do you think that earning a high school diploma in a jail setting is likely to benefit inmates and their communities? Why, or why not?

2. What are the likely barriers to completion of high school in most jails? How might such barriers be overcome?

researchers. Longer-term trends do indicate that the number of adult males in jail from 1990 to 2006 almost doubled while the numbers of adult females and juveniles almost tripled. Percentage increases for women and juveniles are also large: In 1990, women represented only about 9% of jail populations and juveniles about 0.6%, whereas by 2000, women composed 11.3% and juveniles 1.2% of jail populations (Bureau of Justice Statistics, 2000, 2007; see also Table 6.1). However, the percentage of inmates in adult jails who were juveniles has decreased by half from 2000 to 2014 (from 1.0 to 0.5) while the percentage of females has increased by over 3% during that same time period (see Table 6.1).

Across the two largest racial groupings (whites and African Americans) and the largest ethnic grouping (Hispanics), there have been significant increases in jail incarceration. The raw number of whites has increased from 1990 (when there were fewer whites incarcerated in jails than African Americans). Proportionate to their representation in the population, however, African Americans are much more likely to be incarcerated in American jails than are whites or Hispanics. As reported by the Bureau of Justice Statistics (2008), for 2006, "Blacks were almost three times more likely than Hispanics and five times more likely than whites to be in jail" (p. 2). Again, this higher proportional rate of incarceration for African Americans, in particular, can likely be attributed to their greater concentration in impoverished neighborhoods and to the focus of the drug war that has tended to target such living areas and the selling and use of crack cocaine (see the discussion of enhanced sentences for crack cocaine in Chapter 5). But as the drug war has waned, in terms of not only crack cocaine sentences but also marijuana prosecutions, as medical and recreational marijuana are decriminalized and legalized, the number of minorities has decreased as a percentage of jail populations, particularly among African Americans (from 41.3% in 2000 to 35.4% by midyear 2014; Minton & Zeng, 2015, p. 4 [see Table 6.1]).

THE POOR AND THE MENTALLY ILL

The late corrections scholar John Irwin (1985) once referred to the types of people who are managed in jails as the "rabble," by which he meant "disorganized and disorderly, the lowest class of people" (p. 2). These were not just the undereducated, the under- or unemployed, or even the poor and mentally ill. He meant to include all those descriptors as they related to the state of being disorganized and disorderly and as those designations might lead to permanent residence in a lower class, but he also meant that jail inmates tend to be "detached" and of "disrepute," in the sense that they offend others by committing mostly minor crimes in public places.

Mental Illness, Homelessness, Substance Abuse, and Poverty

Certainly, the fact of being homeless puts that person at a greater risk for negative contact with the police; lacking a home, private matters are more likely to be subject to public viewing in public spaces, and this disturbs or offends some community members, which leads to police involvement. Those who are mentally ill are more likely to be homeless, as they are unable to manage the daily challenges that employment and keeping a roof over one's head and food in one's mouth require (McNiel, Binder, & Robinson, 2005; Severson, 2004).

Jails in the United States are full of the mentally ill, the homeless, and the poor. Data from the Bureau of Justice Statistics (BJS) (based on interviews of local-jail inmates in 2002) indicate that about 64% of jail inmates (75% of females and 63% of males) have a mental-health problem (as compared with 56% of state prisoners and 45% of federal prisoners; see Figure 6.3) (James & Glaze, 2006, p. 1). In a later BJS study, it was determined that 26% of jail inmates had symptoms of "serious psychological distress" (Beck, Berzofsky, Caspar, & Krebs, 2013, p. 25). In contrast, about 10.6% of the U.S. population has symptoms of mental illness. Moreover, for virtually every manifestation of mental illness, more jail inmates than state or federal prisoners were likely to exhibit symptoms, including 50% more delusions and twice as many hallucinations (James & Glaze, 2006, p. 2). Of those jail inmates with a mental-health problem, the specific diagnosis included mania (54%), major depression (30%), and a psychotic disorder (24%) (James & Glaze, 2006, p. 2). The specific identification of a mental illness for each inmate by the BJS research team was based on a recent clinical diagnosis or symptoms that fit the criteria of the *Diagnostic and Statistical Manual of Mental Disorders (DSM-IV)*.

A whole host of problems has been found to be associated with mental illness, including homelessness, greater criminal engagement, prior abuse, and substance use (McNiel et al., 2005). Among the findings from this BJS study of jails was that those with a mental illness were almost twice as likely to be homeless as those jail inmates without a mental-illness designation (17%, as opposed to 9%) (James & Glaze, 2006, pp. 1–2). More inmates with a mental-health problem had prior incarcerations than those without such a problem (one quarter, as opposed to one fifth). About 3 times as many jail inmates with a mental-health problem had a history of physical or sexual abuse than those without such a problem (24%, as opposed to 8%). Almost three quarters of the inmates with a mental-health problem were dependent on or abused alcohol or illegal substances (74%, as opposed to 53% of those without a mental-health problem). In short, mental illness, along with poverty, was entangled in a whole array of societal issues for jail inmates.

Further evidence for this supposition was found by McNiel et al. (2005) in their study in San Francisco County. They found that mental illness, substance abuse, and jail incarcerations were inextricably connected as life events. Those who were mentally ill and

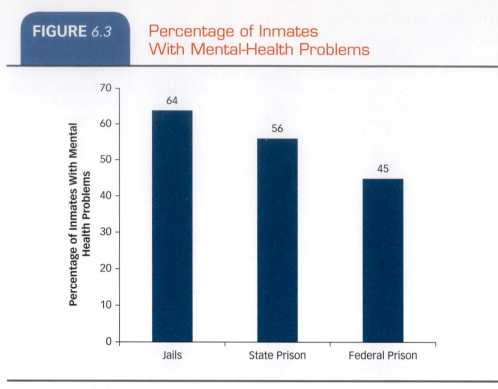

FIGURE *6.3*   Percentage of Inmates
With Mental-Health Problems

Source: James and Glaze (2006).

homeless were also more likely to have a substance abuse problem, and it was also likely for this population that jail incarcerations were part of their existence as well.

Mental Illness and Victimization

Moreover, in the BJS's National Inmate Survey—conducted in state and federal prisons, jails, Immigration and Customs Enforcement detention centers, and military and Indian country facilities and focused primarily on sexual victimization—the researchers found that those who are mentally ill are much more likely to be sexually victimized while incarcerated than inmates who are not (Beck et al., 2013). Among their important findings were the conclusions that inmates with serious psychological distress reported high rates of inmate-on-inmate and staff sexual victimization in 2011 and 2012:

- Among state and federal prison inmates, an estimated 6.3% of those identified with serious psychological distress reported that they were sexually victimized by another inmate. In comparison, among prisoners with no indication of mental illness, 0.7% reported being victimized by another inmate.

- Similar differences were reported by jail inmates. An estimated 3.6% of those identified with serious psychological distress reported inmate-on-inmate sexual victimization,

compared to 0.7% of inmates with no indication of mental illness.

- Rates of serious psychological distress in prisons (14.7%) and jails (26.3%) were substantially higher than the rate (3.0%) in the U.S. noninstitutional population age 18 or older.

- For each of the measured demographic subgroups, inmates with serious psychological distress reported higher rates of inmate-on-inmate sexual victimization than inmates without mental health problems.

- Among inmates with serious psychological distress, nonheterosexual inmates reported the highest rates of inmate-on-inmate sexual victimization (21.0% of prison inmates and 14.7% of jail inmates) (Beck et al., 2013, pp. 6–8).

What we might learn from these findings is that jails hold more inmates with psychological problems than do prisons, and as with prisons, this mental illness makes them more vulnerable to sexual abuse. These data tell us that the likelihood of abuse is also heightened if the inmate is LGBTI (Lesbian, Gay, Bisexual, Transgender, or Intersex) and has serious psychological problems.

Mental Illness and Solitary Confinement

Mental illness also makes jail inmates more likely candidates for the use of solitary confinement and targets of other violent inmates. In a study of the Rikers Island 10-jail complex by New York City, city health officials noted that a disproportionate number of inmates have a mental-health diagnosis (Pearson, 2015). It was reported that the health care workers, who are employed by the city but are bound by medical ethics, are reticent to approve solitary confinement for such inmates, as they know it can exacerbate their already precarious mental-health status. Yet the mentally ill in this jail are more likely to be placed in solitary because of their behavior problems and/or as protection. In an earlier study of the Rikers Island jail complex by the Department of Justice and by the *New York Times*, it was found that a culture of violence was predominant in these jails (particularly those for juveniles) and that too often, the target of this violence was the adult and juvenile mentally ill inmates (Seabrook, 2014).

Calls for Reform in the Care of the Mentally Ill

And the abuse and poor conditions for the mentally ill are not a problem reserved for the Rikers Island jail inmates. As Andrew Cohen (2013) documented in an article in the *Atlantic Monthly*, a number of reports emanating from the Justice Department, the American Civil Liberties Union, and a federal judicial decision indicate that the abuse is widespread and exists in both jails and prisons. "Prison [and jail] officials have failed to provide a constitutional level of care in virtually every respect, from providing medication and treatment to protecting the men from committing suicide" (A. Cohen, 2013, p. 1). In fact, the problematic treatment of mentally ill jail inmates has risen to crisis status for the Council of State Governments. As a consequence, on May 6, 2015, they launched a national initiative to help counties address this issue in their jails (Council of State Governments Justice Center, 2015). Remedies, embodied in what is termed an evidence-based Stepping Up Program, will focus on diversion from jail to other services and the provision of treatment and better care for mentally ill inmates.

••• MEDICAL PROBLEMS

One of the social issues that is particularly problematic for jail inmates and the people who manage them is the relatively poor health of people incarcerated in jails. According to the 2011–2012 study of jail inmates by the BJS (Maruschak, 2015), half of jail inmates reported a chronic medical problem, such as cancer or blood pressure or heart problems. According to an earlier iteration of this study (Maruschak, 2006, p. 1), most of these medical maladies preceded placement in jail and included the following (in order of prevalence): arthritis, hypertension, asthma, heart problems, cancer, paralysis, stroke,

Video 6.1: Health Services Changes in Washington State Department of Corrections diabetes, kidney problems, liver problems, hepatitis, sexually transmitted diseases, tuberculosis, and HIV. A small percentage of inmates (2%) were so medically impaired that they needed to use a cane, walker, or wheelchair. Almost 75% were overweight, and over 60% were morbidly obese (Maruschak, 2015, p.1).

ELDERLY INMATES

Video 6.2:
Elderly Prisoners Up 250 Percent: Should They Be Released to Save Money?

As one might expect, the elderly—and in prisons and jails, due to the premature aging of inmates, that can mean anyone over 50—are much more prone to some of these medical maladies than are younger inmates (Hamada, 2015). In one BJS study, 61% of those over 45 reported a medical problem (Maruschak, 2006, p. 1). With the exception of asthma and HIV, which tended to be more prevalent among younger inmates, the older inmates were much more likely to have the other medical problems tallied in this report; this means that older inmates are more costly to manage in jails because of their greater need for medical care.

FEMALE INMATES

Video 6.3:
Woman Dies While in Custody of Davis County Jail; Family Protests

Like the older inmates, women were much more likely to report medical problems to the BJS researchers (53% for women, as opposed to 35% for men) (Maruschak, 2006, p. 2). They reported a rate of cancer that was almost 8 times that of men (831 per 10,000 female inmates, compared with 108 per 10,000 male inmates), with the most common type of cancer being cervical for women and skin for men. In fact, of every medical problem documented in the study, the women reported more prevalence than the men, with the exception of paralysis, where they were even with men, and tuberculosis, where a slightly greater percentage of men reported more (4.3% for men, as opposed to 4.0% for women) (Maruschak, 2006, p. 2).

JUVENILE INMATES

Incarcerated youth have their own set of potentially debilitating health problems that also present an immediate health risk to communities. In a study of adolescents in a

PHOTO 6.5: Female inmates line up for their medications.

juvenile detention center in Chicago, about 5% of the teens had contracted gonorrhea, and almost 15% had chlamydia (Broussard et al., 2002, p. 8). Girls were over 3 times more likely to have one of these diseases than were boys in this study.

RIGHTS TO MEDICAL CARE

According to the 1976 Supreme Court case, *Estelle v. Gamble*, inmates have a constitutional right to reasonable medical care. The court held that to be *deliberately indifferent* to the medical needs of inmates would violate the Eighth Amendment prohibition against cruel and unusual punishment. The Affordable Care Act of 2010 (ACA, commonly referred to as Obamacare) also requires that jails provide medical and mental-health care within their facilities (Tally, 2015). Needless to say, treating such problems while providing care that meets this new mandate requires that a jail of any size have budgetary coverage for the salaries of nurses; a contract with a local doctor, mental-health provider, and dentist; and an arrangement with local hospitals. Moreover, regular staff need basic training in CPR and other medical knowledge (e.g., to know when someone is exhibiting the symptoms of a heart attack or stroke or the symptoms of mental illness) so that when problems arise, staff recognize how serious they might be and know how to address them or whom to call (Kerle, 2011; Rigby, 2007).

Some jails are addressing these issues by contracting with private companies to provide medical services or using telemedicine as a means of delivering some services. The National Commission on Correctional Health Care recommends that should jails go the route of private provision of services, they make sure that such programs are properly accredited so that the services provided meet national standards (Kerle, 2011). When such matters as obtaining and maintaining quality care are not attended to, as is sometimes the case in jails and prisons (Vaughn & Carroll, 1998; Vaughn & Smith, 1999), jail inmates are likely to suffer the consequences in terms of continued poor health (Sturgess & Macher, 2005). In addition, jails may be sued for failure to provide care, and communities might be exposed to contagious diseases, along with liability for legal bills (J. Clark, 1991; Macher, 2007; Rigby, 2007). Clearly, the provision of decent health care to incarcerated persons is important not just because the Supreme Court mandates it or because it is the moral thing to do for people who are not free to access health care on their own but because the vast majority of jail inmates return to the community, most within a week or two (Kerle, 2011). Therefore, to prevent the spread of diseases and to save lives both inside and outside of jails, basic medical care would appear to be called for. Some jails are evidently expending energy to address this area of incarceration, as 4 in 10 of the inmates in the 2002 BJS study reported that they had had a medical exam since their admission (Maruschak, 2006, p. 1).

SUBSTANCE ABUSE AND JAILS

It is one of those oft-cited assumptions that people in prisons and jails have substance abuse problems, but this is one area of social commentary that actually fits social reality. According to a 2002 BJS study of jail inmates (the latest available data at the time of writing), fully 68% of jail inmates reported substance abuse or dependence problems (Karberg & James. 2005, p. 1). In fact, half of convicted inmates reported being under the influence at the time they committed their offense, and 16% said they committed the crime to get money for drugs. Female and white inmates were both more likely to report usage at the time of the offense (Karberg & James, 2005, p. 5). For convicted offenders who used at the time of offense, alcohol was more likely to be in their system than drugs (33.3% for alcohol, as opposed to 28.8% for drugs). The drugs of choice for abusers and users varied and included, by prevalence of use, marijuana, cocaine or crack, hallucinogens, stimulants (including methamphetamines), and inhalants (Karberg & James, 2005, p. 6). Not surprisingly, those who reported a substance abuse problem were also more likely to have a criminal record and to have been homeless before incarceration. M. D. White, Goldkamp, and Campbell (2006) found in their study conducted in New Mexico that many people who are arrested and subsequently come into contact with the local jail have "co-occurring disorders," such as mental illness and substance abuse problems (p. 303).

Violent offenders were more likely to use alcohol than other substances at the time of the offense. But violent offenders were also least likely, with the exception of public-order offenders, to report being on drugs or alcohol at the time of the offense (Karberg & James, 2005, p. 6).

Fully 63% of those with a substance abuse problem had been in a treatment program before (Karberg & James, 2005, p. 1). Most such programs were of the self-help variety, such as Alcoholics Anonymous or Narcotics Anonymous. However, 44% of these people had actually been in a residential treatment program or a detoxification program, had received professional counseling, or had been put on a maintenance drug (Karberg & James, 2005, p. 8). Treatment for convicted offenders in jails, as of 2002, was at 6%. Notably, provision of treatment in jails is difficult because most inmates are out of the facility within a week, and about 60% are unconvicted, so as people who are presumed innocent, they cannot be coerced into getting treatment. Therefore, treatment programs are usually focused on those who meet all of the following criteria: They have a substance abuse problem, they are convicted, and they are longer-term inmates. Even having said this, the amount of treatment programming in jails does not fit the obvious need (Kerle, 2011).

••• SUICIDES, GANGS, AND SEXUAL VIOLENCE IN JAILS

SUICIDES

AP Video 6.1: Bland Death

As indicated from the data presented above, those incarcerated in jails often enter them at some level of intoxication. Moreover, many have a mental disability, and if this is their first experience with jail, it might be exacerbated by the shock of incarceration. Most who are booked into jails are impoverished, and some are homeless. Also, being booked itself may represent both the mental and physical low point of their lives. Such a combination of conditions may predispose some jail inmates to not just contemplate suicide but to attempt it (Winfree & Wooldredge, 1991; Winter, 2003).

Audio 6.1: The "Shock of Confinement": The Grim Reality of Suicide in Jail

In 1986, the National Center on Institutions and Alternatives (NCIA) did a study of suicides in jails. Twenty years later, in 2006, the National Institute of Corrections funded another NCIA study of the status of jail suicides. Based on 464 suicides that occurred in 2005 and 2006, the NCIA published the following findings regarding suicide victims in jails and characteristics of the suicides:

- Sixty-seven percent were white.

- Ninety-three percent were male.

- The average age was 35.

- Forty-two percent were single.

- Forty-three percent were held on a personal and/or violent charge.

- Forty-seven percent had a history of substance abuse.

- Twenty-eight percent had a history of medical problems.

- Thirty-eight percent had a history of mental illness.

- Twenty percent had a history of taking psychotropic medication.

- Thirty-four percent had a history of suicidal behavior.

- Deaths were evenly distributed throughout the year; certain seasons and/or holidays did not account for more suicides.

- Thirty-two percent occurred between 3:01 p.m. and 9 p.m.

- Twenty-three percent occurred within the first 24 hours, 27% between 2 and 14 days, and 20% between 1 and 4 months after incarceration. (Hayes, 2010, p. xi)

These data indicate that the profile of the suicide-prone inmate in jail is that of someone who is male, white, somewhat young (though the BJS data indicate both younger and older inmates are prone to committing suicide), and in jail on a violent-offense charge, with a history of substance abuse and at the beginning of his jail incarceration. Other data, from the BJS and other sources, flesh out and contextualize these findings (see Figure 6.4).

Data obtained by BJS in a 2-year study (2000–2002) of deaths while in custody also suggest that age, gender, and race are important variables in predicting suicide, along with jail size (Mumola, 2005). White males under 18 and over 35 and those inmates with a more violent commitment history were more likely to commit suicide than African American males or those in other age groups and who were not incarcerated for a violent offense (Mumola, 2005; Winter, 2003). Winter (2003) found in her study of 10 years of suicide data from jails in one midwestern state that those who committed suicide tended to be younger, were arrested for a violent offense, had no history of mental or physical illness, did not necessarily "exhibit suicidal tendencies," and were more likely to be intoxicated with alcohol when admitted (p. 138).

Moreover, according to the authors of the BJS study, the suicide rate for large, primarily urban jails, which tend to hold fewer whites, was about half that of the smaller jails (as cited in Mumola, 2005). Similarly, in a study by Tartaro and Ruddell (2006), the researchers also found that smaller jails (with less than a 100-bed capacity) had a 2 to 5 times greater prevalence of attempted and completed suicides than larger jails did (p. 81). In this study, crowded jails and those with "special-needs and long-term inmates" were also more likely to have a higher suicide completion (Tartaro & Ruddell, 2006, p. 81). The shock of incarceration may be one explanation for jail suicide rates, although why this shock might be greater for those in smaller jails is not entirely clear. The BJS and NCIA data do indicate that about half of the suicides occur within the first 9 days—for women, it was 4 days—and in the cell of the person committing the suicide (Mumola, 2005).

Larger jails, with their greater resources and higher level of training for staff, may be better equipped than their smaller counterparts to monitor and prevent suicides in their facilities. For instance, if the younger inmates are fearful of being housed with and possibly abused by adults, some less crowded and perhaps larger jails may have the luxury of segregating young men from older men and thereby lessening the fear that might precipitate some suicides. Winter's (2003) conclusion, after studying 18 years worth of administrative data on suicides in a midwestern jail, is that keeping and accessing more complete records regarding suicides is critical to preventing them. It is possible that larger, more urban jails are better able to handle this responsibility. In their comparison study of rural and urban jails, Applegate and Sitren (2008) remarked on the greater capacity of urban jails, relative to rural jails, to provide services to inmates, which one assumes would directly and indirectly affect the rate of suicides in these jails.

However, large jails still have their share of problems with suicides. In a study by Selling et al. (2014, p. 163) of suicides in the New York City jail system, the researchers

FIGURE *6.4*   Predictors of Jail Suicide

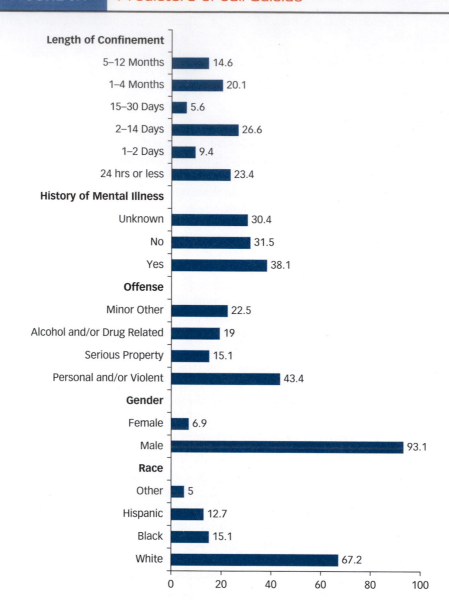

Source: Based on data from Hayes (2010, p. xi).

found that between 2007 and 2011, there were eight deaths resulting from suicide and 2,514 cases of self-injury (out of yearly admissions of 80,000 and an average daily population of about 12,500). The self-injuries had increased in number during this time period. The methods of self-injury included, among others, "lacerations, ligatures tied around the neck, attempted overdose, and swallowed foreign objects" (Selling et al., 2014, p. 163). In response to this research, the jail managers (there are several New York City jails) improved the surveillance system and the electronic health records so they could better watch and document those who would be most likely to need help.

We do know that the rate of suicide among inmates in jails, despite its marked decrease over the last 9 years, is still twice as high as would be true for a comparable group of free citizens (Mumola, 2005). Jails have 3 times the rate of suicides that prisons do, though their homicide rates are comparable (Mumola, 2005). The good news, however, is that jail and prison deaths due to suicide (and homicide) have declined precipitously from 1983 to 2002, with the rate of prison suicides declining by half during this time period and jail suicides by almost two thirds (Mumola, 2005, p. 2). In 1983, jail suicides were the major cause of death for inmates, but by 2002, illness had replaced suicide as the primary reason for death.

GANGS

Gangs present myriad management problems for jail and prison managers. Violence, including robberies, assaults, drug smuggling, and even murders, tends to naturally follow in their wake and prevents the orderly and safe operation of the facility for staff and inmates. Because gangs are more prevalent in large urban areas, they are more of a problem in large urban jails. Yet the estimates of their prevalence in large jail systems ranges from 16% to 25%, depending on the location of the jail (Tapia, 2014, p. 258). However, these estimates are likely to be low, as gang members are usually not forthcoming about their membership in a correctional environment (Ruddell, Decker, & Egley, 2006). It is generally true that larger urban jails have more problems with gangs. As jails are more likely to involve a short-term period of incarceration, however, they may be less likely to hold as many gang members as prisons (Alarid, 2000).

In order to counter the collective influence of gangs, jails will try to separate members in housing units, placing the most disruptive members in segregation (Tapia, 2014). Another tactic is to document those involved in gangs and to track them and their activities throughout the jail system. However, though gang members, by their definition, might appear to present a monolithic adherence to gang orthodoxy, there is some indication that not all gang members agree about how the gang should be operated and the tactics they should employ. For instance, in a study by Tapia (2014) of Latino gangs in Texas, it was found that there were intergenerational disputes on these matters, with younger inmates tending to organize themselves in more autonomous groups, which are as much support groups as criminal enterprises in jails. In that same research, though, the gangs identified by correctional-officer respondents as most prevalent in Texas jails were the Texas Mexican Mafia, the Aryan Brotherhood, Bloods, the Texas Syndicate, Crips, Tango Blast, Tango Orejon, Aryan Circle, and Hermandad de Pistoleros Lainos (Tapia, 2014, p. 262).

SEXUAL VIOLENCE

The **Prison Rape Elimination Act of 2003** mandated that the BJS collect data on sexual assaults in adult and juvenile jails and prisons and that it identify facilities with high levels of victimization. According to the National Inmate Survey for 2011 and 2012 (which included 358 local jails and was conducted by BJS researchers), 3.2% of jail inmates (as opposed to 4.0% of prison inmates) reported experiencing sexual victimization perpetrated by other jail inmates or staff in the previous 12 months (Beck et al., 2013, p. 1). Extrapolating these sample findings to the national population of jail and prison inmates, the BJS researchers estimate that fully 80,600 inmates in prisons and jails experienced sexual victimization during this time period (Beck et al., 2013, p. 8). For jails, it was estimated that there were 25,100 victims: 11,900 were inmate on inmate, and 13,200 were staff on inmate, and of these, 2,400 reported being victimized by both staff and inmates (Beck et al, 2013, p. 8). Notably, some of these victimizations were likely "consensual," though it is legally impossible for inmates, who occupy a powerless positions vis-à-vis staff, to give consent to them.

Female inmates in jails (as well as in prisons) were more than twice as likely as male inmates to experience sexual victimization perpetrated by another inmate (3.6% for females versus 1.4% for males) (Beck et al., 2013, p. 17). Male inmates in jails and

AP Video 6.2:
Prison Abuse

Audio 6.2:
Enforcing Prison
Rape Elimination
Standards
Proves Tricky

....

**Prison Rape
Elimination Act of
2003:** Act that
mandated that the
Bureau of Justice
Statistics collect data
on sexual assaults in
adult and juvenile jails
and prisons and that it
identify facilities with
high levels of
victimization.

ETHICAL ISSUE 6.1 ?

What Would You Do?

You are a correctional officer who works in the booking area of a large urban jail. About once per month, the jail admits one or two transgender inmates. You notice that there is one male colleague named Joe who is particularly abusive of the transgender female inmates (calling them names, strip searching them, making them stand around naked in front of other staff and inmates while making derogatory comments about their body parts, doing unnecessary pat downs that focus inordinately on their breasts and genitals, referring to them by male pronouns, etc.). Though Joe is the primary instigator of this abuse, there are a few others, male and female, who play along and others who try to ignore it (including you). You know your sergeant also has witnessed the abuse and has done nothing to stop it. You are unaware of any complaints being lodged by staff regarding Joe's or the others' behavior, though it is openly practiced in the booking area at least once or twice a month. You have heard that a lawsuit has been filed by a former inmate about Joe's and the other officers' treatment of her. As a booking officer, you are likely to be called to testify about what happened in her case (all of the abuse mentioned above). What will you do if called to testify? How will you explain your failure to report this abuse beforehand? What do you think will be the likely outcomes of the choices you made and make?

prisons were slightly more likely to be victims of staff perpetrators. There was higher victimization among inmates who were two or more races or who were white by other inmates and staff. Generally younger inmates (under age 34) and those with a college degree were targeted more by both inmates and staff for sexual victimization.

As mentioned previously in this chapter, LGBTI inmates were much more likely to be victimized by both staff and inmates in both prisons and jails. In prisons, 1.2% and 2.1% of heterosexual inmates experienced either inmate-on-inmate or staff-on-inmate sexual victimization, as compared with 12.2% and 5.4% of LGBTI inmates. In jails, the figures were similarly startling, with 1.2% and 1.7% of heterosexual inmates who experienced either inmate-on-inmate or staff-on-inmate sexual victimization, as compared with 8.5% and 4.3% of LGBTI inmates (Beck et al., 2013, p. 18). In essence, in jails, the LGBTI inmates were 7 times more likely to experience sexual victimization by other inmates and 2.5 times more likely to experience sexual victimization by staff than were heterosexuals.

Also, as mentioned previously in this chapter, those with a mental illness were much more likely to experience sexual victimization than were inmates without such a malady (Beck et al., 2013). Mentally ill jail inmates experienced more inmate-on-inmate and staff-on-inmate sexual victimization than inmates without mental-health problems.

In the Prison Rape Elimination Act–prescribed surveys of adult correctional authorities in prisons, jails, and other adult correctional facilities, it has been found that the allegations of sexual victimization increased from 2009 to 2011, though the number of substantiated cases (those where an investigation found that the allegation was true) has remained about the same since 2005 (Beck, Rantala, & Rexroat, 2014, p. 1). Notably, in an earlier version of this research, it was explained that most of these allegations were not substantiated, nor were they investigated or found to be supported by evidence, by prison or jail officials (Beck, Harrison, & Adams, 2007). Having said this, however, we should recognize that in most such instances of sexual violence, it would be very difficult to find evidence, as it is in the free world, particularly if the one perpetrating the victimization was a staff member, which, of course, is why the inmate survey data presented first in this section become so important.

More than half of the substantiated staff-on-inmate sexual-misconduct victimization was committed by female staff on male inmates:

> Among all substantiated incidents between 2009 and 2011, the majority (84 percent) of those perpetrated by female staff involved a sexual relationship that "appeared to be willing," compared to 37 percent of those perpetrated by male staff. Any sexual contact between inmates and staff is illegal, regardless of whether it "appeared to be willing." (Beck et al., 2014, p. 1)

Other research has found that female staff were more likely perpetrators in prisons, though we know from research on Texas prisons that when the offense was actual sexual battery, the staff offender was more likely to be male (Marquart, Barnhill, & Balshaw-Biddle, 2001). Male staff were more likely the perpetrators of sexual violence in jails. For instance, in a 2007 case involving the Yuma County, Arizona, jail, three male officers were charged with unlawful sexual conduct with three female inmates (Reutter, 2007).

When the allegation was substantiated, most of the staff were fired (78%), and almost half (45%) were arrested, prosecuted, or convicted (Beck et al., 2014, p. 1). Inmate perpetrators in substantiated cases were more likely to be placed in solitary confinement (73%), and about half (48%) were prosecuted if the act was a nonconsensual sex act (Beck et al., 2014, p. 1).

Researchers at the Urban Institute (e.g., see La Vigne, Debus-Sherrill, Brazzell, & Downey, 2011, p. 3) used a situational crime prevention approach with the hoped for result of reducing violence and sexual assault after studying three jails. Their recommendations were multifaceted and included studying past incidents of violence to determine what characteristics of the situation might be changed to reduce future violence; increasing surveillance cameras outside of cells (having a record of who goes in and out, as cells are a typical locus for violence); ensuring that staff are around consistently; hiring better quality staff; training staff in crisis intervention and about violence, mental illness, suicide, and sexual assault; having an enforceable no-tolerance policy for staff sexual misconduct; developing strategies to reduce violence and sexual assault; reducing the contraband coming into the jail, as this is often linked with violence; and making sure that inmates who need it get their medications and mental-health care, as not getting it on time may precipitate violence.

••• INNOVATIONS IN JAILS

NEW-GENERATION OR PODULAR DIRECT-SUPERVISION JAILS

In the 1980s, a new kind of jail was under construction in the United States, then called a **new-generation** jail and now known as a **podular direct-supervision** jail. Its two key components are a rounded, or *podular*, architecture for living units and the *direct*, as opposed to indirect or intermittent, supervision of inmates by staff; in other words, staff were to be in the living units full time (Applegate & Paoline, 2007; Jay Farbstein & Associates, 1989; Gettinger, 1984; Zupan, 1991). It was believed that the architecture would complement the ability to supervise, and the presence of staff in the living unit would negate the ability of inmates to control those units. Other important facets of these jails are the provision of more goods and services in the living unit (e.g., access to telephones, visiting booths, recreation, and library books) and the more enriched leadership and communication roles for staff.

Not surprisingly, several scholars recognized that the role for the correctional officer in a podular direct-supervision jail would have to change. Zupan (1991), building on the work of Gettinger (1984), identified seven critical dimensions of new-generation jail officer behavior: (1) proactive leadership and conflict resolution skills; (2) building a respectful relationship with inmates; (3) uniform and predictable enforcement of all rules; (4) active observation of all inmate doings

New-generation or podular direct-supervision jails: Jails that have two key components: a rounded, or *podular*, architecture for living units and the direct supervision of inmates by staff.

Courtesy of Bergen County Sheriff's Office/Bergen County Jail

PHOTO 6.6: A female correctional officer operates a new generation jail control pod.

IN FOCUS 6.1

Prison Rape Elimination Act Controversy

As mentioned in the text of this chapter, the Prison Rape Elimination Act (PREA) of 2003 required that the Department of Justice and its subdivisions—the National Institute of Justice and the Bureau of Justice Statistics—study and report on the amount of sexual violence in adult and juvenile prisons and jails. In reaction to this reporting and court cases that indicated that LGBTI inmates were particularly vulnerable to sexual abuse by inmates and staff and after studying the matter, the National Prison Rape Elimination Commission, which was created by the PREA legislation, released its national standards in June 2009. These standards are extensive and require that states train staff differently, monitor inmates differently, report offenses, treat victims and offenders, audit themselves, and collect and keep relevant data related to sexual violence. The U.S. Attorney General was asked to release these standards and require that the Bureau of Prisons and each governor certify compliance with these standards or certify that they were working toward compliance. If governors did not do this, they risked losing 5% of any future DOJ grants (U.S. Department of Justice, 2015). As the date for certification of compliance neared in spring 2014, at least seven states' governors (Arizona, Florida, Idaho, Indiana, Nebraska, Texas, Utah, and the Northern Marianas Islands territory) ignored the certification deadline of May 15 or indicated that they would not certify compliance with these standards, some claiming that they were too cumbersome and expensive to comply with (Reilly, 2014, p. 1). On the other hand, a few states, including New Hampshire and New Jersey, certified compliance, while 46 states or territories promised to use their grant monies from the DOJ to work toward compliance with the federal standards (Reilly, 2014, p. 1). By spring 2016, most states had certified or had promised to move toward compliance.

DISCUSSION QUESTIONS

1. What benefits would flow from certification by states for jail inmates?

2. How might non-LBTQI inmates benefit from certification?

3. Why would states be reluctant to promise certification, and how might that reluctance be overcome?

and occurrences in the living unit; (5) attending to inmate requests with respect and dignity; (6) disciplining inmates in a fair and consistent manner; and (7) being organized and in the open with the supervisory style. Whether officers in podular direct-supervision jails are always adequately selected and trained to fit these dimensions of their role is, as yet, an open research question (Applegate & Paoline, 2007; Nelson & Davis, 1995; Wener, 2006).

New-generation jails, though hardly "new" anymore, became popular in the United States by the late 1980s and through the 1990s (Kerle, 2011; Wener, 2005). Reportedly, in the 21st century, about one fifth of medium and larger jails are said to be new-generation facilities (Tartaro, 2002). Their architecture, though not all features of such jails, can be seen in most new jails and prisons built these days, whether or not they include direct supervision.

It is widely acknowledged by correctional scholars and practitioners that though podular direct-supervision jails or prisons are not necessarily a panacea for all that ails corrections today (e.g., crowding and few resources), they often do represent a significant improvement over more traditional jails (Kerle, 2003; Perroncello, 2002; Zupan, 1991). If operated correctly and including all of the most important elements, they are believed to be less costly in the long run (due to fewer lawsuits), be safer for both staff and inmates, provide a more developed and enriched role for staff, and include more amenities for inmates. This is a big *if*, however, and some research has called these claims of a better environment for inmates and staff and a more enriched role for staff into question, as the implementation of the new-generation model has sometimes faltered or been incomplete in many facilities (Applegate & Paoline, 2007; Stohr, Lovrich, & Wilson, 1994; Tartaro, 2002, 2006). Clearly, more research on new-generation jails is called for to determine their success (or failure) in revolutionizing the jail environment for staff and inmates.

COMMUNITY JAILS

Another promising innovation in jails has been the development of **community jails** (Barlow, Hight, & Hight, 2006; Kerle, 2003, 2011; Lightfoot, Zupan, & Stohr, 1991). Community jails are devised so that programming provided on the outside does not end at the jailhouse door, as the needs such programming was addressing have not gone away and will still be there when the inmate transitions back into the community. Therefore, in a community jail, those engaged in education, drug or alcohol counseling, or mental-health programming will seamlessly receive such services while incarcerated and again as they transition out of the facility (Barlow et al., 2006; Bookman, Lightfoot, & Scott, 2005; National Institute of Corrections, 2008). Whether one is in and out of the facility within a few days or a few months, needs are met and services provided so that the reintegration into the community is smoother for the inmate and the community in question.

Managers of community jails also recognize that they cannot staff or resource the jail sufficiently to address every need of their inmates. Rather, community experts who are regularly engaged in the provision of such services are the appropriate persons to provide them, whether the inmate is in a jail or free in the community; in both instances, it is argued, he or she is a community member and entitled to such services (Barlow et al., 2006; Lightfoot et al., 1991).

Obviously, the development of community jails requires that some resources (particularly space) be devoted to the accommodation of community experts who provide for inmates' needs. Unfortunately, it is the rare jail that has the luxury of excess space for allocation to such programming. Therefore, the solution may lie in inclusion of such space in jail architectural plans, though this certainly is not optimal given the immediacy of inmate needs discussed in the foregoing section.

The second problem that faces jail managers interested in creating community jails is convincing local service providers—and lawmakers, if need be—that people in jails have a right to and a continued need for services and that the continued provision of such services by community experts benefits both those inmates and the larger community. Needless to say, making this case, as reasonable as it might sound, can be a "hard sell" to those social-service agencies that already have scarce resources and to policy makers concerned that more tax dollars might be required to fund such resource provision in jails. For these reasons, larger jails and communities, with their economies of scale and a greater proportion of their populations in need of social services, might be better situated to operate community jails and thus achieve their purported benefits of less crime from the continuous provision of services in jails (Kerle, 2011; Lightfoot et al., 1991).

One interesting development on this front will be how the Affordable Care Act will be implemented in jails. The ACA does not expressly prohibit jail inmates, as long as they

? ETHICAL ISSUE 6.2

What Would You Do?

You are a professor at a university, and you do research on jails. Some of your early research was on new-generation or podular direct-supervision (PDS) jails. One of the jails you profiled in that early research was a model PDS jail, in that it practiced all of the principles of the best of such jails. You happen to visit that jail more than 20 years later, and other than the physical podular architecture, there is no longer anything new or progressive about the jail; there is no evidence that it is a PDS jail anymore. In fact, the supervision practices now seem to you to be abusive. Staff are no longer in the living units 24/7, and inmates are locked up in their double- and sometimes triple-celled small cells (made for one) for up to 23 hours a day. Staff are not trained in how to be leaders in their living units, as they are rarely in them, and inmates are not out of their cells to be led; instead, staff contact with inmates often includes yelling through the steel cell doors or the slight contact staff have with inmates when let out for their 1 hour of exercise. Inmates no longer have the support or services that typified PDS jails—and this jail—in the past. You are aware that fully 50% to 60% of the inmates in this jail have not been convicted of a crime, yet they are treated like they are serious offenders with behavior problems in a supermaximum-security prison. You know how this jail used to be operated, you know how it should be operated, and you know it is not being operated in this way. What would you do, and why? Whom might you talk to? What do you think would be the likely consequences of the action(s) you choose?

Community jails: Jails organized so those inmates engaged in education, drug or alcohol counseling, or mental-health programming in the community will seamlessly receive such services while incarcerated and again as they transition out of the facility.

are not convicted, from being able to sign up for Medicaid or qualified health plans while they are in jail. What this will mean is that a jail can embrace this community function by ensuring that its inmates are signed up. Evidence indicates that mentally impaired inmates with Medicaid coverage who reentered communities from jails were more likely to have a smooth transition to needed care than those who were not so covered (Robertson, 2014).

COEQUAL STAFFING

Another promising innovation in jails that has occurred in the last couple of decades in some sheriffs' departments has been the development of **coequal staffing**, which provides comparable pay and benefits to those who work in the jail with those who work on the streets as law enforcement (Kerle, 2003, 2011). Historically, jails have not been a dumping ground (to use Irwin's [1985] terminology) just for inmates but for staff as well. If a sheriff deemed that a staff person could not "make it" on the streets as law enforcement, he or she was given a job in the jail, where apparently, the individual's lack of skills and ability was not seen as a problem. Moreover, jail staff were (and often still are) paid less and received less training than their counterparts working on the streets (Stohr & Collins, 2009). As a result, jails do find it difficult to attract and keep the best personnel, or even if they can attract the more talented applicants, jail jobs were and are used as "stepping stones" to better-paying and higher-status jobs on the law enforcement side of sheriffs' agencies (Kerle, 2011).

Since the 1980s, however, many sheriffs' departments, though far from a majority, have recognized the problems created by according this second-tier status to those who work in jails (Kerle, 2011). Consequently, they have instituted programs whereby staff who work in the jails, who often are given deputy status, are trained and paid similarly to those who work in the free communities. Some anecdotal evidence from sheriffs' departments indicates that this change has had a phenomenal effect on the professional operation of jails (as they are better staffed) and on the morale of those who labor in them (Kerle, 2011).

REENTRY PROGRAMS FOR JAILS

Journal Article 6.1: Integrated Primary and Behavioral Health Care in Patient-Centered Medical Homes for Jail Releases With Mental Illness

Perhaps the newest "thing" in jails these days (and in prisons, too) is a rethinking about how to keep people out of them. (Reentry will be discussed in greater detail in Chapter 12.) Rather than focusing on deterrence or incapacitation so much (as in the 1980s and 1990s), jail practitioners are studying how to make the transition from jails to the community smoother and more successful so that people do not commit more crime and return (Bookman et al., 2005; Freudenberg, 2006; McLean, Robarge, & Sherman, 2006; Osher, 2007). Research by Wodahl, Boman, and Garland (2015) would indicate that community sanctions for probation and parole violations can be as effective as the use of jail and, at the same time, cost much less, so there is additional impetus for communities to try to move their jail inmates back into the community or to restrict their placement in the jail in the first place.

Coequal staffing: Programs that provide comparable pay and benefits for those who work in the jail to that for people who work on the streets as law enforcement in sheriffs' departments.

Reentry: The process of integrating offenders back into the community after release from jail or prison.

As is indicated by the discussion in the foregoing material of all of the medical, psychological, and social—not to mention educational—deficits that many inmates of jails have, this transition back into the community is likely to be fraught with difficulties. That is why any successful **reentry** program must include a recognition of the problems individual inmates may have (e.g., mental illness, physical illness, joblessness, and homelessness) and address them systematically, in collaboration with the client and the community (Freudenberg, 2006; McLean et al., 2006). In a study by Freudenberg, Mosely, Labriola, and Murrill (as cited in Freudenberg, 2006) conducted in New York City jails, the researchers asked hundreds of inmates what their top-three priority reentry needs were. For adult women, they were housing, substance abuse treatment, and financial support; for adult men, they were employment, education, and housing; for adolescent males, they were employment, education, and financial support (Freudenberg, 2006, p. 15). Spjeldnes, Jung, and Yamatani (2014) also argue that women's and men's reentry needs may differ; these researchers found, in their study of a large urban jail, that more women than men reported chemical dependency and mental-health needs and that the women were more likely to value treatment programming.

Web 6.2: Reentry Programs

Effective interventions to improve reentry, in the New York study, included everything from referral to counseling to drug treatment to postrelease supervision, depending on the needs of the inmate, his or her unique reentry situation, and the services available in the community. Clearly, reentry is a complex process for people with multiple problems, and it requires that jail personnel prioritize the needs they will target and the interventions they will apply and then network with community agencies to provide the package of services most likely to further the goal of successful reentry (Freudenberg, 2006; McLean et al., 2006). In fact, Bookman and her colleagues (2005) would argue that jail personnel should expect to engage in collaborative arrangements with community agencies (sounds a bit like community jails, doesn't it?) if they hope to succeed in the reentry process.

SUMMARY

- Jails in the United States are faced with any number of seemingly intractable problems. They are often overcrowded—or close to it—and house some of the most debilitated and vulnerable persons in our communities. They house the accused, the guilty, and the sentenced, as well as low-level offenders and the serious and violent ones. As with prisons, their mission is to incapacitate (even the untried), to deter, to punish, and even to rehabilitate. The degree to which they accomplish any of these goals is, in large part, determined by the political and social climate that the jail is nested in. Since the 1980s, the political climate has favored "harsh justice" meted out by policy makers and the actors in the criminal justice system and has led to the unrelenting business of filling and building prisons and jails across the country (Cullen, 2006; Irwin, 1985, 2005; Whitman, 2003).

- Jails have also served as a dumping ground for those who are marginally criminal and are unable or unwilling to access social services. Too often, the needs of such persons go unaddressed in communities, and as a result, these unresolved needs either contribute to their incarceration (in the case of substance abuse and mental illness) or make

it likely (such as in the case of homelessness) that they will enter and reenter the revolving jailhouse door.

- Sexual violence in jails remains problematic. It is likely true that the rate of violence between inmates and inmates or between staff and inmates has gone down in recent years. However, increased monitoring of this phenomenon is certainly called for and may serve to further reduce violence through the implementation of violence reduction techniques and training for staff. To that end, the implementation of the Prison Rape Elimination Act of 2003, with its reporting requirement for correctional institutions, represents a positive move.

- Thankfully, there have been some other hopeful developments on the correctional horizon. Jails in a position to do so have expanded their medical and treatment options to address the needs of inmates. Architectural and managerial solutions have been applied to jails in the form of new-generation jails and coequal pay for staff in sheriffs' departments, and some jails have even experimented with community engagement to ensure that the needs of people in communities are not neglected when such folks enter jails or reenter communities.

KEY TERMS

Coequal staffing 142

Community jails 141

Jails 120

New-generation or podular
direct-supervision jails 139

Overcrowding 122

Prison Rape Elimination Act of
2003 137

Reentry 142

DISCUSSION QUESTIONS

1. Why are jails the "dumping ground" for so many people in our communities? What are the consequences of this social policy?

2. What is the best use for a jail? What factors might make it difficult to operate jails so that they are able to focus on this best use?

3. What do you think are the best practices (most effective) in managing medically challenged or potentially suicidal inmates?

4. How can jail managers best reduce or eliminate sexual violence against inmates in jails? What do you think keeps managers from being successful at eliminating such violence?

5. What factors are likely to compromise the ability of podular direct-supervision jails to achieve their promise?

6. Why are jail staff in most facilities and sheriffs' departments still paid less than those on patrol? What argument can be made for the same or even higher pay for jail staff?

7. What are the relative advantages and disadvantages of community jails?

8. How might reentry programs prevent recidivism?

USEFUL INTERNET SITES

Please note that the sites listed can be accessed at edge.sagepub.com/stohrcorrections.

American Jail Association: www.corrections.com/aja

The AJA is an organization that focuses on professionalization in corrections but as it involves jails. Their website provides information about the latest training, trends, and research in jails.

Bureau of Justice Statistics: www.bjs.gov

The BJS provides an incredible wealth of information about all manner of criminal justice topics, including corrections. It is one of our go-to websites when we are investigating a correctional topic (or police or courts, etc.).

National Institute of Corrections: nicic.gov

The National Institute of Corrections provides correctional agencies and managers with directed

research and counsel about how best to operate their facilities. They offer small grants to agencies and researchers to study improved practices with the goal of determining what works in corrections.

Urban Institute Justice Policy Center: www.urban.org/center/jpc

The Urban Institute conducts research on correctional—and other criminal justice—topics that are of interest to policy makers and criminal justice managers and researchers.

Vera Institute: www.vera.org

The Vera Institute has been behind some of the biggest criminal justice reforms of the last 40 years. Check out their website to learn what important reforms and issues are on the correctional horizon.

SAGE edge™

Sharpen your skills with SAGE edge at **edge.sagepub.com/stohrcorrections**. SAGE edge for Students provides a personalized approach to help you accomplish your coursework goals in an easy-to-use learning environment. You'll find action plans, mobile-friendly eFlashcards, and quizzes as well as video, web, and resources and links to SAGE journal articles to support and expand on the concepts presented in this chapter.

7

Special Problem-Solving Courts in Corrections

TEST YOUR KNOWLEDGE

Test your present knowledge of problem-solving courts by answering the following true-or-false questions. Check your answers on page 535 after reading the chapter.

1. Problem-solving courts are designed to take as many people who commit crimes off the streets for as long as possible.

2. Problem-solving courts are treatment oriented.

3. Despite the best intentions, problem-solving courts only reduce recidivism by about 5%.

4. Most people diverted to a problem-solving court do not like it since they are supervised more closely than other probationers.

5. Problem-solving courts abandon, to a great degree, the adversarial system of common law.

6. Most people arrested in major cities have one or more of the problems that are addressed in problem-solving courts.

7. Problem-solving courts include courts for the homeless.

8. Although problem-solving courts do a better job of rehabilitating than traditional methods, they do so at a much higher net cost to the community.

9. Because juveniles require gentler and less punitive handling, there are no problem-solving courts for juveniles.

LEARNING OBJECTIVES

- Identify some of the correctional issues that led to the implementation of problem-solving courts

- Explain how drug courts differ from traditional criminal courts

- Articulate the major difficulties encountered by participants in mental health courts in successfully completing treatment

- Describe key issues veterans courts help address

- Evaluate the success of domestic violence courts

- Identify key influences on the development of the community court model

VETERAN COURTS **IN ACTION**

Around 11:00 p.m. on July 28, 2009, a woman in Boise, Idaho, frantically dialed 911 and told the operator that someone with a gun was pounding on her door. The man fired one round at a lock of an apartment door, trying to kick his way in. When the police arrived, they were confronted with a man holding a gun with a flashlight attached in a stairwell, and they fired 12 rounds without hitting him. The man then surrendered without firing a shot and was charged with six felony counts. The man was 38-year-old sergeant George Nickel, a decorated (Bronze Star and Purple Heart) Iraq War hero who, in 2007, suffered severe wounds in a bomb blast that killed three of his fellow soldiers. He told police that he hadn't slept for three days and had drunk close to a full case of beer that day. He also told them that he was out looking for his dog, which he believed had been stolen and was angrily trying to get it back.

Like many war veterans, Nickel suffered from posttraumatic stress disorder (PTSD) and survival guilt, *and having survived both a horrific a blast in Iraq and gunfire from police, he must have thought, while in his jail cell, that for all intents and purposes, his life was over. However, under a plea agreement, he was allowed to admit to one count of firing a weapon into an occupied residence, and the judgment was withheld. A withheld judgment means that the charge would be purged from his record if he received mental health treatment and cooperated with law enforcement, which he did. Cooperation with law enforcement included sharing his harrowing experiences on videotape, which has been distributed to law enforcement agencies across the United States for training purposes.*

Nickel's case was instrumental in the idea of establishing a veterans court for Idaho, which began in 2009, when judges, law enforcement officials, and veterans' advocates met to discuss hopes of dealing with special cases, such as Nickel's. Nickel subsequently earned a degree in social work from Boise State University and now works with other veterans to try to resolve their problems. Had it not been for the humane intervention of people like former Boise police chief Mike Masterson (who now considers

Nickel his friend) and Judge Deborah Bail, Nickel might have received up to 15 years in prison and still be left with his problems, instead of becoming the upstanding citizen he now is. This is the kind of success story (although few are quite as dramatic) that all special problem-solving courts can claim: lives saved and turned around by considering the problem behind the act(s) that brings unfortunate souls before them. Such problem-solving courts have been one of the very few success stories in American corrections.

••• INTRODUCTION: WHAT ARE PROBLEM-SOLVING COURTS?

AP Video 7.1:
Autism Ruling

Problem-solving courts (sometimes called *specialty courts*) are courts of limited jurisdiction that are designed to help mostly nonviolent offenders with specific problems and needs that have not been adequately addressed in traditional criminal courts. The basic idea behind the problem-solving court model is the notion that instead of merely processing criminals through the legal system and punishing their behavior after the fact, problem-solving courts should seek to prevent crime from happening again by addressing any underlying causes that may have been identified. These courts originated in the late 1980s and early 1990s in response to burgeoning rates of incarceration, the financial costs of incarceration, the realization that many offenders needed treatment rather than jail or prison, and the woeful inability of the social-service system to provide that treatment. The traditional criminal courts have long seen the same individuals with the same problems recycle through them, time after time. Problem-solving courts are designed to address the underlying causes of a person's antisocial behavior under the assumption that it will cease or diminish with the alleged cause under control. These courts largely suspend the adversarial approach to justice in the interest of achieving a therapeutic outcome (Bureau of Justice Assistance, 2008). In other words, the judge, prosecutor, *and* defense attorney are supposed to work together collegially, along with treatment specialists and supervising probation and parole officers, to achieve a common goal: the rehabilitation of the offender. As we shall see, this has been a somewhat major concern of some defense attorneys and legal purists.

Career Video 7.1:
Defense Attorney

The problems addressed in problem-solving courts include substance abuse, mental illness, homelessness, domestic abuse, and many other issues. The courts endeavor to assist offenders to successfully deal with the issues that led to their arrest in ways that will not only help them to lead productive lives but also provide benefits for victims and society at large. (Note the tremendous benefit to society, military veterans, and to Nickel himself from the therapeutic rather than punitive approach). These courts are under direct judicial supervision and combine social work with social control. They provide treatment and counseling services for troubled people lacking resources who might otherwise be incarcerated or placed on probation without their needs and problems being addressed. As John Feinblatt, New York City's criminal justice coordinator, aptly put it, "There's no doubt that, often, courts are the social service agencies of last resort" (in W. Davis, 2003, p. 34).

Problem-solving courts: These are courts of limited jurisdiction meant to address underlying causes of criminal behavior, like drug use, in order to prevent crime.

Bureau of Justice Assistance: A federal agency under the umbrella of the Department of Justice that provides guidance and grants to support state, local, and tribal criminal justice organizations.

Problem-solving courts exist under the umbrella of a branch of the U.S. Department of Justice known as the **Bureau of Justice Assistance** (BJA). The BJA provides guidelines and hands-on assistance to state court systems seeking to implement a problem-solving court. According to the BJA (2014), all problem-solving courts, regardless of the specific problems they may deal with, share these common elements:

- *Focus on Outcomes.* Problem-solving courts are designed to provide positive case outcomes for victims, society and the offender (e.g., reducing recidivism or creating safer communities).

- *System Change.* Problem-solving courts promote reform in how the government responds to problems such as drug addiction and mental illness.

- *Judicial Involvement.* Judges take a more hands-on approach to addressing problems and changing behaviors of defendants.

- *Collaboration.* Problem-solving courts work with external parties to achieve certain goals (e.g., developing partnerships with mental health providers).

- *Non-traditional Roles.* These courts and their personnel take on roles or processes not common in traditional courts. For example, problem-solving courts are less adversarial than traditional criminal justice processing.

- *Screening and Assessment.* Use of screening and assessment tools to identify appropriate individuals for the court is common.

- *Early Identification of Potential Candidates.* Use of screening and Assessment tools to determine a defendant's eligibility for the problem-solving court usually occurs early in a defendant's involvement with criminal justice processing. (n.p.)

Video 7.1: Former Heroin Addict Thanks Drug Court Program for Saving His Life

Drug court: A problem-solving court that specializes in the supervision and treatment of substance-abusing offenders.

Differences in the design and structure of problem-solving courts will, of course, exist, depending on the nature of the problem the court is designed to deal with and the social, political, and economic climate of the community in which it is located. All court programs are implemented at the local level, and thus, any program will reflect the strengths, circumstances, and capacities of each community. Some communities will have abundant resources and dedicated believers in the rehabilitative promise of problem-solving courts and will thus fund them adequate and assure they are run properly; other communities will not be so blessed. Because drug courts are, by far, the most numerous of the problem-solving courts and because other kinds of problem-solving courts are modeled on them, our emphasis is on them.

●●● DRUG COURTS

A **drug court** specializes in the supervision and treatment of substance-abusing offenders. Drug courts are typically referred to as simply drug courts, although they are also involved with offenders with alcohol problems. (Of course, alcohol is a drug, too.) Some jurisdictions have separate DUI ("driving under the influence") courts that deal with offenders whose sole drug of abuse is alcohol, however. The first drug court in the United States was implemented in Miami-Dade County, Florida, in 1989 (Steadman, Davidson & Brown, 2001), and since then, they have spread like wildfire across the American continent. The BJA (2014) graph in Figure 7.1 shows how over 2,800 drug courts dotted the U.S. landscape in 2013. The Miami-Dade County drug court was launched in response to the revolving door of drug-addicted offenders and took an approach that combined drug treatment with offender accountability.

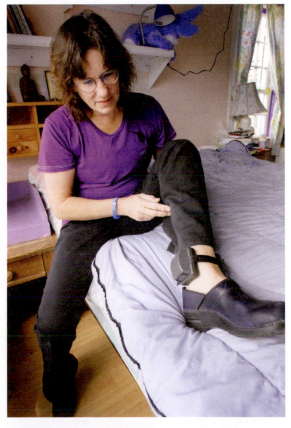

Getty Images/Portland Press Herald

PHOTO 7.1: Melinda Monks, of Cape Elizabeth, wears a SCRAM—Secure Continuous Remote Alcohol Monitor—ankle bracelet, Thursday, September 13, 2007. She was facing a year and a half in jail and is wearing the device in lieu of a jail sentence.

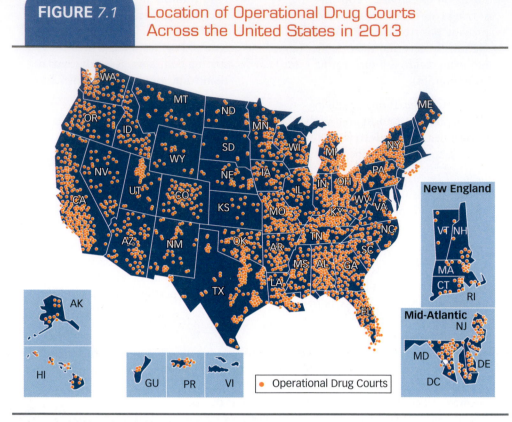

FIGURE *7.1*   Location of Operational Drug Courts Across the United States in 2013

Source: National Institute of Justice (2014).

Web 7.1:
Drug Courts

Drug offenders placed on such programs face strict levels of compliance while on their arduous road to recovery. Because many drug-addicted offenders placed in these programs turn to alcohol as a substitute, there is also strict monitoring of alcohol use. Because alcohol is legal, and testing is not done frequently enough to catch most drinking events, courts have turned to continuous alcohol-monitoring devices to enforce compliance with treatment, such as SCRAM CAM. This is a bracelet-type, tamperproof device worn around the ankle that tests for alcohol use (detected through perspiration) every 30 minutes, around the clock. The use of such devices attests to the level of commitment drug courts have to rehabilitating offenders while still holding them accountable for their behavior.

THE DRUG COURT PROCESS

Journal Article 7.1:
Juvenile Drug
Court Operations

The screening, assessment, and evaluation process for determining eligibility for a drug court treatment program varies from jurisdiction to jurisdiction; what follows is the typical process gleaned from examining the procedures of a number of different state programs. The goal of the process is to access offenders' needs and resolve to change their lifestyles. The drug court processes, from arrest to final outcome (either graduation or termination and incarceration), are graphically shown in Figure 7.2 from the Albany, New York, drug court.

The first stage of the process is a referral to the drug court, which may come from almost anyone, but it typically comes from an offender's attorney. Drug courts are usually managed by a nonadversarial and multidisciplinary team, headed by a judge. With the receipt of the referral, the drug court team (typically a judge, prosecutor, probation officer, and treatment specialist, along with defense counsel) reviews the applicant's criminal history and police reports relevant to the current offense and other pertinent information.

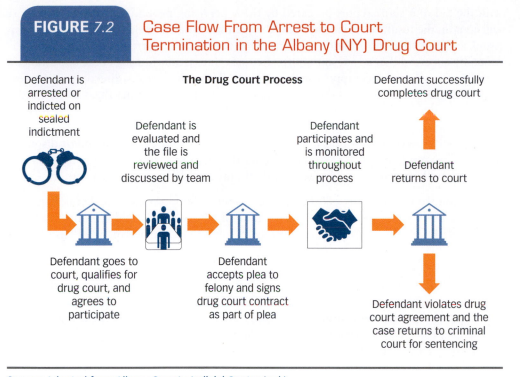

FIGURE *7.2*   Case Flow From Arrest to Court Termination in the Albany (NY) Drug Court

The Drug Court Process

Defendant is arrested or indicted on sealed indictment

Defendant is evaluated and the file is reviewed and discussed by team

Defendant participates and is monitored throughout process

Defendant successfully completes drug court

Defendant returns to court

Defendant goes to court, qualifies for drug court, and agrees to participate

Defendant accepts plea to felony and signs drug court contract as part of plea

Defendant violates drug court agreement and the case returns to criminal court for sentencing

Source: Adapted from Albany County Judicial Center (n.d.).

Violent offenders and offenders who have previously committed the same offense or who have failed other treatment programs before will not be accepted into most drug court programs. A standardized form containing all of the gathered information is sent members of the drug court team for review at a weekly staff meeting. After reviewing a case, members of a drug court team vote to accept or reject an offender's application.

If the offender is accepted, the case is referred to a probation officer, who then performs a prescreening interview. The officer will listen to defendants and observe their behavior and attitudes in order to assess the level of desire to change their lifestyle. The officer will provide a rundown of the drug court program and ascertain an offender's willingness to abide fully with the program's guidelines in order to achieve sobriety. Most offenders, it should be understood, lack the personal skills associated with success in any endeavor, so the prospect of participating in an arduous treatment program in which they will be held strictly accountable is often daunting to them. Offenders who, by their words and actions, give the impression that they do not take responsibility for their behavior and have no desire to change will not be accepted.

One of a number of addiction severity instruments is then administered by a treatment counselor. The candidate may then be interviewed by an employment and family resources counselor to identify the defendant's treatment needs and to develop an overall treatment plan. After further consultation with their attorneys to discuss legal questions, defendants then instruct their attorneys as to whether or not they still wish to enter into the program. If a defendant decides affirmatively, he or she is signed up. The offender's signature on the contract is a significant commitment to the program, and he or she will be constantly reminded of that commitment throughout the program, particularly if compliance is not forthcoming.

Treatment planning should be guided by offender needs, particularly those related to the offense, and goals should be incrementally increased as the offender becomes more familiar and comfortable with the program. The offender will appear before the drug court judge at least once per week. At that time, the judge will assess the defendant's progress, with the aid of a short report prepared by the supervising probation officer. This report will contain the results of urine analyses (UAs), efforts at seeking employment (if this is an issue), and any other information relevant to the defendant's progress in the program. It is generally expected that as a result of their frequent interactions during court appearances, participants will develop rapport with the judge. The judge speaks directly to offenders in an informal way, asking about their progress and either exhorting them to try harder or praising their accomplishments. The judge will also remind them of the obligation to remain drug free and may impose sanctions for ongoing drug use or other behavior that impedes progress toward sobriety. These sanctions may include jail time and/or dismissal from the program, in which case, the offender receives the agreed-upon prison sentence. The judge will ultimately decide the defendant's fate: graduation or incarceration.

Graduation from drug court takes place with as much fanfare as a typical college graduation ceremony. Commenting on the graduation of 54 drug, DUI, and veterans treatment court participants, recognized at a ceremony in Tulsa, Oklahoma, Amanda Bland (2014) wrote,

> Drug Court saved Clark Dagnall's life. In return, the 26-year-old Sand Springs resident took the stage at the program's most recent graduation and promised to pay it forward by helping others. "My goal is just to help the next addict," he told the crowd of graduates' friends and family members. "Maybe I can get through to somebody that nobody else could." (n.p.)

Graduates received certificates of graduation for completing the nearly two-year program. Bland also wrote that the graduates who spoke at the ceremony were grateful for the support and guidance they received in the program, and the drug court staff expressed their pride in the graduates. "'We watch these individuals transform and rise from the ashes,' said Lawrence Gilbert, Action Steps Counseling program coordinator" (Bland, 2014, n.p.).

It goes without saying that given the important role of a drug court judge, he or she should possess special qualities over and above the typical judge. According to Judge Jeffrey Tauber (2009), a former leader in the problem-solving court movement, he or she should be a good communicator who enjoys interacting with people, both the other members of the program staff and the program participants. Tauber (2009) writes,

> For a true DCJ [drug court judge], this is the most fun you can have in a courtroom, outside of the occasional wedding or Christmas party. You get to work in a team with dedicated professionals, engage drugged out, unhealthy substance abusers in treatment, work together as a "community" to change lives, and be there as they are transformed to healthy productive citizens. What's not to like. (p. 4)

A drug court judge must know how to motivate people by letting them know what is expected of them, expressing his or her belief in their ability to succeed, and showing his or her appreciation for their efforts. A drug court judge ditches the stern and somber demeanor of the stereotypical judge and conducts her or his court with an eagerness and friendliness that lets offenders know that he or she is rooting for them to succeed. Tauber (2009) goes on to write these words of advice to drug court judges:

> Don't be afraid to congratulate participants for a job well done. In some instances that may include leading applause for the successful participant; on other occasions ask the participant to come to the bench for a brief conversation and handshake. But don't overdo the cheerleading. Remember the participants are not a TV Quiz Show audience responding to applause cues. Keep the applause and physical contacts to a meaningful level, and they won't seem staged or lifeless. (p. 4)

If, God forbid, you are ever required to participate in a drug court program, wouldn't it be nice to draw someone in the mold of the Honorable Judge Jeffrey Tauber as your judge?

SOME PROS AND CONS OF DRUG COURTS

As with almost anything else, even if something is performing well relative to what went before, there are always those who feel that it is "not the answer," that it could be done better, and that it violates some principle or another. Some see drug courts as net widening and more punitive than traditional criminal courts, and others see the requirement to plead guilty as a condition of entry and the expected cooperation of defense attorneys in the process as an abandonment of the traditional adversarial nature of the criminal justice system. For instance, the Drug Policy Alliance (DPA), a group dedicated to promoting alternatives to the drug war, asserts that drug courts have made the criminal justice system more, not less, punitive:

> In drug court, the traditional functions and adversarial nature of the U.S. justice system are profoundly altered. The judge—rather than lawyers—drives court processes and serves not as a neutral facilitator but as the leader of a "treatment team" that generally consists of the judge, prosecutor, defense attorney, probation officer and drug treatment personnel. The judge is the ultimate arbiter of treatment and punishment decisions and holds a range of discretion unprecedented in the courtroom, including the type of treatment mandated, whether methadone prescription is acceptable (and at what dosage) and how to address relapse. The defense lawyer, no longer an advocate for the participant's rights, assists the participant to comply with court rules. (DPA, 2011, pp. 5–6)

Similarly, there are defense attorneys who fear that their collaboration with the drug court's therapeutic programs, despite any beneficial outcome, violates their obligation to vigorously defend their clients. Drug courts use a carrot-and-stick approach in which defendants sign a contract in which they agree to plead guilty to the charge and to a jail

ZUMA Press, Inc./Alamy Stock Photo

PHOTO 7.2: Former New Mexico secretary of state Dianna Duran (*left*) and her attorney Erlinda Johnson hash out the final wording of a plea agreement with the attorney general's office in First District Court, Santa Fe, October 23, 2015. Duran pled guilty to 6 counts of the 65 counts she was charged with. Duran also resigned from her office.

sentence (usually at least one year) if they fail to complete treatment. For his or her part, the prosecutor agrees to dismiss all charges if the defendant successfully completes the program. This is the primary reason why even defendants who might receive a lesser sentence choose the intensive-treatment option. Drug court graduates avoid a felony conviction, which is a very important consideration for someone who is employed or seeking work or for someone who, at some future date, may be charged with another crime. (He or she will not have the conviction on his or her rap sheet.)

Many legal scholars see this as coerced treatment because defendants have a prison term hanging over their heads if they do not successfully complete the program. The reasoning is, of course, that the prison sentencing lurking in the background is a strong incentive to do well in the program. It is true that the vast majority of people treated for substance abuse have very large boot prints impressed on their backsides. Being involved with the criminal justice system because of substance abuse should be crisis enough to generate motivation in some offenders. Two reviews of the literature on coerced substance abuse treatment in the United States (Farabee, Pendergast, & Anglin, 1998) and United Kingdom (Barton, 1999) concluded that such treatment leads to positive reductions in abuse, even greater reductions in some cases than among voluntary clients. Nevertheless, others remind us that many defense attorneys are uncomfortable with such coercion. Lawrence Vogelman, a board member of the National Association of Criminal Defense Lawyers, tells us that while prosecutors and judges have an obligation to ensure justice is done, "people can't lose sight of the fact that the defense attorney is the only person in the room whose obligation is *not* to do justice" (in W. Davis, 2003, p. 36).

Drug courts appear to do reasonably well meeting the goals set for them, but if they help to salvage the lives of just a small percentage of those who participate in their programs, they have saved the communities in which they operate millions of dollars and millions of hours of anguish and sorrow over the period they have been operating. For instance, John Roman's (2013) study of drug courts in 29 different U.S. jurisdictions, illustrated in Figure 7.3, shows that drug court participants were significantly less likely to test positive for drugs than other probationers (29% versus 46%) and less likely to be rearrested (52% versus 62%). Roman also noted that the costs per drug court participant was significantly higher per year ($15,326) for drug court participants than for comparable probationers ($7,191), but that was offset by lower costs in other areas, such as the costs of

FIGURE *7.3*   Comparison of Drug Court Participants and Probationers on Certain Outcomes

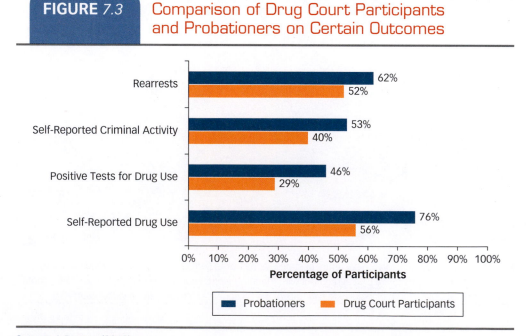

Source: J. Roman (2013).

further crime and victimization. Overall, the net financial benefit per participant spread over all 29 jurisdictions in the Roman (2013) study was $5,680 compared with control probationers. If there were only 100 participants, this would amount to an average saving of $1,360,000 over two years, which is the usual duration of such courts. This is without even considering the emotional costs of criminal victimization. Other studies have found that compared with tradition probation, drug courts reduce overall recidivism by 12.4% and drug-related recidivism by 13% (Mitchell, Wilson, Eggers, & MacKenzie, 2012).

Another meta-analysis of 201 different studies (Sevigny, Fuleihan, & Ferdik, 2013) found that drug courts reduce jail and prison incarceration by 32%. Putting this in a nationwide perspective, the researchers report that this results in 9,911 fewer incarcerations among the estimated 52,777 annual drug court participants across the United States. However, these lower incarceration rates were offset by the longer sentences imposed on participants who failed. Nevertheless, in addition to saving the states many millions of dollars in jail and prison costs, drug courts appear to be quite successful in reducing recidivism. For instance, the Baltimore County Juvenile Drug Court outcome analysis (Mackin, Lucas, & Lambarth, 2010) estimated that the program saved the country $8,762 per participant over 24 months because of lower recidivism rates and saving from incarceration. Figure 7.4

? ETHICAL ISSUE 7.1

What Would You Do?

You are a defense attorney whose client, Janet, wants to avoid a felony conviction and prison sentence by agreeing to enter a drug court program. Because of this, you know you must shed your adversarial courtroom relationship with the prosecution and focus more on the facilitation of Janet's progress in treatment and less on the legalities of her case. Janet has always maintained her innocence, but both you and she recognize that the prosecutor has a good case against her, which is why she pled guilty. After Janet has been in the program about six months and is making good progress with her treatment, you obtain incontrovertible evidence that Janet was indeed innocent. You can do two different things. First, you can do what you are trained to do and have sworn to do: vigorously defend your client. Or, because you know that Janet is doing well in the program, you know that in the long run, she will benefit greatly, and her arrest record will be expunged anyway. Do you sit on the information and let an innocent client remain subject to strict criminal justice supervision "for her own good," or do you do what lawyers are supposed to do and vindicate Janet?

| FIGURE 7.4 | Comparison of Rearrest Rates for Juvenile Drug Court Participants and Nonparticipants at 6 Through 24 Months Postadmittance |

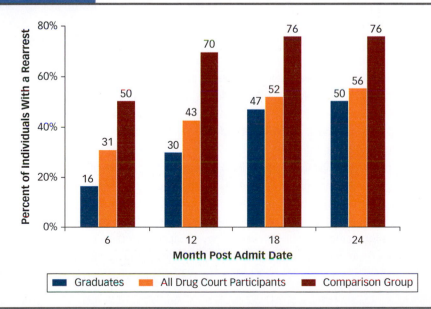

Source: Mackin, J. R., Lucas, L. M., Lambarth, C. H., Herrera, T. A., Waller, M. S., Carey, S., & Finigan, M. W. (2010). Baltimore County juvenile drug court outcome and cost evaluation. Portland, OR: NPC Research. Retrieved from http://www.ndcrc.org/sites/default/files/baltimore_co_juv_dc_outcome-cost_0110.pdf

POLICY AND RESEARCH

Evaluating Drug Court Performance

Policies to control drug usage in the United States have historically been dominated by the efforts of law enforcement efforts to reduce the availability of illegal drugs. As the demand for illegal drugs increased, so did the number of individuals entering prison as drug offenders, who have mainly driven the huge increase in incarceration in the United States. This led to states expending greater proportions of their budgets on prison construction and maintenance and eventually prison overcrowding. It soon became clear that some alternate policy was called for that was both more successful in reducing recidivism and less of a strain on the state coffers, leading to the implementation of drug courts.

The evaluation of drug court programs has attracted researchers in numbers unmatched by any other criminal justice program. Numerous program evaluations have been conducted since 1990, and the findings have been varied, although the overall picture is positive. These evaluations typically examine such things as cost-saving estimates of drug court services versus the costs of adjudication and incarceration and the effectiveness of drug court programs in reducing recidivism and on their impact on the lives of participants compared with drug offenders processed through traditional court proceedings.

Rossman, Roman, Zweig, Rempel, and Lindquist (2011) conducted a longitudinal multisite evaluation of adult drug courts in Florida (2 courts), Illinois (2), New York (8), Pennsylvania (2), North Carolina (2), and Washington (1). Their evaluation was designed to answer these questions: (1) Do drug courts work in reducing substance abuse, crime, and other psychosocial problems? (2) Do drug courts work better for some types of participants than others? (3) What are the mechanisms through which drug courts achieve positive effects? And (4) what are the net benefits of drug courts? They initially interviewed 1,157 drug court offenders and a comparison group of 627 non–drug court drug-abusing offenders in 2005 and 2006. Between 2006 and 2008, they interviewed and drug tested 764 drug court participants and 383 offenders from the comparison group. Seventy-six percent of the comparison group self-reported using any drug during a given period, as opposed to 56% of the drug court offenders, who were less likely than the comparison group to report using "serious" drugs. More importantly,

during the fluids drug test interview, significantly fewer drug court participants than control group offenders tested positive (29% versus 46%). Furthermore, whereas 62% of the comparison group were rearrested over the period, 52% of the drug court offenders were. Rearrest and technical violations were responsible for the attrition rates of both groups over the 3-year period.

There were other benefits for drug court participants. At the 18-month interview, drug court participants reported less need for educational, employment, and financial services, suggesting that the provision of these services may be a major mechanism by which drug courts achieve their success, compared with traditional court processing of drug offenders. However, there were only modest differences in 18-month employment rates, income, and family emotional support between the groups, nor were there any differences in symptoms of depression or homelessness. Violent offenders showed greater reduction in criminal activity than nonviolent offenders, and offenders with mental health problems showed smaller reductions in crime and drug abuse than other offenders. The researchers concluded,

> There is a direct effect of drug court participation on desistance from drug use and criminality; after controlling for all significant individual risk factors, court practices, and theoretical mediators, there remains an independent effect of drug court on improved behavior. Drug courts participants reported fewer subsequent days of drug use and crimes committed per month, on average across all courts, 18 months later, and, they expressed more positive attitudes toward the judge at their 6-month interview, which in turn was associated with lower levels of drug use and crime at their 18-month interview, on average across all courts. (Rossman et al., 2011, p. 4)

Questions remain about the extent to which drug courts reduce substance abuse and recidivism in the long run because most drug courts do not typically monitor the behavior of participants beyond completion of the program. However, they do appear to be a better strategy than the "lock 'em up" mentality of the traditional courts.

DISCUSSION QUESTIONS

1. Why would evaluating drug court programs appeal to so many researchers?

2. By what mechanism would you say drug courts "work": close monitoring, services provided, the perception that someone cares, or another mechanism?

3. Since drug court participants are not monitored after completion, how confident are you that a successful completer will continue to remain drug free?

Reference

Rossman, S., Roman, J., Zweig, J. Rempel, M., & Lindquist, C. (Eds.). (2011). *The Multi-site adult drug court evaluation: The impact of drug courts: Volume 4*. Washington, DC: Urban Institute, Justice Policy Center.

provides an illustration of recidivism outcomes for drug court graduates, participants who did not graduate, and the control group consisting of juveniles who fit the criteria for participation but did not participate. Note that while the likelihood of rearrest increased for all groups over time, the graduates had a lower arrest rate at 24 months than the control group did at 6 months.

NEW JERSEY DRUG COURT PROGRAM: TESTIMONIALS

Although cost–benefit ratio and general-outcome studies are invaluable to practitioners and lawmakers, they seem a pretty cold way to evaluate the usefulness of drug courts for the average person. We all like to hear the emotional story from the "horse's mouth" than from the statistician's cold pen. The New Jersey Judiciary (n.d.) posted a number of testimonials from individuals who successfully completed drug court programs, four of which are presented below.

> I want to thank God, the court, my probation officer. I never really respected judges and probation officers before. But here they treat you like an adult, and you're made to feel part of a larger society. The judge has been very friendly and caring. He was there for me, as well as my probation officer. Life is beautiful, but I avoided life. You can't use mood- or mind-altering chemicals and be part of life. I'm grateful. —Tommy

> This is truly, truly a blessed day. It feels so good being clean. Now, people come to me for help! With drug court, I learned to be a man, not a kid. I'm studying music again. I don't know how to read or write, in English or Spanish, but God gave me the ability to have a band. When I go home, I kiss my instruments, because I can't believe I have this: my music, my apartment. I used to live in abandoned buildings and eat garbage. Now my eyes are open, my mind is clear. People respect me. —Juan

> In '97, I was arrested with crack. I ran and I ran and I ran so hard, until I became the worst person you ever saw on drugs. I felt useless, full of self-pity. I was ashamed. My mother had a double stroke, they came to tell me, and I ran from that, too. Now I have a new life. . . . When I was low, I would remember the words of Psalm 142: I cried unto God with my voice; even unto God did I make my supplication. Consider my complaint; for I am brought very low. . . . O deliver me from my persecutors; for they are too strong for me. Bring my soul out of prison, that I may give thanks unto thy Name. Thank you, God. I love you. —Marcie

ETHICAL ISSUE 7.2 **?**

What Would You Do?

You are a drug court judge who has had many private conversations with Joe, one of the drug court participants. This has given you wide knowledge of his history of prior violations and sanctions during his 18-month participation in the program. After you have given Joe his "last chance," he tests positive for cocaine, and his case is set for a termination hearing, leading to his incarceration. Joe files a motion asking you to recuse yourself (remove yourself from the case) because of a possible conflict of interest or lack of impartiality, alleging it would be a violation of due process for you to preside over the termination proceedings because of your intimate knowledge of his lack of cooperation with the program. Not to recuse yourself is consistent with the policies and goals of the drug court, but not doing so is also in violation of the normal rules of due process. What will you do: grant or deny Joe's motion?

Audio 7.1:
States Try Out
Courts Tailored
for Mentally Ill

I want to thank God for giving me another chance when I had given up on myself. He picked me up. Jail saved my life. This drug court program works. The key is honesty with yourself. —John

••• MENTAL HEALTH COURTS

Mental health courts are modeled on the success of the drug court model and are designed to deal with the special problems of (mostly) nonviolent offenders suffering from **mental disorders** (Steadman et al., 2001). Mental health courts are not nearly as numerous as drug courts. A 2013 study identified only 346 adult and 51 juvenile mental health courts currently operating in the United States (Goodale, Callahan & Steadman, 2013). According to Almquist and Dodd (2009),

> Mental health courts generally share the following goals: to improve public safety by reducing criminal recidivism; to improve the quality of life of people with mental illnesses and increase their participation in effective treatment; and to reduce court- and corrections-related costs through administrative efficiencies and often by providing an alternative to incarceration. (p. v)

THE MENTAL HEALTH COURT PROCESS

Mentally ill offenders pose a particularly difficult set of challenges for the criminal justice system. Mental illness lurks behind many other factors that are linked to criminal behavior, such as substance abuse, lack of education, poor work history, and homelessness. Unlike drug courts, mental health courts often accept felony offenders. Almquist and Dodd (2009) inform us that "according to a 2006 survey of 87 mental health courts around the country, 40 percent accepted only individuals charged with misdemeanor crimes; 10 percent accepted only individuals charged with felonies; and 50 percent accepted both types of charges" (p. 7).

Mental health courts: Special problem-solving courts designed to work with offenders struggling with mental health problems.

Mental disorders: Clinically significant conditions characterized by alterations in thinking, mood, or behavior associated with personal distress or impaired functioning.

Mentally ill offenders under correctional supervision present a particularly difficult treatment problem. Alcoholics and drug addicts ingest substances that alter the functioning of their brains in ways that interfere with their ability to cope with everyday life, although their brains may be normal when not befuddled by drugs. Mentally ill persons also have brains that limit their capacity to cope, but that limitation is intrinsic to their brains rather than attributable to intoxicating substances. Studies around the world have found that mentally ill persons are at least three to four times more likely to have a conviction for violent offenses than persons in general (Fisher et al., 2006). Most mentally ill persons, however, are more likely to be victims than victimizers, and many of them make their problems worse by abusing alcohol and/or drugs (Walsh & Yun, 2013). It is because of their substance abuse and greater propensity for violence, in addition to mental-hospital deinstitutionalization, that the mentally ill are overrepresented in the correctional system.

PHOTO 7.3: It is a sad fact that jails and prisons now house more mentally ill persons than do psychiatric hospitals.

There are a number of antipsychotic drugs on the market today that allow mentally ill offenders to live fairly normal lives while taking them. However, because of side effects or other changes induced by medication, many people do not like to take it. Some will take their medicine for a while but then stop once they begin to feel "normal." It is during these times of nonmedication that a mentally ill person is most in danger of committing crimes. If a person not on his or her medication is arrested, it is recognized that it is mental illness rather than criminality that precipitates offending. The mental health courts recognize this, and thus, their first goal is to get the offender back on prescribed medication voluntarily. If he or she will not take the medicine, then he or she is hospitalized to ensure compliance. Because a judge oversees this process, offenders are likely to receive treatment more quickly than nonoffenders. This "queue jumping" is seen by some as unfairly penalizing mentally ill nonoffenders for not offending (W. Davis, 2003). However, offenders with mental illness are seen as a more immediate threat to themselves and to the community, and thus, their needs are more urgent; the quicker treatment is available, the quicker he or she be stabilized, which is good for everyone.

When offenders have been medically stabilized, they are returned to court and offered entry into a mental health court program in exchange for a plea of guilty to the charges against them. It is assumed that hospitalization has stabilized the individual to the point that he or she is competent to make an informed decision on the offer. If the offer is accepted, an offender is admitted to an intensive, treatment-based probation program that typically lasts for two years. The initial primary goal (unique the mental health courts) is offenders' compliance with their medication regimens. Because medication compliance is a major factor in the offending of the mentally ill, probation officers, judges, and psychiatrists in a mental health court work together to ensure that offenders stay on their prescribed medication.

SOME PROS AND CONS OF MENTAL HEALTH COURTS

Despite all of the problems faced by mental health courts, they have generally shown positive treatment outcomes, although not at the same level as drug courts. A three-year evaluation of 10 mental health courts with 331 graduates in Michigan found the following:

- Almost all mental health court participants graduated with improved mental health and better quality of life.

- Of participants charged with felonies, 39 percent improved their employment status—starting a job or working more hours—while in the program. An additional 18 percent of misdemeanor participants improved their employment status.

- A significant percentage of participants improved their education level—for example, by taking courses toward a GED—while in mental health court. Misdemeanor and felony participants were most likely to improve their education level, at 29 percent and 27 percent respectively.

- Over 90 percent of successful participants were taking their medications upon graduation.

- Graduates of mental health courts averaged over 300 days of continuous sobriety before graduation. (Michigan Supreme Court, 2013, pp. 1–2)

The effects were still in evidence 30 months after graduation, with mental health court graduates having a recidivism rate of 18.9%, as opposed to 43.2% for a comparison group of mentally ill offenders not admitted to a mental health court (Michigan Supreme Court, 2013).

Better-than-average treatment outcomes are perhaps primarily due to the informality and less adversarial methods mental health courts display when compared with traditional criminal courts and due to their elimination of many of the barriers mentally ill offenders usually encounter in receiving treatment. Mental health courts provide the mentally ill with more, better, and faster treatment than they would typically receive. By providing offenders with opportunities for involvement in their own cases and because of the court's more respectful treatment of them, offenders are more likely to perceive the courts as fair and thereby be more compliant with the demands put on them.

Unfortunately, many of the participants in mental health courts are homeless or change their addresses often. It is thus a challenge for the court team to remain in contact with them. This can be a potential threat to ongoing treatment plans and constitutes a threat of removal from the program. There are many other difficulties that mental health courts face that drug courts do not. Drug courts focus on behavior (substance abuse and the crimes that issue from it) while mental health courts focus on mental illness, which is not itself a crime but can lead to it. Mental health courts have to adapt the drug court model to accommodate individuals with a variety of mental health problems, a difficult task indeed. Table 7.1, from the Bureau of Justice Assistance, shows some of the differences between the issues faced by drug and mental health courts.

Audio 7.2: New Minnesota Court Handles Vets Accused of Crimes

●●● VETERANS COURTS

THE VETERANS COURT PROCESS

Veterans courts are basically hybrids of drug and mental health courts. They accept veterans who have been arrested for some crime (typically nonviolent) whose primary diagnosis is substance dependency and/or "mild" mental health issues; that is, issues that do not include one of the major psychoses, such as schizophrenia. If veterans are found to be suffering from severe mental illness, they will be referred to mental health court. The major mental health issues found among veterans are posttraumatic stress disorder (PTSD) and depression. *PTSD* occurs after someone witnesses a traumatic event, such as death or serious injury to oneself or another person, and it can induce extreme anxiety and fear. According to Bass and Golding (2012), "The symptoms of PTSD include reexperiencing the event, hyperarousal (irritability, anger, or hypervigilance, for example), and diminished responsiveness to or avoidance of stimuli associated with the trauma"

Veterans courts: Special problem-solving courts designed to work with military veterans who have committed offenses and are struggling with substance abuse or mild mental health issues.

FIGURE *7.5*   Flowchart for Brooklyn (NY)
Mental Health Court

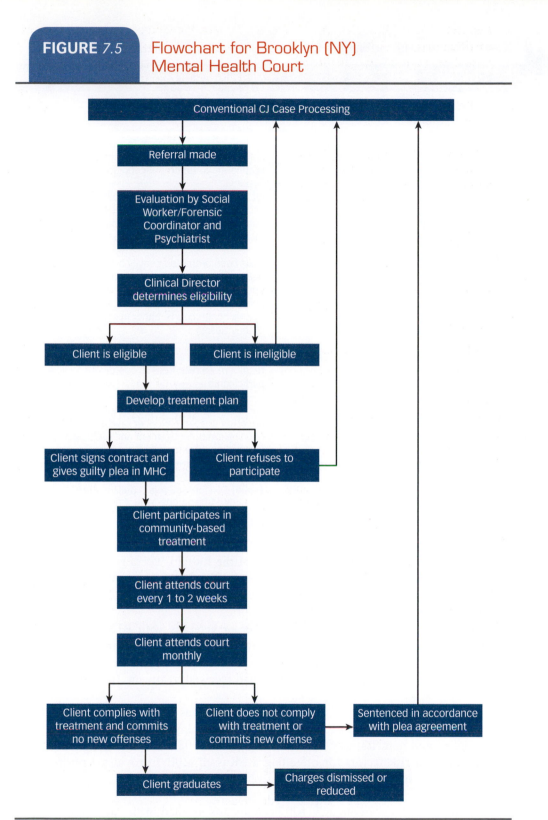

Source: Rossman, Willison, Mallik-Kane, Kim, and Sherrill (2012). Urban Institute report by URBAN INSTITUTE. Reproduced with permission of URBAN INSTITUTE PRESS, in the format Book via Copyright Clearance Center.

(p. 1). Although anyone can suffer from PTSD, it is particularly prevalent among those who have experienced combat and can be viewed as an invisible war wound that may go undiagnosed for years.

TABLE 7.1	Key Differences Between Drug Courts and Mental Health Courts	
PROGRAM COMPONENT	**DRUG COURTS. . .**	**MENTAL HEALTH COURTS. . .**
Charges accepted	Focus on offenders charged with drug related crimes	Include a wide array of charges
Monitoring	Rely on urinalysis or other types of drug testing to monitor compliance	Do not have an equivalent test available to determine whether a person with a mental illness is adhering to treatment conditions
Treatment plan	Make treatment plans structured and routinized; apply sanctioning grid in response to noncompliance, culminating with brief jail sentence	Ensure that treatment plans are individualized and flexible; adjust treatment plans in response to nonadherence along with applying sanctions; rely more on incentives; use jail less frequently
Role of advocates	Feature only minimal involvement from advocacy community	Have been promoted heavily by some mental health advocates, who are often involved in the operation of specific programs; other mental health advocates have raised concerns about mental health courts, either in general or in terms of their design
Service delivery	Often establish independent treatment programs, within the courts' jurisdiction, for their participants	Usually contract with community agencies; require more resources to coordinate services for participants
Expectations of participants	Require sobriety, education, employment, self sufficiency, payment of court fees; some charge participation fees	Recognize that even in recovery, participants are often unable to work or take classes require ongoing case management and multiple supports; few charge a fee for participation

Source: Council of State Governments Justice Center. (2008) *Mental Health Courts: A Primer for Policymakers and Practitioners.* New York: Council of State Governments Justice Center Criminal Justice/Mental Health Consensus Project (for the Bureau of Justice Assistance, Office of Justice Programs, U.S. Department of Justice). https://www.bja.gov/Publications/MHC_Primer.pdf

Video 7.2:
Experimental Housing for Vets Changes Lives, Reduces Violence

Judge Robert Russell (2009), presiding judge of the Buffalo Veterans Treatment Court and creator of its drug court, informs us that as of 2008, 84,000 veterans had been diagnosed with PTSD, but that

> research indicated that the actual number of veterans with PTSD or major depression is around 300,000. In regard to substance abuse, research indicates that in 2001 alone, 256,000 veterans needed treatment for illicit drug use; however, a mere 20 percent of those veterans had received treatment. (p. 130)

Many other veterans are facing numerous other problems that compound their PTSD, depression, and substance abuse, such as chronic unemployment, strained relationships with families, and homelessness (Tanielian & Jaycox, 2008). All of these problems constitute significant risk factors for offending. R. Russell (2009) provides a positive and uplifting analysis of the Buffalo, New York, veterans court:

> To date [2009], approximately 100 veterans are enrolled in Buffalo's veterans treatment court. Fifteen have successfully completed the program, two have voluntarily withdrawn, and two were unsuccessfully terminated. Thus far, graduates of Buffalo's veterans treatment court have experienced drastic positive life changes.
>   They are clean and sober and actively addressing any mental-health needs. All are either employed or pursuing further education. Many have been able to

Video 7.3:
For Veterans in Legal Trouble, Special Courts Can Help

FIGURE *7.6*   Prevalence of Mental Health Issues Among Veterans in Jail

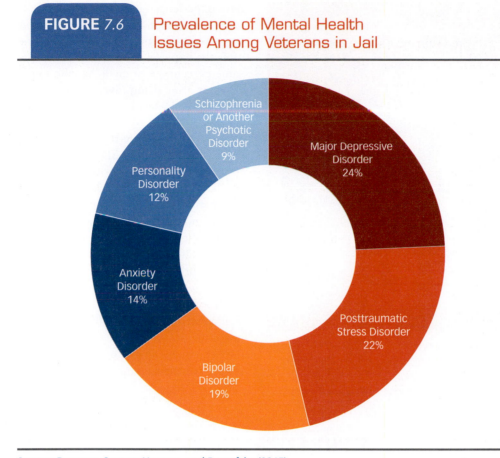

Source: Bronson, Carson, Noonan, and Berzofsky (2015).

mend strained relationships with family and friends, and those who were homeless were able to attain stable housing. To date, graduates of Buffalo's veteran's treatment court maintain a zero percent recidivism rate. Perhaps most significant of all of this is the change in the demeanors and attitudes of these individuals. Graduates leave the treatment court program with a renewed sense of pride, accomplishment, and motivation. (p. 132)

SOME PROS AND CONS OF VETERANS COURTS

There are a number of reasons why veterans courts are particularly successful. One such reason is the extensive use of other military veterans as mentors to offenders before the court. This develops a sense of "someone cares" and camaraderie with the volunteer, one result of which is that veterans in veterans courts keep about 93% of their clinical appointments, versus about 35% at general treatment clinics for offenders (Cartwright, 2011). The close supervision that characterizes all problem-solving courts may be particularly suited to military veterans, who are used to regimentation and close supervision.

As is the case with other specialty courts, veterans courts have their critics. For instance, the American Civil Liberties Union (ACLU) complains that these courts turn veterans into a special class of offenders who warrant a "get out of jail free" card by virtue of having served in the military (Cartwright, 2011). The courts assume that all veterans have experienced combat and may therefore carry war's invisible wounds, which is not always true. Not all veterans have experienced combat, and not all those who

PHOTO 7.4: Hank Pirowski (*right*), Veterans Court Project Director, listens to Guy LaPenna about paperwork concerns after appearing in the Veterans Court session in Buffalo, New York, on June 3, 2008. The veterans' treatment court is the first of its kind in the country, where defendants have all served their country in the military.

have experienced combat have PTSD. It is estimated that about 30% of combat veterans experience PTSD at some time after the experience, which is about the same percentage of civilians who experience it after being involved in serious motor vehicle accidents and other such disasters (Wimalawansa, 2013). There is also a moderate-to-strong genetic risk for developing PTSD when exposed to traumatic events, with some people being affected by relatively minor traumatic events and others requiring severe and protracted stress before succumbing (Stein, Jang, Taylor, Vernon, & Livesley, 2002). Whatever the case may be, we surely owe it to those men and women who have served in the military to afford them some sort of special consideration when they fall afoul of the law if the putative cause of their offending behavior is in any way connected to service for their country.

••• DOMESTIC VIOLENCE COURTS

Web 7.2: Domestic Violence Courts

Domestic violence encompasses a variety of abusive acts (physical, sexual, or psychological) that occur within a domestic setting. Domestic violence is the most prevalent form of violence in the United States today, and most of that is intimate-partner (spouse or lover) violence (Tolan, Gorman-Smith, & Henry, 2006). Except for minor forms of abuse, intimate-partner violence is overwhelmingly committed by males against females, although when females commit such violence, they are more likely to use a weapon to equalize the size and strength difference between the sexes (Smith & Farole, 2009). However, while just over one third of all murders of females in the United States are committed by intimate partners, less than 4% of males are killed by intimate partners (Rennison, 2003). Figure 7.7 indicates the level of risk of domestic violence victimization for different income categories.

THE DOMESTIC VIOLENCE COURT PROCESS

The first thing to note is that compared with other kinds of problem-solving courts, **domestic violence courts** are few and not as well run. A national survey uncovered only 208 such courts and concluded that findings highlighted "an important distinction between domestic violence courts and other problem-solving models, particularly drug and mental health courts, which have a more clearly delineated structure and widely shared set of core goals, policies, and practices" (Labriola, Bradley, O'Sullivan, Rempel, & Moore, 2010, p. ix). Research consistently finds that most abusers that come to the attention of the criminal justice system have other criminal offenses on their record. For example, among 66,759 individuals charged with domestic violence in the state of Washington from 2004 through 2006, the average number of prior non–domestic violence offenses was 4.6. The average age for their first recorded adult offense was 26.3; it was 31.5 years for their first recorded domestic violence offense (George, 2012).

Domestic violence courts: Special problem-solving courts meant to deal with the most prevalent form of violence: domestic violence.

FIGURE *7.7*   Victimization by Annual Household Income of Victims

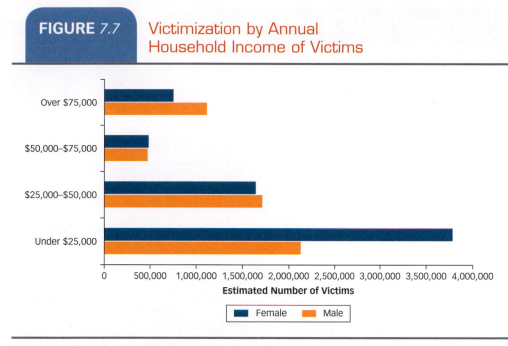

Source: Breiding, Chen, and Black (2014).

Nevertheless, domestic violence courts do seem to do far better than traditional methods of dealing with domestic violence. Cissner, Labriola, and Rempel's (2013) study of New York's domestic violence courts found that "domestic violence courts that prioritize deterrence and that both prioritize and implement specific policies to sanction offender noncompliance, while also addressing the needs of victims, are most effective in reducing recidivism" (p. iv). According to Susan Keilitz (2004), the major goals and achievements of domestic violence courts are as follows:

- Enhanced coordination of cases and consistent orders in different cases involving the same parties.

- More comprehensive relief for victims at an earlier stage of the judicial process.

- Advocacy services that encourage victims to establish abuse-free lives.

- Greater understanding by judges of how domestic violence affects victims and their children.

- More consistent procedures, treatment of litigants, rulings, and orders.

- Greater availability of mechanisms to hold batterers accountable for the abuse.

- Improved batterer compliance with orders.

- Greater confidence on the part of the community that the justice system is responding effectively to domestic violence.

- Greater system accountability. (p. 6)

Because victim and offender in a domestic violence situation typically live together, it is important for the domestic violence court to become involved immediately because of the risk of continued victimization during the pretrial period. Judges must thus take a more active role in monitoring defendants before trial and respond quickly to violations of restraining orders and other court orders with immediate penalties. Strict

PERSPECTIVE FROM A PRACTITIONER

Honorable Judge Robert Russell

Position: Judge of Buffalo treatment courts and acting judge of Erie County Court

Location: New York State Office of Court Administration

Education: Juris doctorate from Howard University, Washington, D.C.

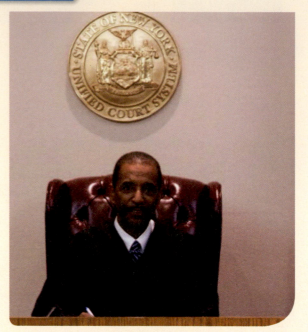

How long have you been in your current position, and what, if any, previous criminal justice experience have you had?

I have served as a judge since 1992. I began Buffalo's drug treatment court in 1995, its mental health treatment court in 2002, and created the country's first veterans treatment court in January 2008.

Prior to serving as a judge, my criminal justice experience included working for the state of Ohio's Attorney General's Office, the state of New York's Attorney General's Office, and the state of New York's Erie County District Attorney's Office.

I served as the past chairman of the Board of Directors of the National Association of Drug Court Professionals (NADCP) and the past president of the New York State Association of Drug Treatment Court Professionals, Inc. In addition, I also serve on the National Advisory Board of the Judges' Criminal Justice/Mental Health Leadership Initiative (JLI). It is a pleasure working with the men and women who've served our country by providing meaningful treatment and ancillary services to reestablish fruitful, healthy lives.

What are the duties and responsibilities of being a judge?

Generally, judges are to interpret the law, assess the evidence presented, and control how hearings and trials unfold in their courtrooms. Judges are required to be impartial decision makers. They are to provide independent and impartial assessment of the facts and how the law applies to those facts. As a treatment court judge, my expanded duties include overseeing a participant's progress in his or her treatment program, imposing incentives and consequences, and working collaboratively with prosecution and defense lawyers, community treatment providers, and other community providers of resources.

Please describe a typical workday.

There is no "typical" workday, but there are memorable days. At the beginning of Buffalo's veterans court, I set aside one day a week for cases of veterans suffering from mental health disorders or substance abuse. I reached out to the local V.A. hospital to ask for volunteer veteran mentors for the program. I remember one sad case of a veteran who attended the required sessions but failed to participate or engage. The man was strongly built and 6 feet, 4 inches tall, but he would slump in the courtroom, avoiding eye contact; nothing was getting through to him. I asked one of my staff, a Vietnam veteran who served in the 82nd Airborne, to go talk with the man during a recess to see if he could motivate him. They returned after 20 minutes, and it looked like a different person entered the courtroom. There was a remarkable distinguishing difference in this veteran's disposition. Standing erect—at what they call *parade rest*, with his feet slightly apart and hands cupped in the back, which is part of the military culture—he looked at me, eye to eye, and he said, "Judge, I'm gonna try harder." This shift made an immediate impact on me. I asked my staff member, "What the heck did y'all do?" He answered simply that they discussed their common service in Vietnam and their military service in general; after that, "they addressed that they wanted him to get better."

This shows the power of mentors who share a common experience with offenders. I am pleasantly surprised that our Buffalo experiment is swiftly become a national model. It is far more successful than jailing drug offenders—70% of enrolled veterans successfully complete the program, and 75% are not arrested within the following two years.

monitoring of offender accountability is of the utmost importance, as is concern for the future safety of victims. This is achieved with rapid coordination with victim advocate services and law enforcement. To ensure victim safety during the pretrial period, the court will typically restrict offenders' contact with their victims before trial, and any violation of such restriction conditions will be punished.

There are two ways the court attempts to decrease (or eliminate) future domestic violence offending: First, it tries to change offenders' beliefs and attitudes toward women (of course, some women commit domestic violence, too) and violence (rehabilitation), and second, it increases the offenders' perceptions about the punitive consequences of reoffending (deterrence) (Labriola et al., 2010, p. 34). In most

PHOTO 7.5: Police officer taking a domestic violence call. Domestic violence is a big problem, and domestic violence courts are designed to reduce the number of such incidents.

domestic violence courts, there is a strict no-exceptions rule for such violations, which result in incarceration. This results in domestic violence courts presenting a different set of concerns for defense attorneys than they do in other problem-solving courts. According to W. Davis (2003),

> While defense attorneys worry that they might lose the chance to advocate for their clients in drug and mental health courts, in domestic violence courts they face the opposite problem: Efforts to get treatment for their clients are secondary to demands for incarceration. (p. 37)

Victim advocates are an essential part of domestic violence courts, helping victims to navigate the complexities of the judicial process and helping them to restore their lives to some sense of normalcy following the abuse. Victim advocates often accompany victims to court and explain this criminal justice system—what is going on and what to expect from the process. They also help with safety planning, such as providing referrals to shelters for battered women or to available housing if the victim does not have a family support group available. Advocates also provide counseling, emphasizing victims' strengths rather than their weaknesses and solution talk over problem talk. Many female victims of domestic violence demonstrate what psychologists call *learned helplessness*, meaning that they tend to have little regard for their self-worth and their ability to survive on their own (often returning, time and again, to their abusers) and may even feel that they are responsible for their abuse (Houston, 2014).

Career Video 7.2: Victim Advocate

••• COMMUNITY COURTS

Community courts are another addition to the ever-growing number of problem-solving courts. The idea of a community court began in the United States with the establishment of the Midtown Community Court in Midtown Manhattan in 1993 (Lee et al., 2013). A community court addresses primarily *quality-of-life crimes*, such as petty theft, vandalism, loitering, graffiti, public drunkenness, and prostitution. A community court should ideally be an integral part of the community and a major force for

Community courts: Special problem-solving courts that work to solve the underlying problems of offenders who have committed quality-of-life crimes while ensuring that offenders compensate the community that they have harmed.

transforming it into a place that is safe and desirable to live in. With the cooperation of local community boards and local police, community courts seek to solve the problems of offenders while using the court's leverage to ensure that they compensate the community for the damage they caused. This compensation is typically in the form of providing community services, such as weeding vacant lots, cleaning graffiti, and general neighborhood cleanup.

THE COMMUNITY COURT PROCESS

An excellent short but comprehensive definition of a community court's philosophy, processes, and goals is provided by Cynthia Lee and her colleagues (2013):

> Two key influences on the development of the community court model were the "broken windows" theory of crime and the related concept of community policing. According to the broken windows theory, visible conditions of disorder in a neighborhood—such as broken windows that are never repaired or misdemeanors that go unprosecuted—serve as a signal that the community does not enforce social norms, inviting further misdemeanor activity that eventually leads to more serious crimes. In accordance with the broken windows theory, community courts typically focus on cleaning up minor "quality of life" crimes . . . on the assumption that this will lead to reductions in other types of crime as well. Building upon the broken windows theory, the community policing model seeks to take police officers out of their patrol cars and integrate them into the fabric of the community, where they can better exercise both formal and informal control over conditions of disorder. In a similar fashion, the community court model aims to relocate the production of justice out of large centralized courts and into the local community. (p. 2)

A flowchart from arrest to disposition for the Midtown Community Court (Lee & Martinez, 1998) is presented in Figure 7.8.

The litmus test of any criminal justice intervention is, of course, the extent to which it reduces recidivism. A particularly good study is a RAND Corporation evaluation of the Community Justice Center in San Francisco (Kilmer & Sussell, 2014). This study looked at all of the offenders arrested who were both geographically (the Tenderloin District) and categorically eligible to go through the community court system who had been processed through the traditional court system before the community court program began and compared them with similar offenders arrested in the same "catchment" area after it was launched. Researchers found that the community court program reduced rearrests for eligible offenses during the period from 2009 (when the community court opened) to 2013 by 8.9% to 10.3%. The researchers attributed this reduction to the speed of processing and the multifaceted interventions the program provided. Rather than appearing in a traditional criminal court a month or more after arrest, offenders had to report to the court within 7 business days, and once accepted into the court, they were provided with quick and easy access to social services, such as job training and substance abuse treatment.

FIGURE *7.8*   Case Flowchart of Midtown Community Court in Manhattan

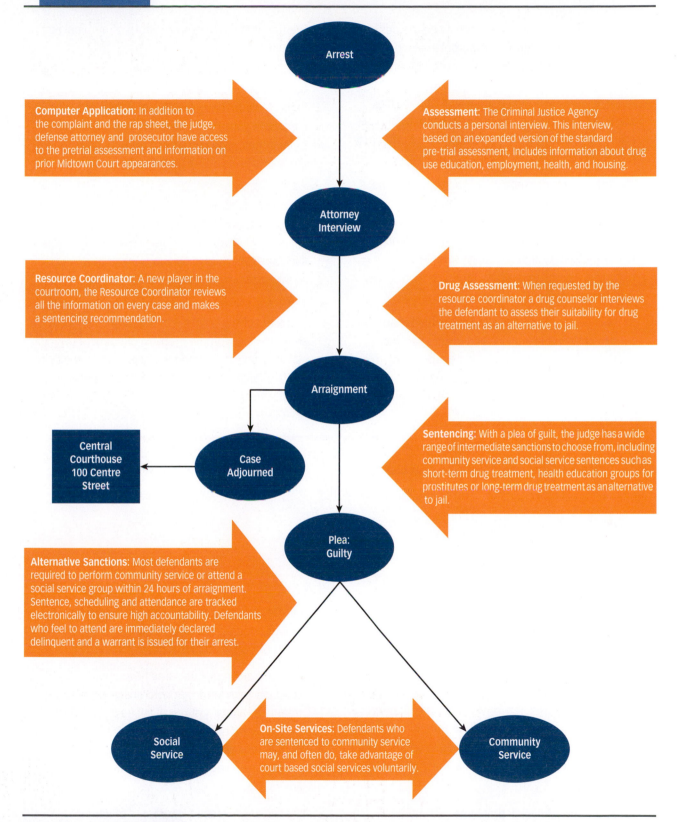

Source: Lee and Martinez (1998).

SUMMARY

- Problem-solving courts are specialty courts designed to help offenders with specific problems and needs that have not been adequately addressed in traditional criminal courts. Problem-solving courts operate with the notion that instead of punishing criminals after the fact, courts should try to prevent crime by addressing any underlying causes that may have been identified.

- The most prevalent problem-solving courts—and the first to be implemented—are drug courts. The selection process and treatment regimen in a drug court is intense and is run by a treatment team under the supervision of a judge, who involves himself or herself in the case far more than traditional judges.

- Some view drug courts as more punitive than traditional criminal courts, and others see the requirement to plead guilty as a condition of entry and the expected cooperation of defense attorneys in the process as an abandonment of the traditional adversarial nature of criminal justice system.

- Mental health courts are modeled on drug courts but are not as numerous or successful. Participants in these courts have multiple problems (e.g., substance abuse and homelessness) in addition to their mental problems. The primary issue in these courts is getting offenders to stay on their medication.

- Veterans courts are also similar to drug courts but limit their clientele to offenders who are military veterans. Many of these offenders have problems such as PTSD, caused by exposure to traumatic events experienced during combat service.

- There are also domestic violence and community problem-solving courts. The first of these courts seeks to deal with the problem of intimate-partner violence, and the second addresses various quality-of-life offenses, such as vandalism and public drunkenness.

KEY TERMS

Bureau of Justice Assistance 148

Community courts 167

Domestic violence courts 164

Drug courts 149

Mental disorders 158

Mental health courts 158

Problem-solving courts 148

Veterans courts 160

DISCUSSION QUESTIONS

1. Discuss the rationale behind problem-solving courts. Is it convincing to you?

2. What would you say is the single greatest benefit to the community of problem-solving courts?

3. Some critics of problem-solving courts condemn them as being more punitive than traditional criminal processing. Why is this, and in your opinion, are the possible benefits worth the greater punitiveness?

4. What are the additional problems that mental health courts deal with, as opposed to drug courts, and do you think people who find themselves in mental health courts would be better served by being placed in mental institutions?

5. One of the complaints some have about veterans courts are that veterans get special treatment and a "get out of jail free" card because they are veterans. What is your opinion of this? Do people who have served their country in the military deserve special consideration? Why, or why not?

6. Explain why we see higher rates of domestic violence among low-income individuals.

USEFUL INTERNET SITES

Please note that the sites listed can be accessed at edge.sagepub.com/stohrcorrections.

Illinois Center of Excellence for Behavioral Health and Justice: www.illinoiscenterofexcellence.org

> The website of the Illinois Center of Excellence for Behavioral Health and Justice has many interesting features about statewide problem-solving courts.

National Drug Court Online Learning System: www .drugcourtonline.org

> This National Drug Court Online Learning System offers easy-to-use lessons on a wide array of topics relevant to adult drug courts.

Council of State Governments Justice Center: csgjusticecenter.org/mental-health-court-project

> This Council of State Governments website for mental health courts provides information on new programs and links to other relevant sites.

$SAGE edge™

Sharpen your skills with SAGE edge at **edge.sagepub.com/stohrcorrections**. SAGE edge for Students provides a personalized approach to help you accomplish your coursework goals in an easy-to-use learning environment. You'll find action plans, mobile-friendly eFlashcards, and quizzes as well as video, web, and resources and links to SAGE journal articles to support and expand on the concepts presented in this chapter.

8 Community Corrections

Probation and Intermediary Sanctions

TEST YOUR KNOWLEDGE

Test your present knowledge of probation by answering the following questions as true or false. Check your answers on page 535 after reading the chapter.

1. Probation in the United States began in the 1800s and was run by volunteers.

2. Probation is a popular punishment option among the American public.

3. Parole is another name for probation.

4. Probation is the most frequent sentence imposed by the courts in the United States.

5. Tough, law enforcement–type probation officers achieve better results from their probationers than social-work-type officers.

6. Work release programs are programs that allow tighter control of probationers than regular probation while allowing them to maintain their employment.

7. Hardened criminals would rather have any form of community supervision than a prison sentence.

8. Boot camps, where offenders are treated with strict discipline, are quite successful, especially with young offenders.

LEARNING OBJECTIVES

- Explain the origins and purpose of probation

- Explain the goals of community-based corrections, as opposed to incarceration

- Analyze the probation officer's role and models of probation supervision

- Describe the benefits of graduated sanctions and of engaging the community in offender rehabilitation

- Identify the various intermediate community sanctions and what they have to offer

BETTY'S REPRODUCTIVE RIGHTS VERSUS THE PROTECTION OF CHILDREN AND SOCIETY

In 1980, a district court in Ohio gave "Betty Smith" (not her real name) a choice of 5 years in prison or 5 years on probation if she agreed to sterilization. Betty had six children out of wedlock by five different men; she admitted to her probation officer she had her children in order to get more welfare. She was facing her fourth conviction for child endangerment, this time for breaking her son's arm. (He was suffering from fetal alcohol syndrome due to Betty drinking while pregnant.) The judge reasoned that it would be unconscionable to allow Betty to continue producing more children for the taxpayer to support and for her to abuse. Betty agreed to the proposition (the judge could not simply order it),

but the American Civil Liberties Union (ACLU) stepped in and prevented it. An aggrieved Betty was thus sentenced to 5 years imprisonment, and her children were made wards of the state.

This case and many others like it (a man who fathered 22 children by 11 different women in court for failure to pay child support was recently ordered not to procreate as a condition of probation) highlight the limits to which the criminal justice system can go in using probation as a tool to coerce offenders into behaving responsibly. For the ACLU and many other groups and individuals, procreation is a basic human right that should not be infringed upon no matter what the reason, and interfering with that right smacks of eugenics (the forced sterilization of "defectives" that was popular in the United States and many other countries in the early 20th century). Although Betty was given a choice, it was a coerced choice. Of course, all conditions of probation are coercive in that they make offenders do things that they don't want to, but the issue is how far can the system travel down that road, and how much freedom to accept or reject the court's "treatment plan" should we afford offenders? Do you believe Betty should have been allowed her choice? If so, is there a slippery slope here to eventually allowing judges to order sterilization regardless of offenders' wishes?

••• THE ORIGINS OF PROBATION

Web 8.1: American Probation and Parole Association

This chapter focuses on community corrections, with an emphasis on probation. The Bureau of Justice Statistics defines **probation** as "a court-ordered period of correctional supervision in the community, generally as an alternative to incarceration. In some cases, probation can be a combined sentence of incarceration followed by a period of community supervision" (Herberman & Bonczar, 2015, p. 2). Probation is thus a sentence imposed on convicted offenders that allows them to remain in the community under the supervision of a probation officer, instead of being sent to prison. The term *probation* comes from the Latin term *probare*, meaning "to prove." Because probation is a conditional release into the community, the probation period is a time of testing a person's character and his or her ability to meet certain requirements mandated by the court. That is, convicted persons must prove to the court that they are capable of remaining in the community and living up to its legal and moral standards. About 90% of all sentences handed down by the courts in the United States are probation orders (Kramer & Ulmer, 2009).

The practice of imprisoning convicted criminals is a relatively modern and expensive way of dealing with them. Up to two or three hundred years ago, they were dealt with by execution; corporal punishments, such as disfigurement or branding; or humiliation in the stocks. All of these punishments took place as community spectacles and even with community participation in the case of individuals sentenced to time in the stocks. Assuming that a convicted person was not executed, he or she remained in the community, enduring the shame of having offended it. (Think of Hester Prynne's punishment in Nathaniel Hawthorne's *The Scarlet Letter*, briefly discussed in Chapter 1). The only kinds of offenders typically subjected to this kind of shaming today are sex offenders, whose pictures are displayed on the Internet and who are frequently identified to their neighbors through community notification orders.

More enlightened ages saw punishments move away from barbaric cruelties and into emerging penitentiaries, where offenders could contemplate the errors of their ways and perhaps redeem themselves while residing there. But as we have seen, penitentiaries were not very nice places, and some kind souls in positions to do so sought ways to spare deserving or redeemable offenders from being consigned to them. This practice had its legal underpinnings in the practice of **judicial reprieve**, sometimes practiced in English courts in former times. A judicial reprieve was a delay in sentencing following a conviction, a delay that most often would become permanent if the offender demonstrated good behavior. In those days, there were no probation officers charged with supervising reprieved individuals; the nosey and judgmental nature of the small communities was more than adequate for that task.

Early American courts also used judicial reprieve, whereby a judge would suspend the sentence, and the defendant would be released on his or her own recognizance. Today, an *own-recognizance release* is the release of an arrested person without payment of bail but with the promise to appear in court to answer criminal charges. In early America, it was granted to persons already convicted as a form of probation, although offenders received no formal supervision or assistance to help them to mend their ways.

Probation: A sentence imposed on convicted offenders that allows them to remain in the community under the supervision of a probation officer, instead of being sent to prison.

Judicial reprieve: British and early American practice of delaying sentencing following a conviction that could become permanent, depending on the offender's behavior.

FOUNDING FATHERS OF PROBATION: JOHN AUGUSTUS AND MATTHEW DAVENPORT HILL

The first real probation system in which a reprieved person was supervised and helped was developed in the United States in the 1840s by a Boston cobbler named John Augustus. Augustus would appear in court and offer to take carefully selected offenders into his own home where he would do what he could to reform them as an alternative to imprisonment. Probation soon became his full-time vocation, and he recruited other civic-minded volunteers help him. By the time of his death in 1859, he and his volunteers had saved more than 2,000 convicts from imprisonment (Schmalleger, 2001). It should be noted, however, that Augustus only worked with first offenders and excluded the "wholly depraved" (Vanstone, 2004, p. 41), a luxury modern probation officers do not enjoy.

In 1878, the Massachusetts legislature authorized Boston to hire salaried probation officers to do the work of Augustus's volunteers, and a number of states quickly followed suit. This legislation grew out of the need to enforce the conditions of a suspended sentence, as well as the need to help offenders to change their lives (Vanstone, 2008). However, the probation idea almost died in 1916 when the U.S. Supreme Court ruled that judges may not indefinitely suspend a sentence (*Ex Parte United States [Killits]*, 1916). In this case, an embezzler was sentenced to 5-years imprisonment, which the judge (federal judge John Killits) suspended contingent on the embezzler's good behavior. What Killits had done was place an offender on probation without there being such a system established by law. However, the Supreme Court recommended the legislative establishment of probation, and because it was such a popular idea with legislators at this time, the **National Probation Act of 1925** was passed, allowing judges to suspend sentences and place convicted individuals on probation if they found that circumstances warranted it.

National Probation Act of 1925: The act that initiated the legal use of probation in the United States.

The probation concept in the United States and in Europe is the brainchild of the Christian missionary and temperance movements of the 19th century and grew rapidly in the late-19th and early 20th centuries. Between 1878 and 1920, probation statutes were in place in countries on every continent in the world (Vanstone, 2008). While John Augustus can rightfully claim the title of "father of probation" (he coined the term for what he was doing), in the very same year (1841), a British magistrate in Birmingham, England, named Matthew Davenport Hill was laying the foundations for probation in Britain. Like Augustus, Davenport Hill was a deeply religious man and an enemy of alcohol. Unlike Augustus, in addition to helping offenders overcome their problems, Davenport Hill also implemented the supervision of offenders and kept records of their behavior in the community. Davenport Hill thus operated in a manner closer to the modern notion of what probation is supposed to be than did John Augustus. He used what were known as *police court missionaries*, who were middle-class volunteers animated by strong Christian and temperance values, and augmented them with appointed police officers (Gard, 2007). The first full-time professional probation officers in England were appointed in 1907 (Gard, 2007). As in the United States, probation is the most common disposition of a criminal case in the UK.

PHOTO 8.1: 1961 Probation Officer Kirk Hills (*left*) and Gilliam at the door of a juvenile probation department. Youngsters could earn probation in 90 days on a work crew, if they did a good job.

••• PROBATION TODAY

According to the Bureau of Justice Statistics, there were 4,708,100 adult Americans (1 in 52 adults in the United States) on probation in 2014 (Kaeble, Maruschak, & Bonczar, 2015). This figure is a decrease of 8% from the previous all-time high of 5,119,000 in 2007. Figure 8.1 shows trends in the number of entries into the probation system from 2000 to 2014. In 2014, there were 2,067,100 entries and 2,130,700 exits. Of those who exited, 35% did so successfully, 8% were incarcerated, and 9% were unsuccessfully terminated (terminated for such things as failure to meet certain conditions, such as fines and restitution, by the end of their probation period). The remainder absconded, died, were deported, or were transferred to another agency. Males constituted about 75% of the adult misdemeanor and felony probation population. Whites were 54% of adult probationers, 30% were black, 13% were Hispanic, and 2% were American Indian, Alaska Native, Asian, or Pacific Islander. Figure 8.2 provides more information on the demographics of individuals on probation (Kaeble, Maruschak & Bonczar, 2015).

Community corrections: A branch of corrections defined as any activity performed by agents of the state to assist offenders in reestablishing functional, law-abiding roles in the community while monitoring their behavior for criminal activity.

••• WHY DO WE NEED COMMUNITY CORRECTIONS?

Community corrections may be defined as any activity performed by agents of the state to assist offenders to establish or reestablish law-abiding roles in the community while monitoring their behavior for criminal activity. In theory, monitoring and assisting offenders while allowing them to remain in the community protects society from criminal predation without taxpayers shouldering the financial cost of incarceration. Because

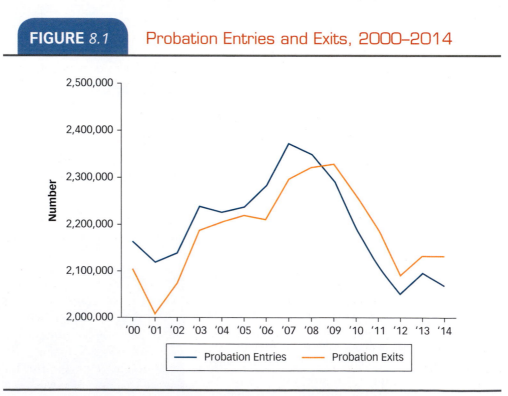

FIGURE *8.1*   Probation Entries and Exits, 2000–2014

Note: Counts rounded to the nearest 100.

Source: Bureau of Justice Statistics, Annual Probation Survey, 2000–2014.

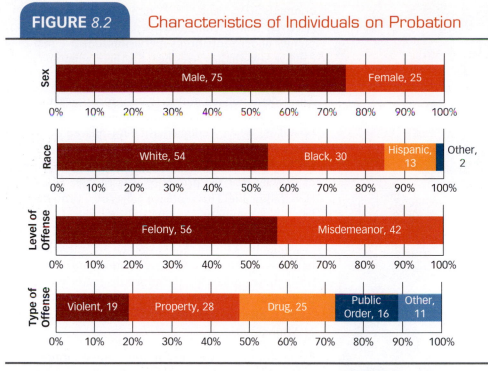

FIGURE *8.2*   Characteristics of Individuals on Probation

Source: Based on data from Bureau of Justice Statistics (November 2015), Annual Probation Survey, 2000–2014. Retrieved from https://www.bjs.gov/content/pub/pdf/ppus14.pdf

of the tough-on-crime policies that followed the huge upsurge in crime in the 1980s and early 1990s, correctional expenditures became a very large part of state and local budgets. Get-tough policies led to mass incarceration, which, in turn, resulted in numerous court orders to limit overcrowding in correctional facilities and in state efforts to decentralize state corrections. In order to do this, a number of states passed legislation known as **community corrections acts** (CCAs). CCAs include the provision of state funds to local governments and community correctional agencies to develop alternative community sanctions in place of incarceration. Mary Shilton (1992) provides three major motivations driving state adoption of CCAs:

1. Most correctional functions are best performed in the area where the offender resides.

2. Community corrections acts offer a better way of handling responsibility for correctional programs through incentives for intergovernmental cooperation, public education, and local management of a range of sanctions.

3. Community corrections acts provide localities with an opportunity to engage citizens in the debate over correctional goals and in the allocation of scarce resources. (p. ix)

In essence, the emergence of CCAs indicated that many states are redirecting funding toward rehabilitative goals in lieu of incarceration, where practicable. But it's not all about finances. Even if, as a society, we were willing and able to bear the monetary cost of imprisoning all offenders, incarceration imposes other costs on the community. These costs can and must be borne where seriously violent and chronic criminals are concerned, but to send every felony offender to prison would be counterproductive. Yet the general public is not well disposed to the idea of probation because "it suffers from a 'soft on crime' image" and is seen as "permissive, uncaring about crime victims, and blindly advocating a rehabilitative ideal while ignoring the reality of violent, predatory

Community corrections acts: Legislation that provides state funds to local governments and community correctional agencies to develop alternative community sanctions in place of incarceration.

PHOTO 8.2: A probation officer meets with a probationer.

criminals" (Petersilia, 1998, p. 30). However, allowing relatively minor felony offenders to remain in the community under probation supervision to prove that they can live law-abiding lives benefits their communities, as well as themselves.

The general public's notion that a probation sentence is "getting away with it" is a notion not shared by many offenders. When a convicted felon is placed on probation, he or she actually receives a prison sentence. This prison sentence is then suspended during the period of proving that the probationer is capable of living a law-abiding life. This sentence hangs over probationers' heads like a guillotine, ready to drop if they fail to provide that proof. It may be for this reason that a number of studies have found that "experienced" offenders who have done prison time, probation time, and parole time often prefer prison to the more demanding forms of probation, such as day reporting and intensive-supervision probation (Crouch, 1993; May, Wood, Mooney, & Minor, 2005).

There are good reasons for this counterintuitive disjunction between what the general public thinks of as severe of punishment and what offenders perceive as severe punishment. First of all, offenders do not live by the same values and norms as the law-abiding public. Probation requires offenders to work, submit to treatment and educational programs, and do many other orderly things that many hardened criminals simply do not have the inclination to do. Numerous interviews with active "street criminals" (e.g., burglars, robbers, and carjackers) show that such things are treated with disdain by them (Jacobs & Wright, 1999; Mawby, 2001; R. Wright & Decker, 1997). Serving time in prison is less of a hassle for many of them, and many know they would end up there anyway because they would not live up to probation conditions (May et al., 2005).

Second, offenders typically come from the lower socioeconomic classes, and thus, we must consider the contrast effect discussed in Chapter 1. Prison does not conjure up the same onerous images of fear and deprivation that it probably does for law-abiding individuals, and many offenders may view it as an occupational hazard of their chosen lifestyles, just like icy roads for truck drivers or cave-ins for miners. As Fleisher (1995) notes, "Prison isn't a risk that worries street hustlers. Things such as limited freedom, loss of privacy, violence, and variant sexual activity, which might frighten lawful citizens, don't frighten them" (p. 164).

Other, less criminally involved offenders prefer a probation sentence so that they can retain their jobs and remain connected to their families and communities. As we saw in Chapter 1, one's perception of the severity of a punishment—and thus, its deterrent effect—is a function of the contrast between one's everyday life and life under punishment conditions (the contrast effect). We have seen that while many fail their probation periods and are incarcerated, the majority succeed. It is surely true, then, that providing nonviolent offenders the opportunity to try to redeem themselves while remaining in the community is sensible criminal justice policy. There are also many benefits for the community in probation.

- Probation costs far less than imprisonment. Note from Figure 8.3, provided by the U.S. Courts (2013), that it costs almost 9 times more (and even more for women, juveniles, and the elderly) for imprisonment than for community supervision. For each person sentenced to probation rather than incarceration in 2012, taxpayers saved over $25,000. Many jurisdictions require probationers to pay for their own costs of supervision, which means that the taxpayer pays nothing. However, while economic considerations are important ones for policy makers, they are not the primary concern of corrections—protecting the community is. Community-based corrections is the solution only for those offenders who do not pose a significant risk to public safety.

- Employed probationers stay in their communities and continue to pay taxes, and offenders who were unemployed at the time of conviction may obtain training and help in finding a job. This adds further to the tax revenues of the community and, more importantly, allows offenders to keep or obtain the stake in conformity that employment offers. A job also allows them the wherewithal to pay fines and court costs, as well as restitution to victims.

- In the case of married offenders, community supervision maintains the integrity of the family, whereas incarceration could lead to its disruption and all the negative consequences such disruption entails.

- Probation prevents felons from becoming further embedded in a criminal lifestyle by being exposed to chronic offenders in prison.

FIGURE 8.3   Community Supervision Costs Versus Incarceration Costs

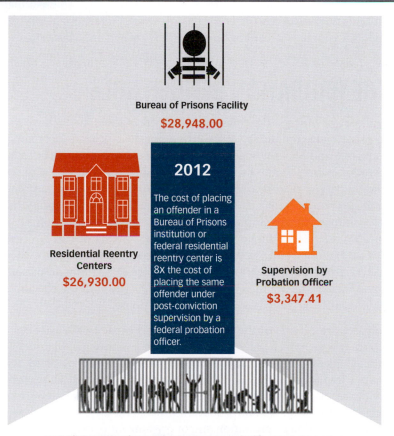

Bureau of Prisons Facility
$28,948.00

Residential Reentry Centers
$26,930.00

2012

The cost of placing an offender in a Bureau of Prisons institution or federal residential reentry center is 8X the cost of placing the same offender under post-conviction supervision by a federal probation officer.

Supervision by Probation Officer
$3,347.41

Pretrial detention for a defendant was nearly 10× more expensive than the cost of supervision of a defendant by a pretrial services officer in the federal system.

Source: U.S. Courts (2013). Supervision costs significantly less than incarceration in federal system. http://news.uscourts.gov/supervision-costs-significantly-less-incarceration-federal-system

Almost all prisoners will leave the institution someday, and many will emerge harder, more criminally sophisticated, and bitterer than they were when they entered. Furthermore, they are now ex-cons, a label that is a heavy liability when attempting to find legitimate employment and reintegration into free society.

● Many more offenders get into trouble because of deficiencies than because of pathologies. Deficits, such as a lack of education, a substance abuse problem, faulty thinking patterns, and so forth, can be assessed and addressed using the methods discussed in Chapter 10 on treatment. If we can correct these deficits to some extent, then the community benefits because it is a self-evident truth that whatever helps the offender to become a productive citizen also protects the community.

We do not wish to appear naive about this; there are people who are unfit to remain in the community and could not lead a law-abiding life even if given everything they needed to start over. We noted in Chapter 1 that for serious and violent offenders, incarceration is cost-effective. Placing dangerous offenders on probation is putting the community at risk, and they will mess up sooner or later and end up in prison anyway. For instance, according to the U.S. Marshals Service (2012), about 95% of those in the witness protection program (a program run by the U.S. Marshals Service to protect threatened witnesses and "snitches" during and after a trial) are criminals, and 17% percent of them commit further crimes under their new identities within a year, despite being given jobs, housing, and basically a new start in life as part of the program. Although the witness protection program is not probation, it is analogous in the sense that participants are free in the community, with greater opportunities and incentives not to reoffend, yet many do. To use a medical metaphor, probation is outpatient treatment for the less seriously criminally afflicted; prison is hospitalization for people who cannot be successfully treated anywhere else.

●●● THE PROBATION OFFICER ROLE

Video 8.1:
Rural Community
Corrections Officers
Go the Extra Mile

Probation and parole officers (the roles are combined in some states) have two common roles: (1) to protect the community and (2) to assist their probationers and parolees to become productive and law-abiding citizens. The dual roles mark them as law enforcement officers (this is their legally defined role in most states) and as social workers. The offenders they supervise may be on probation or parole, depending on their legal status. Probation is typically—but not always—a judicial function, meaning that offenders are under the ultimate supervision of the court. Even where probation is an executive function, because offenders are sentenced by a judge, only he or she can terminate that probation. A probationer may or may not have served jail time prior to community supervision by a probation officer. Offenders who have served time in prison are placed on parole upon release and are under the ultimate supervision of the executive branch of government, typically the state department of corrections.

Probation officers are officers of the court, and in this capacity, they are responsible for enforcing court orders, which may require them to monitor probationers' adherence to programs such as drug and alcohol treatment and to develop plans to assist them to transition into a free society. They are also required to make arrests, perform searches, and seize evidence of wrongdoing. Officers may have to appear in court occasionally to present evidence for violation of probation orders and to justify their recommendations for either termination of probation and imprisonment or continued probation with additional conditions. This is part of the officers' law enforcement role. Probation and parole officers work with criminal offenders who may be dangerous and often live in areas that may also be dangerous, which is why 35 states require their officers to carry a firearm (Holcomb, 2008). Nevertheless, it is important that officers spend a lot of time in those communities, learning about their culture, customs, and values and learning what resources are available to assist with the rehabilitation of offenders.

In a nutshell, a probation (or probation and parole) officer's primary responsibilities are to do the following:

- Provide effective, efficient, and consistent enforcement of court orders

- Provide safety for the community through the diligent supervision of offenders

- Provide rehabilitation and treatment opportunities for offenders (see Chapter 10)

- Administer a standardized risk and needs assessment, using scales to aid them to do this, and determine the level of supervision offenders require (see Chapter 9)

- Provide accurate and timely services to the courts, such as presentence investigation (PSI) and probation violation (PV) reports (see Chapter 5)

- Provide resources to victims of crimes, such as putting them in touch with victims' advocacy services, and include the impact their victimization has had on their lives in a victim impact statement to be presented in the PSI

MODELS OF PROBATION SUPERVISION

As is the case with all occupations, the effectiveness of probation and parole officers' performance ranges from dismal to outstanding. Their job is complex and quite dangerous because of daily contact with offenders and the nature of the contacts they have with them. Probation and parole officers concentrate their efforts on offenders who are at the highest risk of recidivism, and these are the most dangerous. Contacts with offenders include home visits, office visits, and employment checks; offenders are subjected to unannounced home visits, searches of their person and homes, random urine testing, and sometimes polygraph testing to monitor compliance with conditions of supervision. None of these intrusions endear probation and parole officers to the offenders whom they supervise.

One of the biggest problems in probation and parole work is gaining the trust of their probationers and parolees and developing rapport with them. In addition to exercising a very large degree of control over their offenders, probation and parole officers differ greatly from them demographically. Most officers are white and middle class, whereas many of their "clients" are minorities, and while most probationers and parolees are male, about half of probation officers are female (Walsh & Stohr, 2010). It is very difficult for both officers and probationers to overcome the class, race, and gender divides and for each to understand and appreciate where the other is "coming from." Nevertheless, the job must be done as effectively as possible.

The measures of correctional effectiveness are how well the community is protected from the offenders on an officer's caseload (law enforcement role) and how well their offenders are able to resolve their criminogenic problems and become decent, law-abiding citizens (social-work role). There is often tension between these supposedly contradictory roles (Skeem & Manchak, 2008), although there need not be. One chief probation officer referred to this so-called conflict in a question-and-answer session:

? ETHICAL ISSUE 8.1

What Would You Do?

You are a probation officer assigned to write a PSI report on a burglary case that resulted in the loss of over $1,000 in property and in which the house was trashed. Upon reading the police report, you realize that the house is that of a very close friend who was devastated by the experience. You realize that you can slant the report to put the offender in the worst possible light and recommend a stiff sentence for him, thus exacting "revenge" for your friend. Would you do this, or would you still try to be as objective as possible and go ahead and write the report? Alternatively, would you realize your bias, tell your supervisor the circumstances, and request that the report be assigned to another officer?

When I'm asked at a meeting with probation officers, "Are we supposed to be cops or social workers?" I answered with another question—"How many of you are parents of teenagers?" I asked those who raised their hands, "Would you say you are a cop or social worker?" One of those that raised his hand said, "At different times, I was both." Bingo! (as cited in Klingele, 2013, p. 1030)

Some officers take on an exclusively law enforcement role and embrace working values, emphasizing strict compliance with probation conditions and holding offenders strictly accountable. Other officers take on the counselor role, providing offenders with whatever is available in the community to bring about behavior change. The extent to which officers follow these different models depends not only on the personalities and training of the individual officers but also on the overall supervision model dictated by whether their department's philosophy is punitive or rehabilitative, which, in turn, is dictated by the ideology of local politicians.

A third group of officers combines the two roles and follows a "hybrid" approach, which means they follow both the law enforcement and social-work models, when appropriate. Skeem and Manchak (2008) view the law enforcer as authoritarian and the counselor as permissive but see the hybrid officer as authoritative, the kind of parenting style that psychologists tell us the most effective parents adopt (Grusec & Hastings, 2007). Authoritarian officers are inflexible disciplinarians who require unquestioning compliance with their demands. Such a style often leads to hostility and rebelliousness among those to whom it is directed.

Permissive officers set few rules and are reluctant to enforce those that are set. This style often results in the perception among their probationers that the officer is a "pushover," and it practically invites lack of respect and noncompliance. Authoritative officers are hybrids who are firm enforcers but fair, knowing that boundaries must be set and consequences endured for venturing beyond them. They clearly describe those boundaries and the consequences for crossing them (the law enforcement role) but also offer guidance and support to probationers (the social-work role) so that they may be better able to stay within those boundaries.

How well do these different styles do with respect to the dual roles of community protection and offender rehabilitation? One study found that in terms of technical violations such as failure to comply with some condition of probation, 43% of probationers supervised by law enforcement–oriented officers, 5% of probationers supervised by a treatment-oriented officer, and 13% supervised by a "hybrid" officer received a technical violation (Paparozzi & Gendreau, 2005). These findings are as expected: Law enforcers do not tolerate any violations, counselors tolerate almost every violation, and hybrids, like good and concerned parents, tolerate selectively. New criminal convictions are a better measure of supervision effectiveness than technical violations, however, because while technical violations are largely in the hands of officers, new criminal convictions are out of their hands. Offenders with treatment-oriented social-work officers were convicted of new crimes at twice (32% versus 16%) the rate of those supervised by law enforcement officers, whereas only 6% of offenders supervised by hybrid officers were convicted of a new crime.

Further evidence for the effectiveness of the authoritative hybrid model comes from the success of

ETHICAL ISSUE 8.2 ?

What Would You Do?

You are 32-year-old Mary Mitchell's probation officer. She has been on your caseload for almost two years since pleading guilty to shoplifting and drug possession. She has been a model probationer who has maintained employment, never missed an appointment with you, paid all of her fines and court costs, and has never tested positive for drug use. Now she has missed two appointments in a row and has not returned your phone calls. You go to her home to investigate and find her lying on a couch, disheveled and obviously high. She tells you that she is deeply depressed because her mother passed away a month ago and that she cannot face the world without her. She begs you not to violate her probation since she only has two more months to serve. What are your options here, and what do you think you should or will do?

PERSPECTIVE FROM A PRACTITIONER

Brian Fallock, Probation and Parole Officer

Position: Probation and parole agent

Location: Pennsylvania Board of Probation and Parole

Education: BA in administration of justice, University of Pittsburgh

What are your duties and responsibilities?

The primary responsibility of a probation and parole (P&P) agent is to ensure the safety of the community by supervising offenders on parole and probation, released from a state correctional institution or county prison. While doing this, P&P agents also will assist offenders in adequately reentering into society through numerous techniques and programs to hopefully reduce recidivism and provide the offenders with the tools they need to stay out of jail. Agents refer offenders to outside agencies for specialized therapy in order to assist them in dealing with problems that need special attention, such as employment, drugs, alcohol, and sexual and mental-health problems. If an offender does violate, agents are responsible for requesting a warrant for their arrest through a superior and physically taking an offender into custody with the assistance of other agents or police agencies. P&P agents also participate in court proceedings, providing testimony on the adjustment of offenders in the community and answering questions concerning agency policy and procedures so the court can make an accurate decision pertaining to an offender who has violated his or her supervision.

What are the characteristics and traits most useful in your line of work?

Strong interpersonal skills are recommended, as you will be dealing with many offenders from different backgrounds, as well as dealing with the offenders' families on a daily basis. Agents routinely work with various local and state law enforcement agencies, and being able to work with others to achieve a common goal is encouraged. Good time management and organizational skills are a must, as you will consistently have numerous issues to deal with simultaneously and will need to be able to keep track of them. Communication and writing skills are also required, as there are various reports and notes that will need to be submitted on a regular basis.

Please describe your typical workday.

As a field agent, I am required to make field contacts with offenders, whether at their home, job, or elsewhere. Every offender is assigned a level of supervision that dictates policy regarding how often you are required to see that offender in a given supervision period. A typical workday will involve traveling through your assigned area of supervision, making attempts to see your offenders and their families to monitor their adjustment back into society. Agents will also communicate with various treatment agencies to ensure the offender's compliance with the program he or she is enrolled in. If scheduled, agents will attend various court hearings to provide testimony and evidence proving any violations and detailing an offender's history while under supervision. When needed, agents will spend time in the district office writing reports, answering e-mails, and making phone calls.

What is your advice to someone who wants to enter your field?

Being a P&P agent can be challenging. P&P agents are often said to wear numerous hats, depending on the situation. One minute you could be wearing a "law enforcement hat" that will require you to violate offenders (determine they have violated parole) or take them into custody. The next minute you could be wearing a "social-worker hat" where you are referring offenders to other agencies to get any help they need. To be successful in this type of work, you need to be flexible and hardworking. But you also need to keep in mind that these offenders can be dangerous, and you need to be cautious and on your toes at all times. You cannot become complacent, as there is no such thing as a "routine contact." Anything can happen, and you need to be prepared. But along with being challenging, being a P&P officer can be extremely rewarding. You will be able to provide guidance to offenders and give them the tools they need to be a contributing member of society, and hopefully, they will complete their supervision successfully. Reducing recidivism is key, and if the offender is willing to change, P&P agents are on the front lines and can have a great effect on it.

Hawaii's Opportunity Probation with Enforcement (HOPE) program. According to the judge that initiated the program, it is based on the principles of effective parenting and on Beccaria's notion that consequences for misbehavior will be swift, certain, and proportionate to the severity of the misbehavior (as cited in Alm, 2013). HOPE begins with a formal warning that *no* violation of probation conditions will be tolerated, and any violation will *immediately* result in a short jail stay. The program has been shown to be so remarkably successful (it will be examined in greater detail in Chapter 15) that a number of states have implemented similar programs, such as Delaware's Decide Your Time (DYT) program (O'Connell, Visher, Martin, Parker, & Brent, 2011).

PROBATION OFFICER STRESS

Audio 8.2: After Thousands of Inmates Released Early, Probation Officers Will Be Watching

Supervising criminal offenders as a probation and parole officer is not the easiest or most lucrative job in the world, although by today's job standards, the pay and stability are excellent. Unlike police officers and correctional officers, probation and parole officers are almost universally required to hold a bachelor's degree because the job is considered to be more complex. According to the Bureau of Labor Statistics (BLS, 2014), in 2013, probation officers earned a median (half below and half above that figure) salary of $53,360. Experience and location strongly affect salaries. Officers in California had the highest ($78,060) median salary, and officers in Idaho ($37,350) had the lowest. Additionally, federal, state, and local benefits are much better than those typically provided by the private sector and include paid vacations; sick leave; pension plans (a rare thing in private-sector jobs these days); and health, dental, and life insurance plans.

In common with police officers and correctional officers, probation and parole officers are dealing with difficult human beings on a daily basis, often without the tools and support needed to do the job as it should be done. Doing a demanding and sometimes dangerous job under less-than-adequate conditions can and does lead to stress (Slate, Wells, & Wesley Johnson, 2003). For instance, one study of officers in four states found that 35% to 55% reported that they had been victims of threatened or actual violence (Finn & Kuck, 2005). Stress is a physical and emotional state of tension as the body reacts to environmental challenges (stressors). No one can be expected to do a very good job while experiencing stress.

The most important job stressors identified by the officers surveyed by Slate et al. (2003) were poor salaries, poor promotion opportunities, excessive paperwork, lack of resources from the community, large caseloads, and a general frustration with the inadequacies of the criminal justice system. These stressors may eventually lead to psychological withdrawal from the job, which means that probationers—and thus, the community—are getting shortchanged. High stress levels in the department also lead to frequent absenteeism and high rates of employee turnover; thus, it is imperative that the issue of probation and parole officer stress be meaningfully addressed.

Slate et al. (2003) emphasize that attempts to address the problem of probation officer stress should not be one of counseling officers on how to cope with stress because the problem is organizational (inherent in the probation system), not personal. They suggest that participatory management strategies be instituted so that each person in the department participates in the decision-making process and thus feels valued and empowered. The researchers found that personnel who did participate in decision making reported fewer stress symptoms and were happier on the job. Participatory management (workplace democracy) leads to a happier and more productive workforce, even if nothing else changes—"contented cows give better milk."

POLICY AND RESEARCH | The EPICS Model of Probation Supervision

The operating policy of every probation department is contained in its mission statement, which typically contains goals that contribute to community safety through positive offender change aimed at reducing recidivism. Departments are increasingly aware that this must range beyond simply monitoring offenders' behavior, waiting for violations to occur, and then applying sanctions. A number of departments are requiring officers to undergo an innovative training program devised by correctional specialists at the University of Cincinnati called Effective Practices in Community Supervision (EPICS). According to Smith, Schweitzer, Labrecque, and Latessa (2012), "The purpose of the EPICS model is to teach community supervision officers how to translate the principles of effective intervention into practice, and, more specifically, how to use core correctional practices in face-to-face interactions with offenders" (p. 189).

EPICS teaches officers methods to change criminal thinking patterns, decrease their criminal offending, and provide accountability. It shifts resources from low-risk probationers to provide more intensive concentration on medium- and high-risk probationers. It trains officers how to identify criminal thinking, teach prosocial behaviors, reinforce acceptable behavior, and correctly sanction unacceptable behavior. It emphasizes the development of collaborative relationships between officers and offenders by training officers in active listening skills using techniques such as motivational interviewing (to be explained in Chapter 10) and equipping them to teach social and problem-solving skills through providing offenders with carrot-and-stick positive and negative reinforcements.

The four components of the EPICS system are *check-in*, *review*, *intervention*, and *homework*. The *check-in* involves an officer–offender meeting designed to build rapport, hold a discussion about compliance with probation orders, and deal with any difficulties the offender may have. A *review* consists of a discussion about what was said in the check-in session and what the offender has done in response to it. *Intervention* is the process of identifying the offender's risks and needs (this process is examined fully in Chapter 9) and teaching relevant skills or referring him or her to an agency specializing in such matters. The *homework* component consists of assigning the offender to tasks where he or she is to apply any new skill that is to be demonstrated at the next meeting.

EPICS has been shown to be quite effective in a number of studies in terms of compliance and lower recidivism rates compared with offenders not supervised under the model. It has also been shown to increase probation officers' job satisfaction. While EPICS is a relatively new model of community supervision, Smith et al. (2012) state that

preliminary results from several jurisdictions suggest that the use of core correctional practices within the context of community supervision has been associated with meaningful reductions in offender recidivism. This work affirms the role of probation and parole officers as agents of behavioral change, and provides empirical support for the notion that community supervision can be effective. (pp. 189–190)

DISCUSSION QUESTIONS

1. Is it a good idea to shift resources from low-risk offenders in order to concentrate on higher-risk offenders? What impact might this have on low-risk offenders?

2. Do programs such as EPICS turn probation and parole officers into agents of behavioral change (social workers or psychologists) at the expense of their law enforcement roles?

3. What aspects of EPICS do you think contribute most to its apparent success?

References

Bourgon, G. (2010). The role of program design, implementation, and evaluation in evidence-based "real world" community supervision. *Federal Probation, 74,* 2–15.

Smith, P., Schweitzer, M., Labrecque, R., & Latessa, E. (2012). Improving probation officers' supervision skills: An evaluation of the EPICS model. *Journal of Crime and Justice, 35,* 189–199.

© Jessica Miller

PHOTO 8.3: A probation officer's job is highly varied, ranging from interviewing police officers, victims, family members of the defendant, as well as the defendant him/herself, to making midnight raids on a probationer's home.

••• STRATEGIES TO REDUCE RECIDIVISM

AP Video 8.1: TI Court Appearance

PROBATION VIOLATIONS AND GRADUATED SANCTIONS

In these days of severe budget cuts and the concerns of cost-conscious politicians, there has been a tendency to turn to evidence-based research to see what can be done to reduce probation revocations (Klingele, 2013). After all, one of the advantages of probation is supposed to be saving the taxpayer money, and probation is hardly a cost cutter if it is simply a deferred incarceration. We have seen that 15% of probationers were ultimately incarcerated in 2013 (Herberman & Bonczar, 2015), which amounts to almost 600,000 individuals, and probation violators constitute about one third of all individuals admitted to prison each year (Klingele, 2013). Probation officers enjoy a certain amount of discretion as to whether or not to formally violate someone's probation and the reasons why he or she will do so. A formal PV (probation violation) goes before the sentencing judge with a recommendation from the officer regarding whether or not the suspended prison sentence should be imposed.

One of the ways state legislatures and correctional departments have addressed the issue is by turning to actuarial assessment tools devised by criminal justice researchers to determine the circumstances for technical and, in some cases, minor criminal violations of probation. Table 8.1 presents one such tool, used by the Vermont Department of Corrections, that is designed to eliminate costly court appearances and incarcerations for offenders whose violations do not bear directly on their threat to the community or their rehabilitation.

Note that both the violations and the sanctions attached to them have a three-level hierarchy of increasing seriousness of violation and increasing severity of punishment. Under this scheme, offenders are only brought before a judge for technical violations after they reach Level 3 violations and after all appropriate casework interventions have been exhausted. While state legislatures have designed these assessment tools primarily as cost-cutting devices, they also appear to be useful correctional tools by providing officers with a uniform way of responding to violations, thus making authoritarian law enforcement–oriented officers less punitive and permissive social-work-oriented officers less indulgent with offenders' technical violations.

TABLE 8.1   Graduated Sanctions Guideline for Technical Probation Violations

LEVEL 1 VIOLATIONS	LEVEL 1 SANCTIONS
➤ Failure to report as instructed	➤ Graduated Sanction Thinking Report
➤ Out of Place	➤ Apology (verbal or written)
➤ 1st positive drug/alcohol test	➤ Verbal warning
➤ Refusal of drug/alcohol test	➤ Develop Relapse Prevention Plan
➤ Missed treatment/programming group	➤ Written essay/educational activities
➤ Unemployment or failure to seek employment within 45 days	➤ Increase contacts for up to 30 days
➤ Failure to fulfill financial obligations	➤ Increase curfew restrictions for up to 30 days
➤ Failure to follow case plan/ORP	➤ Use of schedules for up to 30 days
➤ Failure to complete community service	➤ DOC work crew
➤ Curfew Violation	

LEVEL 2 VIOLATIONS	LEVEL 2 SANCTIONS
➤ Multiple Level 1 violations	➤ Referral for treatment assessment
➤ Non-compliance with Special Conditions not indicated above	➤ Community Service Work for up to 80 hours
➤ Continued substance abuse or 2nd positive drug/alcohol test	➤ Community Restitution Work Crew for up to 10 days
➤ Continued missed treatment/programming group	➤ Curfew/Restriction to residence
➤ Failure to comply with Level 1 sanctions	➤ Increased reporting as directed for Alco-sensor, drug testing employment search, or other related activity
➤ Contact with restricted persons (Non-Sex Offender/Domestic Violence)	➤ Activities to address risk behaviors (self-help)
➤ Tampering with electronic monitoring equipment	➤ Loss of curfew/placed on schedule
	➤ Modification of the case plan to address risk-related behavior
	➤ Any Level 1 sanction
	➤ Use of Electronic Monitoring Equipment along with Level 1 sanction for up to 60 days

LEVEL 3 VIOLATIONS	LEVEL 3 SANCTIONS
➤ Multiple Level 2 violations	➤ Use of Electronic Monitoring Equipment along with Level 2 sanction for up to 60 days
➤ Failure to comply with Level 2 sanctions	➤ Modified Conditions of Probation (risk-related)
➤ Non-threatening contact with victim	
➤ Suspension or placed on probation in treatment/programming group	
➤ Misdemeanor behavior (Non-risk/Non-violent)	
➤ Out of Place for more than 24 hours	

Source: Vermont Department of Corrections (2010). *Graduated sanctions for technical violation of probation in lieu of court referral*. http://www.doc.state.vt.us/about/policies/rpd/rules/rpd/correctional-services-301-550/335-350-district-offices-general/doc-policy-347-graduated-sanctions-for-technical-violations-of-probation-in-lieu-of-court-referral

ENGAGING THE COMMUNITY TO PREVENT RECIDIVISM

Video 8.2: Offender Credits DOC Course for Changing His Behavior

Although probation began as a voluntary community effort in the United States and Britain, community involvement in offender rehabilitation has faded in those countries with the professionalization of probation. Japan is a country in which probation volunteers still dominate. In Japan, there are about 50,000 volunteer officers but only 800 professional officers (T. Ellis, Lewis, & Sato, 2011).

Western countries probably cannot revive the old level of community involvement, and cultural differences preclude volunteerism at anywhere near Japanese levels. (A volunteer probation officer position is highly sought in Japan because it confers high status [Gardner, 1996].) To achieve the average 2.5 ratio of probationers to volunteer probation officers that is enjoyed in Japan (only about 60,000 adults on probation there in 2010 [T. Ellis et al., 2011]) with our approximately 4 million probationers would require about 1.6 million volunteer officers. Nevertheless, we can engage our communities in the process of offender rehabilitation more than we are doing, realizing that whatever helps the offender helps the community.

Career Video 8.1: Director of IT and Electronic Security

Many probation departments across the United States offer opportunities to volunteer with them. It is an opportunity to give something back to the community and, if you are interested in a career in the field, to get your feet in the door. The Orange County Probation Department in California provides the information in In Focus 8.1 for becoming a volunteer probation officer.

IN FOCUS 8.1

Becoming a Volunteer Probation Officer in Orange County

The Volunteer Probation Officer (VPO) Program offers a unique opportunity to be a part of the exciting and challenging field of criminal justice. VPOs receive 40 hours of classroom training, two on-site visits to the Orange County Probation Juvenile Institutions, and 24 hours of on-the-job training. VPOs are enabled to perform duties similar to those of the department's deputy probation officer. Participants will gain personal satisfaction, work experience, and an opportunity to develop new skills in an exciting and challenging field.

Minimum Requirements for VPO Applicants

- Be at least 21 years old
- Be a U.S. citizen
- Have a valid California driver's license
- Commit to a minimum of 20 hours per month for one year
- Have no felony convictions or history that would disqualify you as a peace officer candidate

- Pass a background investigation and psychological evaluation

Volunteer probation officers work with and under the supervision of deputy probation officers. The Volunteer Probation Officer Program offers a unique opportunity for citizens to be involved. VPOs are provided the opportunity to assist in the following areas:

- Investigation of adult and juvenile cases
- Field monitored caseloads
- Making home, work, and jail visits
- Telephonic compliance checks
- Victim contacts and collateral information
- Residence and employment verification
- Requesting record checks
- Providing bilingual services
- Working with juveniles in drug treatment programs
- And much more!

IN FOCUS 8.2

Community Supervision and Recidivism

It is an article of faith among police officers that it is only a matter of time before a probationer or parolee commits another crime, but little is known about the probability of a person under community supervision being arrested versus someone not under supervision being arrested. An ambitious effort to find out was conducted by the Council of State Governments Justice Center (CSGJC, 2013) based on adult arrests occurring in four California jurisdictions (Los Angeles County, San Bernardino County, Sacramento County, and San Francisco County) from January 2008 to June 2011. Figure 8.4 shows that probationers and parolees, combined, accounted for just over 22% of the total arrests. However, 40% of arrestees not under supervision

at the time had histories of prior criminal justice supervision. The 106,727 people under supervision were about 1% of the combined population of over 14 million people residing in those counties. Thus, factoring out characteristics of individuals not likely to be arrested—such as the very young and the very old—probationers and parolees are, at the very least, 10 times more likely to be arrested than individuals in general. The crimes for which probationers and parolees were most likely to be arrested were drug related.

Source: http://ocgov.com/gov/probation/employment/volunteer/vpo

The criminological literature provides abundant support for the notions that social bonds (Hirschi, 1969) and social capital (Sampson & Laub, 1999) are powerful barriers against criminal offending. Social bonds are connections (often emotional in nature) to others and to social institutions that promote prosocial behavior and discourage antisocial behavior. Social capital refers to a store of positive relationships in social networks on which the individual can draw for support. It also means that a person with social capital has acquired an education and other solid credentials that enable him or her to lead a prosocial life. Those who have opened their social-capital accounts early in life (bonding with parents, school, and other prosocial networks) may spend much of it freely during adolescence but nevertheless manage to salvage a sufficiently tidy nest egg by the time

FIGURE *8.4* Comparing Probationer and Parolee Arrests With Arrests of People Not Under Supervision in Four California Counties, January 2008 to June 2011

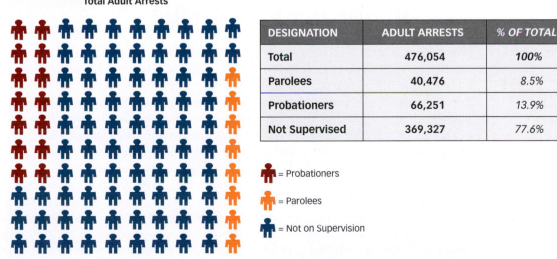

Total Adult Arrests

DESIGNATION	ADULT ARRESTS	% OF TOTAL
Total	476,054	100%
Parolees	40,476	8.5%
Probationers	66,251	13.9%
Not Supervised	369,327	77.6%

= Probationers

= Parolees

= Not on Supervision

Source: Council of State Governments Justice Center (2013). *The impact of probation and parole populations on arrest in four California cities.* http://www.cdcr.ca.gov/Reports/docs/External-Reports/CAL-CHIEFS-REPORT.pdf

they reach adulthood to keep them on the straight and narrow. The idea is that they are not likely to risk losing this nest egg by engaging in criminal activity (the contrast effect again). Most criminals, on the other hand, lack social bonds, and largely because of this, they lack the stake in conformity provided by a healthy stash of social capital.

If we consider the great majority of felons in terms of deficiency (good things that they *lack*) rather than in terms of personal pathology (bad things that they *are)*, we are talking about a deficiency in social capital. The community can be seen as a bank in which social capital is stored and from which offenders can apply for a loan. That is, the community is the repository of all of those things from which social capital is derived, such as education, employment, and networks of prosocial individuals in various organizations and clubs (e.g., Alcoholics Anonymous, churches, hobby or interest centers, and so on). Time spent involved in steady employment and with prosocial others engaged in prosocial activities is time unavailable to spend in idleness in the company of antisocial others planning antisocial activities. The old saying that "the devil finds work for idle hands" may be trite, but it is also very true.

Thus, good case management in community corrections requires community involvement. No community corrections agency is able to deliver services for the full range of offender needs (mental health, substance abuse, vocational training, welfare, etc.) by itself, and thus, officers consider themselves intermediaries or brokers of community services. Probation and parole officers not only must assess the needs of their charges but also must be able to locate and network with the social-service agencies that address those needs as their primary function. In fact, there are those who maintain that the probation and parole officer's relationships with community service agencies are more important than their relationship with their probationers and parolees (Walsh & Stohr, 2010).

Figure 8.5 illustrates the central role of the probation (or parole) officer in community efforts to make the community safe. Officers receive all kinds of information (concerns and complaints) from people in the community that they have to assess and then decide on a method of action. If the officer decides that the concern is beyond his or her expertise, then he or she will refer it to the appropriate agency. Officers must be skilled at networking with the various agencies if they are to help provide offenders with the services they need. This brokerage function can be best achieved with fewer offenders who are intensively supervised on an officer's caseload than with many who are infrequently seen and haphazardly supervised.

••• INTERMEDIATE SANCTIONS

Journal Article 8.1: Extralegal Disparity in the Application of Intermediate Sanctions

Intermediate sanctions: Refers to a number of innovative alternative sentences that may be imposed in place of the traditional prison-or-probation dichotomy.

As we see in Figure 8.6, there are a large number of sentencing options that are intermediate, between prison and simple supervised probation. **Intermediate sanctions** refer to these alternative sentences that may be imposed in place of the traditional prison-versus-probation dichotomy. Such sanctions are considered intermediate because they are seen as more punitive than straight probation but less punitive than prison. However, they are most often part of a probation order and are thus discussed in this chapter. They are a way of easing prison overcrowding and avoiding the financial cost of prison while providing the community with higher levels of safety through higher levels of offender supervision and surveillance than is possible with regular probation. As we shall see, however, these supposed benefits are not always realized. We have already seen that many experienced offenders would choose prison over some of the more strict community-based alternatives. Furthermore, since offenders placed in some sort of alternative sanction program have recidivism rates not much different from offenders released from prison within the first and subsequent years, the costs of state incarceration are deferred rather than avoided (Klingele, 2013; Marion, 2002).

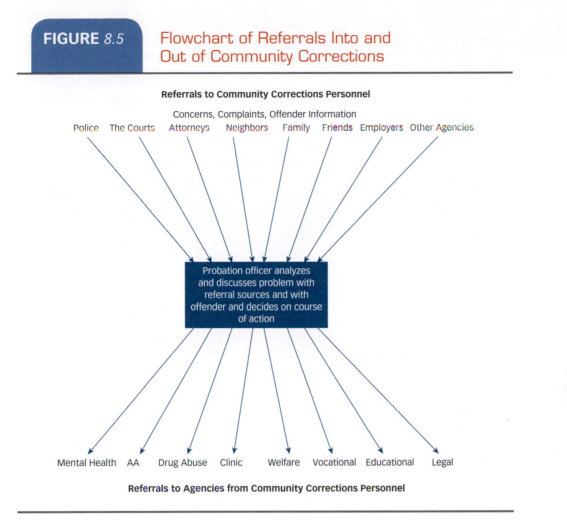

FIGURE 8.5   Flowchart of Referrals Into and Out of Community Corrections

Referrals to Community Corrections Personnel

Concerns, Complaints, Offender Information

Police   The Courts   Attorneys   Neighbors   Family   Friends   Employers   Other Agencies

Probation officer analyzes and discusses problem with referral sources and with offender and decides on course of action

Mental Health   AA   Drug Abuse   Clinic   Welfare   Vocational   Educational   Legal

Referrals to Agencies from Community Corrections Personnel

The first alternative in Figure 8.6 is community detention (jail) and is addressed elsewhere in this book. Split sentencing is simply a period of probation preceded by a jail sentence of up to 1 year. The work release option is the first intermediate sanction we examine. Halfway houses and electronic monitoring are examined in the next chapter.

WORK RELEASE

Work release programs are designed to control offenders in a secure environment while, at the same time, allowing them to maintain employment. Work release centers are usually situated in or adjacent to a county jail, but they can also be part of the state prison system. Residents of work release centers have typically been given a suspended sentence and placed on probation, with a specified time to be served in work release. Work release residents may also be parolees with special circumstances, such as new parolees who need close supervision or parole violators given another opportunity to remain in the community rather than being sent back to prison. Surveillance of work release residents is strict; they are allowed out only for the purpose of employment and are locked in the facility when not working. The advantage of such programs is that they allow offenders to maintain ties with their families and with employers. Such programs also save the taxpayer money because offenders pay the cost of their accommodation with their earnings.

Although offenders given a work release order are generally the least likely of all community-based corrections offenders to be rearrested and imprisoned within 5 years of successful

AP Video 8.2:
Lohan Reports to Jail

Video 8.3:
Inside the Mind of an Offender in the Work Release Program

Work release programs: Programs designed to control offenders in a secure environment while allowing them to maintain employment.

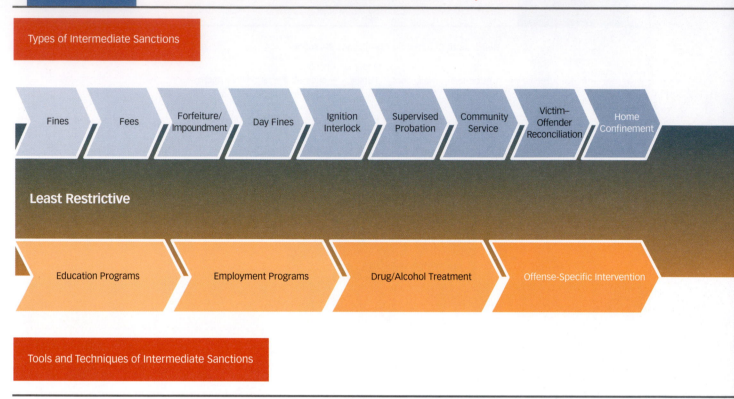

FIGURE *8.6*   The Continuum of Correctional Sanctions by Restrictiveness

Source: Center for Community Corrections (1997). Community corrections call for punishment that makes sense. U.S. Department of Justice.

completion, one study of a number of such programs found that 64% of offenders successfully released and 71% unsuccessfully released had further arrests within 5 years (Marion, 2002). Offenders chosen to partake in work release are typically chosen because, although they have committed a crime deemed too serious for regular probation, they are usually employed, although unemployed probationers can be placed in work release, contingent on their finding employment within a specified time (Abadinsky, 2009). Being employed is incompatible with a criminal lifestyle (although obviously, from the aforementioned statistics, not completely), especially if the offender is a probationer rather than a parolee.

As indicated before, work release is also used for reintegrating parolees. Research with parolees assigned to work release programs finds conflicting outcomes, although most are positive. A study of parolees in Minnesota by Grant Duwe (2014) matched 1,785 parolees assigned as work release participants with a comparison group of 1,785 parolees from the larger pool of inmates released between 2007 and 2010 and assigned normal parole supervision. It was found that work release significantly increased the probability of a parolee being returned to prison for a technical violation, which might be expected due to the rigid supervision of work release. On the other hand, work release significantly reduced the risk of reoffending and significantly increased the odds that parolees found a job, the hours they worked, and the total wages they earned. It was also found that work release produced an estimated benefit to the community $1.25 million overall, or about $700 for each work release participant. This benefit was produced by parolee payment of taxes, the costs of their own supervision, and rent in the work release facility (typically, $25 per day), plus the avoidance of further criminal justice costs because of lower rearrest rates.

Intensive-supervision probation (ISP): Probation that involves more frequent surveillance of probationers and that is typically limited to more serious offenders in the belief that there is a fighting chance that they may be rehabilitated (or to save the costs of incarceration).

INTENSIVE-SUPERVISION PROBATION

Intensive-supervision probation (ISP) is an intermediate sanction that arose in the 1980s out of concerns about growing prison populations and was based on a deterrence perspective

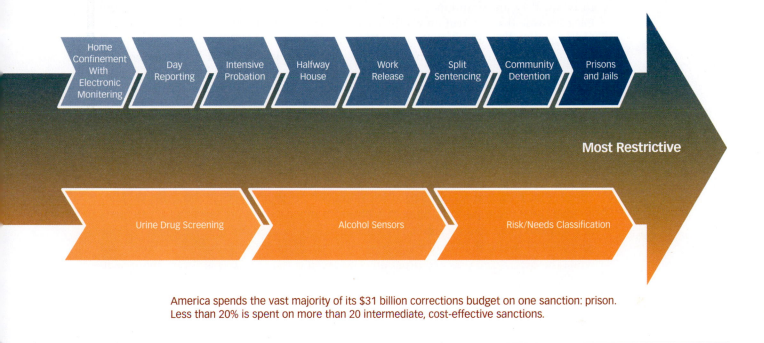

Home Confinement With Electronic Monitering | Day Reporting | Intensive Probation | Halfway House | Work Release | Split Sentencing | Community Detention | Prisons and Jails

Most Restrictive

Urine Drug Screening | Alcohol Sensors | Risk/Needs Classification

America spends the vast majority of its $31 billion corrections budget on one sanction: prison. Less than 20% is spent on more than 20 intermediate, cost-effective sanctions.

("This is your last chance; so behave yourself!") (Lowenkamp, Flores, Holsinger, Makarios, & Latessa, 2010). ISP is usually limited to offenders who probably should not be in the community but have been allowed to remain there, either in the belief that there is a fighting chance that they may be rehabilitated or in an effort to save the costs of incarceration. ISP officers' caseloads are drastically reduced (typically a caseload of 25) to allow officers to more closely supervise offenders, often on a daily basis, with frequent drug testing and surveillance. Burrell (2006) describes ISP officers as "aggressive in their surveillance and punitive in their sanctions" (p. 4). Liberal critics of the tactics of ISP officers describe their model of supervision colorfully as one of "pee 'em and see 'em" or "tail 'em, nail 'em, and jail 'em" (Skeem & Manchak, 2008). This type of law enforcement surveillance is the kind of supervision required with high-risk offenders (Walsh & Stohr, 2010).

A study conducted by MacKenzie and Brame (2001) hypothesizes that ISP coerces offenders into prosocial activities that, in turn, lead to a lower probability of reoffending. Intensive supervision means that probation officers maintain more frequent contact with probationers and intrude into their lives more than is the norm with other probationers. Offenders on ISP are supervised at that level because they have the greatest probability of reoffending and are the most deficient in social capital. (They have high risk and high needs.) Higher levels of supervision allow officers to coerce offenders into a wide variety of educational and treatment programs and other prosocial activities designed to provide offenders with social capital. MacKenzie and Brame (2001) found that ISP does result in offenders being coerced into more prosocial activities and that there was a slight reduction in recidivism. The issue the study left unresolved is whether participating in prosocial activities enabled offenders to acquire skills that provided them with social capital that they could put to good use or if intensive supervision per se accounted for their findings.

The term *coercion* has negative connotations for the more libertarian types among us ("you can lead a horse to water, but you can't make it drink"), but the great majority of people being treated for problems such as substance abuse have very large boot prints impressed on their backsides. Probationers and parolees, almost by definition, will not voluntarily place themselves in the kinds of programs and activities we would like them to be in; they are simply not motivated in that direction. The criminal justice system must provide that motivation via the judicious use of carrots and sticks. Reviews of the U.S. (Farabee, Pendergast, & Anglin, 1998) and UK (Barton, 1999) literature on coerced substance abuse treatment concluded that coerced treatment often has more positive outcomes than voluntary treatment, probably because of the threat of criminal justice sanctions.

Overall, research on deterrence and surveillance ISP programs has found disappointing results. Gendreau, Goggin, Cullen, and Andrews (2000) pooled findings from 47 different ISP programs and found, at best, that they had no effect on recidivism, and at worst, some actually increased it. On a more positive note, a study of 58 different ISP programs by Lowenkamp and his colleagues (2010) found that they can be effective in reducing recidivism, albeit minimally, if they meet certain criteria. They divided these programs into those that provided intensive human services for offenders ($n = 42$) and those that focused on deterrence ($n = 16$) and found that the human service programs showed an overall small but statistically significant reduction in recidivism while the deterrence-oriented programs evidenced a statistically significant increase in recidivism.

SHOCK PROBATION OR PAROLE AND BOOT CAMPS

Shock probation was initiated in Ohio in the 1970s and was designed to shock offenders into desisting from crime by briefly exposing them to the horrors of prison. It was limited to first offenders who had perhaps been unimpressed with the realities of prison life until given a taste. Under this program, offenders were sentenced to prison, released after (typically) 30 days, and placed on probation. In some states, a person may receive shock parole, which typically means that he or she has remained in prison longer than the shock probationer and is released under the authority of the parole commission rather than to the courts. Most of the research on this kind of shock treatment was conducted in the 1970s and 1980s and concluded that shock probationers and parolees had lower recidivism rates than incarcerated offenders not released under shock conditions (Vito, Allen, & Farmer, 1981). This should not be surprising, however, given the fact that those selected for shock probation or parole were either first offenders or repeaters who had not committed very serious crimes.

When we hear of shock incarceration today, it is typically incarceration in a so-called boot camp. **Correctional boot camps** are facilities modeled after military boot camps. Normally, only relatively young and nonviolent offenders are sent to correctional boot camps. They are usually there for short periods (90 to 180 days) and are subjected to military-style discipline and physical and educational programs. Boot camps are the most unpopular sentencing alternative with offenders. In May et al.'s (2005) analysis of exchange rates, discussed earlier, offenders who had served time in prison would only be willing to spend an average of 4.65 months in boot camp to avoid 12 months in prison. Interestingly, judges and probation and parole officers also agree that boot camp is more punitive than prison, estimating that their charges would be willing to serve only 6.19 and 6.05 months, respectively, to avoid 12 months in prison (Moore, May, & Wood, 2008).

Wilson, MacKenzie, and Ngo's (2010) description of the typical boot camp experience may explain why people "in the know" would rather do 2 or 3 times as much time in prison as in a boot camp. In the typical boot camp, participants are required to arise

Correctional boot camps: Facilities modeled after military boot camps, where young and nonviolent offenders are subjected to military-style discipline and physical and educational programs.

early each morning and follow a rigorous daily schedule of activities, including drill, ceremony, and physical training. Correctional officers are given military titles, and participants are required to use these titles when addressing them. Staff and inmates are required to wear uniforms. Punishment for misbehavior is immediate and swift and usually involves some type of physical activity, such as push-ups. Frequently, groups of inmates enter the boot camps as squads or platoons. There is often an elaborate intake ceremony where inmates are immediately required to follow the rules, respond to staff in an appropriate way, stand at attention, and have their heads shaved. Many boot camps have graduation ceremonies for those who successfully complete the program, and family mem-

PHOTO 8.4: Boot camps feature no-nonsense discipline and hard work modeled on military boot camps.

bers and others from the outside public frequently attend these events. The typical boot camp program is 3 months, although some run for 6 months or are part of a longer split sentence.

The idea of boot camps for young-adult offenders was once a popular idea among the general public, as well as among a considerable number of correctional personnel and criminal justice academics. Boot camps conjured up the movie image of a surly, slouching, and scruffy youth forced into the army who, two years later, proudly marched back into the old neighborhood with a crew cut, sparklingly clean and properly motivated and disciplined. Yes, the drill sergeant with righteous fire and brimstone would do what the family and social-work-tainted juvenile probation officers could never do.

Such magical transformations rarely happen in real life. The army merely provided many such youths with new opportunities to offend, and they spent much of their time either avoiding the MPs or lodged in the brig while awaiting their dishonorable discharges. Bottcher and Ezell's (2005) evaluation of offenders sent to correctional boot camp in California revealed the same sorry outcome. Specifically, they found no significant differences between their experimental group (boot campers) and a control group of similar offenders not sent to boot camp in terms of either property crime or violent-crime reoffending. In other words, boot camps have joined the woeful list of correctional programs that have proven ineffective.

VICTIM–OFFENDER RECONCILIATION PROGRAMS

Victim–offender reconciliation programs (VORPs) are programs designed to bring offenders and their victims together in an attempt to reconcile ("make right") the wrongs offenders have caused and are an integral component of the philosophy of **restorative justice**. This philosophy differs from models (retributive, rehabilitative, etc.) that are offender driven (what do we do with the offender?) in that it considers the offender, the victim, and the community as partners in restoring the situation to its previctimization status. Restorative justice has been defined as "every action that is primarily oriented toward justice by repairing the harm that has been caused by the crime . . . [and it] usually means a face-to-face confrontation between victim and perpetrator, where a mutually agreeable restorative solution is proposed and agreed upon" (Champion, 2005, p. 154). Restorative justice is often referred to as a **balanced approach**, in that it gives approximately

Video 8.4:
The Neuroscience of Restorative Justice

Web 8.2:
Restorative Justice

Victim–offender reconciliation programs (VORPs): Programs designed to bring offenders and their victims together in an attempt to reconcile the wrongs offenders have caused.

Restorative justice: A system of justice that gives approximately equal weight to community protection, offender accountability, and offender competency.

Balanced approach: A three-pronged goal of the juvenile justice system: (1) to protect the community, (2) to hold delinquent youths accountable, and (3) to provide treatment and positive role models.

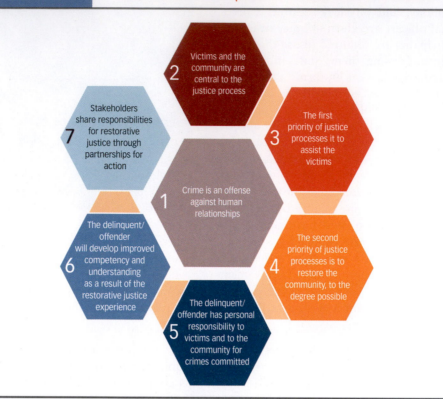

FIGURE *8.7*   The Seven Principles of Restorative Justice

Source: *Restorative Justice: Principles, Practices, and Implementation Training Broadcast.* U.S. Department of Justice, 2002. Available at http://nicic.gov/library/017612.

equal weight to community protection, offender accountability, and offender competency. Figure 8.7 provides the seven major principles or values of restorative justice. Note how it centers primarily on the victim and the community while still holding offenders responsible for their crimes.

Journal Articles 8.2: Effectiveness of Restorative Justice

Many crime victims are seeking fairness, justice, and restitution *as defined by them*, as opposed to revenge and punishment. While we saw in the chapter on sentencing that victims have an opportunity to provide input on a defendant's fate through a victim impact statement, VORPs provide more opportunities for victims to influence outcomes more broadly, which may provide a degree of satisfaction and a feeling that they are no longer the forgotten parties in criminal justice. Central to the VORP process is bringing together the victim and offender in face-to-face meetings mediated by a person trained in mediation theory and practice (Walsh & Stohr, 2010). Meetings are voluntary for both offender and victim and are designed to iron out ways in which the offender can make amends for the hurt and damage caused to the victim.

Victims participating in VORPs gain the opportunity to make offenders aware of their feelings of personal violation and loss and to lay out their proposals for how offenders can restore the situation. Offenders are afforded the opportunity to see firsthand the pain they have caused their victims and perhaps even to express remorse. The mediator assists the parties in developing a contract agreeable to both. The mediator monitors the terms of the contract and may schedule further face-to-face meetings.

VORPs are used most often in the juvenile system but are rarely used for violent crimes in either juvenile or adult systems. Where they are used, about 60% of victims invited to participate actually become involved, and a high percentage (mid- to high 90s) results in signed contracts (Coates, 1990). Mark Umbreit (1994) sums up the various satisfactions reported by victims who participated in VORPs:

1. Meeting offenders helped reduce their fear of being revictimized.

2. They appreciated the opportunity to tell offenders how they felt.

3. Being personally involved in the justice process was satisfying to them.

4. They gained insight into the crime and into the offender's situation.

5. They received restitution.

VORPs do not suit all victims, especially those who feel that the wrong done to them cannot so easily be "put right" and who want the offender punished to the fullest extent of the law (Olson & Dzur, 2004). In addition, the value of VORPs for the prevention of further offending has yet to be properly assessed. Studies do show lower recidivism rates for offenders participating in VORPs, but the problem is that because most programs are voluntary and because typically less serious offenders engage in them, we cannot know if the VORPs per se produced the change or if the experience of being processed through the system was itself enough to prevent further offending. However, strong advocates of this approach insist that the evidence is strong enough to claim that the VORP experience itself can prevent recidivism among a broad range of both adult and juvenile offenders (McAlinden, 2011).

SUMMARY

- Community-based corrections is a way of attempting to control the behavior of criminal offenders while keeping them in the community. Although conditional release (judicial reprieve) was practiced in ancient times, in common law, probation wasn't really established until the 20th century. Although often considered too lenient, community corrections benefits the public in many ways. Probation helps the offender in many ways, and what helps offenders automatically helps the communities they live in.

- There are many things to recommend probation over prison for many offenders, including saving the high cost of incarceration, allowing offenders to maintain family contacts and employment, and preventing them from becoming more embedded in a criminal lifestyle. However, there are many offenders who must be incarcerated for the safety of the community.

- Probation officers are both law enforcement officers and social workers. They follow a supervision style consistent with their department's philosophy and

their own personality. Some emphasize the law enforcement role, some emphasize the social-worker role, and some emphasize one or the other when the occasion arises. The latter supervision style, dubbed the hybrid style, consistently gets the best results.

- Both for cost-cutting and consistency concerns, many probation departments have initiated guidelines to determine officers' responses to technical violations. These guidelines graduate the severity of the sanctions imposed against offenders in accordance with the severity of his or her violations.

- Because of the dangers inherent in the job and officer perceptions of poor salaries, excessive paperwork, and large caseloads, among other things, probation officer stress is a major concern. However, the job can be interesting and exciting, and the median salary is about $10,000 more than the median salary of all occupations requiring a BA or BS in a social science.

- Engaging the community in the task of rehabilitating criminals should be a major concern of community supervision agencies. Engaging the community involves officers paying close attention to concerns and complaints flowing into them about offenders on their caseloads and being aware of the agencies outside their departments that offer services that may help offenders. It also means adopting effective volunteer probation officer programs within their departments.

- Intermediate sanctions are considered more punitive than regular probation but less punitive than prison, although experienced criminals do not necessarily share that view. Some of these programs, particularly work release, show positive results, although this may be more a function of the kinds of offenders placed in them rather than the programs themselves. Most participants in these programs, however, tend to recidivate at rates not significantly different from parolees.

- VORPs are a fairly recent addition to community corrections. They consider the victim, the offender, and the community as equal partners in returning the situation to its previctimization status. This idea of restorative justice is mostly used with juvenile offenders and younger adult offenders.

KEY TERMS

Balanced approach 195

Community corrections 176

Community corrections acts 177

Correctional boot camps 194

Intensive-supervision probation (ISP) 192

Intermediate sanctions 190

Judicial reprieve 174

National Probation Act of 1925 175

Probation 174

Restorative justice 195

Victim–offender reconciliation programs (VORPs) 195

Work release programs 191

DISCUSSION QUESTIONS

1. Looking at all the pros and cons of community-based corrections, do you think probation is too lenient for felony offenders? If so, what do we do with them?

2. In your opinion, what is the single biggest benefit of probation for the community, and what is its single greatest cost?

3. Studies show that about 95% of probation officers' sentencing recommendations to the courts are followed. Why do you think this is so, and is it a good or bad thing that probation officers control the flow of information to judges?

4. Should probation and parole officers carry guns if they are supposed to be social workers, as well as cops?

5. Boot camps have full and total control of offenders for up to 6 months, so why are they not able to change offenders' attitudes and behaviors?

6. Do you think police officers should be given the same powers of search and seizure as probation and parole officers for the purposes of controlling the activities of probationers and parolees?

USEFUL INTERNET SITES

Please note that the sites listed can be accessed at edge.sagepub.com/stohrcorrections.

American Probation and Parole Association: www.appa-net.org/eweb

This website provides a lot of useful information about all aspects of probation and parole.

Bureau of Labor Statistics: www.bls.gov/ooh/Community-and-Social-Service/Probation-officers-and-correctional-treatment-specialists.htm

If you are attracted to corrections work, this website gives you lots of information about pay, conditions, and opportunities, listed by state.

$SAGE edge™

Sharpen your skills with SAGE edge at **edge.sagepub.com/stohrcorrections**. SAGE edge for Students provides a personalized approach to help you accomplish your coursework goals in an easy-to-use learning environment. You'll find action plans, mobile-friendly eFlashcards, and quizzes as well as video, web, and resources and links to SAGE journal articles to support and expand on the concepts presented in this chapter.

9

Prisons and the Correctional Client

TEST YOUR KNOWLEDGE

Test your present knowledge of prisons by answering the following questions. Check your answers on page 536 after reading the chapter.

1. The incarceration rate in the United States remains the highest in the world. (True or false?)

2. Most inmates serve out their sentence in maximum-security prisons. (True or false?)

3. What factors describe a medium-security prison? How is it similar to and different from maximum- and minimum-security prisons?

4. What are *prisonization* and *importation* in the prison context?

5. What are gangs, and what role do they play in the prison subculture?

6. Why does violence exist in prisons?

7. Transgender inmates, particularly in men's prisons, are more likely to be sexually assaulted than any other group of inmates. (True or false?)

LEARNING OBJECTIVES

- Describe the differences between types of prisons

- Describe what factors affect the operation of prisons

- Explain what prisonization, mortification, importation, pains of imprisonment, and mature coping are and how they influence inmate behavior

- Evaluate the roles of inmates, staff, and prison gangs and why they exist in prisons

- Identify the reasons why violence, riots, and sexual assaults occur in prisons and some strategies for their reduction

- Describe the challenges of meeting the needs of aging, physically and mentally ill, and LGBTI (lesbian, gay, bisexual, transgender, and intersex) inmates in prisons

KITCHEN SUPERVISOR **SEXUALLY ABUSES TWO MALE INMATES**

The kitchen supervisor in a federal prison in Phoenix, Arizona, Carl David Evans, sexually abused two male inmates, whom he supervised ("Kitchen Supervisor Gets Prison Time," 2014). He would separately take the two inmates into a food storage area of the kitchen and give one of them a package of cigarettes (which, in turn, they could then sell for as much as $150 to other inmates) in exchange for sex. After the FBI learned of

the abuse of one of these inmates, they placed a video camera in the storage area and caught Evans and the inmates having sex.

Evans pleaded guilty to five of the federal charges against him in February 2013. He was sentenced to 36 months in prison, 3 years on supervised release, and a $5,000 fine ("Kitchen Supervisor Gets Prison Time," 2014, p. 20).

••• INTRODUCTION: THE STATE OF PRISONS

It has become axiomatic to say that correctional programs and institutions are overcrowded, underfunded, and unfocused these days. For the better part of 50 years, the drug war has raged on, mandatory sentencing has had its effect, and probation and parole caseloads and incarceration rates have spiraled out of control. As a consequence, though spending on corrections had, until recently, steadily and steeply climbed, it was and largely still is nearly impossible for most states and localities to meet the needs for programs, staff, and institutions. So they do not. As a consequence, the corrections experience for staff and offenders continues to be shaped by shortages.

However, in the last several years, there has been a reconsideration of the drug war: At the time of this writing (summer 2016), recreational marijuana has been legalized in four states (Alaska, Colorado, Oregon, and Washington) and Washington, D.C., and medical marijuana has been legalized in several others. It is likely that many more states will move to legalize marijuana in the near future. As is discussed in Chapter 5 of this book, a few years ago, Congress reduced the sentencing disparity between crack and powder cocaine. The effect of these two changes—marijuana legalization and reduced sentences for crack cocaine—has been to reduce correctional populations. In addition, several states have rescinded their mandatory sentences for drugs and other crimes (e.g., three-strikes laws), which is also limiting time spent in prisons (Garland et al., 2014). The shift in correctional treatment away from retribution and deterrence as the sole justifications for prisons and other forms of corrections has also reduced populations. (Some things do work for some people, and often, treatment works best in the community.) Finally, the cost of corrections for states and localities, particularly after the recession of 2007 hit, has caused those governmental units to shutter prisons and jails and to rethink the use of prisons, the most expensive correctional option (Cullen, Jonson, & Stohr, 2014). The collective effect of these changes in law and policy has been decarceration in several states and localities.

AP Photo/Brynn Anderson

PHOTO 9.1: A crowded dormitory at the Elmore Correctional Facility in Elmore, Alabama. Crowding makes the lives of inmates much harder, while it makes their supervision by staff more complicated and results in prisons that are much more dangerous.

Having written this and as has been discussed already in this text, it has always been somewhat true that the corrections experience has tended to be shaped by shortages. With the exception of the recent past, if it has been built or, in the case of probation and parole, offered, they will come—because, as with all corrections sentences, they are forced to. Cases in point, almost immediately after the first American prisons were built, Walnut Street Jail (1790), Auburn Prison (1819), Western Pennsylvania Prison (1826), and Eastern Pennsylvania Prison (1829) were full, and within a few years, they were expanded, or new prisons were under construction.

To say that crowding and corrections have always been linked, of course, is not to dismiss the negative effects of overfilling institutions. Certainly, despite some of the decarceration we are seeing across the United States, the combined incarceration rate for jails and prisons remains the highest in the Westernized world, at 690 per 100,000 U.S. residents, as of 2014 (Kaeble, Glaze, Tsoutis, & Minton, 2015, p. 3). By way of comparison, this rate was 748 in 2009 but has decreased since then (West, 2010, p. 4). Though the rate of incarceration is now the same as it was in 2000, at 690, the raw number of inmates in prisons has increased by roughly 167,000 since 2000, as the rate is based on the number of U.S. citizens, which has increased in those 14 years (Kaeble et al., 2015, p. 3; see also Figure 9.1). All of this means that, though we are seeing some decreases in the use of incarceration, the crowding of prisons is not a thing of the past.

In this chapter, we discuss the structure and operation of prisons. The inmate subculture that flourishes in prisons and the violence and gangs that bedevil them will also be reviewed. The nature of the correctional experience for individuals incarcerated in prisons is somewhat different from what those in jails or community corrections encounter, and those differences are explored here.

••• PRISON ORGANIZATIONS

CLASSIFICATION

As inmates enter the prison system from the courts, they are usually assessed at a classification or reception facility based on their crime, criminal history, escape risk, behavioral issues (if any), and health and programming needs. Women and children

Web 9.1:
Prison Security
Levels

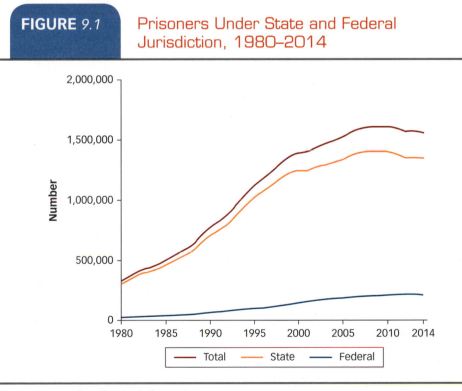

FIGURE 9.1   Prisoners Under State and Federal Jurisdiction, 1980–2014

Source: Bureau of Justice Statistics (n.d.).

are classified in separate facilities from adult males. This assessment includes the review of materials related to the inmate by reception center personnel and tests and observation of the inmate regarding his or her dangerousness and amenability to treatment. After being assessed by prison personnel for a period of weeks or months, inmates are sent to the prison that the personnel believe is the best fit, based first on security needs, followed by space available, and finally the inmate's needs. Inmates generally have no control over which prison they are sent to. Once they have done some time, inmates may request that they be moved to a facility that is closer to their family and friends, but such considerations are not a priority for classification and are more an option for adult males, as the facilities available for transfer for adult females and juveniles are much more limited because there are fewer of them.

Prisons: Correctional facilities used for long-term and convicted offenders.

PRISON TYPES AND LEVELS

Prisons were and are used for long-term and convicted offenders who are to be simultaneously punished (experience retribution), deterred, and reformed (rehabilitated)

POLICY AND RESEARCH

False Imprisonment as a Result of Wage Slavery

Sexual slavery and wage slavery are much in the news these days, as organized crime and criminal entrepreneurs take advantage of desperate and vulnerable people who want to enter the United States and other relatively prosperous nations where demand for low-cost goods, even if that means poverty wages for some, is high. Unfortunately, the United States has allowed such wage slavery and sexual-slavery entities a foothold on our shores, and local, state, and federal law enforcement are engaged in fighting another war on slavery in the 2010s. A key element of both types of slavery is *false imprisonment*, or illegally holding a person against his or her will.

In 2015, the Southern Poverty Law Center (SPLC), along with several firms donating their labor pro bono, won a coordinated lawsuit against a company that engaged in wage slavery. In this case, 500 Indian guest workers were lured to Mississippi in 2006 and 2008 with the promise of a well-paying job and a green card. One prospective worker paid a labor recruiter in India $12,000 for a chance at these opportunities. But when he arrived in the states, he instead discovered the horrific truth:

There would be no green card, but rather a 10-month worker visa. He was packed into a

guarded, isolated labor camp and forced to pay $1,050 a month to bunk with 23 other men in a space the size of a double-wide trailer. Their bags were regularly searched. No visitors were allowed. ("Jury Awards $14 Million," 2015, p. 1)

As these guest workers were paid slave-like wages, housed in slave-like conditions, and prevented from quitting (one man tried to leave and was physically detained), a federal district jury awarded the five men who brought the case $14 million and found that Signal International, its lawyer, and the Indian recruiter had engaged in labor trafficking, forced labor, fraud, racketeering, and discrimination. In one case, they were also found guilty of false imprisonment. The company had reportedly made $8 million by treating the workers this way.

DISCUSSION QUESTIONS

1. What do you think the appropriate sentence should be for people and companies who engage in labor and sex trafficking?

2. Why are such offenses increasing, even in Westernized countries, and what can be done to stop their spread?

while being isolated (incapacitated) from the community and, for most, reintegrated back into that community. As the number of prisons has expanded across the United States, their diversity has increased. Rather than just an all-purpose maximum- or medium-security prison, as was the norm when prisons were first built, there are state and federal prisons with myriad security levels, including supermaximum, maximum, medium, and minimum. There are prisons for men, women, men and women, children, and military personnel. Prisons come in the form of regular confinement facilities but also prison farms, prison hospitals, boot camps, reception centers, community corrections facilities (sometimes known as work release or day-reporting facilities), and others (Stephan, 2008).

By 2013, the number of inmates in federal prisons stood at 205,700, which is 3.7% more than in 2000 but about 2% less than in 2012 (Glaze & Kaeble, 2014, p. 12). Of these federal prisoners, 31,900 were in private facilities, which is over 3 times the number (9,400) from 2000 (Glaze & Kaeble, 2014, p. 12). But most inmates are in state prisons; only 16% are held in federal facilities. Public state prisons held 1,178,700 inmates while private state prisons held another 92,100 in 2013, or about 7% of inmates (Glaze & Kaeble, 2014, p. 12). The number of privately held state inmates was up by 18% from 2000 but down by 5% since 2012. Only 1,400 inmates were held in military prisons in 2013—the same number as in 2012 and about 1,000 less than in 2000 (Glaze & Kaeble, 2014, p. 13).

As indicated in Figure 9.2, as of 2005 (the latest Census of State and Federal Correctional Facilities data available at the time of writing), there were 1,821 state and federal prisons in the United States, 1,406 of which were public and 415 of which were under private contract with either a state or the federal government (Stephan, 2008, p. 2). Most prisons were operated or under contract with the states (1,719) rather than the federal government (102). Although only about one fifth of the prisons in the United States are designated as maximum security, because of their size, they hold about a third of the inmates incarcerated in this country (Stephan, 2008, pp. 2, 4). In contrast, medium-security prisons constitute about one fourth of prisons but hold two fifths of inmates—again, perhaps because of their relatively large size compared with minimum-security prisons, which are about a half of all prisons but hold only about one fifth of inmates

| FIGURE 9.2 | State and Federal Correctional Facilities |

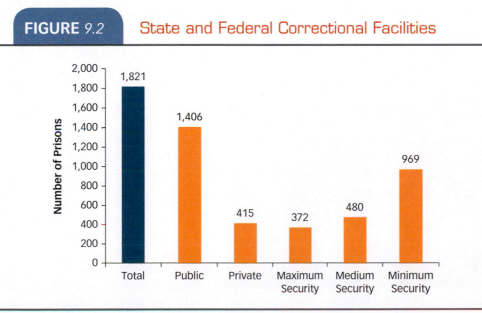

Source: Stephan (2008).

(Stephan, 2008, p. 4). These data do indicate that the popular and academic depictions of maximum-security prisons as the norm in America are incorrect.

Supermax Prisons

Journal Article 9.1: The Theory and Practice of Supermax Prisons

Video 9.1: Life in a Supermax Prison

Supermax prisons: High-security prisons that hold those who are violent or disruptive in other prisons in the state or federal system.

When states were first building prisons, they tended to be a combination of a maximum- and medium-security type (think industrial and big-house prisons). The exterior of these prisons was very secure, but internally, inmates were given some, though restricted, freedom to move about and were often expected to do so for work, dining, and related purposes. **Supermax prisons** (the slang term for supermaximum-security prisons) developed later, and arguably, the first of these was at the federal level, with Alcatraz Prison, which was built in 1934 to hold the most notorious gangsters of the era. Others argue that the first full-fledged supermaxes did not develop until the 1980s and were part of the get-tough-on-crime movement that promoted more severe punishment (e.g., see Mears, 2013). Today, supermax prisons at the federal and state level are not all operated exactly the same way, though certain characteristics do appear to be common (at least in theory): Inmates are confined to their windowless cells for 23 hours a day, except for showers three times a week (where they are restrained) and solo exercise time a couple of times a week. They eat in their cells, and often, the food is some form of nutraloaf (a bland but nutritious food that requires no utensils). If any limited rehabilitation is provided, the treatment personnel stand outside the cell and talk to the inmate within; physical contact is prohibited unless inmates are in restraints (Pizarro & Narag, 2008). Moreover, their confinement is usually lengthy, not for a day, a week, or even a month but for a year or more (Mears, 2013).

Alcatraz closed in 1963, and other federal supermaxes in Marion, Illinois (opened in 1963 to take some of the Alcatraz inmates), and later Florence, Colorado, in 1994, took its place. States began building supermaxes in earnest in the 1980s and 1990s in reaction to the felt need to control more dangerous and disruptive inmates and to "get tough" with them (Mears, 2008, 2013; Olivero & Roberts, 1987; Richards, 2008). It is estimated that a total of 44 states, holding some 25,000 inmates, had some form of a supermax (Mears, 2013, p. 684), though definitions of what a supermax is does vary across the states (Naday, Freilich, & Mellow, 2008). As with Alcatraz, these supermax prisons at the federal and state levels are supposed to hold the most dangerous offenders, violent gang members, those who cannot behave well in lower-security prisons, and those who pose an escape risk.

AP Photo/Brennan Linsley

PHOTO 9.2: The supermax prison in Florence, Colorado, is considered a possible site for housing Guantánamo detainees in the future.

Because of the heightened security requirements, incarceration in a supermax is expensive, at about $50,000 per year, as compared with $20,000 to $30,000 to incarcerate an adult male in a lower-security prison (Richards, 2008, p. 18), and because of the materials used in their construction, they are at least 2 to 3 times more expensive to build than a "regular" prison (Mears, 2008). The research indicates that wardens believe that the presence of a supermax in a prison system deters violent offenders, increases order and control, and reduces assaults on staff in the other prisons in that system, not just in the supermax itself (Pizarro

& Narag, 2008). Several states (e.g., Texas, Colorado, and California) have claimed that violence decreased in their systems once they opened a supermax. Sundt, Castellano, and Briggs (2008) reported that inmate assaults on staff decreased in Illinois once the supermax was opened in that state, though there was no effect for inmate assaults on inmates. Clearly, there is room for more systematic examination of the data, as in this study, for these and other issues as they relate to supermaxes.

For instance, critics and some researchers claim that inmates' mental health is impaired after a stay in a supermax because of the sensory deprivation, and there is some evidence to support this assertion (Mears, 2013). There is also evidence that supermaxes are sometimes used to incarcerate those who are merely mentally ill or who have committed more minor infractions (Mears, 2008; O'Keefe, 2008). In addition, the effect of incarcerating less serious or mentally impaired offenders in a supermax, as King, Steiner, and Breach (2008) note, can be a self-fulfilling prophecy, exacerbating inmate mental and behavioral problems through such secure and severe confinement. (Note the story of the mentally ill inmate held in the Dona Ana County, New Mexico, jail that appears at the beginning of Chapter 6.) On the other hand, there are researchers who have found evidence that such a stay had a calming effect on inmates, allowing them to reflect on their wrongs and how they might change their behavior (e.g., see Ward & Kassebaum, 2009). Pizarro and Narag (2008) note, however, that the evidence is weak on both sides of this argument and that more—and more rigorous—research is merited before we know the true effect of supermaxes on inmates or on prison systems.

ETHICAL ISSUE 9.1

What Would You Do?

You are a correctional officer in a supermax prison in "most states," USA. You understand the stated reasoning for such prisons in your state is "to house the worst of the worst" —inmates with behavioral problems and to separate gang members. You have been on the job for a few years, and you generally like your colleagues and workplace. However, you have noticed that the mental stability of some of the inmates you supervise has deteriorated the longer they stay in this prison. You have reported these problems to the medical officer in charge of the medical unit for the prison, and she and your supervisor have discouraged you from making further reports because the medical unit is already full and understaffed, making the transfer of inmates out of supermax cells difficult. Is there anything else you can do? What do you think would be the best response to this problem, and why?

Maximum Security

State and federal and military laws, traditions, and practices differ on how each type of prison operates, but some generalizations about how prisons with different security levels operate are usually accurate. Those prisons with the greatest internal and external security controls are the supermaximums, and next in security level are the **maximum-security prisons**. Inmates in supermaxes and, to a lesser extent, maximum-security prisons are often locked up all day, save for time for a shower or recreation outside of their cells, and they are ideally in single cells deprived of other sensory stimulation. Visits and contact with the outside are very restricted. The maximum and supermax exterior security consists of some combination of layers of razor wire, walls, lights, cameras, armed guards, and attack dogs on patrol.

As the states that have a supermax usually only have one, maximum-security prisons are responsible for holding most of the serious offenders and those who could not handle themselves in the relatively freer environment of the medium- and minimum-security prisons. The latter type of inmate might be able to qualify for a medium- or minimum-security-level classification but instead is in maximum security because the inmate is unable to control his or her behavior.

AP Video 9.1: Manhunt

Maximum-security prisons: Prisons where both external and internal security are high, and programs and contact with other prisoners and visitors are very limited.

IN FOCUS 9.1

Alcatraz: The United States' First Supermax

As Ward and Kassebaum (2009) note in their book, *Alcatraz: The Gangster Years*, when Alcatraz was first opened as a federal prison in 1934, it was created in response to a perceived national crisis. This crisis involved gangsters and outlaws who were terrorizing communities with kidnappings, bank and train robberies, and organized crime. Moreover, there were a number of scandals where these gangsters and outlaws were effectively corrupting state and federal prison officials and staff through intimidation and with their money, contacts, and infamy.

Corrupt and poorly managed, state and federal prisons of the time were widely perceived as coddling influential felons by permitting special privileges and allowing them to continue involvement in criminal enterprises from behind bars while flaws in their security systems offered inmates opportunities for escape (Ward & Kassebaum, 2009, p. 2).

Al Capone, one of the most notorious gangsters of this era, when incarcerated at Eastern State Penitentiary in Pennsylvania, was provided by the warden with a single cell, furnished like a home; a cushy library clerk job; unlimited visits by family and friends; and use of the telephone to contact his lawyer, crime partners, and politicians. Though he and his gang were implicated in a number of murders and graft of all sorts, he was able to evade prosecution for most of those crimes, and it was a tax evasion conviction that landed him in federal prison.

Alcatraz, on an island in the San Francisco Bay, was created to end the undue influence on incarceration that the "Capones" of the world exerted. "Surrounded by cold ocean currents, it was intended to hold the nation's 'public enemies' to an iron regimen, reduce them to mere numbers, cut them off from the outside world, and keep them locked up securely for decades" (Ward & Kassebaum, 2009, p. 2). News reporters were prohibited from interviewing Alcatraz staff or inmates, and staff were told not to talk to reporters or they would be fired. Visits were limited to a few blood relatives and then only once per month and through a guard-monitored telephone. Inmates were not allowed to talk about their life on the inside during those visits. That life was very controlled and monotonous and consisted of strict adherence to silence at night, work (when earned as a privilege), and not much else. No effort was made to rehabilitate these inmates, as they were supposed to be the most incorrigible troublemakers of all federal prisoners. There was no commissary, so there was no underground economy in goods. Inmates were out of their cells from 6:30 in the morning, if they had a job, until 4:30 in the afternoon. From then on, all they had were small crafts, reading, letter writing, and time for reflection.

In practice, over the 30 years of its existence (it closed in 1963), Alcatraz never lived up completely to the ideal, though Ward and Kassebaum (2009) claim it may have rehabilitated a number of inmates. The maintenance of silence, except at prescribed times, had long since been abandoned. Many inmates had attempted escape, inmates held strikes to protest conditions, and a few inmates and staff were assaulted—including a warden—or killed by inmates in fights and escapes. (It is possible that two men did succeed in escaping, but there is some debate about this.) The internal controls were never as harsh or effective as they were supposed to be, either, though more than one inmate of the early years characterized incarceration there as tantamount to being buried alive (Ward & Kassebaum, 2009). Ex-inmates also talked to reporters once released, and the gunfire, fires, and sirens from the various events were noticed and speculated on by San Francisco reporters across the bay. Moreover, as there were not enough notorious and incorrigible inmates in the federal system to fill Alcatraz, about two thirds of its inmates were less dangerous and influential than had been planned for (Ward & Kassebaum, 2009, p. 459). Yet Alcatraz became the model for other federal and state supermaxes that followed as, for the most part, it had avoided the corruption and violence apparent in other prisons, and it had effectively controlled the gangsters and outlaws of its time (Ward & Kassebaum, 2009).

DISCUSSION QUESTIONS

1. What events spurred the creation of the first supermax prison?

2. What made Alcatraz distinct from other prisons, and why did it become a model prison?

In many states where the death penalty is legal, their death row is located at a maximum-security prison. Death rows are usually wholly separate areas of the prison, sometimes in a different building, and often have their own separate designated staff and procedures. (For a more involved discussion of the death penalty, see Chapter 19.)

Maximum-security prisons may have the same exterior security controls as supermaxes, but inside, inmates are not locked down as much, though the treatment and work programming is much more constricted than in the medium-security prisons. Maximum-security inmates may or may not be double bunked, depending on the crowding in the institution, and unless under some special classification, they have some access to the yard (a large gathering area for inmates), the cafeteria, and the chapel. Visiting and contact with the outside world are less restricted than in the supermax, and inmates are usually not in some kind of restraint when it occurs.

Medium Security

In **medium-security prisons,** the exterior security can be as tight as it is for the supermax and the maximum-security prisons, but internally, the inmate has many more opportunities to attend school, treatment, and church programming and to work in any number of capacities. There is also greater diversity in rooming options, from dormitories to single cells, with the preferred single or double cells used as a carrot to entice better behavior. Visiting and contact with the outside world are less restricted. Some medium-security inmates may even be allowed to leave the institution for work-related deliveries or on furloughs, though this is much more common in minimum-security prisons.

Medium-security prisons will hold a mix of people in terms of crime categories, all the way from the convicted murderer doing life but who programs well, down to the lowly burglar or drug user who is awaiting transfer to a lower-security prison or who is engaged in the substance abuse programming that the prison affords. Medium-security prisons are more likely to have a college campus–type interior, with several buildings devoted to distinct purposes. There might be a separate cafeteria building, a separate programming and treatment building, a separate gym and recreation building, and separate work and housing buildings. Medium-security prisons are heavily engaged in industrial work, such as building furniture, making clothing, and printing license plates for the state. In some cases and states, the goods produced in the prison are sold on the open market.

Minimum Security

Minimum-security prisons have a much more relaxed exterior security; some do not even have a wall or a fence. Inmates are provided with far more programming, either inside the institution or outside, in the community. The housing options are often as diverse as in the medium-security prisons, and inmates can usually roam the facility much more freely, availing themselves of programming, recreation, the yard, the chapel, and the cafeteria at prescribed times. With the recognition that inmates in a minimum-security prison will often be free within a year or two, visiting options are more liberalized so that the transition from prison to the community is smoother. Work is promoted, and inmates are often encouraged or, in the case of work release facilities with a minimum-security classification, are expected to work in the community.

Inmates confined to minimum-security prisons are usually *short timers*, or people who are relatively close to a release date. These could be people who have been classified directly to this prison or work release facility because they received a sentence of a

Medium-security prisons: Prisons that have high external security but less restrictive internal security and more opportunities for programs.

Minimum-security prisons: Prisons with relaxed external and internal security created for lower-level felony offenders who are not expected to be an escape or behavioral problem.

PHOTO 9.3: Inmates in the yard at Mule Creek State Penitentiary in California. Prison yards provide a modicum of freedom for inmates but can be dangerous because the inmate-to-officer ratio is so high.

year or two and because they are not expected to be an escape risk or behavioral problem. Whether they can work might also be a consideration in classification, as this is often a central element of these prisons. Other inmates who might do time in a minimum-security prison or work release facility are more serious offenders who have moved through, or "down," the other classification levels and are relatively close to their release. Minimum-security prisons thus also hold the most serious offenders, including murderers, rapists, and child molesters, along with those convicted of burglary and substance abuse and trafficking offenses. The difference is that in minimum-security prisons, all such offenders, no matter their offense, are believed to be a good risk for behavior and in need of preparation for their imminent release.

PRISON VALUE?

Placing someone in prison is a very expensive decision, costing states and the federal government at least $20,000 per year for adult males and more than double that for women and children (Bureau of Justice Statistics, 2011). In the past, this cost was not always considered by policy makers intent on locking up those who had offended even in relatively minor ways. Instead, as discussed in preceding chapters, prisons and other means of "correcting" were created to achieve retribution, deterrence, incapacitation, rehabilitation, and reintegration. (Note: Cullen and Jonson [2012, pp. 10–12] would add [1] restorative justice, or "reducing harm" for the victim, the community, and the offender, and [2] early intervention, or "saving children," to this list of theoretical goals for correctional entities.)

Whether retribution is achieved by imprisonment and, if so, how much imprisonment is needed to achieve it are philosophical and ultimately subjective matters left to judges, juries, and social commentators. Achieving incapacitation is a much more tangible objective, however. When a person is removed and kept away from a community, as he or she is when incarcerated in a jail or prison or, to a lesser extent, when the individual's movements are restricted on probation or parole, it is obvious that incapacitation has been achieved. There is even evidence that incapacitation is related to reduced criminality in the range of three to six crimes per year for some criminals (Owens, 2009; Sweeten & Apel, 2007).

However, measuring whether corrections has had the effect of deterring or rehabilitating is not always obvious or easy to do. We do know that imprisonment for more than a year has not been consistently linked to reduced crime, and thus, imprisonment does not appear to deter. Instead, it may prove criminogenic, in that it exposes the incarcerated to deviant attitudes and beliefs and stigmatizes the individual, thus limiting his or her future employment and social opportunities (Nagin, Cullen, & Jonson, 2009). However, as will be discussed in the chapter on programming and treatment (Chapter 11), there is solid evidence that when done correctly, some treatment programs, even in prisons, can reduce recidivism. Therefore, any positive "value" of imprisoning must be assessed based on what is a desirable outcome; the research on whether it can be achieved in a prison; and, in these trying economic times, the financial cost of achieving that goal or those goals.

••• ATTRIBUTES OF THE PRISON THAT SHAPE THE EXPERIENCE

TOTAL INSTITUTIONS

Once classified to a given prison, whether maximum or otherwise, the inmate experience is shaped by several factors, including the *operation* of it. One central component of that operation is the "totality" of the organization.

As will also be discussed in Chapter 14 in reference to staff, Erving Goffman (1961) coined the term *total institution* to describe the nature of mental hospitals, as well as prisons, in the United States in the 1950s. For one year, he served as a staff member (athletic director's assistant) and did ethnographic research in a federal mental-health hospital in Washington, D.C. While avoiding sociable contact with staff, he immersed himself in the inmate world as much as he could without being admitted to the hospital, and what he observed allowed him to learn a great deal about that kind of institution and about roles for staff and inmates.

Goffman (1961) defined a **total institution** as "a place of residence and work where a large number of like-situated individuals, cut off from the wider society for an appreciable period of time, together lead an enclosed, formally administered round of life" (p. xiii). Another key component of this total institution is the defined social strata, particularly as that includes "inmates" and the "staff" (Goffman, 1961, p. 7). Specifically, there are formal prohibitions against even minor social interactions between these two groups in a total institution, and all of the formal power resides with one group (the staff) over the other group (the inmates).

This definition is directly applicable to prisons, even today, though it more aptly described both prisons and jails of the past. For prison inmates, the institution is where they live—and often work—with people who are like themselves, not only in terms of criminal involvement but also largely in terms of their social class and other background characteristics. Though there is some ability to visit with others, the mode and manner of this contact with the outside world are quite limited in prisons and are also dependent on the security status of the institution (e.g., whether it is a work release facility or a maximum-security prison). The formal rules of prisons also closely control inmate behavior and movement. As already mentioned, another key formal attribute of total institutions governs interactions between staff and inmates. Simply put, staff are to restrict such interactions to business only and are to parcel out information only as absolutely necessary. As Goffman (1961) put it, "Social mobility between the two strata is grossly restricted; social distance is typically great and often formally prescribed" (p. 7).

How do these aspects of total institutions affect the lives of inmates? In the 1950s, Goffman (1961) believed that total institutions had the effect of debilitating their inmates. As he saw it, upon entrance into the institution, the inmate may become *mortified* (known as **mortification**), or suffer from the loss of the many roles he or she occupied in the wider world (see also Sykes, 1958). Instead, only the role of "inmate" is available, a role that is formally powerless and dependent.

In addition, though each person entering a prison *imports* (known as **importation**) aspects of his or her own culture from the outside, to some extent, inmates are likely to experience **prisonization**, whereby they adopt the inmate subculture of the institution (Carroll, 1974, 1982; Clemmer, 2001). Couple this mortification and subsequent role displacement with prisonization into the contingent inmate subculture, and you have the potential for

Video 9.2: Responding to Offenders' Needs Motivates Behavior Change

Total institution: "A place of residence and work where a large number of like-situated individuals, cut off from the wider society for an appreciable period of time, together lead an enclosed, formally administered round of life."

Mortification: Process that occurs as inmates enter the prison and suffer from the loss of the many roles they occupied in the wider world.

Importation: Occurs when inmates bring aspects of the larger culture into the prison.

Prisonization: The adopting of the inmate subculture by prisoners.

the new inmate to experience a life in turmoil while he or she adjusts inside and some difficulty when reentering the community.

PAINS OF IMPRISONMENT

Web 9.2: Deprivation in Prison

Part and parcel of this inmate world are what Gresham Sykes (1958)—based on his research in a New Jersey maximum-security prison—described as the **pains of imprisonment**. Such pains include "the deprivation of liberty," "the deprivation of goods and services," "the deprivation of heterosexual relationships," "the deprivation of autonomy," and "the deprivation of security" (pp. 63–83).

Deprivation of Liberty

Inmates in a prison (or jail) are not free to leave or even to move about the institution without the permission of their keepers (staff). But for Sykes, the worst of the liberty restrictions meant that inmates were cut off, for the most part, from family and friends. They cannot call whomever they like or visit with whom they want, when they wish to do so. As many inmates are functionally illiterate and poor, they also have difficulty writing letters and affording the postage. This deprivation of contact with family members, particularly their children, is a severe pain that many inmates experience when, as an artifact of their incarceration, they are unable to have regular interactions with their own children or to have any control over their child's environment on the outside (more about this in the chapter titled "Women and Corrections," Chapter 15) (Gray, Mays, & Stohr, 1995; Stohr & Mays, 1993).

Deprivation of Goods and Services

Pains of imprisonment: The deprivation of liberty, goods and services, heterosexual relationships, autonomy, and security.

As to the pain related to goods and services, inmates are required to surrender all of their property upon entrance into the prison system, and in most cases, they cannot have it back until they leave. The property they are allowed to legally possess is very limited and monitored closely by staff. Relatedly, they cannot choose who will cut their hair or where they will get their nails done, nor can they choose their doctor or schedule a visit. As Sykes (1958) noted—and this is perhaps even truer today in many prisons because of

AP Photo/Gerald Herbert

PHOTO 9.4: An inmate's access to significant others is limited to visitations where touching is only minimally sanctioned (e.g., a brief kiss or hug at the beginning of the visit).

court intervention—most inmates' basic needs for food, shelter, space, and health care are met, yet it is the perception of deprivation in this material society that matters, too.

Deprivation of Sexual Relations

In light of the greater knowledge we have regarding sexual orientation of human populations today, as opposed to 50 years ago, we might amend Sykes's (1958) "deprivation of heterosexual relations" to a more generalized *deprivation of sexual relations*. An inmate's access to significant others in the wider world is limited to visiting where touching is only minimally sanctioned (e.g., a brief kiss or hug at the beginning of the visit). Though much is made of conjugal visits for prison inmates, in reality, there are few prisons that allow these, and a miniscule number of inmates even in those prisons are granted access to such visits. Very few prisons allow conjugal visits between inmates and their gay or lesbian partners. Though, as with the free population, there are likely to be 3% to 5% of prison inmates who are gay or lesbian (see a brief discussion related to this topic later in this chapter), sexual intimacy between same-sex inmates is against the rules; however, it does occur. It is illegal, as well, between same- and opposite-sex staff and inmates.

Deprivation of Autonomy

Autonomy for the inmate is also severely restricted in the rule-bound prison world. When, how, where, and with whom they live, eat, work, and play are all determined by the rules of the institution. Inmates can make few choices regarding their lives while imprisoned, and all of those choices are shaped by their imprisonment.

Deprivation of Security

Due to their imprisonment, inmates are thrown together with others, some of whom are aggressive and violent or become so in a prison environment, perhaps particularly in the maximum-security environment that Sykes was studying. Because of the circumstances surrounding incarceration in a supermax but also, to a lesser degree, in medium- and minimum-level prisons, inmates are deprived of their security, a basic human need, as defined by Maslow (1943/2001). Quoting an inmate in his study, Sykes (1958) repeated that "the worst thing about prison is you have to live with other prisoners" (p. 77), meaning that even if one is prone to violence or manipulation (termed an *outlaw inmate* by Sykes), and not all inmates are, it is unnerving for even an outlaw inmate to have to live with others who are also so inclined. This lack of security, according to Sykes, can lead to anxiety on the part of inmates and the belief that at some point, they, whether an outlaw among outlaws or not, are likely to be forced to fight to defend themselves or to submit to the abuse of others.

Effects of Deprivation

Sykes (1958) argued that these pains, though not physically brutalizing, have the cumulative effect of destroying the psyche of the inmate. In order to avoid this destruction, inmates in prisons may be motivated to engage in deviance while incarcerated as a means of alleviating their pain. So bullying other inmates, involvement in gangs, buying items through the underground economy, and sexual relations might all be motivated, in fact, by the need for some autonomy, liberty, security, goods and services, and sexual gratification (Johnson, 2002). Extrapolating from this point, the extent to which female inmates form pseudofamilial relationships may be a means of alleviating the pain experienced due to the separation from children and other close family members (Owen, 1998).

One final note regarding the pains of imprisonment: Sykes (1958) did not believe that all inmates experienced or perceived these pains in the same way. He acknowledged that the way in which one experiences these pains does vary some by individual and by

IN FOCUS 9.2

Prison Debate Project

By Amber Morczek and Roger Schaefer (written while doctoral students at Washington State University)

The Prison Debate Project was created in 2012 by Loretta Taylor and Johannes Wheeldon at Walla Walla Community College and Dr. Faith Lutze at Washington State University. The debate is structured to allow all members of the debate teams to participate in various capacities. Debate teams are composed of university student participants majoring in criminal justice and inmate student participants who work collaboratively to identify, develop, and deliver arguments supporting their side of the debate proposition (Pro or Con). Each team is assigned five speaking roles—introduction, fact, value, policy, and conclusion—that must be supported by research or academic literature. Speaking roles are agreed upon by the team members and approved by course instructors.

The logistics of the program present unique challenges that demand routine coordination between university officials, prison staff and administration, and debate participants. University officials and prison administration work closely to address issues of risk in an effort to ensure safety. Custody and educational staff work together to promote safety while university students are at the prison. Criminal background checks are required for all individuals who enter the prison, including debate participants, as well as university faculty or staff. The success of the prison tours, group meetings, and debate is a direct result of the collaborative work and preparation that occurs long before university students enter the prison.

The Diagrammatic Dialogue and Debate Model, developed and implemented by a group of scholars and instructors at Coyote Ridge Corrections Center in Connell, Washington, has emerged as a unique correctional and educational discourse (see Wheeldon, Chavez, & Cooke, 2013). Using this debate model, both university and inmate students are exposed to the human reality of disagreement and resolution, particularly within a traditionally rigid correctional environment. Within the context of correctional discourse, the Prison Debate Project empowers inmate participants to recognize opposing viewpoints and participate in respectful dialogue. From an educational perspective, the Prison Debate Project invites inmates to engage in an ongoing academic discussion on important social issues (e.g., gun control, gender and justice, or jury selection). Overall, it is the structure of the debate that creates a foundation for prosocial self-actualization through critical thinking and respectful discourse.

DISCUSSION QUESTIONS

1. How might this program reduce the pains of imprisonment for inmates?

2. How might this program benefit the college student participants?

3. How might this program benefit the prison in which it is hosted?

Reference

Wheeldon, J., Chavez, R. B., & Cooke, J. (2013). *Debate and dialogue in correctional settings: Maps, models, and materials*. New York, NY: IDEBATE Press.

background, as well as by the prison in which one is incarcerated. However, he argued that at least among the inmates he studied, there was a consensus that "life in a maximum security prison is depriving or frustrating in the extreme" (p. 63).

••• THE PRISON SUBCULTURE

A *subculture*, or a subset of culture with its own norms, values, beliefs, traditions, and even language, tends to solidify when people are isolated from the larger culture and when members have regular and intense contact with each other for an extended period of time. In other words, it would appear that the total-institution nature of prisons provides the perfect environment for a **prison subculture** to form. Accordingly, the degree to which a correctional environment fits the definition of a total institution will determine the extent to which a client subculture exists. It is also possible that the shared experiences of deprivation, as detailed by Sykes (1958), can further solidify a subculture for inmates.

Thus, research on inmate subcultures has tended to focus on prison inmates and specifically on medium- or maximum-security prison inmates. This is not to say, of course, that those in a jail or a minimum-security prison do not have distinguishable norms, values, beliefs, traditions, and language that set them apart from the wider community, but it is much less likely. By definition, the longer inmates are in an institution, associating with others like them, and the more "total" the institution is in its restrictions on liberty and contact with "outsiders," the more subjected inmates are to the pains of imprisonment, and the more likely they are to become prisonized, in that they adopt the inmate subculture.

ROLES FOR INMATES AND STAFF

Indicators of such a subculture, as identified by prison researchers, include prescribed values and defined roles for inmates (Clemmer, 2001; Owen, 1998). For instance, Clemmer, in 1940 (reprinted in 2001), broadly defined criminal subcultural values, which include "the notion that criminals should not betray each other to the police, should be reliable, wily but trustworthy, coolheaded, etc." (p. 7). Also emphasized among these values are ultramasculinity and displays of toughness and solidarity among inmates and against staff (Lutze & Murphy, 1999; Sykes, 1958). Accordingly, the types of roles (inmate typology) that Sykes and Messinger (1960) and Sykes (1958) described for adult male prison inmates in their own argot, or language, are detailed in In Focus 9.3. Though these researchers identified these roles for inmates in prisons over 60 years ago, current researchers still see them in prisons of today. Of course, any given inmate might be expected to change roles from time to time during his or her incarceration or to engage in more than one role simultaneously.

Video 9.3:
Prison Security
Levels

These roles are played out in the prison in a criminal subculture, which becomes a *convict subculture* for Clemmer (2001) when such inmates seek power and information so that they might get the goods and services they desire to alleviate those pains of imprisonment. Owen (1998) noted that some women engaged in a version of this subculture and these roles, although it might have been tempered by the relationships they had and the goods and services they needed (more about the different roles women inmates adopt in Chapter 15). Notably, both Clemmer and Owen found that a significant portion of inmates in the male and female prisons they studied were not at all interested in being involved in the convict subculture or the "mix" of behavior that can lead to trouble in prisons. Such inmates, in the argot identified by Sykes (1958) and Sykes and Messinger (1960), were *square johns*. These inmates either chose not connect to the inmate subculture, or they held on to more traditional and legitimate values from the larger culture.

Feature Video 9.1:
Pains of
Imprisonment

More recent research confirms that inmates are not as solidly aligned against staff as the early works indicated (Hemmens & Marquart, 2000; J. B. Jacobs, 1977; Johnson, 2002; Jurik, 1985a; Jurik & Halemba, 1984; Lombardo, 1982; Owen, 1998). Many inmates identify with free-world values, as much or more than inmate values and inmate subculture.

Other recent researchers and writers on prisons (e.g., Conover, 2001; Johnson, 2002; and Rideau, 2010) find that staff and inmates engage in more personal and informal relationships with each other than is formally acknowledged, a reality that Sykes (1958) noted as well. The diversification of staff by race, ethnicity, and gender has changed the old dynamic between staff and inmates, making staff less dissimilar to inmates and the inmate world less "masculinized" than it was previously (for a more involved discussion

Prison subculture:
The norms, values, beliefs, traditions, and even language of the prison.

of these matters, see Chapter 15, "Women and Corrections," and Chapter 16, "Minorities and Corrections"), perhaps continuing to break down some of the more formal barriers between staff and inmates in a total institution.

Research, observations, and personal experience as a teacher, student-inmate, attendee, and governor (warden) in a male prison in the United Kingdom led Crewe, Warr, Bennett, and Smith (2014) to theorize that emotionally restrained "tough-guy" depictions of inmates in prisons do not fully describe the *emotional geography* of such places. Rather, these researchers claim there are certain subcultural zones where a wider range of emotions is allowed because the circumstances of such places allow it. One such zone in the prison is the visiting room, where interactions with families require more open emotional exchanges and allow for shows of vulnerability by inmates. Classrooms and the chapel were other areas where comradeship and the sharing of ideas and even personal experiences and beliefs broke down the typical emotional barriers that are present in prisons.

IN FOCUS 9.3

Inmate Roles Identified by Sykes (1958) and Sykes and Messinger (1960)

- **The right guy:** The inmate who fully supports and embraces the inmate code.
- **The rat or squealer:** The inmate who "snitches" on others to staff. Usually, such inmates are despised by other inmates, as they violate the prohibition in the inmate code regarding this sort of behavior. Because they are so disliked, rats are vulnerable to attacks by other inmates.
- **The center man:** The inmate who agrees with the prison rules and procedures either because he is trying to curry favor from staff or because he believes that is the correct way to behave.
- **The tough:** The inmate who is aggressive, has anger issues, and is touchy and so is willing to fight at will.
- **The hipster:** The inmate who aspires to be a tough but who is really all talk and little action. He chooses his victims selectively to be sure he can, in fact, conquer them, whereas the tough will fight both the weak and the strong.
- **The gorilla:** The inmate who may be as aggressive as the tough but uses that aggression—or just the threat of it—to gain something from other inmates.
- **The merchant or peddler:** The inmate who engages in the underground black market to supply illicit goods and services to other inmates for material advantage.
- **The weakling:** The inmate who is vulnerable to exploitation by others and cannot stand up to them. Someone who submits to the coercion—or threatened coercion—of the gorilla.
- **The fish:** The inmate who has just arrived and is not yet adjusted to the ways of the prison.
- **The wolf:** The inmate who aggressively and sexually pursues other inmates. He is believed to play a "masculine" role. There is no emotion or connection in the sexual act for the wolf; rather, he pursues men in the prison and rapes them.
- **The "fag":** The inmate who plays the passive, though not unwilling, role in the sexual relationship with another inmate. He is believed to play a "feminine" role. (Note: The authors of this text acknowledge that the term "fag" is derogatory, and the assumption that male and female roles are tied to aggression and passivity is dated and limiting, but this term and these assumptions are the ones used by Sykes [1958] and Sykes and Messinger [1960], who were repeating the argot used by inmates of the late 1950s. As Sykes explains, inmate argot was often meant to be derogatory and inflammatory as it marked and labeled the roles of others.)
- **The punk:** The unwilling inmate who is coerced or bribed into the passive sexual role vis-à-vis other inmates. This inmate does not adopt the "feminine" role.
- **The ball buster:** The inmate who continually struggles against the system and staff, despite the futility of it, often to the point of foolishness.
- **The innocent:** The inmate who repeatedly claims his innocence of the crime for which he is incarcerated.
- **The square john:** The inmate who does not become prisonized but identifies with the free-world values of staff and the outside community.

GANGS AND THE PRISON SUBCULTURE

Gangs, or groups of people with similar interests who socialize together and who may engage in deviant or criminal activities, are a common phenomenon in jails and prisons. According to the U.S. Department of Justice (2015) website, gangs in prisons and jails are, by definition, engaged in criminal activities and are connected through members and criminal involvement with communities. Prison gangs have a hierarchical organizational structure and a set and often strict code of conduct for members. As reported by the U.S. Department of Justice (2015),

PHOTO 9.5: Mexican mafia tattoo on a member. Such tattoos provide a ready signal to other inmates and to staff what gang an inmate is a member of.

Prison gangs vary in both organization and composition, from highly structured gangs such as the Aryan Brotherhood and Nuestra Familia to gangs with a less formalized structure such as the Mexican Mafia (La Eme). Prison gangs generally have fewer members than street gangs and Outlaw Motorcycle Gangs (OMGs) and are structured along racial or ethnic lines. Nationally, prison gangs pose a threat because of their role in the transportation and distribution of narcotics. Prison gangs are also an important link between drug-trafficking organizations (DTOs), street gangs and OMGs, often brokering the transfer of drugs from DTOs to gangs in many regions. Prison gangs typically are more powerful within state correctional facilities rather than within the federal penal system. (p. 1)

Video 9.4: Prison Gang Violence Reduction Strategy

Correctional scholars and practitioners believe gangs are so ubiquitous in corrections because they meet the needs of inmates for security, goods and services, power, and companionship. They lessen the pains of imprisonment by providing protection in numbers and the potential to respond with force to any threats an inmate might face. They are conduits for the supply of illicit goods, like tobacco, drugs, alcohol, and sex, in prisons and jails. They also provide some substitution for the diminished relationships that inmates have with those family and friends on the outside.

The history of gangs in prisons is a long one. Sykes (1958) noted that the first investigation of the New Jersey State Prison, in 1830, found what they called a "Stauch-Gang," which was firmly entrenched there and engaged in terrorizing both inmates and staff while also planning escapes (p. 92). Ward and Kassebaum (2009) also point out the importation and exportation of gang-related criminal activity between state and federal prisons and the streets in the 1920s. J. B. Jacobs (1977), in his history of the Stateville Prison in Illinois, observed that prison gangs had existed in that state for decades, as imports from the streets of Chicago, though he thought their ferocity and strength increased in the late 1960s and early 1970s.

The prison gangs of today are almost too numerous for correctional authorities to keep track of, but they do tend to have in common a criminal focus. According to the Florida Department of Corrections (FDOC) (2014), most prison gangs these days recruit their membership based on ethnicity or race. Both the federal government and the FDOC report that gangs are much stronger in male prisons, and gangs will conspire with others, even rival gangs, so as to provide protection and increase their criminal reach. (For example, the Aryan Brotherhood might sometimes work with members

Gangs (prison): Groups of people with similar interests who socialize together and support each other but who also engage in deviant or criminal activities. Prison gangs have a hierarchical organizational structure and a set and often strict code of conduct for members.

ETHICAL ISSUE 9.2 ?

What Would You Do?

As an experienced counselor in the prison you work at, you are often given the more "difficult" inmates to work with. You are told by the prison intelligence officers that you may have a number of gang members on your caseload. One younger inmate by the name of Jacob, whom you have spent some time with, has told you of his affiliation with one of the gangs in the prison. He has also emphasized that, though he is a member, he is not involved in any illegal activities. He is programming well and has a responsible job in the facility. As best as you can tell from your contacts with other inmates, Jacob is not involved in any criminal activities. You know that if you tell the intelligence officer about this inmate's affiliation, however, there is a good chance that Jacob will be placed in segregation or moved to another facility. What do you think would be the best response in this instance, and why?

of the Black Guerrilla Family despite the racial hatred of their members for each other if it will increase their drug sales.) The FDOC website identifies the six major prison gangs in the United States as follows:

1. Neta (Puerto Rican American/Hispanic)
2. Aryan Brotherhood (white)
3. Black Guerrilla Family (black)
4. Mexican Mafia (Mexican American/Hispanic)
5. La Nuestra Familia (Mexican American/Hispanic)
6. Texas Syndicate (Mexican American/Hispanic)

Because of their underground engagement in prison crime and the rivalries that develop between gangs, even those with members of the same ethnic backgrounds (e.g., the Mexican Mafia and La Nuestra Familia) are sworn enemies. Moreover, both the Mexican Mafia and La Nuestra Familia are rivals of the Texas Syndicate. Because of these rivalries, jails and prisons constantly have to consider gang membership in classification decisions. Whether it is fights over turf, protection of members, or some other issue, the presence of gangs and gang activities leads to disruption and even murder in prisons. For instance, according to the FDOC (2014), the Aryan Brotherhood (AB) disruptions of prisons include the following:

- The main activities of the AB are centered on drug trafficking, extortion, pressure rackets, and internal discipline.

- Prison activities include introduction of contraband, distribution of drugs, and getting past facility rules and regulations.

- Traditionally, targets have been non-gang inmates and internal discipline.

- From 1975 to 1985, members committed 40 homicides in California prisons and local jails, as well as 13 homicides in the community.

- From 1978 to 1992, AB members, suspects, and associates in the federal system were involved in 26 homicides, 3 of which involved staff victims.

Because of the threat prison gangs present for the security of the institution and the safety of staff and inmates, managers try to control or suppress gang involvement in their facilities. The first step in this process is the identification of gang members and their leaders. Once identified, correctional staff will try to separate members and leaders from each other. However, given the crowding of most prisons and prison systems, it is almost impossible to always employ the separation tactic as a means of control and suppression. Therefore, what they are often left with is the monitoring of gang activity and, as much as possible, punishing deviance or neutralizing gang members and reducing their impact on a given system.

••• VIOLENCE

WHY PRISONS ARE VIOLENT

Violence is endemic to prisons. There is violence in prisons because incarcerated people are there unwillingly, forced to do things they normally would not do, with people they may not like, and most important of all, some of them are inclined to be violent. According to Bureau of Justice Statistics researcher Carson (2014), in 2013, about 54% of the state prison population were incarcerated for violent offenses. As was mentioned earlier, prisons, as a whole, are running at or over capacity. Maximum- and medium-security prisons tend to hold more inmates convicted of violent offenses or who have problems with following the rules in prisons, and as a result, they are more likely to experience violent outbursts. Research by Meade and Steiner (2013), in which they used a representative national sample of adult male inmates, indicates that inmates who were exposed to violence or who were physically victimized prior to incarceration were likely to have more problems with adjustment while incarcerated. The researchers also found that abuse as a child—not an uncommon experience for many inmates—was associated with maladjustment while in prison. Add to this mix the presence of gangs and their willingness to use force to achieve their criminal ends, and the possibility of violence in prisons rises.

AP Video 9.2: Prisons

THE AMOUNT OF VIOLENCE

With the exception of deaths due to violence, it is difficult to determine the exact amount of violence in prisons. Correctional institutions tend to underreport its incidence, and there is variation across facilities about what constitutes violence (Byrne & Hummer, 2008). Relatedly, inmates are reluctant to report the violence they experience or witness to staff. With these caveats regarding official statistics in mind, Stephan and Karberg (2003) found, using data collected from correctional institutions around the United States, that the number of assaults on staff and inmates increased in state and federal prisons from 1995 to 2000 and that the size of the increase was greatest for private institutions. They do note, however, that the rate of assault on staff (or the number of assaults per staff person) decreased slightly during this time period. We also know, based on the Bureau of Justice Statistics (BJS) data, that both the suicide and homicide rates in jails and prisons decreased from 1980 to 2003. More recent BJS data (2000–2013) indicate that the suicide rate in jails has continued to decline, while in prisons, it has remained stable at 2002 levels (Figure 9.3) (Noonan & Ginder, 2013).

SEXUAL ASSAULTS

As was discussed in Chapter 6, the amount of sexual violence in prisons and jails, based on inmate surveys and official statistics, is becoming increasingly clear. The Prison Rape Elimination Act of 2003 (PREA) requires that the BJS collect data yearly on the amount of prison rape that occurs. In 2013, this meant that a 10% sample of the 7,600 jails, prisons, and community-based and juvenile facilities were included (BJS, 2014, p. 1). The findings from this research indicate the following:

Audio 9.2: Prison Rape

- The allegations of sexual victimization increased from 2005 to 2011, more in prisons than in jails.

- Ten percent of the allegations in 2011 were substantiated (meaning were found to be true after an investigation).

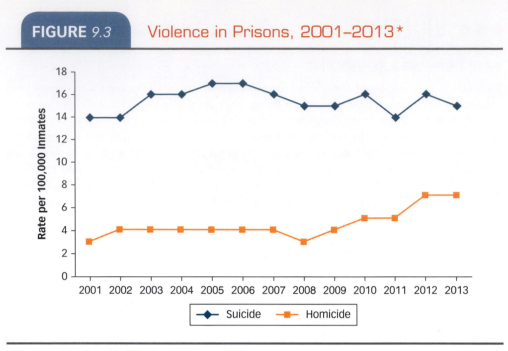

FIGURE *9.3*   Violence in Prisons, 2001–2013*

*Most recent data available.

Source: Noonan, Rohloff, and Ginder (2015).

- Fifty-two percent of the substantiated incidents involved only inmates, whereas the other 48% involved staff and inmates.

- Injuries were reported in 18% of the inmate-only victimizations, whereas

- less than 1% of the staff and inmate victimizations involved injuries.

- Female staff committed more than half of the substantiated incidents of sexual misconduct (BJS, 2014, p. 1).

The data indicate that 4.0% of prison inmates reported experiencing sexual victimization in 2011–2012 (63,400), which was perpetrated by either other inmates or staff (BJS, 2014, p. 3). Whether the number of such assaults is trending upward or downward and why it might be more prevalent in some facilities than others are matters yet to be determined by more longitudinal research. Certainly, though horrific for the inmate experiencing it and keeping in mind the likely underestimation of victimization, a 4% sexual-victimization rate does not fit the "myth" of sexual victimization that many people believe regarding prisons, a myth that predicts that everyone, particularly young males, who goes to prison will be raped (Fleisher & Krienert, 2009).

It might well be that this myth has more than a grain of truth in it, in that prison rapes are underreported or that in the past, it was much more common. The percentage of those raped or sexually assaulted may have declined, the way the rate of prison assaults appears to have done (though not the number) over the years as corrections has become less "total" in its isolation and operation, as the courts have recognized some inmates' rights, and as training of staff has increased. As Byrne, Hummer, and Stowell (2008) note, there are many factors (e.g., staffing levels and crowding) whose effect on violence is not yet established in the research.

Though it might be a myth that all who enter prisons—or even most—will be raped, the research by the BJS indicates that fully 80,600 inmates in prison and jails were victims of

FIGURE *9.4*   Total Allegations of Sexual Victimization, by Type of Incident, 2011*

*Most recent data available.

Source: Beck and Rantala (2014).

sexual violence in 2011–2012 (Beck, Berzofsky, Caspar, & Krebs, 2013, p. 8). And it is true that certain groups are much more likely to be raped in prisons than other groups. As was discussed in the chapter on jails, females, nonheterosexuals, and the mentally ill are much more likely to be victims of sexual assault in prisons and jails than are other inmates.

RIOTING

Rioting is another form of violence. It is group violence. Rioting presents a direct threat to the security of the institution and the inmates in it and is often met with reciprocal force by the staff and administration of the prison. Prison riots have existed as long as there have been prisons—in fact, before there were prisons. Recall the Newgate "prison" of Connecticut (see Chapter 2), where inmates were confined to a copper mine for much of their incarceration. Inmates at Newgate repeatedly rioted throughout the history of its operation. In fact, virtually every maximum- and medium-security prison with any longevity has experienced some form of rioting by inmates. Rioting—and violence in general—is engaged in by inmates to achieve some end, like better food or housing or power, or inmates might riot out of anger or frustration. When violence is used to achieve some end, it is known as *instrumental violence*, but when it is just an angry outburst, then it is known as *expressive violence*. Of course, inmates engaged in violence or a riot could be involved for *both* instrumental and expressive reasons. An inmate who wants to protest the overcrowding of his or her institution may riot to let the world know about the conditions of confinement (instrumental violence), but he or she might also be angry about the effect such crowding has on housing and the ability to sleep and become violent as a means of expressing it. When enough inmates engage in this violence together, it is called a riot.

The two most notorious instances of inmate rioting to date occurred in the **Attica Prison Riot** of 1971 in New York and the **New Mexico Prison Riot** of 1980. At Attica, the riot began with a spontaneous act of violence by one inmate against an officer when the officer tried to break up a fight. The violence spread when other inmates became involved

Attica Prison Riot (1971): The bloodiest prison riot in American history. Ended when the prison was retaken by law enforcement, leaving 10 hostages and 29 inmates dead and 80 inmates wounded.

New Mexico Prison Riot (1980): Prison riot over the conditions of confinement and crowding. The state eventually retook the prison. Over 3 days, 33 inmates were killed by other inmates.

the next day to avenge the punishment of the two fighting inmates (Deane & Bosch, 2000). The riot also spread because inmates were frustrated and angry about the overcrowded conditions and lack of programming for inmates, among other problems with the conditions of confinement; even showering and toilet paper were rationed. There were charges of racism by the mostly African American inmates regarding their treatment by the mostly white staff at Attica as well (Useem & Kimball, 1989). Add to this the student protests against the Vietnam War and the civil rights movement that had roiled the country outside of the Attica prison walls in the late 1960s and early 1970s, and it was clear why there was tension within them.

As the prison staff were unprepared to respond to a riot, the inmates easily took over the Attica prison, burning some buildings and eventually congregating in one yard with their 40 hostages (Deane & Bosch, 2000). In the negotiations between the inmate leaders and the administration, the inmates asked for better food, health care, and the ability to practice their religion. A number of observers, composed of politicians and media members, tried to intervene in the negotiations but to no avail. Some inmates killed three other inmates and one hostage, which also impaired the ability to negotiate. Moreover, Governor Nelson Rockefeller, who was considering a run for the White House at the time, did not want to appear soft on crime by being too soft on the rioting inmates.

In the end, the inmates and administrators could not come to an agreement (the inmates wanted amnesty for the rioters), and eventually, on Governor Rockefeller's orders, the prison was stormed by the state police and by correctional staff. Tear gas was dropped from police helicopters into the occupied yard, and the inmates and their hostages were indiscriminately fired upon with shotguns by the staff and police. As a consequence, 10 hostages and 29 inmates were dead or dying when the prison was secured, and another 80 inmates had gunshot wounds (Useem & Kimball, 1989). It was the bloodiest prison riot in American history. Inmates, even injured ones, were then beaten and humiliated (forced to stand naked in the yard for hours), and medical care was delayed or denied.

The state indicted 60 inmates for a number of crimes, including sodomy and murder, arising out of the riot, but only eight inmates were convicted (Gonnerman, 2001, p. 1). Years of legal wrangling eventually led to the $8 million award by the state of New York to the inmates who were beaten or tortured after the riot (Deane & Bosch, 2000). In 2005, the state paid out another $12 million to the survivors and families of employees killed in the aftermath of the riot (Kirshon, 2010).

In 1980, the New Mexico State Penitentiary also exploded in a riot over the conditions of confinement, which were deplorable, and crowding, which was at epidemic levels. Despite repeated warnings that a riot was going to occur, the administration and staff failed to adequately prepare. When a staff member slipped up in a security measure when locking down a dormitory for the night, he was grabbed, along with his keys, and inmates quickly advanced through the prison, taking control of several cellblocks, including the pharmacy and shops. Drugs and weapons were readily available as a result, and brutal inmate-on-inmate violence ensued. Some of this violence was particularly focused on inmate snitches and child molesters, who were housed in a separate cellblock. Rioting inmates broke into this cellblock, and gruesome and vicious assaults on and murders of these inmates were committed. The state eventually retook the prison without the resulting bloodshed that happened at Attica. However, over the course of 3 days, 33 inmates were killed by other inmates. Numerous other inmates, along with staff hostages, were beaten or raped, and millions of dollars in damage was done (Useem, 1985; Useem & Kimball, 1989). In the aftermath of this riot, New Mexico was sued several times. The state did build a number of medium- and minimum-security prisons following the riot, which eased the overcrowding at the main facility.

SOLUTIONS TO PRISON VIOLENCE

Strategies to Reduce Violence

There are some scholars and social commentators who argue that prisons and jails are naturally violent institutions, essentially for the same reasons that we wrote in the foregoing that they can be incubators for violence (e.g., they hold violent people involuntarily, etc.). But there is evidence that the degree of violence differs markedly from institution to institution and from group to group (Beck et al., 2013). If this is true—that one prison or jail is more or less violent than comparable institutions that hold similar types of inmates (i.e., security level and inmate history of engaging in violence)—then it is implied that it is not that violence is endemic to prisons or jails per se as it is that how the institution operates creates and fosters violence. Therefore, it occurs to us that there are strategies that might be used to reduce violence, such as the following:

Video 9.5: Group Violence Reduction Strategy Shows Positive Results in Washington State Prison

- *Professional subculture:* Promote a professional environment or one where staff are well trained, well educated, and versed in ethical behavior. Promote those who model these values up the career ladder for the institution (see Stohr & Collins, 2014).

- *Personnel:* Hire potentially professional people (people with education and ethical values), train them well, and pay them a wage that will entice them to stay. Training should include the latest research on how to spot and reduce violence in corrections (see Rembert & Henderson, 2014).

- *Supervise:* Promote ethical supervisors who have proven their abilities on the job. Value and facilitate further training, education, and development for them. Then, keep the *span of control* (the number of persons a supervisor is responsible for) within reason so that supervisors can know and influence what is going on around them. Discipline or fire those who violate ethical standards of the institution (see Stohr & Collins, 2014).

- *Classification:* Pay careful attention to inmate histories and proclivities for violence, and separate inmates based on this intelligence. Neutralize criminal gangs so that their influence does not heighten the level of violence in the facility. As much as possible, classify inmates so that their needs can be met (e.g., work

training, proximity to family and their communities, treatment to address their needs, etc.) (see Mears, Stewart, Siennick, & Simons, 2013).

- *Activities:* Provide opportunities for inmates to stay busy in prosocial activities like work, education, treatment, recreation, art, religious engagement, or niches where they are more likely to experience prosocial values. This will benefit them and communities. Also, provide opportunities for inmates to use their talents and abilities (see the discussion of mature coping and niches following, and see also research by Rocheleau, 2013; Wooldredge & Steiner, 2014).

- *Formal grievance procedures:* Ensure that there are formal grievance procedures in place where inmates can report on perceived deficiencies in the operation of the facility and that they can use to vent their concerns. Just having the ability to vent and knowing one is heard can often be enough to alleviate anger and thus violence. Grievance procedures also provide the opportunity for inmates to report on real deficiencies in the prison operations (see Rembert & Henderson, 2014).

- *Ombudsman:* Larger facilities or prison or jail systems may be able to staff an ombudsman position; such a person can investigate serious complaints by staff or inmates and work to resolve them.

- *Open architecture:* When building a new jail or prison or when significantly remodeling them, try to improve the openness of the facility so that sight lines are clearer in living units, as violence is more likely to occur when it cannot be seen (e.g., see the discussion of podular or direct-supervision jails in the chapter on jails, and see research by Wooldredge & Steiner, 2014).

- *Official reporting:* Support the official reporting of violence to auditors at the local, state, or federal level. Note the discussion of PREA in the chapter on jails and the requirement of reporting sexual abuse and assaults in prisons and jails. Sometimes jail and prison managers do not know that their facility is an outlier in terms of the amount of violence that occurs there. Having official reports gets this information out into the sunlight and makes it more likely that there will be efforts to reduce the violence in facilities that have more of it.

- *Involve policy makers and the public:* Keep policy makers and the public apprised of the amount of violence that occurs and why it occurs, and enlist their support and assistance in solutions that would reduce it.

Mature Coping

Prison violence, whether by individuals or groups of rioters, occurs, in part, because some inmates are not capable of interacting or do not know how to interact with others without violence. In his research on corrections, Johnson (2002) noticed that despite the mortification, prisonization, and pains experienced, to different degrees, by incarcerated individuals, some were able to adjust prosocially, even to grow, in a prison setting. Though the exception rather than the rule, he noted that some inmates developed another means of adjusting. This alternative means of handling incarceration—or supervision in the case of probationers and parolees—is **mature coping**. As identified and defined by Johnson,

> Mature coping means, in essence, dealing with life's problems like a responsive and responsible human being, one who seeks autonomy without violating the rights of others, security without resorting to deception or violence, and relatedness to others as the finest and fullest expression of human identity. (p. 83)

As indicated by this definition, the offender needs to learn how to be an adult with some autonomy in an environment where the individual has little formal power (although the informal reality may be different), and his or her status is almost subhuman by wider community standards. Moreover, offenders must accomplish this feat without doing violence to others, though Johnson (2002) allows that violence in self-defense may be necessary, and they need to exercise consideration of others in their environment.

Johnson (2002) notes that mature coping is relatively rare among the inmate population for a number of reasons. He argues that inmates are typically immature in their social relations to begin with, which, of course, is one of the reasons they are in prison in the first place. Because of impoverishment; poor, absent, or abusive parenting; mental illness; abuse of drugs or alcohol at a young age; and schools that fail them or that they fail, offenders enter the criminal justice system with a number of social, psychological, and economic deficits. They are often not used to voluntarily taking responsibility for their actions, as one would expect of "mature" individuals, nor are they typically expected to "empathize with and assist others in need" (p. 93), especially in a prison or jail environment.

Secondly, Johnson (2002) argues that for inmates to maturely cope, it is helpful if they are incarcerated in what he terms a *decent prison*. Such a facility does not necessarily have more programming, staffing, or amenities than the norm, though he thinks it might be helpful if it did; rather, such institutions or programs would be relatively free of violence and would include some opportunities so that inmates might find a *niche* (defined

Mature coping: The ability to adjust prosocially and to respond to problems responsibly and without resorting to violence.

below) to be involved in. In order for inmates to find this niche, however, decent prisons need to include some opportunities for inmates to act autonomously.

Being secure from violence, like autonomy, is basic to human development. In fact, according to Maslow (1998), if the security need is not fulfilled, it will preoccupy offenders and motivate them to engage in behaviors (e.g., bullying or gang activity) that they normally might avoid if they were not feeling continually threatened (Johnson, 2002). Then, assuming that the offender perceives that he is relatively safe, there need to be prosocial activities, including work, school, athletics, church, treatment, or art programs,

IN FOCUS 9.4

The Story of Wilbert Rideau

Wilbert Rideau, an African American, grew up poor to laborer parents in Lawtell, Louisiana, in the 1940s and 1950s. The family moved around the segregated state, from small town to small town, looking for work, eventually settling in Lake Charles, Louisiana. His father drank, womanized, and abused his mother and later the children; he abandoned the family when Wilbert was a teenager, and his family went on welfare.

In the 1950s, Lake Charles was segregated and restricted the opportunities of African Americans to advance in any profession. After he was denied advancement at his low-paying job at a sewing shop, and as a means of leaving town for better opportunities, Wilbert Rideau attempted to rob a nearby bank. The robbery went horribly wrong. He kidnapped three bank employees, killing one and shooting another, in the botched bank robbery attempt. Once caught, almost immediately after committing the crimes, he was nearly lynched instead of being tried, his confession was coerced, the evidence presented was false, and he had inadequate counsel. But he admitted that he had committed the murder, shot another woman, and kidnapped three people.

In 1961, at the age of 19, Rideau was convicted and received a death sentence. He then spent 10 years on death row at the Angola prison in Louisiana. He was eventually released to the general population of the prison when the *Furman v. Georgia* (1972) Supreme Court case invalidated death sentences around the country. He served the rest of his sentence, another 33 years, at the infamous Angola prison and, during most of it, was the editor of *The Angolite*, an inmate newspaper.

In his book, *In the Place of Justice: A Story of Punishment and Deliverance*, Rideau (2010) discusses how, as an inmate, he grew—you might say he maturely coped—by finding a niche at *The Angolite* and doing work that was worthwhile. He won critical acclaim for the uncensored writing about prison life that he was allowed to present to the world by one forward-thinking warden. Once this pattern of an uncensored prison paper had been established, subsequent wardens were reluctant to shut him down, though they tried. Because his writing became known in the outside world, and several wardens even allowed Rideau to leave the prison to talk to community groups, he had a form of power that allowed him access to wardens and directors of prisons. According to Rideau, he used this access to help some inmates, to avert violence against inmates, and to steer wardens in the direction of treatment and programming. He also had plenty of time to regret his crimes and to reflect not only on the racism he had confronted in his life but also on his own racial stereotypes. He observed the workings of the inmate code in prison and learned to walk a fine line between upholding it and staying within the rules.

Rideau was released from prison in 2005 after a court found that his original trial had been mishandled. He had spent a total of 44 years in jails and prisons since his conviction, when the norm for his crime was less than 10. He lives with his wife, whom he met 20 years before on one of his speaking gigs outside of prison. She had spent many years of her life working to free him.

DISCUSSION QUESTIONS

1. How did Rideau "grow" as a human being while incarcerated?

2. How might such growth be increased for all inmates in prisons?

3. What are the chances that Rideau went on to live peaceably once released from prison?

that provide some sort of means for positive-self-value reinforcement. Such places are termed *niches* by Johnson, and the opportunities they afford provide redress for the mortification and pains that offenders, particularly those who are incarcerated, experience.

••• SOCIAL SUPPORT

Social support is a necessary element to successful existence in this world. Humans, for the most part, are social animals in need of the assistance of others, such as families, friends, neighbors, schools, churches, nonprofits, and governments, to grow and thrive. Inmates in prisons and jails perhaps need more social support to succeed than most Americans. They usually come from poor backgrounds where their education was limited, they have few job skills, and socialization in prosocial behavior may have been lacking. Upon release, they will be dependent on family and friends, should they be lucky enough to have some, who are stretched financially and emotionally themselves. Former inmates will leave the prison relatively unskilled, with a GED or less, and the stigma of being an "ex-con." They will have financial obligations for their children and for fines imposed as part of their sentence, and often, they will have to pay for their own supervision in the community. Their needs will be multifaceted and many, and to succeed, they will depend on private and public sources of support.

Lin (1986) defined social support as "the perceived or actual instrumental and/or expressive provisions supplied by the community, social networks, and confiding partners" (p. 18). Cullen (1994) modified this definition to include both formal and informal delivery of this support. *Instrumental support* is material and includes the exchange of goods or money. *Expressive support* is more emotional and is the kind supplied by family and close friends. It is thought that the greater the degree to which inmates experience social support, whether instrumental or emotional, from whatever source while in prisons, the more likely they are to change their behavior while incarcerated (fewer infractions of the rules and less violence) and in the larger community (reduced recidivism) (Woo et al., 2014). Currently, the research in this area is more suggestive than solid, but if evidence indicates that social support reduces the deviance of inmates while incarcerated, then, when released, it would make sense that correctional institutions develop ways to provide social support to inmates or allow others from the community to do so (Beare & Hogg, 2013; Hamilton, Kigerl, & Hays, 2015; Hochstetler, DeLisi, & Pratt, 2010; Lutze, Rosky, & Hamilton, 2013; Mears et al., 2013; Reisig, Holtfreter, & Morash, 2002).

••• SPECIAL POPULATIONS

ELDERLY INMATES

As mentioned in the chapter on jails, the number of elderly people in jails and prisons is increasing at an exponential rate. As America ages, and mandatory sentences and other such laws lengthen sentences, correctional populations are graying. There are a number of collateral consequences that derive from this fact, most of them unintended:

1. The cost of incarceration increases to accommodate the extra medical care needed for older people.

2. Elderly inmates are less able to work in or for the prison, making them a further economic drain on the system.

3. Elderly inmates may require housing that is separate from younger inmates who may prey on them.

4. Elderly inmates, particularly those who have spent much or all of their adult lives in prisons, are less likely to have a supportive family or friends waiting for them on the outside, which makes the development of a parole or reintegration plan even more challenging for them.

As elderly inmates necessarily present such a drain on state and federal correctional budgets, it might make sense for states to rethink the sentencing laws and correctional practices that led to the graying of prison populations nationally (more about this rethinking in the last chapter of the book). To not do so is to support the continued exponential growth in correctional budgets at the expense of all other budget priorities.

PHYSICALLY ILL INMATES

The number of ill people incarcerated in America's prisons and jails has grown in tandem with the number of elderly inmates. At this juncture, about half of inmates in prisons and jails report an illness more serious than a cold or the flu (Maruschak, 2008, p. 1; see also Maruschak, 2006, 2015). According to a 2004 survey of state and federal prison inmates by the Bureau of Justice Statistics, the two most prevalent medical problems for prison inmates were arthritis and hypertension (Maruschak, 2008). Women and elderly inmates in prisons, as in jails, report more medical problems than do other inmates. And heart disease and suicide accounted for most of the deaths in jails while cancer and heart disease claimed over half of those who died in state prisons from 2011 to 2012 (Noonan & Ginder, 2013, p. 1).

The extent of medical care provided for such inmates depends on the jurisdiction, with some larger counties, some states, and the Bureau of Prisons at the federal level providing better care than other jurisdictions. According to that 2004 study, about 70% of the state and 76% of the federal prison inmates with medical problems reported seeing a medical professional at the prison about their illness, and more than 80% reported receiving a medical exam since their admission (Maruschak, 2008, p. 1). However, even in those jurisdictions that can afford to and do provide decent medical care, it is often minimal. Dentistry typically consists of pulling teeth rather than crowning or even filling them. Not much preventive medical care is provided, and the common response to complaints is the provision of medication.

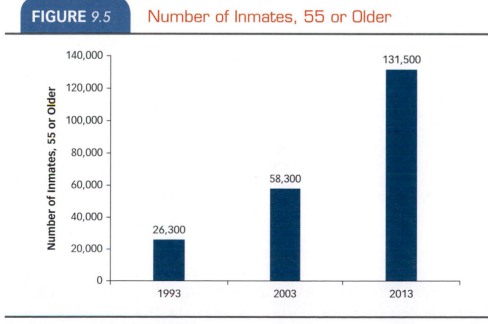

FIGURE *9.5*   Number of Inmates, 55 or Older

Source: U.S. Bureau of Justice Statistics.

Most larger jails have a section devoted to their inmates with medical complaints. Larger prisons or prison systems often have buildings or whole institutions devoted to inmates with medical maladies. The staffing of such sections, buildings, or institutions again varies by jurisdiction and the ability and willingness to pay the high cost for qualified staff (Vaughn & Carroll, 1998; Vaughn & Smith, 1999). Working in a jail or prison medical facility has not usually been the first choice of medical personnel, and so, it is not surprising that it might be hard to recruit and keep the best personnel.

MENTALLY ILL INMATES

The number of mentally ill inmates has also grown in America's prisons, though not to the same extent as it has in the jails (see Chapter 6). As jails became dumping grounds for the mentally ill after mental-health hospitals closed in the 1970s, some of these inmates with chronic mental illnesses have found themselves in a prison environment (Slate & Wesley Johnson, 2008).

The **deinstitutionalization of the mentally ill** in the United States came about as a result of the civil rights movement and the related effort to increase the rights of powerless people (Slate & Wesley Johnson, 2008). Too many people were civilly committed to mental-health institutions for years without any legal recourse or protection, it was thought. In addition, the pharmaceutical company Smith, Kline, & French (now GlaxoSmith-Kline) pushed its drug, Thorazine, as a potential "cure" for some mental illnesses with state legislators who were eager to save money by closing mental-health institutions (Slate & Wesley Johnson, 2008). As legal restrictions on civil commitment of the mentally ill spread across the country and as state legislators believed the claims (which turned out to be unfounded) of the pharmaceutical company, states and counties closed their mental-health hospitals or reduced their capacities significantly. Congress passed the Community Mental Health Act in 1963, which ended much of the federal support for mental-health hospitals. Instead, Congress was to fund less restrictive institutional alternatives, such as halfway houses, but outpatient facilities were either underfunded or shunted away by community members who did not want such facilities in their neighborhoods (Slate & Wesley Johnson, 2008). Thus, an unintended consequence of this deinstitutionalization movement was that there were few public services available in communities to assist the mentally ill and their families. Jails and then prisons became the de facto mental-health patient dumping ground.

Unfortunately, as with those who have major medical problems, most prisons and jails are ill equipped and ill staffed to handle mentally ill inmates. There are difficulties in diagnosis, management of people who do not understand how to behave in a prison, programming and developing appropriate prison employment, and devising a reentry plan (Slate & Wesley Johnson, 2008). Any treatment programming available has a long waiting list. Sometimes staff need to be concerned that the mentally ill inmates require protection from predation, and to protect other inmates, they will need to keep an eye on the violent outbursts of mentally ill patients, as they might injure others (Wood & Buttaro, 2013). Some studies link PTSD with an assault history, propensity for revictimization, violent behavior, substance abuse, and mental illness, so it is no surprise that there needs to be trauma-related treatments available for the mentally ill in prisons as well (Wood & Buttaro, 2013).

Deinstitutionaliza-tion of the mentally ill: This happened in the United States as a result of the civil rights movement and the related effort to increase the rights of people involuntarily committed to mental hospitals.

Needless to say, the cost of providing medical and mental-health care to an aging and ill correctional population is cost prohibitive. However, as these inmates are unable to access such services in communities due to their incarceration, such costs must be borne.

GAY, LESBIAN, BISEXUAL, TRANSGENDER, AND INTERSEX INMATES

The true number of gay, lesbian, bisexual, transgender, and intersex (LGBTI) inmates in corrections is not known. According to Gary Gates (personal communication, March

PERSPECTIVE FROM A PRACTITIONER

Michael Klein, Correctional Officer

Position: Correctional officer (2006–2009)

Location: Indiana Department of Corrections, Wabash Valley Correctional Facility

Education: MA in criminal justice; currently completing a PhD in criminal justice

What is your previous experience in criminal justice?

I have worked as a juvenile correctional officer and in private security and social services.

What are the duties and responsibilities of a correctional officer?

Maintaining the safety and security of the facility, mediating offender disputes, ensuring one's personal security, ensuring the safety of offenders, and ensuring the safety of one's fellow officers.

What are the characteristics and traits most useful for a correctional officer?

Patience, courage, ability to work as a team member, understanding, ability to keep calm in disturbing situations, and a strong stomach

What was your typical workday as a correctional officer?

First, I would enter the facility and go through a security check. I would then arrive at my post, greet the prior shift of officers, and sign into the logbook. I had several different positions within the WVCF, and my activities varied by position. If I worked in a cell house, there would be the initial rush of complaints, concerns, and questions from the offenders. I would then try my best to maintain a smooth shift as 100 offenders milled freely about me. If I worked in segregation, there was less offender contact, but there were a lot more messy situations to contain. The daily activities of a correctional officer are both banal and uncertain. You never really know what to expect.

What is your advice for future correctional officers?

Keep your cool, stay out of bad situations, and ask for help. Working in corrections is something that each officer has to figure out for himself or herself. Just be sure to think things through before making any rash judgments.

14, 2011), a demographer with the Williams Institute at the University of California–Los Angeles School of Law, estimates, based on surveys that query people about their sexual orientation and **gender identity** (the gender one identifies with, rather than the sex of one's genitalia when born), suggest that about 3% to 5% of the free community are gay, lesbian, or bisexual. Gates notes that the percentage of transgender (and likely intersex) people in the community is also unknown, but it is likely 1% or less. In a recent study published by the Williams Institute, the researchers estimate, based on state-level surveys, that about 0.6% of adults identify as transgender, or about 1.4 million people in the United States (Flores, Herman, Gates, & Brown, 2016, p. 1). Based on these estimates, we might reasonably expect that similar percentages for each group are represented in prisons. In addition, as heterosexual relations are formally restricted in prisons, there is some percentage of male and female inmates who engage in homosexual relations while incarcerated, though they may never have done so when they were free. Lieb and his colleagues (2011) found that the percentage of men who have ever had sex with men in the free community ranges around 6.4%. We might expect, therefore, that the percentage of men who engage in sexual relations with other men while in prison is likely around 6% or higher.

As with gays and lesbians, the exact number of transgender and intersex people in communities is unknown, as they often keep their feelings on this matter hidden, knowing

Gender identity:
The gender one identifies with, rather than the gender associated with the genitalia one is born with.

they might be marginalized (Tewksbury & Potter, 2005). In prisons, the number of transgender inmates is also difficult to know, although large male prisons will often house many (Sexton, Jenness, & Sumner, 2010). In their study of transgender female inmates in California prisons, Jenness and her colleagues (2007, as cited in Sexton et al., 2010) found that they are much more likely than other inmates (59%, as compared with 4.4% for nontransgender inmates) to report being sexually assaulted while in prison (a report that is backed up by PREA-inspired research by the Bureau of Justice Statistics [Beck et al., 2013]).

Protecting sexual-orientation and gender identity minorities in prisons presents a challenge for administrators, particularly in male prisons. Male bravado and posturing to show strength and ward off attacks is common in male prisons, which makes males who are unable or unwilling to put on such fronts targets for abuse or predation. If one is a transgender inmate in a male prison or a person who was once biologically male but through dress, hormonal treatment, and/or surgery is now a female, the challenges mount. Not only must administrators be concerned about the safety of the inmate, but they must also figure out a way to accommodate her needs for privacy, medical treatment, and housing. As noted in the chapter on jails, PREA regulations are now requiring greater consideration of the privacy, respect, and medical needs of transgender and intersex inmates, as they have been a particular target for abuse in jails and prisons, particularly transgender women in men's prisons (Routh et al., 2014; Sexton et al., 2010; Stohr, 2014).

In women's prisons, as with racial and ethnic minorities, there appears to be more acceptance of both lesbian and transgender inmates; part of this greater acceptance may have to do with the sense that women inmates have direct experience with marginalization and therefore are more understanding of those who vary from the norm in sexual orientation or gender identity. Or it might have to do with the lesser need of women in prisons to defend themselves physically from the predation of other inmates; the frequency of violent and sexual attacks in women's prisons by other inmates, as far as this can be determined, is much lower than it is in men's facilities (Britton, 2003).

AP Photo/Pat Sullivan

PHOTO 9.6: Transgender and bisexual inmates visit in their specially designated cellblock in the Harris County Jail in Houston, Texas. Separate facilities for transgender female inmates protects their privacy and enhances their safety from assault by male inmates.

PERSPECTIVE FROM A FORMER INMATE

Rex E. Hammond, Former Inmate and Doctoral Student

Location: Indiana Department of Corrections

Education: MA in criminal justice; doctoral student in criminal justice

Previous experience in criminal justice: 27 years in juvenile and adult jails and prisons

Prison and Change
By Rex E. Hammond*

Quite often, people discuss the negative effects of incarceration, and there are a plethora of these to concentrate on: disrespecting prison staff, being treated like an animal by some correctional staff, engaging in fights, stabbings, illegal gambling and drugs, learning new and different ways to commit crimes, and being oppressed, depressed, and separated from family and the larger society. However, I thought I would discuss a couple of the positive effects of spending over 27 years (two as a juvenile and 25 as an adult) behind concrete walls and razor wire fences.

Currently, I am a 51-year-old PhD student. However, prior to this, I was a life course criminal. My crimes as a youth included the following: runaway, truancy, incorrigibility, theft, burglary, and armed robbery. As an adult, I took a deputy hostage in a county jail and was engaged in a series of armed robberies. My first run-in with the law was when I was 9 years old, and my last was at the age of 32; in between, I was repeatedly in and out of juvenile halls or adult jails and prisons. My last incarceration consisted of a 13.5-year stay in prison.

Students and professors may wonder what on Earth I could possibly have to say that is positive about spending over half of my life imprisoned. Well, during a college presentation I gave, a female student asked me a question: Have you ever thought about fate? It was perhaps the best question I have ever been asked.

I had a brother who was two years older than me. He was my idol, and I looked up to him. He was a strong influence in my early life—introducing me to drugs, crime, and an uncontrollable temper; however, he never served prison time. He spent his life in the free community only to become an alcoholic for over 25 years. He was an ex-Marine, suffered from depression, was in and out of volatile relationships, and was heavily addicted to gambling and prescription pills. Four months after my final release from prison, he committed suicide by parking on a country road, putting a handgun to his head, and pulling the trigger. So to answer her question, yes, since my brother's suicide, I have often thought of fate.

You see, had I not spent almost my entire life incarcerated, the opportunities for me to become just like the brother I "idolized" would have greatly increased. I find that prison probably saved my life. Though it took me years to grow, understand, and mature, I was finally able to undergo enough self-reflection that I found the strength and self-determination to succeed. It was after getting my associate's degree in prison (2001), coupled with the cognitive behavioral programming, that I was able to change the way I thought and then my behavior. Maybe this is very elementary, but early in my life, I never knew that I could control the way I thought, thus changing my reactions and behavior. Throughout my life behind bars, I observed this to be true for many repeat or life course criminals. They think that they are reduced to reacting the way they have always reacted. Prison gave me the opportunity to alter my thinking process and to gain better control over my emotions.

When I first entered the adult Indiana prison system in 1983 at the age of 19, there were no college programs or cognitive behavioral programs. In addition, prisons were not designed for controlled offender movement, meaning inmates could move about the prison without accountability, oversight, or a particular schedule. This lack of control created plenty of opportunities for inmates to engage in violent acts against other inmates and other criminal behavior without detection. When I began my prison term, the only programming available was GED classes, vocational training, or work lines. While vocational training affords inmates the opportunity to learn an employment skill, it does nothing to help offenders make it through the strain and stressful situations they will encounter in society. It was not until the 1980s, after Dr. Stanton Samenow and Dr. Samuel Yochelson's studies of violent offenders, that the benefits of cognitive behavioral programming for prisoners became clear. Indiana's Department of Corrections began to adopt this change in the 1990s.

(Continued)

(Continued)

Life is all about being able to change and adapt. I began my incarceration as a young punk: engaging in unruly behavior, gambling, drugs, drinking homemade brew, tattooing, and fighting with prison staff, often finding myself spending months upon months in solitary confinement. Just like my brother, I was spinning out of control as each day passed. However, as the prison environment transformed, I found myself engaging in this adjustment and utilizing the opportunities that prison granted me. It gave me the opportunity to experience great personal growth. I also witnessed firsthand the way the Indiana prison system changed over a quarter of a century. Getting my college degree while imprisoned and participating in various cognitive behavioral programs afforded me the opportunity for self-development. While my brother spent 25 years sinking further into a darkened hole, prison gave me the chance to spend 25 years climbing out of one.

DISCUSSION QUESTIONS

1. Do you think that if Rex (or inmates like him) had been afforded more programming earlier in his prison sentence that this might have changed his behavior earlier? Why, or why not?

2. Is it possible that programming in the community could have been as helpful in changing Rex's behavior as it was in the prison?

3. What do you think would have happened if, instead of 25 years in prison, Rex's sentence was reduced to 15 or 10 years because of his successful completion of programming? In other words, what amount of time was sufficient punishment for his crimes and enough time for him to rehabilitate?

4. What can we learn about redemption and the renewal of one's spirit from Rex's story?

*Rex E. Hammond was a doctoral student in the Department of Criminal Justice and Criminology at Washington State University. He earned his bachelor's and master's degrees from the Department of Criminology and Criminal Justice at Indiana State University. Before that, he spent 27 years as an inmate in juvenile and adult jails and prisons.

SUMMARY

- Prisons come in various shapes and security levels.

- To varying degrees, inmates experience mortification and pain related to their status, and as humans, they will behave in either pro- or antisocial ways to lessen that pain.

- Inmates adopt certain roles and engage in certain behaviors because they are prisonized and adopt the subculture or because they import aspects of the culture from the outside community into the prison.

- *Total institutions* exist to different degrees, depending on the security level and operation of prisons.

- Gangs and violence are one way that inmates "adjust" to their environment and have their needs met and their pain alleviated.

- Strategies to reduce violence exist and can be practiced by agencies interested in reducing violence.

- Mature coping is one way that correctional clients can fruitfully "adjust" and perhaps reform in that environment.

- Social support, even when inmates are on the "inside," may potentially have prosocial effects (e.g., reduce violence) while inmates are in the prison and once they leave.

- Special-population inmates present unique challenges for administrators interested in meeting their needs and keeping them safe in the correctional environment.

KEY TERMS

Attica Prison Riot (1971) 221

Deinstitutionalization of the mentally ill 228

Gangs (prison) 217

Gender identity 229

Importation 211

Mature coping 224

Maximum-security prisons 207

Medium-security prisons 209

Minimum-security prisons 209

Mortification 211

New Mexico Prison Riot (1980) 221

Pains of imprisonment 212

Prison subculture 215

Prisonization 211

Prisons 204

Supermax prisons 206

Total institution 211

DISCUSSION QUESTIONS

1. Which prison, from our history of prison chapters, most reminds you of supermaximum-security prisons? What were the problems with this historical prison? Based on what we know of that prison from our history, what problems do you foresee arising with the supermax prisons of today?

2. Define what a *total institution* is and how it might vary by type of correctional arrangement (e.g., probation, parole, jail, or prison) and inmate status.

3. Inmate subcultures are thought to be related to the concepts of prisonization, importation, and the pains of imprisonment. Discuss how and why this might be so.

4. What are the attributes of gangs that make them appealing to inmates in prisons? How might that appeal be reduced by prison managers?

5. What are some of the difficulties that correctional organizations might face in employing the strategies to reduce violence? Who would you expect to support these strategies, and who would not?

6. How might correctional clients configure their environment to ensure their own reform? How might we, as citizens, assist them in that endeavor?

7. What might be the most effective strategies for managing special populations in prisons?

USEFUL INTERNET SITES

Please note that the sites listed can be accessed at edge.sagepub.com/stohrcorrections.

American Correctional Association: www.aca.org

The ACA is an organization that has, for 146 years, focused on professionalizing corrections in the United States. Their website and materials provide information on the latest training, research, and ideas in corrections.

American Friends Service Committee: www.afsc.org

This is a Quaker organization interested in correctional reform.

Bureau of Justice Statistics: www.bjs.gov

The BJS provides an incredible wealth of information about all manner of criminal justice topics, including corrections. It is one of our go-to websites when we are investigating a correctional topic (or police or courts, etc.).

Federal Bureau of Prisons: www.bop.gov

The Federal Bureau of Prisons website provides information about prisons at the federal level and about the staff who labor in them.

The Sentencing Project: www.sentencingproject.org

The Sentencing Project is a nonprofit organization that has agitated for sentencing reform for decades. It is also a repository for research on sentencing in the United States.

The Williams Institute—UCLA School of Law: www.law.ucla.edu/williamsinstitute

The Williams Institute is a think tank devoted to research on law and public policies concerned with sexual orientation and gender identity.

Vera Institute: www.vera.org

The Vera Institute has been behind some of the biggest criminal justice reforms of the last 40 years. Check out their website to learn what important reforms and issues are on the correctional horizon.

$SAGE edge™

Sharpen your skills with SAGE edge at **edge.sagepub.com/stohrcorrections**. SAGE edge for Students provides a personalized approach to help you accomplish your coursework goals in an easy-to-use learning environment. You'll find action plans, mobile-friendly eFlashcards, and quizzes as well as video, web, and resources and links to SAGE journal articles to support and expand on the concepts presented in this chapter.

10

Classification and Assessment of Offenders

TEST YOUR KNOWLEDGE

Test your present knowledge of the assessment and classification of offenders by answering the following questions, true or false. Check your answers on page 536 after reading the chapter.

1. The subjective judgment of mental-health professionals is superior to statistical data in predicting the future behavior of offenders.

2. Predicting human behavior is fairly easy, given the right tools.

3. Prisons in the past made no efforts to classify inmates by age, gender, or mental health.

4. The primary purpose of assessing and classifying inmates is rehabilitation.

5. In probation and parole, the rehabilitative needs of offenders take precedence over their risk of reoffending.

6. The assessment and classification of offenders lets probation and parole officers make better use of their time.

7. While classification is useful for prison officials, it is not for inmates.

LEARNING OBJECTIVES

• Evaluate the importance of assessment and classification in identifying custody status and offender risk and needs

• Describe the history of offender classification and how it has evolved

• Examine the important items on a classification scale, and discuss why you think they are important

• Correctly score a risk and needs scale according to a hypothetical case

• Describe the limitations inherent in classifying humans

THE CHALLENGES OF CLASSIFICATION

Frank King was a 26-year-old male gainfully employed at a local factory and attending college in Chicago. In 1990, he embarked on a short-lived spree, robbing local fast-food restaurants at gunpoint at closing time. He committed four successful robberies until one night, he was disturbed by police sirens and ran from the store. A police officer pursued on foot and was shot in the leg by Frank, who was able to escape. Unfortunately for Frank, he dropped his backpack containing schoolbooks and other identifying information, which was retrieved by the police. Knowing he had no other choice, Frank turned himself in the next day and was arrested and jailed.

Three months later, Frank pled guilty to one count of armed robbery and one count of aggravated assault and was referred to the probation department for a presentence investigation report (PSI). The investigating officer found that Frank was an entirely atypical criminal. He came from a solidly middle-class, intact home; had an IQ in the bright-to-normal range, was gainfully employed, was attending college, and had no juvenile or adult criminal history. In fact, his college major was criminal justice, and he had recently passed the test to become a

member of the Cook County Sheriff's Department. Frank told the probation officer that the reason he robbed the restaurants was to obtain extra money to spend on his fiancée, Grace, who apparently had expensive tastes. The officer's inquiries determined that Frank was unhealthily obsessed with Grace, to the point that he had a shrine complete with candles and incense dedicated to her set up in his bedroom. But he was also cruel and possessive at times, hanging her pet cat when he suspected Grace of being interested in some other man.

Frank was sentenced to a total of 14 years in prison for both crimes. When he arrived at the penitentiary, Frank was given the usual battery of tests to classify him for custody level within the prison and to determine his rehabilitative needs. When he is paroled, his parole officer will have to do the same thing to determine his supervision level. Given Frank's very serious crimes, combined with his previously exemplary lifestyle, classifying him (putting him in some sort of category with similar others) will be a demanding task. We will refer to Frank's case when discussing the various classification instruments in this chapter.

••• WHAT IS CLASSIFICATION AND ASSESSMENT?

Web 10.1:
Objective Jail
Classification
Systems

Classification and assessment are related but distinct processes that are vital to the just and efficient operation of the correctional system. **Classification** is the process of sorting things into categories according to their shared qualities or characteristics to achieve some purpose. The "things" being classified in the criminal justice system are people, and the purpose for categorizing them into distinct groups is so that we can have some idea what we should do with them (how closely should we supervise them, and what resources should we provide for them?) and how they should respond to what we do. We have already encountered a comprehensive sentencing guideline in Chapter 5 (Figure 5.6) that classifies convicted felons according to the seriousness of their crimes and criminal histories for the purpose of making sentencing decisions. Likewise, prison authorities classify inmates according to dangerousness and escape risk in order to protect staff and other inmates and to determine their security level housing (minimum, medium, and maximum security), and probation and parole authorities classify offenders according to treatment needs and the risk they pose to the community.

Classifying prison inmates is an immensely important function that is never taken lightly. Austin and McGinnis (2004) describe the reason for and purpose of classification as follows:

Web 10.2:
Prisoner Intake
Systems

> During the past decade, prison systems have experienced increased pressure to improve their approaches to classifying prisoners according to custody, work, and programming needs. Litigation and overcrowding have caused classification systems to be viewed as a principal management tool for allocating scarce prison resources efficiently and minimizing the potential for violence or escape. These systems are also expected to provide greater accountability and to help forecast future prison bedspace and prisoner program needs. In other words, a properly functioning classification system is seen as the "brain" of prison management. (p. 1)

Classification is thus about making predictions about how offenders sorted into categories can be expected to behave in prison, on probation, or on parole and what the respective agencies can do to try to assure that they will behave responsibly while in their charge and thereafter. Make no mistake, though; prediction is a very tricky business. As the great physicist Niels Bohr once said (tongue in cheek), "Prediction is hard, especially about the future."

PREDICTING BEHAVIOR

Classification:
Classification is the process of sorting things into categories according to their shared qualities or characteristics to achieve some purpose.

Actuarial method:
A method of making predictions based on statistical analyses of behavior patterns of people similarly situated, averaged over many thousands of cases.

Making predictions about human behavior is difficult, but the best way to predict any person's behavior is what he or she has done in the past—"past is prologue," wrote William Shakespeare. However, the correctional system's aim is to change a person's criminal behavior, so predictions based solely on previous behavior are inadequate; we need to be forward looking, as well as backward looking. We can also make predictions based on expert diagnosis and evaluation, such as a psychologist or psychiatrist might make, although such judgments have been found inferior to actuarial predictions. The **actuarial method** of making predictions is based on statistical analyses of behavior patterns of people similarly situated, averaged over many thousands of cases. The comprehensive sentencing guideline is an example of using actuarial data to make important decisions. In forging the makeup of the guidelines, researchers examined previous decisions of Ohio judges over a period of two years and included in the guidelines information that the typical judge considered important. According to Gottfredson and Moriarty (2006), actuarial methods are a big improvement over clinical judgments because "in virtually all decision-making situations . . . actuarially developed predictions outperform human judgments." (p. 180). Like all rules, however, there are exceptions. Most assessment instruments provide room for being overridden in exceptional circumstances, as we will see when we apply them to Frank King.

PHOTO 10.1: Jail Booking photographs an inmate being booked at the Saline County Sheriff's Office, Nebraska.

Any classification process dealing with human beings and their predicted behavior is obviously prone to error, which is why we try to take as much subjectivity out of the process as possible. Even so-called "objective" classification instruments contain a great deal of potential for error. We talk about two types of prediction errors: *false positive* and *false negative*. A false positive prediction is one in which we predict a high level of offender risk when there is no risk, and a false negative is predicting a low level of offender risk when there is actually a considerable risk. Classification errors tend more often to be false positive than false negative, indicating the tendency of classification instruments to err on the side of caution (Bench & Allen, 2003). There are obvious problems associated with classification errors. If offenders who pose a real risk to the prison population are not classified as such (false negative), prison security and order are threatened. On the other hand, if we err and deprive offenders of rights and privileges because they are wrongly classified as high risk (false positive), we become excessively punitive. There is very little we can do about this except to continually strive to produce better classification instruments.

ASSESSING RISKS AND NEEDS

Assessment is the process of making a judgment about something or someone based on certain criteria. For instance, a student's academic progress is assessed by his or her grades on a variety of tests and how they may have improved with tutoring. If we wish to go beyond academic achievement to assess (evaluate) his or her social and emotional development, we require other methods. In the correctional field, assessment is the process of subjecting offenders to a formal evaluation and analysis of their deficiencies and needs and the risks they pose to the community so that prison treatment specialists and probation and parole officers can develop realistic plans and strategies to help them to walk the straight and narrow. To accomplish assessment, correctional workers use well-researched and tested instruments that document the knowledge, skills, attitudes, beliefs, strengths, weaknesses, needs, deficiencies, and many other things that may have precipitated an offender's criminal behavior and that may help or be a hindrance in the rehabilitative process. Attempting to supervise, counsel, advise, and otherwise help an offender without a thorough assessment is

Journal Article 10.1:
Sex Offender Risk Assessment

Audio 10.1:
The Hidden Discrimination in Criminal Risk-Assessment Scores

Assessment: The process of making a judgment about something or someone based on certain criteria.

rather like a physician performing surgery without first conducting a thorough diagnostic workup of a patient.

••• THE HISTORY OF CLASSIFICATION AND ASSESSMENT

As we have seen in previous chapters, societies have historically responded to criminal acts almost exclusively from a retributivist stance. Punishment was always backward looking, focusing on what the offender had done, rather than forward looking, focusing on what he or she might do in the future. Punishment was swift and cruel, so there was no need to concern oneself with how best to house, supervise, or treat those convicted of crimes. In later periods, if convicts were consigned to prison, they typically were rat-infested human warehouses in which no concern was paid to anything other than keeping them there. Early jails and prisons did not even classify inmates according to age or gender, throwing males, females, adults, and children together with highly dangerous and mentally unstable inmates (Clement, 1993).

EARLY ATTEMPTS AT CLASSIFICATION

There were some attempts to differentiate among offenders in the early United States, but this form of "classification" was designed to be mostly punitive in nature, and there was no meaningful assessment of their risk and needs. For instance, Philadelphia's Walnut Street Prison inaugurated a system that separated serious offenders from less serious offenders. Those classified as serious offenders were placed in isolation and were not allowed to work or interact with other prisoners. In the early 1800s, the Charlestown Prison in Massachusetts established a trilevel system of classification based on prior convictions. Distinctive uniforms identified each of the three strictly segregated groups. Offenders were assigned quarters, prison work, and differential access to various amenities based on their classification. First-time offenders received the best quarters, job assignments, and food. Second-time offenders were allowed only two meals per day and performed less desirable work, and third-time, or habitual, offenders did the most menial tasks and received the worst food and accommodation (Walsh & Stohr, 2010).

Alexander Maconochie's mark system (to be discussed in Chapter 12) was a sort of classificatory system. Inmates on Norfolk Island could earn "tickets of leave" and eventual release by earning "marks" by displaying good character and demonstrating the willingness to work hard at accomplishing tasks. Other early penal pioneers, such as Walter Crofton in the United Kingdom and Zebulon Brockway in the United States, implemented similar systems that could be construed as classification. Similarly, the American Prison Association's (now the American Correctional Association, or ACA) 1870 *Declaration of Principles* saw classification almost identically to the way Alexander Maconochie did: "The progressive classification of prisoners, based on character and work on some well-adjusted mark system, should be established in all prisons above the common jail." That is, prisoners should be classified according to how well they behave in prison, which essentially meant that the prisoners classified themselves by their behavior. This is simply a wait-and-see strategy determined solely by the inmate's behavior, to which prison authorities reacted by awarding them with marks if they behaved well and worked hard. In modern times, correctional authorities go beyond simple reaction to proactively classify offenders so that prison and probation and parole professionals can securely and safely manage offenders and assist them in becoming law-abiding citizens.

In response to the growing lawlessness in the United States during Prohibition, President Herbert Hoover established the National Commission on Law Observance and Enforcement (otherwise known as Wickersham Commission) in 1929. Although primarily concerned with law enforcement, the commission blamed the large number of prison riots that occurred in the 1920s on "inmate idleness, arbitrary rules and punishments, and the failure of rehabilitation" (McShane & Williams, 1996, p. 385). Among other things, the commission recommended individualized treatment based on proper classification in the context of indeterminate sentences. However, its main concerns were obviously prison security, staff safety, and public protection, which are rightfully the primary considerations in any criminal justice classification system.

Any useful advances in proper classification had to wait for a federal court ruling in *Morris v. Travisono* (1970). This case was brought by inmates at a Rhode Island prison, filing under 42 USC §1983 ("Section 1983"), which is a civil rights claim filed for some deprivation-of-rights grievance. The inmates alleged that they had been discriminatorily segregated from the general prison population and placed in a control unit, where they were denied opportunities to work, attend church, and engage in other prison activities. The complaint addressed the constitutionality of the classification and disciplinary procedures in the prison and eventually led to a federally mandated set of procedures for classifying prisoners, to be overseen by the federal courts. The functions and benefits of proper classification are amply noted in the following excerpt from the decision in *Morris v. Travisono:*

> Classification contributes to a smoothly, efficiently-operated correctional program by the pooling of all relevant information concerning the offender, by devising a program for the individual based upon that information, and by keeping that program realistically in line with the individual's requirements. It furnishes an orderly method to the institution administrator by which the varied needs and requirements of each inmate may be followed through from commitment to discharge. Through its diagnostic and coordinating functions, classification not only contributes to the objective of rehabilitation but also to custody, discipline, work assignments, officer and inmate morale, and the effective use of training opportunities. Through the data it develops, it assists in long-range planning and development, both in the correctional system as a whole and in the individual institution. (at 865)

••• CLASSIFICATION TODAY

Classification takes precedence over needs assessment in institutional corrections. The courts have thus charged correctional administrators with placing each offender in the least restrictive setting consistent with the safety and security goals of the institution and with the needs of the offender. Inmate classification is perhaps the most involved aspect of inmate supervision because it addresses issues of security, treatment, and other issues of concern to the safe and smooth operation of the prison. As Bartollas (2004) remarks, "The classification of inmates is important in a humane prison. Proper classification can do much to provide a safe and secure facility" (p. 156).

Figure 10.1 provides an overview of the typical process of inmate classification. It is clear that classification is a valuable management tool devised for both the benefit of correctional administrators and offenders. It "profiles" offenders so that resources can be allotted where they are most needed. Because it serves such a function, proper classification aids in the adjustment and rehabilitative goals of offenders, whether they are in prisons, jails, or residing in the community. Because it also classifies offenders according to the risks they pose to others, proper classification protects other inmates and correctional

Career Video 10.1:
Division Chief

AP Video 10.1:
Inmates Fires

Video 10.1:
Modern
Classification
Systems

FIGURE *10.1*   Overview of Inmate Initial, Internal, and Reclassification Systems

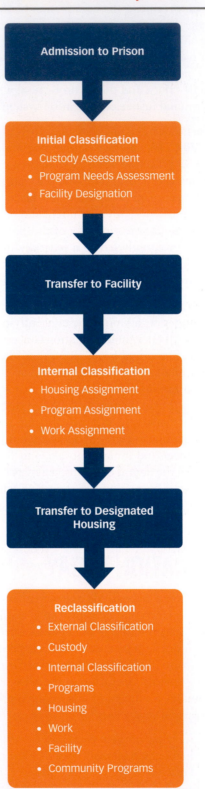

Source: Hardyman, Austin, Alexander, Johnson, and Tulloch (2002). National Institute of Corrections.

staff, as well as members of the general public, from the predations of the dangerous of offenders.

Following a sentence of imprisonment, offenders are transported to the designated facility. Upon arrival at the institution, all offenders are considered close-custody (closely watched and guarded) inmates pending initial classification at a part of the prison usually called the reception and diagnostic unit. The function of the security staff, at this point, is to instill the reality of prison security in the newly committed inmate. During inmates' stay at the reception and diagnostic unit, security and programming staff closely observe their adjustment and behavior, and these observations are forwarded to the classification committee for inclusion in their assessments and evaluations.

According to Hardyman, Austin, and Peyton (2004), all institutions conduct a standard "core" of prison intake functions, and the standard stay at an intake or reception facility is 40 days for males and 31 days for females. The identified intake functions include the following:

1. Identifying the prisoner (photographing, fingerprinting, and so forth)

2. Developing the prisoner's record

3. Performing medical and mental-health assessments

4. Determining the prisoner's threat to safety and his or her security requirements

5. Identifying security threat groups

6. Identifying sex offenders, sexual predators, and vulnerable inmates

Figure 10.1 identifies the various assessment and classification tasks, those responsible for these tasks, and the instruments and/or processes by which these tasks are accomplished.

Once pertinent tests and examinations have been completed and consolidated, new inmates are then given a classification interview in which the factors that establish risk and custody levels are explained to them. The psychological, educational, and vocational needs that have been identified during the assessment period also are explained, and inmates are informed about available programs and how they may access them.

The next step is to determine if there are any override considerations. An *override* means that factors not addressed in classification instruments are considered important enough to overrule the custody level indicated by them in favor of another custody option. Areas of concern related to security and order maintenance include gang or organized-crime affiliations. Areas of concern related to custodial safety include consideration of suicidal gestures, the protection of any inmates known to be informants, and the protection of inmates whose crimes make them targets for abuse, such as child molesters. The override option provides for both objective and subjective considerations, and committee chairpersons are usually required to justify the reasons for overriding the classification instrument in writing.

ETHICAL ISSUE 10.1

What Would You Do?

You are the chairperson of the classification committee in a state penitentiary. Among the new arrivals at the reception and diagnostic center is one Calvin Morgan, who has been convicted of manslaughter. Calvin is put through the usual battery of assessment and classification tests and his score puts him in maximum-custody housing, due primarily to the nature of his offense. (He also has one prior conviction for assault.) However, the prison chaplain knew Calvin on the outside, as a member of his congregation, and tells you that he is a thoroughly decent religious person, except when he is drinking, and wants you to override his custody placement and place him in medium custody, "away from the influence of really bad and Godless inmates." You are also a deeply religious person and are friendly with the chaplain and don't want to offend him. On the other hand, religion is not supposed to be a factor in classification, and prison safety and security is supposed to come before all other considerations. Would you heed the chaplain's request or deny it?

Audio 10.2: Supreme Court Weighs Legality of Strip Searches

Video 10.2: Laws That Allowed Escaped Murderer Outside Prison Walls

PERSPECTIVE FROM A PRACTITIONER

Sheila Gibson, Assessment and Classification Specialist

Position: Assessment and classification specialist

Location: Texas Department of Criminal Justice

Education: BA in general business, Sam Houston State University

What, if any, previous criminal justice experience do you have?

My previous criminal justice experience is as a clerk typist for four years and purchaser for two years.

What are your primary duties and responsibilities?

The primary responsibility of an assessment and classification specialist (ACS) is to interview newly received offenders and review official records to gather sociological data. Official records include but are not limited to Texas Crime Information Center (TCIC) and National Crime Information Center (NCIC) arrest records; court documents, such as judgments and sentences; jail conduct reports; offense or police reports; prior incarceration records; disciplinary cases; medical and mental-health evaluations; and numerous assessments for IQ, educational achievement, drug and alcohol use, and risk factors for recidivism. An ACS identifies offenders that are known or suspected gang members, offenders with enemies on assigned units, and offenders that are an escape risk, as well as offenders requiring special housing as a result of at-risk behavior, aggressive or vulnerable characteristics, or medical or mental-health conditions. This information is then compiled and used to classify offenders and ensure appropriate unit, custody, and housing assignments. An ACS may provide a first offender with referrals and information about intake and the classification process.

What are the characteristics and traits most useful in your line of work?

Good communication skills and intuition are very useful, as you will be interviewing many offenders from various backgrounds and socioeconomic statuses. Being able to obtain the information you need often depends on how well you are able to adapt the interview and ask follow-up questions based on the cues you receive. This skill is employed throughout the interview and allows you to glean additional information and details not originally volunteered. Time management skills are also very important, as new offenders come in on a daily

basis and must be processed through intake in a timely manner. You must have efficient note-taking and writing skills. As you conduct an interview, you are constantly taking notes that you must later be able to go back and turn into a cohesive and comprehensive profile of the offender.

Please describe a typical workday.

As an assessment and classification specialist, I am required to interview up to eight offenders each day. A typical workday involves a preliminary review of available documents before an offender is called to be interviewed. I then conduct an interview with each offender in which I gather information that will then be used to classify the offender. After my interviews are complete, I then begin a more comprehensive assessment of an offender's previous criminal history to locate the disposition of every arrest and incarceration since he was a juvenile. This includes a thorough examination of previous institutional behavior, focusing on violent acts of misconduct, gang involvement, or past indicators of escape, weapons possession, and so forth. All of this information is then compiled, computerized, and presented in a format known as a *travel card*, which will follow the offender throughout his or her incarceration. An ACS specialist is also responsible for creating a detailed summary of the present offense(s) and noting any significant comments from victim impact statements.

What is your advice to someone who wants to enter your field?

Being an assessment and classification specialist can be challenging. We are often placed in situations with offenders who are very unpredictable. To be successful, you must be able to gauge the situation you are in to know how to handle each individual offender. Some are new to the system and don't know the process or what to expect while others have been in and out of the system numerous times. You can never allow yourself to become complacent while working as an ACS. Anything can happen inside a prison facility, and you always need to be prepared. Although challenging, being an assessment and classification specialist can also be rewarding. You are an important segment in the offender intake process, helping to ensure the safety and security of all offenders and staff.

THE NATIONAL INSTITUTE OF CORRECTIONS CUSTODY CLASSIFICATION MODEL

As we see from Figure 10.1, the first concern of inmate classification is custodial level. **Custodial level** refers to the prison housing area inmates are assigned to and the degree of supervision they receive, which can be minimum, medium, or maximum. Access to programs and activities, such as educational and vocational opportunities, counseling services, and recreational and hobby activities, is largely determined by custody level, regardless of inmates' needs—safety must always be the major classificatory concern.

The **National Institute of Corrections Model for Custody and Need** instrument identifies eight areas of assessment that provide for objective custodial placement. To accurately assess the new inmate, the classification committee refers to the detailed classification manual that accompanies the instrument. Based on the offender's record, points are assessed according to whether or not he or she has ever exhibited any of the behaviors listed below. After becoming thoroughly familiar with the manual and instrument, committee members need to refer to the manual only to verify adherence to and use of appropriate criteria (Hardyman et al., 2002). Figure 10.2 is a custody classification form used by the Federal Bureau of Prisons, after which almost all state forms are modeled. As we go through the custody classification sections, we will apply them to Frank King using the information in the opening vignette to this chapter.

1. *History of Institutional Violence. Assault and battery* is any overt act toward another person, including another inmate, in which contact was made and injury attempted. If a weapon was used or serious injury occurred, this section is scored 7. In the event of two similar offenses, only the more serious is scored. Frank had no previous institutional history. Therefore, unless he assaulted someone at the reception center, he would have a score of 0.

2. *Severity of Current Offense.* A severity-of-offense scale is provided in Figure 10.2. Although an inmate may be committed for several offenses, only the most severe is scored, for a maximum of 6 points. Frank would get 6 points assessed against him because he committed armed robbery and shot the police officer; either offense earns him 6 points.

3. *Prior Assaultive Offense History.* This section reflects offenders' propensity for frequent violent behavior. Attempts to commit battery (simple assault) are scored regardless of the degree of contact or injury. The maximum score is 6. Frank's assaultive history is minimal in terms of frequency. However, shooting a police officer to avoid capture is extremely serious and indicates that Frank can be dangerous when cornered. In light of the seriousness of his assault, he gets 6 points.

4. *Escape History.* Any documented escape or attempt within the time framework provided is scored. Any adjudication by an institutional disciplinary-hearing committee is sufficient for assessment regardless of any court prosecution. The maximum score is 7. Frank has no escape history, so he gets 0 points.

The first four areas are the primary indicators of the risk that an inmate presents to the security of the institution and the welfare of other inmates and staff. A maximum score of 26 may be obtained. A score of 10 or more requires that the inmate initially be classified to close-custody (maximum) supervision. A score of 9 or less on the first four classification criteria requires that the last four areas (Criteria 5–8) be scored. Frank has 12 points assessed against him. Thus, he initially will be placed in maximum custody, but assume, for the purposes of the exercise, that he had 9 or fewer points, and score him on the following.

5. *Alcohol or Drug Abuse.* Abuse causing occasional legal and social-adjustment problems is defined as any abuse that has resulted in five or fewer misdemeanor convictions or interruption of employment within the last three years. Six or more alcohol

Custodial level: Custodial level refers to the prison housing area inmates are assigned to and the degree of supervision they receive, which can be minimum, medium, or maximum.

National Institute of Corrections Model for Custody and Need: A correctional tool that identifies eight areas of assessment that provide for objective custodial placement.

FIGURE *10.2* Classification Form Used by the Federal Bureau of Prisons

BP-A0338
JUNE 10

CUSTODY CLASSIFICATION CDFRM

U.S. DEPARTMENT OF JUSTICE   **FEDERAL BUREAU OF PRISONS**

A. IDENTIFYING DATA

1. INSTITUTION CODE	2. UNIT	3. DATE

4. NAME	5. REGISTER NUMBER

6. MANAGEMENT VARIABLES	**A** – NONE **B** – JUDICIAL RECOMMENDATION **D** – RELEASE RESIDENCE/PLANNING **E** – POPULATION MANAGEMENT	**G** – CIMS **I** – MED/PSYCH TREATMENT **N** – PROGRAM PARTICIPATION **M** – WORK CADRE	**S** – PSF WAIVED **U** – LONG TERM DETAINEE **V** – GREATER SECURITY **W** – LESSER SECURITY	

7. PUBLIC SAFETY FACTORS	**A** – NONE **B** – DISRUPTIVE GROUP (males only) **C** – GREATEST SEVERITY OFFENSE (males only) **F** – SEX OFFENDER **G** – THREAT TO GOVERNMENT OFFICIALS **H** – DEPORTABLE ALIEN	**I** – SENTENCE LENGTH (males only) **K** – VIOLENT BEHAVIOR (females only) **L** – SERIOUS ESCAPE **M** – PRISON DISTURBANCE **N** – JUVENILE VIOLENCE **O** – SERIOUS TELEPHONE ABUSE	

B. BASE SCORING				
1. TYPE OF DETAINER	**0** = NONE **1** = LOWEST/LOW MODERATE	**3** = MODERATE **5** = HIGH	**7** = GREATEST	
2. SEVERITY OF CURRENT OFFENSE	**0** = LOWEST **1** = LOW MODERATE	**3** = MODERATE **5** = HIGH	**7** = GREATEST	
3. MONTHS TO RELEASE				
4. CRIMINAL HISTORY SCORE	**0** = 0–1 **2** = 2–3	**4** = 4–6 **6** = 7–9	**8** = 10–12 **10** = 13 +	

5. HISTORY OF ESCAPE OR ATTEMPTS		NONE	>15 YEARS	10–15 YEARS	5–10 YEARS	<5 YEARS	
	MINOR	0	1	1	2	3	
	SERIOUS	0	3(S)	3(S)	3(S)	3(S)	

6. History of Violence		NONE	>15 YEARS	10–15 YEARS	5–10 YEARS	<5 YEARS	
	MINOR	0	1	1	3	5	
	SERIOUS	0	2	4	6	7	

7. VOLUNTARY SURRENDER STATUS	**0** = NOT APPLICABLE	**(–3)** = VOLUNTARY SURRENDER	
8. AGE	**0** = 55 and over **2** = 36 through 54	**4** = 25 through 35 **8** = 24 or less	
9. EDUCATION LEVEL	**0** = Verified High School Degree/GED **1** = Enrolled in and making satisfactory progress in GED Program **2** = No verified High School Degree/GED & not participating in GED Program		
10. DRUG/ALCOHOL ABUSE	**0** = Never/>5 Years	**1** = <5 Years	
11. BASE SCORE (ADD § B. ITEMS 1 – 10)			0

C. CUSTODY SCORING			
1. PERCENTAGE OF TIME SERVED	**3** = 0–25% **4** = 26–75%	**5** = 76–90% **6** = 91+%	
2. PROGRAM PARTICIPATION	**0** = POOR	**1** = AVERAGE	**2** = GOOD	
3. LIVING SKILLS	**0** = POOR	**1** = AVERAGE	**2** = GOOD	
4. TYPE & NUMBER OF MOST SERIOUS INCIDENT RPT	**0** = ANY GREAT (100) IN PAST 10 YRS **1** = > 1 HIGH (200) IN PAST 2 YRS **2(A)** = 1 HIGH (200) IN PAST 2 YRS **2(B)** = > 1 MOD (300) IN PAST YR	**3(A)** = 1 MOD (300) IN PAST YR **3(B)** = >1 LOW MOD (400) IN PAST YR **4** = 1 LOW MOD (400) IN PAST YR **5** = NONE	
5. FREQUENCY OF INCIDENT REPORTS (IN PAST YEAR)	**0** = 6+ **1** = 2 THRU 5	**2** = ONE **3** = NONE	
6. FAMILY/COMMUNITY TIES	**3** = NONE OR MINIMAL	**4** = AVERAGE OR GOOD	
7. CUSTODY TOTAL (ADD § C. ITEMS 1 – 6)			0
8. CUSTODY VARIANCE (FROM APPROPRIATE TABLE ON TABLE ON BP-338, PAGE 2)			
9. SECURITY TOTAL (ADD OR SUBTRACT CUSTODY VARIANCE (§ C.8) TO BASE SCORE (§ B.11))			0
10. SCORED SECURITY LEVEL		11. MANAGEMENT SECURITY LEVEL	

Source: Federal Bureau of Prisons.

or drug convictions during an offender's lifetime or commitment to jail or treatment facilities within the last three years for substance abuse is considered serious abuse. The maximum score is 3. Frank's PSI indicated no history of drug or alcohol abuse causing him legal and social-adjustment problems. He gets 0 points here.

6. *Current Detainer.* A detainer is a legal hold that another jurisdiction has placed on an inmate. Prior to releasing the inmate on parole or at the expiration of a sentence, the institution notifies the jurisdiction that holds the detainer so that the agency that issued the detainer can make arrangements to transfer the inmate to its jurisdiction. The maximum score is 6. Frank has no detainers. He gets 0 points here.

7. *Prior Felony Convictions.* This is a simple summation of prior felony convictions. Do not include the current offense. The maximum score is 4. Again, Frank is not assessed any points since the current offense is his first.

8. *Stability Factors.* Each item should be verified prior to scoring. This is the only area in which the scores are cumulative, thus resulting in a possible score of –4. Frank would receive the maximum points for stability factors. He was 26 or older at the time of his offense (–2), he is a high school graduate (–1), and he had been employed for more than six months at the time of his arrest (–1). If this section were scored regardless of the custody score, Frank would have a total of 8 points (12 – 4). This would place him in medium rather than maximum custody. The classification committee might decide to override the custody classification score and place him in medium custody.

After Criteria 1 through 8 of the instrument have been completed, the obtained scores determine custody level. Recall that a score of 10 or more points in Criteria 1 through 4 results in maximum security classification. If the score in Criteria 1 through 4 is 9 or less, the score is totaled with the scores in Criteria 5 through 8. If the final score is 7 or more, the inmate will be assigned to medium custody. If the score is 6 or less, the assignment will be to minimum custody. As seen in Table 10.1, the degree of freedom inmates are afforded, as well as the privileges, depend on their assessed custody level.

PHOTO 10.2: Plumes of smoke rise from the yard and recreation building of Reeves County Detention Center 1 unit in Pecos, Texas. The fires came five days after inmates set fires to other parts of the RCDC I and II units during a riot blamed on complaints about inadequate health care and food.

| TABLE 10.1 | Degrees of Supervision and Privileges by Custody Level |

ACTIVITY	CUSTODY LEVEL		
	MINIMUM	MEDIUM	MAXIMUM
Observation by staff	Occasional; depends on situation	Frequent and direct	Always supervised when outside cell
Day movement inside facility	Unrestricted	Observed periodically by staff	Restricted: directly observed or escorted when outside cell
Movement after dark After evening lockdown	Intermittent observation Intermittent observation	Restricted, with direct supervision Escorted and only on order of watch commander	Out of cell only in emergencies; in restraints when outside cell or as approved by watch commander
Meal periods	Intermittent observation	Supervised	Directly supervised or in cell
Access to jobs	Eligible for all, both inside and outside perimeter	Inside perimeter only	Only selected day jobs inside perimeter or directly supervised within the housing unit
Access to programs	Unrestricted, including community-based activities	Work and recreation inside perimeter; outside perimeter only as approved by CEO	Selected programs/ activities inside the facility perimeter as approved by CEO
Visits	Contact; periodic supervision indoor and outdoor	Contact, supervised	Noncontact or closely supervised
Leave the institution	Unescorted/escorted	Direct staff escort; handcuffs with chains and leg irons (optional); armed escort (optional)	Minimum of two escorts, with one armed; full restraints; strip search prior to departure and upon return
Furlough	Eligible for unescorted day pass and furlough*	Eligible for staff-escorted day pass or furlough	Not eligible

*A furlough authorizes an overnight absence from the prison; a day pass only authorizes absence during daylight hours.

Source: Walsh and Stohr (2010). Used with permission.

ADULT INTERNAL MANAGEMENT SYSTEM (AIMS)

According to Seiter (2005), the most widely used internal classification system is the **Adult Internal Management System (AIMS),** developed by Herbert C. Quay. This instrument differs substantially from the National Institute of Corrections' model. Quay's model relies on observable behavior patterns, as assessed by correctional staff, and integrates the documented behavioral history addressed by the NIC model. According to Austin and McGinnis (2004),

> AIMS relies on two instruments to identify inmates who are likely to be incompatible in terms of housing and those who are the most likely to pose a risk to the safe and secure operation of a facility. The first instrument, the Life History Checklist, focuses on the inmate's adjustment and stability in the community. The second instrument, the Correctional Adjustment Checklist, is designed to create a profile of an inmate's likely behavior in a correctional setting. (p. xii)

The AIMS model establishes five groups based on the behavioral characteristics of inmates. These groups are identified as Groups I and II ("heavy"), Group III ("moderate"), and Groups IV and V ("light"). The terms heavy, moderate, and light allude to

Adult Internal Management System (AIMS): This correctional instrument differs from the National Institute of Corrections' model because it relies on observable behavior patterns, as assessed by correctional staff, and integrates the documented behavioral history addressed by the NIC model.

| TABLE 10.2 | Major Components of Prison Intake Processing | | | |

TASKS	CONDUCTED BY STATES (%)	MANDATORY IN STATES (%)	PERSONNEL RESPONSIBLE FOR TASK	INSTRUMENT (S) AND/OR PROCESS(ES) USED
Identification	100	100	Security staff	Fingerprints
Medical screen within 24 hours	100	98	Nurses	Screen
Mental health screen within 24 hours	98	74	Nurses and mental health staff	Screen
Physical examination	100	90	Physician or nurse practitioner	Physical
DNA testing	90	14	Medical staff	Blood test
Criminal history	100	94	Records and classification staff and case manager	National Crime Information Center (NCIC), state courts, presentence investigation, department of corrections' management information system
Social history	94	88	Classification staff and case manager	Interview
Custody level	94	92	Classifications staff	Initial classification form
Internal classification	66	54	Classifications staff	Initial classification form
Prisoner separation	96	82	Classification, security threat group, and mental health staff	Interview and court documents
Gang membership	96	74	Security threat group coordinator	Tattoos and self-report
Victim notification	80	32	Records staff	Victim request
Academic achievement	98	86	Education staff	TABE and WRAT
IQ tests	68	50	Education and mental health staff	WRAT and WAIS
Vocational aptitude	50	28	Education staff	Variety
Substance abuse testing	100	88	Classification and substance abuse treatment staff	SASSI, TCUDDS, ASI, and interview
Psychological testing	96	58	Mental health staff	Millon (e.g., MCMI), MMPI, WAIS, and interview

Source: Hardyman, Austin, & Peyton (2004). National Institute of Justice.

prison slang that describes a perceived risk, threat, or the propensity to victimize other inmates ("heavies") or to be victimized ("lights"). The basic idea behind the AIMS model is that classifying inmates according to behavioral characteristics can greatly enhance differential treatment modalities.

Under the risk classification model already examined, all five of the AIMS groups may be represented in each custody level. The assumption behind custody classification based on type of crime is that those who commit similar crimes are similar in terms of more

POLICY AND RESEARCH

Assessment and Classification of Sex Offenders

State and federal policies on sex offenders are strict. Many sex offenders may be classified (or may ask to be classified) to administrative segregation, where they often remain in their cells 23 hours a day and are thus not able to take advantage of various programs. Federal law requires states to classify sex offenders into tiers of decreasing seriousness for purposes of sex offender registries. Tier III is the most serious classification and includes offenders convicted of rape, abusive sexual contact against a minor under age 13, the kidnapping of a minor, or sexual offenses committed while classified as a Tier II offender. Tier III sex offenders must register for life. A Tier II sex offender is someone convicted of offenses such as sex trafficking, coercion and enticement, using a minor in pornography, soliciting a minor for prostitution, producing or distributing child pornography, or committing a sexual offense while classified as a Tier I offender. Tier II offenders must register for 25 years. Tier I offenders are those convicted of a less serious sex offense not included in the other tiers and must register for 15 years (Reinhart, 2006).

Relative to the "typical" offender, sex offenders have a much wider variety of backgrounds. We don't see teachers, priests, engineers, physicians, and judges robbing convenience stores or 65-year-old men burglarizing houses, but sex offenders are found among all occupations, ethnic groups, educational levels, and ages. Sex offenders usually score in the low range on risk assessment instruments because such instruments do not address most areas indicative of risk for sexual offending. Given this, more sophisticated physiologically based assessment tools are used (discussed in the next chapter).

One physiological measure of sexual interest is the amount of viewing time spent looking at sexual image measured by a computer-based system called the Abel Assessment for Sexual Interest (AASI). The AASI consists of a questionnaire assessing a person's sexual preferences, among other things. The AASI measures visual reaction time (time viewing) while the person views 160 slides on a computer that show clothed children, teens, and adults, and the person is asked to rate his or her level of sexual arousal to the slides

on a scale of 1 to 10. These self-reported responses to visual stimuli are compared with the amount of time the subject spent viewing the slides, which was recorded on the computer. The recorded viewing time is taken as the offender's level of sexual interest in the type of person depicted in the slides.

A standard paper-and-pencil assessment tool for sex offenders is the Sex Offender Risk Appraisal Guide (SORAG). The SORAG is a 14-item scale that uses items to predict violent criminal recidivism in general; these items include family, school, and work history; alcohol or drug problems; criminal history score for nonviolent and violent offenses; prior probation or parole failure; and age at present offense. It adds sex-specific items to these general items, such as age of victim and number of prior sex offenses. The guide also incorporates psychiatric and psychological diagnoses of any personality disorder and psychopathy. Research has found that among four widely used instruments, SORAG was one of two that significantly predicted sexual and violent recidivism (Bartosh, Garby, Lewis, & Gray, 2003).

DISCUSSION QUESTIONS

1. Why is the federal government so concerned with sex offenses?

2. Why do you think sex offenders come from all walks of life, even from prestigious occupations that are so valued that their occupants would never risk committing any other type of crime?

3. Do you think you can judge someone's sexual preference by measuring the amount of time viewing clothed subjects?

References

Bartosh, D., Garby, T., Lewis, D., & Gray, S. (2003). Differences in the predictive validity of actuarial risk assessments in relation to sex offender type. *International Journal of Offender Therapy and Comparative Criminology, 47,* 422–438.

Reinhart, C. (2006). Federal law on classifying sex offenders. Office of Legislative Research. Retrieved from http://www.cga.ct.gov/2006/rpt/2006-r-0765.htm

general behavioral traits. At all custody levels, there is a wide variety of behavioral types. There are those who are victimized and those who victimize. The vast majority of inmates, however, are found between these extremes. Also, within each custody level, it is necessary to provide programs that are duplicated at other levels. AIMS classification is an attempt to discriminate more meaningfully among prisoners so that mixing victimizers and victims does not occur and so that programs are not unnecessarily duplicated. This should result in a reduction of prison violence and an increase in program effectiveness.

NEEDS ASSESSMENT AND CLASSIFICATION

Identification of inmate needs is based on all gathered data and the inmate's own perceptions of his or her programming needs. During initial assessment interviews and testing, staff elicit from inmates their ideas of what they need to become productive citizens. Areas of primary concern are educational, vocational, and medical needs; mental abilities; psychological problems; and substance abuse problems. The needs instrument reflects the fact that an individual's perception of his or her needs is somewhat subjective. For this reason, it is imperative that a high-quality classification interview is conducted by personnel thoroughly trained in the process. Inmate needs are determined by an instrument not significantly different from the one used in community corrections, shown in Figure 10.3. Note that the list of needs includes almost everything that anyone needs to lead a productive and law-abiding life, but just because such needs are determined, it does not mean that correctional agencies have either the finances or trained staff to provide them. However, with the help of outside agencies, they do the best job that they can.

Following the risk and needs classifications, the classification committee will summarize the findings. Included in the summary will be the custody level and score, any override considerations and justifications for them, a final custody level assignment, and program and job assignment recommendations.

PSYCHOPATHY CHECKLIST–REVISED

Although not routinely administered to all inmates, an instrument widely used around the world to identify the most troublesome and dangerous of criminals is **Hare's Psychopathy Checklist–Revised (PCL-R)**, developed by Robert Hare, the leading expert in psychopathy in the world today (Bartol, 2002). Psychopaths are callous individuals who lack the social emotions of guilt, shame, and embarrassment and are relatively fearless (Walsh & Wu, 2008). Psychopaths are mercifully small in number (about 1% of the general population), but they make up 15% to 25% of the prison population (Hare, 2003), which make it important to identify them. To make a clinical diagnosis of an individual using the PCL-R, the diagnostician must be a doctoral-level clinician with special training with the instrument. Diagnostic interviews may last two hours or more, and on the basis of information gleaned during that time and on the basis of file data, clinicians rate patients as either having or not having each of 20

ETHICAL ISSUE 10.2

What Would You Do?

You are an assessment and classification specialist working in the reception center of a large state prison. Among the newcomers you have to classify and assess is Charlie Finkbiener. Charlie has been incarcerated on a sole count of armed robbery, to which he plead guilty. Part of Charlie's plea bargain was the prosecutor's agreement to drop a child molestation charge against him in exchange for his guilty plea. You tell Charlie that you will classify him as a sex offender so that he can take advantage of a new sex offender program. Charlie vehemently objects, stating that it is wrong for you to classify him on the basis of a crime for which he was not convicted. Charlie knows that a sex offender classification is severely stigmatizing, but you want to put him in the program and cannot do so unless Charlie is classified as a sex offender. Do you ignore Charlie's point that it is wrong to classify him in a manner unrelated to his conviction history and do so, or do you classify him only according to his conviction history?

Hare's Psychopathy Checklist–Revised (PCL-R): The PCL-R is an instrument widely used around the world to identify the most troublesome and dangerous of criminals: the psychopath.

PHOTO 10.3: A prisoner speaks with Connecticut governor Dannel Malloy (D), and Connecticut correction commissioner Scott Semple, at the new DUI unit of the Cybulski Community Reintegration Center on April 1, 2016, in Enfield, Connecticut. Malloy's "Second Chance" bill, which he signed into law in July 2015, has been described as at the cutting edge of criminal justice reform efforts nationwide. The DUI unit is designed to prepare nonviolent inmates convicted of driving under the influence of drugs or alcohol for reintegration into society at the end of their prison sentences. The initiative is also supported by Mothers Against Drunk Driving.

traits. Ratings are made on a three-point scale, ranging from 0 (does not apply) to 1 (applies somewhat) to 2 (definitely applies), and persons receiving a score of 30 or higher, out of a possible 40, are considered psychopaths. To put this number in perspective, offenders, in general, have an average PCL-R score of 22, and nonoffenders have an average score of 5 (Hare, 1996).

The assessed factors are then subjected to a statistical technique called factor analysis, which takes a large number of interrelated factors and reduces them to a smaller number that cluster together. Factor analysis of the PCL-R reveals that psychopathy comprises two main factors: one describing a constellation of personality traits that point to insensitivity to the feelings of others and the second describing a generally unstable, impulsive, and deviant lifestyle (Hare, 1996). These factors are shown in Table 10.3.

While these two factors sometimes exist independently, they are often present together in the same individuals. It is frequently found that the brain anomalies associated with psychopathy correlate with high scores on Factor 1 (personality traits) but not necessarily with Factor 2 (unstable and antisocial lifestyle) and that low IQ correlates with high scores on Factor 2 but not on Factor 1 (G. Harris, Skilling, & Rice, 2001). The PCL-R strongly predicts recidivism, violent recidivism, and treatment response and clearly discriminates among prison inmates with high, medium, and low PCL-R scores in terms of involvement in violent incidents while imprisoned. Most impressive of all is that brain-imaging studies (PET, fMRI, etc.) find significant differences in the brains of psychopaths and those of control subjects. Kiehl (2006) sums up the reliability and validity of the PCL-R in these words: "The replicability and consistency of the neurobiological findings are a further testament to the psychometric robustness of the PCL-R and the construct of psychopathy in general" (pp. 123–124).

••• ASSESSMENT AND CLASSIFICATION IN COMMUNITY CORRECTIONS

Video 10.3: Offender Change at Washington State Department of Corrections

The need for proper risk and needs assessment may be even more important for community corrections than for institutional corrections since probationers and parolees mingle with the general public, the safety of whom is the paramount responsibility of all correctional agencies. Probation officers use them during the presentence process to determine offenders' suitability for probation. Just as was the case in institutional

| TABLE 10.3 | Personality and Behavioral Traits Measured by Hare's PCL-R |

FACTOR	EXAMPLES
Factor 1: Personality	Grandiose sense of self-worth Pathological lying Cunning/manipulative Lack of remorse or guilt Emotionally shallow Callous/lack of empathy Failure to accept responsibility for actions
Factor 2. Behavior/Lifestyle	Need for stimulation/proneness to boredom Parasitic lifestyle Poor behavioral control Promiscuous sexual behavior Lack of realistic, long-term goals Impulsiveness Irresponsibility Juvenile delinquency Early behavioral problems

Source: Adapted from Hare (2003).

corrections, in the early days of modern corrections, offender assessment was mostly based on the clinical judgment of correctional psychiatrists, psychologists, and social workers. This was the first generation of assessment. In the 1970s, a shift to objective actuarial methods based on known risk factors to predict treatment needs occurred. Because actuarial assessment used historical data (criminal record, history of drug and alcohol use, employment history, and so on), all risk factors were static, and thus, there was no way of gauging diminished or increased risk under treatment. The limitations of this second generation led to the third generation of assessment tools in the 1980s, which were more evidence based and dynamic. These tools took into account offenders' constantly changing situations (family dynamics, criminal friends, treatment progress, and so forth). They were thus sensitive to an individual offender's changing risks and needs.

We are now in the era of fourth-generation classification. Fourth-generation assessment tools (like third-generation tools) are based on the risk-need-responsivity principle. We will be discussing this this principle at greater length in the chapter on treatment, but for now, we will simply say that this principle maintains that if offenders are to respond to treatment in meaningful and lasting ways, those charged with their care must be aware of their different development stages and learning styles and their need to be treated with respect and dignity (Andrews & Dowden, 2007). Fourth-generation instruments are more theory driven; they both fine-tune older instruments and address additional risk and needs factors.

The **Level of Service/Case Management Inventory (LS/CMI)**, developed by Canadian researchers, is the best current example of a fourth-generation instrument, but very few American agencies are using it at present because it is relatively expensive in comparison to other instruments. It contains eight factors (see below) addressed by 43 items. The LS/CMI is a research-based condensation of the 10-factor, 53-item forerunner called the Level of Service Inventory–Revised (LSI-R)

- Criminal History (8 items)

- Education/Employment (9 items)

- Family/Marital (4 items)

- Leisure/Recreation (2 items)

Level of Service/ Case Management Inventory (LS/CMI): A Canadian fourth-generation instrument that contains eight factors addressed by 43 items to determine risk, needs, and supervision level of offenders.

- Friends/Companions
  (4 items/concerns)

- Procriminal Attitude/Orientation
  (4 items)

- Alcohol/Drug Problems
  (8 items)

- Antisocial Patterns
  (4 items)

Brenda Vose, Francis Cullen, and Paula Smith (2008) summarized the research of 47 studies conducted between 1982 and 2008 evaluating the predictive validity of the LSI among adult, juvenile, male, and female samples and found that 46 of them showed a positive relationship between total LSI score and recidivism. They concluded that the LSI was a valid predictor of recidivism across all groups of offenders, regardless of the measures of recidivism used. The LSI is thus a theoretically and empirically supported assessment tool for gauging the amenability of offenders of different ages and both genders to supervision and treatment, as well as for predicting recidivism. There were, of course, plenty of false positives and false negatives scattered throughout these studies; no instrument predicting human behavior comes anywhere near perfection.

THE CLIENT MANAGEMENT CLASSIFICATION ASSESSMENT INSTRUMENT

Keiser (2003) lists a number of assessment instruments in use in the United States, some of which are commercially marketed and expensive. According to a National Institute of Justice survey (Hubbard, Travis, & Latessa, 2001), the most widely used instrument is the **Case Management Classification (CMC) System**, used by 36.1% of responding agencies. The next most popular instruments are the risk and needs assessments, which are an integral part of the CMC System but are used alone by 26.3% of agencies. The LSI-R, used by 15%, is next, followed by many other lesser-known instruments. The CMC performs in roughly the same way as the LSI-R, and it is a tried and true instrument in the public domain, and thus, departments are free to use it without charge.

The CMC contains an interview schedule and risk and needs scales and is scored so that probation and parole officers can assign offenders to one of four supervision levels (discussed later). This scoring is complicated, and probation and parole officers attend three-day workshops and receive extensive follow-up training before they are able to use this system efficiently. Explaining the system in its entirety is well beyond the scope of this book. As mentioned previously, the risk and needs scales that are part of the CMC are used by themselves in many departments. We now discuss these scales.

RISK AND NEEDS ASSESSMENT SCALES

The risk and needs assessment scales to be discussed are part of the CMC and are designed to be used in conjunction with the CMC interview schedule. Risk assessment is done by assigning numerical scores to the offender on variables known to correlate with recidivism. The earlier one begins a criminal career, the more involved one is in it; the more one turns to chemical substances, the less one is legitimately employed; and the more negative one's attitude is, the more likely one is to reoffend. The more likely offenders are to reoffend, the greater their risk to the community, so they must be more closely supervised. The risk and needs instrument consists of two separate scales that assess offender risk and offender needs. **Offender risk** refers to the probability of reoffending and/or the threat the offender poses to the community. Risk factors are of two types: static and dynamic. Static factors are those that cannot be changed, such as age,

Case Management Classification (CMC) System: The most widely used instrument in the U.S. for offender assessment by probation departments to identify supervision levels.

Offender risk: The probability of reoffending and/or the threat the offender poses to the community. Risk factors are of two types: static and dynamic.

sex, criminal history, and family background. Factors associated with recidivism that can be changed are called **criminogenic needs**.

The term *needs* refers to programming needs to provide offenders with something they lack that may be responsible for their offending. For instance, a major predictor of recidivism is unemployment, and if an offender's educational deficiencies impair his or her ability to secure and retain employment, then education is a criminogenic need. However, if an offender's educational level does not adversely affect his or her ability to secure and retain employment, education is not a criminogenic need. Other criminogenic factors that can be changed through treatment include substance abuse, alcohol dependency, anger or hostility issues, poor social skills, poor attitudes toward work or school, poor family dynamics, low self-control, and criminal values and thinking patterns. Some programming for offenders with serious mental problems is the domain of mental-health staff; other programming needs addressing such things as criminal thinking patterns, problem-solving skills, coping with stress, anger management, impulsive decision making, substance abuse, and risk-taking behavior are dealt with by prison treatment specialists.

To further help us understand the sometimes confusing difference between criminogenic risks and needs, Latessa and Lowenkamp (2005) compare them with the risk of having a heart attack. The risks include age (over 50), being male, genetic factors, high blood pressure, weight, lack of exercise, high cholesterol, smoking, and stress. You cannot change your age, sex, or genetic inheritance, so these factors are referred to as *static*; all other factors are referred to as *dynamic* because they can change. In their own words, "To *understand* your risk you would factor in all of them; to *affect*—and lower—your risk you would focus on the dynamic ones" (p. 15). Thus, everything known to be associated with criminal reoffending is a criminogenic risk, but only those things that can be changed are criminogenic needs.

A perusal of the risk and needs scales contained in Figure 10.3 will reveal that they address the major nonbiological risk factors for offending identified by multiple researchers and summarized by Weibush, Baird, Krisberg, and Onek (1994). These major factors are as follows:

AP Video 10.2: US Jails Mentally Ill

1. Age at first adjudication or conviction

2. Criminal history (number and type of arrests, incarcerations, and probation and parole periods prior to the current offense)

3. History and extent of drug and alcohol use

4. Education and vocational skills

5. Employment history and potential

6. Family stability

7. Emotional stability

8. Intellectual ability

If used in conjunction with the CMC, the probation and parole officers also will be able to identify offenders' friends and social network, as well as their attitudes and beliefs regarding crime and life in general. It remains to be seen if fourth-generation instruments will outperform these third-generation instruments.

Criminogenic needs: Factors associated with recidivism that can be changed—that is, dynamic risk factors.

FIGURE 10.3 — Typical Risk and Needs Scale in Probation and Parole

DEPARTMENT OF CORRECTIONS: PROBATION & PAROLE DIVISION

Client No._____ Client Name _____ Officer No. _____

CLIENT RISK ASSESSMENT	CLIENT NEED ASSESSMENT
1. TOTAL NUBMER OF PRIOR FELONY CONVICTIONS a. none (enter 0) b. one (enter 2) c. two or more (enter 4)	**1. ACADEMIC/VOCATIONAL SKILLS** a. high school or above (enter 0) b. vocational training, no additional training needed (enter 1) c. some skills, additional needed or desired (enter 3) d. no skills/training needed (enter 5)
2. PRIOR NUMBER OF PROBATION/PAROLE SUPERVISION PERIODS (include juvenile, if known) a. none (enter 0) b. one or more (enter 4)	**2. EMPLOYMENT** a. satisfactory employment for one year or more (enter 0) b. employed, no difficulties reported; or homemaker/student/retired/ disabled and unable to work (enter 4) c. part-time, seasonal, unstable employment; OR needs additional employment; OR unemployed but with a skill (enter 4) d. unemployed and virtually unemployable, needs training (enter 7)
3. PRIOR PROBATION/PAROLE REVOCATION (adult only) a. none (enter 0) b. one or more (enter 4)	**3. FINANCIAL STATUS** a. longstanding pattern of self-sufficiency (enter 0) b. no current difficulties (enter 1) c. situational/minor difficulties (enter 4) d. severe difficulties (enter 6)
4. AGE AT FIRST KNOWN CONVICTION OR ADJUDICATION a. 24 or older (enter 0) b. 20 through 23 (enter 2) c. 18 or younger (enter 4)	**4. LIVING ARRANGEMENTS (within last six months)** a. stable and supportive relationships with family/living group (enter 0) b. living alone or independently within a household (enter 1) c. occasional, moderate interpersonal problems with living group (enter 4) d. frequent and serious interpersonal problems with living group (enter 6)
5. AMOUNT OF TIME EMPLOYED IN LAST 12 MONTHS a. 7 months or more (enter 0) b. 4 - 8 months (enter 1) c. under 4 months (enter 2) d. N/A (enter 0)	**5. EMOTIONAL STABILITY** a. no symptoms of instability (enter 1) b. symptoms limit but do not prohibit adequate functioning (enter 5) c. symptoms prohibit adequate functioning (enter 8)
6. HISTORY OF ALCOHOL ABUSE a. no history of abuse (enter 0) b. occasional abuse or prior abuse (enter 2) c. frequent and/or current abuse (enter 4)	**6. ALCOHOL USAGE (currently)** a. no interference with functioning (enter 1) b. occasional abuse, may need treatment (enter 4) c. frequent abuse, serious disruption, needs treatment (enter 7)
7. HISTORY OF OTHER SUBSTANCE ABUSE a. no history of abuse (enter 0) b. occasional abuse or prior abuse (enter 1) c. frequent and/or current abuse (enter 2)	**7. OTHER SUBSTANCE USAGE (currently)** a. no interference with functioning (enter 1) b. occasional abuse, may need treatment (enter 4) c. frequent abuse, serious disruption, needs treatment (enter 6)
8. AGENT IMPRESSION OF OFFENDER ATTITUDE a. motivated to change, receptive to assistance (enter 0) b. dependent/unwilling to accept responsibility (enter 3) c. rationalizes behavior, is negative, does not show motivation to change (enter 5)	**8. REASONING/INTILLECTUAL ABILITY** a. able to function adequately (enter 1) b. some need for assistance, potential for adequate adjustment (enter 4) c. limited ability to function independently (enter 7)
9. RECORD OF CONVICTION FOR SELECTED OFFENSES a. burglary/theft/auto theft/robbery (add 2) b. forgery/deceptive practices (fraud, bad checks, drugs) (add 3) c. none of the above (enter 0)	**9. HEALTH** a. physically sound, seldom ill (enter 1) b. handicap or illness interferes with functioning on recurring basis (enter 2) c. serious handicap or chronic illness, needs medical care (enter 3)
10. ASSAULTIVE OFFENSES (circle YES or NO) Assaultive Offenses are crimes against persons that include use of weapon, physical force, threat of force, sex crimes, and vehicular homicide	**10. AGENT'S IMPRESSION OF CLIENT'S NEEDS** a. none (enter 0) b. low (enter 1) c. moderate (enter 4) d. high (enter 6)
Total score (number between 6 and 34)	Total Score (number between 5 and 61)

SCORING AND OVERRIDE

Instructions: circle appropriate categories.
SCORE-BASED SUPERVISION LEVEL: Maximum/Medium/Minimum
OVERRIDE: yes/no (Explanation of Override if Yes: _____)

FINAL CATEGORY OF SUPERVISION: Maximum/Medium/Minimum
_____

APPROVED (Supervisor's Signature and Date)

Date Supervision Level Assigned

MO	DAY	YR

••• THE CMC AND SUPERVISION LEVELS

The average caseload of a probation officer is around 139 (Finn & Kuck, 2005), which means that there is precious little time to devote to each offender, especially given that there are other duties an officer must perform, such as conducting pre-sentence investigations and attending court. This is why we need some method of organizing officers' time so that they do not find themselves floundering all over the place, and this is a major reason why correctional agencies use instruments such as the CMC. Some offenders need more services and higher levels of monitoring than others, and to treat them all as equals in this regard would be both counterproductive and wasteful. The CMC places probationers into the four supervision level categories, which are outlined next.

SELECTIVE INTERVENTION

These are low-risk and low-needs offenders; that is, they are minimally criminally involved, and they have a stake in conformity. These offenders require little of the officers' time or resources, which means that there are more available for others that need them. There is evidence that low-risk offenders actually become worse if they are over-supervised and subjected to treatment modalities that they do not need (Lowenkamp & Latessa, 2004). Placing such offenders in the same restrictive programs as high-risk offenders exposes them to bad influences and may disrupt the very factors (family, employment, and prosocial activities and contacts) that made them low risk in the first place. Officers are advised only to intervene in the lives of such people *selectively*—that is, only in very special circumstances, such as a new arrest or if any information arises about the offender from concerned others (such as family members or the police) that requires attention.

ENVIRONMENTAL STRUCTURE

These offenders are on the low end of medium risk and require regular supervision. Officers work with these individuals to channel them into a number of services, such as educational, vocational, and substance abuse programs. These are not necessarily people deeply embedded in a criminal lifestyle but rather people with a number of social deficits that can be corrected. The typical probation or parole goals for these offenders are to develop and/or improve intellectual, social, and work skills, to find alternatives to associations with criminal peers, and to increase impulse control. This type of offender probably constitutes the majority of probationers and perhaps a few parolees.

PHOTO 10.4: A probation officer talking with and advising an ex offender.

© iStockphoto.com/menmetaliertek

CASEWORK AND CONTROL

These offenders are at the high end of medium risk or the low end of high risk. These offenders tend to be more entrenched in the criminal lifestyle and more likely to have severe drug and/or alcohol problems. They require intensive casework, and their activities should be closely monitored. The treatment goals for this group are much the same as those for the environmental-structure offenders, but they are more difficult to achieve because of their higher levels of substance abuse and greater emotional problems. These offenders require a great deal of officer time and considerable coordination of auxiliary programs in the community. They also require the same educational and occupational services as environmental-structure probationers, but they are less likely to benefit from them.

LIMIT SETTING

Offenders in this category are firmly bedded in a criminal lifestyle and are thus at high risk for probation or parole failure. These offenders are typically placed in special intensive-supervision units whose officers usually have small caseloads, enabling them to devote the time necessary to supervise high-risk offenders. Protection of the community through surveillance and strict control (often with the aid and cooperation of the police) of offenders is of primary concern with offenders of this type.

SUMMARY

- Correctional classification is the process of sorting offenders into similar "classes" so that correctional authorities are better able to house, supervise, and treat them. Classification is also about making predictions about future behavior based on actuarial data. Proper classification contributes greatly to the smooth and efficient operation of correctional facilities and is essential to running a humane prison.

- Correctional assessment is the art of making judgments about offenders' strengths, weaknesses, and needs and the risk they pose to the community by reoffending. Assessment is also based on actuarial data and is used to determine supervision level and treatment needs.

- The first concern of inmate classification is the level of custody: maximum, medium, or minimum. This is based on a variety of factors listed in the National Institute of Corrections Model of Custody and Need.

- Sex offender classification and assessment is more intense and utilizes physiological measures, as well as the usual instruments used with non–sex offenders. These physiological measures are devices like the polygraph ("lie detector").

- Another widely used instrument is the Adult Internal Management System. This prison classification instrument is designed to create a profile of an inmate's likely behavior in a correctional setting. It establishes five groups based on the behavioral characteristics of inmates: Groups I and II ("heavy"), Group III ("moderate"), and Groups IV and V ("light"). The primary concern here is prison safety.

- Hare's Psychopathy Checklist–Revised is not routinely administered to all inmates but is used to identify the very worst type of criminal: the psychopath. This instrument is used around the world and is fairly highly corrected with biological measures of psychopathy, such as brain imaging.

- Assessment and classification in community corrections uses a number of instruments to determine offenders' level of supervision and their amenability to treatment. The Level of Service/Case Management Inventory (LS/CMI), a fourth-generation assessment instrument, is considered the best one today, but the Case Management Classification (CMC) System is most widely used because it is in the public domain.

KEY TERMS

Actuarial method 238

Adult Internal Management
System (AIMS) 248

Assessment 239

Case Management Classification
(CMC) System 254

Classification 238

Criminogenic needs 255

Custodial level 245

Hare's Psychopathy Checklist–
Revised (PCL-R) 251

Level of Service/Case Management
Inventory (LS/CMI) 253

National Institute of Corrections
Model for Custody and Need 245

Offender risk 254

DISCUSSION QUESTIONS

1. What is the main function of any kind of classification instrument?

2. Discuss why you believe or do not believe that cold actuarial data outperform clinical assessment most of the time.

3. Why does efficiently running the prison trump offender rehabilitation needs in prison classification instruments?

4. Discuss the impact of *Morris v. Travisono* on correctional classification procedures.

5. Obtain a recent scholarly article that assesses to predictive usefulness of any of the scales discussed here, and share the results with the class.

6. Score Frank King on the probation and parole risk and needs scale, and assume he is on probation. What supervision category will you place him in, and why?

USEFUL INTERNET SITES

Please note that the sites listed can be accessed at edge.sagepub.com/stohrcorrections.

National Institute of Corrections (NIC): http://nicic.gov

This website provides training, technical assistance, information services, and policy or program development assistance to federal, state, and local corrections agencies regarding a variety of correctional practices, including treatment operations nationwide in areas of emerging

interest and concern to correctional executives and practitioners, as well as public policy makers.

Center for Sex Offender Management (CSOM): http://www.csom.org

This website is for the national clearinghouse and technical assistance center that supports state and local jurisdictions in the effective management of sex offenders.

$SAGE edge™

Sharpen your skills with SAGE edge at **edge.sagepub.com/stohrcorrections**. SAGE edge for Students provides a personalized approach to help you accomplish your coursework goals in an easy-to-use learning environment. You'll find action plans, mobile-friendly eFlashcards, and quizzes as well as video, web, and resources and links to SAGE journal articles to support and expand on the concepts presented in this chapter.

11 Correctional Programming and Treatment

TEST YOUR KNOWLEDGE

Test your present knowledge of correctional programming and treatment by answering the following questions, true or false. Check your answers on page 536 after reading the chapter.

1. Trying to rehabilitate criminals is mollycoddling them and costs society too much; therefore, we should stop trying.

2. Programs to treat offenders and prevent recidivism are the biggest budget items in corrections after salaries.

3. Even the best-run treatment programs reduce recidivism by only about 5%.

4. Personal experience will give you a better understanding of what will or will not work with criminals.

5. Because addiction is a brain disease, the major way of attacking it in corrections is through pharmaceutical means.

6. Sex offenders are less likely to reoffend than almost any other type of offender.

7. Most people arrested in major cities test positive for some kind of illegal drug.

8. There are more mentally ill individuals in U.S. jails and prisons than in mental hospitals.

LEARNING OBJECTIVES

- Explain what rehabilitation is and why it is imperative

- Describe the principles of evidence-based practices (EBP) and the risk, needs, and responsivity (RNR) model of treatment

- Discuss the use of cognitive behavioral therapy (CBT) in corrections

- Identify the various substance abuse programming used in correctional institutions

- Evaluate the special treatment modalities applied to sex offenders

- Describe the treatment options for mentally ill offenders

LIFE'S TURNING POINTS

Kathy Gardener was born to an "all-American" family in Dayton, Ohio. Her parents sent her to a Catholic girls' school, where she did well in her studies. All seemed to be going well for Kathy until she was 16 years old, when she went to a local air force base with two older friends from the neighborhood to meet the boyfriend of one of the girls. The boyfriend brought along two of his friends, and the six of them partied with alcohol, drugs, and sex. It was Kathy's first time experiencing any of these things, and she discovered that she liked them all. Thus, began a nine-year spiral into alcohol, drug, and sex addiction and into all of the crimes associated with

these conditions, such as drug trafficking, robbery, and prostitution.

When she was 25 years old, she was involved in a serious automobile accident in which she broke her pelvis, both legs, and an arm and suffered a concussion. She was charged with a probation violation, drunken driving, and possession of methamphetamine for sale. Kathy spent 10 months recuperating from her injuries, during which she was drug, alcohol, and sex free. Because of her medical condition, she was placed on probation. Her probation officer (PO) was a real "knuckle-dragger," who demanded full and immediate compliance with all conditions of Kathy's probation but who also became something of a father figure to her. While she was recuperating, she was often taken care of by a male nurse she described as "nerdy but nice." Her parents, who had been estranged from her for some time, became reacquainted with her, and her PO and nurse taught her to trust men again. She also occupied her time taking online college courses on drug addiction and counseling. She eventually married her "nerdy nurse," with her parents blessing, and one of the guests was the "knuckle dragger."

Kathy's story illustrates some core ideas in this chapter. No matter how low a person sinks into antisocial behavior, he or she is not destined to continue the downward spiral. There are a number of treatment programs available for all sorts of problems that get people into trouble with the law. Of course, not everyone is confronted with such a dramatic turning point in his or her life as a major automobile accident, leaving him or her plenty of time to ruminate about life and where he or she is going. Kathy's addictive personality got her into all kinds of trouble, and she knew it. People must come to this realization, and when they do, there must be programs in place to help them turn their lives around, or else, they will probably fail, and the community will suffer.

••• THE RISE AND FALL (AND RISE AGAIN) OF REHABILITATION

As we have seen, there are five primary goals of the correctional system: deterrence, incapacitation, retribution, rehabilitation, and reentry. This chapter deals with the fourth of these goals: rehabilitation. The term rehabilitation means to restore or return to constructive or healthy activity (habilitation), but many offenders never experienced anything close to habilitation in the first place, so there is little to restore. Correctional treatment or programming has to begin at the beginning and try to provide some of the things previously missing from the lives of offenders. Such programming obviously cannot supply the warmth and nurturing so critical in the early years of life, nor the deep sense of attachment and commitment to social institutions that comes from such experiences. However, programming and treatment can provide some of the concrete rewards, such as an education and job training, that most of us have had largely thanks to the attachments to family and other social institutions we enjoyed as children, and it can do its best to change the destructive thinking patterns that infect criminal minds.

We try to rehabilitate criminals with the realization that whatever helps offenders helps the community. As former U.S. Supreme Court chief justice Warren Burger opined, "To put people behind walls and bars and do little or nothing to change them is to win a battle but lose a war. It is wrong. It is expensive. It is stupid" (as cited in Schmalleger, 2001, p. 439). In this chapter, we look at various ways in which treatment personnel have been fighting the war. When reading this chapter, keep in mind that the vast majority of money assigned to correctional agencies is spent on surveillance and control functions. According to the National Center on Addiction and Substance Abuse (2010), among the 1.5 million inmates in jails and prisons nationwide in 2006, only 11.2% had received professional treatment since admission.

The American Prison Association (now the American Correctional Association [ACA]) declared its commitment to rehabilitation in its *Declaration of Principles*, written almost a century and a half ago (see In Focus 11.1).

IN FOCUS 11.1

The American Correctional Association's 1870 Declaration on Treatment

Corrections is responsible for providing programs and constructive activities that promote positive change for responsible citizenship.

Opportunity for positive change or "reformation" is basic to the concept of corrections because punishment without the opportunity for redemption is unjust and ineffective. Hope is a prerequisite for the offender's restoration to responsible membership in society.

Sound corrections programs at all levels of government require a careful balance of community and institutional services that provide a range of effective, humane, and safe options for handling juvenile and adult offenders.

Corrections must provide classification systems for determining placement, degree of supervision, and programming that afford differential controls and services for juvenile and adult offenders, thus maximizing opportunity for the largest number.

Corrections leaders should actively engage the community to assist in the restoration and reintegration of the offender.

Offenders, juvenile or adult, whether in the community or in institutions, should be afforded the opportunity to engage in productive work, participate in programs including education, vocational training, religion, counseling, constructive use of leisure time, and other activities that enhance self-worth, community integration, and economic status.

Source: American Correctional Association (2013).

Influenced by British pioneers Alexander Maconochie and Walter Crofton, rehabilitation was the goal of the early American prison reformers such as Zebulon Brockway. The ideal of rehabilitation reached the pinnacle of its popularity from about 1950 through the 1970s, when the medical model of criminal behavior prevailed. The medical model viewed crime as a moral sickness that required treatment, and prisoners were to remain in custody under indeterminate sentences until "cured." Consistent with the switch from a punishment role to a more rehabilitative corrections role, classification systems, individual and group counseling, therapeutic milieus, and college classes were added to the usual rehabilitative fare of labor, basic education, and vocational training (Cullen & Gendreau, 2001).

The rehabilitative goal was questioned and then fell apart with the publication, in 1974, of Robert Martinson's article, "What Works?—Questions and Answers About Prison Reform," in which he concluded that "with few and isolated exceptions, the rehabilitative efforts that have been reported so far have had no appreciable effect on recidivism" (p. 25). Unfortunately, the rhetorical question, "What works?" got translated into a definitive, "Nothing works," and became a taken-for-granted part of corrections lore. Before we can decide if something does or does not work, we have to define thresholds for what we mean. If we demand 100% success, then we can be sure that "nothing works." A program designed to change people is not like a machine that either works or does not. Human nature being what it is, nothing works for everybody; some things work for some people some of the time, and nothing will work for everybody all of the time. High failure rates existed in many fields at their inception, but as practitioners in those fields learned from their mistakes and their successes, failure rates inevitably dropped.

THE SHIFT FROM "NOTHING WORKS" TO "WHAT WORKS?"

Many correctional programs Martinson surveyed sought to change behaviors unrelated to crime, used programs that were not intensive enough, and used inadequately skilled staff. Few programs were based on the proper assessment of offender risks and needs and were often faddish "let's see what happens" programs, including everything from acupuncture to Zen meditation. While both of these practices are beneficial in their own right, they are hardly useful for changing criminal lifestyles. One probation department actually insisted that male offenders should "get in touch" with their feminine side by requiring them to dress in female clothes, and another required "poetry therapy" (Latessa, Cullen, & Gendreau, 2002). Correctional resources are scarce and should only be expended on programs that have proven themselves useful in reducing recidivism.

How have Martinson's conclusions stood up over the last 30 years? Gendreau and Ross (1987) reviewed a number of studies of treatment programs and concluded, "It is downright ridiculous to say that 'Nothing works' . . . much is going on to indicate that offender rehabilitation has been, can be, and will be achieved" (p. 395). Others have stated that properly run community-based programs could result in a 30% to 50% reduction in recidivism (Van Voorhis, Braswell, & Lester, 2000), although on the basis of major literature reviews, reductions in the 10% to 20% range are more realistic expectations (Cullen & Gendreau, 2001). A *success rate* is the difference in recidivism between a treatment and a control group. A review of studies from prison, jail, probation, and parole settings conducted by Pearson, Lipton, Cleland, and Yee (2002) found that 55.7% of the subjects in treatment groups did not reoffend, versus 43.3% of control group subjects. On

PHOTO 11.1: The goal of correctional programing and treatment is to break the revolving door of inmates being imprisoned, released, reoffending, and then incarcerated again.

average, this difference translates into about a 22.3% decrease in offending for treatment group members (.557 − .433 = .124 ÷ .557 = .223, or 23.3%). Although there are still plenty of failures, if treatment programs managed only half of this success rate, the financial and emotional savings to society would be truly enormous.

Mark Lipsey and Francis Cullen (2007) reviewed numerous studies of a variety of correctional intervention programs conducted from 1990 to 2006 and concluded that treatment works moderately well in reducing recidivism. Lipsey and Cullen believe the biggest problem in offender treatment is not that "nothing works" but that correctional systems do not use the available research to determine what works and then implement it. Rather, they tend to rely on convenience ("Who is available, and what methods do they use?"), custom ("We've always done it this way and see no reason to change"), and ideology ("Criminals are scumbags; why waste time and money on them?").

ETHICAL ISSUE 11.1

What Would You Do?

You are the chairperson of your state's financial appropriation committee. The director of state corrections is again asking for a substantial increase in the prison budget for new treatment counselors in the state's five prisons. You know that there is a desperate need for rehabilitation, but given a realistic reduction in recidivism of about 10% achieved by most programs and given other pressing needs the state has, you have deep reservations about providing corrections with more money when the health, education, law enforcement, and infrastructure needs of the state are urgent. You know, however, that there are two "bleeding hearts" on the committee who might swing the vote in favor of hiring prison counselors. Would you recommend appropriating the money or simply deny the request without taking it to the committee?

●●● EVIDENCE-BASED PRACTICES

Moving from the medical to the just-deserts or risk management model in corrections did not mean the death of the rehabilitation goal, but terms such as *assessment* and *programming* have replaced medical terms such as *diagnosis* and *treatment*. The main concern of corrections is to reduce the risk that offenders pose to society, not improving offenders' lives. Of course, the two goals are not incompatible; if more offenders can be taught to walk the straight and narrow, the risk of community members being victimized by them is reduced proportionately. Even though programs are run on a financial shoestring, prison officials like programming because it keeps inmates busy and out of trouble. Inmates also like it because it gives them something to do outside of their cells and looks good on their parole board records.

Video 11.1: Using Evidence-Based Corrections in Washington State Department of Corrections

The movement to a "what works" frame of mind has resulted in the most progressive agencies moving to **evidence-based practice (EBP)**. EBP is the use of peer-reviewed research based on the best available data to guide policy and treatment decisions such that outcomes for offenders, victims and survivors, and communities are improved. In other words, EBP simply means that in order to reduce offender recidivism, corrections must implement practices that have consistently been shown by rigorous empirical assessment to be effective in that endeavor. Extensive research has identified the following eight principles of evidence-based programming, as formulated by the National Institute of Corrections (n.d.) and illustrated in Figure 11.1.

1. *Assess Actuarial Risk/Needs*—Assessing offenders' risk and needs (focusing on dynamic and static risk factors and criminogenic needs) at the individual and aggregate levels is essential for implementing the principles of best practice.

2. *Enhance Intrinsic Motivation*—Research strongly suggests that "motivational interviewing" techniques, rather than persuasion tactics, effectively enhance motivation for initiating and maintaining behavior changes. Motivational

Evidence-based practice (EBP): EBP means that in order to reduce recidivism, corrections must implement practices that have consistently been shown to be effective.

©REUTERS/Lucy cholson

PHOTO 11.2: Women participate in a nutrition class at the Los Angeles County women's jail in Lynwood, California, April 26, 2013. The Second Chance Women's Re-entry Court is one of the first in the United States to focus on women and offers a cost-saving alternative to prison for women who plead guilty to nonviolent crimes and volunteer for treatment. Of the 297 women who have been through the court since 2007, 100 have graduated, and only 35 have been returned to state prison.

interviewing is a method of prompting behavior change by helping clients to explore and resolve discrepant thinking; that is, the ambivalent feelings of wanting, and not wanting, to change. The task of the counselor is to facilitate and engage intrinsic motivation on the assumption that if people can resolve the ambivalence themselves they will value it more than if it is resolved by others, and they will develop a "can-do" attitude.

3. *Target Interventions*
   a. *Risk Principle*—Prioritize supervision and treatment resources for higher risk offenders.
   b. *Needs Principle*—Target interventions to criminogenic needs.
   c. *Responsivity Principle*—Be responsive to temperament, learning style, motivation, gender, and culture when assigning to programs.
   d. *Dosage*—Structure 40% to 70% of high-risk offenders' time for 3 to 9 months.
   e. *Treatment Principle*—Integrate treatment into full sentence/sanctions requirements. Taking a proactive approach to treatment using CBT.

4. *Skill Train With Directed Practice*—Provide evidence-based programming that emphasizes cognitive-behavior strategies and is delivered by well-trained staff.

5. *Increase Positive Reinforcement*—Apply four positive reinforcements for every one negative reinforcement for optimal behavior change results.

6. *Engage Ongoing Support in Natural Communities*—Realign and actively engage prosocial support for offenders in their communities for positive reinforcement of desired new behaviors.

7. *Measure Relevant Processes/Practices*—An accurate and detailed documentation of case information and staff performance, along with a formal and valid mechanism for measuring outcomes, is the foundation of EBP.

8. *Provide Measurement Feedback*—Providing feedback builds accountability and maintains integrity, ultimately improving outcomes. (n.p.)

FIGURE *11.1*	Integrated EBP Model Illustrated

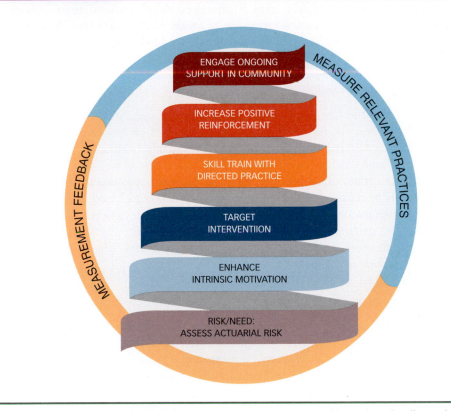

Source: United States Department of Justice. (2009). *Implementing evidence-based policy and practice in community corrections*. http://b.3cdn.net/crjustice/ac1468136a4b5a4c4fp2m6bf5bl.pdf

Taking a closer look at some of these principles, the psychosocial assessment of offenders typically begins with the **risk, needs, and responsivity (RNR) model**. The RNR model is the premier treatment model in corrections today in the United States and in many other countries (Ward, Melser, & Yates, 2007). The **risk principle** refers to an offender's probability of reoffending, and those with the highest risk are targeted for the most intense treatment ("Dosage" under Principle 3). Criminologists have documented numerous individual and environmental factors that put a person at risk for criminal behavior and recidivism. As we discussed in the previous chapter, criminogenic risk factors are divided into dynamic and static categories. Static factors are those that cannot be changed, such as age, sex, criminal history, and family background. Factors associated with recidivism that can be changed are called criminogenic needs. The **needs principle** refers to programming needs to provide offenders with something they lack that may be responsible for their offending. For instance, a major predictor of recidivism is unemployment, and if an offender's educational deficiencies impair his or her ability to secure and retain employment, then education is a criminogenic need. However, if an offender's educational level does not adversely affect his or her ability to secure and retain employment, education is not a criminogenic need. Other criminogenic factors that can be changed through treatment include substance abuse, alcohol dependency, anger or hostility issues, poor social skills, poor attitudes toward work or school, poor family dynamics, low self-control, and criminal values and thinking patterns. Some programming for offenders with serious mental problems is the domain of mental-health staff; other programming needs, addressing such things as criminal thinking patterns, problem-solving skills, coping with stress, anger management, impulsive

Risk, needs, and responsivity (RNR) model: A treatment correctional model that maintains that offenders and the community are better served if offenders' risks for reoffending and their needs (their deficiencies, such as lack of job skills) are addressed in a way that matches their developmental stage.

Risk principle: A principle that refers to an offender's probability of reoffending and maintains that those with the highest risk should be targeted for the most intense treatment.

Needs principle: A principle that refers to an offender's prosocial needs, the lack of which puts him or her at risk for reoffending, and that suggests these needs should receive attention in program targeting.

decision making, substance abuse, and risk-taking behavior, are dealt with by prison treatment specialists.

The **responsivity principle** maintains that if offenders are to respond to treatment in meaningful and lasting ways, counselors must be aware of their different development stages, motivation, and learning styles, as well as their need to be treated with respect and dignity (Andrews, Bonta, & Wormith, 2006). The crux of these three principles is that we can no longer rely on one-size-fits-all models and that treatment must be tailored to individual offenders' risks and needs.

Offender risk (defined in Chapter 10) and **offender needs** are assessed by two separate scales: one for risk and one for needs. These scales are used to make predictions about offenders' success or failure based on **actuarial data** (Principle 1)—that is, what has actually occurred and been recorded over many thousands of cases. As we saw in the previous chapter, it has been found time and time again across many professions that decisions made on the basis of actuarial statistical norms trump decisions based on the insight of individuals the great majority of the time (Andrews et al., 2006). Table 11.1 identifies and describes risks and dynamic needs that must be addressed; note that identifying needs mirrors the identification of risk. The other principles of EBP are either self-explanatory of addressed elsewhere in this book.

MOTIVATIONAL INTERVIEWING

As noted earlier in Principle 2 of evidence-based practices, motivational interviewing is something that research has shown to be very effective in dealing with offenders' treatment issues. The objective of **motivational interviewing** is to increase offenders' motivation for positive behavioral change by the exploration and resolution of the ambivalence about changing assumed to exist in offenders. It can be used as a formal plan for several sessions of assessment and feedback or as a one-time response to something an offender has done. For example, if an offender fails a UA (urinalysis), the probation and parole officer may ask the offender to explore the positive and negative aspects of drug abuse *as the offender sees it* to assess his or her ambivalence about quitting (Thigpen, Beauclair, Brown, & Guevara, 2012).

Motivational interviewing is the blending of two strands of counseling thought. According to Burke, Arkowitz, and Menchola (2003), "Motivational interviewing is a relatively new and promising therapeutic approach that integrates the relationship-building principles of humanistic therapy with more active cognitive-behavioral strategies targeted to the client's stage of change" (p. 843). Motivational interviewing is humanistic in its assumption that the solution to people's problems lie within themselves and in its emphasis on building rapport between treatment provider and offender. It is also confrontational—but with a difference. Rather than the treatment specialist or probation and parole officer confronting an offender, he or she is trained to guide the offender to confront himself or herself.

There are two stages in motivational interviewing: the contemplative and the action stages. The first stage involves strategies employed by the treatment specialist or probation and parole officer designed to get offenders actually thinking about the desirability of change, and the second stage implements plans of action to put that desire into practice. The contemplative stage involves empathy and developing discrepancy, and the action stage involves rolling with resistance and supporting self-efficacy. The concepts are briefly described below.

Empathy

The prerequisite for all counseling is the development of a positive and trusting relationship between the treatment provider and the offender. If the offender does not have

---

Responsivity principle: A principle maintaining that if offenders are to respond to treatment in meaningful and lasting ways, counselors must be aware of their different developmental stages, learning styles, and need to be treated with respect and dignity.

Offender needs: Refers to deficiencies in offenders' lives that hinder their making a commitment to a prosocial pattern of behavior.

Actuarial data: Data relating to what has actually occurred and been recorded over many thousands of cases. Evidence-based treatment modalities are based on actuarial data.

Motivational interviewing: Attempts to increase offenders' motivation for positive behavioral change by exploring and overcoming the ambivalence about changing assumed to exist in offenders.

TABLE *11.1*   Major Risk and/or Need Factors and Promising Intermediate Targets for Reduced Recidivism

FACTOR	DYNAMIC NEED	RISK
History of antisocial behavior	Early and continuing involvement in a number and variety of antisocial acts in a variety of settings.	Build noncriminal alternative behavior in risky situations.
Antisocial personality pattern	Adventurous, pleasure seeking, weak self-control, restlessly aggressive.	Build problem solving skills, self-management skills, anger management, and coping skills.
Antisocial cognition	Attitudes, values, beliefs, and rationalizations supportive of crime; cognitive emotional states of anger, resentment, and defiance; criminal versus reformed identity.	Reduce antisocial cognition, recognize risky thinking and feeling, build up alternative less risky thinking and feeling, adopt a reform and/or anticriminal identity.
Antisocial associates	Close association with criminal others and relative isolation from anticriminal others; immediate social support for crime.	Reduce association with criminal others; enhance association with anticriminal others.
Family and/or marital	Two key elements are nurturing and/or caring and monitoring and/or supervision.	Reduce conflict, build positive relationships, enhance monitoring and supervision.
School and/or work	Low levels of performance and satisfaction in school and/or work.	Enhance involvement, rewards, and satisfactions.
Leisure and/or recreation	Low levels of involvement and satisfaction in anticriminal leisure pursuits.	Enhance involvement, rewards, and satisfactions.
Substance abuse	Abuse of alcohol and/or other drugs.	Reduce substance abuse; reduce the personal and interpersonal supports for substance-oriented behavior; enhance alternative to drug abuse.

Source: Andrews, Bonta, & Wormith (2006, p. 11).

the necessary trust, the rest of the process will be unworkable. To develop that trust, the treatment provider must display empathy by active, reflective, and accepting listening to what offenders are saying. According to Thigpen et al. (2012), this is the most challenging part of motivational interviewing because it requires "expressing accurate empathy to clients by using reflections that convey an understanding of clients' words and meaning" (p. 15). Motivational interviewing stresses that the counselor must accept that an offender's ambivalence about change is normal (a reflection of the self-consistency motive) and not pathological defensiveness.

Developing Discrepancy

If the offender appears comfortable and trusting, the activity can move on to the process of developing discrepancy. As previously noted, an assumption of motivational interviewing is that offenders are ambivalent about changing their lives; they want to, and they do not want to, at the same time. Discrepancy development is about helping offenders identify their ambivalent feelings between how they are presently and how they would like to be. The counselor or officer strives to increase psychological discomfort (*cognitive dissonance*) in offenders so that they will become motivated to reduce it. As Miller and Rollnick (in M. Clark, 2005) put it, "MI [motivational interviewing] considers 'confrontation to be the goal, not the counselor's style.' That is, the goal of helping is to create a 'self-confrontation' that prompts offenders to 'see and accept an uncomfortable reality'" (p. 25). If offenders can be guided to confront a reality that is disquieting to them by themselves, rather than having the counselor or officer point it out, they are more likely to accept it and become motivated to do something about it: "People are more persuaded by what they hear themselves say than by what other people tell them" (Miller & Rollnick, 2002, p. 39). And as Thigpen et al. (2012) opine, "The key to developing discrepancy is trusting and supporting the client in doing his/her own discovery, rather than pointing out and advising him/her on how to discover something that could be meaningful" (p. 64).

Roll With Resistance

The counselor or officer is most likely to meet with resistance during the process of developing discrepancy. The motivational-interviewing system says that you must "roll with resistance"; that is, you must avoid arguments by reflecting feelings back on offenders and by turning problems back on them to work out for themselves.

> Rolling with resistance describes the ability to avoid getting 'hooked' or caught up in a client's demonstration of resistance, regardless of the form it takes (e.g., rebellious, rationalizing, reluctant, resigned). Rolling with resistance implies taking the client's manifestation of resistance seriously as a signal for changing tactics, but not taking it personally. (Thigpen et al., 2012, p. 70)

Too much resistance probably means that the process has moved into the action phase (see Figure 11.2) prematurely, and you should return to the contemplative stage and try another strategy.

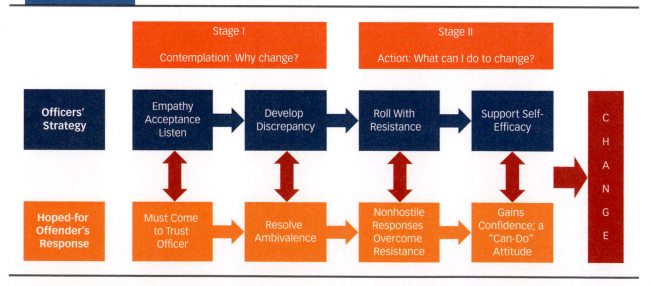

FIGURE *11.2*   The Basics of Motivational Interviewing: Officer's Strategy Above; Hoped-For Offender Responses Below

Support Self-Efficacy

Self-efficacy is the extent to which a person believes in his or her ability to complete tasks and achieve goals. To support self-efficacy means "to be willing to pay close attention and either create or use available opportunities for reinforcing the client's sense of capacity or confidence for achieving (prosocial) goals" (Thigpen et al., 2012, p. 71). Self-efficacy is essentially the confidence persons have in themselves to successfully accomplish what they set out to do. Counselors or officers must reinforce any positive statements made by offenders that indicate a can-do attitude. The basics of the process of motivational interviewing are presented in schematic form in Figure 11.2.

••• COGNITIVE BEHAVIORAL THERAPY

The therapeutic concepts and methods that proponents of the RNR model find most useful in addressing offender risks and needs are cognitive behavioral (Ward et al., 2007). Most of today's programming consists of **cognitive behavioral therapy (CBT)**. CBT is an approach that tries to solve dysfunctional cognitions, emotions, and behaviors in a relatively short time through goal-oriented, systematic procedures, and it has been called "the most overtly 'scientific' of all major therapy orientations" (McLeod, 2003, p. 123). There are a number of different treatment models that fall under the CBT model; they include moral reconation, reasoning and rehabilitation, rational emotive behavior therapy, and, of course, motivational interviewing. We cannot go into the fine nuances that differentiate these models but must be content with outlining the commonalities of all CBT approaches. What these models have in common is that they attempt to change dysfunctional thinking patterns by improving empathy, moral reasoning, planning, and problem-solving skills, and CBT combines the principles of operant psychology, cognitive theory, and social-learning theory. Operant psychology asserts that behavior is determined by its consequences (rewards and punishments). Cognitive theory asserts that at a more proximal level, self-defeating behaviors are the result of unproductive thought patterns relating to our history of rewards and punishments (D. Wilson, Bouffard, & Mackenzie, 2005). We can do nothing about past experiences (they are static risk factors), but we can do something to put the way we think about those things into proper perspective. (Thinking is dynamic—open to change.) Finally, social-learning theory is a sociological view of socialization that asserts that behavior is learned by modeling and imitation, as well as our history of rewards and punishments.

Albert Ellis (1989) claims that the great religious leaders of the past were cognitive behavioral therapists because they were trying to get people to change their behavior from self-indulgence to temperance, from hatred to love, and from cruelty to kindness by appealing to their rational long-term self-interest. The common message imparted by religion is the need for personal change and the rewards that such change brings with it: "Do these things, and you will feel good about yourself now, and you will be eternally rewarded." This is what CBT tries to do: change offender's antisocial and self-destructive behavior into prosocial and constructive behavior by changing the way they think and by showing them that it is in their best interests to do so.

CBT AND CRIMINAL THOUGHT

The first lesson of CBT is that criminals think differently from the rest of us. Yochelson and Samenow (1976) and Samenow (1999) pioneered treatment theories based on challenging criminal thinking errors when they realized that modalities based on "outside circumstances" theories did not work. The task is to understand how criminals perceive and evaluate themselves and their world so that we can change them. Criminal thinking

Cognitive behavioral therapy (CBT): A counseling approach that tries to address dysfunctional cognitions, emotions, and behaviors in a relatively short time through goal-oriented, systematic procedures using a mixture of operant psychology, cognitive theory, and social-learning theory.

is destructive; it lands them in trouble with family, friends, employers, and the criminal justice system. Habitual offenders tend to perceive the world in fatalistic fashion, believing that there is little that they can do to change the circumstances of their lives. To illustrate this fatalism and other criminal thinking patterns, Boyd Sharp (2006) cites a cartoon in which one of the characters named Calvin says,

> I have concluded that nothing bad I do is my fault. . . . I'm a helpless victim of countless bad influences. An unwholesome culture panders to my undeveloped values and it pushes me into misbehavior. I take no responsibility for my behavior. I'm an innocent pawn of society. (p. 3)

Criminals think like Calvin, in the context of a society where many people prefer to claim victimhood rather than personal responsibility. (McDonald's made me fat, cigarette companies made me smoke, and so on.) Many mainstream criminological theories locate the blame for crime on external factors, such as poverty and peer pressure, rather than allowing criminals the dignity of owning responsibility for their behavior. Criminals are eager to jump on authoritative pronouncements that excuse their behavior, and defense lawyers are equally quick to argue them in court. All of this reinforces the patterns of criminal denial that treatment providers find so frustrating (B. Sharp, 2006; Walsh & Stohr, 2010). Challenging and changing maladaptive thought patterns takes on a central role in treatment, as corrections workers strive to impress on offenders that whatever influences external factors may have on behavior, before they can affect behavior, they have to be evaluated by individuals. The frustrations we experience in everyday life certainly do influence our behavior, but they just as certainly do not determine it. The important thing is not the presence of stresses, strains, and frustrations but whether we deal with them constructively or destructively. The task of correctional workers is to teach criminals to stop blaming outside circumstances for their problems, how to take responsibility for their lives, and how to deal constructively with adversity.

CBT methods are used to address issues relating to self-control, victim awareness, relapse prevention, critical reasoning, and anger control (Vanstone, 2000). CBT therapy literally "exercises the thinking areas of the brain and thereby strengthens the [neuronal] pathways by which the thinking brain influences the emotional brain" (Restak, 2001, p. 144). If you receive a high enough "dosage" of CBT, it can literally reorganize the brain's wiring patterns (Vaske, Galyean, & Cullen, 2011). A number of brain-imaging studies show that CBT changes brain processes exactly the way that drugs such as Prozac do (Linden, 2006). A systematic review of brain-imaging studies revealed neurobiological changes in people undergoing cognitive behavioral therapy. These studies show that cognitive behavioral therapy modifies the brain circuits involved in the regulation of negative emotions and fear extinction in treatment subjects. In short, CBT is able to change dysfunctions of the brain (Porto et al., 2009). However, these studies have only been conducted with individuals with problems such as depression, anxiety, and obsessive–compulsive disorder, in which patients, unlike most criminals, are intensely motivated to overcome their problems.

• • • SUBSTANCE ABUSE PROGRAMMING

Career Video 11.1: Police Captain

Alcohol is, at the same time, our most popular and most deadly way of drugging ourselves. Police officers spend more than half their law enforcement time on alcohol-related offenses. One third of all arrests (excluding drunk driving) in the United States are for alcohol-related offenses, about 75% of robberies and 80% of homicides involve

POLICY AND RESEARCH

Can Psychopaths Be Treated?

Many of you have seen the movie *The Silence of the Lambs*, featuring the manipulative and charming Dr. Hannibal Lecter—a psychopath. While psychopaths are only about 1% of the general population, they compose 15% to 25% of prison inmates (Kiehl & Hoffman, 2011). Psychopaths have been found to have brains that do not make proper connections between areas governing the rational and emotional components of behavior in hundreds of brain-imaging studies (reviewed in Raine, 2014). The tend to make decisions based almost entirely on rationality ("How do I maximize benefits for myself?"), without those decisions being moderated by the social emotions of empathy, guilt, shame, and embarrassment. ("How will my decisions impact others, and how will that make me feel?")

The conventional wisdom has been that treatment makes psychopaths worse. A study of psychopaths treated in a therapeutic community had a higher violent recidivism rate than untreated psychopaths (Hare, 1993). Treatment provides psychopaths with new information that they use to become better at manipulating others. As one psychopath remarked, "The programs are like finishing school. They teach you how to put the squeeze on people" (Hare, 1993, p. 199). This, as well as the strongly genetic nature of psychopathy, led to the conventional wisdom in corrections that psychopaths are impossible to treat (Polaschek, 2014).

Attitudes about treating psychopaths are beginning to change with the emergence of new techniques. The new thinking is that instead of treating psychopathy in general, we should target specific subtraits of the syndrome: cognitive, emotional, and behavioral (Felthous, 2015). Felthous recommends medication with an anti–impulsive aggression agent (a selective serotonin reuptake inhibitor such as Prozac), which he says has been shown to be highly effective in a number of studies.

There are new approaches specifically designed for psychopaths that are much more intensive than traditional methods. One such method is *decompression therapy* (DT). DT is based on positive reinforcement alone because punishment tends to make psychopathy worse and more resistant. (Nearly all of the boys in the program were deemed uncontrollable at the other institutions.) Group members are monitored continuously by staff for any sign of positive behavior, and when it occurs, it is reinforced with some sort of reward. Rewards are scaled; that is, the longer their good behavior persists, the greater the rewards become. Rewards can be a kind word or pat on the back, which can graduate to a candy bar and then to the right to play video games. The treatment program is intense, requiring several hours per day and lasting at least six months. The basic idea behind psychological decompression treatment is similar to the physical decompression a deep-sea diver undergoes during the ascent from a dive. The psychological analog of the physical process is to methodically build (or rebuild) the kind of social connections that are absent in psychopaths and to reduce toxic thoughts and behaviors.

One study of DT followed 248 incarcerated "unmanageable" boys for an average of 54 months after release and showed that 56% of the 101 youths who received the DT recidivated, versus 78% of those who received traditional group therapy who were rearrested. The recidivism rate for violence was 18% for the decompression group, versus 36% for the traditional therapy group (Caldwell & Rybroek, 2005). According to Kiehl and Hoffman (2011), although decompression treatment costs $7,000 more per inmate than traditional treatment, when compared with the costs associated with recidivism and incarceration, the initially high cost of decompression treatment provides an overall positive cost–benefit ratio for taxpayers of about $43,000 more per inmate.

DISCUSSION QUESTIONS

1. How would the poor connections between the rational and emotion areas of the brain be useful to psychopaths in pursuit of their goals?

2. Are the time and costs of DT worth it?

3. Why do you think this rewards-only, no-punishment program apparently has some positive effects with psychopaths?

References

Caldwell, M., & Van Rybroek, G. (2005). Reducing violence in serious and violent juvenile offenders using an intensive treatment program. *International Journal of Law & Psychiatry, 28*, 622–636.

Felthous, A. (2015). The appropriateness of treating psychopathic disorders. *CNS Spectrums, 20*, 182–189.

Hare, R. (1993). *Without conscience: The disturbing world of the psychopaths among us*. New York, NY: Pocket Books.

Kiehl, K., & Hoffman, M. (2011). The criminal psychopath: History, neuroscience, treatment, and economics. *Jurimetrics, 51*, 355–397.

Polaschek, D. L. (2014). Adult criminals with psychopathy: Common beliefs about treatability and change have little empirical support. *Current Directions in Psychological Science, 23*, 296–301.

Raine, A. (2014). *Psychopathy: An introduction to biological findings and their implications*. New York: New York University Press.

PHOTO 11.3: Substance abuse often contributes to poor decision making and criminal engagement for inmates.

a drunken offender and/or victim, and about 40% of other violent offenders in the United States were drinking at the time of the offense (Mustaine & Tewkesbury, 2004).

Alcohol is a very powerful and addictive drug and is the biggest curse of the criminal justice system, despite the system's current obsession with illegal drugs. Illegal-drug usage presents almost as big a problem, with about 67% of state and 56% of federal prisoners being regular drug users prior to their imprisonment (Seiter, 2005). Clearly, mind-altering substances, both legal and illegal, are strongly associated with criminal behavior, and as such, the tendency of many criminals to overindulge in them must be addressed by correctional agencies.

Substance abuse problems are extremely difficult to treat because individuals most at risk for becoming addicted share many of the same traits associated with chronic criminal behavior, with many of these traits being strongly genetic (Vaughn, 2009). For instance, alcoholism researchers divide alcoholics into two types: Type I and Type II. Type II alcoholics start drinking and using other drugs earlier, become more rapidly addicted, and exhibit many more character disorders, behavior problems, and criminal involvement, both prior and subsequent to their alcoholism, than Type I alcoholics (Crabbe, 2002). Genetic researchers maintain that genes are much more heavily involved in Type II than in Type I alcoholism (Crabbe, 2002).

AP Video 11.1: Drug Treatment

Audio 11.1: In 2016, States Expected to Ramp Up Ideas to Solve Opiate Abuse

It has been shown that drug addiction and criminality are part of a broader propensity to engage in many forms of deviant and antisocial behavior (Fishbein, 2003; Vaughn, 2009). For instance, the U.S. government's Arrestee Drug Abuse Monitoring (ADAM) Program collects urine samples from arrestees across the country to test for the presence of drugs. Figure 11.3 shows the percentage of adult arrestees in five large U.S. cities who tested positive for illicit drugs over a 3-year period. The numbers show that illicit-drug abuse is clearly strongly *associated* with criminal behavior, but the association is not necessarily a *causal* one. A large body of research indicates that drug abuse does not appear to *initiate* a criminal career, although it does increase the extent and seriousness of one (Menard, Mihalic, & Huizinga, 2001). In other words, research seems to point to the fact that chronic drug abuse and criminality are part of a broader tendency of some individuals to engage in a variety of deviant and antisocial behaviors. Numerous studies have shown that traits characterizing antisocial individuals, such as conduct disorder, impulsiveness, and psychopathy, also characterize drug addicts (Fishbein, 2003; McDermott et al., 2000). The large body of research indicating a strong genetic vulnerability to alcoholism and drug addiction helps to explain why the many millions who drink and/or experiment with drugs do not descend into the hell of addiction and why others are "sitting ducks" for it (Walsh, Johnson, & Bolen, 2012).

DRUG TREATMENT WITH SWIFT CONSEQUENCES FOR FAILURE: HAWAII'S HOPE PROGRAM

The state of Hawaii has a drug treatment program highly touted by the National Institute of Justice (NIJ, 2012) called Hawaii's Opportunity Probation with Enforcement

(HOPE). The results of this program are based on 493 drug-using probationers with an elevated risk of violating probation, two thirds of whom were randomly assigned to the HOPE program and the rest to regular supervision. The program emphasizes a "no nonsense" delivery of both treatment and "swift and certain" punishment for violations. HOPE probationers are more closely monitored for drug usage and other violations than control probationers. Figure 11.4 shows that this program had very positive results after 12 months. For instance, HOPE participants were 55% ($47 - 21 = 26 \div 47 = .553$, or 55.3%) less likely to be arrested and 72% less likely to have used drugs. This experiment needs to be repeated in other locations with larger samples, and if results of any further studies come close to Hawaii's, there is real cause for optimism.

Web 11.1: Drug Treatment Programs

PERSPECTIVE FROM A PRACTITIONER

Margaret Jackson, Drug Treatment Specialist

Position: Drug treatment specialist

Location: Phoenix, Arizona

Education: BS in criminal justice, Northern Arizona University; MA in criminal justice administration, Boise State University; drug and alcohol counseling courses at Rio Salado University

What are the primary duties and responsibilities of a drug treatment specialist?

My primary duties are to provide drug abuse treatment to inmates in the federal prison system. I provide individual and group counseling and therapy to drug- and alcohol-addicted inmates incarcerated in the federal prison system. The Federal Bureau of Prisons provides a voluntary but criteria-based program called the Residential Drug Abuse Program (RDAP), a 9-month (a minimum of 500 hours of direct treatment) modified therapeutic community (TC). I provide clinical services using CBT techniques and introduce community as method to the inmates and develop a working system of a therapeutic community. The first step in working with inmates in this process is to determine their eligibility to receive counseling and therapy; one of the tools I use for this is a psychosocial assessment. If an inmate is eligible for treatment, I will use the psychosocial assessment to create an individual treatment plan for the inmate. Once eligibility has been determined and an assessment for treatment has been conducted, a team of three other therapists and I are responsible for providing residential treatment to the offenders. The inmates are assigned a series of workbooks and attend daily meetings. I construct the inmate's individual therapeutic treatment plans, reviews, and recommendations for further treatment upon release from federal prison.

What are the qualities or characteristics that are most helpful for one in a probation or parole career?

- Be fair and consistent
- Have good judgment
- Be aware of population at hand
- Know your craft well
- Be reliable
- Be a team worker
- Be able to communicate with multiple agencies
- Be attentive to detail when writing reports and preparing inmate charts

Describe, in general, a typical day for a drug treatment specialist in corrections.

Monday through Friday, the TC starts with a morning meeting called *community meeting*. This meeting is an inmate-run, self-help meeting, with drug treatment staff supervising. During the treatment meetings and groups, inmates are learning and demonstrating therapeutic language and actions in a public "community" setting. After community meeting, inmates are

(Continued)

(Continued)

separated into their appropriate phase group based on the date they entered treatment. RDAP, similar to other TCs, uses a hierarchal form for the 9 to 12 months they are in treatment. Program participants typically have 3.5 hours of treatment daily; during this time, I am working directly with the inmates, providing therapy. Therapy consists of using their RDAP workbooks and a facilitator guide to treat the inmate's addictions and behaviors. In RDAP, there are three phases of treatment, with new inmates entering treatment every 3 months (approximately 25 inmates per phase). With inmates phasing in and out of treatment, creating individual treatment plans, reviews of progress, and treatment summaries for each inmate are my responsibility to maintain and develop.

What is your advice to someone either wishing to study or now studying criminal justice to become a practitioner in this career field?

It would be important to understand the population for which you are providing therapy. In this regard, being an intern in a correctional setting would be beneficial to someone becoming a practitioner, due to the nature of working inside a prison. Finally, practice development and presentation of lectures and seminars to groups, as this will be a skill used often when providing group therapy.

Disclaimer: Opinions expressed in this article are those of the author and do not necessarily represent the opinions of the Federal Bureau of Prisons or the Department of Justice.

THERAPEUTIC COMMUNITIES

Video 11.2: Teaching Social Skills to Prison Inmates

Therapeutic communities (TCs) are residential settings for drug and alcohol treatment that use the community spirit generated by the influence of peers and various group processes to help individuals overcome their addition and develop effective social skills. Most such communities offer long-term (typically 6 to 12 months) residence, in which opportunities for attitude and behavioral change operate on a hierarchical model, whereby treatment stages reflect increased levels of personal insight and social responsibility. The interactions of the residents are both structured and unstructured but always designed to influence attitudes and behaviors associated with substance abuse (Litt & Mallon, 2003). TCs provide dynamic *mutual self-help* environments, in which residents transmit and reinforce one another's acceptance of and conformity with the highly structured and stringent expectations of the TC and of the wider community. Life in a TC is extremely hard on people who have never experienced any sort of disciplined expectations from others, and as a consequence, there are many dropouts; some residents withdraw voluntarily, and others are removed by TC staff for noncompliance.

TCs also operate within prison walls and are most often known as **residential substance abuse treatment (RSAT)** communities. These RSATs typically last 6 to 12 months and are composed of inmates in need of substance abuse treatment and whose parole dates are set to coincide with the end of the program. RSAT inmates are separated from the negativity and violence of the rest of the prison, are provided with extensive cognitive behavioral counseling, and attend Alcoholics Anonymous (AA) and Narcotics Anonymous (NA) meetings, as well as many other kinds of rehabilitative classes (Dietz, O'Connell, & Scarpitti, 2003). Most participants in these RSATs are positive about most aspects of their experience, with most inmates listing cognitive self-change programs as the most positive aspect of their treatment (Stohr, Hemmens, Shapiro, Chambers, & Kelly, 2002). Dietz et al. (2003) also found that most inmates in prison-based TCs were positive about the program and that they had significantly fewer rule violations and rates of grievance filing than inmates in the general population.

Therapeutic communities (TCs): Residential communities providing dynamic mutual self-help environments and offering long-term opportunities for attitude and behavioral change and learning constructive, prosocial ways of coping with life.

Residential substance abuse treatment (RSAT): These RSATs typically last 6 to 12 months and provide various forms of substance abuse treatment to inmates separate from the general prison population.

FIGURE *11.3*   Percentage of Arrestees Testing Positive
for Drugs in Five U.S. Cities, 2007–2013

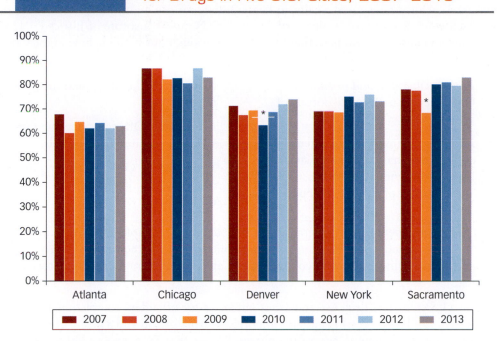

*Differences between each year and 2013 are significant at the 0.05 level or less.

Note: Most recent data available.

Source: Office of National Drug Control Policy (2014).

FIGURE *11.4*   Comparison of Outcomes Between
HOPE and Control Probationers

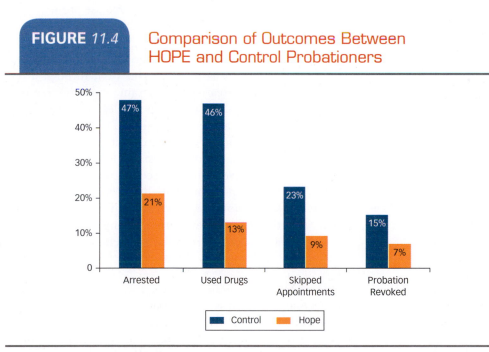

Source: National Institute of Justice (2012).

Video 11.3:
Dog Training
Program
Encourages
Interaction,
Changes Lives at
Washington State
Penitentiary

An interesting program implemented in a prison setting and transitioning into the community is the Delaware Multistage Program (Mathias, 1995). In Phase 1, offenders spend 12 months in a prison-based TC called Key; in Phase 2, they spend 6 months in a prerelease TC called Crest; and finally, in Phase 3, they receive an additional 6 months of counseling while on parole or in work release. The National Institute of Justice (2015a) lists several phases of treatment that offenders go through during their time in the Crest program after release from prison:

- *Entry, evaluation, and orientation*: Offenders get used to life outside of prison.

- *Primary*: Counselors and offenders explore the challenges and issues faced by individual offenders and prepare appropriate responses

  to minimize the likelihood of relapse.

- *Job seeking*: Offenders develop job-seeking and interviewing skills.

- *Work release*: Offenders maintain residence at Crest while working in the community.

The final component of the program, after offenders have completed Crest, is aftercare while on parole and living full-time in the community. They are required to return weekly to an assigned center for group counseling and are subject to random mandatory drug testing.

Figure 11.5 compares drug use and arrest outcomes for offenders completing all phases (Key, Crest, and Key-Crest) 18 months after release from prison and a group of offenders who did not participate in any of the phases. We see that 76% of Key-Crest members remained drug free, and 71% remained arrest free, compared with only 19% and 30%, respectively, of the control group. Put another way, 3 times as many Key-Crest participants were drug-free after 18 months than the comparison group, and 2.37 times more Key-Crest participants were arrest free than the comparison group.

ETHICAL ISSUE 11.2

What Would You Do?

You are the chief psychologist in the largest state prison in the state. One of your counselors hasn't recommended any inmate be put on a program of prerelease in 6 months, and you get a lot of complaints about his "hard-nosed" attitude. The counselor tells you he operates from a therapeutic theory with a "no nonsense, no excuses" framework and that he's not going to let these "trailer trash out of here until they've completed their full minimums." What would be your response to this counselor?

Inciardi, Martin, and Butzin (2004) followed this same group 5 years after release from prison. As expected, the greater the time lapse between treatment and evaluation, the greater the relapse rate. Over the 5-year period, it was found that 71% of drug abusers who went through a residential treatment program and who received additional treatment upon release (the Key-Crest group) had relapsed, and 52% had been rearrested. However, the contrast with the comparison group still makes the Key-Crest program impressive. Among the comparison subjects, 95% had relapsed, and 77% had been rearrested. This study shows how extremely difficult it is to battle addiction, even after a long period of forced abstinence and extensive psychosocial treatment.

PHARMACOLOGICAL TREATMENT

Allan Leshner (1998) informs us that addiction is a brain disease and a "prototypical psychobiological illness, with critical biological, behavioral, and social context elements" (p. 5). As **addiction** is basically a brain chemistry problem, pharmacological treatment with drug antagonists (drugs that work by blocking the effects of other drugs) stabilizes brain chemistry and renders addicts more receptive to psychosocial counseling. Proponents of pharmacological treatment emphasize that it is not a magic bullet and that it augments, not replaces, traditional treatment methods.

Addiction: A psychobiological illness characterized by intense craving for a particular substance.

FIGURE 11.5   Delaware Multistage Correctional Treatment Program 18 Months After Release From Prison

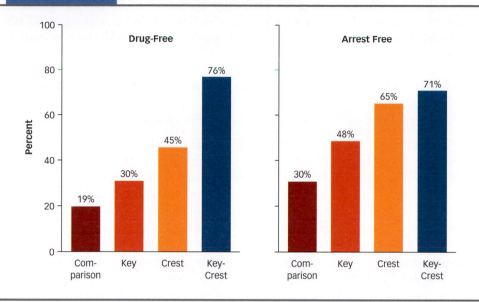

Source: Mathias (1995).

There are many drug antagonists, but only one has claimed success in curbing both alcohol and drug addiction: naltrexone. Naltrexone reduces craving among alcohol- and drug-abstinent addicts and reduces the pleasurable effects of those who continue to use (Schmitz, Stotts, Sayre, DeLaune, & Grabowski, 2004). A study of drug addicts on federal probation found that about one third of probationers who received naltrexone plus counseling relapsed, as opposed to two thirds of those who only received counseling (Kleber, 2003). A new drug called Vivitrol is a slow-release (it releases the drug into the blood stream slowly over a period of days) version of naltrexone that controlled clinical trials have shown to be effective in preventing not only drug abuse relapse but also to diminish the cravings that drive it. "Vivitrol is the first non-narcotic, non-addictive, extended release medication approved for the treatment of opioid dependence—marking an important turning point in our approach to treatment" (Volkow, 2010, n.p.).

Proponents of pharmacological treatment claim that the effects of such treatment are more effective and immediate and wonder why the correctional system is relatively uninterested in pharmacological treatment (Kleber, 2003). It could be that corrections professionals received their training primarily in the social sciences, and there are some who have genuine ethical problems regarding chemical treatments for behavioral problems. However, according to the National Institute on Drug Abuse (2006), while medication is important for treating many addicts because medication helps them to stabilize their lives, it must be combined with counseling.

••• ANGER MANAGEMENT

A central component of many treatment programs in corrections is anger management, particularly in violent, drug, and sex offender treatment programs. **Anger management**

Anger management programs: Programs that consist of a number of techniques by which someone with problems controlling anger can learn the causes and consequences of anger, to reduce the degree of anger, and to avoid anger-inducing triggers.

programs consist of a number of CBT techniques by which someone with problems controlling anger can learn the causes and consequences of anger, to reduce the degree of anger, and to avoid anger-inducing triggers. Anger is often central to violent criminal behavior, and given the frustrations resulting from being in custody or under correctional supervision in the community, it often leads to violence. Anger is a normal and often adaptive human feeling that is aroused when we feel that we have been offended or wronged in some way. The tendency to undo that wrongdoing by retaliating is motivated by anger and is adaptive in the sense that it warns those who have offended or wronged you that you are not to be treated that way. The problem, however, is not anger per se but rather the inability of some to manage it. These individuals often become excessively angry over minor real or imagined slights, to the point of rage.

Anger management classes are taught in groups and designed to increase offenders' responsibility for ownership of their emotions (anger) and their reactions to them. Offenders often become frustrated and angry because they think life is not fair to them ("I'm a victim of circumstances") and the world owes them a living. This kind of destructive thinking must be challenged and replaced by individual responsibility. Anger management classes also teach such skills as rational thinking ("Did this person really mean to dis me?") to increase offenders' ability to react to frustration and conflict in assertive rather than aggressive ways and to develop effective communication skills (Jolliffe & Farrington, 2009). There appears to be a growing consensus that properly conducted anger management programs reduce inmate violence and reduce violent recidivism for program completers versus control subjects by about 8% to 10% (Jolliffe & Farrington, 2009; Serin, Gobeil, & Preston, 2009). Although this seems like a small return on a corrections investment, even an 8% reduction in violent offenses prevents much needless suffering and saves millions of dollars in expenses.

Journal Article 11.1: Effectiveness of Sex Offender Treatment for Psychopathic Sexual Offenders

••• SEX OFFENDERS AND THEIR TREATMENT

The American public harbors all sorts of very negative images of sex offenders. We lock them up under civil commitment orders after they have completed their prison terms, and all 50 states have sex offender registration laws (Talbot, Gilligan, Carter, & Matson, 2002). However, the term *sex offender* defines a very broad category of offenders, ranging from "flashers" to true sexual predators, just as property offenders include everyone from petty shoplifters to career burglars. At least 98% of all sex offenders are either in the community on probation or parole or will be some day (Carter & Morris, 2002), making the issue of sex offender treatment of the utmost importance.

Although it is part of popular lore that sex offenders are untreatable and will never stop their offending, as a category of offenders, they are actually less likely to reoffend than any other category. A review of 61 studies of sex offender recidivism found an average rate of reconviction for sexual crimes of 13.4% over a 4- to 5-year follow-up (Hanson &

© iStockphoto.com/Alina Solovyova-Vincent

PHOTO 11.4: Group work is often used in offender programming, both inside and outside of correctional facilities.

FIGURE *11.6*   Recidivism Rates at 5-Year, 10-Year, and 15-Year Follow-Ups for Child Molesters

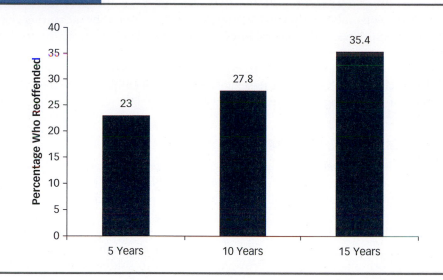

Source: Przybylski (2015).

Bussière, 1998). Perhaps the most instructive study of recidivism conducted to date was a study by the Bureau of Justice Statistics, whose researchers tracked 9,691 sex offenders released from prisons in 15 states in 1994 (Langan, Schmitt, & Durose, 2003). Over the 3-year period of the follow-up, sex offenders had a lower rearrest rate (43%) than 272,111 non–sex offenders released at the same time in the same states (68%). Rearrest rates included all types of crimes and technical violations, such as failing to register as a sex offender or missing appointments with their parole officers. Only 3.5% of the sex offenders were reconvicted of a new sex crime during the follow-up period. Because recidivism rates include only those offenders who have been caught, in common with other types of offenders, the above figures should be considered bare minimums.

State-of-the-art treatment of sex offenders must include a thorough assessment of psychosocial problem areas, deviant arousal patterns, and polygraph assessment (Marsh & Walsh, 1995). A number of states have made polygraph testing mandatory for sex offenders on probation or parole to determine if offenders are engaging in noncompliant behavior. The polygraph is also used for the purpose of obtaining a complete sexual history of the offender for treatment purposes and for offenders in denial of the offense or who minimizing its seriousness or their responsibility for it. ("She wanted it." "I was drunk.") Monitoring examinations are administered typically every 6 months. Counselors are in agreement that effective treatment is impossible until the full extent of the offender's sex-offending history is acknowledged by him or her and known to treatment personnel (Walsh & Stohr, 2010). But sex offenders are notorious for hiding their sexual histories, so polygraph assessment is needed to access their sexual histories. Comparing self-reports before and after polygraph testing across two decades of research, it has been found that child molesters underreport the number of sex crimes they have committed by about 500% and overreport their own childhood sexual victimization (the "I'm a victim too" excuse) by about 250% (Hindman & Peters, 2001). The polygraph may therefore be seen as a very useful tool if the first goal of treatment is to honestly acknowledge one's sexual history.

Another useful tool in the assessment of sex offenders is the penile plethysmograph (PPG). The PPG measures blood flow in the penis by a placing a small, expandable,

Video 11.4:
Reality Check:
Minnesota's Sex
Offender Treatment
Program

pressure-sensitive rubber gauge filled with mercury at the base of the penis. This gauge sends information to a machine that relays information about the level of expansion of the penis as the offender is exposed to sexually suggestive pictures and videos. Machine readings then enable treatment professionals to determine the offender's level of sexual attraction to various subjects (boys, girls, rape, sadism, and so on) by measuring changes in his erectile responses. This enables an evaluation of offenders' attraction to deviant sex relative to consensual adult sex by creating a measure dividing the level of penile arousal to deviant stimuli to arousal to consenting sex. Hanson and Bussière's (1998) meta-analysis showed PPG response to sexual depictions of children to be the most accurate method of identifying sexual-recidivism risk.

PHARMACOLOGICAL TREATMENT

Unlike treatment for other problems in corrections, there has been a great deal of interest in the pharmacological treatment of sex offenders. Numerous researchers have concluded that optimal treatment (following a thorough psychosocial and physiological assessment) combines the biomedical with cognitive behavioral approaches (Walsh & Stohr, 2010). The biomedical approach involves so-called **chemical castration**. There are a number of medications that are used for chemical castration, but the most widely used is a synthetic hormone called Depo-Provera, which is also sold as a method of female birth control. Depo-Provera works in males to reduce sexual thoughts, fantasies, and erections by drastically reducing the production of testosterone, the major male sex hormone. (Other medications used to treat sex offenders affect testosterone receptor sites rather than reducing its production.) Depo-Provera prevents testosterone production, and it is testosterone activating a part of the brain called the hypothalamus that controls the male sex drive. Depriving the brain of testosterone allows offenders to concentrate on their psychosocial problems without distracting sexual fantasies and urges (Marsh & Walsh, 1995). A review of 11 meta-analyses covering 353 separate studies, from 1943 to 2009, found that surgical castration had the strongest effect on recidivism, followed by chemical castration (Kim, Benekos, & Merlo, 2016). Insight-oriented therapies such as psychoanalysis had essentially no effect, but cognitive behavioral therapy had a significant effect, though much less if not combined with some form of antitestosterone medication.

Following the state of California in 1997, several states now mandate chemical castration ("castration" is reversible upon withdrawal from the drug) for repeat offenders. Not all sex offenders should be treated with this drug because there are sometimes negative side effects, and treatment can only be provided by a medical doctor. However, a number of reviews of the literature from Europe and America show that antiandrogen drugs such as Depo-Provera result in recidivism rates for repeat rapists and child molesters that are remarkably low (in the 2% to 3% range) when compared with offenders treated with only psychosocial methods (Maletzky & Field, 2003).

Chemical castration: A biomedical treatment for chronic sex offenders in which a synthetic hormone called Depo-Provera is administered. Depo-Provera works in males to reduce sexual thoughts, fantasies, and erections by drastically reducing the production of testosterone, the major male sex hormone.

●●● MENTALLY ILL OFFENDERS

As graphically indicated in Figure 11.7, from the Council of State Governments Justice Center (2013), mental illness lurks behind many factors that are linked to criminal behavior. Mentally ill offenders under correctional supervision present a particularly difficult treatment problem. Alcoholics and drug addicts ingest substances that alter the functioning of their brains in ways that interfere with their ability to cope with everyday life, although their brains may be normal when not artificially befuddled. Mentally ill persons also have brains that limit their capacity to cope, but that limitation is intrinsic to their brains, not attributable to intoxicating substances. Studies around the world have found that mentally ill persons (mostly schizophrenics and manic depressives) are at least 3 to 4 times more likely to have a conviction for violent offenses than persons in general (Fisher et al., 2006). Most mentally ill persons, however, are more likely to be victims than victimizers, and many of them make their problems worse by abusing alcohol and/or drugs (Walsh & Yun, 2013). It because of their substance abuse and greater propensity for violence, in addition to mental-hospital deinstitutionalization, that the mentally ill are overrepresented in the correctional system.

Torrey and his colleagues (2014) tell us that there were an estimated 356,268 inmates with severe mental illness in prisons and jails in the United States in 2012 and approximately 35,000 severely mentally ill patients in psychiatric hospitals. In addition, the David L. Bazelon Center for Mental Health Law (2008) estimates that about 16% of individuals on probation or parole have some form of mental illness. This state of affairs results from the deinstitutionalization of all but the most seriously ill patients from mental hospitals that occurred in the 1960s. For instance, there were 559,000 persons in U.S. mental hospitals in 1955; in 2000 (with a U.S. population about 80% greater), there were only 70,000 (Gainsborough, 2002), and as we have seen, it was down to 35,000 in 2012. Deinstitutionalization of the mentally ill from mental hospitals has shifted to their institutionalization in jails and prisons, which, in essence, has resulted in the criminalization of mental illness (Lurigio, 2000). Table 11.2 presents the highlights of a Bureau of Justice Statistics report on the mental-health problems of prison and jail inmates (James & Glaze, 2006).

Mentally ill offenders in jails and prisons are often victimized by other inmates, who call them "bugs" and exploit them sexually and materially (stealing from them), although most inmates seek to avoid them. Mentally ill offenders are also punished by corrections

AP Video 11.2:
NYC Jail Deaths

Video 11.5:
Marion County
Sheriff Runs the
Largest Mental
Illness Facility in
Indianapolis

| FIGURE *11.7* | Mental Illness Lurks Behind Many Other Problems |

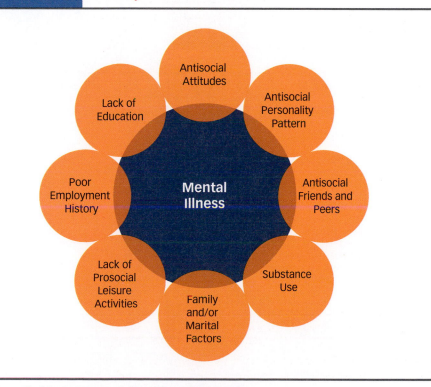

Source: Council of State Governments Justice Center (2014).

officers for behavior that, though not pleasant, is symptomatic of their illness. These behaviors include such things as excessive noise, refusing orders or medication, self-mutilation, and poor hygiene. Obviously, correctional facilities are not the ideal place for providing mental-health treatment, even assuming that the staff is aware who the mentally ill are among their charges. Few correctional or probation and parole officers have any training about mental-health issues, and one nationwide survey of probation departments found that only 15% of them operated special treatment programs for the mentally ill (Lurigio, 2000). It is not that anyone expects correctional workers to become treatment providers because that's a job for psychologists and psychiatrists. However, they should be expected to recognize signs and symptoms of mental illness, should know how to effectively deal with situations involving mentally ill persons, and should have a basic understanding of the causes of and treatment for the major mental illnesses.

Treatment for the mentally ill in prisons and jails consists primarily of antipsychotic and antidepressive medication, typically administered by a nurse. Many mentally ill individuals, especially paranoid schizophrenics, often refuse to take their medication. It is permissible in a number of states to forcibly treat mentally ill inmates if they meet state-specific criteria, which is typically if inmates pose a risk to others or themselves. This is determined on a case-by-case basis by a review committee composed of correctional and medical professionals (Torrey et al., 2014). Of course, just because such procedures are authorized by the state does not mean that they are utilized or that the inmate will be treated. According to Torrey and his colleagues (2014),

| **TABLE** 11.2 | Prevalence of Mental-Health Problems Among Prison and Jail Inmates |

| | PERCENTAGE OF INMATES IN . . . | | | |
| | STATE PRISON | | LOCAL JAIL | |
SELECTED CHARACTERISTICS	WITH MENTAL PROBLEM	WITHOUT	WITH MENTAL PROBLEM	WITHOUT
Criminal record				
Current or past violent offense	61%	56%	44%	36%
Three or more prior incarcerations	25%	19%	26%	20%
Substance dependence or abuse	74%	56%	76%	53%
Drug use in month before arrest	63%	49%	62%	42%
Family background				
Homelessness in year before arrest	13%	6%	17%	9%
Past physical or sexual abuse	27%	10%	24%	8%
Parents abused alcohol or drugs	39%	25%	37%	19%
Charged with violating facility rules*	58%	43%	19%	9%
Physical or verbal assault	24%	14%	8%	2%
Injured in a fight since admission	20%	10%	9%	3%

*Includes items not shown.

Note: Most recent data available.

Source: James and Glaze (2006).

Given the many legal difficulties in providing treatment for individuals with serious mental illness in prisons and jails, it is not surprising that many of them, including those who are most severely ill, receive no treatment whatsoever. This leaves corrections officers with few options for controlling mentally ill inmates' psychotic, often violent behavior. One option is seclusion, which often makes the inmate's mental illness worse. (pp. 104–105)

What is both morally and fiscally required of the criminal justice system is to provide offenders with mental illness the support and structure they need to avoid further criminal behavior. One of the ways this is attempted is through mental-health courts, which are modeled on drug courts in use across the nation (and discussed earlier). As with drug courts, mental-health courts seek to divert offenders from jails and prisons by facilitating their access to services, providing intensive judicial monitoring, and promoting collaboration between the court, probation, and mental-health service and social-service providers.

EDUCATIONAL AND VOCATIONAL PROGRAMS

In addition to psychological treatment issues addressed here, prisons also provide academic education leading to the GED and/or provide English literacy classes. Inmates who were too bored with formal education as teenagers or were more attracted to other things may be more open to such programs now that there are far fewer other things to occupy their minds. These programs are sorely needed because, when compared with the general population, inmates are severely undereducated. The lack of education limits their job prospects and their ability to handle common tasks that confront them in everyday life. Inmates who earn a GED may also have the opportunity to further their education, possibly provided by volunteers from local colleges or by taking advantage of free MOOCs (*massive open online courses*), if they have computer privileges.

Audio 11.2: Inmates' Jobs, From Call Centers to Paint Mixing

Studies have demonstrated that inmates who go beyond the GED and participate in postsecondary education (PSE) have lower recidivism rates. One meta-analysis of 15 studies found that 14 showed that overall, recidivism rates for ex-inmates who had participated in PSE were about 46% lower than for ex-inmates who did not (Chappell, 2004). Of course, we cannot discount the motivation and intelligence of those who self-select into PSE and thus were probably less likely to recidivate anyway. This is a problem encountered with all

Web 11.2: Prison Education Project

kinds of prison programs; they are voluntary, and volunteers may be more likely to be motivated to change. On the other hand, an inmate's voluntary participation in a program may be motivated by a desire to impress the parole board or to just get out of the cell for a while. Once in the program, however, an inmate may come to value it for its own value.

When individuals are not randomly assigned to a treatment (correctional education), it is necessary to use a comparison group and use statistical controls to try to eliminate the self-selection factor. A Rand Corporation meta-analysis of 58 studies using comparison groups concluded, "After examining the higher-quality studies, we found that, on average, inmates who participated in correctional education programs had 43 percent lower odds of recidivating than

PHOTO 11.5: In this February 11, 2014, photo, Willie Walker cuts the hair of Nathaniel Tucker in the barber school at the Stateville Correctional Center in Crest Hill, Illinois. The barber training program has been part of the prison for more than 30 years, but in November 2013, inmates who complete the program became eligible to be licensed by the state.

inmates who did not" (Davis, Bozick, Steele, Saunders, & Miles, 2013, p. 57). The study also suggests that prison education programs are cost-effective. It was estimated that for each $1 invested in prison education, incarceration costs were reduced by $4 to $5 during the first three years after release. Unfortunately, the 2008 recession cut deeply into prison treatment budgets, and many educational programs were cut. However, Davis et al. (2013) indicate that there has been an uptick in prison education budgets since about 2011, as states have come to understand the long-term budgetary advantages of providing prisoners with minimal educational tools.

Prison education programs have their strongest effect indirectly via the increased probability of employment. The Rand study found that prisoners who participated in vocational programs were 28% more likely to gain employment upon release than individuals who had not participated in vocational training. Those who participated in academic programs (GED and postsecondary education) had only 8% higher odds of obtaining employment after release than individuals who did not participate in academic programs. However, even the successful completion of the GED should favorably affect inmates' sense of agency and self-esteem and offer them a glimmer of hope that they can make it in the legitimate world. Further discussion of vocational programs is deferred until the next chapter on parole and reentry.

SUMMARY

- Although the vast majority of the correctional budget is spent on security, rehabilitation efforts have not completely ceased. The success rates of many rehabilitation programs are low, but outcomes are significantly better for treated offenders than for similarly situated offenders who did not receive treatment.

- Successful treatment programs implement EBPs that proceed by conducting a thorough assessment of offenders' risks and needs and then address these issues using the principles of responsivity. This model is best begun using the techniques and guidance of motivational interviewing.

- The major programming and counseling model used in corrections is cognitive behavioral therapy (CBT). CBT is used to address and change criminal thinking patterns and to get them to take responsibility for their own lives.

- Treatment is best accomplished for severe substance abusers in therapeutic communities,

although even then, there is a significant percentage of failure. Much of this failure has to do with the intense psychological craving for the substance of abuse, which is something that may be significantly alleviated by certain alcohol and drug antagonists, such as naltrexone.

- Similar observations were made about sex offenders, who have difficulty refraining from acting out their sexual fantasies with inappropriate targets. Repeat sex offenders treated with Depo-Provera combined with cognitive behavioral counseling have much lower recidivism rates compared with offenders treated only psychologically.

- Mentally ill individuals are represented in the correctional system by a factor of at least 3 or 4 times their prevalence in the general population. The correctional system is not equipped to deal with mentally ill people, who are often victimized by other jail or prison inmates or disciplined by corrections officers for exhibiting behavior that is basically part of their mental disease.

KEY TERMS

Actuarial data 268

Addiction 278

Anger management programs 279

Chemical castration 282

Cognitive behavioral therapy (CBT) 271

Evidence-based practice (EBP) 265

Motivational interviewing 268

Needs principle 267

DISCUSSION QUESTIONS

1. In your estimation, are the time, effort, and finances spent on rehabilitative efforts worth it, given the low success rates? Would longer periods of incarceration better protect the public?

2. Cognitive behavioral approaches stress thinking and rationality. How about emotions? Do you think that human behavior is motivated more by emotions than by rationality?

3. Given the greater involvement of genes in Type II alcoholism, in what ways would you treat Type II alcoholics differently from Type I alcoholics if you were a treatment provider? How about if you were a probation and parole officer?

4. Should all sex offenders undergo Depo-Provera treatment? What are the ethical problems of such invasive treatment?

5. Discuss the various component parts of the responsivity principle.

USEFUL INTERNET SITES

Please note that the sites listed can be accessed at edge.sagepub.com/stohrcorrections.

Center for Evidence-Based Practices: www.ohiosamiccoe.cwru.edu

> The center's website provides consulting, training, evaluation for service innovations that improve quality of life and other outcomes for people with mental illness and substance use disorders.

Information on Risk and Needs: www.riskandneeds .com

> This site offers everything you ever wanted to know about assessing risk and needs. It also provides a chat room.

Treatment of Sexual Offenders: www.atsa.com

> A site with much information about policy, prevention, research, and evaluation of sexual offenders.

The Prison Studies Project: prisonstudiesproject.org/ why-prison-education-programs/#_ftn17

> This is a directory of nationwide postsecondary programs in U.S. prisons, by state, that is searchable and continually updated.

$SAGE edge™

Sharpen your skills with SAGE edge at **edge.sagepub.com/stohrcorrections**. SAGE edge for Students provides a personalized approach to help you accomplish your coursework goals in an easy-to-use learning environment. You'll find action plans, mobile-friendly eFlashcards, and quizzes as well as video, web, and resources and links to SAGE journal articles to support and expand on the concepts presented in this chapter.

12 Parole and Prisoner Reentry

TEST YOUR KNOWLEDGE

Test your present knowledge of probation by answering the following questions as true or false. Check your answers on page 537 after reading the chapter.

1. Parole began in an Australian penal colony in the 1830s.

2. Parole and probation are both under court supervision.

3. Parolees are always scrutinized by a parole board to determine eligibility.

4. Most parolees reoffend within three years of release.

5. The parolees most likely to recidivate are property offenders.

6. Researchers agree that incarcerating too many people from the same neighborhood is detrimental because it causes more crime in the long run.

7. Parole success is determined similarly in all states; that is, success means that there is no recidivism.

8. Sanctions such as halfway houses and electronic monitoring cut costs and increase parolee surveillance.

LEARNING OBJECTIVES

- Describe the history and purpose of parole

- Summarize the roles and duties of parole officers and parole board members

- Describe the issues involved in prisoner reentry into the community and parolee recidivism

- Analyze what factors make for a successful reentry

- Identify and discuss halfway houses, house arrest, and electronic monitoring

- Evaluate what is meant by parole "success"

THE PERILS **OF PAROLE**

On the 29th of July, 1994, parolee Jesse Timmendequas lured 7-year-old Megan Kanka into his New Jersey home, where he beat, raped, and murdered her. Timmendequas, who was 33 years old at the time, had two previous convictions for sexually assaulting two young girls: One was 5 years old, and the other was 7 years old. He was given probation on his first conviction but sentenced to prison on his second. After his release from prison, Timmendequas lived with two other convicted sex offenders in Kanka's neighborhood. He confessed to investigating officers the next day and was arrested. He was subsequently convicted of kidnapping, aggravated assault, rape, and murder and was sentenced to death (commuted to life without parole in 2007, when New Jersey abolished the death penalty). The murder led to the introduction of Megan's Law, requiring law enforcement to disclose the location of registered sex offenders on probation or on parole.

What really upset people about this case (in addition to the brutal and needless death of a young girl) was that Timmendequas was a parolee who many thought should never have been released given his criminal record. It was cases such as this that led to efforts to eliminate parole, but short of locking each and every offender up until death, we have to have some way of reintegrating them into the community. The recognition of this brute fact and the need to protect the community from predators such as Timmendequas is the daunting task of parole board members and parole officers. How do the authorities deal with conflicting public demands for protection and for less tax money being spent on corrections, and how do they deal with the vexing problems of trying to turn around the lives of parolees who have demonstrated their inability to control their behavior, time and time again? These are some of the frustrating and troublesome problems we will discuss in this chapter.

●●● WHAT IS PAROLE?

This chapter is about parole and reentry. Parole and reentry are essentially the same thing, although parole refers to the legal status of a person under conditional release from prison while reentry refers to the practical problems facing a person who has that status. The term *parole* comes from the French phrase *parole d' honneur*, which literally means "word of honor" in English. In times when a person's word really meant something, parole was used by European armies to release captured enemy soldiers on the condition (their word of honor) that they would take no further part in hostilities (Seiter, 2005). The practice also existed for a brief time in the American Civil War, but it was soon realized that neither side was honoring it because paroled soldiers were back in the fight weeks after release (CivilWarHome.com, 2002*)*. Modern **parole** refers to the release of convicted criminals from prison under the supervision of a parole officer before the completion of their full sentences on their promise of good behavior. Parole is different from probation in two basic ways. First, parole is an administrative function practiced by a parole board that is part of the executive branch of government while probation is a typically a judicial function. Second, parolees have spent time in prison before being released into the community, whereas probationers typically have not. In many states, both parolees and probationers are supervised by state probation and parole officers or agents; in others, they are supervised by separate probation or parole agencies.

A BRIEF HISTORY OF PAROLE

The philosophical foundation of parole, as applied to convicted criminals, was laid by the superintendent of the Norfolk Island penal colony off the coast of Australia in the 1830s. The superintendent was a former British naval officer and geography professor named Alexander Maconochie, who had experienced imprisonment himself as a captive of the French during the Napoleonic Wars after his ship was wrecked (Morris, 2002). The horrendous conditions in the colony offended the compassionate and the deeply religious Maconochie, who was a firm believer in the primacy of human dignity. As prison superintendent, he operated on three basic principles: (1) Cruel and vindictive punishment debases both the criminal and the society that allows it, making both worse; (2) the purpose of punishment should only be the reformation (today we would say rehabilitation) of the convict; and (3) criminal sentences should not be seen in terms of time to be served but, rather, in terms of tasks to be performed. To implement his programs, Maconochie required indefinite prison terms rather than fixed determinate terms so that convicts would have an incentive to work toward release. As we have seen, the type of sentence Maconochie advocated is known today as an indeterminate sentence.

Parole: The release of prisoners from prison before completing their full sentence.

PHOTO 12.1: The Norfolk (Australia) penal colony's superintendent in the 1830s, Alexander Maconochie, laid out the philosophical foundation of parole, as applied to convicted criminals.

Maconochie was a conservative realist, not a bleeding-heart idealist, whose correctional philosophy is best stated by himself:

> I am no sentimentalist. I most fully subscribe to the right claimed by society to make examples of those who break its laws, that others may feel constrained to respect and obey them. Punishment may avenge, and restraint may, to a certain limited extent, prevent crime; but neither separately, nor together, will they teach virtue. That is the province of moral training alone. (Cited in Morris, 2002, p. xviii)

Maconochie's point is that retribution may deter some offenders, and incapacitation is a temporary

© Steve Daggar

hold on a criminal career, but the real goal of corrections should be to correct or, in Maconochie's words, "teach virtue." With respect to the third principle (tasks performed rather than time served), Maconochie devised a *mark system* involving credits earned for the speedy and efficient performance of these tasks, as well as for overall good behavior. When a convict had accumulated enough credits, he could apply for a *ticket of leave* (TOL), which was a document granting him freedom to work and live outside of the prison before the expiration of his full sentence. TOL convicts were free to work, acquire property, and marry, but they had to appear before a magistrate when required, and church attendance was mandatory. Maconochie's system appeared to have worked very well. It has supposedly been determined that only 20 out of 900 of Maconochie's TOL convicts were convicted of new felonies (many more crimes were felonies in the 19th century than today), a recidivism rate of 2.2% that modern penologists are scarcely able to comprehend and many dismiss as too good to be true (R. Hughes, 1987). Nevertheless—and perhaps predictably—when Maconochie returned home to England and tried to institute his reforms there, he was accused of coddling criminals and relieved of his duties.

Nevertheless, the TOL system was adapted to the differing conditions in Britain under Walter Crofton, who devised the so-called **Irish system**. This system involved four stages, beginning with a 9-month period of solitary confinement, the first 3 months with reduced rations and no work. This period of enforced idleness was presumed to make even the laziest of men yearn for some kind of activity. The solitary period was followed by a period in which convicts could earn marks through labor and good behavior to enable their transfer to an open prerelease prison when enough marks had been accumulated and, finally, to receive a TOL. TOL convicts were supervised in the community by either police officers or civilian volunteers (forerunners of the modern parole officer), who paid visits to their homes and attempted to secure employment for them (Foster, 2006). Of the 557 men released on TOL under the Irish system in the 1850s, only 17 (3.05%) were revoked for new offenses (Seiter, 2005); again, if true, this is an extraordinary level of success.

Elements from both Maconochie's and Crofton's systems were brought into practice in the United States in the 1870s by Zebulon Brockway, superintendent of the Elmira Reformatory in New York. Brockway's system required indeterminate sentencing so that *good time* earned through good conduct and labor could be used to reduce inmates' sentences (Roth, 2006). However, there were no provisions for the supervision of offenders who obtained early release until 1930, when the U.S. Congress established the U.S. Board of Parole. Eventually, parole came to be seen not as a humanistic method of dealing with "reformed" individuals but, rather, as a way of maintaining order in prisons by holding out the prospect of early release if convicts behaved well. It has also become a way of trying to reintegrate offenders back into the community by offering programs to prepare them for life outside the walls and as a partial solution to the problem of prison overcrowding. Because of these functions, parole became an essential and valued part of the American correctional system.

THE MODERN PAROLE SYSTEM

There were 856,900 state and federal parolees in the United States in 2014, 88% of whom were males. As shown in Figure 12.1, by race/ethnicity, 43% were white, 39% were black, 16% were Hispanic, and 2% were "other" (Herberman & Bonczar, 2014). Drug offenses were the most serious offenses for 31% of these parolees, followed by violent crime (31%), property (22%), and other (12%) offenses. Figure 12.2 shows that close to 460,200 adults entered parole in 2014, and about the same number exited parole (451,900 individuals). The decline in both entries and exits from 2013 to 2014 reflects the decrease in inmates being conditionally (as opposed to unconditionally) released. Of those who exited parole, 33% successfully completed it, 14% were reincarcerated, 3% absconded, and the remainder exited for a variety of other reasons (Kaeble, Maruschak, & Bonczar, 2015).

Irish system: A prison system used in the 19th century. This system involved four stages, beginning with a 9-month period of solitary confinement, the first 3 months with reduced rations and no work.

FIGURE *12.1*   Characteristics of Parolees

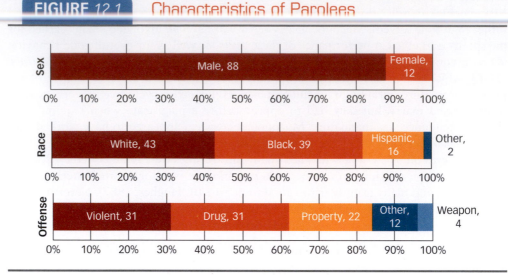

Source: Kaeble, Maruschak, and Bonczar (2015). Bureau of Justice Statistics.

The skyrocketing crime rates in the 1970s, 1980s, and early 1990s, much of it committed by offenders on probation or parole, led to the tough-on-crime approaches to punishment discussed in the last chapter. The heinous kidnapping, rape, and murder of 13-year-old Polly Klaas by parolee Richard Davis and of 7-year-old Megan Kanka by parolee Jesse Timmendequas (in this chapter's opening vignette) led to calls for the abolition of parole from a fearful public and their representatives. Further fueling the fire was the case of Willie Horton. Horton was serving a life sentence in Massachusetts for murder, supposedly without the possibility of parole. In 1986, Horton was granted a weekend furlough (a temporary leave of absence from prison) that he used to commit an armed robbery, rape, and assault. (He is now serving two life sentences, plus 85 years, in Maryland.) With public outrage at a fever pitch, the federal government and a number of states abolished parole, substituting the return of the fixed determinate sentence that Maconochie so disliked. This system means that essentially prisoners are unconditionally released after the completion of their sentences, without supervision or reporting requirements. This type of release is known as **unconditional release**. Inmates who are either required to "max out" their time or who choose to max out rather than be placed on parole have less incentive to enter rehabilitation programs or to abide by prison rules. A number of states had already made the switch to mandatory sentences for their own reasons prior to these hideous crimes committed by Davis, Timmendequas, and Horton.

Abolishing parole sounds very tough and goes over quite well politically, but the reality is something different. Prisoners are still released early for reasons of overcrowding and budgetary concerns, but there is much less rational control today over who is released than there was in the past. It is discretionary parole that has really been abolished in favor of mandatory parole in some states. **Discretionary parole** is parole granted at the discretion of a parole board for selected inmates who are deemed to have earned it. Prisoners earn discretionary parole by avoiding disciplinary infractions and engaging in programs that prepare them for reentry into the community. Discretionary parole also allows parole board members to assess the probability of a given offender's risk to society based on the crime for which he or she was incarcerated and on his or her criminal history, prison behavior, and psychological assessments.

Mandatory parole, on the other hand, is automatic parole for almost all inmates in states that have a system of determinate (i.e., fixed) sentencing (Petersilia, 2000). This system is

Unconditional release: A type of release from prison for inmates who have completed their entire sentences. They are released unconditionally—with no parole.

Discretionary parole: Parole granted at the discretion of a parole board for selected inmates who have earned it.

Mandatory parole: Automatic parole after a set period of time for almost all inmates.

FIGURE *12.2*   Number of Parole Entries and Exits, 2000–2014

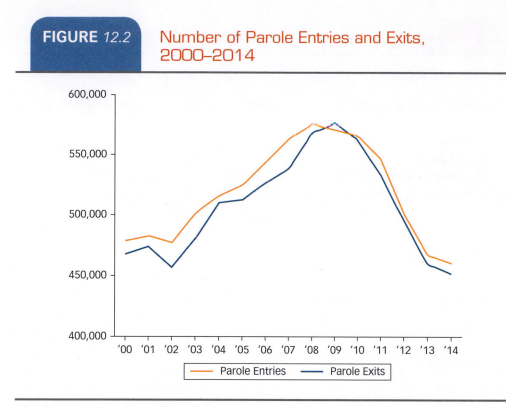

Note: Counts rounded to the nearest 100.

Source: Kaeble, Maruschak, and Bonczar (2015). Bureau of Justice Statistics.

used by the federal government and about half of the states. Mandatory parole still has provisions for earning good-time credits. Tragically, both Davis and Timmendequas were granted mandatory parole determined by mathematical norms generated by a computer based solely on time served—that is, without any kind of consideration of the risk these individuals posed to society. Had their cases gone before a parole board, where board members can peruse parole applicants' criminal history and target violent and dangerous criminals for longer incarceration, odds are that neither man would have been released (Petersilia, 2000). Davis, for instance, had been released after serving only one half of his 16-year sentence because of his supposed "good behavior" while institutionalized for a previous kidnapping, robbery, and assault of a woman (Skolnick, 1993). On the other hand, there is no such thing as mandatory furloughs, so what kind of "rational" discretion led to the decision to grant a vicious murderer like Willie Horton a weekend of freedom to go on a crime spree?

As we see from the graph in Figure 12.2, the percentage of offenders released on mandatory parole is dropping while discretionary-parole releases are increasing. In 2012, 41% entered parole through discretionary release versus 35% who entered through mandatory release (Maruschak & Bonczar, 2013). This reverses the trend from 1980 to 1999, when mandatory-parole releases exceeded discretionary releases by about 22% (T. Hughes, Wilson, & Beck, 2001). Both discretionary- and mandatory-release parolees are supervised after release, but those 17% to 18% of inmates who are released at the expiration of their sentences (unconditional release) are not supervised. The graph in Figure 12.3 supports those who favor discretionary parole and the elimination of mandatory parole. Note that in 1999, about 52% of discretionary parolees successfully completed parole while only about 32% of mandatory parolees did. This discrepancy was still very much in evidence in 2008 (Paparozzi & Guy, 2009).

IN FOCUS 12.1

Example of Parole Conditions

When prisoners are released from prison and placed on parole, there are a number of strict conditions they must follow. Below are examples of these conditions from the state of Nevada. Conditions are pretty standard in all states, but the extent to which parolees are held to them and the severity of consequences for not doing so vary from jurisdiction to jurisdiction.

State of Nevada

Board of Parole Commissioners

PAROLE AGREEMENT

On the day of _____ _____ was sentenced by_____, District Judge of the _____ Judicial District Court in and for the County of _____, State of Nevada, to imprisonment in the Nevada State Prison System, for the crime of _____ for a term of _____.

The Board of Parole Commissioners, by virtue of the authority vested in it by the laws of the State of Nevada, hereby authorizes the Director of the Department of Prisons to allow said on the day of, or as soon thereafter as a satisfactory program can be arranged and approved by the Division of Parole and Probation, to go upon parole outside the prison buildings and enclosure, subject to the following conditions:

Reporting/Release: Upon release from the institution, you are to go directly to the program approved by the Division of Parole and Probation, and shall report to the Supervising Officer or other person designated by the Division. You are required to submit a written Monthly Report to your Supervising Officer on the first of each month on forms supplied by the Division of Parole and Probation. This report shall be true and correct in all respects; in addition, you shall report as directed by your Supervising Officer.

1. Residence: You shall not change your place of residence without first obtaining permission from your Supervising Officer, in each instance.

2. Intoxicants: You shall not drink or partake of any alcoholic beverages (whatsoever) (to excess). Upon request by any Parole or Peace Officer, you shall submit to a medically recognized test for blood/breath alcohol content. Test results of .10 blood alcohol or higher shall be sufficient proof of excess.

3. Controlled Substances: You shall not use, purchase nor possess any narcotic drugs, nor any dangerous drugs, unless first prescribed by a licensed physician; you shall immediately notify your Supervising Officer of any prescription received. You shall submit to narcotic or drug testing as required by any Supervision Officer.

4. Weapons: You shall not possess, own, carry, or have under your control, any type of weapon.

5. Associates: You shall not associate with individuals who have criminal records or other individuals as deemed inappropriate by the Division. You shall not have any contact with persons confined in a correctional institution unless specific written permission has been granted by your supervising officer and the correctional institution.

6. Cooperation: You shall, at all times, cooperate with your Supervising Officer and your behavior shall justify the opportunity granted to you by this parole.

7. Laws and Conduct: You shall comply with all institutional rules, municipal, county, state and federal laws, and ordinances; and conduct yourself as a good citizen.

8. Out-of-State Travel: You shall not leave the State without first obtaining written permission from your Supervising Officer.

9. Employment/Program: You shall seek and maintain legal employment, or maintain a program approved by the Division of Parole and Probation and not change such employment or program without first obtaining permission.

10. Supervision Fees: You shall pay monthly supervision fees while under supervision of the Division.

11. Fines/Restitution: You shall pay all Court-ordered fines, fees and restitution on a schedule approved by the Division.

12. Special Conditions: _____

13. Search: You shall submit to a search of your person, automobile, or place of residence, by a Parole Officer, at any time of the day or night without a warrant, upon reasonable cause as ascertained by the Parole Officer.

14. Your Parole Expiration Date is:

15. Credits: You shall receive no credit, whatsoever, on this sentence should you be absent from supervision at any time and be considered an absconder.

This parole is granted to and accepted by you, subject to the conditions stated herein, and with the knowledge that the Board of Parole Commissioners have the power, at any time, in case of violation of the conditions of parole to cause your detention and/or return to prison. Your right to vote has been revoked and may be restored upon Honorable Discharge from parole.

APPROVED BY THE BOARD OF PAROLE COMMISSIONERS

Chief Parole Officer _____ **Dated:** _____

AGREEMENT BY PAROLEE

I do hereby waive extradition to the State of Nevada from any state in the United States, and from any territory or country outside the continental United States, and also agree that I will not contest any effort to return me to the United States or the State of Nevada.

I have read or had read to me, the conditions of my parole, and I fully understand them and I agree to abide by and strictly follow them. I fully understand the penalties involved should I, in any manner, violate the foregoing conditions.

Parolee _____

Officer Witness _____ **Dated:** _____

PAROLEE RECIDIVISM

A nationwide study of parolee recidivism looked at almost 300,000 parolees from 15 states released from prison in 1994 (Langan & Levin, 2002). Within 3 years of release, 67.5% were rearrested for a new offense, with the entire sample accumulating

FIGURE *12.3*   Percentages of Parolees Successfully Completing Parole by Release Type

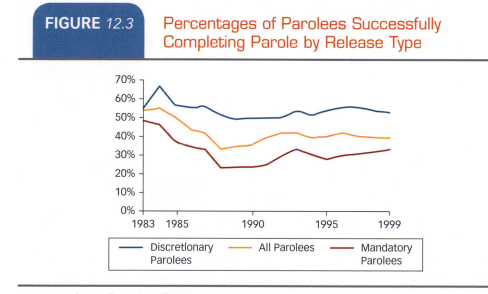

Source: Hughes, Wilson, & Beck (2001).

an astounding 744,000 new offenses in those 3 years. New arrests included 2,871 for murder; 2,444 for rape; 21,245 for robbery; and 54,604 for assault. Property offenders (over 70%) had the highest rate of recidivism while murderers (40.7%) and sex offenders (41.4%) had the lowest recidivism rates. These rates do not mean, for instance, that 40.7% of murderers committed another murder—they mean a further arrest for any type of crime.

A Bureau of Justice Statistics study (Durose, Cooper, & Snyder, 2014) of recidivism among the 405,000 state prisoners released in 30 states in 2005 and followed for a 5-year period found almost identical results. Among the results were the following:

- About two-thirds (67.8%) of released prisoners were arrested for a new crime within 3 years, and three-quarters (76.6%) were arrested within 5 years.

- Within 5 years of release, 82.1% of property offenders were arrested for a new crime, compared to 76.9% of drug offenders, 73.6% of public order offenders, and 71.3% of violent offenders.

- More than a third (36.8%) of all prisoners who were arrested within 5 years of release were arrested within the first 6 months after release, with more than half (56.7%) arrested by the end of the first year.

- Two in five (42.3%) released prisoners were either not arrested or arrested once in the 5 years after their release.

- A sixth (16.1%) of released prisoners were responsible for almost half (48.4%) of the nearly 1.2 million arrests that occurred in the 5-year follow-up period.

- An estimated 10.9% of released prisoners were arrested in a state other than the one that released them during the 5-year follow-up period. (p. 1)

Amy Solomon, Kachnowski, and Bhati (2005) analyzed a subset of 38,624 parolees for whom the type of release was known. There were surprisingly few differences between the parolees, other than the fact that discretionary-release parolees had a lower average number of prior arrests (7.5) than mandatory- (9.5) or unconditional-release (9.6) parolees. Among those rearrested after release, the unconditionally released were rearrested an average of 9.9 months after release; mandatory parolees, an average of 10.4 months; and discretionary parolees, an average of 11.5 months. The average time served, as one would expect, was also noticeably different, with the unconditionally released serving an average of 32 months; mandatory parolees, 18.5 months; and discretionary parolees, 21.3 months. This suggests that supervision is particularly vital at the early stages of the parole process, when parolees are still struggling to find their way back into their communities and are thus most susceptible to returning to their criminal ways.

Figure 12.4 provides an example of a mandatory-parole release form showing the "word of honor" promises that parolees are supposed to abide by in Alaska. The listed conditions are fairly standard from state to state and are indistinguishable from the conditions set for probationers. These are general conditions with which all parolees must comply, but often, there are additional conditions set for individual offenders. These conditions may be things such as requiring alcoholics or drug addicts to enroll in and attend certain programs or requiring sex offenders to stay away from all contact with children or to refrain from Internet pornography. These additional conditions will likely be set by the parole board and/or by each individual parole officer after reviewing each parolee's case. It is then the responsibility of the parole officer to make sure that the parolee follows the conditions that have been mandated.

FIGURE *12.4* Example of a Mandatory Parole Form

STATE OF ALASKA   **DEPARTMENT OF CORRECTIONS**

ORDER OF MANDATORY PAROLE

Parolee: _____ DOB: _____ OTIS# _____ Released: _____ Supv. Expires: _____

****

The following terms and conditions are effective on the release date shown on the CERTIFICATE OF GOOD TIME AWARD (AS 33.20.030) for all prisoners released pursuant to AS 33.16.010 or AS 33.20.040. I understand I am required by law to abide by the conditions imposed, whether or not I sign these conditions. The Parole Board may have me returned to custody at any time when it determines a condition of parole has been violated.

CONDITIONS OF MANDATORY PAROLE

1. REPORT UPON RELEASE: I will report in person no later than the next working day after my release to the P.O. located at: _____ and received further reporting instructions. I will reside at: _____
    _____

2. MAINTAIN EMPLOYMENT/TRAINING/TREATMENT: I will make a diligent effort to maintain steady employment and support my legal dependents. I will not voluntarily change or terminate my employment without receiving permission from my Parole Officer (P.O.) to do so. If discharged or if employment is terminated (temporarily or permanently) for any reason, I will notify my P.O. the next working day. If I am involved in an education, training, or treatment program, I will continue active participation in the program unless I received permission from my P.O. to quit. If I am released, removed, or terminated from the program for any reason, I will notify my P.O. the next working day.

3. REPORT MONTHLY: I will report to my P.O. at least monthly in the manner prescribed by my P.O. I will follow any other reporting instructions established by my P.O.

4. OBEY LAWS/ORDERS: I will obey all state, federal and local laws, ordinances, and court orders.

5. PERMISSION BEFORE CHANGING RESIDENCE: I will obtain permission from my P.O. before changing my residence. Remaining away from my approved residence for 24 hours or more constitutes a change in residence for the purpose of this condition.

6. TRAVEL PERMIT BEFORE TRAVEL OUTSIDE ALASKA: I will obtain the prior written permission of my P.O. in the form of an interstate travel agreement before leaving the State of Alaska. Failure to abide by the conditions of the travel agreement is a violation of my order of parole.

7. NO FIREARMS/WEAPONS: I will not own, possess, have in my custody, handle, purchase or transport any firearm, ammunition or explosives. I may not carry any deadly weapon on my person except a pocket knife with a 3" or shorter blade. Carrying any other weapon on my person such as hunting knife, axe, club, etc. is a violation of my order of parole. I will contact the Alaska Board of Parole if I have any questions about the use of firearms, ammunition, or weapons.

8. NO DRUGS: I will not use, possess, handle, purchase, give or administer any narcotic, hallucinogenic, (including marijuana/THC), stimulant, depressant, amphetamine, barbiturate or prescription drug not specifically prescribed by a licensed medical person.

9. REPORT POLICE CONTACT: I will report to my P.O., not later than the next working day, any contact with a law enforcement officer.

10. DO NOT WORK AS AN INFORMANT: I will not enter into any agreement or other arrangement with any law enforcement agency which will put me in the position of violating any law or any condition of my parole. I understand that the Department of Corrections and Parole Board policy prohibits me from working as an informant.

Source: State of Alaska.

••• PAROLE BOARDS

Parole boards are only required in states that employ a discretionary system of granting parole. A **parole board** is a panel of people presumably qualified to make judgments about the suitability of a prisoner to be released from prison after having served some specified time of his or her sentence. This is termed an inmate's *parole eligibility date*, which is the earliest possible time that he or she can be released from prison. Board members are appointed by the governor for a fixed (renewable) term in most states. Some states mandate that a board appointee be well versed in criminology and corrections while other states have no such requirement. Although many board members serve on a part-time basis and collect a minimal salary and per diem expenses, chairpersons and vice chairpersons are full-time, salaried individuals in almost all states (Abadinsky, 2009).

In making their decision whether to grant or deny parole, board members assess a variety of information about the inmate and interview him or her at a parole hearing to discuss the assessed information and to gain some face-to-face insight about the inmate. Among the information considered by the parole board to help them make their decision are the following:

- The nature of the offense for which the inmate is currently incarcerated
- The criminal history of the inmate
- Indications by word and/or deed that the inmate is repentant
- The inmate's mental health via psychological and psychiatric reports
- The original presentence investigation report
- Reports of institutional conduct, including disciplinary reports
- and participation in religious and rehabilitative programs
- The inmate's parole plan—that is, where does the inmate plan to reside, does the inmate have guaranteed or possible employment waiting, and does the inmate enjoy a good support system in the community?
- Statements made by others supporting (family members, counselors, or ministers) or opposing (the victim, prosecutor, or other criminal justice officials) the inmate's request for parole

Parole board: A panel of people presumably qualified to make judgments about the suitability of a prisoner for release from prison after having served some specified time of his or her sentence.

PHOTO 12.2: Parole board hearing at the Community Corrections Center (CCC L) in Lincoln, Nebraska. This board will determine whether or not this inmate is ready to reenter society.

PERSPECTIVE FROM A PRACTITIONER

Lisa Growette Bostaph, Parole Commissioner

Position: Parole commissioner

Location: Idaho Commission on Pardons and Parole

Education: PhD in criminal justice, University of Cincinnati

What previous criminal justice experience do you have?

My full-time position is an associate professor of criminal justice and graduate program coordinator for the Department of Criminal Justice at Boise State University in Boise, Idaho. Earlier in my career, I worked as a team member in a batterer treatment program; ran a crime scene crisis intervention program for victims of domestic violence, sexual assault, and child abuse; and worked as a victim/witness coordinator for a prosecutor's office, all in Minnesota.

What are the duties and responsibilities of being a parole commissioner?

A parole commissioner is charged with reviewing all applicable case material (police reports, presentence investigation reports, criminal history, previous supervision periods, institutional behavior, treatment case notes, and any applicable evaluations and/or assessments) in preparation for making a decision regarding parole during an open hearing with the offender. In addition, we review all offender requests for reconsideration of previous decisions and commutation of sentences, plus all requests for pardons.

What are the characteristics and traits most useful in your line of work?

In terms of reviewing all of the documents, anyone serving on the commission needs to have a good attention span and be detail oriented, empathetic, and nonjudgmental. Offenders come from all walks of life, backgrounds, and demographic categories. To be fair, you must be able to withhold any preconceived notions or stereotypes about people in any of these categories. This also applies to conducting the interviews during the hearings. To be a successful interviewer, you must be a good listener. Asking questions is not the most important aspect of interviewing; the ability to *hear* what is being said and respond appropriately is of utmost importance.

Please describe your typical workday.

In Idaho, the Parole Commission is a part-time body. There are five of us who serve in rotation on three-person panels hearing cases for 2 weeks of every month. Parole commissioners in Idaho review case materials for all offenders eligible for parole and then conduct interviews of the offenders during open hearings. We also hear from supporters for the offender and from the victim(s) of the crime at these hearings. Once the interview and statements are completed, we deliberate in private to reach a unanimous decision regarding parole for the offender. We may make one of the following decisions: offer a parole date, deny parole and set another hearing at a later date for reconsideration, or deny parole and pass the offender to his or her full-term release date (meaning he or she serves the entire sentence in prison). After reaching a decision, we reconvene the open hearing and announce our decision. In one day, we generally hear 25 cases, which translates into roughly 125 cases in the one week that each three-person panel handles during a month. If we cannot reach a unanimous decision, the hearing is continued to our quarterly hearing, when all five commissioners hear cases. (Majority decision prevails in these hearings.)

What is your advice to someone who wants to enter your field?

For most parole commissions or boards, you must be appointed by the governor, so it is not something that they advertise or for which you apply. That being said, performing well in whatever your chosen career is and serving on criminal-justice-related boards and committees will demonstrate your commitment to the field.

ETHICAL ISSUE 12.1 ?

What Would You Do?

As a probation and parole agent, you become aware that one of your colleagues with whom you have a good relationship is sexually preying on his female probationers and parolees. He essentially waits for them to commit violations, such as nonpayment of fines, missed appointments, or providing dirty urine samples, and then hints around that he will not violate their probation or parole status if they are forthcoming with sexual favors. You learn that he has been quite successful with this strategy and that he overlooks numerous violations. Would you (1) ignore this as none of your business, (2) talk to him and counsel him on the dangers of doing this and tell him to stop or you will report him (it is a crime for someone with legal authority over another to demand sexual favors), or (3) report him to his supervisor?

Feature Video 12.1: Reentry Challenges

Of course, parole boards comprise human beings who have their own reasons for granting or denying parole. Although a majority vote wins the day, there are always members (especially chairpersons) who wield more influence than others. They can never be certain who will or will not fail on parole, but they know that on average, about two thirds will fail. They are thus likely to err on the side of caution (not releasing someone who would have made it successfully) than to endanger the public and embarrass themselves by releasing someone who then proceeds to commit heinous and highly publicized crimes, such as those committed by Davis and Timmendequas.

••• WHAT GOES IN MUST COME OUT: PRISONER REENTRY INTO THE COMMUNITY

Numerous commentators of all political persuasions consume an incredible amount of space writing about America's imprisonment binge, but rarely, outside of the academic literature, do we find much concern about the natural corollary of the binge: What goes in must come out. Jeremy Travis (2005) introduces us to the idea of prison reentry:

> Reentry is the process of leaving prison and returning to society. Reentry is not a form of supervision, like parole. Reentry is not a goal, like rehabilitation or reintegration. Reentry is not an option. Reentry reflects the iron law of imprisonment: they all come back. (p. xxi)

"They all come back," refers to prisoners returning to the communities from which they came.

Understanding the process of prisoner reentry and reintegration into the community is a very pressing issue in corrections. In 2012, 609,800 offenders entered American state and federal prisons, and 637,400 left them (Carson & Golinelli, 2013). Except for those few who leave prison in a pine box or who make their own clandestine arrangements to abscond, all prisoners are eventually released back into the community. Unfortunately, among this huge number, one in five will leave with no postrelease supervision, rendering "parole more a legal status than a systematic process of reintegrating returning prisoners" (J. Travis, 2000, p. 1). Pushing convicts out the prison door with $50, a bus ticket to the nearest town, and a fond farewell is a strategy almost guaranteeing that the majority of them will return. With the exception of convicts who max out, prisoners will be released under the supervision of a parole officer charged with monitoring offenders' behavior and helping them to readjust to the free world.

Because parolees have been in prison and are thus, on average, more strongly immersed in a criminal lifestyle, we should expect them to be more difficult to supervise than probationers—and they are—and to have lower success rates—and they do. While Glaze and Palla (2005) indicate a success rate of 60% for probationers in 2004, the same figure for successful completion of parole was only 46% (although note the difference between the success rates of discretionary- versus mandatory-release parolees in Figure 12.3 and the 58% success rate in 2012 noted earlier in this chapter).

The longer people remain in prison, the more difficult it is for them to readjust to the outside world. Inmates spend a considerable amount of time in prison living by a code that defines as "right" almost everything that is "wrong" on the outside. Adherence to that code brings them acceptance by fellow inmates as *good cons*. Over time, this code becomes etched into an inmate's self-concept, as the prison experience becomes his or her comfort zone. When inmates return to the streets, they do not fit in, they feel out of their comfort zone, and their much-sought-after reputation as a good con becomes a liability rather than an advantage. As prison movie buffs are aware, these readjustment problems were dramatically presented in the suicide of Brooks in *The Shawshank Redemption* and in the final crazy hurrahs of Harry and Archie in *Tough Guys*.

Brooks, Harry, and Archie were all old men who had served very long periods of incarceration and who had thoroughly assimilated into the prison subculture by the time of their release into an alien and unaccepting world. Thus, one recommendation might be to reduce the length of prison sentences so that those unfortunate enough to be in prisons do not have time to become *prisonized*. Such a recommendation gains support from statistics showing that the shorter the time spent in prison, the greater the chance of success on parole (J. Travis & Lawrence, 2002). But if we are looking for

PHOTO 12.3: A prison gate stands open both to admit new inmates and to allow them to leave when they have completed their time.

something causal in those statistics, we are surely sniffing around the wrong tree. Shorter sentences typically go to those committing the least serious crimes and who have the shortest arrest sheets; such people are already less likely to commit further crimes than those who commit the more serious crimes and have long rap sheets. It is not for nothing that former U. S. attorney general Janet Reno called prisoner reentry "one of the most pressing problems we face as a nation" (as cited in Petersilia, 2001, p. 370).

THE IMPACT OF IMPRISONMENT AND REENTRY ON COMMUNITIES

Because crime is highly concentrated in certain neighborhoods, a disproportionate number of prison inmates come from and return to those same neighborhoods. There are those who believe that though high incarceration rates may reduce crime in the short run, the strategy provides only a temporary reprieve and that it will eventually lead to higher crime rates by weakening families and communities and reducing the supervision of children (DeFina & Arvanites, 2002). According to this body of literature, the loss of individuals concentrated in certain communities reduces community organization and cohesion, disrupts families economically and socially, and adds many other problems that will eventually lead to more crime than would have occurred if offenders had been allowed to remain in the community. Clear, Rose, and Ryder's (2001) interviews of residents of high-incarceration neighborhoods is in this tradition. They hypothesize that when public control (incarceration) occurs at high levels, private control (informal control) functions at low levels and ultimately results in more crime. Clear, Rose, and Ryder do not deny that neighborhood residents are better off and safer when the bad apples are pulled from the shelf and shipped off to prison. This implies the opposite of their hypothesis, however. ~~That is, when private control functions at low levels, public control occurs at high levels.~~

There can definitely be many negative impacts on the community, especially the financial impact on families, when working fathers are removed from it. However, a Bureau of Justice Statistics report (Mumola, 2000) showed that 48% of imprisoned parents were never married, and 28% of those who were ever married were divorced or separated, and very few men lived with their children prior to imprisonment. Moreover, the majority of parents had been convicted of violent or drug crimes, and 85% had drug problems, which makes it difficult to see how the presence of antisocial fathers in the community somehow contributes to private control rather than detracts from it (Rodney, & Mupier, 1999). For instance, a longitudinal study of 1,116 British families showed that the presence of a criminal father in the household strongly predicted the antisocial behavior of his children and that the harmful effects increased the longer he spent with the family (Moffitt, 2005). Another large-scale study found that when an antisocial father resides with a mother and offspring, there is more risk to children than when the father does not because "children experience a double whammy of risk for antisocial behavior. They are at genetic risk because antisocial behavior is highly heritable [greatly influenced by genetic factors]. In addition, the same parents who transmit genes also provide the child's environment" (Jaffee, Moffitt, Caspi, & Taylor, 2003, p. 120).

THE PROCESS OF REENTRY

Reentry is a process of reintegrating offenders back into their communities regardless of whether or not they were integrated into it in a prosocial way before they entered prison. Part of that process is preparing offenders to reenter by providing them with various programs that target the risks they pose to the community (e.g., anger management classes) and their needs (e.g., educational and vocational programs). Unfortunately, one of the prices we have paid for prison expansion in recent years is "a decline in preparation for the return to the community. There is less treatment, fewer skills, less exposure to the world of work, and less focused attention on planning for a smooth transition to the outside world" (J. Travis & Petersilia, 2001, p. 300). Yet there is always an abundance of suggestions about what we should be doing to prepare inmates to reenter free society. If these programs were to be actually implemented and if they do what they are supposed to, parolees may have a fighting chance of remaining in the community. The United States Department of Justice (A. Solomon, Dedel Johnson, Travis, & McBride, 2004) lists three programmatic phases believed necessary for reentry with a chance of success:

Phase 1—Protect and Prepare: The use of institution-based programs designed to prepare offenders to reenter society. These services include education, treatment for mental health and substance abuse issues, job training, mentoring, and a complete diagnostic and risk assessment.

Phase 2—Control and Restore: The use of community-based transition programs to work with offenders prior to and immediately following their release from jail or prison. Services provided in this phase include, education, monitoring, mentoring, life-skills training, assessment, job-skills development, and mental health and substance abuse treatment.

Phase 3—Sustain and Support: This phase uses community-based long-term support programs designed to connect offenders no longer under the supervision of the justice system with a network of social-service agencies and community-based organizations to provide ongoing services and mentoring relationships.

This three-phase programming strategy is an ideal rather than a reality most of the time, but many offenders released from incarceration do have access to some parts of each of

TABLE 12.1	Evidence-Based Parole Policy and Practices and Their Rationales	
	PAROLE POLICY AND PRACTICE	**RATIONALE**
Guiding Philosophy	Offenders' likelihood of success can be increased by aligning the intensity and type of prison and community interventions with assessed risk level. Postrelease supervision offers an opportunity to address criminogenic needs, monitor offenders' community adjustment, and address risk factors prior to release from criminal justice control.	Ninety-five percent of all incarcerated offenders will eventually be released from prison. A large body of knowledge is available to support decisions that are demonstrated to reduce the likelihood of reoffense.
Risk Assessment	1. Determinations regarding the timing of parole release and requirements of release are guided by clear policy that incorporates an assessment of risk as well as a structured consideration of other factors as defined by the sentencing structure of the jurisdiction. 2. Offenders at lower risk of reoffending are identified for parole *review* and consideration as early in the sentence as possible, in light of other sentencing considerations. Where the law directs the paroling authority to give primary consideration to public safety and the reduction of the likelihood of future crime, offenders at lower risk levels should be identified for release as soon as possible.	Research demonstrates that it is possible to identify individuals who are most—and least—likely to reoffend. Furthermore, research demonstrates that all categories of offenders (high, moderate, and low risk) are more successful when interventions are tailored to address their risk level.
Prison-Based Interventions	3. Requirements for in-prison treatment are based on assessed criminogenic needs. 4. In-prison programming is prioritized for higher risk offenders and used only selectively with lower risk offenders.	In-prison programming is costly and limited. Reserve these resources for those who can benefit from them most. Community-based programming is not only less expensive, but research demonstrates it can also be more effective than in-prison programming.
Parole Supervision	5. Parole supervision intensity is based on assessed level of risk. 6. Terms and conditions of supervision are individually tailored and based on assessed criminogenic needs. 7. Parole officers devote their time and attention to addressing offenders' criminogenic needs. 8. Parole supervision practices align with other evidence-based supervision approaches. Paroling authorities with responsibility for supervision practices are aware of and adhere to this body of knowledge. Those without this responsibility are nonetheless familiar with these findings.	Assessment tools enable professionals to determine both the level of recidivism risk and the specific factors likely to result in reoffense. Research demonstrates that tailoring interventions—both in terms of intensity and type—to these findings offers the greatest recidivism reduction potential. Furthermore, a body of knowledge exists that provides specific guidance with regard to reducing reoffense through the nature and type of interactions between supervision officers and offenders.
Community-Based Interventions	9. Three to eight criminogenic needs are targeted for programming and services with moderate- and high-risk offenders (both in prison and in the community). 10. Paroling authorities and supervision agencies are familiar with the body of research on effective interventions and engage with providers to ensure that this body of knowledge is integrated into therapeutic practice.	Research demonstrates that the rate of recidivism among moderate- and high-risk offenders is reduced when interventions are matched is assessed criminogenic needs, when multiple criminogenic needs are addressed, and when the interventions themselves are evidence—based (e.g., they use appropriate program methodologies and are delivered by skilled staff in research-supported doses).
Responding to Violations	11. Violations of conditions of supervision are responded to swiftly by parole supervision officers and, where appropriate, boards. 12. Responses to violations are proportional and aimed at reducing future noncompliance/criminal behavior rather than punishment alone.	Many offenders will violate their conditions of supervision one or more times. Research demonstrates that responses are most effective when they are delivered quickly and when the actions taken seek to positively change, rather than punish, behavior.

these phases, and some manage to successfully complete parole. To be successful in Phase 1, offenders have to be willing to apply themselves to the training and programming offered to them. They have to make a conscious decision to set long-term goals and convince themselves that a criminal career is not for them. Obviously, these are decisions that are typically only made by individuals not fully immersed in the criminal lifestyle. In Phase 2, they have to implement those decisions in the real world, where it counts, and not get sidetracked by either the frustration generated by the monitoring they are subjected to by their parole officers or by the criminal opportunities that may present themselves. Phase 3 may be the most difficult of all for offenders who rely on authoritative figures to give their lives direction. This is why it is so important for community corrections officers to plug their clients into agencies outside of the criminal justice system that are able to address parolee needs prior to termination of supervision. Table 12.1 provides evidence-based parole practices and policies that are more specific than the Department of Justice's three phases.

U.S. assistant attorney general Karol Mason (2016), in a guest column in the *Washington Post*, noted that the use of words like *convict* or *felon* to describe ex-inmates had the unintended effect of psychologically harming, through labeling, those trying to make a successful reentry into their community. Her recommendation originates from a recognition that people making the transition from prison to a community are in a vulnerable place as they try to become full community members, and words that denigrate them or that reinforce negative self-concepts just make that change harder. Instead, she recommended that correctional staff involved in guiding the reentry refer to their charges as a *person who committed a crime* and as an *individual who was incarcerated*, rather than the more pejorative terms. Do you think this is a difference that makes a difference?

THE ROLE OF EMPLOYMENT FOR SUCCESSFUL REENTRY

Video 12.3: Offenders Chart Path to Good Jobs With CAD Training

Perhaps the most important tool for the successful reintegration of offenders who want to go straight is employment. Many of you are familiar with the old saying, "The devil finds work for idle hands." Being involved in legitimate endeavors denies us the time and the energy to engage in illegitimate endeavors, even if we have the inclination to do so. Criminologists have long told us that commitment to a prosocial career is incompatible with a criminal lifestyle (Hirschi, 1969). It follows, therefore, that one of the most important factors in a successful reentry process is finding legitimate employment. Without employment, ex-convicts are 3 to 5 times more likely to recidivate than are those who gain employment (Sonfield, 2009). Le'Ann Duran, Plotkin, Potter, and Rosen (2013) explain its critical role:

> Employment can make a strong contribution to recidivism-reduction efforts because it refocuses individuals' time and efforts on prosocial activities, making them less likely to engage in riskier behaviors and to associate with people who do. Having a job also enables individuals to contribute income to their families, which can generate more personal support, stronger positive relationships, enhanced self-esteem, and improved mental health. For these reasons, employment is often seen as a gateway to becoming and remaining a law-abiding and contributing member of a community. Employment also has important societal benefits, including reduced strain on social service resources, contributions to the tax base, and safer, more stable communities. Of course, finding employment for parolees is more difficult today than it was a couple of generations ago when well-paying jobs requiring little education or training were plentiful. We have sent many of these jobs overseas and have automated many of those that remain. Then there are the attitudes toward work of many offenders themselves. Many are not prepared temperamentally or intellectually for the studied discipline of a nine-to-five, 5-days per week routine. Adding to this misery, employers are understandably reluctant to hire ex-convicts because of such concerns as liability for employees' actions, reliability, and simple fear of how they will behave in

general. One survey found that only 40% were willing to hire an ex-convict, and 92% said that they conducted criminal background checks as a normal process in their hiring. (p. 2)

Unfortunately, the typical offender is not prepared for much other than a low-skill manufacturing job, the kind of job that the United States has been losing in truly staggering numbers due to technological advances and companies moving operations overseas. Job prospects are thus fairly limited unless offenders can improve themselves educationally. Amy Solomon and her colleagues (2004) report that 53% of Hispanic inmates, 44% of black inmates, and 27% of white inmates have not completed high school or obtained a GED, as opposed to 18% of the general population. In addition to their general lack of preparedness, employers are understandably reluctant to hire ex-convicts. Even taking into consideration lack of preparedness and employer reluctance to hire offenders, economists find that incarceration reduces employment opportunities by about 40%, wages by about 15%, and wage growth by about 33% (Western, 2003). There is no doubt that once offenders embark on a criminal career, it is extremely difficult for them to desist.

Nevertheless, parolees are required to demonstrate efforts to seek employment as a condition of their parole, and a significant number of them manage to do so, albeit usually in low-paying occupations. Employers are less reluctant to hire parolees with prior work experience and those who were incarcerated for property or drug-related offenses than those with no proven work history or with a record of violent offenses (Visher, Debus-Sherrill, & Yahner, 2015). Visher et al.'s (2015) longitudinal study of 740 parolees from prisons in Illinois, Ohio, and Texas found that 31% were employed between 76% and 100% of the time since their release eight months earlier, with a median income, however, of only $700 per month. Of the remainder, 35% had not found any employment at all, and 34% were employed intermittently for brief periods. They also found that unemployed individuals were 3 times more likely to be returned to prison (23%) than individuals making more than $10 an hour (8%).

For motivated offenders, one very promising solution to the difficulties faced by ex-convicts in obtaining employment is to start their own business. This is not as utopian as it might sound since a number of states have started what are known as *prison entrepreneurship programs* (PEPs). The first such program began operations in 2004 in the Cleveland Correctional Facility in Cleveland, Texas. The Houston-based PEP is a nonprofit organization that pioneered programs that connect the nation's top executives, entrepreneurs, and MBA students with convicted felons; it provides an "entrepreneurship boot camp" and reentry programs to minimize recidivism while maximizing self-sufficiency. The program is run on a budget of about $2 million from private donations (not the public coffers) and claims more than 1,100 graduates who have launched 165 businesses, with at least two of them grossing more

© iStockphoto.com/Juanmonino

PHOTO 12.4: Once they are released from prison, it is difficult for individuals to find employment, though this is often a condition of parole.

POLICY AND RESEARCH

Offenders' Attitudes Toward Parole

Little is known about offenders' attitudes about parole. We would like to know how they feel about parole, why many inmates reject parole and prefer to "max out," and what those who accept it see as the major barriers to parole success. A significant proportion of prisoners reject parole, and from an inmate's point of view, it is often a rational decision. In 2007 and 2008, 45% of Canadian federal prisoners waived their right to parole consideration (Beauchamp, Cabana, Emeno, & Bottos, 2009), as did 40% of prisoners in New Jersey (Ostermann, 2011). This is not a function of the attractions of prison life, so it must be fear of the prospect of freedom under the watchful eye of a PO.

In Best, Wodahl, and Holmes's (2014) study of prisoners who refused parole, 76% said they turned it down because prison is easier than parole, and 36% said their fear of parole revocation motivated their refusal. As one inmate put it: "It's easier to do time when you're older and you've experienced it before. . . . When you've been in before, you've had time to mature, and this place doesn't seem as unpredictable as parole." Predictability is a major benefit of prison to these people: "At the end of the month you don't have to worry about if you will still have a place to stay or food to eat. Being in here is predicable—out there, everything constantly changes." Another said that it's scary and hard to go back outside because in prison, "you're guaranteed meals and shelter and everything is planned out for you." Others spoke of their fear of revocation and returning to prison: "I don't trust myself not to violate. I do things on the spur of the moment. I like to move around. And you can't do that when you have to register."

Interviews of 740 parolees (Yahner, Visher, & Soloman, 2008) found that compared with ex-prisoners not on parole, parolees had an increased likelihood of being employed and being drug free and crime free, but they also had an increased likelihood of being returned to prison. This was primarily due to technical violations, so the fears of inmates who turned parole down appear to ring true. However, the interviewed parolees had a good opinion of their POs; 92% remarked that they acted professionally, 93% agreed that they treated them with respect, 82% said their PO was trustworthy, and 63% said that they were helpful in their transition to the free world.

Bahr, Armstrong, Gibbs, Harris, and Fisher (2005) found that the dysfunctional families many parolees came from contributed a lot to their inability to successfully complete their parole. As one parolee remarked,

> I think the biggest, a big part of these people that get out of prison is all their uncles and brothers smoke or drink or do drugs or are violent. So really they don't have a choice, and then you're paroled with all them people; you're, you're gonna go back, unless you're strong enough and you have your mind set [against it]. (p. 255)

Another parolee remarked that his family was "toxic" but that he had found alternative sources of social support:

> My family members to me is, uh . . . if I would follow suit with what they expected, I'd be back in prison already. What has helped me most is the positive people that I have surrounded myself with, keeping careful not to hang around with toxic people, people that are doing things wrong. (p. 256)

It is noteworthy that 50 of the 51 parolees in this study were initially firm in their desire to change in their lives, but within 6 months, 10 (20%) were reincarcerated. This study points to the importance of social support in making a successful transition from prison to the community and how difficult the process is.

DISCUSSION QUESTIONS

1. Why is prison a more attractive option than parole, and what can be done to change this?

2. Why is it important to pay attention to what offenders think and believe about the criminal justice system?

3. Did it surprise you that most parolees had positive attitudes about their POs?

References

Bahr, S. J., Armstrong, A. H., Gibbs, B. G., Harris, P. E., & Fisher, J. K. (2005). The reentry process: How parolees adjust to release from prison. *Fathering: A Journal of Theory, Research, and Practice About Men as Fathers, 3*(3), 243–265.

Beauchamp, T., Cabana, T., Emeno, K., & Bottos, S. (2009). *Waivers, postponements, and withdrawals: Offenders, parole officers, and Parole Board of Canada perspectives*. Ottawa: Parole Board of Canada.

Best, B., Wodahl, E., & Holmes, M. (2014). Waiving away the chance of freedom: Exploring why prisoners decide against applying for parole. *International Journal of Offender Therapy and Comparative Criminology, 58*, 320–347.

Ostermann, M. (2011). Parole? Nope, not for me: Voluntarily maxing out of prison. *Crime & Delinquency, 5*, 686–708.

Yahner, J., Visher, C., & Solomon, A. (2008). *Returning home on parole: Former prisoners' experiences in Illinois, Ohio, and Texas*. Washington, DC: Urban Institute.

than $1 million. According to the PEP website (https://www.pep.org), the recidivism rate of graduates is less than 7%.

Applicants for this PEP are recruited from throughout the Texas prison system. If accepted, they are transferred to Cleveland State Prison (PEP's "boot camp"), where they receive an intense, four-month business education from volunteer corporate executives and MBA students (an excellent example of engaging the community in offender rehabilitation). Upon being paroled, graduates are provided with assistance from volunteers and are required to attend 20 more workshops at local universities, followed by mentoring by business executives and the receipt of a $500 start-up stipend. A 2009 study found that within four weeks of release, 97% of graduates were employed (Sonfield, 2009).

It should be noted that the program does not "stack the deck" by recruiting only well-educated prisoners with minimal criminal histories. Sonfield (2009) tells us, "Most selected inmates are either drug dealers or violent felons; most are repeat offenders; they average a ninth-grade education" (p. 76). He also informs us that "drug dealers, and their employees, often display the same entrepreneurial and managerial skills as successful owners and employees of legitimate business operations" (2009, p. 70).

••• DETERMINING PAROLE SUCCESS

Although one would not think so, defining *parole success* is difficult because there is no agreed-upon standard by which we can judge success. Does it mean (1) a completed crime-free and technical-violation-free period of parole, or does it mean (2) that the offender was released from parole without being returned to prison despite his or her behavior while on parole? It obviously means vastly different things in different states because parole "success" rates ranged from 19% in Utah to 83% in Massachusetts in 1999 (J. Travis & Lawrence, 2002). Does this mean that Utah's criminals are over 4 times more resistant to taking the straight-and-narrow road than Massachusetts's criminals, or that Massachusetts has much better programming and professional parole officers? Of course not; it most likely means that conservative Utah follows our first definition of success while liberal Massachusetts follows our second definition. Given the national average success rate of 42% that year, it is plain that many parolees are forgiven many technical violations—or perhaps even a petty arrest or two—in most states. Thus, *success* has as much or more to do with the behavior of the parole authorities in different jurisdictions as it does with the behavior of parolees. When we speak of *success*, then, we are generally speaking in middle-of-the-road terms in which certain parolee misbehaviors are forgiven occasionally in the interest of maintaining them on a trajectory that is at least somewhat positive.

Video 12.4:
Offenders Hone
Interview Skills With
Help From Real
Employers

PAROLE VIOLATIONS

In these days of tight budgets, a factor that may have played a large part in the increase in parole success rate—from 46% in 2004 to 58% in 2012, noted earlier—is the increasing reluctance of states to reincarcerate offenders for minor infractions than was heretofore the case. We saw in Chapter 8 that departments are taking a similar approach with probationers and are developing guidelines for officers to follow that are uniform across all officers' supervision styles. Figure 12.5 presents the Minnesota Department of Corrections's guidelines for restructuring parole conditions or for parole revocation.

Note that parole officers can restructure the conditions of parole without a formal hearing for any of the parole violations listed as Severity Level I or II, although if there

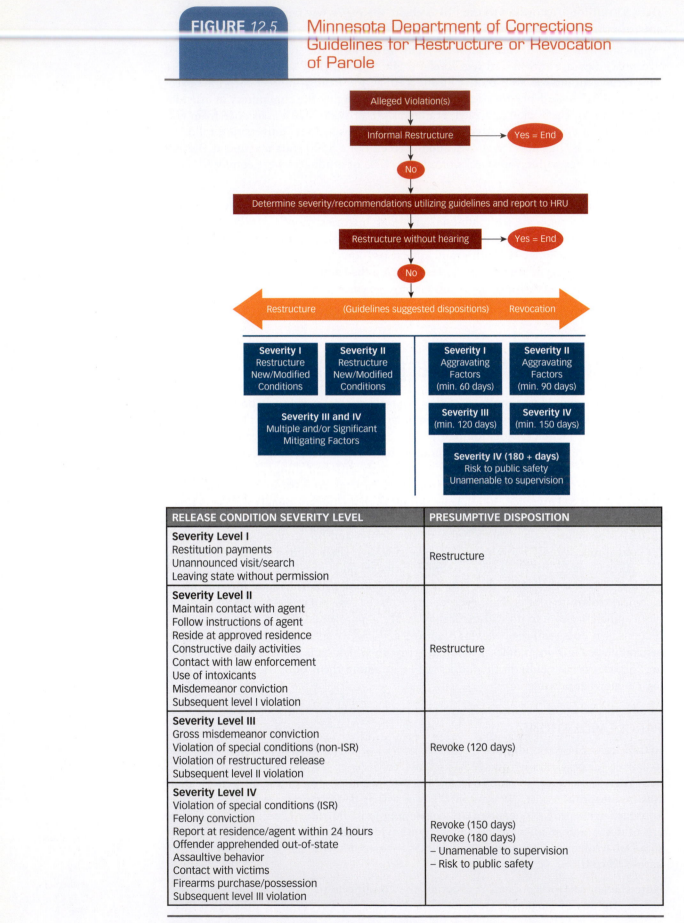

FIGURE *12.5*   Minnesota Department of Corrections Guidelines for Restructure or Revocation of Parole

RELEASE CONDITION SEVERITY LEVEL	PRESUMPTIVE DISPOSITION
Severity Level I Restitution payments Unannounced visit/search Leaving state without permission	Restructure
Severity Level II Maintain contact with agent Follow instructions of agent Reside at approved residence Constructive daily activities Contact with law enforcement Use of intoxicants Misdemeanor conviction Subsequent level I violation	Restructure
Severity Level III Gross misdemeanor conviction Violation of special conditions (non-ISR) Violation of restructured release Subsequent level II violation	Revoke (120 days)
Severity Level IV Violation of special conditions (ISR) Felony conviction Report at residence/agent within 24 hours Offender apprehended out-of-state Assaultive behavior Contact with victims Firearms purchase/possession Subsequent level III violation	Revoke (150 days) Revoke (180 days) – Unamenable to supervision – Risk to public safety

Source: Minnesota Department of Corrections (2009).

are aggravating factors involved, parole may be revoked and the offender incarcerated for the times indicated. Severity Levels III and IV automatically lead to revocation unless there are "multiple and/or significant mitigating factors." As noted in our discussion of the Vermont probation revocation guidelines in Chapter 7, the impetus to develop these guidelines was financial, but they are also useful correctional tools in that they provide officers with a uniform way of responding to violations, making authoritarian officers less punitive and permissive officers less tolerant of offender misbehavior.

••• APPROACHES TO PAROLE

HALFWAY HOUSES

An additional problem facing efforts to reintegrate parolees into their communities is knowing what works best, why, and for whom. Examining 32 studies that analyzed the process of prisoner reentry, Richard Seiter and Karen Kadela (2003) identified programs that work, that do not work, and that are promising in helping prisoners in the long process of successfully reentering the community. In their research, they looked at transitional community programs, such as halfway houses and work release programs, and programs that initiated treatment for inmate deficits (drug dependency, low education, poor life skills, etc.) while they were in prison and continued in the community after release. Programs that worked best were concrete programs that provided offenders with skills to compete in the workforce and intensive drug treatment programs. Programs that were located in the community were more effective than prison-based programs.

As the name implies, **halfway houses** are transitional places of residence for offenders that are, in terms of strictness of supervision, "halfway" between the constant supervision of prison and the much looser supervision in the community. As with probation and parole, early halfway houses were organized and run by private religious and charitable organizations designed to assist released prisoners in making the transition back into free society. The earliest such home was set up in New York City in 1845 by Quaker abolitionist Isaac T. Hopper (Conly, 1998). Also, as with probation and parole, federal and state governments adopted the principles of halfway houses as a good idea. Many states use halfway houses as transition points between prison and full release into the community, and the federal prison system releases about 80% of its inmates into halfway houses ("Director Addresses Changes Within BOP," 2006).

In addition to being a transition between prison and the community, such places (also referred to as **community residential centers**) may serve as an intermediate sanction for offenders not sent to prison but needing greater supervision than straight probation or parole. The rationale behind halfway houses is that individuals with multiple problems, such as substance abuse, lack of education, and a poor employment record, may have a better chance to positively tackle these problems and to comply with court orders if they are placed in residential centers where they will be strictly monitored while, at the same time, being provided with support services to address some of the problems that got them there. Halfway houses may be operated by corrections personnel, but they are also likely to be operated by faith-based organizations, such as the Salvation Army and Volunteers of America. Nevertheless, residents are still under the control of probation and parole authorities and may be removed and sent to prison if they violate the conditions of their probation or parole.

In times of rising costs and prison overcrowding, cost-conscious legislators tend to view community-based alternatives to prisons like diet-conscious beer drinkers—"prison lite." Community-based residential programs supposedly provide public safety at a fraction of

Audio 12.2: Minnesota Judge Considers Sending ISIS Recruits to Halfway House

Halfway houses: Transitional places of residence for correctional clients who are "halfway" between the constant supervision of prison and the much looser supervision in the community.

Community residential centers: Places where offenders (usually parolees) reside when correctional authorities deem them not yet ready to live completely freely.

the cost while allowing offenders to remain in the community and at work, earning their own keep, and best of all, they are assumed to reduce recidivism. Halfway houses are also a valuable resource in that they provide offenders released from prison who would otherwise be homeless with an address for employment purposes.

Nancy Marion (2002) questions some of these assumptions and generally paints a disappointing picture for those who believe that keeping offenders out of prison aids in rehabilitation. She sees programs such as halfway houses admitting individuals who would not have gone to prison anyway, which means such programs increase rather than decrease correctional budgets. Many residents are *unsuccessfully released* from halfway houses because they used alcohol or drugs while there, and even among those successfully released in Marion's multiyear study, between 10.8% and 50.6% (depending on the year of release) were later imprisoned. However, Lowenkamp and Latessa's (2002) more comprehensive examination of 38 such facilities in Ohio found that while not all were effective, most were. They found that community-based programs were of no use for low-risk offenders (indicating that they didn't need them in the first place) but that the majority of them were effective in substantially reducing recidivism among medium- and high-risk offenders. Another review of the relative success of halfway houses concluded, "Relative to individuals discharged into the community without supportive living environments, those men and women who found residence in halfway houses had better substance abuse, criminal justice, and employment outcomes" (Polcin, 2009, p. 11).

Halfway houses should not be viewed as another way of coddling criminals. The *exchange rate* (that is, how much time in an alternative sanction an offender is willing to serve to avoid 12 months in prison) for halfway-house placement in the study by May, Wood, Mooney, and Minor (2005) was an average of 12.77 months for offenders who had served time in prison (14.42 months for all offenders). "Experienced" offenders therefore see it as almost as punitive as prison, despite the relative freedom that halfway residency affords offenders to reintegrate themselves into the community. Much of this has to do with the level of responsibility expected of residents of halfway houses. Living in a halfway house, offenders are expected to take more responsibility for their lives than prison inmates. Halfway-house residents are expected to be in programming and working or looking for work and are subjected to frequent and random testing for drug and alcohol intake, and some halfway houses augment all of this with electronic monitoring. None of these expectations are "suffered" by prison inmates (Shilton, 2003).

HOUSE ARREST

House arrest:
Programs that require offenders to remain in their homes except for approved periods to travel to work, school, or other approved destinations.

House arrest is a program used by probation and parole agencies that requires offenders to remain in their homes at all times except for approved periods, such as travel to work or school and occasionally for other approved destinations. As a system of social control, house arrest is typically used primarily as an initial phase of intensive probation or parole supervision, but it can also be used as an alternative to pretrial detention or a jail sentence. As is the case with so many other criminal justice practices, house arrest was designed primarily to reduce financial costs to the state by reducing institutional confinement.

ELECTRONIC MONITORING AND GLOBAL POSITIONING SYSTEMS

Electronic monitoring (EM): A system by which offenders under house arrest can be monitored for compliance using computerized technology, such as an electronic device worn around the offender's ankle.

House arrest did not initially gain widespread acceptance in the criminal justice community because there was no way of assuring offender compliance with the order short of having officers constantly monitoring the residence. It was also viewed by the public at large as being soft on crime—"doing time in the comfort of one's home." However, house arrest gained in popularity with the advent of **electronic monitoring (EM)**. EM is a system by which offenders under house arrest can be monitored for compliance using computerized technology. In modern EM systems, an electronic device worn around the offender's ankle sends a continuous signal to a receiver attached to the offender's house phone. If the offender moves beyond 500 feet from his or her house, the transmitter records it and relays the information to a centralized computer. A probation and parole officer is then dispatched to his or her home to investigate whether the offender has absconded or removed or tampered with the device. As of 2004, almost 13,000 offenders were under house arrest, with 90% of them being electronically monitored (Bohm & Haley, 2007).

An even more sophisticated method of tracking offenders is **global positioning system (GPS) monitoring**. GPS monitoring requires offenders to wear a removable tracking unit that constantly communicates with a nonremovable ankle cuff. If communication is lost, the loss is noted by a Department of Defense satellite that records the time and location of the loss in its database. This information is then forwarded to criminal justice authorities so that they can take action to determine why communication was lost. Unlike EM systems, a GPS device can be used for surveillance purposes, as well as detention purposes. For instance, it can let authorities know if a sex offender goes within a certain distance of a schoolyard or if a violent offender is approaching his or her victim's place of residence or work (Black & Smith, 2003). As of 2007, 28 states had legislation calling for some form of electronic monitoring of sex offenders (Payne, DeMichele, & Button, 2008).

PHOTO 12.5: House arrest is certainly preferable to spending time in jail, but as this young woman's expression shows, it can be pretty boring.

Payne and Gainey (2004) indicate that detractors of electronic monitoring tend to criticize it as intruding too much into the realm of privacy and even as barbaric. Of course, it is intrusive; that is the point. But it is far less intrusive than prison, and Payne and Gainey (2004) state that offenders released from jails or prisons and placed in EM programs are generally positive about the experience (not that they enjoyed it but rather that it was better than the jail or prison alternative). Their findings mirror those from a larger sample of offenders on EM programs in New Zealand (Gibbs & King, 2003). Many see it as a jail or prison time simply served in a less restrictive and less violent environment (so much for the charge that it is barbaric), and although the average experienced offender would exchange 11.35 months on EM for 12 months in prison, offenders overall would exchange 13.95 months on EM for 12 months in prison (Moore et al., 2008). It would seem that from this and similar studies that inveterate offenders tend to prefer prison over virtually any other correctional sentence other than straight probation.

Researchers are positive about the alleged rehabilitative promise of allowing offenders to serve time at home and thus maintain their links to family. A large study comparing 5,000 medium- and high-risk offenders on EM to 266,000 not on EM found a 31% decline in the risk of failure among EM offenders (National Institute of Justice, 2011). On the downside, although successful completion rates for EM programs are high, recidivism rates *after release from EM* were not any better than for probationers and parolees not on EM programs matched for offender risk in several Canadian provinces (Bonta, Wallace-Capretta, & Rooney, 2000). This may be viewed positively, however, as a function of the greater ability to detect noncompliance with release conditions among those under EM supervision.

An additional problem with EM is that because its low cost relative to incarceration is alluring to politicians, it may be (and is) used without sufficient care being taken as to

Journal Article 12.1: The Electronic Monitoring of Offenders Released From Jail or Prison: Safety, Control, and Comparisons to the Incarceration Experience

Global positioning system (GPS) monitoring: A system of probation and parole supervision whereby probationers and parolees are required to wear a tracking unit that can be monitored by satellites.

who should be eligible for it. While offenders can be monitored and more readily arrested if they commit a crime while on EM, EM does not prevent them from committing further crimes. Several high-profile crimes, including rapes and murders, have been committed by offenders who succeeded in removing their electronic bracelets (Reid, 2006). When cases such as these are reported, the public (which, by and large, would rather see iron balls and chains attached to offenders rather than plastic bracelets) responds with charges of leniency. This is unfortunate because EM does appear to have a significant impact on prison overcrowding and on reducing correctional costs. Of course, EM can only be considered to reduce correctional costs if it is used as a substitute for incarceration, not as an addition to normal probation and parole, in which case, it is an added cost.

ETHICAL ISSUE 12.2 ❓

What Would You Do?

You are a parole agent. Vice squad police officers with whom you have enjoyed a good relationship in the past have approached you to enlist your aid in setting up a parolee they badly want off the streets. Because you have more leeway than the police to enter his home and conduct searches, they want you to conduct an early morning raid on his house. They tell you that even if you don't find drugs, you should plant drugs that they will provide for you. You know this parolee has been a major dealer in the past and that he has employed violent tactics to protect his territory. Although he hasn't given you any real trouble on parole so far, you agree that this man should not be on the streets. Discuss your options and what you believe you would end up doing.

Several European nations have turned to EM to ease the burden of overcrowded prisons over the past two decades. The successful completion rates are fairly consistent across countries, and they are refreshingly high. This is possibly a function of the lower-risk offenders that are typically placed on EM in Europe. It is generally required that for an offender to be placed on EM, he or she must have a suitable residence with functional phone line and be working (Havercamp, Mayer, & Levy, 2004). There is also a wide range of times to be served on EM, ranging from about three months in England and Wales for probationers to 13 to 23 months for parolees in France (Wennerberg & Pinto, 2009). One large-scale study of parolees released under home detention curfew using electronic monitoring for enforcement conducted in Britain provided very positive results (Dodgson et al., 2001). Six months after release, only 9.3% (118 out of 1,269) of the EM parolees were reconvicted of a new crime, compared with 40.4% (558 out of 1,381) of the prisoners who were unconditionally released. Of course, all of this difference cannot be attributed to the EM program because the groups were not matched for criminal history, and those on the program were already considered to have a lower risk of reoffending. Nevertheless, the EM group was positive about the program (it got them early release from prison), and the net financial savings to the prison service over 12 months was estimated to be £36.7 million (about $60.9 million). The consensus in the European literature reviewed seems to be that electric monitoring "works" and that it is here to stay.

••• CONCLUDING REMARKS ON REENTRY AND RECIDIVISM

We have learned that reentry into the community, whether on supervised parole or not, is an extremely difficult process. Everything appears to be working against offenders' successful reintegration, not the least of these factors being the offenders themselves. Many criminals are committed to their lifestyles and simply cannot or will not lead law-abiding lives. Numerous lines of evidence show that work and other normal responsibilities that go with the straight life do not mesh well with their "every night is Saturday night" lifestyles (B. Jacobs & Wright, 1999; Mawby, 2001; Rengert & Wasilchick, 2001). Nevertheless, correctional work is premised on the assumption that people can change, and not all criminals, by any means, are totally resistant to change. Although many offenders seem hell-bent on thwarting the best efforts of all to turn their lives around, many others can be reformed. When we find the best reentry programs (programs that have been shown repeatedly and empirically to significantly reduce recidivism) and implement them, what kind of success can we expect? Joan Petersilia (2004), the preeminent reentry researcher today, sums up the combined Canadian and American reentry "what works" literature and states,

> They took place mostly in the community (as opposed to institutional settings), were intensive (at least six months long), focused on high risk individuals (with risk level determined by classification instruments rather than clinical judgments), used cognitive-behavioral treatment techniques, and matched therapist and program to the specific learning styles and characteristics of individual offenders. As the individual changed his or her thinking patterns, he or she would be provided with vocational training and other job-enhancing opportunities. Positive reinforcers would outweigh negative reinforcers in all program components. Every program begun in jail or prison would have an intensive and mandatory aftercare component. (pp. 7–8)

Pertersilia (2004) goes on to suggest that if we could design programs that combined all of these things, we might be able to reduce recidivism by about 30%. So with all of the best methods currently available, caring and knowledgeable counselors, and legislators willing to provide a budget sufficient to meet the needs of all of the identified programs, the best we can hope for is a 30% reduction in recidivism. Even this 30% figure is a "best guess" premised on Petersilia's faith in the efficacy of rehabilitative programs. As much as we would all love to find a way to turn offenders into respectable citizens, Petersilia's estimate reminds us that human beings are not lumps of clay to be molded to someone else's specifications. Although correctional workers might regret that they cannot mold their charges' minds as they might wish to, the fact that they cannot do so without their owner's consent is a vindication of human freedom and dignity.

SUMMARY

- Parole is the legal status of a person who has been released from prison prior to completing his or her full term. The concept can be traced back to the 19th century, with Maconochie's ticket-of-leave system in Australia and Walter Crofton's Irish system. Parts of these systems were brought to the United States in the 1870s by Zebulon Brockway, superintendent of the Elmira Reformatory in New York. Brockway's system required indeterminate sentencing so that good time earned through good conduct and labor could be used to reduce inmates' sentences.

- In the modern United States, we have two systems of parole: discretionary and mandatory. Discretionary parole is parole granted by a parole board based on their perceptions of the inmate's readiness to be released; mandatory parole is based simply on a mathematical formula of time served. Discretionary parolees are significantly more likely to successfully complete parole than mandatory parolees.

- The reentry of prisoners into the community is a very difficult process. The ex-con stigma makes getting employment problematic, and the period of absence makes it tough to reestablish relationships. Successful reentry depends on several factors, not the least of which are the policies of the parole authorities, as the huge gap between the Massachusetts and Utah success rates indicates. Nevertheless, providing parolees with concrete help, such as job skills and drug rehabilitation programs, can go a long way in helping them to remain crime free. This effort may be particularly fruitful if it is made in some form of community-based residential program.

- EM and GPS-monitoring technology are increasingly used in corrections. It helps by increasing the level of offender monitoring and apprehension, but it cannot altogether prevent additional crimes while on the program, which is why candidates for this type of supervision must be chosen carefully. In sum, few programs can be said to work for most offenders if we define working unrealistically. Human nature is complicated, often ornery, and resistant to change. Even "ideal" programs, such as those defined by Petersilia (2004), could only be expected (according to her) to reduce recidivism by about 30%.

KEY TERMS

Community residential centers 309

Discretionary parole 292

Electronic monitoring (EM) 310

Global positioning system (GPS) monitoring 311

Halfway houses 309

House arrest 310

Irish system 291

Mandatory parole 292

Parole 290

Parole board 298

Unconditional release 292

DISCUSSION QUESTIONS

1. Compare the recidivism rates claimed for the TOL parolees with those of modern American recidivism rates of parolees. What do you think may account for the huge differences?

2. Explore and discuss why it is that we still continue to utilize mandatory parole in the face of evidence that discretionary parole is a safer bet?

3. Consider a parolee who has just been released after serving 5 years. What do you think may be the single most difficult problem to overcome in order to stay out of trouble?

4. Would it be a good thing to have a number of community-based residential facilities located in high-crime communities so that some of the problems noted by Clear et al. (2001) might be avoided?

5. Given that expert opinion says a 30% reduction in the recidivism rate is about the best we can accomplish if all treatment conditions were optimal, do you think that trying to rehabilitate criminals is a waste of time and that the money would be better spent on keeping them locked up?

USEFUL INTERNET SITES

Please note that the sites listed can be accessed at edge.sagepub.com/stohrcorrections.

American Probation and Parole Association: www.appa-net.org

This site covers contemporary and historical aspects of probation and parole and offers synopses of important research.

Reentry Court Solutions: www.reentrycourtsolutions.com/tag/national-reentry-resource-center

Provides insights into the resources available to parolees to help them transition back into society.

$SAGE edge™

Sharpen your skills with SAGE edge at **edge.sagepub.com/stohrcorrections**. SAGE edge for Students provides a personalized approach to help you accomplish your coursework goals in an easy-to-use learning environment. You'll find action plans, mobile-friendly eFlashcards, and quizzes as well as video, web, and resources and links to SAGE journal articles to support and expand on the concepts presented in this chapter.

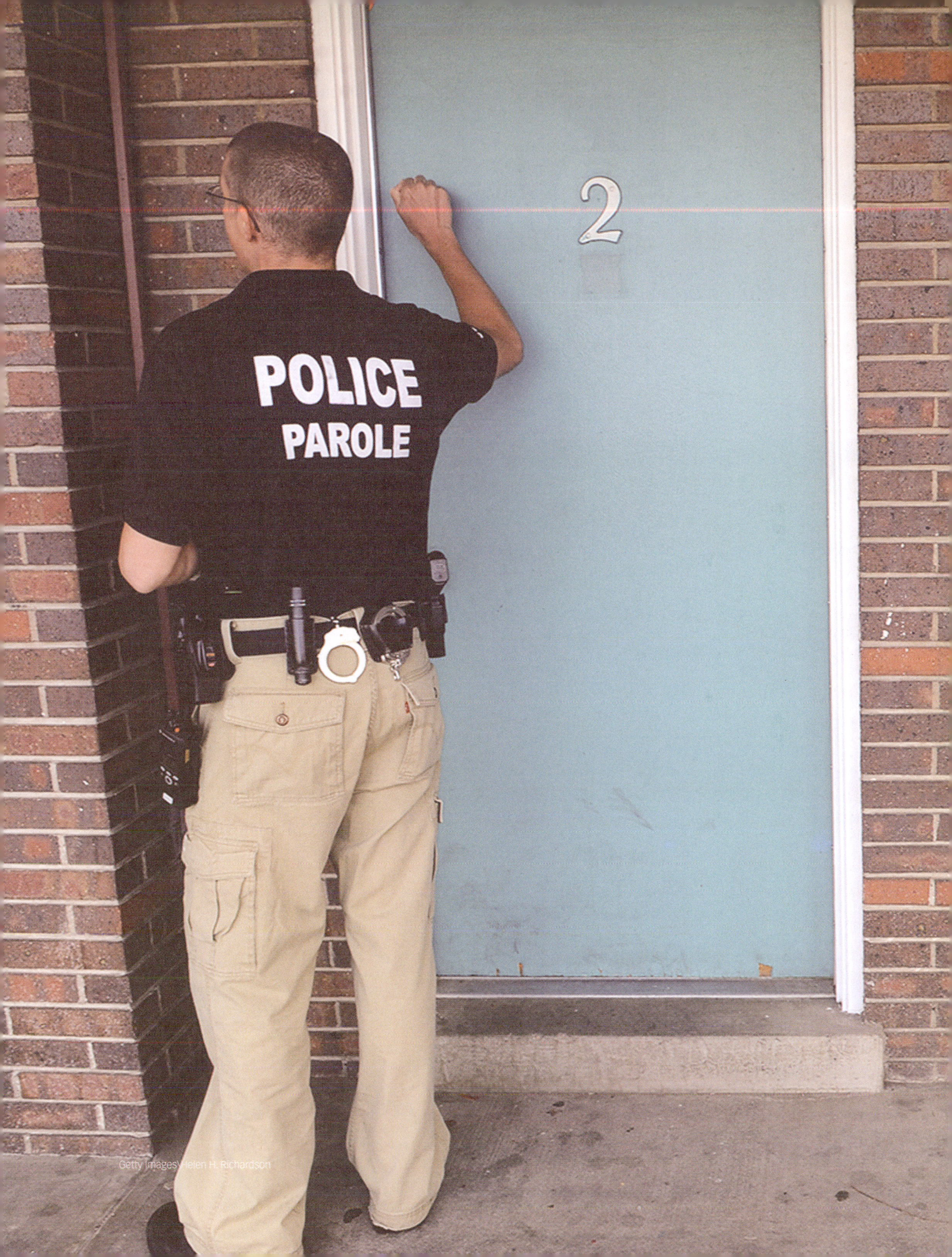

Getty Images/Helen H. Richardson

13 Correctional Organizations and Their Management

TEST YOUR KNOWLEDGE

Test your present knowledge of correctional organizations by answering the following questions as true or false. Check your answers on page 537 after reading the chapter.

1. Bureaucracies, as a form of organization, can be very efficient.

2. Closed institutions are better at innovation.

3. Prisons are more likely to fit the descriptor of *total institution* than are jails.

4. Organizations have both a formal and an informal side.

5. Theory X organizations fit the descriptor of *traditional organizations*.

6. Theory Y organizations fit the descriptor of *human-relations organizations*.

7. Theory Z organizations combine elements of Theories X and Y.

8. Learning organizations tend to be "closed off" to their environment.

9. Leadership in corrections these days occurs only at the top of the organizational chart.

LEARNING OBJECTIVES

- Define what the terms *bureaucracy*, *closed institution*, and *total institution* mean and how they relate to corrections

- Explain how both traditional and human-relations theories of management apply to corrections

- Examine what leadership styles are and why leaders often have to adjust their styles to fit the circumstances they face

- Identify what a subculture is and how it affects the workplace

RESPONSES TO **REALIGNMENT**

In 2011, Governor Brown ordered a major realignment in corrections in California in response to a lawsuit about the overcrowding of prisons in the state. It was not just state-level prisons that were asked to change drastically by downsizing their number of inmates, but county jails were obligated to care for thousands more low-level inmates who would normally have done their time in prisons. Some monies were provided to smooth this transition. In Sacramento County alone, the already overcrowded jail was forced to house almost 500 more inmates in the first year of the realignment. In response, the Sacramento Sheriff's Department developed "strategies for success" focused on "creating additional evidence-based programs to reduce recidivism and expanding our alternative custody programs" (S. Jones, 2013, p. 2). The strategies were developed by key stakeholders familiar with the system and the community, and the approaches and programs were evidence-based, targeted the real needs of the clientele and those who were high risk, and involved the coordination of support services from several agencies and job partnerships with businesses. Whether their strategies were successful in helping the department achieve its goals is an open question that can only be answered by their built-in evaluation process and over a period of time. However, this vignette of what happened and is happening in California provides an example of forces in the larger political environment that can wreak havoc on the orderly operation of a correctional institution (in this case, virtually all of the jails and prisons in California). How the Sacramento Sheriff's Department management approached this problem is instructive because it appears, at least from a distance, that they took what could have been a devastating change of circumstances for the jail and turned it into a positive—or took the proverbial lemons and turned them into lemonade!

••• INTRODUCTION

People tend to think that all jails, probation and parole departments, and prisons are alike, and the truth is that they are not. Organizationally speaking—and that is what we are doing in this chapter—they might look alike, they might have staff and clients or inmates who seem similar, and their organizational charts might appear to be roughly the same. (For example, at the top of the organizational chart for a prison, you will find a warden, but at the top of the organizational chart for a jail, you will most often find a sheriff.) But there are many, many differences between them, and those differences are the reasons you have some correctional organizations with more complaints by staff and inmates, more lawsuits, and more eruptions of violence than others. Many of these differences have to do with the support that a correctional agency gets from its community—yes, in the form of funding but in other ways, too. But correctional organizations differ in their leadership, in their communication paths and protocols, and in the management theory or theories they embrace. They differ in how they approach problems (see, for instance, the discussion of Sacramento County's proposed response to a pending realignment in corrections at the beginning of this chapter).

Try this: Do a litmus test the next time you visit a few jails, prisons, or community corrections agencies. (And since you are interested in criminal justice, you probably have visited correctional institutions or want to do so!) Pay attention to how the organizations operate. Pay attention to who has power, whether the institution offers programs, if staff and inmates or clients appear happy. (Maybe *happy* is too much to expect for incarcerated and supervised people but at least not angry and maybe even polite!) Note whether the floors are clean and whether the staff know the clients' names. Notice if the inmates or clients appear fearful. If you visit more than one agency, you are likely to notice discrepancies between them, and sometimes those differences will be huge, and they can be explained by all of the concepts covered in this chapter (along with the next one on staff).

Management:
Management may refer to one or more persons who have formal control over an organization or the act or process of operating the organization.

You will be equipped to apply your litmus test because in this chapter, we will explore the nature, structure, and theoretical underpinnings of correctional organizations and their management. **Management**, for our purposes, refers to one or more persons who have formal control over an organization or the act or process of operating the organization (Stohr & Collins, 2014, p. 25). We will review how communication and leadership operate, are linked to management, and might be improved in corrections. An examination of organizational culture, a concept that explains all of those differences you would find from your visits, will finish out the chapter. So here is the litmus test after visiting those correctional institutions: Ask yourself which of the correctional organizations, holding the security level of their clients or inmates constant, you would want to be supervised by or incarcerated in, and then, think about why that is. Part of the answer to the *why* question, we expect, will be the management of the organizations you will observe.

PHOTO 13.1: An old prison fallen into decay.

••• ORGANIZATIONAL-LEVEL FACTORS THAT AFFECT CORRECTIONAL OPERATIONS

BUREAUCRACIES

It is often forgotten that people created organizations and that they can change them, if need be. Organizations can be reconfigured to suit workers (and clients) so that they are more satisfied with, less stressed by, and more challenged by their work.

A **bureaucracy** is a kind of organizational structure typically used in corrections. Most correctional institutions and programs are shaped like a bureaucracy. Bureaucracies were created to increase the efficiency of workers and the uniformity of their work. A bureaucracy, as defined by the German theorist and philosopher Max Weber (1946), can be distilled down to these three elements of its structure: hierarchy, specialization, and rule of law. The hierarchy refers to the pyramidal shape of the organization, with one person, the leader, at the top and an expanding number of people below him or her at each level of the organization. Most of the formal power of a bureaucratic organization resides in the uppermost portions of the bureaucracy (e.g., see Figure 13.1, Utah Department of Corrections Organizational Chart), and most of the formal communications come from the top-level administrators and travel down to the lower-level administrators and then the workers. Specialization occurs in a bureaucracy when the sectors of the pyramid below the leader are segmented to concentrate on different aspects of the work, particularly as that work becomes more complicated and requires specific skills and abilities. The rule-of-law element of a bureaucracy refers to the formal rules, procedures, and laws that govern agency operations. Such regulations, whether imposed by an outside governmental agency, such as a legislature, a court, or the executive branch, or whether internally created for the organization, are formal and usually prescribe how the organization works and how the employee should react when faced with given circumstances.

Working in a bureaucracy, as most of us do even outside of corrections, has the effect of making our work routine and predictable. Community corrections officers, working with adults in larger bureaucratic organizations, will specialize in work with either parolees or probationers—with more serious offenders or first-time felons. Their work will be governed by both legal requirements and court decrees, as well as rules and procedures created by their organization. They will report to and be accountable to supervisors, who will report to other supervisors, who will, in turn, report to managers, all the way up to the director or secretary of corrections in the state, who is usually a political appointee of the governor.

CLOSED AND OPEN INSTITUTIONS

In addition to being bureaucratic organizations, corrections agencies, particularly prisons and jails and less so community corrections, are thought to be partially **closed institutions** in that they are separated from their outside environments and unaffected by those environments, to some extent. This closed nature of corrections is much reduced from the past, when inmate visits and outside contacts were more restricted; when staff behavior, even off the job, was controlled; and when what went on inside of the institution was kept secret from the general public, let alone the courts and the media. Of course, however, even in the early prisons and jails, this "closed" characteristic was never absolutely descriptive of those institutions, as inmates would have visitor contact (albeit usually much less than these days), and they would get out eventually. Also, most staff did go out and about in the community, even if, in some cases, they slept at the institution. Moreover, outside factors, like changing laws, funding, technology, and even weather, affected

Video 13.1: Five Years of Struggle, Success at Washington State Penitentiary

Career Video 13.1: Corrections Sergeant

Journal Article 13.1: An Examination of Organizational Justice Among Correctional Officers in Adult Prisons

Web 13.1: Prison Bureaucracies

Bureaucracy: A type of organizational structure that includes these three elements: hierarchy, specialization, and rule of law.

Closed institutions: Institutions separated from their outside environments and, to some extent, unaffected by those environments.

FIGURE 13.1

The Utah Department of Corrections Organizational Chart

Utah Department of Corrections

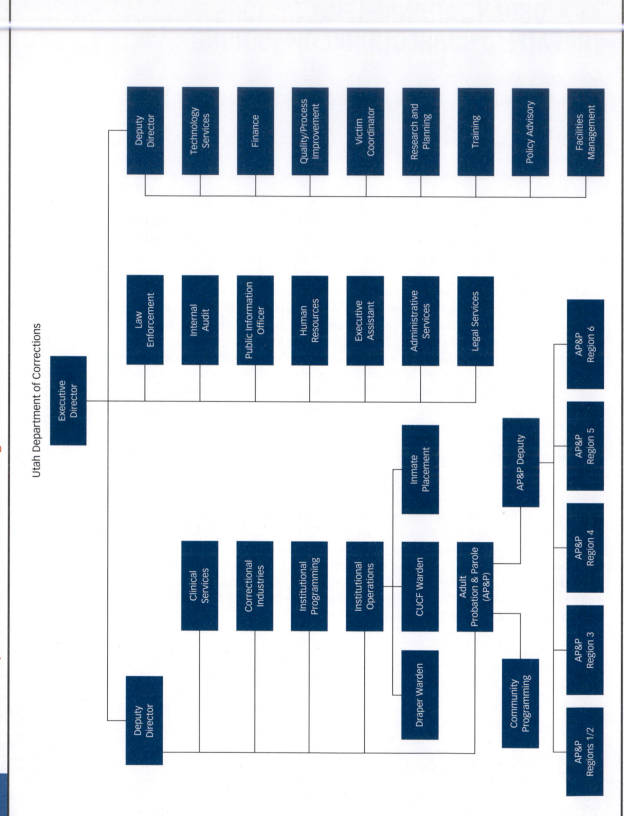

Source: State of Utah Organizational Charts.

the operation of such facilities (Stohr & Collins, 2014). **Open institutions** are those that are fully part of their communities, both dependent on and responsive to them, and that are affected by their outside environment, such as changes in laws, norms, and values in their communities.

But the point here is that the extent to which an organization is open or closed affects the work of employees. If open, the employees are free to discuss their work with members of the outside world, and they are free to gather information, research, and seek assistance that might improve their work. The more closed the organization is to the outside world, the less employees are free to garner these materials and resources.

TOTAL INSTITUTIONS

A related aspect of correctional organizations—and again, this applies more to prisons and jails than it does to community corrections—is the creation of a total institution. Goffman (1961) defined a total institution as a place where

> First, all aspects of life are conducted in the same place and under the same single authority. Second, each phase of the member's daily activity is carried on in the immediate company of a large batch of others, all of whom are treated alike and required to do the same thing together. Third, all phases of the day's activities are tightly scheduled, with one activity leading to a prearranged time into the next, the whole sequence of activities being imposed from above by a system of explicit formal rulings and a body of officials. Finally, the various enforced activities are brought together into a single rational plan purportedly designed to fulfill the official aims of the institution. (p. 6)

This quote leads us to believe that in a total institution, (1) all aspects of life (e.g., eating, sleeping, working, etc.) are conducted under one figurative roof, (2) people's lives are led in groups with others like them, and they are treated like other group members, (3) all activities are scheduled and controlled by rules and procedures and officials, and (4) all such controlled activities are part of a plan that is meant to achieve predictable outcomes. In addition, Goffman (1961) argues that total institutions have two other characteristics: (5) They have formal and distinct roles for staff and inmates that are sacrosanct, and each must stay separate from the other, and (6) staff are invested with formal power, and inmates must not be given any or allowed to exert any of their own. Of course, in reality, even the most locked-down maximum-security prison is not a total institution, nor is it a model of a bureaucracy or completely closed off from the community. Correctional institutions fit these descriptors by degrees, and there are no absolutes. But by necessity and practice, a maximum-security prison is more likely to fit these descriptors than is a probation agency in the community.

FORMAL AND INFORMAL ORGANIZATIONS

Jails, prisons, and community corrections agencies, much like most other public- or private-sector organizations, have both a formal and an informal side. The **formal organization** is the public face of the organization and includes its mission statement, what's on its official website, its rules and procedures, its training manual and curriculum and memorandums by its leaders (either in hard-copy of e-mail form), and anything officially sanctioned by its leaders (Blau & Scott, 1962/2001; Stohr & Collins, 2014). The **informal organization** is often hidden from the public, even clients, but known, at least in part, by its employees and includes how it really operates (no matter what the official statements about that are). The informal organization can be found in the stories

Audio 13.1: What Does the Justice Department's Decision to End Private Prisons Mean for the Future?

Open institutions: Those institutions that are fully part of their communities, both dependent on and responsive to them, and that are affected by their outside environment, such as changes in laws, norms, and values in their communities.

Formal organization: The public face of the organization, including its mission statement; what's on its official website; its rules and procedures; its training manual, curriculum, and memorandums by its leaders (either in hard copy of e-mail form); or anything officially sanctioned by its leaders.

Informal organization: Often hidden from the public, even clients, but known, at least in part, by its employees and includes how it really operates.

© Jeffrey Wickett/Alamy Sto :: Photo

PHOTO 13.2: Aerial picture of a private prison in Michigan. How are prisons examples of total institutions?

Web 13.2:
Private Prisons

AP Video 13.1:
Idaho Prison
Abuse

Audio 13.2:
In Wake of Riot,
Arizona Governor
Fires For-Profit
Prison Firm

Video 13.2:
Motivational
Interviewing
in Intensive
Management
Units

and jokes told by employees about the work, the management, other employees, and clients and the unofficial orders and requests by supervisors that do not fit the official rules, among other activities outside of what is regarded as officially sanctioned by the organization and its leaders. The formal side of correctional agencies prescribes what is legal and what is publicly accepted behavior for staff. The informal side of correctional agencies, on the other hand, is not necessarily prescribing illegal behavior by staff, though sometimes it can.

For instance, if the formal rules of the organization require that community corrections officers write-up or violate a probationer every time he has a dirty urinanalysis, but an officer doesn't always do this, as she prefers to consider extenuating circumstances, the question is, Has she violated the formal rules of the organization? Yes, she has, and consequently, she might be disciplined or fired if her supervisor finds out that she has not followed the rules. More importantly, the offender may continue to engage in substance abuse and put himself or others in danger when he drives a car. On the other hand, the CO might be convinced that the dirty UA is understandable and may have been told unofficially by her supervisor that in rare instances, when she thinks it justified, she can ignore them. Our point here is not to explore whether or not the officer made the correct decision but just to illustrate the point that underneath the surface of every organization is its informal operation. It is not necessarily a negative thing for there to be both this formal and informal organization. It only becomes detrimental to the organization and its clients and employees when the gap between what is official and unofficial is large, as that will lead to deviance and possibly illegal behavior by staff when they ignore the rules and make up their own.

••• MANAGEMENT THEORIES

There are a number of organizational theories that prescribe how an agency best operates. Most of these have been developed for private-sector businesses, and so, the focus is on the most efficient manufacture of a product and on the best way to motivate workers to make sure this happens. Whole books have been devoted to management theories, but for brevity's sake, here, we will only focus on the ones most relevant to correctional organizations.

TRADITIONAL THEORIES OF MANAGEMENT

A more traditional theory of management, Frederick Taylor's **scientific management** determines, through observation, who is the "first-rate" worker who does the work in the "one best way," meaning the person who does the most the fastest, also known as the most efficient worker (F. Taylor, 1911). Such a worker, for Taylor, is motivated by money and so will do his or her work best when he or she is paid by the product produced, or by *piece rate*. Scientific management assumes that workers labor in bureaucracies, as described by Weber, and so possess little power but do what they are told by those higher up the chain of command. Under scientific management, workers are analogous to machines, expected to do their work consistently and swiftly, and when they can no longer perform up to standards, they are replaced.

As was mentioned in the foregoing, correctional organizations are structured as bureaucracies, and staff at the bottom (correctional officers particularly but also counselors and probation and parole officers) have had little power to determine how to do their job; they are expected to take orders in these paramilitary organizations and do what they are told. Traditionally, they have been expected to be cold and impersonal in their relations with clients and to maintain a distance from them. Their products are the people they supervise; they are expected to process clients impersonally, like a machine, and they are thought to be incentivized by the pay. This belief about how best to manage correctional organizations is still practiced to some extent today but was even more true in the past. As management theories for businesses have developed since Taylor first proposed scientific management in 1911, so too have their operations and inevitably some of those newer theories been applied to the public sector, including the management practices used in corrections.

HUMAN-RELATIONS THEORIES OF MANAGEMENT

Prisons, jails, and community corrections organizations are still bureaucracies, but it is no longer assumed that people are just motivated by money nor that they can treat people as products to be processed (meaning completely controlled, supervised, and molded). Of necessity, people under correctional supervision must be controlled and supervised, and rehabilitation is all about molding them to be prosocial citizens. But newer management theories posit that organizations run best and staff are more motivated to do their work when the organization is flatter (less hierarchical), and they have a say in how their work should be done (fatter). In **flatter and fatter organizations, human-relations theories of management** posit that people are motivated to do their best work because power is more distributed across positions; management listens to workers, who know their jobs; people work in teams; communication is open, and ideas are freely disseminated; people are allowed to make mistakes, and their colleagues are encouraged to learn from them; and clients are allowed to provide feedback that is relevant to the improvement of the services they receive (see Figure 13.2).

Many of the newer theories of management (and some of these "newer" theories are more than 70 years old) are framed by **Maslow's hierarchy of needs** and are known as human-relations theories. Maslow (1943/2001; 1961/1998) argued that people are first motivated by lower-level needs, such as physiological (food, water, and sex) and security (physical safety, security, provision for old age, etc.) needs, and then by higher-level needs, such as love (the need to belong, the need to give and receive love, and the need to be accepted by associates), self-esteem (also known as self-respect—the need for achievement, recognition, importance, and confidence and the desire for reputation or prestige),

Career Video 13.1: Corrections Sergeant

Scientific management: Management determines, through observation, who is the "first-rate" worker who does the work in the "one best way" (i.e., the fastest and most efficient worker) and presumes that workers are motivated by money.

Flatter and fatter organizations: Organizations with less hierarchy and more distribution of power and responsibility among the members.

Human-relations theories of management: Posit that people are motivated to do their best work in organizations where the power is more distributed across positions.

Maslow's hierarchy of needs: A concept developed by Maslow, who argued that people are first motivated by lower-level needs, such as physiological and security needs, and then by higher-level needs, such as love, self-esteem, and self-actualization.

FIGURE *13.2*   Power Distribution in Management

Theory X: Under this theory by McGregor (1957), workers are assumed to be passive and to not like to work. Therefore, their behavior is controlled by management to achieve organizational ends.

Theory Y: Under this theory by McGregor (1957), workers are assumed to be naturally self-motivated, and it is management's role to provide the organizational conditions so that workers can achieve their own goals that align with the organization's objectives.

Participatory management: Occurs when employees are allowed to have a say in what they do and how they do their work.

Theory Z: Under this theory by Ouchi (1981), the production needs of Theory X and the human needs recognized by Theory Y are combined, along with an understanding of the influence that the larger environment has on the organization and those who labor in it.

and self-actualization (the need to be creative, to fulfill one's potential, and to become what one is meant or fitted to be) (see Figure 13.3). Maslow believed that workers who had these needs met were the most creative and resilient people, but he thought a precondition to the fulfillment of these needs was freedom (Maslow, 1943/2001, p. 172). Management's job under Maslow's theory is to provide the freedom, environment, and work tasks that allow workers to meet these needs because if they do so, then workers will be motivated to produce more and better products.

McGregor (1957/2001) based his Theory Y on Maslow. **Theory X**, on the other hand, was based on traditional theories of management and posits that workers do not like to work; they are naturally lazy and stupid, prefer to be led, and are motivated by money. In other words, Theory X is the traditional theory of management, as represented by

FIGURE *13.3*   Maslow's Hierarchy of Needs

Source: Adapted from Maslow (1943/2001).

scientific management and bureaucracy (Taylor and Weber). Under **Theory Y**, however, a worker likes to work and wants both lower- and higher-level needs (ala Maslow's hierarchy of needs) met in the workplace. Theory Y posits that people want to work, to have a say in that work, to do interesting things in their work, and to make a difference with their work. Under Theory Y, it is management's job to arrange the organization and its operation so that people can achieve their goals and meet their needs. By doing so, workers will be motivated to do their work well. McGregor (1957/2001; Heil, Bennis, & Stephens, 2000) recommends that managers decentralize decision making, delegate work, make work meaningful for workers, and allow workers to have a say in what they do and how they do it (an approach called **participatory management**).

There has been some criticism of these early versions of human-relations theories, including the observation that a focus on efficiency, as scientific management does, "works" in terms of achieving organizational ends (Stohr & Collins, 2014) and that maybe organizational ends are more important than the individual workers' goals. Others have said that the focus on group work that emanates from a Theory Y focus can have the effect of suppressing individuality. Then there is the assumption under Theory Y that people are, at their core, basically good and kind, and critics don't believe this is true, thinking instead that Theory X is correct and that people are really lazy and selfish. This latter point is at the heart of the centuries-old debate about the nature of human nature. But despite these criticisms of human-relations theories, most newer theories of management are based on a Theory Y view of the best way to motivate people to achieve organizational goals. Theory Z, teams, total quality management, management by objectives, and learning organization theories all hold as their basic premise a human-relations approach to management. But interestingly enough, these newer theories, like most organizations, including most correctional and criminal justice organizations, include elements of traditional theories, too. Most correctional organizations are bureaucratic, and scientific management still pervades many aspects of their operation. Management of correctional organizations today is really an amalgamation of traditional and human-relations theories.

PHOTO 13.3: According to Theory X, this would be an example of a lazy employee who is not excited by his job.

PHOTO 13.4: In contrast, according to Theory Y, employees who are excited by their jobs are much more productive.

COMBINING TRADITIONAL AND HUMAN-RELATIONS THEORIES

Theory Z, proposed by Ouchi (1981) combines some elements of both traditional and human-relations theories of management. It acknowledges the production needs of X, along with the human needs of Y (Klofas, Stojkovic, & Kalinich, 1990). What it adds to those theories, however, is that it recognizes the importance of the larger environment in influencing and motivating human behavior at work. Ouchi centers the organization in the larger social, political, and economic environment and understands that the organizations must and do adapt to the environment.

Total quality management (TQM) is an extension of Theory Z because proponents argue that the greater the involvement of workers or teams in developing and delivering on organizational goals, the higher their level of commitment to the achievement of those goals. Some remnants of traditional theories live on in TQM too, however, as it also is assumed that workers are motivated by rewards and that there is a need for accountability by workers and managers as regards their productivity (Gordon & Milakovich, 1998).

Management by objections (MBO) is a yet another theory of management that contains elements of both traditional and human-relations theories of management (Drucker, 1954; Fink, Jenks, & Willits, 1983). Under MBO, workers collaboratively set their work objectives with management. The idea is that people will work harder to achieve goals they had a hand in choosing.

The term **learning organizations** is given to organizations that encourage education and training for their workers, promote risk taking and the publication of mistakes by members so that all might learn from them, and open up their doors to evaluation by outside entities so that they might critically assess how they do their work. It is understood that organizations, whether public or private, operate in a dynamic and changing environment where much adaptation and innovation is necessary to survive. It is thought that organizations that embrace change by preparing their staff for it (through education, training, risk taking, and assessment) are most likely to survive and succeed at achieving their goals. We see the application of all of these theories with human-relations elements to corrections when agencies encourage group problem solving, invite outside stakeholders to engage with staff so they are cognizant of and responsive to their environment, develop their staff professionally through educational requirements and training (more about this in Chapter 14), allow their workers to take creative risks without undue punishment, and encourage evaluation by outside entities. Notably, the Sacramento County Sheriff's Department's adaptation to the realignment requirement for county jails in California, as described at the beginning of this chapter, would appear to be a perfect example of a correctional organization operating as a learning organization.

Video 13.3: Motivating Offender Change

Total quality management (TQM): A theory that values worker involvement but also recognizes that workers are motivated by rewards and must be held accountable for their productivity by management.

Management by objections (MBO): Under this theory, workers set their work objectives with management, as it is believed they will work harder to achieve goals they helped set.

Learning organizations: Organizations that encourage education and training for their workers, promote risk taking and the publication of mistakes by members so that all might learn from them, and open up their doors to evaluation by outside entities so that they might critically assess how they do their work.

••• ELEMENTS OF EFFECTIVE ORGANIZATIONS

COMMUNICATION

Communication in any organization is central to its effective function. In corrections, management needs to communicate with staff and outside stakeholders (e.g., governor's office, county commissioners, media outlets, or citizens' groups), staff need to communicate with inmates and each other, and inmates need to communicate with staff and other inmates. If communication is blocked or garbled, then the smooth operation of the facility—and perhaps its safety—is compromised.

Yet communications in correctional organizations is complicated and, strangely enough, facilitated by their bureaucratic structure. Hierarchy promotes communication from the top of the organization down to the bottom, but it stymies communication from the bottom up. The specialization required of a bureaucracy also makes communication from one subset of the organization to the other difficult, but it concentrates the expertise and, thus, the transference of knowledge within that sector of the organization quite well (Stohr & Collins, 2014). Other barriers to communication across organizations include the specialized language and acronyms that make communication within the organization easier but difficult for outsiders to understand. Communication to the outside by inmates is necessarily restricted and monitored, and staff are legally constrained in what they can communicate to people on the outside.

PERSPECTIVE FROM A PRACTITIONER

Teri Herold-Prayer, Veteran Services Manager

Position: Veteran services manager

Location: Washington Department of Corrections and Washington Department of Veterans Affairs

Education: MA in criminal justice and MA in political science from Washington State University

What previous criminal justice experience do you have?

I served for 1.5 years as a higher education research analyst for the Washington Association of Sheriffs and Police Chiefs and for four years as a research manager at the Washington State Department of Corrections (WA DOC). What are your primary duties and responsibilities?

As the veteran services manager, my responsibilities are focused on the incarcerated veterans and those who enter work release and field community supervision under WA DOC supervision. The position is dually supported by WA DOC and the Washington Department of Veterans Affairs (WDVA), which is the first of its kind in the history of WA DOC. This position reports to both agencies about work focused on assisting incarcerated veterans with their reentry needs. This unique population has benefits not available to the general prison and field population. The efforts are to streamline the access to state and federal veterans benefits in an effort to support reentry into the community and to better serve incarcerated veterans in understanding their eligibility for benefits prior to entering the community.

What are the characteristics and traits most useful in your line of work?

There needs to be a passion to assist while, at the same time, understanding the limitations that exist for offenders returning to the community. Veteran offenders face not only the struggles of having a felony on their record, but they also harbor shame for dishonoring their service to their country. The ability to collaborate with those public and private resources is essential to successfully serving this population. Being a visionary has allowed me the opportunity to establish the first dedicated veteran living units within the prison system.

Please describe a typical workday.

There is no typical workday in my position. My position takes me out of the office and into the community to serve on various offender reentry committees on the western side of the state. When I'm not in the community or in the office answering e-mails, I might be visiting the prisons across the state, meeting with veteran offenders to hear their concerns or meeting with prison staff to educate them on the veteran initiative aimed to better serve veteran offenders.

I consult with staff who supervise and counsel the veterans in the dedicated living units. I assist with the development of programs that are veteran centric in an effort to provide an opportunity for veteran offenders to give back to the veteran community. These programs are important, for they give the veterans something they can be proud of. They tap into their military culture of service.

It is important that executives and staff gain an awareness of the statistics that describe the veteran population since it is roughly 9% of the entire population. Writing reports and preparing PowerPoints is vital to furthering the understanding of this population.

What is your advice to someone who wants to enter your field?

This position requires one's ability to be passionate, process oriented, and a good communicator to those who are at the offender level, staff level, leadership level, and professional level. To have a broad understanding of whom the audience is you are speaking to or listening to is paramount to gaining the support of those who exist at the various levels. *Support* is the key word to the success of my position.

Secondly, this work wouldn't be possible without a vision and the ability to put that vision into motion. The most important attributes are to be open-minded—to look outside the box and challenge the norm—and to accept that change in corrections is slow. Change can happen but not without resistance, which only makes you a better employee and respected professional.

Corrections and other criminal justice organizations have adopted ways to improve communications through the use of teams (e.g., for classification, training, problem solving, forecasting, etc.). Some have promoted the use of cross-rank teaming as a means of subverting the restrictions of a hierarchy, developed newsletters and mass e-mails to ensure that information is widely distributed, developed their websites to ensure that the public is more fully informed of their operation, and invited university researchers and other public-interest-group researchers in to review their operations. All of these efforts, of course, are in line with the more recent efforts to manage from human-relations, TQM, MBO, and learning perspectives. One clear example of an organization seeking to promote a learning ethic in its culture was when the Washington State Department of Corrections, in perhaps an unprecedented move about five years ago, opened up all of their inmate data to researchers at Washington State University. One of the authors also witnessed the Oregon Youth Authority offering the same kind of access to researchers from several universities in 2015. The likely outcome of this openness, beyond the organizational self-assessment that is likely to improve services for its clients, is the communication of important knowledge about practices and lives that will advance the field of corrections.

LEADERSHIP AND WHY IT MATTERS

Because most criminal justice organizations are populated by public-service employees with some civil-service protection, any given leader is not all powerful in such workplaces. Nor are police chiefs, sheriffs, judges, wardens, prosecutors, probation and parole district managers—or leaders of criminal justice organizations—completely responsible for the actions of their employees or how successful the organization is at accomplishing its goals. Still, those leaders at the top of the organizational chart are people whose position is invested with the power to hire and fire (although this power is constrained somewhat for public employees by laws, rules, and procedures—i.e., civil-service protections), and they are the people who ultimately decide which policies to pursue or how and whether to implement them. Should their decisions not be acceptable to the political actors who supervise them or to the public who elects them (as they do with sheriffs, prosecutors, or judges), they, too, can be let go. But before that happens, they are free to make important decisions about the direction of the organization and how the workplace operates. They are also the people who interact with politicians, funding entities, and the public, and for this reason, they are in the best position to garner resources and support for their decisions. Therefore, leadership in correctional organizations matters a great deal because it affects all areas of their operation.

But what is leadership exactly? Scholars have defined it in a number of ways. For our purposes, we will use the following definition from Stohr and Collins (2014), as it synthesizes a number of definitions and seems to fit the modern organizational milieu of criminal justice agencies best: "**Leadership** is an ongoing process of activity involving organizing, decision making, innovating, communicating, team building, culture creation and molding that is engaged in by workers and supervisors to achieve organizational goals" (p. 184). Note that this definition melds what leaders do with what they are and recognizes that to some extent, everyone in the organization has a leadership role to play. This acknowledgement of the role of all in leadership best fits the human-relations theories mentioned in the preceding. Under traditional theories of management, a leader was thought to rule from the top of the organizational chart, with all power and communication flowing from him to the underlings down below. Though in criminal justice organizations, there are such leaders formally and according to the organizational chart (e.g., the sheriffs, prosecutors, wardens, etc.), their "underlings" have some formal power to make decisions about how they do their

Video 13.4: White House Drug Czar Describes Prison Program as National Leader

Leadership: "An ongoing process of activity involving organizing, decision making, innovating, communicating, team building, culture creation and molding that is engaged in by workers and supervisors to achieve organizational goals" (Stohr & Collins, 2009, p. 184).

work according to law and procedure, and they have informal power over whether to be responsive to leadership commands. Of course, there may be repercussions if they are not responsive, as they have less power than the formal leader, but they still have power. It is in recognition of this fact that modern leaders in criminal justice organizations will often involve lower-level workers in participatory management or shared decision making about some aspects of their job and about initiatives the organization is involved in.

It is also for this reason that most managers in public-service agencies will sometimes employ leadership styles that allow more involvement by those who are supervised (Klofas et al., 1990; Stohr & Collins, 2014). It is thought that the most effective leaders are those who adjust to the situation they face. If followers are new to the job or if there is an emergency, a leader will tend to be more directive about what must be done, or in other words, he or she will give orders. If there is no emergency, the leader might consider trying to persuade followers as to the benefits of one given action over another. If there is no emergency, and the followers are well versed in how to do the job, then a leader might consider allowing them to make the decisions about how to do their work. If there is no emergency, and the followers are experienced and well versed in best practices for a job, the leader might consider taking a step back from supervising at all and completely trusting the workers to make all decisions about how to do their work.

••• ORGANIZATIONAL CULTURE

Every organization has its own culture that makes it distinct and that helps to define how the work is done. When visiting a given organization for any length of time, even for a day, and after talking to the staff and clients, interviewing the manager or leader, and observing how things are done, you can get an inkling of what this culture is like, whether positive or negative or something in between. Though they have the same bureaucratic structure and have closed and total attributes, correctional organizations, even when residing in the same state or county, may have vastly different organizational cultures.

For our purposes, **organizational culture** may be defined here as the norms, values, beliefs, history, traditions, and language held and practiced in a given organization. (Note that this definition is the same as that of a *subculture* [defined in the foregoing], with the exception that an organizational culture is organization-wide rather than just referring to a group of people within a population, as is true with a subculture). The organizational culture becomes apparent both formally and informally. Formally, the statutes that govern the organization, the arrangement of staff (either hierarchically, as in corrections, or not), the policies and procedures, and the memorandums that are exchanged are part of the official or formal culture. The informal culture manifests itself in the stories, jokes, cautionary tales, gossip, and rumors that are told. The informal organizational culture may not be written down, except perhaps in e-mails and texts, but it is often as powerful in determining how an organization is operated as the formal culture is.

Prisons, jails, and community corrections organizations are no different than any other in that their culture is affected by such factors as how ethical members are, how satisfied they are with their work, whether the organization promotes participatory management and learning, how leadership shapes the organization and sets the tone, whether the staff perceive that their job has "enriching" characteristics (e.g., it is meaningful, interesting, and stimulating), whether respect is practiced both between staff and between

Video 13.5: In the Gay Wing of Los Angeles Men's Central Jail, It's not Shanks and Muggings but Hand-Sewn Gowns and Tears

Organizational culture: The values, beliefs, history, traditions, and language held and practiced in a given organization.

PHOTO 13.5: A correctional officer providing clothing to an inmate. Officers' jobs include the provision of goods and services to inmates.

ETHICAL ISSUE 13.1

What Would You Do?

You are a brand-spanking-new director of a community corrections (aka probation and parole) district. You have been brought in by the director of corrections for the state to "clean house," as the district is perceived as failing to achieve organizational goals. Moreover, central office has fielded numerous complaints by staff and client advocates, not to mention some pending client lawsuits that the courts are not dismissing, about the treatment of staff and inmates. Staff morale, from what you can tell, is low; clients are resentful and noncompliant; and there does not appear to be much community stakeholder engagement from the agency. In other words, as best you can tell, you have been assigned to lead a failing organization where unethical behavior by administrators and staff, though not the norm, is all too common. Knowing what you know about leadership styles and management theory, what approach would you take to change the organizational culture and, as a result, the work outcomes of this agency?

staff and their clients, and how staff think the public views their work (as a partial determinate of how proud they are of it) (Stohr et al., 2012). Other factors in the correctional environment that might influence the culture include the degree to which violence is promoted or discouraged between staff and inmates and between inmates; whether respect for the rights and dignity of inmates and clients are emphasized and practiced; the degree to which the practices of corrections are open for review by the public; and, a more recent consideration, how much the culture is guided by scientific evidence of best practices in corrections.

As you can imagine, it is hypothesized that the organizational culture affects staff turnover, stress, and burnout (Finney, Stergiopoulos, Hensel, Bonato, & Dewa, 2013; Garner, Knight, & Simpson, 2007). It affects how staff, clients, and citizens are treated. It affects whether suspects or inmates are safe in police custody or in correctional institutions. It affects whether evidence is fully considered in a court setting and whether police investigations or correctional treatment are successful. It ultimately affects whether the public is supportive of policing, corrections, or courts. In other words, it affects everything.

Correctional organizations, like any other, have both an overall organizational culture and then subcultures within that larger culture. Typically, there is an administration subculture comprising the formal leaders in the organization, the subculture of the staff who deliver services (and this is usually divided into at least security and treatment staff), and the client and inmate subculture, which is divided by race/ethnicity, age, time under supervision and incarcerated, and so on. Notably, subcultures require that their members be in continuous contact over a period of time in order to transmit those values and beliefs, so there is less likely to be a strong client subculture for those on probation or parole as there is for inmates in a jail and especially those in a prison. Continuous contact between subcultural members over a period of time allows socialization into the subculture to occur. (There will be more about this socialization for staff in Chapter 14.).

A review of the scholarly literature on organizational cultures reveals that (1) there are attributes of an organizational culture that are associated with positive outcomes and that (2) those attributes are identifiable, particularly by those at the lower levels of the organization (Stohr et al., 2012). For instance, in research on the organizational culture of a jail setting by Stohr and her colleagues (2012) using an organizational-culture instrument that was devised for jails, they found that there was some indication that staff were not always content with their pay, training, or promotional opportunities, though, in general, their assessment of their workplace was quite positive. The leader (sheriff) of the studied jail, when questioned about his perceptions, however, was not aware that staff felt this way about their training or promotional opportunities (though he knew the pay was not where it should be).

We found that the dimensions of an organizational culture are not always easily identifiable. As the literature did indicate (e.g. Jung et al., 2009; Scott et al., 2003), there are many aspects to a culture that define and distinguish it.

POLICY AND RESEARCH

Management of Correctional Organizations

Management of any organization of any size is very difficult. As you can tell from this short review of the management of correctional organizations in this chapter, there are so many factors to consider and so many ideas and people to accommodate. Among them are the people you manage and work with (colleagues and clients) and the community you manage them in. The research on the management of correctional organizations is relatively sparse, but two people who have been heavily involved in it over the years are Eric Lambert (professor and department chair at the University of Mississippi) and his research collaborator, Nancy Hogan (professor and graduate program coordinator at Ferris State University). They and their colleagues and students have likely published hundreds of articles about personnel and management issues in correctional organizations. Taken in total, their findings indicate that when organizations are managed so that stress for staff is limited (stress from the job but also that created by management), job satisfaction is high (because the job is enriched but also because management provides the working conditions to make it so), and participatory management is practiced (because management facilitates it), then you are likely to reap a number of benefits organizationally, like less stress and more job satisfaction (both predictably!) but also less turnover of staff and a better work product. For political actors, this means that good management of corrections ensures that money is not only saved but well spent.

DISCUSSION QUESTIONS

1. What factors would make management of corrections more doable?

2. Why do you think all managers don't practice a human-relations style of management?

3. Do you think that the management of correctional institutions is qualitatively different from the management of other public or private organizations? If so, how?

SUMMARY

- Correctional organizations tend to be bureaucratic, closed, formal, and total institutions to a great extent. Yet research, reality, and theory tell us that these descriptors are far from absolute. In truth, such organizations are not always top down in terms of their hierarchy (others in the organization also have power and engage in management); they are open in the sense that they are influenced by their environment, they have informal operations and networks that function beneath their more formal surface, and they are no longer as "total" as they once were.

- Management theories have changed the organizational landscape in the business world, and those changes have influenced the operation of public-sector entities such as correctional organizations, too. Today's correctional organization is as much a Y or Z organization as it is an X in operation. These management changes are also evident in communication and leadership styles that are less dictatorial and more participatory in focus. As theory, communication, and conceptions of leadership change, so does the organizational culture.

- The material presented here would indicate that there are organizational factors that can be manipulated to improve this experience for staff and clients or inmates so that they and their organization can realize their promise. Also, better pay, benefits, and training can be used to foster the greater development of professional attributes, such as education, and the consequent reduction in role ambiguity, turnover, and stress and increase in job satisfaction. (See Chapter 14 for a developed discussion of these topics.) The organizational culture can also be assessed to determine if certain characteristics are making it a more or less positive work environment for staff and a safe, secure, and developmental one for clients and inmates.

KEY TERMS

Bureaucracy 319

Closed institutions 319

Flatter and fatter organizations 323

Formal organization 321

Human relations theories of management 323

Informal organization 321

Leadership 328

Learning organizations 326

Management 318

Management by objections (MBO) 326

Maslow's hierarchy of needs 323

Open institutions 321

Organizational culture 329

Participatory management 325

Scientific management 323

Theory X 324

Theory Y 325

Theory Z 325

Total quality management (TQM) 326

DISCUSSION QUESTIONS

1. Explain how theories of management are related to communication practices in an organization.

2. Explain how theories of management are related to leadership styles in an organization.

3. Bureaucracies, as an organizational type, have been around for some time now. What are the benefits of such a type for corrections?

4. What are the drawbacks of a bureaucratic organizational structure for corrections?

5. The authors argue that it is more than just the "head" of the organization who functions as a leader in corrections. Explain how other organizational members in corrections engage in both formal and informal leadership.

USEFUL INTERNET SITES

Please note that the sites listed can be accessed at edge.sagepub.com/stohrcorrections.

American Correctional Association: www.aca.org

The ACA is an organization that has, for 146 years, focused on professionalizing corrections in the United States. Their website and materials provide information on the latest training, research, and ideas in corrections.

American Jail Association: www.corrections.com/aja

The AJA is an organization that also focuses on professionalization in corrections but as it involves jails. Their website provides information about the latest training, trends, and research in jails.

American Probation and Parole Association: www.appa-net.org

The APPA is an organization that focuses on the professionalization of probation and parole or community corrections. From their website, you can learn about the best research and training and the newest ideas about practices in community corrections.

Bureau of Labor Statistics: www.bls.gov/ooh/Community-and-Social-Service/Probation-officers-and-correctional-treatment-specialists.htm

This government bureau provides information on employment, unemployment, and earnings in all sectors of the U.S. economy.

Vera Institute: www.vera.org

The Vera Institute has been behind some of the biggest criminal justice reforms of the last 40 years. Check out their website to learn what important reforms and issues are on the correctional horizon.

$SAGE edge™

Sharpen your skills with SAGE edge at **edge.sagepub.com/stohrcorrections**. SAGE edge for Students provides a personalized approach to help you accomplish your coursework goals in an easy-to-use learning environment. You'll find action plans, mobile-friendly eFlashcards, and quizzes as well as video, web, and resources and links to SAGE journal articles to support and expand on the concepts presented in this chapter.

14

The Corrections Experience for Staff

Kim Hairston/MCT/Newscom

TEST YOUR KNOWLEDGE

Test your present knowledge of work in corrections by answering the following questions. Check your answers on page 537 after reading the chapter.

1. Correctional officers are not called guards anymore. (True or false?)

2. Name three of the five characteristics of a profession.

3. Generally speaking, which job do you think pays the most and the least of these three (and why): police officer, correctional officer, or probation and parole officer?

4. Generally speaking, which job do you think requires the most education and which requires the least (and why): police officer, correctional officer, or probation and parole officer?

5. Television programs and movies tend to depict corrections work accurately. (True or false?)

6. A *role* is what a person does on the job every day. (True or false?)

7. What factors likely cause stress for correctional officers?

8. Unionized correctional officers make more money than non-unionized correctional officers. (True or false?)

LEARNING OBJECTIVES

- Compare what makes work a profession as opposed to just a job

- Describe the effect of growth in staff and clients or inmates

- Explain the importance of education and training in the correctional field

- Describe how and why demographic factors affect corrections

- Identify what correctional roles are

- Describe the influence of subculture and socialization on correctional officers

- Discuss why correctional staff might abuse power and experience stress and burnout

JOHN'S TRAGIC **STORY**
Mary K. Stohr

John was about 22 when I first met him as an inmate on my caseload at the adult male prison I worked at in the 1980s. I was his classification counselor and only a few years older than him at the time. He had a tragic life up until that point: He was abandoned, for the most part, by his father; his mother was hauled away to a mental institution in front of him when he was 5; and foster care homes and struggling family members took care of him for the rest of his childhood. He was in and out of juvenile facilities, mostly for property crimes and joy riding, though he admitted that he had a problem controlling his temper. He received very few visits, as the people he loved (his girlfriend and sister) were poor and unable to make the trip often. His instant offense was one of those crimes (robbery) that was technically serious, but the facts indicated it was really burglary. It was the 1980s, and the talk was all about being "tough on crime" and that meant criminals like John, too.

He would come in and talk to me at length once or twice a week about his life and his hopes (e.g., getting a job once released, staying out of prison, and reuniting with his off-and-on estranged girlfriend). He seemed sincere and in need of a friend, but a correctional staffer can never cross the line or be "friends" with inmates, though he or she can be friendly, to a point. One time, he came in to talk, and it was clear he had been crying; his dad was presumed to have killed himself by driving his truck into a lake on purpose and drowning. John was distraught, feeling that he had let the father who had pretty much abandoned him down. I talked to John for some time, and though upset, he seemed rational. Security staff wanted to put him in segregation, but I successfully argued against it. John continued to come to see me and seemed to need someone to talk to. Then, all of a sudden, about a month after his dad died, he stopped coming by. It was a Friday night, and I was getting ready to leave for the weekend and tracked *him down at a bingo game in the cafeteria. He was with one of his buddies, and when I asked him why I hadn't seen him in the last couple of weeks, he was noncommittal and uncharacteristically standoffish. I suspected something was wrong. In retrospect, I should have probed further and have always wondered if things would have turned out differently if I had.*

The next morning, I came in and was told what had happened. John had escaped from the prison during

the night (it was a restricted, minimum-custody prison, with no fence) and stolen a motorcycle, ostensibly to try to see his girlfriend, who had recently broken up with him. He drove the bike wildly in downtown Vancouver, Washington, and attracted the attention of a police officer, who then gave chase. John refused to stop for the officer and instead sped up and seemingly purposefully drove straight into a concrete wall. He died instantly.

••• INTRODUCTION: WHAT IS A PROFESSION?

Web 14.1: Career as a Correctional Officer

Work in corrections has changed a great deal from the *shire reeves* (the Old English name for sheriffs) who ran the jails in England in the Middle Ages and the guards who staffed the first Pennsylvania and Auburn prisons. For one thing, security staff in correctional facilities are no longer referred to as *guards*, as that title is thought to reflect a more primitive role, and are instead formally referred to as *correctional officers*, perhaps a reflection of the move to professional status for these staff.

Yet the public does not generally see corrections work as a profession. Other than probation and parole work (which, not coincidentally, usually requires more education and pays more), most college students do not identify work in jails or prisons as their career goal either. Also, despite a century of effort by some determined correctional administrators, corrections organizations (such as the American Correctional Association, the American Jail Association, and the American Probation and Parole Association), and academicians, many correctional jobs are not structured like a profession. A **profession** is typified by five characteristics: (1) prior educational attainment involving college, (2) formal training on the job or just prior to the start of the job, (3) pay and benefits that are commensurate with the work, (4) the ability to exercise discretion, and (5) work that is guided by a code of ethics (Stohr & Collins, 2014). Yet most jobs in corrections still do not adequately meet the first three of these criteria for professional status, and though most correctional workplaces either have their own code of ethics or are nominally guided by that of a corrections organization (e.g., see the American Correctional Association's Code of Ethics in In Focus 14.1), there is no enforcement of this code as there is for medical doctors with the American Medical Association or for lawyers with the American Bar Association.

In this chapter, we will explore the nature of correctional work as it has evolved and as it is shaped by professionalism, the requirements of the job, and clients and inmates. We will review the factors that lead to stress and turnover for officers and how those might be addressed. Though correctional work is often not the first choice of a college graduate, it does have its own appeal, and we will discuss why that might be so and how it has grown in the last three decades.

Profession: Regarding the positions of corrections officers and staff, a profession is distinguished by prior educational attainment involving college, formal training on the job or just prior to the start of the job, pay and benefits that are commensurate with the work, the ability to exercise discretion, and work that is guided by a code of ethics.

••• THE STATE OF THE WORK IN CORRECTIONAL INSTITUTIONS AND PROGRAMS

GROWTH IN STAFF AND CLIENTS OR INMATES

In addition to exploding inmate and offender populations, the number of employees in corrections, albeit often undereducated, undertrained, and underpaid for their work, has grown astronomically in the last 24 years. From 1982 to 2007, there was almost a 600% increase in direct expenditures for all criminal justice agencies (i.e., police, courts, and corrections). (For the latest data available at the time of this publication, see Figure 14.1.) During that same time period, just the expenditures for corrections increased by 660%. Surprisingly, employment in corrections more than doubled, from 300,000 to 765,466, during this time period, with the majority of those employees being correctional officers (66%) working in state and local correctional facilities and programs, both public and private (K. Hughes, 2006; Perry, 2008; Stephan, 2008, p. 4). By 2014, over 686,000 people worked in state and local corrections alone (U.S. Census Bureau, 2014b, p. 1). At the state level, where most prisons and most adult probation and parole agencies are operated and funded, three quarters or more of the correctional budget was spent on correctional institutions through 2011 (Kyckelhahn, 2014, p. 2). Given the recession that began in 2007 and ended about three to four years later and the decarceration we are seeing at the state and federal levels (Kaeble, Glaze, Tsoutis, & Minton, 2016), it is likely that these increases have not continued, however. In fact, as indicated by Figure 14.2, by far, most employees of state and local governments are employed in education (either K–12 or higher education) or by hospitals or the police.

Of these employees, in 2005 (the latest date for which we have figures), the majority, particularly those who work directly with inmates as correctional staff, were males by a 3-to-1 ratio (Stephan, 2008, p. 2). In federal facilities, the gender differences were largest, with 87% of correctional officers being male and only 13% being female. The smallest gender employment difference was in the 400-plus private facilities, where 52% were male, and 48% were female. In the more numerous state correctional facilities, there were 74% male correctional officers compared with 26% female (Stephan, 2008, p. 2).

Web 14.2: Applying for a Correctional Officer Position

Audio 14.1: States Face Correctional Officer Shortage Amid a Cultural Stigma

---

FIGURE *14.1*   Direct Expenditure by Criminal Justice Function, 1982–2007

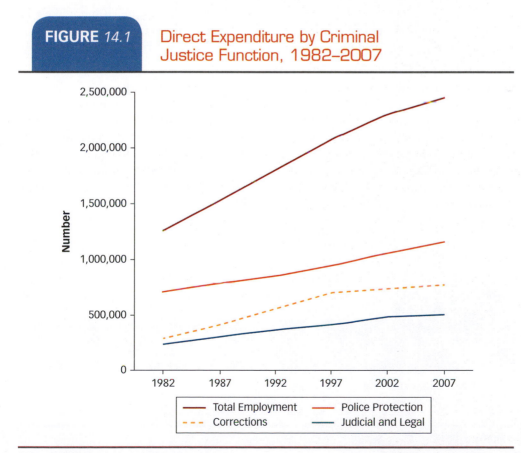

Note: Most recent data available.

Source: Bureau of Justice Statistics (2008).

FIGURE *14.2*   State and Local Government Employees by Field of Work

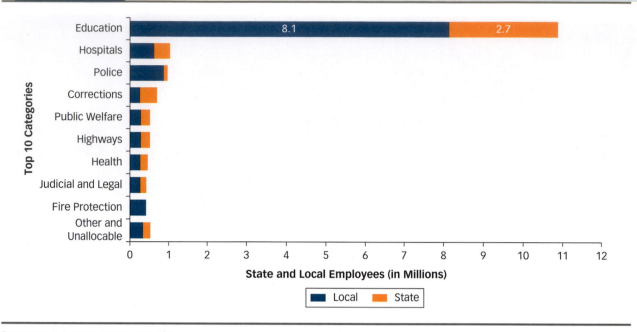

Source: U.S. Census Bureau (2014b).

Notably, these gender differences by level and type of facility very closely align with pay differences. Among prisons, federal correctional officers, who are much more likely to be male, are the best paid, and private-facility correctional officers, who are almost as likely to be female, are paid the least (see Table 14.1 regarding private versus public pay for correctional work).

Even with this growth in staff numbers overall, whether male or female, the proportional growth in inmates has been much larger. As a result, the ratio of inmates to staff in prisons grew significantly from 2000 to 2005, with the most inmates to correctional staff in federal prisons (10.3 in 2006 but decreasing to 4.4 in 2015) and private prisons (6.9, versus 5.0 in public) in 2005, as compared with state prisons (4.9) (Davidson, 2015, p. 1; Stephan, 2008, p. 5). Likewise, jails continue to hold in the neighborhood of 82% of their capacity (Minton & Golinelli, 2014, p. 3), and the caseloads of parole officers at the state level (data on state or federal probation officer caseloads and parole officer caseloads at the federal level were not available) range around 38 per officer (Bonczar, 2008, p. 1). Simply put, staff working in corrections are stretched very thin despite the growth in their numbers. Also, as is indicated in Figure 14.3, the employment of correctional

TABLE *14.1*   Median Annual Pay for Full-Time Workers

	CORRECTIONAL OFFICERS AND JAILERS	PROBATION OFFICERS AND TREATMENT SPECIALISTS	POLICE AND SHERIFFS
Public local, state, and federal	$45,320*	$54,080*	$61,270*
Private	$21,216^	Not available	$45,594^

*Data from 2015.

^Data from 2010.

Source: U.S. Department of Labor. Data taken from Tables 6 and 7.

officers in prisons and jails varies somewhat by state, with states with larger populations employing the most.

Given these numbers of inmates and clients, one can appreciate the organizational problems that develop for correctional managers seeking to hire, train, and retain the best employees to do this difficult work. Perhaps, in part, because of this recognized need to get and keep the best employees, the management of correctional institutions and programs has shifted over the years as efforts to professionalize, democratize (allow more say in the work by those doing it), and standardize work in corrections have had some success.

In general, compensation that is commensurate with job requirements and skills is a clear indication of the value given to a particular profession. It is true that it would be difficult to regard some correctional institutions or programs or their staff as *professionals* because they do not meet the educational, training, or pay requirements of a profession. However, there are a number of correctional institutions and programs that have made much progress in this area, though the path to professionalization and the creation of a work environment that is conducive to employee growth and welfare are not always achieved.

So if we were to imagine a continuum of correctional professionalism across the field, we could probably generalize that community corrections officers (probation and parole officers) and their work are more professionalized—defined as having more education, training, and pay—than are prison and jail correctional officers (see Table 14.1). (We will discuss ethics separately at the end of the chapter, and it was also covered in Chapter 4.) Next along that continuum would come correctional officers who work in public prisons and then those who work in public jails. Of course, these generalizations do not hold true for every institution or every locality. For instance, in some larger city jails, officers might be paid and trained as well as or better than prison officers or even adult probation

| FIGURE *14.3* | Employment of Correctional Officers and Jailers by State, 2015 |

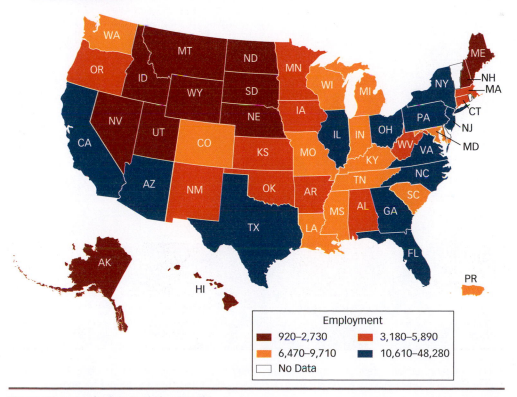

Employment
- 920–2,730
- 3,180–5,890
- 6,470–9,710
- 10,610–48,280
- No Data

Source: Bureau of Labor Statistics (2016b).

and parole officers. Typically, jail officers in large counties are paid more than those in small counties and often are paid less than—but not always—state- and federal-level correctional officers. Usually, federal-level community corrections officers make more than prison officers at their level of government (e.g., at the federal or state level) (Stohr & Collins, 2014). These data do indicate that attempts to professionalize corrections, as it pertains to pay, needs more effort in some areas than in others.

Note that police officers at both the state and local levels are paid about $18,000 more per year than correctional officers and more than $8,000 more than probation and parole officers in any given state (see Table 14.1). Therefore, it is not surprising that both local and state police officers, along with probation and parole officers, are more likely to require at least some college and possibly a college degree. Students of criminal justice tend to recognize this difference in that when asked what they want to do when they graduate, they are more likely to identify police or community corrections (probation and parole) jobs as desirable over work in a prison or jail.

Notably, the push to privatize correctional and law enforcement work since the 1980s has not resulted in better pay for staff. In fact, as is illustrated in Table 14.1, privately employed correctional and law enforcement officers' median pay is about $24,000 less for the former and $14,000 less for the latter than for comparable jobs in the public sector. (Notably, these data were not collected for the same year, and that might account for some of the difference.) If better pay is correlated with a more professional workforce, then we can conclude that the privatization efforts are not moving us in that direction.

PERCEIVED BENEFITS OF CORRECTIONAL WORK

There are many reasons why people who work in corrections might find it gratifying. For one, people are attracted to correctional work because it has been a booming business for a number of decades, creating thousands of jobs in the process. Correctional work also provides a steady, if not lucrative, paycheck (U.S. Census Bureau, 2010a; see Table 14.1).

© Marmaduke St. John/Alamy Stock Photo

PHOTO 14.1: Correctional staff in the control center at the Santa Ana, California, city jail. Control center staff members have the challenging job of monitoring several screens at once and are responsible for the electronic unlocking and locking of most doors in the facility.

People who want to make a difference in other people's lives, to end the tragic circumstances that tend to produce a cycle of street-level criminals, might choose to work with juveniles in corrections or in treatment programming with adults or juveniles on community supervision or in institutions. When they see someone change for the better and know they might have contributed to that change, this is when correctional work can be personally fulfilling.

It is also possible that those who are attracted to correctional work are curious about the human psyche and how it operates. Working with people who have engaged in seriously deviant behavior enhances the understanding about why people behave the way they do. Some might also find it rewarding to be engaged in keeping these seriously deviant and violent offenders off the streets and, in that sense, to be part of the justice-dispensing machinery that is corrections.

COLLECTIVE BARGAINING

Correctional staff moved to unionize as a means of gaining power vis-à-vis administrators. As we know from our history of corrections, the wardens of earlier prisons (and this is still true, to some extent, today in some correctional institutions) often acted like dictators over their fiefdom, the prison (Bergner, 1998; Rideau, 2010). And it was not only inmates who were their subjects but also staff, who were relatively powerless to voice their concerns or to earn a decent and livable wage. By unionizing, correctional staff working at the state and local levels were able to gain some collective power to bargain with administrators to improve their own work conditions. A *union worker* is defined by the U.S. Department of Labor (2010) as follows:

> Any employee in a union occupation when all of the following conditions are met: a labor organization is recognized as the bargaining agent for all workers in the occupation; wage and salary rates are determined through collective bargaining or negotiations; and settlement terms, which must include earnings provisions and may include benefit provisions, are embodied in a signed, mutually binding collective bargaining agreement. A nonunion worker is an employee in an occupation not meeting the conditions for union coverage. (p. 1)

A number of concerns regarding unionization have been raised, however, and these include the belief that unionization restricts the ability of administrators to fire incompetent people, that union contracts are too restrictive regarding the work that people can do, and that, in some cases, unions have worked to increase incarceration as a means of increasing job opportunities. Although some of these concerns may have merit, it is also true that those states with unionized correctional staff pay those staff more and provide more benefits for them (see Table 14.2), which is likely to increase the ability of those states to attract and keep better and more professional workers. If it is harder for administrators to fire incompetent unionized workers, it is also harder for administrators to fire people based on their politics or simply because they do not like them. Such contrarian voices in the workforce (those who disagree with administrative practices) often provide an important check on the power of administrators, and unions give such people protection from the wrath of those administrators who might want to retaliate against "contrarians."

Though the union for correctional officers in California did lobby to increase the number of institutions and jobs in corrections in that state in the 1990s, it is possible that they were just representing the sentiments of their membership. Correctional staff tend to be somewhat conservative regarding crime issues and so would tend to support, like the general public of the 1980s, 1990s, and 2000s, the creation of more correctional institutions.

TABLE 14.2	Mean Hourly Wages of Union and Nonunion State and Local Correctional Workers and Law Enforcement	
	UNION	**NONUNION**
Probation and parole	$27.69	$21.00
Correctional officers and jailers	23.36	14.74
Police	30.42	20.97

Source: U.S. Department of Labor (2010). Data taken from Table 13.

••• WHY REQUIRE MORE EDUCATION AND TRAINING?

First of all—and unfortunately—most correctional institutions and programs do not have prior educational requirements that would elevate them to the level of a profession. Though it is true that many probation and parole officers must have a college degree or at least some college to qualify for the job, most jails, prisons (with the exception of federal correctional officers, who must have a bachelor's degree and experience), and even juvenile institutions, even those with a greater emphasis on rehabilitative programming, do not often require such a qualification from applicants.

STANFORD PRISON EXPERIMENT

Yet the oft-cited **Stanford Prison Experiment** provides a powerful argument for the value of formal education and training for correctional staff. In this 1971 experiment, volunteer students, with no training as officers and only their own expectations and beliefs to guide them, were divided into officers and inmates in a makeshift "prison" (Haney, Banks, & Zimbardo, 1981). The "officers" were outfitted in uniforms, including reflective sunglasses, and given nightsticks. The "inmates" were given sack-like attire. Neither "officers" nor "inmates" were told of any rules or policies to guide or restrict their behavior. Predictably, a few of these "officers" or "guards" engaged in verbal and psychological abuse of the "inmates." In the end, about a third of the "officers" engaged in the abuse, and others stood by while it was going on. The experiment was stopped after a few days and is often referenced as an example of how correctional work and the subcultures that develop as part of the job can foster corrupt behavior by officers.

The problem with the experiment, however, was that the "officers" were never given any education or training in corrections work. They were directed to exercise their discretion in controlling the inmates, but it was a discretion that was not necessarily anchored to any history or knowledge of "best practices" in corrections. Rather, the "choices" made by the officers in the absence of any education and training were likely shaped by the movies and popular-press depictions of corrections that tended to reinforce the stereotypes of the institutions, programs, and work. Not knowing how best to "get people to do what they otherwise wouldn't" (Dahl's [1961] definition of **power**), the "guards" used what knowledge of corrections they had, even if it was all wrong.

ABU GHRAIB

The **Abu Ghraib** scandal of 2004, in which prisoners were tortured by mostly untrained "correctional officers" in the American-operated Abu Ghraib military prison in Iraq, tends

Stanford Prison Experiment: A 1971 experiment conducted at Stanford University that utilized volunteer students, divided into officers and inmates in a makeshift "prison." In the end, about a third of the "officers" engaged in the abuse of "inmates," and other officers stood by while it was going on.

Power: The ability to "get people to do what they otherwise wouldn't" (Dahl, 1961).

Abu Ghraib: An Iraq prison operated by the American military during the war in which prisoners were tortured by mostly untrained "correctional officers."

to reinforce the lessons of the Stanford Prison Experiment, even contrived as those circumstances were. At Abu Ghraib, some correctional officers made inmates sleep naked, crawl on the floor, and pose in pyramids naked (while staff took pictures). A number of officers also deprived inmates of food and basic necessities and engaged in physical torture. The U.S. Army's investigation of the abuses at Abu Ghraib found that officers engaged in the following:

> Breaking chemical lights and pouring the phosphoric liquid on detainees; pouring cold water on naked detainees; beating detainees with a broom handle and a chair; threatening male detainees with rape; allowing a military police guard to stitch the wound of a detainee who was injured after being slammed against the wall in his cell; sodomizing a detainee with a chemical light and perhaps a broom stick, and using military working dogs to frighten and intimidate detainees with threats of attack, and in one instance actually biting a detainee. (Hersh, 2004, p. 1)

Though the army wanted to blame the abuses that occurred at Abu Ghraib on untrained and rogue staffers at the prison (and six of them were prosecuted), the blame for the abuses extended up the chain of command to the Army Reserve brigadier general in charge of all Iraqi prisons, though she had had no previous experience or training in running prisons (she was relieved of command), and perhaps as high as defense secretary Donald Rumsfeld.

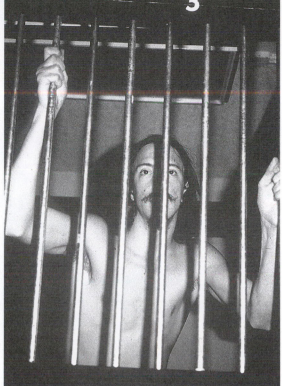

PHOTO 14.2: Stanford Prison Experiment "inmate."

> As the international furor grew, senior military officers, and President George W. Bush, insisted that the actions of a few did not reflect the conduct of the military as a whole. Taguba's report [Major General Antonio M. Taguba investigated what happened at Abu Ghraib], however, amounts to an unsparing study of collective wrongdoing and the failure of Army leadership at the highest levels. The picture he draws of Abu Ghraib is one in which Army regulations and the Geneva conventions were routinely violated, and in which much of the day-to-day management of the prisoners was abdicated to Army military-intelligence units and civilian contract employees. Interrogating prisoners and getting intelligence, including by intimidation and torture, was the priority. (Hersh, 2004, p. 4)

Video 14.1:
Stanford Prison Experiment Continues to Shock

Simply put, the lesson from these incidents and countless corrections scandals over the years that have involved the systematic abuse of inmates by staff is that some people will not act professionally—or even decently—especially when they have no education or training in that profession. The training and education will not necessarily prevent all such abuses (at least two of the officers involved in Abu Ghraib had prior experience as correctional officers in Virginia and presumably some training in that state), but they will at least provide the officers with the knowledge and skills to do the job the way it should be done.

Correctional work often does not resemble other professions because the formal training provided for many new hires, including the number of hours required and the quality of that training, does not approach the level of other professions, which may schedule months of training (e.g., police departments with an average of 761 hours, or 19 weeks, of training for new recruits [Reaves, 2009]) or extensive internships, months or years in duration, in other fields (e.g., teachers, social workers, and doctors).

PHOTOO 14.3: Inmate at the Abu Ghraib prison being terrorized by a staff dog.

The typical correctional job has lesser requirements for formal training or structured experience. For instance, in a *Corrections Compendium* (Clayton, 2003) survey, the researchers found that 31 of the reporting U.S. agencies required at least 200 hours of preservice training for those planning to work in a correctional institution. Likewise, in a quick survey of 150 directors and staff trainers, with responses received from 13 states or agencies in April 2004, the Juvenile Justice Trainers Association found that about 140 to 180 hours of preservice, academy-like training are required for most new hires in juvenile facilities (personal correspondence with B. Collins, May 2004).

Moreover, in some professions, the requisite college or professional degree is geared toward the work itself (e.g., computer programming, law school, or a master's in social work). Yet when a college degree is *required* for a job in corrections, it is rarely specifically a criminal justice degree but is typically one or more of the social-science degrees, which may include no classes on corrections or the criminal justice system at all.

Of course, these deficits in formal education and knowledge base and in training leave correctional workers less suited to perform their job in anything approaching a historical or present-day, research-based context. When they have not studied corrections or been provided with sufficient training, they may not understand the reason some practices are undertaken or why others are abandoned. They do not have the requisite tools to suggest changes or the background in research to know whether something "works" or not. Their ability to behave and develop as a professional is limited. So when they use their *discretion* (defined here as the ability to make choices and to act or not act on them), they could be making ill-informed choices that are not based on knowledge or experience and are overly influenced by their personal ideology, politics, or the media (Merlo & Benekos, 2000).

ETHICS

Not surprisingly and as was discussed in this chapter and the chapter on ethics, there have been numerous instances of documented ethical abuses by staff that include sexual assaults—beatings and rapes of clients on probation and parole, as well as of inmates in jails and prisons in the United States (Amnesty International, 2004; Bard, 1997; Schofield, 1997; Serrano, 2006). As a means of preventing such abuses, correctional agencies will often adopt an ethics code, such as those promulgated by the American Correctional Association (ACA; see In Focus 14.1), the American Jail Association, or others, and train people on what is right and wrong behavior in corrections.

The importance of training correctional workers initially and throughout their careers on what constitutes ethical behavior cannot be overemphasized. Just as important as the training, however, is ensuring that ethical people work in the organization. To do this, managers might consider using selection instruments and practices geared toward weeding out those who have little understanding of what is right and wrong and promoting only those people who exhibit that understanding in their daily work.

CORRECTIONAL WORK IS LITTLE UNDERSTOOD

It is possible that students and the general public may not view correctional work as a desirable career choice because they do not understand it. The truth is that few people outside of correctional work (or academe) probably know how institutions and community supervision actually operate, nor do they hold the roles of staff working in those agencies in very high regard. Students are acculturated by a media preoccupied with violence that tends to depict correctional institutions as dark, corrupt places peopled by abusive or, at a minimum, cynical and distant "guards" (Conover, 2001; R. Johnson, 2002; O'Sullivan, 2006). In the movies and television specials, prisons are almost always maximum security, old, and noisy; jails are crowded and huge monstrosities; and juvenile facilities are depressing and havens for child predators. Perhaps as discouraging, community corrections, which is arguably—based on our criteria here—the most professionalized sector of corrections, is rarely depicted in the mass media at all (Lutze, 2014).

Video 14.2: Community Corrections Officer of the Year Marko Anderson

Unfortunately, the mass media are not alone in misleading the public and students of criminal justice and criminology about corrections and correctional work. Academics have also tended to focus much of their attention on only the biggest and the "baddest" of correctional institutions and programs and the labor of their staff. Maximum-security institutions and, to a lesser extent, metropolitan city jails have been showcased, though they are not the norm for most corrections in this country (e.g., see Conover, 2001; Hassine, 1996; J. B. Jacobs, 1977; R. Johnson, 2002; Morris, 2002; Sykes, 1958). Research on these institutions tends to focus on the negative, or what the institutions or staff are doing wrong, rather than on what is working well. Of course, it is understandable that the "negative" shines through when these particular institutions and their type are the center of attention: Given the makeup of their inmate population and the likelihood that they are overcrowded and understaffed, there is much that is amiss in such places.

Predictably, work in probation and parole, much like the study of jail staff, receives short shrift by academics who tend, like the media, to be preoccupied with what is "sexy," violent, and controversial (Lutze, 2014). Given these depictions by the media and academics, it is hard to discern the truth about correctional institutions and programs and work in them because it is clear that the work is underappreciated, little understood, and hampered by misguided perceptions of it.

IN FOCUS 14.1

ACA Code of Ethics

Preamble

The American Correctional Association expects of its members unfailing honesty, respect for the dignity and individuality of human beings, and a commitment to professional and compassionate service. To this end, we subscribe to the following principles.

1. Members shall respect and protect the civil and legal rights of all individuals.

2. Members shall treat every professional situation with concern for the welfare of the individuals involved and with no intent to personal gain.

3. Members shall maintain relationships with colleagues to promote mutual respect within the profession and improve the quality of service.

4. Members shall make public criticism of their colleagues or their agencies only when warranted, verifiable, and constructive.

5. Members shall respect the importance of all disciplines within the criminal justice system and work to improve cooperation with each segment.

6. Members shall honor the public's right to information and share information with the public to the extent permitted by law subject to individuals' right to privacy.

7. Members shall respect and protect the right of the public to be safeguarded from criminal activity.

8. Members shall refrain from using their positions to secure personal privileges or advantages.

9. Members shall refrain from allowing personal interest to impair objectivity in the performance of duty while acting in an official capacity.

10. Members shall refrain from entering into any formal or informal activity or agreement which presents a conflict of interest or is inconsistent with the conscientious performance of duties.

11. Members shall refrain from accepting any gift, service, or favor that is or appears to be improper or implies an obligation inconsistent with the free and objective exercise of professional duties.

12. Members shall clearly differentiate between personal views/statements and views/statements/positions made on behalf of the agency or Association.

13. Members shall report to appropriate authorities any corrupt or unethical behaviors in which there is sufficient evidence to justify review.

14. Members shall refrain from discriminating against any individual because of race, gender, creed, national origin, religious affiliation, age, disability, or any other type of prohibited discrimination.

15. Members shall preserve the integrity of private information; they shall refrain from seeking information on individuals beyond that which is necessary to implement responsibilities and perform their duties; members shall refrain from revealing nonpublic information unless expressly authorized to do so.

16. Members shall make all appointments, promotions, and dismissals in accordance with established civil service rules, applicable contract agreements, and individual merit, rather than furtherance of personal interests.

17. Members shall respect, promote, and contribute to a work place that is safe, healthy, and free of harassment in any form.

Source: Reprinted from the ACA website (www.aca.org), with permission from the American Correctional Association.

••• INDIVIDUAL-LEVEL FACTORS THAT AFFECT THE CORRECTIONAL WORKPLACE

RACE OR ETHNICITY AND GENDER

Clearly, people should not be hired who are unqualified for a job, but if two people are roughly comparable in terms of skills and abilities, should the employer look for other personal features, such as race, gender, military background, or age, to determine who would be the best hire for the organization? Whether people will admit it or not, such matters do enter the calculus of who gets hired and promoted in organizations. (The topics of gender and race will be explored in greater detail in Chapters 15 and 16.) Left to their own devices and without the pressure that courts brought, the hiring of minorities and women did not occur in most criminal justice agencies to any extent until after the Civil Rights Act (CRA) of 1964 was passed and modified in 1972 to include gender (Stohr & Collins, 2014). Before the passage of this law and its modification, most employees in criminal justice agencies were very homogeneous in terms of race/ethnicity and gender, and today, about 40 years later, this is still true in some organizations but to a much lesser extent or not true at all in others. Correctional organizations, like other criminal justice agencies, did not hire women (except to work with other women and then for less pay) or minorities until they were forced to by the CRA and sometimes by lawsuits. One of the authors of this book worked as a correctional officer for an adult male prison in Washington State in 1983, and she was only the second woman hired there; the other had been hired only a month before. The warden told her he had fought central office for years about hiring any minorities or women. When promoted to the counselor position the next year at that same prison, she was the first woman in the history of that institution to work as a counselor. At the time she worked there, only one Hispanic officer was employed, and the warden did not want him there. The warden told the author that he would never hire a black man or woman for a correctional position. Fast-forward 30 years, and women and minority group members have integrated the correctional workplace at all levels and in every position. There are women correctional officers in maximum-security prisons and working as juvenile probation officers. There are minority group members who serve as wardens and directors of corrections and who serve on the line in medium-security prisons. Is corrections fully integrated? The answer to that question is no, not fully, but the law and courts have made it possible for all qualified applicants to work in correctional organizations so that they better reflect the composition of their communities.

As the correctional workplace has diversified, so has the importance of race, as it might affect workers' perceptions of each other and their labor (Camp, Steiger, Wright, Saylor, & Gilman, 2013). Employees of different racial and ethnic groups perceive that their job opportunities are shaped by their race or ethnicity and the race or ethnicity of others in their workplace. Managers, therefore, need to be cognizant of these perceptions and sensitive to them as they hire, train, and promote people.

As much as race, the change in gender composition of the employee workplace has had an effect on correctional-worker attitudes, perceptions, and behavior. We will discuss the effect of gender much more in Chapter 15, but suffice it to say here that some research has found that female staff are as capable as males and bring a different supervisory style to the work from that of men (Britton, 2003; Jurik & Halemba, 1984). When one of the authors first started in corrections, she had several inmates and officers who approached her and remarked on how the language had become less harsh by staff and inmates since she and another woman had integrated the correctional-officer workforce. She and the other female officer had done nothing to change the language; rather, those around them thought the language should change because of their presence.

As regards sexual harassment in the correctional workplace, the research indicates that women workers are more likely to be harassed by male coworkers or supervisors than are male workers to be similarly harassed by females (Stohr, Mays, Beck, & Kelley, 1998). However, when inmates are harassed by staff, the harassment is not merely restricted to female victims and male offenders, nor is it limited to just staff (Marquart, Barnhill, & Balshaw-Biddle, 2001). Recent research indicates that female officers are much more involved, particularly in the more minor and "consensual" versions of sexual harassment of male inmates, than are their male counterparts. In an example of a serious *boundary violation* in this regard, a female McNeil Island Prison (Washington State) nurse, hired in 2005, was fired in 2006 for allegedly having an intimate sexual relationship with a violent sex offender. Yet she continued to call him and have phone sex with him and visit

Journal Article 14.1: The Sexualized Work Environment: A Look at Women Jail Officers

him after her firing and that was not even the worst of her behavior vis-à-vis this inmate: "In 2007 and 2008, she reportedly smuggled in 50 pornographic movies to the inmate and delivered crack cocaine to him 11 times" (Glenn, 2010, p. A4).

AGE

Correctional agencies will also consider the age of the applicant when making a hiring decision. None will hire below age 18, and many will require that the applicant be at least 21. Correctional agencies do not typically have an upper age limit for hiring, as police departments legally do; rarely will police departments hire people in their 30s, unless they have prior experience, and almost never will departments make a first hire of an officer who is in his or her 40s or older. Most of the time, the initial hires in corrections are people in their 20s and 30s. Depending on the job specified and the correctional clients worked with, correctional work can be a physically taxing and stressful job, which is why agencies will tend to target younger workers. When the job has fewer physical requirements (e.g., counseling and treatment programming or work as a probation or parole officer), the agency is much more likely to hire a worker in his or her 40s and older. What correctional and police agencies may fail to realize, however, is that more mature workers are able to bring a level of human experience and wisdom that might compensate for what they lack in physical agility in the management of inmates and clients.

PRIOR MILITARY SERVICE

Another personal characteristic, beyond race or ethnicity and gender, of workers that tends to shape the correctional environment is prior military service. Such experience is usually considered favorably by correctional agencies seeking to hire. Some agencies will state such a preference explicitly, and others will provide extra points for military service when applications are assessed. Whether such military service better prepares workers to handle jobs in corrections is not a settled matter either, although the militaristic accoutrements of correctional work (i.e., the uniform, military titles, command structure, etc.) would certainly make ex–military officers feel at home in some correctional workplaces.

© Marmaduke St. John/Alamy Stock Photo

PHOTO 14.4: A correctional officer addressing inmates. Correctional staff are often called upon to lead inmates and to instruct them on how the organization works.

••• CORRECTIONAL ROLES

THE ROLE DEFINED

Another aspect of the work that affects staff is the correctional role. The **role** of those working in a correctional workplace—or any other—is determined by what that person does on the job every day. The role of staff in corrections is determined by their job description, their assigned duties, and the type of organization and clientele they work with. Therefore, correctional officers working in a living unit in a medium-security prison have a different role from that of probation officers working with lower-level offenders in the community. The first role involves constant supervision and interaction with inmates who live a very restricted lifestyle in a secure institution. The second role, that of probation officer, also involves supervision and interaction (though it is less intense, as they are likely to see their clients less than daily), but also formally includes assistance to those they supervise. Both the prison and the probation officers usually work with convicted felons, but the prison inmates are more likely to be repeat felons and are usually convicted of more serious offenses. Though the first role involves the maintenance of both safety and security, for the prison officer, that usually means safety and security for other staff and other inmates, whereas for the probation officer, it usually means he or she is concerned about community members the officer's clients interact with. Both are likely involved in facilitating programming, but the prison officer is most often watching inmates engaged in it or escorting them to it—though in some prisons, officers help deliver it—whereas the probation officer might recommend it or even run treatment groups. The prison officer might make recommendations regarding a person's placement in housing or work assignments in the secure facility, whereas a probation officer will monitor a probationer's engagement in them or counsel him or her about how to find them.

Both roles involve paperwork—loads of it—and both involve interactions with supervisors and accountability for what they do. For prison officers, they must adhere to the formal and informal rules that shape prison work, as those are provided by state law, policies and procedures, their administrators, and the subcultural values of coworkers and clients (Lipsky, 1980). For probation officers, they also must work within these formal and informal strictures, but in addition, they are often in constant contact with court actors, prosecutors, police officers, and jail workers, and these contacts, plus the clients on their caseload and their families, can shape the role they play on the job.

We clearly have overgeneralized in our comparison here of how a correctional-officer role in a medium-security prison and that of a probation officer role in the community might differ and be similar. In those states and institutions where treatment is emphasized, some correctional officers are very engaged in providing treatment, not just supervising an inmate's involvement in it, for instance. Moreover, the role of some probation officers, particularly those who have an intensive-supervision caseload with more serious offenders, may involve as much direct supervision as correctional staff provide in a prison. The point is that a role for staff is determined by many things, and it is defined by what people actually do in their work.

STREET-LEVEL BUREAUCRATS

A **street-level bureaucrat** (SLB) is what everyone who wants to work in a criminal justice agency starts out as. They are, according to Lipsky (1980), who first defined them, entry-level public-sector workers with too much work to do, too few resources to do it, and some discretion to choose how to do it. Police officers, public prosecutors and defenders, probation officers, and juvenile and adult correctional officers, along with teachers, social workers, and many other like jobs, are SLBs. They often have clients who are poor, uneducated, and relatively powerless who need public services. Though clients

Video 14.3: Correctional Officers on the Front Lines in Evidence-Based Programs

Career Video 14.1: Public Defender

Role: What a person does on the job every day.

Street-level bureaucrat: A public-sector worker with discretion who has too many clients with too many needs and not enough resources to meet those needs.

in the correctional environment are often involuntary, they still need the assistance of correctional staff in communities and institutions.

The reason we are mentioning SLBs here is that the concept encapsulates the struggles correctional staff face. Though they have discretion, they often have to make Solomonic choices because their resources (time, treatment programming, space, etc.) are limited, and yet, they have so many clients in need. Many of us would then argue that we should just increase the resources that correctional staff have, and consequently, there would be enough for all of the clients. Lipsky (1980), however, would argue that there will never be enough public-sector resources to meet all of the demand because other forces in the larger environment of corrections will obstruct this increase (e.g., taxation reduction groups). So demand will never be met by supply, and that puts the SLB in an untenable position, forced to choose whom to provide resources to and whose needs to ignore while they do it.

HACK VERSUS HUMAN SERVICE

Video 14.4: Driving Results With Staff Feedback

The public may be less inclined to support the increased **professionalization** of correctional staff when they think their role is limited to the use of brute force, a role termed a *guard* in old-style Big House prisons and defined as a **hack** by current scholars (Farkas, 1999, 2001; R. Johnson, 2002). If a correctional officer is viewed by the public as a hack, or as a violent, cynical, and alienated keeper of inmates in a no-hope warehouse prison, then there would appear to be little need to encourage education or provide the training and pay that would elevate such officers to professional status. Yet there is reason to believe that most officers in prisons, jails, juvenile facilities, and community corrections actually regularly engage in **human service**, which serves as an alternative, more developed, and more positive role for correctional workers (Lombardo, 2001; R. Johnson, 2002).

Robert Johnson (2002) defines human-service correctional officers as those who provide "goods and services," serve as "advocates" for inmates when appropriate, assist them with their "adjustment" to prison, and use "helping networks" of staff to facilitate that adjustment (pp. 242–259). Such goods and services might involve food and clothing or medication, and advocacy might include helping inmates find jobs or apply for different housing or roommates while adjustment assistance could include counseling them about how to handle difficult people or situations. Clearly, these kinds of activities are not necessarily in the job description of most officers who work in institutions, but they are often very much a part of what they do in reality and require that the officer be skilled and knowledgeable. When the public does not know about and the correctional organization does not recognize the alternate human-service work role performed by correctional or juvenile justice officers and probation and parole officers, then, again, there is no perceived need to provide the training and pay that would be commensurate with that more developed professional role.

Professionalization: Professionalization in corrections includes the enforcement of professional standards for their new hires, such as a required college-level educational background, sufficient training, pay that is commensurate with job requirements, training that sufficiently prepares people for the job, and a code of ethics that drives the work practice.

Hack: A correctional officer in a prison who is a violent, cynical, and alienated keeper of inmates.

Human service: A correctional officer who provides goods, services, advocacy, and assistance to help inmates adjust.

••• THE SUBCULTURE AND SOCIALIZATION

The staff subculture in corrections, much like the roles, varies by facility and by type of organization. A subculture might be defined as the norms, values, beliefs, history, traditions, and language held and practiced by a group of people. (As indicated in Chapter 13, a subculture is just a subset of a larger organizational culture.) In corrections, those aspects of a subculture are shaped by what kind of facility or organization you have, what kind of clientele you are dealing with, and how isolated the group of people is from the rest of the community. The more isolated and the more exclusive the interaction of the group, the more likely it is that the subculture's norms, values, and beliefs are distinct from the larger community.

Historically, staff literally lived on the prison grounds with the inmates, in prisons that were not open to the public or the media (Ward & Kassebaum, 2009). In such institutions, a distinct subculture was more likely to form than it is in today's prisons, jails, or community corrections entities, where staff come and go with shifts and where visitors, lawyers, and the media have much more access than they did in years past. However, though correctional organizations of today are less likely to have as strong a staff subculture as they did in years past, this is not to say that they do not have a subculture.

SUBCULTURAL VALUES

Subcultural values in the correctional setting are likely to have an effect on what staff do. Even today, correctional organizations and the people who work in them are somewhat cut off from the larger society by the nature of what they do and the need to keep some matters private for legal and security reasons. Moreover, staff in corrections have very intense experiences together, involving violence and strong emotions, experiences that are likely to bind staff together in an us-versus-them stance toward their clients and the larger society. It is for this reason that the role of staff in corrections is likely, for better or worse, to be influenced by the subcultural values of the group (e.g., see the discussion of subcultural values in Chapter 4).

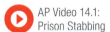

AP Video 14.1:
Prison Stabbing

Some subcultural values are positive in that they facilitate the ability of officers to do their work well (e.g., aiding your coworker and doing your own work). However, other subcultural values sound exactly like those expressed by inmates (e.g., "never rat" and the us-versus-them mentality) and serve to isolate the work and the workers, making them more likely to either participate in corrupt activities or to turn their heads when they witness these activities, and to reinforce negative attitudes toward clients and the work.

••• STAFF INTERACTIONS WITH INMATES

THE DEFECTS OF TOTAL POWER

Many of those subcultural values are shaped by the power relationships between staff and inmates. In a classic work by Gresham Sykes (1958), he describes the relationship between staff and inmates in a maximum-security prison. Sykes notes that staff at this prison or any prison need inmates to comply with orders, as it would be difficult, if not impossible, to force inmates to do "what they otherwise wouldn't" (the definition of power mentioned earlier; Dahl, 1961). Use of force to get inmates to comply with basic commands or orders would be inefficient, impossible, and counterproductive. For instance, if an inmate refused to make his bed or several inmates refused, it would be difficult for an officer to call in the emergency response team every time this happened, as it would mean that these team members would be pulled from their own duties. It would also make the officer in question, the one who could not get the inmate to do something as simple as make his or her bed, appear like he or she could not handle the supervision of inmates. Moreover, force is sometimes impossible to use, at least daily, as the inmates outnumber staff in living units by sometimes as much as 50 or 100 to 1. There are ways to lock down living units and use gas and other measures to suppress disruptions, but if this had to be done on a regular basis, the prison would be in a constant uproar. And if force were used regularly for such trivial matters as making a bed, it is likely that inmates would align themselves more in opposition to staff, thus making the use of force counterproductive and perhaps requiring the greater use of it.

It is for these reasons that Sykes (1958) found that staff *needed* inmate compliance in prisons as much as inmates needed staff assistance. However, gaining compliance from inmates is not always easy. Staff, according to Sykes, have relatively little that they can give to

ETHICAL ISSUE 14.1

What Would You Do?

As a district manager of a probation and parole district, you notice that several of your staff seem burned out and stressed by their work. There are many more sick calls and more turnover than is normal for this size of workplace. You have a bachelor's and master's degree in criminal justice, and you know some of the research around these issues. You convene a meeting and note that your staff are reluctant at first to tell you what is wrong but then start complaining about working conditions and about how they are treated, not by inmates but by management and other staff. What do you think would be the best approach to alleviate the stress and burnout by staff? Will this involve the need for you and other supervisors to give up some power in the workplace? What obstacles do you anticipate getting in the way of any change? Despite these obstacles, should you still do it?

inmates to motivate them. They can sometimes get inmates better work or housing assignments, but the amount of these rewards is limited and their power to garner rewards for inmates may be likewise so. Moreover, staff do not have the ability to reward inmate compliance with what inmates want most: their freedom. Therefore, according to Sykes, given these realities, staff and inmates tend to engage in a "corrupted" relationship, whereby inmates comply with staff orders as long as staff overlook some violations, usually minor ones, by inmates. Such a relationship is most likely to develop between staff and those inmates who have the most power to control and gain compliance from other inmates.

Of course, Sykes was only describing the dynamics of the staff–inmate relationship in a New Jersey maximum-security prison in the 1950s, and much has changed since then, even in the most secure prisons. However, the informal side of the relationship between staff and inmates or clients in corrections is still there, and the need for an exchange relationship between the two is still part of that dynamic. In another classic work on public-service workers generally, Michael Lipsky (1980) also recognized the fact that formally, staff control inmates, but informally, in prisons, schools, and social-welfare departments, clients, even ostensibly powerless ones, also exercise some power over staff. By not complying with orders, failing to review information, or complaining about the service they receive, clients—even inmate clients—are able to force staff to adjust their behavior.

THE CORRECTIONAL ROLE WHEN SUPERVISING CHILDREN

An example of the variability of the correctional role would be the form it takes when officers and counselors supervise children. Inderbitzin (2006) found, in a 15-month

PHOTO 14.5: Correctional officer working with youth in a Toledo, Ohio, detention center.

ethnographic study of staff members supervising a cottage of boys in a juvenile training facility (the juvenile version of a prison), that they "serve as their adolescent inmates' guardians, keepers, counselors, and role models" (p. 431). Noting that the work with these serious and sometimes violent juveniles could be "frustrating, dangerous, often amusing, and occasionally rewarding" (p. 439), she noted that officers and counselors needed to be flexible and energetic in order to best cope with a volatile mix of duties that each day would bring. The tactics used by staff to gain the boys' cooperation and to supervise them effectively ranged from the more punitive disciplinary actions all the way to reasoning with or cajoling them and using humor. Some staff members tended to emphasize certain tactics over others, and some staff members tended to vary their own

POLICY AND RESEARCH

Staff Stress, Burnout, and Turnover

Work in corrections can be taxing and troublesome. Most correctional work in institutions is shift work and, when first started, involves late nights, sometimes all-night shifts, and weekend and holiday work. Even parole and probation officers are often called upon to visit clients in the evenings or on weekends. Needless to say, late-night shifts and weekend work play havoc with family life and children's school schedules, making family obligations challenging to meet.

It does not help matters that the people correctional staff supervise are often angry and upset or immature (R. Johnson, 2002). They are usually unhappy about being supervised and sometimes unpleasant to those correctional staff engaged in supervision.

Relatedly, people who are incarcerated or supervised in the community have often led impoverished and tragic lives, riddled with alcoholism, drug abuse, child abuse and neglect, unemployment, early deaths of loved ones, and homelessness. Many have inflicted serious harm on others, including their victims but also family and community members, and the guilt and regret they shoulder only exacerbate the negativity that surrounds them. Collectively, these tragic lives weigh heavily on the people experiencing them and can create a negative environment for themselves and for those who work with them (R. Johnson, 2002).

Correctional staff immersed in this environment and required to get unwilling people to do things they are not inclined to do often experience stress and the related consequences of it: burnout and turnover (Lambert, Hogan, & Tucker, 2009; Leip & Stinchcomb, 2013; Slate & Vogel, 1997; Stohr, Lovrich, & Wilson, 1994; Tewksbury & Collins, 2006). In a meta-analysis of studies on stress in prisons, Dowden and Tellier (2004)

found that those who adopted a more human-service-work attitude experienced less stress on the job than those who had a more punitive (i.e., hack) and custody orientation. In a study of five jails by Stohr, Lovrich, Menke, and Zupan (1994), the authors found that those jails that invested in training and pay and who allowed staff to have a voice in how to do their work—all factors related to professionalism that we discussed earlier—were more likely to have greater job commitment by staff and less stress and turnover among them. Leip and Stinchcomb (2013) also discovered, in their analysis of data from a national survey of 1,924 line staff, that intention to turnover was reduced when the organizational climate was positive; relationships between colleagues and supervisors were strong when correctional staff felt they had a voice in how their workplace operated. Relatedly, in a study of a large county correctional system (nine facilities), Paoline, Lambert, and Hogan (2006) found that adherence to policies and standards (of the American Correctional Association, which emphasize professionalism, safety, and humanity in supervision) and positive and noncompetitive work relations with coworkers decreased the stress of workers. In their review of the literature on stress and burnout in correctional work, Finney, Stergiopoulos, Hensel, Bonato, and Dewa (2013) found that the organizational structure and climate had the greatest effect on stress and burnout in corrections.

DISCUSSION QUESTIONS

1. Why would the organizational structure and climate have an effect on stress and burnout?

2. Why would having a voice in how your job is done reduce stress?

3. How can correctional managers reduce stress for staff?

PERSPECTIVE FROM A PRACTITIONER

Michael Klein, Correctional Officer

It was a curious bit of the informal slang that makes up the diction of prison life. I first heard it when I was a new officer. I think that I had been out of training for maybe one or two weeks at the time, and I was working a cell house. It was time for nightly cell searches. I walked into my ordered cell, and I started to search. Contraband. Nothing major. The offenders in the cell had eight hardboiled eggs. It doesn't seem like a big deal to have eight hardboiled eggs, but that amount of hardboiled eggs could only have been smuggled out of the dining hall. I gathered up my booty and exited the cell. To be honest, I wasn't going to write the offenders up. I was just going to trash the eggs. So there I was, walking through the dayroom and holding my inconsequential find. All eyes were on me. One hundred offenders stared. I didn't really think much of it. I was new. I was used to offenders staring at me and sizing me up. An offender that we called "Shady" moseyed up to my work station where I had just set the eggs.

"You're taking their food?" he asked.

I shrugged. "I guess."

"Why?"

"Because they're not supposed to have it."

Shady sighed.

"They don't have any money. They don't get any other zoom-zooms or wham-whams."

"What's that mean?" I asked.

"You know. Cakes. Commissary. Treats. Food. They don't get no other food. Don't take their eggs, man."

I then looked around the room. The offenders were staring at me in their curious way of looking while not looking.

It was my turn to sigh. "OK."

Shady smiled, picked up the eggs, and walked them back to the cell. I could feel a ripple of approval flowing through the room. In training, they would tell us that the offenders would try to "fish" or scam us. I don't think that's what happened. I don't think they were trying to scam me. I think that the offenders approved of me giving back the eggs because Shady was right. The offenders in that cell had no family or friends. They had no one to send them money for zoom-zooms and wham-whams. The offenders approved because I had treated the offenders like *people*, not inmates. It was the first time I realized that the offenders in the prison weren't animals or monsters. They were just people. They just wanted a cake, a cookie, or an egg. They just wanted that one moment of daily sweetness. We all need zoom-zooms and wham-whams. There are a lot of epiphanies when you work with offenders, and these sudden moments of realization come out of nowhere. Training may not prepare you, but I found that if you just realize that the offenders are people caught in a bad situation, it will make the job a whole lot easier.

behavior as the situation required. Inderbitzin (2006) concluded that the staff who were most successful in their work, in that they were able to effectively supervise their charges, were those who took on a "people worker" (p. 442) role, or the human-service role that was described earlier in this chapter (Farkas, 2000). Such staff members were also the most flexible, kind, creative, and respectful in their work with the adolescents.

AP Video 14.2: Manhunt

Audio 14.2: New York Corrections Officers Convicted in Inmate Assault

ABUSE OF POWER

There are plenty of instances, both historically and currently, of correctional staff abusing their power over inmates and clients. We discuss such instances in some depth in several chapters in this book. It is important to mention here, however, that the abuse of power is more likely to occur in environments where staff behavior is not supervised closely enough by administrators or those outside the work environment, where inmates have little or no ability to contact the outside, where staff are not sufficiently trained, where there is a higher concentration of young and inexperienced staff, and where there is a higher concentration of disruptive inmates (Antonio, Young, & Wingeard, 2009; Rideau, 2010; Stohr & Collins, 2009).

USE OF FORCE

The actual use of force—or being prepared to use such force—is part of correctional work. Correctional administrators interested in channeling its use in appropriate and legal ways ensure that staff are trained on when to escalate or de-escalate its use based on the situation (Hemmens & Atherton, 1999). In such training, the officer is taught to pay attention to cues that will tell him or her when to increase the force level and when not to do so.

Having said this, the use of force in any correctional environment depends on the type of institution or agency, the clients or inmates served, and the way they are managed. Generally speaking, there is less call for force in probation and parole work with adults or juveniles, though when engaged in arrests, it is not uncommon for community corrections officers to have to use force. Minimum-security prisons for adults or juveniles generally have less cause for use of force; inmates in such institutions are classified as less prone to violence and/ or are on their way out of the system and so are more likely to rein in any violent inclinations. As one proceeds up the correctional-security ladder, from minimum to medium and then to maximum, the need to use force increases, given the types of inmates incarcerated and the need to maintain stricter controls. It should also be mentioned, however, that in some prisons, under some wardens, the use of force is resorted to more frequently than under other wardens of similar prisons (Rideau, 2010). As Rideau observes after his 44-year incarceration in the Angola prison in Louisiana and observing the management style of many wardens (see the description of Rideau's experience in

ETHICAL ISSUE 14.2

What Would You Do?

As an experienced counselor in a private, nonprofit juvenile halfway house, you notice that a few of the staff (whom you are buddies with) tend to denigrate some of the kids at the facility by calling them names (e.g., "little criminals" and worse), using profanity in reference to them, and even writing them up for minor issues when they try to object. You notice that a few of these kids seem depressed and lethargic lately, and you wonder if it could have anything to do with how they are treated at the home. You don't think the supervisor of the house (who also supervises other houses around the state) is aware of what is going on. You need this job and don't want to alienate your friends, but you don't want to continue to work at a place where kids are abused. What do you think would be the best course of action in such a situation? What do you think would be the likely consequences of your action or inaction?

AP Photo/Trent Nelson

PHOTO 14.6: A demonstration of the use of force in a jail by the emergency response team in Montgomery County, Pennsylvania. Such teams are often called upon to subdue violent or disruptive inmates.

Video 14.5: Alarming Number of Corrections Officers Driven to Suicide

Chapter 9), those wardens who allow more openness between staff and inmates and the outside and who have more transparency about their management decisions are less likely to experience the need for the use of force in their facility. The more ready resort to force may be spurred by the type of inmates held (e.g., more violent) or the conditions of the facility (e.g., more crowded), but it could also just be a management tactic adopted by some wardens, as Rideau and others have argued (e.g., see Reisig, 1998).

SUMMARY

- The correctional experience for staff is fraught with challenges and much promise. It involves a diverse role that encompasses work with juvenile and adult inmates in institutions, as well as with offenders in the community. It is not as narrow a role, as is commonly perceived by the public, and it includes many opportunities to effectuate a just incarceration or community supervision experience for inmates and clients.

- Though many have worked long and hard to professionalize correctional work, there is every indication that most jobs in this area do not meet standard professional criteria.

- When correctional workers do not receive the requisite professional training and education they need to do their job in an appropriate manner, both clients and the community are likely to suffer.

- Many who labor in corrections undertake the *human-service role*, focusing on the provision of goods and services; advocating for inmates, offenders, or clients; and assisting in their adjustment (R. Johnson, 2002).

- The research presented here and in Chapter 13 would indicate there are organizational factors that can be manipulated to improve this experience for staff so that they and their organization can realize their promise. Also, better pay, benefits, and training can be used to foster the greater development of professional attributes, such as education, and the consequent reduction in role ambiguity, turnover, and stress and increase in job satisfaction. The organizational culture can also be assessed to determine if certain characteristics are making it a more or less positive work environment for staff and a safe, secure, and developmental one for inmates.

- This research also indicates that the organization can do much to reduce the problems associated with the greater diversification of its staff. It can be open in its promotion practices so that false impressions regarding unfair advantage are not perpetuated and do not have a demoralizing effect on the workforce. It is also within the correctional organization's power to prevent most sexual harassment, whether practiced by staff or inmates. In short, the promise of a positive correctional experience for staff is achievable, and as that perception seeps into the public consciousness, a correctional officer is much more likely to be perceived as a professional.

KEY TERMS

Abu Ghraib 342

Hack 350

Human service 350

Power 342

Profession 336

Professionalization 350

Role 349

Stanford Prison Experiment 342

Street-level bureaucrat 349

DISCUSSION QUESTIONS

1. Explain why work in corrections is often not regarded as *professional* in comparison to other commonly referenced professions.

2. Note which jobs in corrections are most sought after and why. Discuss how all correctional work might become more appealing to educated workers.

3. Review the events surrounding the Stanford Prison Experiment. If you were going to conduct such an experiment now, how would you go about it? What questions would you like to address with the experiment?

4. Explain and discuss the "hack" versus the human-service role for staff. Which role do you think the public typically ascribes to correctional staff? Which role do you think is most commonly undertaken by staff?

5. Explain how the correctional organization can provide the right environment to reduce stress, turnover, and harassment of its staff.

6. Why is ethical behavior such a challenge in correctional work?

7. Consider the benefits and drawbacks of working in corrections. Do you plan on working in corrections? Why, or why not?

USEFUL INTERNET SITES

Please note that the sites listed can be accessed at edge.sagepub.com/stohrcorrections.

American Correctional Association: www.aca.org

The ACA is an organization that has, for 146 years, focused on professionalizing corrections in the United States. Their website and materials provide information on the latest training, research, and ideas in corrections.

American Jail Association: www.corrections.com/aja

The AJA is an organization that also focuses on professionalization in corrections but as it involves jails. Their website provides information about the latest training, trends, and research in jails.

American Probation and Parole Association: www.appa-net.org

The APPA is an organization that focuses on the professionalization of probation and parole or community corrections. From their website, you can learn about the best research and training and the newest ideas about practices in community corrections.

Bureau of Labor Statistics: www.bls.gov/ooh/Community-and-Social-Service/Probation-officers-and-correctional-treatment-specialists.htm

This government bureau provides information on employment, unemployment, and earnings in all sectors of the U.S. economy.

Vera Institute: www.vera.org

The Vera Institute has been behind some of the biggest criminal justice reforms of the last 40 years. Check out their website to learn what important reforms and issues are on the correctional horizon.

$SAGE edge™

Sharpen your skills with SAGE edge at **edge.sagepub.com/stohrcorrections**. SAGE edge for Students provides a personalized approach to help you accomplish your coursework goals in an easy-to-use learning environment. You'll find action plans, mobile-friendly eFlashcards, and quizzes as well as video, web, and resources and links to SAGE journal articles to support and expand on the concepts presented in this chapter.

TEST YOUR KNOWLEDGE

Test your present knowledge about women working in corrections and those under correctional supervision by answering the following questions as true or false. Check your answers on page 538 after reading the chapter.

1. The number of men and boys under correctional supervision almost always has exceeded the number of women and girls.

2. In early prisons, the correctional experience for women did not significantly differ from that of men.

3. Race shaped the incarceration of men and women in southern and northeastern prisons before and after the Civil War.

4. Female matrons were first hired, in part, to protect female inmates from sexual assault in prisons.

5. Street crimes are usually committed by women and girls and less commonly by men and boys.

6. Women are often considered *double deviants*.

7. Feminists have played an important role in improving corrections for women and girls.

8. A liberal feminist is someone who believes that women and girls should have the same jobs and educational opportunities as men and boys.

9. Male inmates' right to privacy has triumphed against women's equal employment rights in the courts.

CHAPTER OBJECTIVES

- Summarize the history of women in corrections

- Identify how the experience of female correctional clients differs from that of males

- Describe the special challenges faced by women and girls in corrections

- Discuss the challenges that female staff have overcome in corrections and how they did so

SUPERVISING IS DIFFERENT **FOR WOMEN**

Mary K. Stohr

This is a story I often tell my students because it was an instance where merely my gender made such a difference in others' aggressive behavior in the correctional environment. The scene is a male-prison control room. The sergeant is a very capable man who believes in the power of talking, as in "talking inmates down" from anger and aggression rather than using brute force. An inmate has been called to the office for the purpose of throwing him in segregation for suspicion that he has been "bull dogging" (I reported him for taking other inmates' desserts at dinner [actually, the other inmates gave him their desserts when he came up to stand by their tables]), and the sergeant admits him to the control room with two other male officers present,

in case there is trouble. And there is trouble. This inmate, we'll call him "Casey," is huge—as large as a door, with muscles bulging in his arms. Despite his size, he is not known to be the smartest of men and is prone to anger. The sergeant is wielding all of his verbal skills to reason with Casey, to no avail. Once the inmate refuses to enter segregation willingly and his fists are balling against his sides as he backs away from the sergeant and up against a wall, the sergeant begins calling in reinforcements.

A male counselor and I are in the backroom watching this through a glass window. (The sergeant wanted me out of the way in case the inmate directed his anger at me.) When we can see, however, that things are getting out of hand and knowing that the prison is understaffed, I move into the control room and face Casey. I don't say a word, but my plan is to grab and hold one of his limbs as we jointly wrestle him into segregation. But this plan doesn't become necessary, as Casey takes one look at me, unclenches his fists, and puts his hands out in front of him for the handcuffs. He goes peacefully to segregation. I am stunned, the sergeant is shocked, and the male correctional officers are staring at me as if I had some magic mojo, when all I had was the fact that I was female. I don't know why, but I believe that Casey didn't want to fight with or in front of a female, and for that, we were all very grateful!

••• INTRODUCTION

As far back as anyone can remember, there have been fewer women and girls incarcerated or under correctional supervision than there have been men or boys. Of course, there have been exceptions for some crimes (e.g., prostitution for adult and juvenile females or status offending for girls), but correctional populations have always included more males. Though the percentage of women and girls in those populations has increased in recent years, it is still true that the vast majority of those under correctional supervision in the United States are male.

What this numerical "minority" status for girls and women has meant is that institutions and programming are and have been typically geared toward boys and men. As discussed in Chapter 2, the first prisons were built for men, though sometimes a section of them was set aside for women. The U.S. history of institution building illustrates this fact. What Young (1994) found from her research on the construction of juvenile facilities in the southern portion of the United States following the Civil War was that males, particularly white males, were much more likely to have juvenile prisons constructed specifically for them than were females. Women and girls accused (in the case of jails) or sentenced (in the case of jails or prisons) were much more likely to "do their time" in male facilities, initially as part of those facilities (e.g., in bridewells and other poorhouses) and later in separate sections of jails and prisons or completely distinct facilities and houses of refuge (Baunach, 1992; Belknap, 2001; Chesney-Lind & Shelden, 1998; Kerle, 2003; Pollock, 2002b, 2014; Rafter, 1985).

Part of what shaped the treatment of women and girls in the past was the numerical fact that they constituted fewer offenders and inmates than men and boys. As those numbers have increased, however, and as feminist beliefs regarding the value of women and girls have changed attitudes, concerns about how females are treated as clients and what their needs are and about female staff and their rights have reshaped correctional practice. In this chapter, we will explore all of these issues, but we will begin with a brief history of the female correctional experience.

••• HISTORY AND GROWTH

THE HISTORY OF WOMEN IN PRISONS

As mentioned in Chapter 2, the first American correctional facility—though it is not generally acknowledged as the first American prison—to hold felons only was Newgate Prison in Greenwich Village, New York City. Opened in 1797, it had a separate wing for women inmates, where they were housed in a group setting. As Rafter (2009) notes, putting the women together, though they had no matron, helped provide protection from "lascivious turnkeys" or guards (p. 51). All indications are that the women at Newgate washed and sewed for the prison (while the male inmates were engaged in the production of goods for sale) and were situated close to other inmates.

When Newgate Prison closed, and the inmates were scheduled for transfer to the congregate but silent and strict-discipline prisons of Auburn and Sing Sing, neither prison wanted to take the women, stating that they were difficult to manage (Rafter, 2009). While the matter was debated, the female inmates from New York City were held at the city's Bellevue Penitentiary, where the conditions in terms of food, housing, supervision, and classification were poor. Moreover, the silent requirement, so popular at the men's prisons, could not be enforced because of the congregate housing and the lack of a female matron. When a cholera epidemic hit the prison, 8 women died, and 11 escaped (Rafter, 2009).

The New York women outside of New York City were sent to the new Auburn Prison in 1825 (Rafter, 2009). However, their treatment there was also subpar, as they were housed in a cramped, unventilated attic above the kitchen, without a matron until one was hired in 1832. Because of the congregate nature of their living and working conditions (they were engaged in sewing), it was once again difficult to enforce the silence requirement.

After discipline by the lash was used on a five-months-pregnant inmate (who got pregnant while in prison) who later died, the state constructed a separate prison at Mount Pleasant for the women in 1839, the first women's prison in the United States (Rafter, 2009).

PHOTO 15.1: A prison officer examines the knitting of an inmate.

Though it was close to Sing Sing prison and was, in part, administered by it, **Mount Pleasant Prison** had its own buildings, staff, and administrator. This prison was built behind Sing Sing and overlooked the Hudson River. It was an Auburn-like building with Auburn- and Sing Sing–like sensibilities. It had a room for lectures, a chapel, and a nursery. The matron's quarters were also in the prison.

Mount Pleasant Prison: The first separate women's prison constructed in the United States (1839). It was ultimately overseen by Sing Sing but had its own buildings, staff, and administrator. Ohio's development of prison facilities for women was similar to New York's (Rafter, 2009). At first, they were held in less secure facilities, along with the men. Then, in 1834, Ohio built an Auburn-like prison called the Ohio Penitentiary, and in 1837, the state housed the women in a separate annex from the men. However, the standards for prison operation in Ohio were even worse than in New York, and disease and corruption were rampant. The annex for the women became crowded and fell into serious disrepair. The women had no matron, and thus, discipline was nonexistent; moreover, they were subject to sexual attack by male staff.

Among Tennessee prisons, when the first opened in Nashville in 1831, there was a progressive attitude toward standards and care, more like the New York model (Rafter, 2009). Women, however, were imprisoned in such small numbers before the Civil War that they were housed right with the men and worked with them in mines and on railroads. There were no matrons to protect them, and there were no separate accommodations for women in Tennessee prisons until the 1880s, and then, they were placed in small, overcrowded quarters in the Nashville prison, with no room for work or exercise.

Mount Pleasant Prison: The first prison constructed for women in the United States. Built in 1839 close to the Sing Sing (New York) prison for men, it was, in part, administered by it but had its own buildings, staff, and administrator.

RACE IN EARLY PRISONS

Maryland opened its first prison, the Maryland State Penitentiary, in 1811 in Baltimore (Young, 2001). From its inception, it housed the women in a congregate fashion, in the same prison with the men, until 1921, although they were separated. At first, the races were not separated, but by the 1830s, black men and white men were separated at the prison, and later, so were the women. As Maryland was a *border state*—a slave state, though one caught between the slaveholding South and the free North before the Civil War—administrators of its penitentiary wrestled with issues of slavery and free and enslaved blacks. The research on incarcerated black women indicates that they were disproportionately incarcerated in the Northeast and Midwest before the Civil War but that there were few blacks, male or female, incarcerated in the South before the war. After the war, however, black men and women were also disproportionately incarcerated in all prisons but particularly in southern prisons, where slavery-like treatment and work requirements were imposed (Oshinsky, 1996; Rafter, 2009; Young, 2001).

In her study of the Maryland State Penitentiary between the years 1812 and 1869, Young (2001) found that 72% of the incarcerated females were black and that as the Civil War drew to a close, the proportion of black women only increased. This was also true regarding the incarceration of black women around the Civil War, especially during the antebellum stage, in Texas, Kansas, and Missouri. It is possible that a Maryland law, passed in 1858, that made black women who committed larceny subject to "sale" rather than prison resulted in less incarceration of black women before the Civil War in that state (Young, 2001).

Both black and white women in the United States of the 19th century tended to be incarcerated for property crimes, particularly larceny (Rafter, 2009; Young, 2001). Very few women were incarcerated for violent crimes, about 3% to 4% (Young, 2001). White women did tend to be incarcerated for "offenses against morality" more than black women were, perhaps because they were more "visible" to the police in white areas of town or because the police were more attentive to them (Young, 2001). But there were also convictions for other felonies, miscellaneous offenses, and vagrancy. Young (2001) also found that black female inmates were required to serve a greater proportion of their sentence than were white female inmates, and they tended to be pardoned less and die more often while incarcerated than white female inmates.

DISCIPLINE IN WOMEN'S PRISONS

As with male prisons during the 1800s, methods of discipline moved from the severe to the soft depending on the availability of supervision, the facilities, the number of women incarcerated, and the inclinations of the keepers. Rafter (2009) reports that rarely was the lash used at Mount Pleasant Prison for women, but the gag was used all of the time. At the Ohio prison, for instance, by the 1870s, the discipline of women was quite severe, and women were beaten or placed in solitary confinement to enforce it (Rafter, 2009). By 1880, the "hummingbird" punishment was used in Ohio; it "forced the naked offender to sit, blind-folded, in a tub of water while steam pipes were made to shriek and electric current was applied to the body" (Rafter, 2009, p. 53).

HIRING OF FEMALE MATRONS

A serious problem for many of the first prisons was the absence of a female matron to supervise and, in some cases, protect the women. Writing in 1845 (reprinted in 1967), after visiting several primarily male facilities that housed women, the reformer Dorothea Dix noted that matrons had been hired in several prisons where women were housed (e.g., Connecticut Prison, Sing Sing, Eastern Penitentiary, and Maryland Prison) but not in many county jails or other prisons.

HOUSES OF REFUGE FOR GIRLS AND BOYS

Developed in tandem with the adult prisons were juvenile facilities in larger states for delinquent, neglected, abandoned, and abused children. **Houses of refuge** were part of the Jacksonian movement (named after President Andrew Jackson) of the early 1800s to use institutions as the solution for social problems. The first was opened in New York in 1825, the second in Boston in 1826, and the third in Philadelphia in 1828 (Beaumont & Tocqueville, 1833/1964, p. 136). Their stated purpose was to remove impressionable youth, mainly boys but also girls, from the contamination that association with more hardened adult prisoners might bring. As Harris (1973) comments, such facilities for younger inmates had existed in Europe, particularly Holland, since the 17th century. The difference she notes between the American experiment with houses of refuge and the Dutch experiment was that the Dutch houses were used only for the delinquent and those thought likely to become so without intervention, and they were devised to achieve reform among their inmates.

From the first, the American house of refuge was a private institution. Such institutions were developed through private charity and subscription and operated by people hired by private subscribers. The states sanctioned their development this way and paid "some pecuniary assistance" to them, but they had no part in their administration (Beaumont & Tocqueville, 1833/1964, p. 137).

The early American houses of refuge were to be a mix of prison and school. The keepers in such houses were guardians, and such guardianship continued until the children reached the age of 20. In some of the houses, the children were separated at night and worked or went to school together during the day. In others, they were in congregate situations both at night and during the day. The requirement of silence, imposed on adult institutions of the time, was not visited on the children, as it was thought to be impossible to keep them completely quiet. In the New York and Philadelphia houses, the children labored in a workshop making shoes or cloth and as carpenters for 8 hours a day and spent another 4 hours in school. In the Boston house, they spent only 5.5 hours in the workshop, 4 hours in school, and 1 hour in religious study, and there were a few hours for play (Beaumont & Tocqueville, 1833/1964, p. 142). The workshops in the houses were operated by private contractors. Notably, the girls did all of the domestic work around the houses, including the cleaning, cooking, and sewing of clothes for themselves and the boys. The discipline used in the houses varied from deprivation of recreation, to solitary confinement, to restrictions on food and water, and sometimes to the use of corporal punishment or the use of stripes (lashes with a leather belt).

Since the children placed in houses of refuge were not always sent there for punishment, it was thought that their time had to be indeterminate, as a magistrate could not tell at the beginning how long it would take to reform or correct the children. It was left to those who operated the institutions to decide when a child was ready to leave them. Moreover, if he or she did not do as well as was hoped when released and if under age 20, the staff at the institution were still his or her guardians and had the right to call the child back into the house. Beaumont and Tocqueville (1833/1964) acknowledged that these absolute rights to deprive liberty might have led to abuse, but they pointed out that judges and parents did have some rights to oversee and protest the incarceration of these children in the courts.

In a recidivism study of the New York House of Refuge conducted by Beaumont and Tocqueville in 1831 (1833/1964), the authors found that of over 500 children released, more than 200 of the boys and girls had been "saved from infallible ruin" (p. 151). As to the other 313 children released, they found that their behavior since release was either doubtful, "bad," or "very bad" (p. 151). Of course, lacking a control group for these

Houses of refuge: Their stated purpose was to remove impressionable youth, mainly boys but also girls, from the contamination that association with more hardened adult prisoners might bring.

releasees, it is difficult to know how to interpret these findings, but it was an admirable attempt by these French observers to try to find evidence as to the effectiveness of such early houses of refuge.

Dorothea Dix (1845/1967—whose own research is described more fully in Chapter 3) also visited houses of refuge in Boston, New York, Philadelphia, and Baltimore and a farm school for children on Long Island. Her impression of these facilities, 14 years after Beaumont and Tocqueville visited some of them, was generally favorable. She liked that the children were employed in useful work, that the facilities were clean, and that the children were generally in good health. She noted that many houses of refuge provided schooling, training, and apprenticeships that would allow the children to succeed once they were able to leave. Some of the reports from the facilities that she reviewed indicated that children as young as 6 were incarcerated in these houses and that possible offenses that led to placement were being "stubborn" or "idle," along with other, more common but usually minor criminal offending (Dix, 1945/1967, p. 91). Boys were often apprenticed to farmers and girls to domestic work once they reached their age of majority and so were able to leave the institution.

GROWTH IN NUMBERS OF WOMEN AND GIRLS

Audio 15.1: Number of Incarcerated Women on Rise

As mentioned in the foregoing, the number of incarcerated and supervised women under the correctional umbrella has never been larger, but it was not always so. In the past, the number of women inmates and supervisees was proportionately smaller. For instance, we know from U.S. Census reports that women constituted 3% or 4% of state and federal prison populations from 1910 through the 1970s (Cahalan, 1986, p. 65). In 1980, that proportion had risen to 5% and has only increased since. If you add in reformatories, women and girls accounted for, on average, about 5% of those incarcerated in correctional facilities from 1910 through 1959 (p. 66). Jail inmates were anywhere from 5% to 9% female from 1910 to 1983 (p. 91). Juvenile institutions averaged about 21.2% female residents (aged 15–19) from 1880 to 1980 (p. 130). Unfortunately, a gender breakdown of parolees and probationers is not available, but given the overall increase in the percentage of incarcerated women generally and women and girls on probation or parole currently, it is likely that historically, they were not as subject to the criminal justice system as they are today either.

© Marmaduke St. John/Alamy Stock Photo

PHOTO 15.2: A female correctional officer searches a male inmate. Most correctional facilities try to perform same-sex searches, but that is not always possible.

The best explanation for the historically low number of female offenders in the U.S. criminal justice system (as compared with males) has been the fact that they commit fewer street crimes that would garner this distinction. Most murders, robberies, rapes, burglaries, and even larcenies are committed by men and boys (Federal Bureau of Investigation [FBI], 2014). Even among corporate, or white-collar, and environmental crimes, the more likely offender is male, if for no other reason than the fact that more males are in a position to commit such crimes than females. As mentioned in other chapters, the drug war of the last 30 years has brought more female offenders into the system, and this fact has resulted in their greater proportional growth among correctional populations, but even with this sort of offense, they are in the clear minority.

••• WOMEN AND GIRLS IN CORRECTIONS TODAY

FEMALE CORRECTIONAL CLIENTS

More recently and by any measure, however, the number of women and girls as inmates or supervisees in corrections has grown exponentially over the last several years (see Figure 15.1).

In 2000, women composed 11.4% of jail populations, but by 2014, that figure was almost 15% (Minton & Golinelli, 2014; Minton & Zeng, 2015, p. 2). In 2000, women composed 6.4% of prison populations, and by 2014, that figure was over 7% (Carson & Golinelli, 2013, p. 23; Carson, 2015, p. 2). Girls confined in residential facilities increased from 13.6% of all juveniles in 1997 to 15.1% in 2003, though by 2010, they accounted for 13% again (Hockenberry, 2013, p. 11). But the largest growth, as far as correctional populations are concerned, has come in probation. Women constituted 22% of probation and 12% of parole caseloads in 2000, and by 2013, that percentage had increased to 25% for probation, though for parole, it had stabilized at 12% by 2013 (Herberman & Bonczar, 2015, pp. 17, 20). Though some of these percentage increases seem small (along with a few decreases), they represent increases, in the case of probation, of thousands of women on probation, as total caseloads in 2006 included 5 million people. For girls on probation, the increases do not even seem small. In 1985, girls constituted 19.3% of juveniles on probation, and by 2004, that percentage had grown to 27.2% and remained at 27% by 2009 (Livsey, 2012, p. 2; Puzzanchera & Kang, 2007). As indicated by the data contained in Figure 15.1, the overall number of adult females under correctional control remained steady from 2010 to 2014; the only exception has been the relatively large increase in women in local jails (an increase of 18.1%). Despite this increase, the majority of inmates for all correctional populations are still largely male, as shown in Figure 15.2.

Audio 15.2:
Female Prison Inmates Trained to Start Businesses

Web 15.1:
National Resource Center on Justice Involved Women

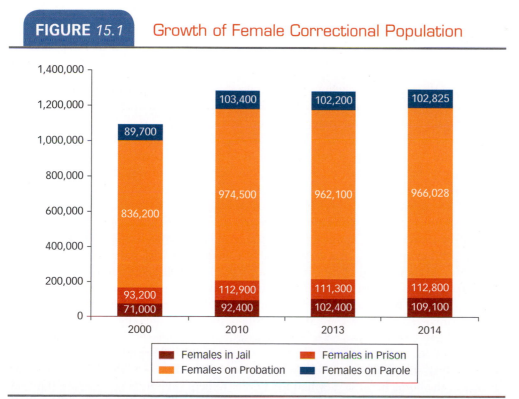

FIGURE *15.1*   Growth of Female Correctional Population

Legend: Females in Jail; Females in Prison; Females on Probation; Females on Parole

Data points:
- 2000: Parole 89,700; Probation 836,200; Prison 93,200; Jail 71,000
- 2010: Parole 103,400; Probation 974,500; Prison 112,900; Jail 92,400
- 2013: Parole 102,200; Probation 962,100; Prison 111,300; Jail 102,400
- 2014: Parole 102,825; Probation 966,028; Prison 112,800; Jail 109,100

Source: Beck and Harrison (2001); Bureau of Justice Statistics (2001); Carson (2014, 2015); Glaze and Bonczar (2011); Glaze and Kaeble (2014); Guerino, Harrison, and Sabol (2012); Herberman and Bonczar (2015); Kaeble, Glaze, Tsoutis, and Minton (2016); Kaeble, Maruschak, and Bonczar (2015).

FIGURE 15.2   Percentage of Male Versus Female Inmates, 2014

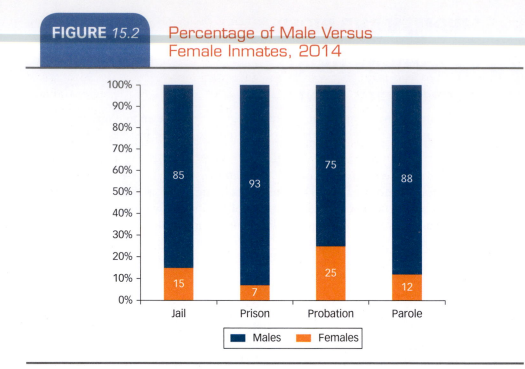

Source: Carson (2015); Kaeble, Maruschak, and Bonczar (2015); Minton and Zeng (2015).

FEMINISM

AP Video 15.1:
Female Inmates

Web 15.2:
Women's Prison
Association

Liberal feminist:
One who believes that the problem for girls and women involved in crime lies more with the social structure around them and that the solution lies in preparing them for an alternate existence so that they do not turn to crime.

Double deviants:
Women and girls are often seen as doubly deviant when they engage in crime because they have violated societal gender role expectations, and they have committed a crime.

Women staff would not be employed at the level they are, and female inmates would not have the attention and programming they do, albeit usually less than men and boys, if not for the sustained efforts of feminist scholars and practitioners agitating for their rights and their needs (Pollock, 2002b, 2014; Rafter, 1985; Smykla & Williams, 1996; Stohr, 2006; Young, 1994; Zimmer, 1986, 1989; Zupan, 1992). As indicated by Rafter (1985), the proponents of change in female corrections in the last half of the 1800s and first half of the 1900s tended to be of two minds, as represented by the moralists and the **liberal feminists.**

There were those *moralists,* who were sometimes *social feminists,* as Rafter terms them, who believed that women and girls involved in the criminal justice system were, in effect, morally impaired and therefore in need of religious and social remedies (prayers, efforts to keep them chaste, etc.). Women were crudely classified by these moralists as either "good," thus acting in conformance with societal expectations for their gender role (labeled the *madonna*), or as "bad," thus acting in opposition to their expected gender role (labeled the *whore*). This conceptualization and limited view of the possibilities for women and girls and its focus on sexuality were also shaped by social class and race/ethnicity. Those women who were of a higher class and who were white were believed to more closely approximate the madonna category, until, that is, they violated societal expectations that they be docile homemakers with nary a thought in their heads. Should they violate these expectations regarding their gender role and social and legal prohibitions against the commitment of crime, then they were **double deviants.** (Rather than just being deviants, as men and boys who committed crime were, women and girls involved in crime were also deviants in terms of societal gender role expectations [Belknap, 2001].) Women of lower classes, but particularly women of color, were not expected to attain this madonna status. Women in the lower and even in the working classes, which described most women in the late 1800s and early 1900s, often worked outside of the home because they had to in order to help support their families; thus, the belief—really a myth—that most women used to work only in the home applied only to the middle-class and wealthier women, not to the majority of women. Women of color, disproportionately represented in the lower classes, then and now, were seen as more sexual in nature, perhaps as a justification for their exploitation in this manner, and so could not even aspire to madonna status (Belknap, 2001).

There were others, those who espoused a *liberal feminist* perspective, who believed that the source of the crime problem for female offenders lay more with the social structure around these women and girls (e.g., poverty and lack of sufficient schooling or training, along with patriarchal beliefs) (Daly & Chesney-Lind, 1988). Liberal feminists believed the solution to female crime lay in preparing those inclined to engage in it for an alternate existence—for work—and sometimes, this involved "traditional women's work" so that they would not turn to crime (Rafter, 1985). Some of these early feminists believed, as liberal feminists do today, that men and women are inherently equal, and as such, women and girls are entitled to the same rights, liberties, and considerations (e.g., in corrections, this would be programming, quality of institutions, and equal employment as staff) as men and boys (Belknap, 2001; Daly & Chesney-Lind, 1988).

The moralists triumphed, though not completely, in the argument over what lay at the heart of female criminality. As a consequence, we have had over a century of correctional operation that has tended to be overly concerned with the sexuality of females (Giallombardo, 1966; Hefferman, 1972; Owen, 1998; Rafter, 1985). Another consequence of this triumph was that reform efforts were directed at training female inmates to be proper wives and mothers while forgetting that as members of the lower classes, they would need to make a living for themselves and their children once they reentered their communities. Despite this morals-of-the-fallen-woman focus—the "soiled dove," if you will—feminist women and men were able to agitate for and sometimes get separate facilities for women and girls, as well as other services (e.g., educational and job training) that were geared toward helping women and girls become independent and self-supporting in the free world (Hawkes, 1998; H. Yates, 2002).

One societal obstacle to achieving equal treatment in corrections has been **patriarchy**. Patriarchy involves the attitudes, beliefs, and behaviors that value men and boys over women and girls (Daly & Chesney-Lind, 1988). Members of patriarchal societies tend to believe that men and boys are worth more than women and girls. They also believe that women and girls, as well as men and boys, should have certain restricted roles to play and that those of the former are less important than those of the latter. Therefore, education and work training that help one make a living and attain better pay are more important to secure for men and boys than for women and girls, who are best suited for more feminine—and by definition, in a patriarchal society, less worthy—professions. Feminist scholars have determined that many cultures, even today, hold such beliefs and engage in the practices that derive from them.

In the United States, much effort has been expended over the centuries, by male and female feminists, to address the patriarchal belief system, and there has been some success in this regard (Dworkin, 1993; S. Martin & Jurik, 1996; Morash, 2006; Whittick, 1979). In terms of corrections, feminists have been instrumental in pushing for more and better programming for incarcerated and supervised women and girls, for a reduction in the incarceration of girls for status offenses, for attention to the sexual abuse of women and girls while incarcerated, and for the greater employment of women in adult male and female correctional institutions.

AP Video 15.2: Prisons and HIV

MEETING FEMALE INMATES' NEEDS AND PROVIDING PROGRAMMING

In an article published in *American Jails Magazine*, Ney (2014) succinctly summarizes some of the basic facts and differences between men and women in jails, with substantial application to prisons:

1. "Women pose a lower safety risk than men." What this means is that women do not riot and don't assault each other or staff as much, and when they do, they do less damage. They are less likely to be incarcerated for violent offenses.

Video 15.1: Issues Related to the Modern-Day Female Offender Population

Patriarchy: Involves the attitudes, beliefs, and behaviors that value men and boys over women and girls.

Journal Article 15.1:
Prison and Female
Mental Health

2. "Women's pathways to criminal justice are different than men's." They are much more likely to be prior victims of abuse and to be impoverished before incarceration than men. They are more likely to have substance abuse problems and to have this problem intertwined with abuse and mental illness.

3. "Women's engagement in criminal behavior is often related to their connections with others." They commit crimes with crime partners, and usually, those are the men in their lives.

4. "Women entering jails and prisons often report histories of victimization and trauma, and continue to be vulnerable to victimization within correctional settings." This history makes them more susceptible to substance abuse, mental illness, and targeting by predators as future victims.

Video 15.2:
Why Offer
Gender-Specific
Items in the
Commissary?

5. "Correctional policies and practices have largely been developed through the lens of managing men, not women." This means that the risk, needs, and responsivity issues that are so key to constructing programming that "works" are not adequately addressed for women.

6. "Jail and prison classification systems can result in unreliable custody designations and over-classification of female inmates." As a result, women will be held in more secure facilities and sections of facilities than is necessary.

7. "Gender-informed risk assessment tools can more accurately identify women's risk and needs." Some research is indicating that assessment might be more accurate—and thus result in more effective programming—if it fits the reality of women rather than men.

8. "Women are more likely to respond favorably when jail (and prison) staff members adhere to evidence-based, gender-responsive principles."

9. "Transition and reentry from jail to the community can be challenging for women." Reentry programming should therefore be geared to address their particular needs, which are often similar to men's but not always.

10. "The cost of overly involving women in criminal justice is high." Not only are we incarcerating or overly supervising people who are in less need of it, we are stymieing the ability of these women to grow and develop in a prosocial manner, we are depriving children of their mothers, and we are costing the taxpayers approximately twice the amount of money it takes to incarcerate men for someone who is usually less of a threat to the community. (pp. 8–10)

As a practical matter, then, if not just because women and girls have historically been valued less by this society (patriarchy) but perhaps because crime has generally been the purview of men and boys, correctional facilities and correctional practices have tended to focus on men. This focus led to disparate treatment that disadvantaged women and girls from the beginning and resulted in little concern for their needs, then or now, as Ney's (2014) summary indicates (Muraskin, 2003).

Yet women and girls are more likely to have mental- and physical-health problems than incarcerated men and boys (Morgan, 2013; Schaffner, 2014). They are also more likely to have substance abuse problems than their male counterparts. Moreover, they have the same kinds of educational and job-training deficits and needs as men and boys (Gray, Mays, & Stohr, 1995; Morash, Haarr, & Rucker, 1994; Owen & Bloom, 1995; Pollock, 2002b). Their need for gainful employment is likely as great as, if not greater than, that of men and boys, as they most often have to support themselves and their children, whereas fewer men have custody of their children before they are incarcerated (Owen, 2006); about 70% of women have custody of their children at the time of their incarceration (Henriques, 1996, p. 77). Moreover, a greater percentage of women, perhaps as high as 60%, were the victims of sexual abuse in the past, and this is likely to negatively shape their self-concept and their relations with others, thus necessitating more programming (Belknap, 2001; Blackburn, Mullings, & Marquart, 2008; Comack, 2006; Morash, 2006; Pollock, 2002b).

IN FOCUS 15.1

Orange Is the New Black (or Not)

The popular Netflix show *Orange Is the New Black* loosely features the sometimes hilarious and sometimes tragic experience of one woman (Piper) in jails and then a federal prison as a result of her drug courier involvement. In later episodes in the first and second seasons, the experience and life circumstances of several women in the same prison as Piper are also chronicled. The color orange in the title refers to the traditional color of the jumpsuit given to women (and men) in American jails (but rarely prisons), though, in reality, their garb in jails varies depending on their security level and the preferences of that facility, typically from orange, to white, to yellow, to red, to striped jumpsuits of various colors against a white background. And in prisons, it is more likely that you'll find the women inmates in jeans and T-shirts than in an orange (or other colored) jumpsuit. Of course, the color black in the title refers to the classic color for women's wear (*basic black*), and so, the title *Orange Is the New Black* might signify that imprisonment of women and the attendant orange wear is becoming much more common in our everyday lives than is the basic black of a woman in the free world. Or put another way, as per this show and the statistics cited in this chapter, prison is becoming a much more common experience for women, even white women with an upper-middle-class background like Piper, but particularly for all

PHOTO 15.3: Some of the cast of the show *Orange Is the New Black*.

of the working-class or poor women of color, as well as those who are white, who are also featured in the show.

DISCUSSION QUESTIONS

1. Why has the number of women in jails and prisons increased (metaphorically making orange the new black)?

2. Why do you think shows about imprisonment are so popular these days?

Given all of these needs and assuming that policy makers would not want women and girls to reenter the system, if for no other reason than that they cost much more to incarcerate (because of their needs and a reduction in economies of scale—separate female institutions house fewer inmates but require almost the same number of administrative and support staff as much larger male institutions), one would think that all of their needs would be met with adequate programming and health care. Unfortunately, this has been far from the case in most jurisdictions. Though there has been some recognition by the federal government of the need to develop programming that fits the needs of women and girls, it is unclear how much this has spread to state and local facilities (Morash, 2006; Morgan, 2013; Schaffner, 2014).

Though most of these needs are far from met in correctional environments, and far less than a majority of women are involved in meaningful programming, Pollock (2002b) notes that some states have made renewed efforts to address the needs of women and girls for educational, vocational, parenting, and substance abuse issues and their histories of past victimization. However, the numbers of these programs and their quality (very few are rigorously evaluated in terms of desired outcomes) leave much to be desired (Pollock, 2002a). In a longitudinal study of prison industries in federal women's prisons, Richmond (2014) found that involvement in this work had no effect on reducing rearrest or recommitment to federal prison. The authors speculated that this lack of effect might be due to the fact that the work program was not suited to women and their needs. In a review of 155 programs designed to meet the reentry needs of women on community supervision in the 10 largest metropolitan areas, the researchers (Scroggins & Malley, 2010, p. 146) found that the programs were inadequate. The sad truth is that most women and girls who need programming in corrections are not able to access it, or if they are, it is sometimes of dubious worth (Morgan, 2013).

Researchers find that women and girls have programmatic needs and styles that determine whether some rehabilitative approaches are more effective than others (Loper & Tuerk, 2006; Staton-Tindall et al., 2007; E. M. Wright, Salisbury, & Van Voorhis, 2007). One type of programming with particular relevance for women, given that most had physical custody of their children prior to incarceration, is parenting programs. Loper and Tuerk found in their research on such programming that it is delivered in several prisons, but its purported value in terms of helping mothers and fathers become better parents has not been rigorously studied (see also Pollock, 2002a; Surratt, 2003). Craig (2009), in her past-to-present review of mother-and-child programs in prisons, found that many states and localities have had programs where infants or very small children may stay with their mothers, at least initially. However, most correctional facilities where women are housed do not have such programs, and the qualifications for their use, even in states that have them, vary widely.

Video 15.4: Parenting in Prison

In an interesting study of male and female inmates in 20 substance abuse treatment programs, Staton-Tindall and colleagues (2007) found that the females reported more psychosocial dysfunction (e.g., anxiety and depression), less criminal thinking (e.g., cold-heartedness, entitlement, and irresponsibility), and greater involvement in programming (e.g., willingness to participate and receptivity to input) than did the males. The authors maintain that these findings support other research that indicates programming for women must be shaped to fit their abuse histories and mental-health needs.

Relatedly, in a study of 272 incarcerated women offenders in Missouri, Emily Wright and her colleagues (2007) found that gender-responsive problems related to parenting, child-care, and self-concept affect prison misconduct. Brown (2006), in her study of native and non-native Hawaiian women imprisoned in Hawaii, developed the alternate but parallel idea of *pathways* women traverse that can lead to crime. A pathway strewn with violence, trauma, and addiction, coupled with discrimination based on race, gender, and class, is more likely to end in criminal engagement for women. Such a pathway, Brown (2006) explains, may be related to poorer treatment outcomes for incarcerated women.

The health care needs of incarcerated women are tied up in needs specific to gender and in the particular pathway that many poor women tread. Women in jails and prisons have numerous gynecological, obstetrical, psychological, and psychiatric health ailments that are more specific to their gender, along with health problems that are common to both genders. As the health care needs of poor women and children in communities are going unmet, it is not surprising that similar circumstances apply to incarcerated women. Predictably, then, Moe and Ferraro (2003) found from their interviews of 30 women incarcerated in an Arizona jail that while basic needs were met in this jail, when the care required was of the long-term, extensive, or individualized type, it was lacking.

ABUSE

Unfortunately, abuse does not necessarily end at the corrections door. One of the primary reasons that women and girls were removed from facilities for men and boys in the 1800s and 1900s, and female staff were hired to supervise them, was that they were targets of sexual abuse by correctional staff and male inmates (Henriques & Gilbert, 2003). Though separation from male inmates has reduced their abuse, the sexual abuse by male staff, though likely much less prevalent than it once was, in part because of the inclusion of more female staff, has not been eliminated.

One of the authors of this volume had occasion to serve as an expert witness for the plaintiffs in a civil suit in 2004 against a city in New Mexico whose judge and a few correctional officers for the local jail were involved in the sexual abuse of female inmates (*Salazar et al. v. City of Espanola et al.* [2004]). The male judge and a few male correctional staff had an arrangement whereby female offenders whom the judge found attractive would be placed in the jail (whether their alleged offense merited it or not), and then, the judge would have access to them when they were sent over to "clean" his chambers. Inevitably, he would make passes at them, using the threat of more jail time, denied privileges, or a lengthened sentence as a way to coerce them into sexual activity with him. Meanwhile, a few of the correctional staff were harassing the female inmates, such as watching and commenting on their bodies as they showered, making sexual advances toward them, and touching them inappropriately. Two male officers were even involved in removing a few females from their cells and having sex with them in the control room at night, when no one else was around. There were no female staff on duty at the time of these sexual assaults and this abuse. After this kind of activity occurred for a period of time and due to the concerted efforts of several ex-inmates and their attorneys, the judge was convicted of rape, and the judge, correctional staff, and city lost a million-dollar lawsuit (*Salazar et al. v. City of Espanola et al.* [2004]).

In an even bigger case, *Tracy Neal v. Michigan Department of Corrections*, the plaintiffs alleged more than two decades of sexual abuse of women inmates in Michigan prisons (Culley, 2012, p. 206). The history of abuse was compelling, as the combined jury verdicts in the case awarded $30 million for the plaintiffs and a settlement of $100 million.

Unfortunately, the sexual abuse of female inmates by male staff is not limited to adult facilities. In 2003, the American Civil Liberties Union (ACLU) investigated reports of

FIGURE *15.3*   Prevalence of Sexual Victimization Among Adult Inmates

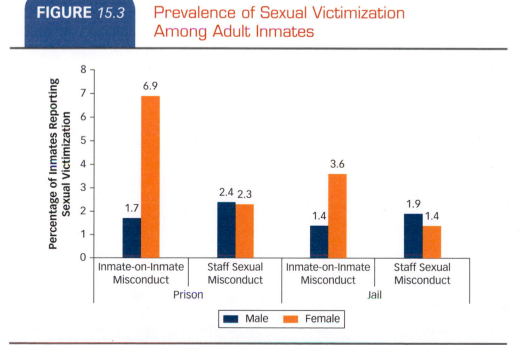

Source: Beck, Berzofsky, Caspar, and Krebs (2013).

the abuse of juvenile girls by male staff in the Hawaii Youth Correctional Facility and reported that male staff observed the girls using the toilets and showers, made comments about their bodies, and threatened to rape them, and in fact, several girls did have sex with the officers in exchange for cigarettes (Chesney-Lind & Irwin, 2006). A year later, one officer pled guilty to three counts of sexual assault and to threatening a female ward. A key circumstance that came out in the ACLU report was that there were no female officers on duty at night, when much of the abuse of the girls took place.

Such abuse is particularly damaging when one considers that over half of incarcerated women and girls have experienced some form of sexual abuse in the past (ACLU, 2015; Gray et al. 1995; Henriques & Gilbert, 2003). The Ninth Circuit Court, though not the Supreme Court, recognizing this fact, put some restrictions on body searches of female inmates by male staff, noting that such searches may serve to revictimize the women with sexual-abuse histories (*Jordan v. Gardner* [1993]).

Efforts to reduce sexual abuse in correctional institutions have centered on ensuring that staff have the proper training and are supervised sufficiently to prevent abuse. Moreover, the value of disciplinary measures to reinforce appropriate practices cannot be overstated. Clearly, staff who violate the rights of their charges in a way that is as serious as sexual abuse should be fired and prosecuted, and there is some evidence emanating from the reporting required by the Prison Rape Elimination Act (PREA) that this may be occurring (see the discussion of PREA in preceding chapters on jails and prisons).

The hiring of more women officers to cover living units is another way that correctional agencies have worked to keep sexual predators from gaining access to relatively powerless female victims. There is no question, however, that lawsuits have been successful in spurring some of these needed changes in correctional practice. But the problem with lawsuits is that their application is hit or miss at best, and the success of plaintiffs is always iffy. For instance, though the *Neal* case referenced earlier was ultimately a success in the end, it took a 15-year battle to get the abuse to stop (Culley, 2012). Therefore, the best preventative measures are those that focus on hiring competent people, training them to behave professionally, supervising them carefully, rewarding them when they behave professionally, and punishing them (up to and including firing and prosecuting them) when they do not.

ADJUSTMENT, MISCONDUCT, AND PSEUDOFAMILIES

Women's adjustment in corrections is associated with their sometimes problematic personal relationships; separation from children; greater propensity for mental-health problems; and the fact that in prisons, women tend to be charged with infractions for more minor offenses (Owen, 2006). As Van Tongeren and Klebe (2010) found in their study of female-inmate adjustment in a maximum-security prison in Colorado, adjustment is a multidimensional concept that encompasses an inmate's particular circumstances and environment, as well as his or her criminal thinking and adoption of the prison subculture. For instance, in a study

FIGURE *15.4*   Prevalence of Sexual Victimization Among Juvenile Inmates

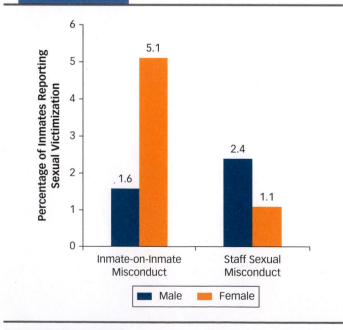

Source: Beck et al. (2013).

of co-occurring disorders, or COD (mental illness and substance use disorder), of women inmates in Pennsylvania prisons, Houser and Welsch (2014) found that those inmates with COD were more likely to engage in misconduct than inmates without COD.

Beyond the mental-illness and substance use disorders that some women prison inmates have, another circumstance they find themselves in, in most states, is being far from family and friends. There is still only one women's prison in most states, which is often located away from urban centers where most of the women come from. As a result, it is difficult to maintain familial relationships and friendships when a woman has a lengthy sentence. Poor families will find it much more difficult to visit their incarcerated family member, as they will not have reliable or inexpensive transportation available. Moreover, incarcerated women do not have access to cell phones or computers to contact family and friends. The pay phones they do have access to are expensive to use for poor families, who must pay for the collect calls (even local calls). As many of these women are incapable of writing a letter, and their children may be unable to read or be unreachable to these women, the ability to maintain contact is further impaired. The separation from children is particularly acute, as the mothers lose control over their children's housing and care. Often, the children are placed with family members who have a history of abuse or in the foster care system, which, in most states, is overwhelmed (S. F. Sharp & Marcus-Mendoza, 2001).

ETHICAL ISSUE 15.1

What Would You Do?

You are a female probationer living in the community. Your probation officer keeps coming on to you, but you aren't interested. Last week, at a family birthday, you had a beer, and the next day, your officer ordered a urinanalysis. It came back "dirty" for alcohol. Now, your probation officer is saying that in exchange for sexual favors, he won't violate your probation. What do you think you should do? What are the likely consequences of any action you take?

© iStockphoto.com/akajeff

PHOTO 15.4: Visits by family members are much appreciated by inmates of correctional facilities.

As with males, females incarcerated or supervised in corrections must grapple with the pains associated with that status and find some way to adjust to its strictures. Early researchers in women's prisons (e.g., see Giallombardo, 1966) reported on the formation of *pseudofamilies* as a way for women to meet their needs for companionship, support, and love, as well as sexual gratification. It was thought that women were importing these familial roles from traditional family structures and playing them out in the prison setting. In any given pseudofamily, there were inmates who took on the roles of fathers, mothers, grandmothers, daughters, aunts, and cousins. More recent research has shown that some women do indeed form "families" while in prison, but the strength of these relationships is perhaps more casual than was first reported (Owen, 1998). Moreover, as might be expected, women incarcerated for longer periods of time and

POLICY AND RESEARCH

Gender Pathways to Community Corrections, Jails, and Prisons

For several years now criminal justicians and criminologists have been researching and writing about the types of circumstances and choices that typify the life course of someone entangled in the criminal justice system. For girls and women, such circumstances include childhood poverty, low levels of education, poor neighborhoods and schools, abuse and neglect as a child and abuse as an adult, mental illness, substance abuse, and involvement with criminally engaged partners (Bloom, Owen & Covington, 2003; Brown, 2006; De-Hart, 2008; Owen, 1998; Simpson, Yahner & Dugan, 2008). The effect of victimization on subsequent offending for such women is clear: Those who experience more victimization as children are also more likely to be involved in the criminal

justice system—including corrections—earlier and are more likely to continue their own criminal engagement into adulthood.

DISCUSSION QUESTIONS

1. Why would victimization as a child and as an adult lead to more involvement in crime?

2. Are men and women likely to differ in their pathways to crime? Why, or why not?

3. What can be done to change the path to criminal involvement for girls and women?

who are farther from their release date may be more likely to maintain their pseudofamilial relations than those who are not as immersed in the subculture due to a shorter incarceration.

••• FEMALE CORRECTIONAL OFFICERS

FEMALE STAFF

Video 15.5: Female Correctional Officers

The trajectory of employment of female correctional officers has not been as steep or as steady as it has been for those women and girls under correctional supervision. As already mentioned, women were employed as matrons, to a limited degree, to work with females in some of the earliest prisons and jails (Pollock, 2002b; Stohr, 2006; Zupan, 1992). However, they did not make significant inroads into the correctional profession until the 1964 Civil Rights Act was amended in 1972, and women began using that law to sue in courts to gain employment in both female and male correctional institutions. According to the Bureau of Labor Statistics (2016a, p. 4), in 2015, women occupied about 23.8% of correctional officer jobs in jails and prisons. As of 2005, only 13% of correctional officers in federal prisons but 48% of correctional officers in private prisons were women (Stephan, 2001, p. 8; 2008, p. 4). As was mentioned in Chapter 11, it is probably no coincidence that the prisons that pay the most (federal) employ the fewest women as officers, and the prisons that pay the least (private) employ the most.

Career Video 15.1: Probation Officer

Staff demographic statistics regarding probation and parole officers for adults and children are not always readily available. According to a recent BJS report, 49% of all state-level parole agency staff are women, but this figure includes all staff, not just parole officers (Bonczar, 2008, p. 3). Unfortunately, the BJS does not supply

PERSPECTIVE FROM A PRACTITIONER

Kay Heinrich, Correctional Program Manager

Position: Correctional program manager

Location: Washington State Department of Corrections

Education: MA in counseling and education, MA in criminal justice, and PhD in criminal justice

What are your primary duties and responsibilities?

The Prison Division (PD) correctional program manager (CPM) is an integral part of the division's management team. This person is responsible for implementation of evidence-based principles (EBP) policies that impact the PD. This includes assisting with staff development related to evidence-based interventions. The CPM provides operational oversight for evidence-based units and institutions, focusing on resource utilization and staff-training needs and operationalizing evidence-based practices within the Washington State Department of Corrections (WSDOC) intensive-management, close-custody, medium, and minimum units.

This position contributes to the mission of the Department of Corrections (DOC) by assuring PD delivers EBP consistent with resource allocations and established principles. These principles target offenders' risks and needs in order to achieve the DOC performance goals of improved public safety, decreased recidivism, and the operationalization of core correctional practices (CCP). CCPs provide staff with tools to hold offenders accountable through effective interventions that contribute to changing offender behavior. The CPM position is responsible for assisting facilities in the operationalization of these principles. In coordination with established chains of command and other divisions, this position supports the fidelity of the EBP structure and delivery within the prisons by assessing data, observing operations at program sites, and interacting with staff and offenders.

Previously, for the WSDOC, the CPM (Ms. Heinrich) worked for 17 years as the clinical supervisor for the WSDOC Chemical Dependency Unit researching evidence-based practices, simultaneously designing, facilitating training for, and implementing chemical dependency (CD) programming treatment, including therapeutic communities, intensive outpatient programs, and a reentry continuum to the community for the incarcerated, chemically addicted offenders.

What are the characteristics and traits most useful in your line of work?

- Perseverance and flexibility
- Honesty and integrity
- Practice what you preach.
- Collaboration and communication skills
- Open minded
- Ability to admit defeat and continuing on while maintaining integrity
- Trustworthy
- Strong work ethic and ability to meet with staff during all three shifts
- Healthy boundaries between and within personal, professional, and offenders' borders
- Understanding of organizational development, culture, attitudes, and the stages of change within the institution and individuals, including offenders
- Getting along with others, which includes a diverse population of staff and offenders
- No matter how competent you are, if you cannot fit in, you will not be promoted.
- Dealing with offenders' criminal histories and crimes, with the ability to remain objective in dealing with the offenders on a daily basis
- Dealing with offenders and managing staff

Please describe a typical workday.

There is no typical workday. Each day depends on the prison's level of security and the immediate needs of the institution to meet the safety and security of staff and offenders. For example, you may have meetings and training sessions planned, treatment groups scheduled, and individual priorities; however, if count is not cleared, there is an act of violence in the units or yard, or a medical or mental-health emergency occurs, everything stops to accommodate correctional officers' responsibilities to maintain control and management of the prison.

When the prison is under "normal" status, responsibilities include traveling to the prisons where the evidence-based programs are facilitated to ensure adequate staff are available and trained, plus that staff are supported for working

(Continued)

(Continued)

in a therapeutic role versus a custodial role. Labor unions, shift work, and a paramilitary environment are additional considerations that influence program implementation and facilitation, which make each day atypical. The prisons are scattered throughout Washington State, so travel is extensive, and use of GPS is mandatory. This position requires knowledge of each prison's administrative and management personnel and style, to include the political, hierarchical expectations from headquarters.

A CPM must have the ability to maintain neutrality in order to ensure that EBP are facilitated with integrity and adherence to the model's curriculum. Neutrality extends toward each of the diverse offender populations (maximum to minimum offender classification),

management styles, and cultures of every prison served according to the personalities, values, and attitudes of the superintendent and executive management team.

What is your advice to someone who wants to enter your field?

Stay away from the naysayers and negative staff. Don't get caught up in the politics at the prison or headquarters level. Don't get personally or intimately involved with fellow employees. Stick to your value system and the important role each position brings to achieving the overarching goal of offender change and public safety. Never lose your sense of humor, belief that people (staff and offenders) can change, hope in humanity, and belief that good always overcomes evil.

this level of information regarding probation officers at the state or federal level. However, the Bureau of Labor Statistics (2016a, p. 3) reports that in 2015, 55.4% of probation officers and correctional treatment specialists in the country were women.

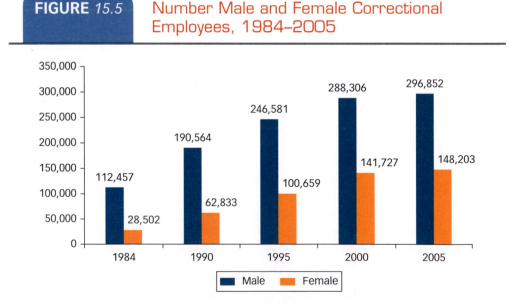

FIGURE 15.5 Number Male and Female Correctional Employees, 1984–2005

Note: Most recent data available. The data from the 1984 Census (Stephan, 1987) was for "state adult correctional facilities"; federal institutions were excluded.

Source: Stephan (1987, 1992, 1997, 2008); Stephan and Karberg (2003).

OVERCOMING EMPLOYMENT OBSTACLES

As with the accused and convicted women in the system, women have always constituted a minority in terms of correctional staff. Though one would expect that women might compose a greater percentage of staff given their representation in the larger community, the current figures actually represent a significant improvement over 30 or 40 years ago. At that time, women—with exceptions allowed for matrons in women's and girls' facilities working for lower pay than men working in male facilities—were prohibited by practice, tradition, or law from working in the more numerous men's and boys' correctional institutions or in probation and parole.

Though they were often prohibited from having an official and paid role in working with correctional clients, women were true partners in the work in America's early and rural jails. In what were termed *mom-and-pop jails*—rural jails from 1900 to 1970—Ruddell and Leyton-Brown (2013) found from their content analysis of newspaper articles covering the period that sheriffs' wives "admitted and supervised arrestees, thwarted jail escapes, apprehended escapees, and challenged lynch mobs" (p. 270).

However, as was mentioned earlier, it was not until the Civil Rights Act of 1964 was passed and amended in 1972 that women were given the legal weapon to sue for the right to work and be paid and promoted in all prisons, jails, detention centers, juvenile facilities, and halfway houses and in community corrections. Many women did, in fact, sue; they had to if they wanted the same kinds of jobs and promotional opportunities then available only to men in corrections, policing, and law (Harrington, 2002; Hawkes, 1998; Stohr, 2006; H. Yates, 2002). As a result of this agitation and advocacy, slowly, the available jobs and promotional opportunities became open to these pioneering women, resulting in the more diverse correctional workforce we see today.

CURRENT STATUS

As the number of women employed in corrections has increased, three issues have been particularly problematic for them in the workplace:

1. Whether women's rights to equal employment in male correctional facilities are more important than male inmates' rights to privacy in those same facilities

2. Whether women are physically and mentally suited to do correctional work with men

3. How to deal with sexual and gender harassment—primarily from other staff—while on the job

Equal Employment Versus Privacy Interests of Inmates

As mentioned before in this section, women achieved the legal right to equal employment in corrections through the law and lawsuits. Most of the jobs in institutional corrections or in communities are in dealing with male inmates or offenders. On the other hand, one can certainly understand the male-inmate perspective that they would like some privacy when engaged in intimate bodily functions, such as using the toilet or showering. The courts, in this matter, however, have tended to side with the female employees' or prospective female employees' right to equal protection over the male inmates' right to privacy (Farkas & Rand, 1999; Maschke, 1996). Their reasoning was likely as much influenced by the fact that inmates in the United States have very limited rights while incarcerated, with no real right to privacy, as by the fact that correctional staff should be respectful and professional, no matter their gender, in their dealings with inmates.

ETHICAL ISSUE 15.2 ?

What Would You Do?

As a new female correctional officer in a male prison, you are finding it difficult to gain acceptance from some of your older male colleagues. Of particular concern is whether you are tough enough to lead people who may not respect you as an officer. An older female officer advises you to act disrespectfully toward a few of the less well-regarded inmates (i.e., sex offenders) in front of those doubtful staff as a way of establishing your "toughness" credentials. Although you can appreciate that doing so may alleviate concerns by a few of these staff, it also requires you to do something you find abhorrent. What would and should you do in this instance?

Qualifications for the Job

The issue of whether women are physically and mentally qualified to work with male inmates has generally become a settled matter in most institutions, agencies, and states: They are. But when they were first making inroads into the correctional workplace, there were plenty of doubts about the ability of women to handle the work (Jurik, 1985b, 1988; Jurik & Halemba, 1984; Zimmer, 1986, 1989). Even as regards their propensity to use aggression in the course of their work, men and women correctional staff are similar (Tewksbury & Collins, 2006). However, the Supreme Court has left open the possibility that if there were a bona fide job requirement that women could not fulfill in a male prison, they could be excluded from that work (Bennett, 1995; Maschke, 1996).

In a qualitative study of female parole agents in California, Ireland and Berg (2006) noted that these agents reported subtle harassment in the form of less desirable shifts or assignments because of their gender. The women also felt that they were overlooked for promotions and an administrative career track. One 40-year veteran of the department observed that it was not the clients who harassed the women agents but their colleagues, who "often questioned her competence and treated her unprofessionally" (p. 140). In response to such bias and views, the women reported that they overcompensated, or did more than was expected of males on the job. Some female parole agents adapted by taking on stereotypically feminine roles, such as acting helpless and in need of male assistance, flirtatious, or maternal. Still another adaptation by these agents was to refuse to acknowledge that there was any bias at all in the workplace; this latter group of women did not think that considerations of gender or race/ethnicity had hampered their ability to advance in their career.

Clearly, because of their biology, most women are not as physically strong as most men, and sometimes, strength is called for in dealing with an unruly inmate. However, the use of brute force is rather rare in most correctional institutions and in the community when functioning as a probation or parole agent. (Note the discussion of violence in corrections in an earlier chapter.) Second, there are defensive (and offensive) tactics that give a trained and armed woman some advantage in a physical altercation with a male inmate. Third, there is some evidence that female staff may have a calming effect on male-inmate aggression because they are more inclined to use their interpersonal and communication skills and are less likely to be seen as a threat (Jurik, 1988; Jurik & Halemba, 1984; Lutze & Murphy, 1999; Zimmer, 1986).

Some research has indicated that both male and female correctional officers value a service orientation over a security orientation in their work, so their work styles and preferences may be more similar than dissimilar (Farkas, 1999; Hemmens, Stohr, Schoeler, & Miller, 2002; Stohr, Lovrich, & Mays, 1997; Stohr, Lovrich, & Wood, 1996). Research in one state indicated that women correctional officers in prisons might be more fearful of victimization by inmates than are their male colleagues (Gordon, Proulx, & Grant, 2013). In research on attitudes of 192 male and female jail officers in a southwestern state's jail system regarding conflict resolution with inmates, Hogan and her colleagues (Hogan, Lambert, Hepburn, Burton, & Cullen, 2004) found that the genders reacted somewhat similarly in this area as well. When the gender of the inmate was female, male and female officers were likely to react equally aggressively. However, female officers perceived a greater physical threat from male inmates and were more likely to use force than male officers.

In research by Kim and colleagues (Kim, DeValve, DeValve, & Jonson, 2003) on the attitudes of male and female wardens, they found that 90 of the female wardens (out of a total of 641 male and female wardens surveyed) were more inclined to value programming and amenities in their prisons that promoted health, education, and other programming for inmates than were their male colleagues. However, these researchers also found that there were many more similarities than differences between the two genders as they viewed and appreciated their work.

Taken in total, what all of this research on women's ability to do the work and on the differences and similarities in work styles between men and women indicate is that men and women mostly view and do correctional work similarly; that some women, perhaps more than some men, can calm an agitated inmate; and that some men, perhaps more than some women, are better at physically containing an agitated inmate.

Sexual and Gender Harassment

Unfortunately, the problem with gender and sexual harassment of female staff by male staff has not become a settled matter. This is not to say, of course, that male staff are not harassed by female staff. This does happen and can be as debilitating for the male employee as it is for the female. But a number of studies have shown, over a period of years, that females are much more likely to be the victims of male harassment by bosses and coworkers in the workplace and that when men are victims, they are as likely to be harassed by other men as by women (Firestone & Harris, 1994, 1999; Mueller, De Coster, & Estes, 2001; O'Donohue, Downs, & Yeater, 1998; Pryor & Stoller, 1994). Male institutions, in particular, with their smaller percentages of women employees and managers and their traditions aligned with male power in the

PHOTO 15.5: Two female officers confer in a jail.

workplace, are more susceptible to this kind of behavior than are other correctional workplaces (Lawrence & Mahan, 1998; Lutze & Murphy, 1999; Pogrebin & Poole, 1997). The types of harassment that occur can be **quid pro quo sexual harassment** (something for something, as in you give me sexual favors, and you get to keep your job) or the less serious but still workplace-stultifying **hostile environment** (when the workplace is sexualized with jokes or pictures or in other ways that are offensive to one gender).

Thankfully, there are remedies, imperfect and cumbersome though they might be, that can be employed to stop or at least significantly reduce such harassment. Initially, women had to sue in order to stop the harassment because many managers of their workplaces simply would not do anything to stop it. In one mid-1990s case, one of the authors of this book served as an expert witness for the plaintiff against the State of California's San Quentin Prison. The female victim won over a million dollars for enduring harassment by several male staff and one inmate that started in the 1970s and ended when she quit in frustration in the 1990s; it was never stopped by the prison administration (*Pulido v. State of California et al.* [1994]). As successful as this case was, there was incontrovertible evidence of the harassment (as provided by memos, diaries, staffing logs, and witnesses), evidence that is usually not available to support most victims' stories. Moreover, the female victim, an African American woman, lost her job and had to endure almost two years of an uncertain legal battle before the case was tried, and the judge ruled. Even then, the State of California appealed, and it took another year before the matter was finally settled in the plaintiff's favor.

What this story illustrates is that there are few true "winners" when sexual and gender harassment cases go to trial. Most such cases fail, as there is not sufficient evidence of the abuse, beyond a he-said, she-said scenario. Victims of such abuse suffer untold harm in terms of their psychological and physical well-being, both during the abuse and as they relive it during the legal process. Even when cases are successful at trial, taxpayers (not just the instigators of the abuse, who often do not have the "deep pockets" of their governmental employer) have to pay for the illegal practices of their own governmental entities and actors.

In other words, there has got to be a better way—and there is. Researchers and correctional practitioners have agreed that there are proactive steps that managers and other employees can take to prevent or stop sexual and gender harassment in the correctional workplace. Such steps would involve hiring, training, firing, and promoting based on respectful treatment of other staff and clients. Training, in particular, can reinforce the message of a no-tolerance policy regarding harassment. But to be effective, employees need to see that people are rewarded when they do or punished when they do not adhere to the policy.

As a discussion of the current status of female staff working in corrections would indicate, women have made some significant advances in these workplaces. They have not just made gains in employment, but female supervisors and managers are also no longer anomalies in most states. Though nowhere near matching the numbers of men as staff and management in corrections and while still grappling with the pernicious problem of sexual and gender harassment, nonetheless, they have come a long way since the days of working as matrons, with lower pay and less respect, attributes that typified their work for most of the history of corrections.

Quid pro quo sexual harassment: Involves something for something, as in you give your boss sexual favors, and he allows you to keep your job.

Hostile environment: Occurs when the workplace is sexualized with jokes or pictures or in other ways that are offensive to one gender.

SUMMARY

- The study of women and girls in corrections was not always a priority for scholars (Flavin & Desautels, 2006; Goodstein, 2006; Mallicoat, 2011). Patriarchal perceptions and beliefs, along with women's status as numerical minorities, have served to shape organizational and scholarly priorities in a way that favors men and boys. Since the 1970s, however, there has been more scholarly focus on the reality of women and girls who work, live, or are supervised under the correctional umbrella.

- Part of this shift in focus has occurred as the result of feminist efforts to equalize the work for women and the living and supervision arrangements for women and girls under correctional supervision.

- Recent research on women and girls under correctional supervision has highlighted the outstanding needs they have for educational, substance abuse, work-training, parenting, and abuse survivor programming. Unfortunately, it has also shown that little programming is provided, in either jails, prisons, or the communities, to meet these needs.

- Female correctional officers have also faced a number of legal and institutional barriers to their full and equal employment in corrections.

- For the most part, many of these formal barriers have been removed, as female officers have demonstrated their competencies in handling correctional work.

- Some researchers have even found a feminine style to officer work that employs the successful use of interpersonal-communication skills to address inmate needs.

- However, there is still evidence that sexual and gender harassment and the sexual abuse of female inmates continues in some correctional environments. Though organizational remedies exist to "deal" with such abuse, they are not always employed by managers.

- Taken in tandem, the research presented in this chapter should shift our perspective from the much more numerous and normative studies of males over to females. By shifting our gaze to the female side, we are as likely to see the sameness of the genders as the contrasts that distinguish them (Rodriguez, 2007; Smith & Smith, 2005). We might also see that the life course of a woman or girl entangled in the criminal justice system (e.g., see Brown [2006] and E. M. Wright et al. [2007]) forms a predictable pattern that might be fruitfully addressed if we only had the will to do so.

KEY TERMS

Double deviants 366

Hostile environment 380

Houses of refuge 363

Liberal feminist 366

Mount Pleasant Prison 361

Patriarchy 367

Quid pro quo sexual harassment 380

DISCUSSION QUESTIONS

1. In what ways have women and girls occupied a minority status in corrections? How has that status affected how they are treated in the system?

2. What is feminism, and what do feminists advocate? How have they had an effect on the work of women and their (and girls') experience with incarceration?

3. What is patriarchy? What kind of effect did and does patriarchy have on corrections for women and girls? How might it negatively affect the experience of men and boys?

4. What sorts of factors are likely to lead to the greater abuse of female inmates in correctional institutions? How might such abuse be prevented?

5. What sorts of factors are likely to lead to sexual and gender harassment in correctional work? How might such harassment be stopped or prevented?

6. How might female officers' supervision styles differ from those of male officers? What might be the advantages of hiring women to work with men and boys in corrections? What might be the advantages of hiring men to work with women and girls in corrections?

USEFUL INTERNET SITES

Please note that the sites listed can be accessed at edge.sagepub.com/stohrcorrections.

American Correctional Association: www.aca.org

This site includes some of the latest information on correctional practices.

American Jail Association: www.corrections.com/aja

This site includes some of the latest information on correctional practices in jails and detention facilities.

American Probation and Parole Association: www.appa-net.org

This site includes some of the latest information on community corrections practices.

Bureau of Justice Statistics: http://bjs.ojp.usdoj.gov

This site includes governmental statistics on any number of criminal justice agencies and actors, including prisons and jails and their staff.

National Organization for Women: www.now.org

This site includes information about a powerful advocacy group for women and about some of the discriminatory issues women still face in the workplace.

$SAGE edge™

Sharpen your skills with SAGE edge at **edge.sagepub.com/stohrcorrections**. SAGE edge for Students provides a personalized approach to help you accomplish your coursework goals in an easy-to-use learning environment. You'll find action plans, mobile-friendly eFlashcards, and quizzes as well as video, web, and resources and links to SAGE journal articles to support and expand on the concepts presented in this chapter.

16

Minorities and Corrections

TEST YOUR KNOWLEDGE

Test your present knowledge about minority groups in this country and their experiences as staff and inmates in corrections by answering the following questions. Check your answers on page 538 after reading the chapter.

1. The race of a person is determined by his or her biology. (True or false?)

2. The ethnicity of a person is determined by his or her culture. (True or false?)

3. Explain what happened in the Scottsboro case and why is it considered emblematic of how African Americans were handled by the criminal justice system in the earlier half of the 20th century.

4. Name at least three facts that would indicate that racism still exists in the criminal justice system of today.

5. Very few Native Americans were in the Americas when Columbus landed. (True or false?)

6. Chinese and Japanese American immigration was widely supported in the 19th and 20th centuries. (True or false?)

7. Describe the reasoning for the internment of Japanese Americans in 1942. Why weren't German Americans also placed in such camps?

8. There is a connection between class, race/ethnicity, and crime. (True or false?)

9. The drug war has led to the increased incarceration of Hispanics and blacks in the United States. (True or false?)

10. Crack cocaine and powder cocaine are pharmacologically different. (True or false?)

11. Research shows that blacks and Hispanics use more drugs than whites. (True or false?)

LEARNING OBJECTIVES

- Define *race*, *ethnicity*, *disparity*, and *discrimination*

- Describe some of the history of minority group members in this country

- Identify the connection between class, race/ethnicity, and crime

- Explain the special challenges faced by minority group members in corrections

- Discuss how the criminal justice system has not been race neutral in its treatment of minorities

UNDOCUMENTED WORKERS AND THEIR SIDE OF THE STORY

One of the largest groups of cases before the federal courts and in some form of federal corrections (jails and prisons) involves unauthorized immigrants from Mexico and Latin America (Light, Lopez, & Gonzalez-Barrera, 2014). Yet though they violate U.S. immigration laws, De La Torre (2013), in her ethnographic research on Mexican migrants and their version of their immigration story, found that these immigrants do not see themselves as criminals at all; rather, they see themselves as moral actors confronting impossible circumstances that require crossing the border in order to provide for themselves and their families. One can well imagine that refugees fleeing war-torn Syria for Europe in 2015 and 2016 would likely make the same argument.

The immigrants, in interviews, characterized coming to the United States as a moral act necessitated by the lack of decent living conditions and sparse opportunities *in Mexico. As it was, they were unable to support their families in Mexico and did not see a future there.*

For instance, Juan Carlos, in his mid-20s, came to work in Chicago because he wanted a better economic position that would allow him to afford necessary things, among them, milk to feed his newborn daughter. His opportunities were limited as he struggled to provide for his family while living in Acapulco. Women also recounted how they had to sacrifice to feed families, raise their children, and take care of their elderly parents and relatives while engaged in paid work. For example,

Araceli, in her early 30s, came to the USA because she was the only provider in her household, as her elderly parents could no longer work and her younger siblings started college in Guanajuato. In coming to the USA she sacrificed her own chance to attend college in Mexico. (p. 272)

But coming to the U.S. carries its own hazards and risks. One of them is incarceration and then expulsion from this country. As Light and his colleagues (2014) document, "Among federal sentenced offenders in 1992, 12% were unauthorized immigrants. By 2012, that share had increased to 40%" (p. 1).

••• INTRODUCTION

The races and ethnicities of America's population have shaped its law and practice from the beginning. At the very writing and ratification of the Constitution, full citizenship was denied to those who were not white and, for many decades, those who were not male and in possession of significant amounts of property. The institution of slavery, the forcible seizure of American Indian lands, and the limitations on the immigration of nonwhites and their rights while in the United States have all marked and marred this country. Accordingly, police agencies, courts, correctional institutions and programs, and their actors have historically treated people differently based on their race and ethnicity.

Minority group members were more likely in some parts of the country to be incarcerated when they were innocent or sentenced for periods that were longer than their white brothers and sisters. Once in the correctional system, minority group members were sometimes segregated into separate institutions, sections of institutions, and programs. At times, they were given less desirable jobs and housing in jails and prisons and were prevented from working in such places. Whether such discriminatory treatment continues today is a matter of some debate, but there are indications that some laws, police, courts, and correctional practices have the effect of maintaining a separate and unequal

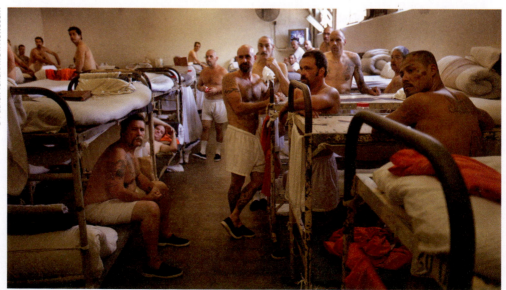

PHOTO 16.1: California inmates in Chino State Prison sitting in mixed-race groups.

system for minority group members. In this chapter, we briefly discuss this history and use it as a context for current practices and experiences in corrections.

••• DEFINING RACE, ETHNICITY, DISPARITY, AND DISCRIMINATION

RACE

Race is a term that refers to the skin color and features of a group of people. The extent to which different racial groups truly differ biologically is still being determined by scientists. Scientists are still putting together the collective pieces of our human history. However, the genotyping of the whole human race indicates that our species likely originated in Africa (Diamond, 1997; McAuliffe, 2010). Waves of migration then occurred, beginning at least 50,000 years ago and continuing over thousands of years, to Europe and Asia, resulting in variation in skin color and other features of racial groups, who, in turn, migrated to other continents and islands (Mann, 2006; McAuliffe, 2010). It is worth noting that even as these physical distinctions developed, there has been much intermingling, both historically and currently, among groups, resulting in populations that are substantially mixed, rather than distinct in their "racial" heritage. For this reason, using racial designations, such as white or black or Asian, might be necessary to ensure that one group is not advantaged over another, but we should recognize that they can be somewhat arbitrary designations, as true racial differences, though visible to the eye, may be measured more in gradations rather than in clear distinctions, particularly in the most racially mixed communities.

ETHNICITY

Ethnicity, on the other hand, refers to the differences between groups of people based on culture. An ethnic group will often have a distinct language, as well as distinct values and traditions and a shared religion and history. Ethnic groups may be made up of several races and have a diverse national heritage. For instance, the term *Hispanic* is applied to an ethnic group in the United States that includes white, black, and Asian racial groups whose ancestors may hail from Cuba, Puerto Rico, Mexico, or Central or South America. Descendants of Italians, Irish, French, German, and other ancestral ethnic Europeans who immigrated to the United States are usually racially white but not always, as while in Europe or after immigrating to the United States those groups may have intermingled with Africans and Asians. For instance, people known as Creoles are both ethnically and racially differentiated by their white and African racial background and the French ethnic cultural influences in Louisiana. And who are "black Irish" Americans but primarily white ethnic Irish people who intermingled with Spanish Moorish people while in Europe (who were at least partially from North Africa) and who then immigrated as Irish to the United States. Among black people in the United States, there are distinct ethnic differences between those whose ancestors have been in the country for hundreds of years, either as free people or as those forcibly brought here through slavery, and those whose families are more recent immigrants from Africa or predominantly racially black areas of the world (e.g., immigrants from Caribbean Islands like Haiti). More recent immigrants from the Sudan, Nigeria, or Kenya are different ethnically; that is to say, they have a distinct culture, as well as nationality, from each other and from those blacks whose families have been in the United States for generations.

DISPARITY AND DISCRIMINATION

Clear, Cole, and Reisig (2011) define **disparity** as "the unequal treatment of one group by the criminal justice system, compared with the treatment accorded other groups"

Race: Refers to the skin color and features of a group of people.

Ethnicity: Refers to the differences between groups of people based on culture. An ethnic group will often have a distinct language, as well as particular values and traditions and a shared religion and history.

Disparity: Occurs when one group is treated differently and unfairly by governmental or other actors, as compared with other groups.

Web 16.1:
Racial Disparity

(p. 527). In turn, they define **discrimination** as "differential treatment of an individual or group without reference to the behavior or qualifications of the same" (p. 527). We would add that disparity can happen in many organizations and entities and is not just restricted to the criminal justice system, and often, discrimination is linked in law to classes of people distinguished by race, ethnicity, gender, age, disability, religion, nationality, sexual orientation, and income.

••• A LEGACY OF RACISM

The legacy of *racism* (or discriminatory attitudes, beliefs, and practices directed at one race by another) runs long and deep in the United States. Notably, sometimes the term racism is also applied when one ethnic group holds discriminatory attitudes or beliefs or engages in discriminatory practices against another ethnic group. Correctional institutions and programs, as social institutions, are products of their larger social, political, and economic environments, and therefore, the legacy of racism has affected and continues to affect their operation.

AFRICAN AMERICANS

In the United States, slavery historically involved the involuntary servitude of black Africans by white Europeans and was practiced almost from the settling of the United States (K. C. Davis, 2008). Many of the founding fathers were slave owners, and the practice of slavery was protected in the Constitution (through the three-fifths designation of slaves in Article I [the worth that slaves had for states that wanted to count them for representation in Congress] and Article IV [which caused fugitive slaves to be returned to the slave owner]).

Slavery was a lucrative business for ship owners in the colonial United States, both Northern and Southern, and for plantation owners in the South, as it provided the back-breaking agricultural labor that built the Southern economy. Though slavery officially ended with the Civil War between the Northern and the Southern states and the subsequent adoption of the 13th Amendment in 1865, it lived on in civil society and law for 100 years through discriminatory laws and practices (see the discussion of Jim Crow laws later in this chapter).

Correctional institutions, particularly in the South following the Civil War, were devised to maintain the slave system, with newly freed and often unemployed blacks incarcerated for minor or trumped-up charges. Once incarcerated, their labor was leased out to Southern farmers for work on the same plantations on which they or their brethren had been slaves (Oshinsky, 1996; Young, 2001). In the same time period, in the North and Midwest, African American inmates were sometimes segregated from whites in prisons and jails and given substandard housing and the least desirable work assignments (Hawkes, 1998; Joseph & Taylor, 2003).

The Scottsboro case exemplified the racist attitudes of communities and how those attitudes were translated into discriminatory practices by law enforcement, courts, and corrections (Walker et al., 1996; see In Focus 16.1). The lynching of black men, fueled by mob rule and widespread Ku Klux Klan hate group activity, was also practiced in many states and communities following the Civil War and well into the 1900s (Keil & Vito, 2009). Lynching reinforced a culture of fear that prevented African Americans from achieving an equal and decent footing in communities. The Klan's avowed purpose was to target and persecute Catholics, Jews, and nonwhites, especially blacks, particularly in the South and in the midwestern states. Membership was widespread among public and criminal justice officials in the first half of the 1900s and even included those who rose to such lofty heights as Supreme Court justices (e.g., Supreme Court justice Hugo Black

Discrimination:
Occurs when a person or group is treated differently because of who they are (e.g., race, ethnicity, gender, age, disability, religion, nationality, sexual orientation or identity, or income) rather than because of their abilities or something they did.

IN FOCUS 16.1

The Scottsboro Case

Nine African American teenage boys were hoboing in 1931 on a freight train headed to Memphis, Tennessee. The train was stopped, and they were arrested and accused of the rape of two white girls on the train. The case was first tried in Scottsboro, Alabama, where the boys received little representation, and the trial was rushed. All of the boys in this first trial, except the youngest (a 12 year old), were convicted of rape and sentenced to death.

The case was appealed and made it all the way to the Supreme Court. In the famous decision *Powell v. Alabama* (1932), the Supreme Court ruled that the due process rights of the accused—in this case, their right to counsel in a capital case, particularly as these teenagers were indigent and illiterate—were violated. The Court reversed their convictions and sent their case back for retrial.

In the second trial, seven of the eight convictions were upheld by all-white juries. (Black voters in Alabama were purposefully excluded from lists for juries.) The reconvictions happened despite the fact that the case was moved to Decatur, Alabama, for retrial, and one of the two victims recanted her story, claiming that the story was made up and that the boys never touched either of them.

The Supreme Court, in 1935, again reheard the case in light of the all-white jury composition; the Court reversed again. The Alabama judge set aside the verdict and scheduled a new trial, where the accused were again found guilty.

Eventually, charges were dropped for four of the nine defendants, but the others received sentences of 75 years to death, and three of those five served prison time. The one who was sentenced to death was eventually pardoned, in 1976 (Walker, Spohn, & DeLone, 1996). This case is widely regarded by legal scholars as a gross miscarriage of justice and as emblematic of the way African

PHOTO 16.2: The Scottsboro accused meeting with their lawyer in jail.

NY Daily News Archive via Getty Images

Americans were treated in racist sectors of this country well after slavery was abolished.

DISCUSSION QUESTIONS

1. Do you think the time and place of this event affected its outcome?

2. How does this case and how these teenage boys were treated compare with how young black men and boys are treated by the police today?

3. Is there room for improvement in race relations between the police and African American community members?

4. Why is it so difficult for racial and ethnic groups in this country to, as Rodney King asked, "just get along"?

was a member in the 1920s) or members of Congress (e.g., Senator Robert Byrd of West Virginia was a member and defender of the Klan well into the 1950s).

There is little doubt that up until the civil rights movement and the implementation of laws and practices that reduced racism in public and private organizations, there was *institutional racism*—or racism practiced by many, if not most, institutional members—in criminal justice and other organizations. In correctional institutions, it was not until the civil rights movement morphed into the *prisoner rights movement* in jails

IN FOCUS 16.2

Fourteen Examples of Racism in the Criminal Justice System

By Bill Quigley*

The biggest crime in the U.S. criminal justice system is that it is a race-based institution where African Americans are directly targeted and punished in a much more aggressive way than white people.

Saying the U.S. criminal system is racist may be politically controversial in some circles. But the facts are overwhelming. No real debate about that. Below I set out numerous examples of these facts.

The question is—are these facts the mistakes of an otherwise good system, or are they evidence that the racist criminal justice system is working exactly as intended? Is the U.S. criminal justice system operated to marginalize and control millions of African Americans?

Information on race is available for each step of the criminal justice system—from the use of drugs, police stops, arrests, getting out on bail, legal representation, jury selection, trial, sentencing, prison, parole and freedom. Look what these facts show.

1. The U.S. has seen a surge in arrests and putting people in jail over the last four decades. Most of the reason is the war on drugs. Yet whites and blacks engage in drug offenses, possession and sales, at roughly comparable rates—according to a report on race and drug enforcement published by Human Rights Watch in May 2008. While African Americans comprise 13% of the U.S. population and 14% of monthly drug users, they are 37% of the people arrested for drug offenses—according to 2009 Congressional testimony by Marc Mauer of The Sentencing Project.

2. The police stop blacks and Latinos at rates that are much higher than whites. In New York City, where people of color make up about half of the population, 80% of the NYPD stops were of blacks and Latinos. When whites were stopped, only 8% were frisked. When blacks and Latinos are stopped 85% were frisked according to information provided by the NYPD. The same is true most other places as well. In a California study, the ACLU found blacks are three times more likely to be stopped than whites.

3. Since 1970, drug arrests have skyrocketed, rising from 320,000 to close to 1.6 million according to the Bureau of Justice Statistics of the U.S. Department of Justice. African Americans are arrested for drug offenses at rates 2 to 11 times higher than the rate for whites—according to a May 2009 report on disparity in drug arrests by Human Rights Watch.

4. Once arrested, blacks are more likely to remain in prison awaiting trial than whites. For example, the New York State Division of Criminal Justice did a 1995 review of disparities in processing felony arrests and found that in some parts of New York, blacks are 33% more likely to be detained awaiting felony trials than whites facing felony trials.

5. Once arrested, 80% of the people in the criminal justice system get a public defender for their lawyer. Race plays a big role here as well. Stop in any urban courtroom and look at the color of the people who are waiting for public defenders. Despite often heroic efforts by public defenders, the system gives them much more work and much less money than the prosecution. The American Bar Association, not a radical bunch, reviewed the U.S. public defender system in 2004 and concluded, "All too often, defendants plead guilty, even if they are innocent, without really understanding their legal rights or what is occurring. . . . The fundamental right to a lawyer that America assumes applies to everyone accused of criminal conduct effectively does not exist in practice for countless people across the U.S."

6. African Americans are frequently illegally excluded from criminal jury service according to a June 2010 study released by the Equal Justice Initiative. For example in Houston County, Alabama, 8 out of 10 African Americans qualified for jury service have been struck by prosecutors from serving on death penalty cases.

7. Trials are rare. Only 3 to 5 percent of criminal cases go to trial—the rest are plea bargained. Most African American defendants never get a trial. Most plea bargains consist of promise of a longer sentence if

a person exercises their constitutional right to trial. As a result, people caught up in the system, as the American Bar Association points out, plead guilty even when innocent. Why? As one young man told me recently, "Who wouldn't rather do three years for a crime they didn't commit than risk twenty-five years for a crime they didn't do?"

8. The United States Sentencing Commission reported in March 2010 that in the federal system black offenders receive sentences that are 10% longer than white offenders for the same crimes. Marc Mauer of The Sentencing Project reports African Americans are 21% more likely to receive mandatory minimum sentences than white defendants and 20% more likely to be sentenced to prison than white drug defendants.

9. The longer the sentence, the more likely it is that non-white people will be the ones getting it. A July 2009 report by The Sentencing Project found that two-thirds of the people in the U.S. with life sentences are non-white. In New York, it is 83%.

10. As a result, African Americans, who are 13% of the population and 14% of drug users, are not only 37% of the people arrested for drugs but 56% of the people in state prisons for drug offenses (Marc Mauer, May 2009 Congressional Testimony for The Sentencing Project).

11. The U.S. Bureau of Justice Statistics concludes that the chance of a black male born in 2001 of going to jail is 32% or 1 in 3. Latino males have a 17% chance and white males have a 6% chance. Thus, black boys are five times and Latino boys nearly three times as likely as white boys to go to jail.

12. So, while African American juvenile youth [are] but 16% of the population, they are 28% of juvenile arrests, 37% of the youth in juvenile jails, and 58% of the youth sent to adult prisons. (2009 Criminal Justice Primer, The Sentencing Project.)

13. Remember that the U.S. leads the world in putting our own people into jail and prison. The *New York Times* reported in 2008 that the U.S. has 5 percent of the world's population but a quarter of the world's prisoners, over 2.3 million people behind bars, dwarfing other nations. The U.S. rate of incarceration is five to eight times higher than other highly developed countries and black males are the largest percentage of inmates according to ABC News.

14. Even when released from prison, race continues to dominate. A study by Professor Devah Pager of the University of Wisconsin found that 17% of white job applicants with criminal records received call backs from employers while only 5% of black job applicants with criminal records received call backs. Race is so prominent in that study that whites with criminal records actually received better treatment than blacks without criminal records!

So, what conclusions do these facts lead to? The criminal justice system, from start to finish, is seriously racist.

DISCUSSION QUESTIONS

1. Have recent events involving videos of unarmed or lightly armed minority group members being shot by the police changed your mind about whether there are racist elements in the criminal justice system?

2. If so, what are the biggest challenges to changing that system?

*Author's Note: Bill Quigley is legal director for the Center for Constitutional Rights and a law professor at Loyola University New Orleans College of Law. This excerpt was taken from an article he wrote for the Huffington Post (www.huffingtonpost.com/bill-quigley/fourteen-examples-of-raci_b_658947.html). Reprinted with permission.

and prisons that these practices were changed, and African American and white inmates were treated more similarly or were legally required to be so treated in correctional institutions (Belbot & Hemmens, 2010). But despite these reforms, African Americans constituted about 35% of total state inmates in 2013, though they only composed about 13% of the general population that year (Carson, 2014, p. 15; U.S. Census Bureau, 2014a, p. 1).

NATIVE AMERICANS/AMERICAN INDIANS

American Indians are another group of people who have been victims of racism in this country. Note the terms *Native American* and *American Indian* are both used to describe the peoples who lived in the Americas when Columbus landed on an island in the Bahamas in 1492. Columbus mistakenly thought he was in India and thus dubbed the native peoples "Indians." The name stuck, giving rise to the more recent use of the name *Native Americans* by those not wishing to associate these native peoples with Columbus. Other terms often used for native peoples in the United States are *indigenous peoples* or *first peoples*. The problem is that sometimes people who are not Indians have adopted the Native American term and might adopt the term indigenous people, as they were born in the United States. The term *first peoples* is not much used in the United States, though it has gained currency in other countries as a term to describe indigenous peoples. However, the most common names used by natives and non-natives in the United States are American Indians and Native Americans, and they will be used interchangeably in this book (Mann, 2006).

At the time of the arrival of the first of Columbus's ships and the subsequent growth in European expansion to North, Central, and South America, there were reportedly as many as 20 million native people residing in North America (Colbert, 1997; K. C. Davis, 2008; Diamond, 1997; Mann, 2006). Emerging archeological evidence has established that complex cities and agriculture flourished in the Americas, particularly in South and Central America, thousands of years before this wave of Europeans arrived. (There are theories and some evidence that Africans, other Europeans, and Asians all made trips to the Americas and did so many times over the millennia and well before this latter foray by the Spaniards and Columbus [Awes & Awes, 2010; Mann, 2006].) Within a few short decades, those populations had been decimated by disease (smallpox mostly), wars, and massacres. Over the course of a few hundred years, only a small percentage of those original peoples survived, and they were overwhelmed by the influx of European immigrants who, through wars and treaties, relocated American Indians, often forcibly, off of their lands and onto reservations.

Such reservations, at least initially, were, in essence, forms of correctional institutions whose purpose it was to incarcerate a whole people on a piece of land by restricting their movement away from the reservation. Such land was usually less desirable than the land the tribe originally resided on and often inadequate to support the survival of that tribe. As a consequence, American Indian reservations of the 1800s and 1900s were populated by poor, underfed, and undereducated people with few prospects for regaining their land, wealth, or status (Blalock, 1967; Kitano, 1997; Stannard, 1992). Federal policy regarding American Indian tribes has shifted over time, from efforts to segregate them from white communities, to efforts to integrate tribal members into the larger community, to more current efforts to respect their identity, independence, and cultures.

As a result of this complicated history, the interplay of tribal and federal and state law is complex and depends on the time period and the state and tribe involved. Currently, there are 566 federally recognized tribes in the United States, and there are a number of tribes that have not received or sought this recognition (Bureau of Indian Affairs, 2014, p. 1943). On large reservations, more minor criminal offending by tribal members falls under the jurisdiction of that tribe, whereas felony offenses or off-the-reservation criminal activity by tribal members might be handled by the tribe, the state, or the federal government. Larger reservations maintain their own jails for tribal members accused of crimes, for minor offenders, and for those with shorter sentences of incarceration. Despite the existence of these separate legal and correctional systems on larger reservations, at least as regards less serious offending, the number of Native Americans in federal and state prisons is often disproportionate to their representation in the larger population of that state (Perry, 2004).

As reported in a recent Bureau of Justice Statistics publication regarding Indian jails (Minton, 2015, p. 1), there were 79 jails in Indian country in 2014, and the number of inmates confined in those jails has been increasing, although admissions decreased slightly between 2013 and 2014, and the percentage of people held for violent offenses also decreased in Indian jails.

HISPANICS/LATINOS/LATINAS

As mentioned previously, the term *Hispanic* is used to designate an ethnic group that spans many races and nations of origin, to the point where it may not be descriptive (Martinez, 2004). For this reason, other monikers are often used to describe Hispanics that may better represent who they are, such as the more general Latinos/Latinas (which can be used to describe those who originally hailed from Latin America or whose ancestors did) or terms that identify a particular national heritage—specifically, Mexican Americans, Cuban Americans, and so forth. Each of these groups of people has a history, with a distinct American experience. Sometimes, that history has included discrimination by criminal justice actors during incarceration.

The history of Mexican Americans, the largest subgroup of Hispanics or Latinos/Latinas in the United States, has been one in which they and their land were forcibly made part of the American Southwest. As a result of the Mexican–American War, which lasted from 1846 to 1848, Mexico lost almost half of its land—the area that has become the American Southwest, from Texas to California and all of the states in between. However, there is evidence that at least some of the Mexicans in these

POLICY AND RESEARCH

Documented Lynchings of Mexican Americans

Lynching in America: Confronting the Legacy of Racial Terror, a publication of the Equal Justice Initiative (EJI) details an investigation into lynching in the South after the Civil War and up to World War II. There were 3,959 lynchings in Southern states during this time period (1877–1950) (EJI, 2015, p. 1). According to the authors of this publication, the lynchings were public events, widely attended by whites, tolerated by state and local officials, and "used to enforce racial subordination and segregation" (EJI, 2015, p. 1). "Crimes" might include "bumping into a white person, or wearing their military uniforms after World War I, or not using the appropriate title when addressing a white person" (EJI, 2015, p. 1).

In a 2015 *New York Times* editorial, William D. Carrigan and Clive Webb describe a little-known dirty American secret (derived from the same publication): "Blacks weren't the only victims of violence by white mobs" (p. A23). Though blacks were the most likely targets of lynching in America's past, particularly in the South, the authors note that Mexicans and, to a lesser extent, Native Americans, Italians, and Chinese were also singled out in other parts of the country. From seven Mexican shepherds hanged by white vigilantes near Corpus Christi, Texas, in 1878; to 547 newspaper-documented cases of lynchings of Mexicans and Mexican Americans in Arizona, California, New Mexico, and Texas from 1848 to 1928; to thousands killed by Texas Rangers and other law enforcement and vigilantes along the Mexican border from 1915 to 1918, the practice was reportedly widespread in the southwestern United States.

DISCUSSION QUESTIONS

1. What do you think spurs people to lynch other people?

2. What makes the people who commit such atrocities, termed *acts of terror* by the EJI, think they can get away with it?

territories were willing to become citizens of the United States (Espinosa, Komatsu, & Martin, 1998).

Today, in border states, the number of Mexican Americans and Cuban Americans is so high, and their assimilation into the culture is so thorough (e.g., in New Mexico, Arizona, parts of Texas, California, and Florida) that the existence of a clear racial or ethnic majority group has disappeared or has become the Hispanic/Latino/Latina group itself. The increased numbers of Mexican Americans in these states and the immigrants crossing over the southern border into the United States have sparked the political debate over recent Mexican immigrants and whether or not they should be accorded citizenship rights. At the center of the debate is the passage by the state of Arizona of an immigration law that allows law enforcement there to demand papers from any person whom they *suspect* might be in the country illegally, without further cause (Archibold, 2010). Civil libertarians and civil rights groups allege that this law has resulted in discrimination against Hispanics in Arizona and creates the potential to fill jails, if not prisons, in that state. In the Supreme Court case *Arizona v. United States* (2012), the Court upheld the requirement that law enforcement verify immigrant status during lawful stops but struck down three other provisions of the law (National Conference of State Legislatures, 2012).

Whether in Arizona or in other states, however, and as with American Indians and African Americans, the representation of Hispanics in American prisons and jails is already disproportionate to their representation in the general population. In 2013, Hispanics constituted 21% of state inmates, when their representation in the larger population was estimated at 17% for that year (Carson, 2014, p. 15; U.S. Census Bureau, 2014a, p. 1). Looking at just the number of inmates incarcerated tells an important story (Figure 16.1), but it is the rate of incarceration (Figure 16.2) that demonstrates more clearly the disparity in our correctional system.

ASIAN AMERICANS

As with most immigrants to America in the 1800s and 1900s, Japanese and Chinese immigrants (who collectively represent the largest group of Asian Americans but certainly not the only group [space prevents us from sufficiently exploring the Korean, Cambodian, Vietnamese, Pacific Islanders, or other East Asian experiences, for example]) were looking for a better life for themselves and their families. Though they found such a life in varying degrees, their experience, like that of the other ethnic and racial minorities mentioned in this chapter, was tinged with racism. Originally settling primarily in western states in the 1800s and early 1900s, Chinese and Japanese immigrants were heavily involved in mining and agriculture in pioneer communities.

Chinese labor was crucial to the construction of the first transcontinental railroad (1863–1869). Later barred from owning property in some states and from voting in others, Chinese people made do by engaging in service professions (e.g., laundries, restaurants, and herb shops) and settling together in parts of cities for both comfort and safety (J. C. Jones, 2016; Lennon, Angier, Tsui, & Cheng, 2003; Wei, 1999). When economies soured in some of those cities or states, Asian immigrants were blamed for taking jobs from poor whites—much like the way blacks

PHOTO 16.3: A cartoon that appeared in *Harper's Weekly* regarding the "Chinese Question," which depicts Lady Justice defending a Chinese man being persecuted by a racist mob.

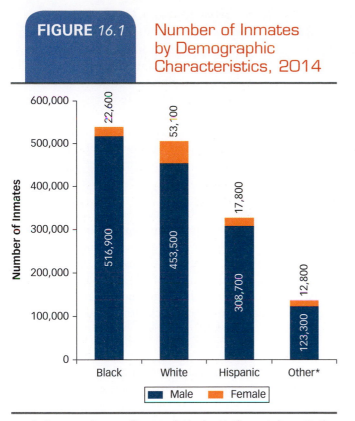

FIGURE 16.1 Number of Inmates by Demographic Characteristics, 2014

*Includes American Indians and Alaska Natives; Asians, Native Hawaiians, and other Pacific Islanders; and persons of two or more races.

Source: Carson (2015), Table 10.

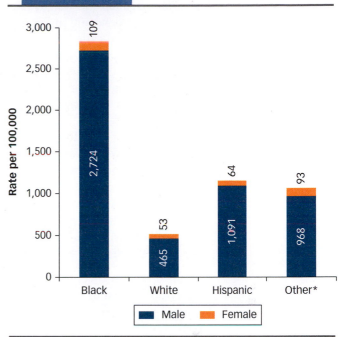

FIGURE 16.2 Rate of Imprisonment by Demographic Characteristics, 2014

*Includes American Indians and Alaska Natives; Asians, Native Hawaiians, and other Pacific Islanders; and persons of two or more races.

Source: Carson (2015), Table 10; U.S. Census Bureau, Population Division (2016).

were blamed by poor whites in the South after the Civil War or recent Mexican immigrants are blamed by poor whites in the West today—and they were often run out of town. They were literally placed on ships and sent home, even though they and their families may have lived in the United States for decades, if not generations.

The first restrictive immigration law in the country, the Chinese Exclusion Act of 1882, was directed at reducing immigration from China (J. C. Jones, 2016; Wei, 1999). This act was not repealed until 1943. Some of the first drug laws, laws against opium dens dating from the 1870s onward, were passed because Chinese immigrants were thought to be corrupting the white population by spreading the use of the drug; such laws were ironic, as opium was first introduced to China by Westerners (Lennon et al., 2003).

Much like Chinese immigrants, Japanese immigrants provided cheap labor, as they were employed in the construction of railroads, as well as agriculture, restaurants, and many other businesses, primarily in the American West. In fact, when Chinese immigrants were excluded, Japanese immigrants filled the gap, beginning in the 1880s, until their own immigration was also restricted in 1908. Barred from owning their own land, many Japanese Americans earned their living in the late 1800s and early 1900s by leasing land and growing beets in Oregon and Idaho, for instance. As their economic strength grew, however, they were regarded as a threat by the local white population, and there were numerous instances where they were forcibly run off of their land and out of town (Mercier, 2010).

Despite the Issei's [another word for the first Japanese immigrants] hard work in the early twentieth century, envy and racial discrimination led to increasing anti-Japanese attitudes on the West Coast, much as the sentiment had developed against perceived Chinese competition. Residents of Mountain Home, Nampa, and Caldwell, Idaho, drove out Japanese workers, and white mobs near Coeur d'Alene and in Portland threatened Japanese railroad workers. Tensions led to the so-called "Gentleman's Agreement" between the U.S. and Japan that effectively limited after 1908 the numbers of laborers that could emigrate from Japan. Instead, the two governments allowed wives and brides to join earlier male immigrants in the United States, changing the character of the immigrant community. (Mercier, 2010, p. 10)

The internment of 120,000 Japanese Americans in 1942 in 10 inland concentration camps during World War II, along with the confiscation of their property, was not based on the actual threat they presented to the safety of western states—or at least no more, say, than the German Americans who were scattered all over the United States at the time and who were not incarcerated (Mercier, 2010, p. 1). The internment of whole Japanese American families in prison camps was instead based on racially tinged beliefs about who could be trusted and on ignorance regarding the allegiance that such citizens felt for this, their country.

As far as the incarceration of most Asian Americans these days goes, they tend to be underrepresented in correctional organizations in relation to their representation in the general population. It is not clear why such underrepresentation exists, but it is likely related to their tight-knit and supportive families and communities and the value those cultures have placed on education and achievement, resulting in higher incomes and education for many Japanese and Chinese American citizens (Mercier, 2010). Notably, successful integration into American society, as measured by economic and educational achievements, is not uniform across all Asian Americans. Those emigrating from war-torn Cambodia and Vietnam in the latter half of the 20th century were not always as "successful" or able to stay out of the criminal justice system and its correctional institutions.

••• THE CONNECTION BETWEEN CLASS AND RACE/ETHNICITY

Americans are often averse to recognizing the existence of a class system in the United States. In part, this dislike of class labels springs from our history of revolution, which was spurred, in part, by a desire to separate ourselves from the rigidity of the class system in England and Europe. Also, our economic, political, and social systems have allowed people in lower classes to advance through ingenuity, education, or drive—or some mix of those—to the middle or upper classes. However, this upward mobility is hampered in any number of ways by poverty and related ills, such as poor nutrition and schools, limited access to health care, and parents who are absent or neglectful. When poverty is combined with long-term and systematic discrimination against a people, such that their families are destroyed, as occurred with the social institution of slavery and the continued discrimination against African Americans, recovery of communities can take generations. Not surprisingly, illegal drug use catches on in such poor communities, as do other forms of involvement in street criminality.

Certain racial and ethnic minorities are more likely to be poor and thus caught up in the criminal justice system and overrepresented in correctional institutions and programs (see Table 16.1). Race and traditions of discrimination against African Americans have stymied their ability to assimilate in many cases. Language barriers and discrimination

TABLE 16.1 Number and Percentage of People in Poverty by Different Poverty Measures, 2014**

	NUMBER IN THOUSANDS	OFFICIAL				SPM				DIFFERENCE	
		NUMBER		PERCENTAGE		NUMBER		PERCENTAGE		NUMBER	PERCENTAGE
		ESTIMATE	MARGIN OF ERROR† (±)	ESTIMATE	MARGIN OF ERROR† (±)	ESTIMATE	MARGIN OF ERROR† (±)	ESTIMATE	MARGIN OF ERROR† (±)		
All people	316,168	47,021	854	14.9	0.3	48,390	868	15.3	0.3	*1,369	*0.4
Sex											
Male	154,815	20,883	441	13.5	0.3	22,497	438	14.5	0.3	*1,614	*1.0
Female	161,353	26,138	525	16.2	0.3	25,893	517	16.0	0.3	−245	−0.2
Age											
Under 18 years	73,920	15,904	401	21.5	0.5	12,360	369	16.7	0.5	*−3,545	*−4.8
18 to 64 years	196,254	26,527	533	13.5	0.3	29,401	570	15.0	0.3	*2,874	*1.5
65 years and older	45,994	4,590	176	10.0	0.4	6,629	223	14.4	0.5	*2,039	*4.4
Type of Unit											
Married couple	189,603	13,696	499	7.2	0.3	17,878	575	9.4	0.3	*4,182	*2.2
Female householder	64,008	18,442	559	28.8	0.7	18,366	537	28.7	0.7	−76	−0.1
Male householder	34,075	6,105	266	17.9	0.7	7,420	292	21.8	0.7	*1,315	*3.9
New SPM unit	28,482	8,779	337	30.8	0.9	4,726	305	16.6	1.0	*−4,053	*−14.2
Race and Hispanic Origin											
White	244,468	31,305	640	12.8	0.3	33,346	683	13.6	0.3	*2,042	*0.8
White, not Hispanic	195,352	19,797	523	10.1	0.3	20,943	568	10.7	0.3	*1,147	*0.6

(Continued)

TABLE 16.1 [Continued]

	NUMBER IN THOUSANDS	OFFICIAL				SPM				DIFFERENCE	
		NUMBER		PERCENTAGE		NUMBER		PERCENTAGE		NUMBER	PERCENTAGE
		ESTIMATE	MARGIN OF ERROR† (±)	ESTIMATE	MARGIN OF ERROR† (±)	ESTIMATE	MARGIN OF ERROR† (±)	ESTIMATE	MARGIN OF ERROR† (±)	NUMBER	PERCENTAGE
Black	41,226	10,870	360	26.4	0.9	9,662	346	23.4	0.8	*–1,208	*–2.9
Asian	17,796	2,142	209	12.0	1.2	2,999	247	16.8	1.3	*856	*4.8
Hispanic (any race)	55,614	13,214	422	23.8	0.8	14,129	442	25.4	0.8	*915	*1.6
Nativity											
Native born	273,984	39,227	771	14.3	0.3	38,379	762	14.0	0.3	*–848	*–0.3
Foreign born	42,184	7,795	287	18.5	0.6	10,011	355	23.7	0.7	*2,216	*5.3
Naturalized citizen	19,733	2,349	146	11.9	0.7	3,467	184	17.6	0.8	*1,118	*5.7
Not a citizen	22,451	5,446	242	24.3	0.9	6,544	282	29.1	1.0	*1,098	*4.9

†The margin of error (MOE) is a measure of an estimate's variability. The larger the MOE in relation to the size of the estimate, the less reliable the estimate. The MOE is the estimated 90 percent confidence interval. The MOEs shown in this table are based on standard errors calculated using replicate weights. For more information, see "Standard Errors and Their Use" at ftp://ftp2.census.gov/library/publications/2014/demo/p60-252sa.pdf.

*An asterisk preceding an estimate indicates change is statistically different from zero at the 90 percent confidence level.

**Latest data available at the time of this writing

SPM = Supplemental Poverty Measure

Source: Short (2015).

regarding race have also prevented some Hispanics, American Indians, and Asians from moving to the middle and upper classes. Cultural differences have created a similar barrier for these groups. The drug war, which is discussed more fully in the following, has tended to target illegal drugs and their use and has had a disparate impact on minority groups, such as Hispanics and African Americans. The drug war has led to the phenomenon of disproportionate representation by these minority groups in correctional organizations.

●●● MINORITIES: POLICIES AND PRACTICES THAT HAVE RESULTED IN INCREASED INCARCERATION

As has been mentioned in other chapters in this book, African Americans and Hispanics, particularly, but also American Indians are disproportionately represented as the accused or convicted in jails, prisons, and community corrections in the United States. Asian Americans are overrepresented in federal prisons. As already mentioned, most of these minority groups are also overrepresented among the poor in the United States and among those accused or convicted of street crimes (see Table 16.1). In the 1950s, an estimated 70% of the inmates in America's prisons were white, but by the year 2013, about 56% of inmates in prisons were African American (35%) or Hispanic (21%) (Carson, 2014, p. 15). Yet according to the 2013 U.S. Census, only 13% of the population as a whole were black or African American, and 17% were Hispanic or Latino of any race, whereas 78% were white (with other races constituting Asian [4.9%], Native Hawaiian or Pacific Islander [0.2%], or two or more races [2.3%]) (U.S. Census Bureau, 2014b, p. 1).

Web 16.2: NAACP

Stated another way, among the largest racial and ethnic groups in 2013, black, non-Hispanic males had an imprisonment rate that was 6 times higher than white, non-Hispanic males and 2.5 times higher than Hispanic males (Carson, 2014, p. 8). Likewise, black, non-Hispanic females were imprisoned at twice the rate of white, non-Hispanic females in 2013 (though the former's numbers had decreased from 2012) (Carson, 2014, p. 8). All of this means that no matter how one views the data, blacks or African Americans and Hispanics/Latinos are disproportionately incarcerated in the United States when compared with their population composition.

THE DRUG WAR: THE NEW JIM CROW?

The rhetoric for the modern drug war was initiated by President Richard Nixon. He ran on a hardline law enforcement platform for president and, as a consequence, was interested in implementing tough-on-crime policies and practices. His efforts, however, were stymied by the fact that law enforcement was (and still is) primarily a responsibility of the states and their counties and cities. Ronald Reagan was the next president interested in enlarging the reach of the federal government into the states' business regarding law enforcement. His administration was responsible for declaring a war on drugs and for asking Congress to allocate money for prisons and law enforcement. Therefore, President Reagan is often credited (or blamed, depending on one's perspective) for starting the modern drug war.

Riding this popular tough-on-crime rhetoric of the 1980s and 1990s, Presidents (G. H. W.) Bush, Clinton, (G. W.) Bush, and Obama each continued to fund—and, at times, expand the reach of—the federal drug war. The practical effect of this modern war, if not the intent of its architects, has been to incarcerate unprecedented hundreds of

ETHICAL ISSUE 16.1 ?

What Would You Do?

You are a black male correctional officer in a jail, working in a living unit for inmates who are new to the facility. It is usually referred to as a *classification unit*, as inmates in it are classified to other units by their conviction status, perceived dangerousness, and programming needs. After working in the unit for a few years, you notice that there are a few other staff, though not most, who treat minority group inmates with less respect than white inmates. You also notice that some minority group inmates are classified with a higher security ranking than similar white inmates, and this means that minority inmates do not have as much access to reentry programming and to placement in the work release facility as do white inmates. What would you do to make sure that minority group inmates are treated and classified in the same way as other inmates?

thousands of minority men and women, primarily African Americans and Hispanics, who would otherwise not be incarcerated in the correctional system (Lurigio & Loose, 2008).

Michelle Alexander (2010), in her book *The New Jim Crow: Mass Incarceration in the Age of Colorblindness*, asserts that the modern drug war has been focused on the poor and minorities while ignoring the fact that most drug users and drug dealers are white. She notes that in 2004, an estimated 75% of those incarcerated for drug offenses were black or Latino while the majority of the drug users and dealers were white (p. 97). She argues the case that the drug war, as executed, has the practical effect of reinstating Jim Crow laws in the United States. She maintains this is so because of the police sweeps of poor and minority neighborhoods, the law enforcement focus on small-time marijuana possession offenders, and the law's nonsensical emphasis on crack cocaine over powder cocaine, though they are similar in addiction and pharmacologically the same (see the following discussion of this topic and Chapter 5 on sentencing). Moreover, the implementation of the drug war has led to the erosion of civil-liberties protections regarding search and evidence.

Jim Crow laws were devised by Southern states following the Civil War, starting in the 1870s and lasting until 1965 and the civil rights movement, to prevent African Americans from fully participating in social, economic, and civic life. These laws restricted the rights and liberties of black citizens in employment, housing, education, travel, and voting. Interestingly enough, voter disenfranchisement, or preventing African Americans from voting, was a key part of the Jim Crow laws back then (M. Alexander, 2010). Today, a felony offense, gained through even a relatively minor drug possession conviction, can mean the loss of employability, access to public housing or food stamps, and the right to vote—much the same effect as the Jim Crow laws of a century ago.

CRACK VERSUS POWDER COCAINE

The concern over crack cocaine started in the 1980s. The sentencing disparity that occurred when crack cocaine possession was treated as 100 times worse than possession of powder cocaine in federal law was tied to the race and class of the persons associated with each drug (M. Alexander, 2010; Sentencing Project, 2011). Poorer and disproportionately black and Hispanic people tended to use the cheaper crack cocaine, whereas richer and disproportionately white people tended to use the more expensive powder cocaine. Though there was never any real evidence that crack was more harmful or addictive than powder cocaine, there were a number of stories sensationalizing news of "crack babies" and mothers—portrayed as *black* babies and their mothers—in the 1980s, when the Reagan administration promoted the disparate sentencing. M. Alexander (2010) reports that the Reagan administration used the emergence of crack as a means of justifying the drug war and its focus on poor and minority people:

Jim Crow laws:
Laws devised by Southern states following the Civil War, starting in the 1870s and lasting until 1965, to prevent African Americans from fully participating in social, economic, and civic life.

They hired staff whose job it was to find reports of inner-city crack users, crack dealers, crack babies, and crack whores and to feed those stories to the media. The media saturation coverage of crack was no accident. It was a deliberate campaign that fueled the race to incarcerate. Legislators began passing ever harsher mandatory-minimum sentences in response to the media frenzy. (Cited in A. Cooper, 2011, p. 7)

IN FOCUS 16.3

Harsh Justice and the Scott Sisters

In 1993, two sisters, Jamie Scott, 22, and her pregnant 19-year-old sister, Gladys, were convicted of using three teenage boys to set up the armed robbery of two men (Pitts, 2010). The Scott sisters supplied the shotgun to the teenagers. Eleven dollars was stolen during this robbery, and the victims were unharmed. For this crime, the sisters, who had no prior criminal history, were each given a double life sentence and, as of November 2010, had served 16 years of it.

The teenage boys, two of whom testified against the sisters as part of their plea bargains, received 2-year sentences, which they completed years ago. The Scott sisters claimed and still claim they are innocent. The mother of the sisters argues that the harsh sentences were revenge for the family's willingness to testify against a corrupt sheriff (Pitts, 2010). As news columnist Leonard Pitts (2010) explains,

> Whatever the proximate cause of this ridiculous sentence, the larger cause is neon clear: The Scott sisters are black women in the poorest state in the union. And as report after report has testified, if you are poor or black (and God help you if you are both), the American justice system has long had this terrible tendency to throw you away like garbage. Historically, this has been especially true in the South. . . . How many other Scott sisters and brothers are languishing behind bars for no good reason, doing undeserved hard time on nonexistent evidence, perjured testimony, prosecutorial misconduct or sheer racial or class bias. (p. B6)

The Scott sisters did, finally, get some relief from their sentences. Due to the advocacy of Pitts and others, such as the NAACP, the original prosecutor of the sisters, the governor of Mississippi, Haley Barbour, suspended the sisters' sentences as long as Gladys donated a kidney to her sister Jamie, whose kidneys have failed (Diaz-Duran, 2010). They were released from prison in January of 2010.

DISCUSSION QUESTION

1. In what ways does the Scott sisters' treatment by the criminal justice system seem similar to and different from that experienced by the Scottsboro Boys?

The harsher sentencing for crack cocaine possession is another example of a current criminal justice policy that even the United States Sentencing Commission concedes has had the practical and discriminatory effect of vastly increasing the incarceration of African Americans and Hispanics. Though the federal law was changed in 2010, crack cocaine sentences at the federal level are still much harsher than powder cocaine, by a factor of 18 to 1 (rather than 100 to 1, as they were under the 1986 law). Even so, the U.S. Sentencing Commission (2011) estimated that 12,811 federal inmates would be affected by the retroactive application of the reduced sentences for crack cocaine and that 85% of those affected will be African Americans (p. 19). In 2016, at the time of this writing, the U.S. Senate is considering the Sentencing Reform and Corrections Act, which would further reduce the sentencing disparity between crack and powder cocaine and would be retroactively applied to those offenders previously sentenced under the old provisions. However, state laws may still treat crack cocaine use more harshly than powder cocaine, which results in disproportionate incarceration of minority group members for this drug offense in state prisons.

RACIAL PROFILING AND DRIVING WHILE BLACK OR BROWN

In addition to the drug war and its effect on increasing minority involvement as the accused or convicted in corrections, scholars note that racial profiling by the police can have a similar effect. DWB, which stands for **driving while black or brown**, refers to the police practice of focusing law enforcement attention on black- or brown-skinned drivers. The research in this area has been mixed, with some researchers finding that this practice affects arrests while others are unable to establish the existence of this practice

Video 16.1: Is "Driving While Black" a Systemic Problem?

Driving while black or brown (DWB): Refers to the practice of police focusing law enforcement attention on black- or brown-skinned drivers.

AP Video 16.1:
Ferguson QA

Video 16.2:
Activists Want
New Law to Curb
Racial Profiling

(Rice, Reitzel, & Piquero, 2005). Lundman's (2010) research also raised questions about the validity of police reports on the race or ethnicity of stopped drivers, noting that there were unaccounted for missing data on drivers from predominately poor and minority neighborhoods in some research.

Police officers will tend to stop older vehicles, and such cars are often owned by poorer and minority group members. Having said this, Langan and colleagues (Langan, Greenfield, Smith, Durose, & Levin, 2001) found, in a review of Bureau of Justice Statistics data from a police and public national contact survey, that blacks and Hispanics were more likely to report being stopped by the police than were whites. Notably, in a presentation at the annual conference of the International Association of Chiefs of Police in October 2015, President Obama stated that he had been stopped for DWB. The researchers also found that minority group members were more likely to report negative criminal justice outcomes for themselves, such as being ticketed, arrested, handcuffed, searched, or subjected to the use of force by officers when stopped. Rice and colleagues (2005) found, in their study of the perceptions of 700 randomly selected young-adult (aged 18–26) New Yorkers, that the nuances of these stops might hinge on what shade one's skin is (p. 63). They found that blacks and black Hispanics were more likely to report that racial profiling was widespread and that they were racially profiled than were whites or nonblack Hispanics.

In a study of drug arrests in Seattle, Washington, Beckett and colleagues (Beckett, Nyrop, Pfingst, & Bowen, 2005) found that the disparity in arrests between minorities and whites can be explained by racialized justice. The drug problem there was seen as a dangerous crack problem, which, in turn, was seen as a problem of use by blacks and Hispanics, despite comparable use of illegal drugs by whites. More minorities were therefore stopped by the police, as they were seen as more involved in illegal drug use.

Of course, the more such stops one is subjected to, the more likely that one is to run afoul of the law and to enter a correctional institution, such as a jail, or to find oneself on probation (Hawkins, 2005). Relatedly, these experiences are also more likely to result in the building of a record, which, later, should one become entangled in the system again, might be used to justify a conviction or a more severe sentence.

© Mikael Karlsson/Alamy Stock Photo

PHOTO 16.4: A white officer stopping a black driver. Critics argue that black and brown drivers are stopped more by the police than white drivers and that they are treated more harshly when they are stopped.

EVIDENCE-DRIVEN PUBLIC HEALTH PROSECUTION USED TO REDUCE MINORITY GROUP CORRECTIONAL POPULATIONS

Prosecutors play a key role in determining what to charge and whether an offense will lead to significant jail or prison time for the offender. In recognition of this fact, the twice-elected district attorney for Milwaukee County, Wisconsin, John Chisholm, has adopted what he terms an evidence-driven public-health model for prosecution with a focus on the question, "What's the most effective way to keep a community healthy?" (Toobin, 2015, p. 27). Rather than being wholly concerned with winning or losing cases, this model puts primacy on keeping the public safe from violent offenders, but then, for the more minor offenders, the model shifts to an effort to keep them out of the system. Proponents of the model argue that low-level offenders are likely to be harmed by placement in corrections and to bring that harm back into their communities in the form of more petty crimes by those who are low-skilled and undereducated, who are likely to remain unemployed and impoverished, along with their families. A disproportionate number of these low-level offenders in Milwaukee and the nation are minority group members.

In the Milwaukee experiment, an early intervention program in the prosecutor's office was established to assess whether the accused is a low-level offender and whether he or she is likely to reengage in crime (based on an eight-question assessment and a review of the rap sheet and police report) (Toobin, 2015). Respondents who score low on this assessment are given probation, and if they successfully complete it, they walk away with no record. Those who score high are further assessed and may garner a criminal record if convicted, but their charges might still be reduced. Other efforts related to the model include evaluations of repeat offenders, much like in a drug or other specialty court, and their program progress to determine if new charges are warranted when violations of probation occur or if they just need other assistance to stay out of crime.

As a result of these efforts, there are far fewer prosecutions of African Americans and whites for low-level drug offenses, including possession of drug paraphernalia, in Milwaukee County since the experiment began in 2006. The number of misdemeanor prosecutions has dropped by over a third, and the number of African Americans sent to state prison from Milwaukee County has dropped by half (Toobin, 2015, p. 32). But the number of murders in Milwaukee and serious violent crimes like it have remained unusually high, and this, the district attorney concedes, is due to factors outside of his and his office's control, as it includes larger societal problems, such as "poverty, hopelessness, lack of education, drug addiction, and the easy availability of guns" (Toobin, 2015, p. 32).

••• MINORITIES: EXPERIENCING INCARCERATION

Victor Hassine (2009), a writer and inmate doing life since 1980 in Pennsylvania prisons for a capital offense, comments that race was and is an integral part of the prison life he has experienced and does experience. Segregation in housing and by gangs (both voluntary) and racial bias in treatment by staff were common in Graterford Prison, where he was an inmate during the 1980s. Most of the inmates in this prison were black while most of the staff were white. (Notably, in the 1980s, in Graterford Prison, the only choices for self-identifying inmate race *or* ethnicity were white and black.) Most of the staff in this prison identified as Christian while a sizable proportion of the black inmates were Muslim. Added to these differences based on race and religion was their place of origin: Many inmates tended to come from urban areas while many staff were raised in more rural settings. Such differences between staff and inmates led to a difficult adjustment for minority inmates (see the following discussion of minority staff) and were cited as one of the complaints by inmates in the 1971 riot at Attica Prison in New York.

AP Video 16.2: Holder Ferguson

Journal Article 16.1: Inmate Racial Integration: Achieving Racial Integration in the Texas Prison System

Audio 16.1: DOJ Report Finds Biased Law Enforcement Tactics in Baltimore

Wilbert Rideau (2010), in his first-person account of incarceration in Louisiana prisons, describes the setting for his third trial and the racial politics of the day in Baton Rouge, Louisiana, in this way:

> In 1970, at the time of my third trial, the Klan was using the kind of intimidation for which it was famous. It invaded North Baton Rouge—the black part of town—and plastered the utility poles and other upright surfaces with signs showing a rearing white-hooded horse carrying a hooded white rider, his left hand holding aloft a fiery cross. Beneath the horse's feet was the Klan's motto: FOR GOD AND COUNTRY. The poster was dominated by the horse and rider and by the big, bold print in the upper left corner that read SAVE OUR LAND, and beneath the picture it read JOIN THE KLAN. (p. 61)

Audio 16.2: One Lawyer's Fight for Young Blacks and "Just Mercy"

Rideau (2010) encountered racism from some staff and inmates over the course of his long incarceration, but he noted that it lessened in degree and frequency as the years went on. Today, the racial mix of staff is more likely to reflect that of the community where inmates come from, which has tended to reduce race as a source of conflict between staff and inmates. However, Ross and Richards (2002) note that a "color line" still divides prison inmates into at least these groups: blacks, whites, and Hispanics. Between and among these groups, there are different styles of living and means of surviving.

VICTIMIZATION BY RACE AND ETHNICITY

As regards victimization in prisons, Wolff, Shi, and Blitz (2008) found that African Americans were more likely to report sexual or physical violence from staff than from other inmates, non-Hispanic whites were more likely to report victimization by other inmates than by staff, and Hispanics had above-average reporting of victimization by both staff and other inmates. When both types of victimization were accounted for, though, all three groups reported about the same amount of victimization, just from different sources.

ETHICAL ISSUE 16.2 ?

What Would You Do?

You are a white female counselor working in a privately owned juvenile detention facility, and you are interested in hiring a more racially and ethnically diverse staff to better match your community and clientele. Your company has an equal employment opportunity policy in place, but it has rarely been implemented in practice, as almost all of the staff are white, whereas almost all of the clients are black or Hispanic. You are on the selection team for a new position at the facility. After several interviews, you notice that at least one other member of the team—and possibly more—is not interested in hiring a minority group member, as this person consistently ranks such applicants' resumes and interviews lower than white applicants, even though you do not think they merit it. The vote on the applicants is approaching, and there are three top candidates for the job who all seem similarly qualified for it. One of those applicants is a Hispanic male, and the other applicants are white. What would you do to ensure that this vote is fair and that the best applicant for the job gets the position?

PROBATION OR PRISON?

Some research indicates that black offenders may prefer prison over community alternative sentencing, whereas white offenders express the opposite preference. In a study by Wood and May (2003), the authors note that blacks and whites "differed in their willingness to participate in alternative sanctions, in their preference for prison over alternatives, and in the amount of these alternatives they were willing to serve" (p. 624), with blacks less willing to participate in alternatives or the number of alternatives and more likely to prefer prison over alternatives. There are several explanations for these differences discovered by these and other researchers.

Crouch (1993) argued that blacks might be more able to accept prison and adjust to it over alternatives because they are more likely to find people they know housed there and are less likely to be threatened by prison life than whites, given that they have suffered the violence and deprivations of the cities already. Wood and May (2003) add that it is possible that blacks may also prefer prison because the alternatives to it in the community may subject them to abuse and harassment and ultimate

PERSPECTIVE FROM A PRACTITIONER

James Watkins, Classification Counselor

Position: Classification counselor (3), Washington State Department of Corrections

Location: Airway Heights Correction Center, Spokane, Washington

Education: North Idaho College and Spokane Community College

What previous criminal justice experience do you have?

I previously served as a correctional officer for 4.5 years, a sergeant for one year, and a classification counselor (2) for four years.

What are your primary duties and responsibilities?

- Supervise counselors on a behavior change unit
- Work with offenders to assure correct classification levels
- Complete offender needs assessment per RNR (risk, need, responsivity) model of offender classification
- Facilitate program services to include mental-health services, education, chemical dependency, and evidence-based programs, when available
- Provide inmates with information about reentry and release resources
- Engage offenders with programs to increase success upon release
- Connect families through the facilitation of increased communication with families
- Mentor language, role-modeling prosocial behaviors for effective communication with staff and offenders
- Manage a caseload of adult criminal offenders whom I am responsible for counseling and informing regarding community resources and problems they might encounter in their transition to work release, parole, or release
- Work with internal and external entities to facilitate offender reentry into the community; enforce court ordered conditions and impose DOC conditions
- Participate in risk management with a multidisciplinary team

- Maintain communication with offenders to assist with attorney calls, child custody and child support hearings with DSHS and courts, and family contact through crisis/emergency situations
- Arrange translator services
- Evaluate offenders for early release
- Regularly review and update offender plans, needs assessment, and programming prioritization
- Make recommendations for offender program progression, earned time, and other incentives
- Exercise sound judgment, aligned with department policy, in decisions concerning sanctions, treatment, and education referrals

What are the characteristics and traits most useful in your line of work?

- Effective communication skills
- Honesty and integrity
- Flexibility and dependability
- Strong time management skills
- Stability, willingness to change, adaptability, and humor
- Do not take things personally, and be understanding of clientele.
- Thick skinned—withstand more than the average individual
- A superior mindset
- Understand that clients and staff are a diverse group of individuals and that inmates and staff come from huge variety of social and economic backgrounds.
- Ability to accept individuals' beliefs that are far from your own and still be able to deal with those individuals
- Be levelheaded, not reactionary.
- Develop an ability to stand alone, stand on your morals and beliefs, and be very independent.
- Have positive avenues of relief outside the job environment.
- Ability to deal with difficult situations appropriately
- Be more rooted and grounded in who you are to overcome perceptions of others' beliefs about who you are.
- Ability to take the higher ground—as a minority, you have to show it more than others
- Be independent because of the cultural perception of how you treat offenders within your same culture and race; you are under the spotlight more.
- Overcome the perception of giving preferential treatment to the same culture, race, and minority. That

(Continued)

(Continued)

stereotype is always in the back of your mind—how others perceive your treatment of a minority and offenders of the same race.

- Do not compromise the self, and act even more professional. Coming from the Spokane area and becoming a part of the criminal justice system while living in the same community and having to withstand scrutiny and stereotyping, I had to maintain values, integrity, and goals regardless of my culture or race.
- Ability to deal with direct and indirect prejudicial statements from staff and references toward race, politics, community, and family
- Ability to deal professionally and maturely with the assumptions, stereotypes, and direct racism and indirect racist undertones

Please describe a typical workday.

- Come to work and check mail messages and calendar for the day
- Return phone calls and e-mails from DOC staff, offender families, offenders, criminal justice system attorneys, and judges
- Check with custody and classification staff passed down from previous shifts that concern any information pertaining to safety and security of unit staff offenders
- Check list for classification case management issues and offender reviews and release dates
- EBC and unit responsibilities include program schedules, class facilitation, and specific unit and prison meetings
- Meet with offenders; attend to classification issues, reentry/release, and security release; address offender jobs and programming
- Deal with insubordinate staff and offenders

- Maintain safety and security of unit in collaboration with unit supervisor

What is your advice to someone who wants to enter your field?

- Make sure to understand who you are. This is a job you want to perform well, but it isn't your life.
- Be prepared every day.
- Be very aware of who you are going to work for and what the job responsibilities are.
- You have to be very aware of the clientele with whom you are dealing on a day-to-day basis on both sides of the spectrum—that is, both the staff and the offenders.
- You need to be aware of how you will be perceived: Go against the stereotype.
- You need to be aware of the stereotypes—for example, how you dress "like a gang member" versus going golfing; wearing identical clothes but being perceived differently; and how you conduct yourself at work and away from work. Stereotypical perceptions include that one is uneducated, is athletic, has low writing and language skills, or has an STG (security threat group, aka gang) affiliation.
- Prove that you are above the stereotypes; you may have to be patient. You want people to judge you on work performance, not by your race and culture.
- Unfortunately, the bigger burden is that how you conduct yourself influences others' perspectives of African Americans.
- Always take the high road. Fair isn't an option. You cannot think about what fair is or should be. You just have to follow your values, integrity, and beliefs and take the high road at all times.
- Have a "superior mindset"—Professor Jigoro Kano, founder of judo.

revocation of their probation anyway. Therefore, it is not likely true that blacks or whites "prefer" prisons or the alternatives (e.g., probation or other programming); they just disagree about which is the lesser evil.

MINORITIES WORKING IN CORRECTIONS

As with women, the employment of minority group men and women in correctional organizations did not increase until the Civil Rights Act of 1964 was passed, and affirmative action plans were developed to encourage their employment. Today, however, the number of minorities employed in corrections, though not always reflecting their representation in the community, particularly as this regards minority group women, has increased substantially. Though data in this area are not always consistent or up to date, we do know from the *Sourcebook of Criminal Justice Statistics* (Pastore & Maguire, 2000 [Table 1.104]; Pastore & Maguire, 2005 [Table 1.101, Table 1.107]) that black non-Hispanics accounted for 23.7% of local-jail correctional officer employees in 1999 (when their representation in the general population was at about 12.2%, according to the U.S. Census for 2001); 19.5% of all employees in state, federal, and private prisons in 2004; and 24.3% of correctional officers in federal prisons in 2004. On the other hand, non-Hispanic whites and Hispanics are underrepresented among staff, when compared with their representation in those communities. In 2001, whites constituted about 69.0% of the U.S. population, and Hispanics constituted about 12.9% (U.S. Census Bureau, 2001). In these same data, whites were still the majority racial-group employee (59.3%, 63.3%, and 60.6%, consecutively) in these jails and prisons, and Hispanics constituted a substantial ethnic minority (7.7%, 7.3%, and 12.4%, consecutively).

PHOTO 16.5: An inmate being cuffed by an officer. Inmates in transit between institutions or who present a danger to staff are cuffed before they are removed from cells.

SUMMARY

- American history contains a racist past, which has affected the operation of correctional entities and the criminal justice system generally.

- Those who fall below the poverty line in the United States are also more likely to be enmeshed in street criminality. Some racial and ethnic groups who are more likely to be poor (e.g., African Americans and Hispanics) are also more likely to be engaged in street crime.

- Police, courts, and correctional practices have had the effect of increasing the disproportionate incarceration of minority group members. DWB, the drug war generally, and the harsh sentencing for crack cocaine specifically, along with the

- disenfranchisement that comes with a felony conviction (and in some states, stays with a felony conviction), all serve to reinforce the disparity in treatment of racial and ethnic minorities by the criminal justice system.

- Physical and sexual victimization in prisons varies by type of victimization and by race and ethnicity, though the total amount of such victimization appears to be similar for these groups.

- The numbers of racial and ethnic minorities working in corrections has increased substantially over the years, and for African Americans, at least, it appears that they mirror their numbers in the community in a number of jurisdictions.

KEY TERMS

Discrimination 388

Disparity 387

Driving while black
or brown (DWB) 401

Ethnicity 387

Jim Crow laws 400

Race 387

DISCUSSION QUESTIONS

1. What sorts of criteria differentiate race and ethnicity? Why might it not always be clear what race or ethnicity a person is? Are there reasons to make such distinctions?

2. What evidence is there of disparity and discrimination against racial and ethnic minorities in the United States in the past?

3. What evidence is there of disparity and discrimination against racial and ethnic minorities in the United States currently?

4. How and why is adjustment in corrections affected by one's race and ethnicity?

5. Discuss how we might reduce the amount of disparity and discrimination against minorities in the United States? What specific steps can be taken in this direction? What are the likely barriers to accomplishing these changes?

USEFUL INTERNET SITES

Please note that the sites listed can be accessed at edge.sagepub.com/stohrcorrections.

American Civil Liberties Union (ACLU): www.aclu.org

This site provides information about ACLU activities, what civil liberties are, and how they are currently under threat.

National Association for the Advancement of Colored People (NAACP): www.naacp.org

This site provides information about NAACP activities and current threats to the rights of minority groups in the United States.

The Sentencing Project: www.sentencingproject.org

This site includes facts, figures, research, and editorials on sentencing practices.

Southern Poverty Law Center: www.splcenter.org

This site provides information on hate groups in the United States.

United States Sentencing Commission: www.ussc.gov

This site provides information on sentencing laws and the USSC actions taken regarding sentencing.

$SAGE edge™

Sharpen your skills with SAGE edge at **edge.sagepub.com/stohrcorrections**. SAGE edge for Students provides a personalized approach to help you accomplish your coursework goals in an easy-to-use learning environment. You'll find action plans, mobile-friendly eFlashcards, and quizzes as well as video, web, and resources and links to SAGE journal articles to support and expand on the concepts presented in this chapter.

17 Juveniles and Corrections

TEST YOUR KNOWLEDGE

Test your present knowledge of juvenile delinquency and juvenile corrections by answering the following questions as true or false. Check your answers on page 539 after reading the chapter.

1. Juveniles commit a disproportionate number of criminal acts.

2. Juvenile antisocial behavior is normal, in that most adolescents engage in it.

3. Special juvenile courts began in England.

4. The ultimate source of responsibility for a juvenile's behavior is the state.

5. Juveniles can be tried in adult courts and sent to adult prisons in some circumstances.

6. Juveniles have always enjoyed the same rights as adults in criminal courts.

7. Juveniles can be sentenced to LWOP for any offense.

8. In the United States, it was never permissible to execute those who committed murder while they were juveniles.

LEARNING OBJECTIVES

- Describe the differences between delinquency and crime

- Evaluate why we see the age–crime curve in terms of adolescent brain development

- Summarize the history and philosophy of juvenile justice

- Discuss the court cases that led to extending due process to juvenile offenders and other key elements of processing juvenile offenders

- Identify community and institutional juvenile corrections practices

TOO YOUNG FOR LIFE

Joe Harris Sullivan was a 13-year-old tearaway when he and two other boys broke into the home of a 72-year-old woman in Pensacola, Florida, and stole jewelry and coins. One of the boys returned later and beat and raped her. Sullivan was convicted of the rape on the testimony of the other two boys (who received light sentences) and sentenced to life without the possibility of parole (LWOP). Sullivan's presentence report showed that he had committed 17 offenses (some serious, some not) prior to the burglary and rape. He was a troublemaker while in juvenile detention for previous offenses and assaulted other juveniles. Under Florida's sentencing guidelines, Sullivan scored 263 points above the minimum required to impose a life sentence.

In July of 2003, 16-year-old Terrance Jamar Graham and two accomplices attempted to rob a restaurant in Jacksonville, Florida. He was charged as an adult and placed on probation after he pled guilty. In December of 2003, Graham was arrested for a number of home invasion robberies and sentenced to LWOP for the robbery and probation violation when he was 17.

In both the Sullivan and Graham cases, the sentencing judges made certain remarks indicating that they were certain the boys were beyond hope of rehabilitation. Both boys were raised in abusive and neglectful homes (Graham's parents were both crack addicts) and lived in the worst ghettoes of their respective cities. While these circumstances cannot excuse their behavior, it makes it understandable. In appealing these boys' cases, their attorneys made much of neuroscience evidence relative to the immaturity of the adolescent brain. We all know that adolescence is a time of rebellion, but most of us limit that revolt to being a little experimental with our lives and being—from a parental point of view—a pain in the rear.

We will see, however, that there is a small subset of people who begin committing antisocial acts prior to adolescence and continue to do so over the life course.

Is LWOP the only solution for such predators, or can their deficiencies be addressed and the community be protected some other way? Should Sullivan and Graham have been sentenced in adult court anyway? Are individuals who commit rapes and armed robberies "children," as we think of them, and should they be treated differently from adults? These are some of the things to think about as you read about the differences between the adult and juvenile justice systems in the United States.

••• INTRODUCTION: DELINQUENCY AND STATUS OFFENDING

Video 17.1: When Kids Get Life

Delinquents:
Juveniles who commit acts that are criminal when committed by adults.

Status offenses:
Offenses that apply only to juveniles, such as disobeying parents or smoking.

Status offenders:
Juveniles who commit certain actions that are legal for adults but not for children, such as smoking and not obeying parents.

The juvenile justice system generally falls under the broad umbrella of the civil law rather than criminal law. This placement emphasizes the distinction that the law makes between adults and juveniles who commit the same illegal acts. Juveniles who commit acts that are criminal when committed by adults are called **delinquents** rather than criminals, conveying the notion that the juvenile has *not* done something he or she *was* supposed to do (behave lawfully), rather than that the juvenile has *done* something he or she *was not* supposed to do (behave unlawfully). This difference is a subtle one that reflects the rehabilitative, rather than punitive, philosophy of American juvenile justice.

Juveniles are subject to laws that make certain actions that are legal for adults, such as smoking, drinking, not obeying parents, staying out at night to all hours, and not going to school, illegal for them. These acts are called **status offenses** because they apply only to individuals having the status of a juvenile, and they exist because the law assumes that juveniles lack the maturity to appreciate the long-term consequences of their behavior. Many of these acts can jeopardize juveniles' future acquisition of suitable social roles because they may lead to defiance of all authority, inadequate education, addiction, and teenage parenthood (Binder, Geis, & Bruce, 2001). If parents are unwilling or unable to shield their children from harm, the juvenile justice system becomes a substitute parent. Status offenses constitute the vast majority of juvenile offenses and consume an inordinate amount of juvenile court time and resources (Bynum & Thompson, 1999). Because of this, some states have relinquished court jurisdiction over status offenses to other social-service agencies, where terms such as *child in need of supervision* (CHINS) or *person in need of supervision* (PINS) are used to differentiate **status offenders** from juveniles who have committed acts that are crimes when committed by adults. In this chapter, we will discuss the extent of juvenile delinquency and status offending, the likely causes of it, the history of dealing with children in corrections, and current processing of delinquents in the system.

PHOTO 17.1: Immaturity of adolescent behavior is matched by the immaturity of the adolescent brain.

© iStockphoto.com/Nikada

••• THE EXTENT OF DELINQUENCY

Figure 17.1 shows the juvenile proportion of all reported arrests in 2014. Juveniles (youths under 18) accounted for 11% of all violent-crime arrests and 15% of all property crime arrests. Figures such as these are troubling, but antisocial behavior is normative (although not welcome) for juveniles; juveniles who do *not* engage in it are statistically abnormal (Moffitt & Walsh, 2003). Adolescence is a time when youths are "feeling their oats" and temporarily fracturing parental bonds in their own personal declaration of independence. Looking at data from 12 different countries, Junger-Tas (1996) concluded that delinquent behavior is a part of growing up and that the peak ages for different types of crimes were similar across all countries (16–17 for property crimes and 18–20

Video 17.2: Montgomery v. Louisiana

AP Video 17.1: Fears that Juvenile Crime Will Increase in the Future

Audio 17.1: Juvenile Incarceration Rates Are Down; Racial Disparities Rise

FIGURE *17.1*   Juvenile Proportion of Arrests by Offense, 2014

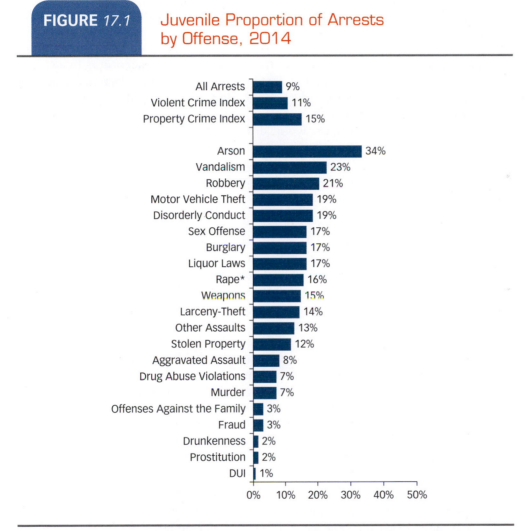

Note: The Violent Crime Index includes the offenses of murder and non-negligent manslaughter, rape, robbery, and aggravated assault. The Property Crime Index includes the offenses of burglary, larceny-theft, motor vehicle theft, and arson. Running away from home and curfew and loitering violations are not presented in this figure because, by definition, only juveniles can be arrested for these offenses.

*The new definition of rape went into effect in 2013. The revised definition expands rape to include both male and female victims and reflects the various forms of sexual penetration understood to be rape, especially nonconsenting acts of sodomy and sexual assaults with objects.

Source: National Institute of Justice (2015b).

for violent crimes). Biologists tell us that adolescent rebellion is an evolutionary design feature of all social primates. Fighting with parents and seeking out age peers with whom to affiliate "all help the adolescent away from the home territory" (Powell, 2006, p. 867). As Caspi and Moffitt (1995) put it, "Every curfew broken, car stolen, joint smoked, or baby conceived is a statement of independence" (p. 500). The juvenile courts are thus dealing with individuals at a time in their lives when they are most susceptible to antisocial behavior.

••• THE JUVENILE BRAIN AND JUVENILE BEHAVIOR

Figure 17.2 shows prevalence rates for criminal behavior over the life course from different times and different countries. This pattern is known as the **age–crime curve**. The age–crime curve is formed from the statistical count of the number of known crimes committed in a population over a given period according to age. The curve reflects a sharp increase in offending beginning in early adolescence, a peak in mid-adolescence, and then a steep decline in early adulthood, followed by a steadier decline thereafter. The peak may be higher or lower at different periods, and the peak age may vary by a year or two at different times or in different places, but the peak remains. This pattern has been noted throughout history for all cultures around the world and has been called "the most important regularity in criminology" (Nagin & Land, 1993, p. 330) and a "law of nature" (Gottfredson & Hirschi, 1990, p. 124).

NEUROSCIENCE RESEARCH

The age–crime curve has long puzzled criminologists. Hirschi and Gottfredson (1983) note, "The age distribution of crime cannot be accounted for by any variable or combination of variables currently available to criminology" (p. 554). However, with the tremendous advances made by the neurosciences over the past three decades, we are in a much better position to understand adolescent offending. Neuroscience research has thrown light on why there is a sharp rise in antisocial behavior in adolescence across time and cultures, and some very important court decisions in juvenile justice (such as the abolition of the juvenile death penalty) have been influenced by this research (Garland & Frankel, 2006). What has emerged from this research is that the immaturity of adolescent behavior is matched by the immaturity of the adolescent brain. Aaron White's (2004) summation of the key messages from the 2003 conference of the New York Academy of Sciences (NYAS) makes this quite clear:

1. Much of the behavior characterizing adolescence is rooted in biology intermingling with environmental influences to cause teens to conflict with their parents, take more risks, and experience wide swings in emotion.

2. The lack of synchrony between a physically mature body and a still maturing nervous system may explain these behaviors.

3. Adolescents' sensitivities to rewards appear to be different than in adults, prompting them to seek higher levels of novelty and stimulation to achieve the same feeling of pleasure.

4. With the right dose of guidance and understanding, adolescence can be a relatively smooth transition. (p. 4)

Age–crime curve:
Formed from the statistical count of the number of known crimes committed in a population over a given period, mapped according to age.

FIGURE 17.2 Illustrating the Age–Crime Curve in Different Countries and Times

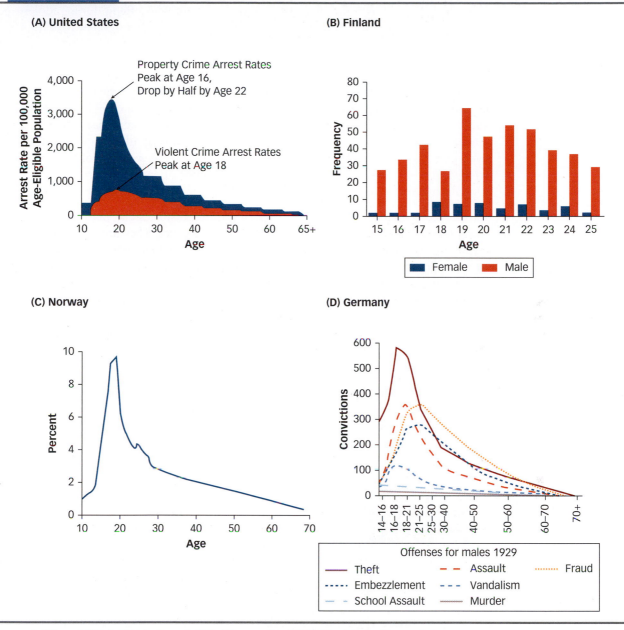

Source: L. Ellis and Walsh, *Criminology: A Global Perspective* (2000). Reprinted with permission.

BRAIN DEVELOPMENT

The onset of puberty also brings with it a 10- to 20-fold increase in testosterone, a hormone linked to aggression and dominance seeking in males (L. Ellis, 2003), and brain chemicals that excite behavior increase in adolescence while chemicals that inhibit it decrease (Collins, 2004; E. Walker, 2002). Many other events are reshaping the adolescent's body and brain during this period that lead to the conclusion that there are *physical* reasons why adolescents often fail to exercise rational judgment and why they tend to attribute erroneous intentions to others. When the brain reaches its adult state, a more adult-like personality emerges, with greater self-control and conscientiousness (Blonigen, 2010). It is important to understand these biological processes, and it is especially important to note the last of the NYAS's messages: "With the right dose of guidance and understanding, adolescence can be a relatively smooth transition" (as cited in A. White, 2004, p. 4). Indeed, by the age of 28, about 85% of all former delinquents have desisted from offending (Caspi & Moffitt, 1995).

It has long been known that the vast majority of youth who offend during adolescence desist and that only a small number continue to offend in adulthood. Terrie Moffitt (1993) calls the former adolescent-limited (AL) offenders and the latter life-course-persistent (LCP) offenders. LCP offenders begin offending prior to puberty and continue well into adulthood. It is typically found that LCP offenders are saddled with neuropsychological and temperamental deficits that are manifested in low IQ, hyperactivity, inattentiveness, negative emotionality, and low impulse control that arise from a combination of genetic and environmental effects on brain development. LCP offenders constitute only about 7% of all delinquents but are responsible for at least 50% of all delinquent acts. Moreover, LCP offenders tend to commit serious crimes, such as assault, robbery, and rape, whereas AL offenders tend to commit relatively minor offenses, such as petty theft and vandalism (Moffitt & Walsh, 2003).

AL offenders, on the other hand, have developmental histories that place them on a prosocial trajectory that is temporarily derailed at adolescence. They are not burdened with the neuropsychological problems that weigh heavily on LCP offenders; they are "normal" youths adapting to the transitional events of adolescence and whose offending does not reflect any stable personal deficiencies. More teens than in the past are being diverted from their prosocial life trajectories because better health and nutrition have lowered the average age of puberty while the average time needed to prepare for participation in an increasingly complex economy has increased. These changes have resulted in about a 5- to 10-year maturity gap between puberty and entry into the job market.

FAMILY DEMOGRAPHICS

Demographically, a National Center for Juvenile Justice report (Sickmund & Puzzanchera, 2014) notes that delinquency rates perfectly track with the percentage of single-parent homes among races and ethnicities. Note from Figure 17.3 that 86% of Asian juveniles,

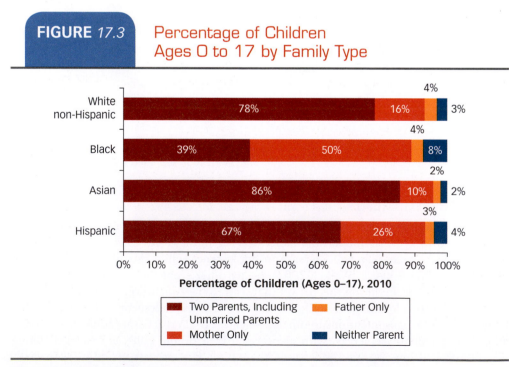

FIGURE *17.3*   Percentage of Children Ages 0 to 17 by Family Type

Source: Sickmund and Puzzanchera (2014).

who are less frequently arrested than juveniles from other racial or ethnic groups, live with two parents, compared with only 39% of black juveniles, who commit the most. In addition to individual characteristics, it is thus also very important, then, to examine the rearing environment of children to understand their behavior. For instance, Kruk (2012) reports,

> Eighty-five percent of youth in prison have an absent father, 71% of high school dropouts are fatherless, 90% of homeless and runaway children have an absent father, and fatherless children and youth exhibit higher levels of depression and suicide, delinquency, promiscuity and teen pregnancy, behavioral problems and illicit and licit substance abuse, diminished self-concepts, and are more likely to be victims of exploitation and abuse. (p. 49)

••• HISTORY AND PHILOSOPHY OF JUVENILE JUSTICE

Until about 300 years ago, the concept of childhood was not recognized; children were considered not much different from property, and no special allowances for children were recognized in matters of determining culpability and punishment. The minimum legal age of criminal responsibility was defined in early English common law as 7. In the United States today, it ranges from 6 in North Carolina to 10 in Arkansas, Colorado, Kansas, Pennsylvania, and Wisconsin, as it is in modern England (Snyder, Espiritu, Huizinga, Loeber, & Petechuck, 2003). Under the increasing influence of Christianity, English courts in the Middle Ages began to exempt children below the age of 7 from criminal responsibility, and children between the ages of 7 and 14 could only be held criminally responsible if it could be shown that they were fully aware of the consequences of their actions. Fourteen was the cutoff age between childhood and adulthood for the purpose of assigning adult criminal responsibility because individuals were considered rational and responsible enough at this age to marry (Springer, 1987).

Ever since the formation of the English chancery courts in the 13th century, there has been movement toward greater state involvement in children's lives. Chancery courts adopted the doctrine of **parens patriae,** which literally means "father of his country" but practically means "state as parent." Parens patriae gave the state the right to intercede *in loco parentis* ("in the place of parents") and act in the best interest of the child or any other legally incapacitated person, such as someone who is mentally ill. This meant that the state, not the parents, had the ultimate authority over children and that children could be removed from their families if they were being delinquent and placed in the custody of the state (Hemmens, Steiner, & Mueller, 2003).

Despite parens patriae, the family was still considered the optimal setting for children to be reared in, and as such, orphans or children with inadequate parents were assigned to foster families through a system known as *binding out*. Children whose parents could not control them or who were too poor to provide for them were apprenticed to richer families, who used them for domestic or farm labor. This period saw the establishment of the first laws directed specifically at children, including laws that condemned begging and vagrancy (P. Sharp & Hancock, 1995). The concern over vagrancy led to the creation of workhouses, in which "habits of industry" were to be instilled. The first one, called Bridewell, was opened in 1555, and in 1576, the English Parliament passed a law establishing *bridewells*, or workhouses (also discussed in Chapter 2), in every English county (Whitehead & Lab, 1996). These places were generally dank, harsh, and abusive, but the idea behind them was that if vagrant youths were removed from the negative influences of street life, they could be reformed by discipline, hard work, and religious instruction.

Web 17.1: Juvenile Justice

Parens patriae: A legal principle giving the state the right to intercede and act in the best interest of the child or any other legally incapacitated persons, such as the mentally ill.

The Protected Art Archive/Alamy Stock Photo

PHOTO 17.2: Juvenile court, 1910. An 8-year-old boy charged with stealing a bicycle. Do you think a court would be more or less lenient on this boy today?

CHILDHOOD IN THE UNITED STATES

Web 17.2:
Office of Juvenile
Justice and
Delinquency
Prevention

American notions of childhood and how to deal with childhood misconduct were imported whole from England. Based on the bridewell model, the New York House of Refuge was established in 1825 to house orphans, beggars, vagrants, and juvenile offenders. Several other cities, counties, and states soon established their own homes for "the perishing and dangerous classes" (Binder et al., 2001, p. 202), as they were thought of. Children in houses of refuge lived highly disciplined lives and were required to work at jobs that brought income to the institution. The indeterminate nature of children's residence allowed the institutions a great deal of latitude in their treatment. Children were required to work long hours, often received little or no training, and were frequently mistreated (Whitehead & Lab, 1996).

It was a frequent practice for poor parents to place their children in residence for idle and disorderly behavior, making it clear that the courts would have to create standards for admission. The courts did this in *Ex Parte Crouse* (1838). (An *ex parte* decision is one made by a judge without requiring all parties involved to be present.) The subject of the case was a child named Mary Ann Crouse, who was placed in the Pennsylvania House of Refuge by her mother against the wishes of her father. Mary's father argued that it was unconstitutional to incarcerate a child without a jury trial, but the Pennsylvania Supreme Court ruled that parental rights are superseded by the parens patriae doctrine. This landmark decision established parens patriae as settled law in American juvenile jurisprudence (Del Carmen, Parker, & Reddington, 1998).

THE BEGINNING OF THE JUVENILE COURTS

Greater concern for children's welfare in the 19th century created an impetus for change in the way juvenile offenders were handled, as it became increasingly obvious that adult criminal courts were not equipped to apply the spirit of the parens patriae doctrine. In

TABLE *17.1*   Comparing Procedural or Event Terminology in Adult and Juvenile Court Systems

PROCEDURE OR EVENT	ADULT SYSTEM	JUVENILE SYSTEM
Police take custody of offender	Placed under arrest	Taken into custody
Official who makes initial decisions about entry into the court system	Magistrate or judge	Intake officer
Place accused may be held pending further processing	Jail	Detention
Document charging the accused with specific act	Indictment or information	Petition
Person charged with illegal act	Defendant	Respondent
Accused appears to respond to charge(s)	Arraignment	Hearing
Accused verbally responds	Enters a plea of guilty, not guilty, or no contest	Admits or denies
Court proceeding to determine if accused committed the offense	Public jury trial	Nonpublic adjudicatory hearing
Decision of the court as to whether accused committed offense	Verdict of jury	No jury; not public; adjudication by judge
Standard of proof required	Beyond a reasonable doubt	Beyond a reasonable doubt
Court proceeding to determine what to do with person found to have committed offense	Sentencing hearing	Dispositional hearing
Institutional confinement	Prison	Juvenile correctional facility
Community supervision	Probation; parole if had been imprisoned	Probation; aftercare if had been confined to juvenile correctional facility

1899, Cook County, Illinois, enacted legislation providing for a separate court system for juveniles, and by 1945, every state in the union had established a juvenile court system (Hemmens et al., 2003). These courts combined the authority of social control with the sympathy of social welfare in a single institution and afforded judges a great deal of latitude in determining how the best interests of the child could be realized. The creation of a separate system of justice for juveniles brought with it a set of terms describing the processing of children accused of committing delinquent acts that differentiated it from the adult system. These terms reflect the protective and rehabilitative nature of the juvenile system, in contrast with the punitive nature of the adult system. Table 17.1 lists the terms used to describe each procedure or event, from initial contact with authorities to the last, in both the adult and juvenile justice systems today.

••• PROCESSING JUVENILE OFFENDERS

Figure 17.4 illustrates the flow of juvenile cases through the juvenile courts in the United States in 2013 (Hockenberry & Puzzanchera, 2015). We see that only 55% of the juveniles taken into custody ("arrested") or otherwise referred to juvenile court were petitioned (formally charged). Among those not petitioned, most had their cases dismissed, some were placed on informal probation (probation without a formal adjudication

FIGURE 17.4 Juvenile Court Case Processing, 2013

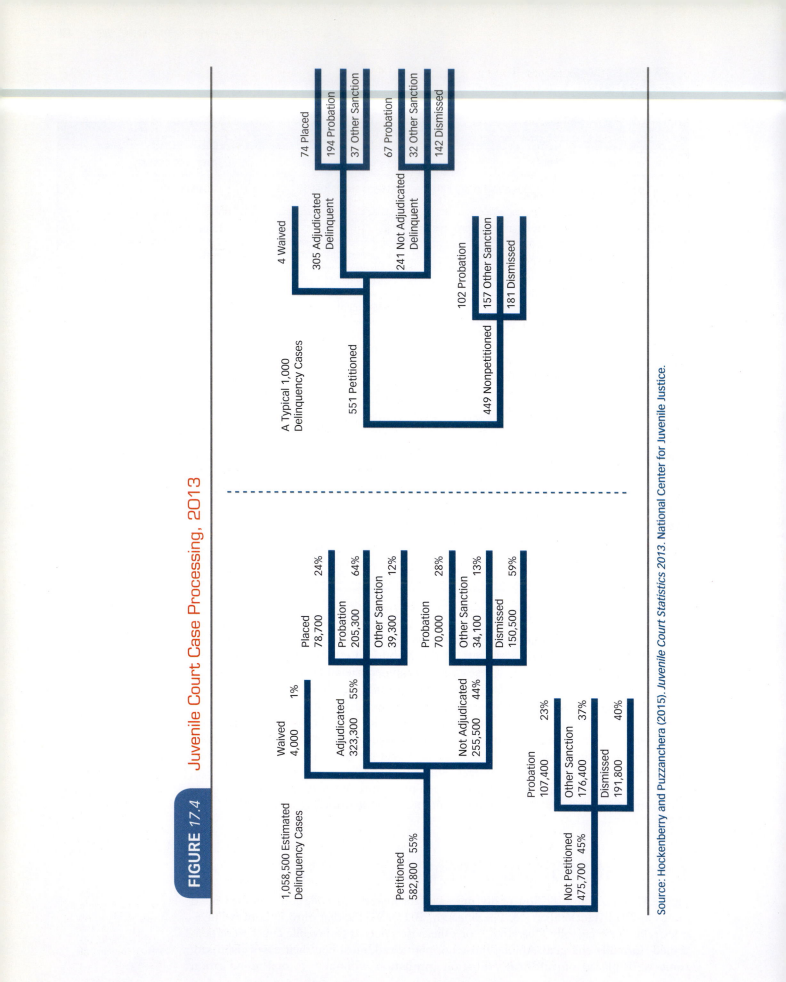

A Typical 1,000 Delinquency Cases

551 Petitioned

- 4 Waived
- 305 Adjudicated Delinquent
  - 74 Placed
  - 194 Probation
  - 37 Other Sanction
- 241 Not Adjudicated Delinquent
  - 67 Probation
  - 32 Other Sanction
  - 142 Dismissed

449 Nonpetitioned
- 102 Probation
- 157 Other Sanction
- 181 Dismissed

1,058,500 Estimated Delinquency Cases

Petitioned 582,800 55%

- Waived 4,000 1%
- Adjudicated 323,300 55%
  - Placed 78,700 24%
  - Probation 205,300 64%
  - Other Sanction 39,300 12%
- Not Adjudicated 255,500 44%
  - Probation 70,000 28%
  - Other Sanction 34,100 13%
  - Dismissed 150,500 59%

Not Petitioned 475,700 45%
- Probation 107,400 23%
- Other Sanction 176,400 37%
- Dismissed 191,800 40%

Source: Hockenberry and Puzzanchera (2015). *Juvenile Court Statistics 2013*. National Center for Juvenile Justice.

of delinquency, sometimes known as diversion), and some were given "other sanctions"—this could range from something as minor as a written apology to something as serious as placement in a mental institution.

When a petition has been filed by the juvenile court prosecutor, the court has to decide if it should take jurisdiction of the case. In about 99% of the cases, the court does accept jurisdiction, and about 55% of the time, the juvenile is adjudicated delinquent (found guilty). Note that in the 44% of the cases without a finding of adjudication, 41% of those cases were not outright dismissed. In adult court, a finding of not guilty always means that the defendant is now a free person. Under the principle of parens patriae, however, the juvenile court has the power to intervene in a child's life as a proactive measure, even though he or she has been found not guilty of any wrongdoing. If the juvenile court does not accept jurisdiction, it means that the case is waived to adult court, which is one of the most controversial issues in juvenile justice.

PHOTO 17.3: Meagan Grunwald (*right*) enters court for her preliminary hearing. She faces murder charges for helping her boyfriend, who fatally shot a Utah deputy. What rights would she have during this preliminary hearing?

JUVENILES WAIVED TO CRIMINAL COURT

As noted earlier, juveniles can sometimes be *waived* (transferred) to adult criminal court, where they lose their status as minors, become legally culpable for their alleged crime, and are subject to criminal prosecution and punishments. A transfer to adult court is called a **waiver** because the juvenile court waives (relinquishes) its jurisdiction over the child to the adult system. Waivers are designed to allow the juvenile courts to transfer juveniles over a certain age who have committed particularly serious crimes or who have exhausted the juvenile system's resources in trying to rehabilitate chronic offenders to a more punitive system. Juveniles become increasingly more likely to be waived if they are chronic offenders approaching the upper age limit of their state's juvenile court's jurisdiction. Note from Figure 17.4 that far less than 1% of juvenile cases nationwide are waived to the criminal courts.

There are three primary (non–mutually exclusive) ways in which juveniles can be waived to criminal court:

1. **Judicial waiver:** A judicial waiver involves a juvenile judge deciding, after a full inquiry, that the juvenile should be waived. (Forty-eight states, at present, use this judicial discretionary model.) In some states, there are *mandatory waivers* for some offenses, but juvenile judges are involved in determining if the criteria for a mandatory waiver are met. Twelve states use a system of *presumptive waivers*, in which the burden of proof is on juveniles to prove that they are amenable to treatment and therefore should not be waived; the burden is not on the prosecutor to prove that they should.

Journal Article 17.1: Juveniles Committing Adult Crimes

AP Video 17.2: Slenderman

Waiver: Refers to a process by which a juvenile offender is "waived" (transferred) to an adult court because he or she has committed a particularly serious crime or is habitually delinquent.

Judicial waiver: Involves a juvenile judge deciding, after a full inquiry, that the juvenile should be waived to the adult system.

Audio 17.2:
Treatment of
Juveniles

Prosecutorial discretion: Allows prosecutors to file some cases in either adult or juvenile court.

Statutory exclusion: These are waivers in cases in which state legislatures have statutorily excluded certain serious offenses from the juvenile courts for juveniles over a certain age, which varies from state to state.

2. **Prosecutorial discretion:** This model allows prosecutors to file some cases in either adult or juvenile court. In such cases (usually limited by age and seriousness of the offense), the prosecutor can file the case directly with the adult court and bypass the juvenile court altogether. Fourteen states and the District of Columbia allow prosecutorial-discretion waivers.

3. **Statutory exclusion:** These are waivers in cases in which state legislatures have statutorily excluded certain serious offenses from the juvenile courts for juveniles over a certain age, which varies from state to state. These automatic waivers are found in 38 states.

EXTENDING DUE PROCESS TO JUVENILES

Contrary to the best-interests-of-the-child philosophy, juvenile courts often punished children in arbitrary ways that would not be tolerated in the adult system, as illustrated in some famous juvenile cases discussed in the paragraphs that follow. Critics argued that the parens patriae doctrine allowed too much latitude for courts to restrict the rights of juveniles and that because the courts could remove juvenile rights to liberty, juveniles should be afforded the same due process protections as adults. Supporters of parens patriae countered that it was suitable and proper for the treatment of children and that

POLICY AND RESEARCH   Consequences of Juvenile Waivers

Sentencing policy is influenced by public opinion, which is influenced by crime rates. The huge surge in youthful offending beginning in the late 1960s and peaking around the mid-1990s was largely responsible for current juvenile waiver policy. Prior to 1970, only eight states had automatic waiver laws; by 2000, 38 states did (Griffin, Addie, Adams, & Firestone, 2011). Additionally, many states lowered the age of eligibility for waivers, expanded the list of offenses eligible for waivers, and limited the discretion of juvenile courts in matters of waivers (Redding, 2010). As crime rates rose, so did states' punitive responses, and so did the punitive attitudes of the general public. A study of a representative sample of 953 respondents from the National Opinion Survey of Crime and Justice found that the public generally held punitive attitudes toward juvenile offenders (Jan, Ball, & Walsh, 2008). Factors such as political ideology, gender, or political party did not influence attitudes about waivers, but those who believed that the purpose of sentencing was punishment were more supportive of juvenile waivers than were those who believed the purpose was rehabilitation. Eighty-seven percent of respondents agreed that juvenile offenders should be tried as adults if they commit violent crimes, 70.4% agreed they should be tried as adults for drug crimes, and 65% agreed they should be tried as adults for serious property crimes.

A waiver to adult court does not necessarily guarantee a more punitive disposition. Waived juveniles who commit violent crimes are likely to be convicted and incarcerated, but juveniles waived for property and drug offenses often receive more lenient sentences than they would have received in juvenile courts (Butts & Mitchell, 2000). As for deterrence, studies show that juveniles waived to adult courts are more likely to recidivate than youths adjudicated for similar crimes in juvenile court (Redding, 2010). Examining the results of a number of different studies, Redding (2010) reports that 24% of violent offenders waived to adult court reoffended during the study period versus 16% of the violent offenders retained in juvenile court. The corresponding percentages for drug offenses were 11% versus 9%, and for property offenders, they were 14% and 10%.

Redding (2010) reported some reasons given by various researchers for why waived juveniles have higher recidivism rates:

- The stigmatization and other negative effects of labeling juveniles as convicted felons.
- The sense of resentment and injustice juveniles feel about being tried and punished as adults.
- The learning of criminal mores and behavior while incarcerated with adult offenders.

- The decreased focus on rehabilitation and family support in the adult system. (p. 7)

Of course, juveniles waived to adult court tend to have committed more serious crimes and have lengthier records and are thus more likely to continue their errant ways regardless of which court they appear before, but this may not always be the case (Redding, 2010). If a juvenile has the potential for rehabilitation, he or she is more likely to realize that potential in a treatment-oriented juvenile facility than in an adult prison, where the focus is always on security above all else. Additionally, juveniles in adult prisons have to adapt to the inmate code, and they learn a lot about criminal values and activities from older cons. A study found that compared with youth in juvenile facilities, juveniles incarcerated in adult prisons were 5 times more likely to be sexually assaulted, 8 times more likely to commit suicide, 2 times as likely to be attacked with a weapon, and 2 times as likely to be beaten by staff than in a juvenile facility (Beyer, 1997). The overall conclusions of studies examining the consequences of juvenile waivers are that they have little or no deterrent effect and sometimes result in a less retributive effect. For those juveniles who are incarcerated in adult prisons, their experiences there can be traumatic and ultimately criminogenic.

References

Beyer, M. (1997). Experts for juveniles at risk of adult sentencing. In P. Purirz, A. Capozello, & W. Shang (Eds.), *More than meets the eye: Rethinking assessment, competency and sentencing for a harsher era of juvenile justice* (pp. 1–22). Washington, DC: American Bar Association, Juvenile Justice Center.

Butts, J., & Mitchell, O. (2000). Brick by brick: Dismantling the border between juvenile and adult justice. In National Institute of Justice (Ed.), *The nature of crime: Continuity and change* (Vol. 2). Washington, DC: Author.

Griffin, P., Addie, S., Adams, B., & Firestone, K. (2011). *Trying juveniles as adults: An analysis of state transfer laws*. Washington, DC: U.S. Department of Justice, Office of Juvenile Justice and Delinquency Prevention.

Jan, I.-F., Ball, J., & Walsh, A. (2008). Predicting public opinion about juvenile waivers. *Criminal Justice Policy Review*, *19*, 285–300.

Redding, R. (2010). *Juvenile transfer laws: An effective deterrent to delinquency?* Washington, DC: U.S. Department of Justice, Office of Juvenile Justice and Delinquency Prevention.

any problems concerning juvenile court operations were problems of implementation, not philosophy (Whitehead & Lab, 1996).

The U.S. Supreme Court maintained a hands-off policy with regard to the operation of the juvenile courts until 1966, when it agreed to hear *Kent v. United States*. In 1961, 16-year-old Morris Kent broke into a woman's apartment, raped her, and stole her wallet. Because of Kent's chronic delinquency and the seriousness of the offense, he was waived to adult court. The adult court found Kent guilty of six counts of housebreaking and robbery, for which he was sentenced to 30 to 90 years in prison. Had Kent remained in juvenile court, he could have been sentenced to a maximum of 5 years (the remainder of his minority, which was until age 21 at the time). Kent appealed, arguing that the waiver process had not included a "full investigation" and that his counsel had been denied access to the court files.

The Supreme Court remanded Kent's case back to district court, with Justice Abe Fortas stating,

> There is no place in our system of law for reaching a result of such tremendous consequences without ceremony—without hearing, without effective assistance of counsel, without a statement of reasons. . . . The admonition to function in a "parental" relationship is not an invitation to procedural arbitrariness. (n.p.)

ETHICAL ISSUE 17.1 ?

What Would You Do?

You are an intake officer at juvenile court and have processed a 16-year-old boy named John, who has an IQ of 80 and is charged with a string of burglaries. The prosecutor has offered him a plea bargain, stating that if he admits to the burglaries, he will receive 6 months of detention, followed by probation until he reaches adulthood at age 18. If John refuses to admit to the charges, the prosecutor indicates that she will seek a waiver to adult court, where the presumptive sentence would be in the range of 36 to 48 months of imprisonment. In your professional judgment, John would be better off taking the plea, but he is adamant that he will not admit anything, which is his absolute right. You are convinced that his diminished capacity is contributing to his decision because all of the evidence shows that he did commit the burglaries. John's defense lawyer is ethically bound to abide by his decision to seek a waiver and be tried in adult court, but you are not sure if you are similarly bound. How far will you go, if at all, to try to convince John to take the plea to save him from adult prison?

Justice Fortas also noted that under the parens patriae philosophy, the child receives the worst of both worlds: "He gets neither the protections accorded to adults nor the solicitous care and regenerative treatment postulated for children" (n.p.). The *Kent* decision determined that juveniles must be afforded certain constitutional rights and thus began the process of formalizing the juvenile system into something akin to the adult system (Hemmens et al., 2003).

The Supreme Court heard a second case concerning juvenile rights one year later in *In re Gault* (1967). In 1964, 15-year-old Gerald Gault was adjudicated delinquent for making obscene phone calls and sentenced to 6 years in the State Industrial School. An adult convicted of the same offense would have faced a $5 to $50 fine and a maximum of 60 days in jail. The Supreme Court used this case to establish five basic constitutional due process rights for juveniles: (1) the right to proper notification of charges, (2) the right to legal counsel, (3) the right to confront witnesses, (4) the right to privilege against self-incrimination, and (5) the right to appellate review, all of which had been denied to Gault.

A third significant juvenile case is *In re Winship* (1970). In 1967, 12-year-old Samuel Winship was accused of stealing $112 from a woman's purse, taken from a locker. Winship was adjudicated delinquent based on the civil law's preponderance-of-the-evidence standard of proof (i.e., is it more likely than not that the person committed the act he or she is charged with?) and was sent to a state training school. Upon appeal, the Supreme Court ruled that when the possibility of commitment to a secure facility is a possibility, the beyond-a-reasonable-doubt standard of proof must extend to juvenile adjudication hearings.

 Career Video 17.1: Legal Assistant

In *McKeiver v. Pennsylvania* (1971), the sole issue before the Court was, "Do juveniles have the right to a jury trial during adjudication hearings?" The Supreme Court ruled that they do not. The Court did not rule that the states cannot provide juveniles with this due process right, only that they are not constitutionally required to do so. And in *Breed v. Jones* (1975), the Supreme Court ruled that the prohibition against double jeopardy applied to juveniles once they have had an adjudicatory hearing (which is a civil process and not technically a trial). Breed had an adjudicatory hearing and was subsequently waived to adult court. The Court ruled that he had been subjected to the burden of two trials for the same offense and therefore the double jeopardy clause of the Fifth Amendment had been violated.

In the case of *Schall v. Martin* (1984), the issue before the Supreme Court was whether the preventative detention of a juvenile charged with a delinquent act is constitutional. The Court ruled that it was permissible because it serves a legitimate state interest in protecting both society and the juvenile from the risk of further crimes committed by the person being detained while awaiting his or her hearing. This ruling established that juveniles do not enjoy the right to bail consideration and reasserted the parens patriae interests of the state.

Another major juvenile case involves the two boys highlighted in this chapter's opening vignette: Sullivan and Graham. Their cases were consolidated as *Graham v. Florida* (2010), in which the majority opinion of the U.S. Supreme Court overturning the imposition of life without the possibility of parole for juveniles who have not committed homicide stated,

> The Constitution prohibits the imposition of a life without parole sentence on a juvenile offender who did not commit homicide. A State need not guarantee the offender eventual release, but if it imposes a sentence of life it must provide him or her with some realistic opportunity to obtain release before the end of that term. (n.p.)

PERSPECTIVE FROM A PRACTITIONER

Skyler Brouwer, Juvenile Probation Officer

Position: Juvenile probation officer

Location: Omaha, Nebraska

Education: Degree in criminal justice from the University of Nebraska at Omaha

What are your primary duties and responsibilities?

My responsibilities are to effectuate positive behavior change in an effort to reduce the likelihood of offenders recidivating; to confirm that offenders are in compliance with their court orders through face-to-face contact and from collateral information from treatment and mental-health providers, drug testing, and school information; to assist offenders and their families with finding resources in the community that they can benefit from while on probation and to motivate the offenders to lead law-abiding and successful lives by building and maintaining positive rapport with the offenders, their family members, and the community support systems; and to update the court on progress or lack of progress through court reports, memos, emails, petitions, and face-to-face contact.

What are the characteristics and traits most useful in your line of work?

- Honesty
- Confidence
- Being able to think outside the box
- Empathetic
- Innovative
- Excellent writing and communication skills
- Consistent
- Motivating
- Fair
- Resilience

Please describe a typical workday.

A typical day includes conducting office and field visits with offenders, treatment providers, school administrators, counselors, and teachers to monitor compliance or noncompliance with court orders. Writing predispositional (presentence) and other reports occupies a considerable portion of a juvenile probation officer's time. Our department uses assessment instruments such as the Youth Level of Service/Case Management Inventory and the Adolescent Chemical Dependency Inventory. These instruments assist the probation officer with assessing the offenders' major needs, strengths, and barriers. The assessment breaks down into the following categories: prior and current offenses, education, substance abuse, family, personality/behavior, leisure and recreation, and attitudes/orientation. The Adolescent Chemical Dependency Inventory is an assessment that is a self-report test. This assessment obtains a lot of information in a short amount of time. The assessment screens the following: substance abuse and use, overall adjustment, and troubled-youth concerns. Other duties include attending court hearings; communicating with formal and informal supports of the offender through voice mails, phone calls, e-mails, and memos; and ensuring the safety of the community and of the offenders through the officer's efforts to assist them in their rehabilitation.

What is your advice to someone who wants to enter your field?

Be able to use your passion to think outside the box and assist people in becoming role models in their communities.

The final relevant juvenile case is *Miller v. Alabama* (2012). Evan Miller, age 14, was sentenced to life without the possibility of parole for murder after he and another boy robbed and murdered a neighbor after indulging in alcohol and marijuana. The boys beat their victim with a baseball bat after robbing him and returned later and set fire to his trailer to destroy evidence. The Court's majority opinion held that mandatory life without parole for juveniles violates the Eighth Amendment's prohibition on cruel and unusual punishment. *Miller* extended *Graham*, which explicitly excluded murder, to include juvenile murderers. Note that the Court did not invalidate all life-without-parole sentences for juveniles. It only ruled that LWOP sentences should not be mandatory and that judges must assess a juvenile's potential for rehabilitation and how his or her age might have influenced the perpetration of the criminal act.

Career Video 17.2:
Juvenile Court
Counselor

JUVENILES AND THE DEATH PENALTY

The justices have also had to wrestle with the moral issue of imposing the death penalty on individuals who committed their crimes as juveniles. From 1973 to 2003, a total of 22 juvenile offenders were executed in the United States (Streib, 2003). The death penalty has only been applied to juveniles who have murdered in particularly heinous and depraved ways.

The first such case was *Eddings v. Oklahoma* (1982). In 1977, 16-year-old Monty Lee Eddings and several companions stole an automobile. The car was stopped by an Oklahoma Highway Patrol officer, and when the officer approached the car, Eddings shot and killed him. At Eddings's sentencing hearing, the state presented three aggravating circumstances to warrant the death penalty, but the judge only allowed Eddings's age in mitigation. The Supreme Court vacated Eddings's death sentence, ruling that in death penalty cases, the courts must consider all mitigating factors (e.g., Eddings had been a victim of abusive treatment at home) when considering a death sentence.

Thompson v. Oklahoma (1988) involved 15-year-old William Thompson, who was one of four young men charged with the murder of his former brother-in-law. All four were found guilty and sentenced to death. Thompson appealed to the Supreme Court, claiming that a sentence of death for a crime committed by a 15-year-old is cruel and unusual punishment. The Court agreed, and using the evolving-standards-of-decency principle, it drew the line at age 16, under which execution was not constitutionally permissible.

Sixteen years later, in *Roper v. Simmons* (2005), the Court redrew the age line at 18, under which it was constitutionally impermissible to execute anyone. Christopher Simmons was 17 when he and two younger accomplices broke into a home, kidnapped the owner, beat her, and threw her alive from a high bridge into the river below where she drowned. Simmons had told many of his friends before the crime that he wanted to commit a murder, and he bragged about it to them afterward. His crime was a "classical" death penalty case—premeditated, deliberate, and cruel—and he was totally unremorseful. Nevertheless, his sentence drew condemnation from around the world, with **amicus curiae briefs** ("friend of the court" briefs presented to the Court, arguing in support of one

Amicus curiae briefs: "Friend of the court" briefs presented to the court, arguing in support of one side or the other, by interested parties not directly involved with the case.

FIGURE 17.5 Supreme Court Cases Altering the Nature of Juvenile Court Proceedings, 1966–2012

1966 — **Kent v. United States:** Courts must provide essentials of due process when waiving juveniles to adult system.

1967 — **In re Gault:** In hearings that could result in institutional commitment, juveniles have four basic constitutional rights.

1970 — **In re Winship:** The state must prove guilt beyond a reasonable doubt in delinquency matters.

1971 — **McKeiver v. Pennsylvania:** Jury trials are not required in juvenile court hearings.

1982 — **Eddings v. Oklahoma:** All mitigating factors should be considered in deciding to apply the death sentence to juveniles.

side or the other, by interested parties not directly involved with the case) being filed in favor of Simmons by the European Union, the American and British Bar Associations, and the American Medical and Psychological Associations, along with 15 Nobel Prize winners, among others.

In a 5–4 opinion, Justice Anthony Kennedy noted the growing body of evidence from neuroscience about the immaturity of the adolescent brain. The majority opinion also cited *Atkins v. Virginia* (2002). In noting that the Court in *Atkins* had ruled the execution of the mentally disabled to be cruel and unusual punishment because of the lesser degree of culpability attached to the mentally challenged, it reasoned that such logic should be applied to juveniles. The Court also pointed out that the majority of states (30) either bar execution for juveniles or have banned the death penalty altogether, thus citing state legislation as part of the impetus behind its decision.

? ETHICAL ISSUE 17.2

What Would You Do?

You are an assistant district attorney who has been assigned a heinous murder case. In this case, a young man was burglarizing a house at night when the occupants were sleeping. The man of the house confronted the youth with a baseball bat, but the youth shot him. The man's wife screamed and ran into the bedroom to call the police, but the youth caught up with her, beat her, raped her, and then shot her also. The young man, who committed the offense on his 18th birthday, was caught later that night. You now have to decide whether you are to seek the death penalty, which is being demanded by an outraged community. Because the young man was only hours into adulthood when he committed the crime, you are urged by an anti–death penalty colleague not to seek it. What will you do, and why?

Figure 17.5 presents a summary of important Supreme Court cases regarding juveniles' due process rights. Taken as a whole, what these cases essentially mean is an erosion of the distinction between juvenile and criminal courts. On the positive side, these rulings have helped to create a juvenile court system that more closely reflects the procedural guidelines established in adult criminal courts. On the negative side, they have, in effect, criminalized juvenile courts. In order to gain due process rights enjoyed by adults, juveniles have surrendered some benefits, such as the informality of solicitous treatment they nominally enjoyed previously. Only time will tell if this convergence of systems results in more just outcomes for juveniles than they received under unmodified *parens patriae*.

••• JUVENILE COMMUNITY CORRECTIONS

As seen from Figure 17.6, juvenile corrections mirror the adult system in that the majority of adjudicated delinquents are placed into some form of community-based corrections, and just over a quarter are sent to residential facilities. Juvenile community corrections offer a wide variety of options, all ostensibly designed to implement the three-pronged goal of the juvenile justice system: (1) to protect the community, (2) to hold delinquent youths accountable, and (3) to provide treatment and positive role models for youths. This is known as the *balanced approach to corrections* (K. Carter, 2006).

1984 — *Schall v. Martin:* Pretrial preventive detention of juveniles is permissible under certain circumstances.

1989 — *Sanford v. Kentucky:* It is constitutionally permissible to impose the death penalty on 16- and 17-year-olds.

2005 — *Roper v. Simmons:* Death penalty for juveniles is unconstitutional.

2010 — *Graham v. Florida:* Life without possibility of parole is unconstitutional for juveniles.

2012: *Miller v. Alabama:* Life without possibility of parole unconstitutional for juvenile murderers.

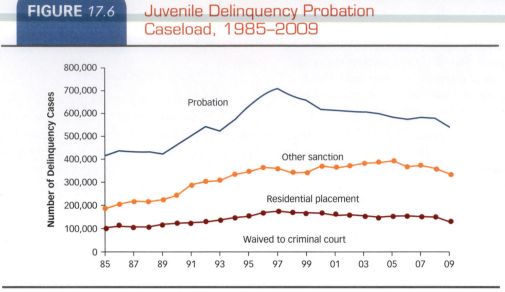

FIGURE *17.6*   Juvenile Delinquency Probation Caseload, 1985–2009

Note: Due to rounding, totals are not exact. Most recent data available.

Source: Livsey (2012).

When juveniles are taken into custody, a complicated process of determining how to best deal with them with the aforementioned goals in mind is initiated. Juveniles may be released to their parents or detained in a detention center until this determination is made. The most lenient disposition of a case is known as deferred adjudication. Depending on the jurisdiction, a **deferred adjudication** decision can be made by the police, the prosecutor, a juvenile probation officer, or a juvenile magistrate or judge. A deferred adjudication means an agreement is reached between the youth and a juvenile probation officer, without any formal court appearance, that the youth will follow certain probation conditions. This form of disposition is only used for status offenses or minor property offenses, and as long as the juvenile has no further charges, he or she is discharged from probation within a short time period. No formal record of the proceedings of the case is made in deferred adjudications.

Other juveniles may be placed on formal probation after adjudication in court by a juvenile judge. In such cases, there are records of the proceedings, and probationers are more strictly monitored. As in the adult courts, juvenile judges typically make their dispositional decision based on recommendations made by probation officers. Juvenile probation officers write **predisposition reports** (analogous to the adult presentence investigation report) and will have a variety of classification instruments very similar to those used in the adult system and discussed in Chapter 9 to help them to formulate their recommendations.

Once a youth is placed on probation, under the doctrine of parens patriae, the probation officer becomes a surrogate parent to the youth. But with probation officers being saddled with a nationwide average of around 42 cases (Taylor, Fritsch, & Caeti, 2007), they can do very little "parenting." Probation officers may see their charges only once a month for perhaps 30 minutes, whereas the juveniles' natural parents see them (or should) every day. Juvenile probation officers therefore insist on parental support in working with their children because parental involvement in the rehabilitative effort of juveniles is considered a *must* (Balazs, 2006). It is a must because while probation serves the positive

Deferred adjudication: A decision made by certain criminal justice personnel to delay or defer formal court proceedings if a youth follows probation conditions.

Predisposition report: A report done in juvenile courts that is analogous to a presentence investigation report in adult courts.

goal of keeping youths in the community and thus avoiding the stigma of institutionalization and the exposure to other seriously delinquent youths, the potential danger is that the probationer may view the disposition as a slap on the wrist and return with more confidence to the old ways that led to his or her adjudication.

If the child comes from an antisocial family rife with substance abuse and criminality, officers are not likely to get any sort of positive support. Even if juvenile probationers come from prosocial two-parent families, there is often resistance by parents to juvenile authorities "poking their noses" into family affairs and "picking on" their children, who, of course, are victims of "bad company" (Walsh & Stohr, 2010, p. 457). If parents are eager to help their children, however, there are some excellent parental-effectiveness-training programs out there. The relatively short-term *Prosocial Family Therapy System* described by Bleckman and Vryan (2000) is a good comprehensive system with some very encouraging results reported.

PHOTO 17.4: Young adult males use reach-and-pick-up tools to pick up trash as part of their community service in downtown Austin, Texas.

INTENSIVE PROBATION

There will always be some juveniles who require more extensive supervision and treatment than others. To meet their needs and the needs of community protection, a variety of methods have been devised. One such method is intensive-supervision probation (ISP), described in Chapter 8. ISP is usually imposed on youths as a last chance before incarceration. Juvenile probation officers with an ISP caseload typically supervise only 15 to 20 juveniles and may carry a gun (Taylor et al., 2007). Officers may make daily contact with their charges, visiting them at home, school, and work to monitor their behavior and progress in these settings. Officers will also enlist the help of other agencies that can provide probationers with more specialized and concrete help of the kind outside the purview of the juvenile court. These agencies will include mental-health clinics, substance abuse centers, educational and vocational guidance centers, and welfare agencies (to help juveniles' families). ISP officers know that they cannot possibly provide for all of the needs of their probationers themselves and that efficient case management consists of their delivering services by using networks of collaborative providers. Delany, Fletcher, and Shields (2003) point out the importance of collaborative efforts to assist youths with multiple problems: "Without some level of collaboration among agencies, the odds of relapse and recidivism, which often leads to repeated institutionalization, are high" (p. 66).

Other forms of more intense supervision include electronic monitoring and/or house arrest. These sanctions were discussed in Chapters 8, 10, and 12, and since they operate for juveniles exactly as they do for adults, they will not be discussed again here.

Youths who commit property crimes are frequently made to pay restitution to their victims to compensate for the victims' losses. This both compensates the victim and holds the youth accountable for his or her actions. To compensate the community as a whole, adjudicated delinquents may receive a **community service order,** which is part of a disposition requiring the probationer to work a certain number of hours doing some kinds of tasks to help their communities. This work can range from cleaning graffiti from walls to picking up trash along highways or in parks. Restitution and community service orders can go a long way to help juveniles to develop a sense of responsibility and the ability to accept the consequences of their actions without rancor. For these reasons, community service and restitution have been called "integral components of the restorative justice philosophy" (Walsh & Stohr, 2010, p. 455).

Restorative justice may be defined as "every action that is primarily oriented toward justice by repairing the harm that has been caused by the act" and "usually means face-to-face confrontation between victim and perpetrator, where a mutually agreeable restorative solution is proposed and agreed upon" (Champion, 2005, p. 154). Restorative justice defines *delinquency* as an offense committed by one person against another rather than against the state and, by doing so, personalizes justice by engaging the victim, the offender, and the community in a process of *restoring* the situation to its preoffense status. Restorative justice thus gives equal weight to the needs of offenders, victims, and the community and focuses equally on each of these rather than being driven solely by offenders ("What do we do with them now?") (K. Carter, 2006). Victims or their representatives are included in the justice process, with the sentencing procedure addressing the needs of the victims, including their need to be heard and to be restored to wholeness again, as far as possible.

Just as the retributive model reemerged after the alleged failure of the medical model, the restorative-justice model has emerged with the apparent failure of get-tough programs (Welch, 1996). However, the restorative model may not suit all victims because many victims understandably feel that things cannot be "put right" so easily and want the offender punished. However, it would be a mistake to see it as a New Age "touchy-feely" approach to corrections. It holds offenders fully accountable for their actions by applying appropriate punishment and adds additional dimensions by requiring offenders to accept responsibility for taking action to repair the harm done (Bazemore, 2000).

A meta-analysis found that restorative-justice programs had a weak-to-moderate positive effect on victim satisfaction, a weak positive effect on offender satisfaction and recidivism, and a moderate effect on restitution compliance (Latimer, Dowden, & Muise, 2005). These findings should be viewed in light of the fact that both victims and offenders select themselves into such programs.

RESIDENTIAL AND INSTITUTIONAL JUVENILE CORRECTIONS

One of the dispositional sanctions that can be imposed on adjudicated delinquents is placement in some sort of program in a residential facility. A *residential facility* or *residential treatment center* is not analogous to an adult prison but rather more like a halfway house. Boot camps, discussed in Chapter 8, are one example of such facilities. Another one is *wilderness programs* or *survival programs*. These are more like self-discipline programs, designed to test delinquents' characters and coping skills by providing them with structured challenges. Overcoming these challenges is said to build youths' confidence and self-esteem, showing them they are capable and not simply victims of circumstance. In such programs, there are no drill instructors bawling and spitting in their faces and belittling them; rather, there are guides who set adventurous challenges for them and provide encouragement. Wilderness programs do seem to be better than boot camps at reducing recidivism, although it is probably true that on the whole, fewer serious offenders are assigned to wilderness programs than to boot camps.

Video 17.3: Neighborhood Corrections Initiative

Community service order: Part of a disposition requiring probationers to work a certain number of hours doing tasks to help their communities.

Nevertheless, one review of 22 studies of wilderness effectiveness found that wilderness participants recidivated at a rate of 29%, versus 37% for comparison subjects (S. Wilson & Lipsey, 2000).

Another alternative is a group home. *Group homes* are typically operated by private organizations that contract with juvenile authorities. These group homes tend to specialize in some form of programming, such as drug treatment or treatment for "troubled girls." Youth in these homes remain in their communities and attend school and all the other normal functions of school-age children but live with perhaps 10 to 30 other youth at the home.

Commitment to a juvenile institutional-corrections facility is a serious matter and is typically the disposition reserved for juveniles who have committed violent offenses or for chronic repeat offenders. There are two broad categories of institutional correctional facilities: long term and short term. Short-term facilities include youth shelters and reception and detention centers (the equivalent of adult jails), where children may be held while awaiting release to parents or court adjudication. Long-term facilities are those used for housing juveniles after adjudication. They include secure detention centers, like training schools (the equivalent of an adult prison) and boot camps, and less secure youth centers, like ranches and adventure forestry camps.

Juveniles sent to long-term secure correctional facilities tend to have committed very serious delinquent acts or are chronic offenders. A study of juveniles sent to long-term secure facilities found that 35% were committed for violent offenses, and the remaining 65% were committed for property, drug, or status offenses (Sickmund & Wan, 2003). Minority youths are even more overrepresented in secure juvenile correctional facilities than minority adults are in adult prisons. Gus Martin (2005) reports that whereas there are about 204 white juveniles per 100,000 in secure facilities, there are 1,018 per 100,000 African American juveniles, and about 70% of juveniles held in custody for violent offenses are minorities (p. 247).

Steiner and Giacomazzi (2007) examined recidivism among juveniles waived to adult court and placed into a boot camp program and compared them with a control group of juveniles who were also waived to adult court but placed on probation rather than in a boot camp. They found no difference between the boot camp and control groups on rates of recidivism, but boot camp juveniles were significantly less likely to be reconvicted, which may be one bright spot in the otherwise poor performance of boot camps.

Other important differences between juvenile and adult facilities are that juvenile facilities are almost always much smaller (rarely more than 250 juveniles), the costs associated with incarceration are considerably higher, and much more money is spent on programming relative to security (Taylor et al., 2007). For instance, the California Youth Authority spends 52% of its budget on academic and vocational training, case planning, counseling, and skills training, as opposed to only 13% on

PHOTO 17.5: Juveniles in the cafeteria of a secure detention facility.

© Bill Gentile/CORBIS/Getty Images

custody and security (Taylor et al., 2007). Nevertheless, many of the same problems seen in adult prisons are also seen in juvenile facilities, especially in the larger institutions with a low staff-to-resident ratio. As in adult prisons, gangs form along racial/ethnic and neighborhood lines, and there is always the danger of violence and sexual assault against the unaffiliated (G. Martin, 2005).

SUMMARY

- The juvenile justice system in the United States is based on civil law and deals with status offenses (those applicable only to juveniles) and delinquency (crimes if committed by adults).

- Juveniles commit a disproportionate number of both property and violent crimes, and this has always been true across time and cultures. Recent scientific evidence relates this situation to the hormonal surges of puberty and a brain undergoing numerous changes. Although most adolescents commit antisocial acts, only a small proportion continue to do so after brain maturation is completed.

- The history of juvenile justice has three distinct periods. Originally, Western culture relied heavily on parents to control children. As society has changed, so have the expectations regarding juvenile delinquency. Institutional control of wayward youth was the model from the mid-1500s until the inception of the juvenile courts in the United States in the late 1800s and early 1900s. The juvenile court follows the doctrine of parens patriae, but recently, there has been a movement away from the broad discretion formerly accorded to juvenile courts to a model more closely reflecting the constitutional protections afforded

adult offenders. Much of this change has issued from the increased waivers of juveniles to adult courts and from the often arbitrary control juvenile justice authorities have exercised over juveniles.

- The juvenile justice system in the United States has gradually changed from a totally paternalistic system governed by civil-law procedures to one that now affords juveniles the same rights as adults. However, some have seen this as criminalizing the juvenile justice system. The greatest success of neuroscience research into the adolescent brain has been the elimination of the juvenile death penalty. We have also seen how the U.S. Supreme Court has ruled LWOP to be unconstitutional for juveniles who have not committed murder.

- Much of what constitutes juvenile corrections mirrors what we have written about in other sections in this book; thus, we have only briefly highlighted differences between the juvenile and adult systems. Major differences include a greater emphasis on rehabilitation, as exemplified by the ratio of programming to security spent in juvenile correctional facilities and the lesser likelihood of juveniles being sent to secure facilities relative to adults.

KEY TERMS

Age–crime curve 414

Amicus curiae briefs 426

Community service order 430

Deferred adjudication 428

Delinquents 412

Judicial waiver 421

Parens patriae 417

Predisposition reports 428

Prosecutorial discretion 422

Status offenders 412

Status offenses 412

Statutory exclusion 422

Waiver 421

DISCUSSION QUESTIONS

1. Discuss the development of the concept of childhood in Western culture.

2. Discuss the doctrine of parens patriae in relation to the development of the juvenile court system in the United States.

3. Do you think that restorative justice is workable? In what circumstances would it be or not be?

4. Which of the models of juvenile justice outlined by Reichel (2005) do you favor? Give your reasons.

5. Do you think that a highly dangerous person, such as Terrance Jamar Graham, should ever be released back into the community just because he committed his crimes as a juvenile?

USEFUL INTERNET SITES

Please note that the sites listed can be accessed at edge.sagepub.com/stohrcorrections.

Juvenile Boot Camps: www.crimesolutions.gov/PracticeDetails.aspx?ID=6

Good information on the purpose, practices, and outcomes associated with boot camps.

National Association of Youth Courts: www.youthcourt.net

This is the website of a nonprofit organization that advocates restorative justice and early intervention for youth offenders. It provides information, training, assistance, and resources for youth courts across the country. Their site contains numerous publications and other learning resources on this topic.

The Office of Juvenile Justice and Delinquency Prevention: www.ojjdp.gov

This site offers many wonderful publications pertinent to the juvenile justice system.

Restorative Justice: www.restorativejustice.org

Everything you always wanted to know about restorative justice, from its history to research studies.

$SAGE edge™

Sharpen your skills with SAGE edge at **edge.sagepub.com/stohrcorrections**. SAGE edge for Students provides a personalized approach to help you accomplish your coursework goals in an easy-to-use learning environment. You'll find action plans, mobile-friendly eFlashcards, and quizzes as well as video, web, and resources and links to SAGE journal articles to support and expand on the concepts presented in this chapter.

© iStockphoto.com/DNY59

TEST YOUR KNOWLEDGE

Test your present knowledge of legal issues pertaining to the rights of people under correctional supervision by answering the following questions, true or false. Check your answers on page 539 after reading the chapter.

1. Prison inmates were not afforded any legal protections until the mid-20th century.

2. The First Amendment freedom of religion is as absolute for prisoners as it is for the rest of us.

3. The majority of lawsuits filed by inmates today have to do with claims of innocence.

4. Prison inmates have no Fourth Amendment protections against unreasonable search and seizure.

5. The mortality rate of prison inmates is lower than that of the U.S. population as a whole.

6. Prisoners are the only group of individuals in the United States with a constitutional right to medical care.

7. Sex offenders can be involuntarily placed in mental institutions after serving their full prison sentence.

8. Probationers and parolees are pretty much subjected to the same curtailment of rights as prison inmates.

Check your answers on page 539 after reading the chapter.

LEARNING OBJECTIVES

- Explain the relevance Packer's (1997) two models of criminal justice have for prisoners' rights

- Identify the different legal periods in terms of prisoners' rights

- Identify issues and cases involving the First, Fourth, Eighth, and Fourteenth Amendments

- Analyze the pros and cons of civil commitment for sex offenders

- Explain how and why prisoners' petitions have been curtailed

- Explain the rights of probationers and parolees during the revocation process

PRISON WITHOUT LAW

Prisons are not nice places; they were never meant to be. This does not mean that society is ever justified in treating prisoners in less-than-humane ways. This message never reached at least two of Arkansas's state prison farms that used inmates' labor to produce crops and dairy products, bringing in average yearly profits of $1.4 million. In 1967, a report was released detailing horrifying conditions at the Tucker and Cummins state penal farms, which included widespread sexual assault, floggings, and extortion by the armed prisoners who were placed in positions of power by prison authorities to save spending money on correctional officers. A federal judge hearing a case stemming from Arkansas prison conditions called the entire Arkansas prison system a "dark and evil world." In addition to such medieval tortures as having testicles crushed and needles inserted under the fingernails, a more "modern" *method of torture was the Tucker telephone. The use of this device involved a prisoner being wired by the big toe and the genitals and an electric current being applied by cranking an old-fashioned telephone. Depending on the offense, an inmate would receive a "local" or "long-distance" call.*

Worse yet, a number of bodies of former inmates who had been listed as "successful escapees" were dug from unmarked graves on the orders of the new warden, Tom Murton (played by Robert Redford in the movie Brubaker, based on the scandal). The scandal eventually became too much for the state governor as more bodies were exhumed, and Murton was fired and told that he had 24 hours to leave the state or be arrested for grave robbing. Thus, even prison reform–minded administrators such as Governor Winthrop Rockefeller circle the wagons and block further investigations and reforms if they become threatening to the authorities.

Who will protect inmates from exploitation, torture, and even murder if the executive branch of government will not? Only an independent body, relatively free of concerns about the personal consequences of doing the morally right thing, can be trusted to safeguard the rights of prisoners. As you read this chapter and perhaps become annoyed at what you may consider legal mollycoddling of "dirtbags," think about how the prison system would be without some sort of judicial oversight, which is precisely the way it was in the not-so-distant past.

••• INTRODUCTION

Winston Churchill once said that a civilization could be judged by the way it treated its prisoners (Morris, 2002). We do not treat them very well and never have, but many members of the public see them getting better treatment than they deserve, as summed up in the line, "If you can't do the time, don't do the crime." Convicted criminals are perhaps the most despised group of people in any society since they are generally viewed as evil misfits who prey on decent people, so why worry about what happens to them while in custody, paying their debt to society? With an estimated 1 in every 100 adults in jails or prisons in the United States in 2008 (Robertson, 2010), however, issues relating to how these people are treated while incarcerated become more pressing. The only system capable of monitoring the treatment of people under criminal justice supervision, other than the criminal justice system itself, is the court system. The courts have changed their attitudes toward the treatment of prisoners over the history of the United States. These attitudes have ranged from complete indifference to almost attempting to micromanage a state's entire prison system. In this chapter, we review how convicted prisoners in prisons and jails and unconvicted detainees awaiting trial in jails were legally viewed in the past, up to how they are legally protected today. Though much as changed in this regard, the trend, in recent years, has been to remove some of those legal protections and access to courts that inmates gained in the latter half of the 20th century.

••• THE RULE OF LAW

Video 18.1:
How I Defend the
Rule of Law

When we discussed Packer's (1997) crime control and due process models of criminal justice in Chapter 1, we were essentially asking, How do we best achieve justice for all concerned—that is, both for society and those who offend against it? The only way we can be reasonably assured that justice resides within a legal system is to determine the extent to which it adheres to the **rule of law**. The idea of the rule of law first appears in Plato's *Laws* (2008, Book IV), written some four centuries before the birth of Christ. Plato wants to determine what constitutes a just state and concludes, "I see that the state in which the law is above the rulers, and the rulers are the inferiors of the law, has salvation, and every blessing which the Gods can confer" (p. 89). In other words, the law should be the supreme authority in a state and should constrain the behavior of government officials. The rule of law involves the notion that every member of society, including lawmakers, presidents, and prime ministers, is subject to the law. The rule of law has been called "the most important legal principle in the world" (Goff, 1997, p. 760), and according to Reichel (2005), it contains three irreducible elements:

1. A nation must recognize the supremacy of certain fundamental values and principles.

2. These values and principles must be committed to writing.

3. A system of procedures to hold the government to these principles and values must be in place.

Rule of law: The principle that laws, not people, govern and that no one is above the law.

All organized societies recognize a set of fundamental values that they hold supreme, whether the ultimate principles are secular or religious. Likewise, all literate societies put these values and principles in writing in their holy books or national constitution. However, the third element is more problematic because it shows whether or not a country honors its fundamental values in practice as well as in theory. The law is just words on paper if it is not respected by human actors. If the law is to be consistent with justice, it can only be so if the procedures followed by its agents are perceived as just by everyone. The procedures designed to hold the government to its written principles are articulated by the concept of due process.

When we speak about something that is due to us, we are referring to something to which we are rightly entitled. Due process of law is owed to all persons whenever they are threatened with the loss of life, liberty, or property at the hands of the state. It is essentially a set of instructions informing agents of the state how they must proceed in their investigation, arrest, questioning, prosecution, and punishment of individuals who are suspected of committing crimes. The individuals charged with monitoring the behavior of agents of the state with respect to their adherence to due process principles compose the judiciary. If the judiciary is corrupt, lax, or the puppet of politicians or public opinion, then the rule of law, especially as it applies to society's

PHOTO 18.1: During the hands-off period, inmates often resided in dilapidated and overcrowded facilities, where they might be overworked, underfed, and mistreated by the state and correctional officials.

least valued citizens, is likely to be ignored. This was the case in the United States until the early 1960s.

THE HANDS-OFF PERIOD, 1866–1963

The general public's attitude of indifference has also been the general attitude of the courts throughout much of American history, as is evident in their so-called **hands-off doctrine**. This doctrine basically articulated the reluctance of the judiciary to interfere with the management and administration of prisons—to keep their "hands off." The doctrine rested primarily on the status of prisoners who suffered a kind of legal and civil death upon conviction. Most states had **civil-death statutes,** which meant that those convicted of crimes lost all citizenship rights, such as the right to vote, hold public office, and—in some jurisdictions—the right to marry. The philosophical justification for civil-death statutes, ironically, came from the text of the Thirteenth Amendment to the United States Constitution, which abolished slavery in the United States. The Thirteenth Amendment reads,

> Neither slavery or involuntary servitude, except as a punishment for a crime whereof the party shall have been duly convicted, shall exist within the United States, or any place subject to their jurisdiction.

Thus, slavery was abolished "except as a punishment for crime." This enabled prison officials (such as those in Arkansas in the opening vignette) to lease prisoners to local businesses for profit and to use them as unpaid labor to maintain the financial self-sufficiency of prisons—in short, to treat them like property (Call, 2011).

In affirming the ruling of a lower court in *Ruffin v. Commonwealth* (1871), the Virginia Supreme Court made plain the slave-like status of convicted offenders:

Video 18.2: Four Ways to Fix a Broken Legal System

Hands-off doctrine: An early American court-articulated belief that the judiciary should not interfere with the management and administration of prisons.

Civil-death statutes: Statutes, in former times, mandating that convicted felons lose all citizenship rights.

For the time being, during his term of service in the penitentiary, he is in a state of penal servitude to the State. He has, as a consequence of his crime, not only forfeited his liberty, but all his personal rights except those which the law in its humanity accords to him. He is for the time being the slave of the State. He is *civiliter mortuus* [civilly dead]; and his estate, if he has any, is administered like that of a dead man. (n.p.)

Ruffin was a state case and thus not binding on other states, but the case was consistent with the earlier U.S. Supreme Court case *Pervear v. Massachusetts* (1866). *Pervear* was the foundational case that first clearly enunciated the lack of concern for prisoners' rights contained in the hands-off doctrine (which was the de facto practice long before 1866). Pervear had been sentenced to 3 months hard labor and a large fine for failing to obtain a license for his liquor store and challenged his sentence on the basis of the "cruel and unusual" clause of the Eighth Amendment. The Supreme Court also made plain the slave-like status of prisoners, ruling that they did not even enjoy the protections of the Eighth Amendment. Convicted felons thus found themselves at the mercy of prison officials and fellow prisoners, without any constitutional protection provided by judicial oversight.

The hands-off doctrine also prevailed because the courts viewed correctional agencies as part of the executive branch of government and did not wish to violate the Constitution's separation-of-powers doctrine. Correctional officials were considered quite capable of administering to the needs of prisoners in a humane way, without having to deal with the complicating intrusions of another branch of government. Besides, if prisoners had been stripped of any rights under civil-death statutes, there was nothing that the courts had to monitor and protect.

THE PRISONERS' RIGHTS PERIOD, 1964–1978

Web 18.1:
Prisoners' Rights

The convict-as-slave approach slowly gave way to the approach by the courts that prisoners did retain a modicum of constitutional rights, but it was the business of the executive and legislative branches of state government to honor them. States' rights and fear of an overbearing federal government were more deeply felt concerns in the past than they are today, and the federal courts were still reluctant to move too far in the direction of limiting states' rights or further fueling citizens' distrust of the federal government.

We have to realize that, initially, the Bill of Rights was intended only to apply to actions of the federal government and was added to the Constitution to appease the fears of supporters of states' rights. It was not until the 20th century that federal courts began to apply the rights in the Bill of Rights to state actions in a process known as incorporation (Walsh & Hemmens, 2014). Incorporation essentially means that due process rights, such as free speech, which formerly had to be respected only by the federal government, now had to be respected by the states as well.

As part of a growing trend toward an overall greater respect for individual rights in the mid-20th century, as African Americans, women, gays and lesbians, and other disadvantaged groups strongly agitated for them, the courts began to enter into the area of prisoners' rights. The major issue in prisoner litigation has been the conditions of confinement, but the first significant case was *Ex parte Hull* (1941), which dealt with the denial, by prison officials, of a Michigan inmate's petition for an appeal of the legality of his confinement. (The term *ex parte* refers to situations in which only one party appears before the court.) Although Hull's petition was denied (Hull had committed a statutory sexual offense, had violated his parole, and was returned to prison to serve out his original sentence), the U.S. Supreme Court ruled that inmates had the right to unrestricted access to federal courts to challenge the legality of their confinement. This ruling was the

PERSPECTIVE FROM A PRACTITIONER

Barbara Beldot, Attorney

Position: Professor at the University of Houston, Downtown

Through the 1980s and 1990s, the Texas state prison system (TDCJ) operated under several court orders issued by federal judge William Wayne Justice in the case *Ruiz v. Estelle*, a lawsuit in which prisoners successfully challenged living conditions in TDCJ-ID. Judge Justice created a special team to monitor the state's progress in implementing the reforms he mandated. I served as an attorney on that team, the Office of the Special Master, from 1986 to 1990. My assignment was to monitor progress related to conditions in administrative segregation, including how inmates were assigned to that status, the inmate disciplinary system, and conditions on death row.

I spent countless hours meeting with administrative-segregation and death row inmates, walking up and down cellblocks and talking with them through their cell doors, as well as meeting with correctional officers assigned to those blocks. I reviewed paperwork and attended meetings related to assigning inmates to administrative segregation. I observed hundreds of disciplinary hearings. I received thousands of letters from inmates requesting I investigate their specific complaint. Our team had open access to all state prison units and could come and go any time of

day. We could speak to anyone we determined could help us gather relevant information.

I met scary prisoners who had committed violent crimes and notorious prison gang members, as well as inmates who had done something stupid and were doing their time as best they could. I met correctional staff who were consummate professionals and those stuck in a job they obviously didn't like.

After spending several days at a prison, I wrote a long, detailed report to the judge documenting the unit's progress toward meeting the court mandates that I monitored. Other team members monitored health care delivery, access to courts, use of force, job safety, and issues related to overcrowding.

Court orders are meaningless unless they're implemented. That takes a long time, especially for a shift in the culture of a complex organization such as a prison system; it took almost 20 years for TDCJ. The staff in the Office of the Special Master served as the judge's eyes and ears during those years.

It was the most fascinating job I've ever had.

beginning of the end for the hands-off doctrine, although, as we shall see, there is growing evidence of its return (Federman, 2004).

The technical term for a challenge to the legality of confinement is a writ of **habeas corpus.** Habeas corpus is a Latin term that literally means "you shall have the body" and is basically a court order requiring that an arrested person be brought before it to determine the legality of his or her detention. Habeas corpus is a very important concept in common law, which precedes even the Magna Carta of 1215, although its precise origins are unknown. It has been called the "Great Writ" and was formally codified into English common law by the Habeas Corpus Act of 1679. Indicative of the respect the Founding Fathers had for habeas corpus is that it is only one of three individual rights mentioned in the U.S. Constitution. (The other two are the prohibition of *bills of attainder*—imposing punishment without trial—and the prohibition of *ex post facto laws*—legislation making an act criminal after the fact). The other individual rights that Americans enjoy were formalized in the first 10 amendments to the Constitution (the **Bill of Rights**), almost as an afterthought. A writ of habeas corpus is not a direct appeal of a conviction but rather an indirect appeal regarding the legality of a person's confinement. In *Coffin v. Reichard* (1944), the Sixth Circuit Court of Appeals widened habeas corpus hearings to include conditions of confinement as well, but this had little impact for 20 years.

Career Video 18.1: Professor

Habeas corpus: Latin term meaning "you have the body." It is a court order requiring that an arrested person be brought before it to determine the legality of detention.

Bill of Rights: The first 10 amendments to the U.S. Constitution.

Web 18.2:
Prisoner Health
and Human
Rights

Two cases signaled the end of the hands-off period: *Jones v. Cunningham* (1963) and *Cooper v. Pate* (1964). In *Jones*, the Supreme Court went further than it did in *Hull* and ruled that prisoners could use a writ of habeas corpus to challenge the conditions of their confinement, as well as the legality of their confinement. This went beyond the original meaning of habeas corpus, which was only meant to address the preconviction issue of the legality of a petitioner's detainment. In *Cooper*, the Court went even further and ruled that state prison inmates could sue state officials in federal courts under the Civil Rights Act of 1871, which was initially enacted to protect Southern blacks from state officials. This act is now codified and known as 42 USC § 1983, or simply as **Section 1983 suits**, and any deprivation-of-rights grievance filed under it is called a **civil rights claim**. The relevant part of the act reads as follows:

> Every person who under color of any statute, ordinance, regulation, custom, or usage of any state or territory, subjects or causes to be subject, any citizen of the United States or other person within the jurisdiction thereof to the deprivation of any rights, privileges, or immunities secured by the Constitution and laws, shall be liable to the party injured in an action at law.

What was a mere trickle of habeas petitions before *Pate* quickly became a flood that threatened to drown the federal courts with grievances ranging from the petty to the deadly serious. The most serious petition led a federal appeals judge to declare the entire prison system of Arkansas unconstitutional and a "dark and evil world" when he placed it under federal supervision (*Holt v. Sarver*, 1969). As we saw in the opening vignette, Arkansas's institutions were horrific places where inmates were routinely subjected to brutal conditions. This case gave birth to what has come to be known as a *conditions-of-confinement lawsuit*. From then on, the federal courts became very much involved in the monitoring and operation of entire prison systems. The vast majority of habeas corpus grievances filed today are about the conditions of confinement, not the legality of an inmate's confinement. Inmates filing a petition challenging their confinement face an uphill battle because the state's defense against such a claim is based on inmates' convictions, which is the obvious legal basis for their confinement!

THE DEFERENCE PERIOD, 1979–PRESENT

Convicted criminals are no longer considered civilly dead while under correctional supervision. However, after a short time in which prisoners' rights were granted and extended, there began an era that correctional scholars have called the **deference period**. This time period was a partial return to the hands-off period and basically refers to the courts' willingness to defer to the expertise and needs of prison authorities. The courts have come to the conclusion that it is necessary to place restrictions on prisoners' rights that do not apply to nonoffenders because of the need to balance the rights of offenders and the legitimate needs and concerns of correctional authorities, particularly the safety and security needs of prisons and jails. In other words, prisoners' rights must be secondary to the maintenance of institutional order and security and the safety of inmates and staff. The basic stance of the U.S. Supreme Court on this matter has not changed since it was first enunciated in *Bell v. Wolfish* (1979), the case widely considered to be the one signaling the onset of the deference period:

> Simply because prison inmates retain certain constitutional rights does not mean that these rights are not subject to restrictions and limitations. There must be a "mutual accommodation between institutional needs and objectives and the provisions of the Constitution that are of general application." Maintaining institutional security and preserving internal order and discipline are essential goals that may require limitation or retraction of the retained constitutional rights of both convicted prisoners and pretrial detainees. (n.p.)

Section 1983 suits: A mechanism for state prison inmates to sue state officials in federal court regarding their confinement and their conditions of confinement.

Civil rights claim: A Section 1983 claim that a person has been deprived of some legally granted right.

Deference period: The period of time when there was a partial return to the hands-off approach; it refers to the courts' willingness to defer to the expertise and needs of the authorities.

We begin by looking at certain fundamental rights guaranteed by the First, Fourth, and Fourteenth Amendments to the Constitution and how they apply to convicted felons.

••• CONSTITUTIONAL RIGHTS

FIRST AMENDMENT

The First Amendment to the Constitution reads,

> Congress shall make no law respecting an establishment of religion, or prohibiting the free exercise thereof; or abridging the freedom of speech, or of the press; or the right of the people peaceably to assemble, and to petition the government for a redress of grievances.

The **First Amendment** thus guarantees freedom of religion, speech, press, and assembly. It goes without saying that in a prison setting, these freedoms cannot extend to activities and materials that jeopardize prison safety or security. The *Cooper v. Pate* (1964) case discussed earlier was essentially a First Amendment issue because Cooper, a member of the Nation of Islam (NOI), alleged that he was denied certain religious publications solely on the basis of his religion. Prison authorities claimed that NOI literature was dangerous and jeopardized the safety and security of the prison because it preached violent revolution and sought to recruit new members. The Supreme Court acknowledged that such literature may have an incendiary effect but ruled that Cooper's right to free exercise of his religion trumps what might result in security problems. Such free access to written materials need not extend to nonreligious materials, such as a manufacturer's guide to prison security locks, pornographic materials, or hate literature.

Religious freedom cannot extend to demanding alcohol or exotic foods to satisfy real or invented religious requirements. But the law is more an ideological exercise than a science. As if to prove our point, two federal circuit courts came to opposite conclusions in the same year (2008) regarding Muslim inmates' right to a *halal* diet (a diet which prohibits eating pork and shellfish and in which animals must be slaughtered in a certain way—closely akin to a Jewish kosher diet). The Eighth Circuit Court ruled that the nonprovision of a *halal* diet did not place an undue burden on the inmate and that there were alternative means of obtaining such a diet. The more liberal Ninth Circuit Court ruled, in a different case, that the prison's refusal to supply a Muslim inmate with a *halal* diet impinged on the free exercise of religion protected by the First Amendment (Robertson, 2010).

Brian Vander Brug/Los Angeles Times/Getty Images

PHOTO 18.2: Inmates retain some First Amendment rights, including the right to practice their religious beliefs if doing so does not unduly interfere with prison security.

Restrictions on inmates' rights to free speech can exceed those necessary to assure safety and security. In *Smith v. Mosley* (2008), the plaintiff made a statement in a grievance that prison authorities saw as insubordinate and false for which he received disciplinary sanctions. The inmate sought relief in federal court, claiming

First Amendment:
Guarantees freedom of religion, speech, press, and assembly.

IN FOCUS 18.1

Muslim Inmates Agitate for Their Rights

As the civil rights movement, fueled in part by Malcolm X and the Nation of Islam, helped raise the political consciousness of African Americans, black prisoners were affected. Correctional officials were threatened by the language and attitudes of such inmates and banned the practice of Islam in prisons (Belbot & Hemmens, 2010). Muslim inmates could not worship together or receive religious materials from the outside community. In 1962, Thomas Cooper sued the officials at the Stateville Prison in Illinois, claiming that he was denied benefit of religious clergy and religious literature, including the Koran, access that he claimed was protected by the First Amendment to the Constitution. Though he initially represented himself in court, the Nation of Islam took up his cause, and in 1964, the U.S. Supreme Court decided the case in Cooper's favor. This case, *Cooper v. Pate* (1964), set a precedent for the expansion not just of religious rights of all prisoners but of other rights as well.

DISCUSSION QUESTION

1. Why was it important that an issue involving religion opened up the rights of prisoners?

---

that he had been punished for exercising his right to free speech. The court disagreed, ruling that while filing a grievance is considered protected speech, the statements made within it were not, and therefore, the imposition of sanctions was constitutionally permissible. Freedom of speech or expression can also be limited on moral or ethical grounds. For instance, inmates can write and publish their thoughts or sell personal memorabilia, but "notoriety-for-profit" statutes enacted by the federal government and most states forbid inmates from profiting monetarily from those activities (Walsh & Hemmens, 2014).

The right of assembly allows for attendance at religious services and for visitation from family and friends, but it obviously cannot be construed as allowing inmates to assemble at a tattoo conference outside of the prison walls. Federal courts have also ruled that while Nation of Islam groups had the right to assemble for worship, their right to hold religious services could be denied if prison administrators considered such services to constitute potential breaches of security (Inciardi, 2007).

FOURTH AMENDMENT

The **Fourth Amendment** reads,

> The right of the people to be secure in their persons, houses, papers, and effects, against unreasonable searches and seizures, shall not be violated, and no warrants shall issue, but upon probable cause, supported by Oath or affirmation, and particularly describing the place to be searched, and the persons or things to be seized.

The right to privacy is a paramount concern of the Fourth Amendment, and so it guarantees the right to be free from unreasonable searches and seizures. Does this mean that inmates have the same right to privacy in their cells—to be "secure in their houses, papers, and effects"—that people on the outside have and that corrections officers should obtain warrants before searching their cells for suspected contraband and/or weapons? What is reasonable inside prison walls is, of course, quite different from what is reasonable outside them. For all practical purposes, inmates have no Fourth Amendment protections since their prison cells are not "homes" of personal sanctuary deserving of privacy (*Hudson v. Palmer*, 1984).

Fourth Amendment: Guarantees the right to be free from unreasonable searches and seizures.

The one area in which Fourth Amendment rights have not been completely extinguished for inmates is that involving opposite-sex body searches. The courts have had to wrestle with conflicting claims on this issue. One is the equal employment claim of female corrections officers who want to work in male institutions where, because of their size and scope, promotion prospects are greater than they are in female prisons. Working in all-male prisons necessarily means that women officers will occasionally view inmates undressed or using toilet facilities, and sometimes, they may be required to perform pat downs and visual body cavity searches. (Physical searches of body cavities may only be performed by medical personnel.) A frequent inmate claim is that cross-gender searches are "unreasonable" within the meaning of the Fourth Amendment.

Bennett (1995) notes that the great majority of cross-gender search complaints are filed by males, which is not surprising since males constitute about 94% of all state prison inmates (Bohm & Haley, 2007). On the other hand, it is surprising given the frequent complaints from female officers that some male inmates seem to take every opportunity to expose themselves and to behave in a sexual manner in their presence (Cowburn, 1998). Of course, this does not mean that many inmates are not genuinely embarrassed and offended by having to bear the indignity of female officers observing them using the toilet. However, ever since the doors were opened in *Hull*, the filing of all sorts of complaints has become a sort of inmate hobby for some that serves the purpose of relieving boredom, getting "one over" on prison authorities and possibly a ride or two into town to attend court (McNeese, 2010). There are many legitimate prisoner complaints, but Dilworth (1995) reports that 75% of prisoner petitions are dismissed by the court's own evaluation, 20% are dismissed in a grant of a state's motion, and about 2% result in a trial, in which fewer than half result in a favorable verdict for the prisoner. Thus, less than 1% of prisoner complaints are considered legitimate. Examples of some frivolous and malicious petitions are given in In Focus 18.2.

In *Turner v. Safley* (1987), the Supreme Court enunciated what has come to be known as the *balancing test*, which means that the courts must balance the rights of inmates against the interests of penological concerns of security and order. In deciding that lower courts were wrong in applying the strict-scrutiny standard of review (a standard of review used by the courts if a "fundamental right"—anything in the Bill of Rights—or a "suspect classification"—race, religion, or national origin—is involved) to inmates' constitutional complaints, the Court ruled that these cases require a lesser standard and involve the issue of whether a prison regulation that impinges on inmates' constitutional rights is "reasonably related" to legitimate penological interests. This *reasonableness* revolves around a number of factors, including whether there is a valid and rational connection between the regulation and a legitimate government interest that is justified in the name of staff and inmate safety and security.

PHOTO 18.3: Such a dank and sparse environment in which to live out one's life is certainly not conducive to rehabilitation.

According to the balancing test, then, viewing opposite-sex inmates without clothing is constitutionally valid "if it is reasonably related to legitimate penal interests." Bennett (1995) tells us how lower courts have interpreted *reasonableness* and concludes that while female officers conducting or observing strip searches of male inmates is tolerated in emergency situations, similar observation and searches by male officers of female inmates are considered unreasonable. This double standard has been justified on two grounds: (1) Males do not experience loss of job opportunities if they are forbidden to frisk female inmates, and (2) intimate touching of a female inmate by a male officer may cause psychological trauma because many female inmates have histories of sexual abuse.

IN FOCUS 18.2

Any Complaints This Morning?

"Any complaints this morning?" was the drill sergeant's daily cynical question to newly drafted soldiers during World War II. Of course, none of the draftees confined in the sweltering barracks were ever bold enough to make any complaint, although living conditions were such that they would not be tolerated by the courts if they existed in our prisons today. We wonder what these old soldiers would say about the following.

In dismissing a lawsuit in one case, the Supreme Court noted that the majority of prisoner petitions are frivolous and/or malicious, cost taxpayers millions of dollars, and waste precious court time. Florida attorney general Bob Butterworth (1995) asserts, "My office spends nearly $2 million a year defending that state against inmate suits, most of which contain ridiculous charges or demands" (p. 1). Similarly, Idaho deputy attorney general Timothy McNeese (2010) notes that fully 27% of all litigation in Idaho's federal district courts involve inmate petitions, most of which are "meritless," "downright frivolous," and "no doubt are filed by inmates out of frustration and anger and desire to get even with a correctional employee or the 'system'" (p. 321). Presented below are some examples of frivolous and/or malicious petitions gleaned from Butterworth and McNeese that judges must wade through to get to prisoner petitions that are really deserving of attention. The sheer audacity of these examples may raise a smile on your face, but they are no laughing matter to the courts, prison administrators, the taxpayers, or the prisoners with real grievances whose petitions are lost in the pile.

Prisoner starts a riot, shatters glass in his cell, and files an Eighth Amendment suit claiming cruel and unusual punishment because he cut his foot on the glass.

Prisoner sends for information about prison security and locks and sues because the warden refused to give him the mail containing the information.

Prisoner sues because his ice cream was half melted when it was served to him.

Prisoner sues over unsatisfactory haircut.

Prisoner sues because jailers cut her sausage into small pieces because she had been caught previously masturbating with a whole sausage.

Prisoner sues because he was required to eat off a paper plate.

Prisoner files over 140 actions in state and federal court over finding gristle in his turkey leg.

Prisoner sues to receive fruit juice at meals and an extra pancake at breakfast.

Prisoner who murdered five people sues because he had to watch network TV programs after lightning knocked out the prison's satellite dish. These programs contained violent material that this multiple murderer said was objectionable.

Prisoner sues over the inferior brand of sneakers issued to him.

Prisoner loses a suit claiming his rights as a Muslim were violated because the prison put "essence of swine" in his food, then converts to Satanism and demands tarot cards and "doves' blood."

Prisoner sues because the disciplinary cell he was placed in had no electrical outlet for his TV.

Farkas and Rand (1999) also support gender-specific standards for cross-gender searches on the basis of prior sexual abuse that an inmate may have suffered and state, "Cross-gender searches have the very real potential to replicate that suffering in prison" (p. 53), and further abuse would constitute cruel and unusual punishment. This raises the question of the possible legal validity of complaints about same-sex body searches if the complainant can show prior sexual abuse by a same-sex person. For instance, will such a person then be in a position to demand an opposite-sex body search?

Inmates' privacy rights have allowed them the freedom to file fraudulent tax returns claiming millions of dollars in refunds. In 2004, over 18,000 false tax returns were filed claiming $68.1 million in refunds, which rose to almost 45,000 filed in 2009 claiming $295 million. The Internal Revenue Service (IRS) catches most of these frauds, but refunds issued to these prisoners in 2009 amounted to over $39 million (Department of the Treasury, 2010). Some prisoners (such as those working in prison industries) earn income and thus must file an annual income tax return with the IRS. Because this income information is considered private, prison officials cannot inspect returns for fraudulent claims.

ETHICAL ISSUE 18.1

What Would You Do?

You are a prosecutor in a jurisdiction that is determined to stamp down hard on crime. You have a case before you of a one-legged man charged with stealing the left boot of a pair of cowboy boots worth $300, making the theft a felony. The defendant has two prior felony convictions, and this would be his third if convicted. You want to dispose of the case quickly via a plea bargain, and you offer to reduce the charge to a misdemeanor if the defendant will plead guilty. You also tell him that if he does not take the plea, you will charge him as a habitual offender under the states' three-strikes law. The defendant refuses to plea, saying the theft should be a misdemeanor anyway since he only stole one boot. What will you do? After you have decided, take a look at *Bordenkircher v. Hayes* (1978), and see what the prosecutor chose to do and how this case was actually decided by the Supreme Court. (Yes, it actually happened.)

EIGHTH AMENDMENT

The **Eighth Amendment** reads,

> Excessive bail shall not be required, nor excessive fines imposed, nor cruel and unusual punishments inflicted.

The pertinent part of the amendment for us is the part that addresses cruel and unusual punishment. According to the U.S. Supreme Court, cruel and unusual punishment is punishment applied "maliciously and sadistically for the very purpose of causing harm" (*Hudson v. McMillian*, 1992), although the inmate is responsible for proving that the punishment was so applied. Eighth Amendment protections are denied by prison officials not only doing something to inmates that they should not but also failing to do something that they have a duty to do. Prison officials must provide inmates with the basic amenities of life, such as food and medical attention, and they must provide them with protection from the physical and sexual predations of other inmates, many of whom have histories of "maliciously and sadistically" causing harm to others.

AP Video 18.1: Lethal Inject QA

Liability attaches to prison officials for inmate-on-inmate assaults if officials display deliberate indifference to an inmate's needs (Vaughn & Del Carmen, 1995). The courts have struggled to make plain what deliberate indifference means, but basically, it occurs when prison officials know of but disregard an obvious risk to an inmate's health or safety (*Wilson v. Seiter*, 1991). In other words, prison officials must not turn a blind eye to situations that obviously imperil the health or safety of inmates entrusted to their care. Purposely placing a slightly built and effeminate young male in a cell with a known aggressive sexual predator is an example of a violation of the deliberate indifference standard for which prison authorities would be liable for any injuries suffered. For

Eighth Amendment: Constitutional amendment that forbids cruel and unusual punishment.

inmates to prevail in suits involving deliberate indifference claims, they must prove that (1) they suffered an objectively serious deprivation or harm, and (2) prison officials were aware of the risk that caused the alleged harm, and they failed to take reasonable steps to prevent it. *Wilson* is seen as a key decision favoring correctional agencies because of these stringent proof requirements.

AP Video 18.2: Firing Squad

Audio 18.1: Bill of Rights Series: The Eighth Amendment

Despite movie depictions and public perceptions of jails and prisons as places where sexual assault is rife, the rate of sexual assault in prisons is 0.40 per 1,000 inmates, which is much lower than sexual violence rates on the outside (Beck & Harrison, 2007). The forcible-rape rate in 2012 in the free community was at 0.53 per 1,000 females (FBI, 2013a), and this does not include all other sexual-misconduct offenses of the kind included in the Beck and Harrison (2007) report. The Beck and Harrison (2007) report also noted that 38% of the allegations involved staff misconduct, sometimes referred to as "romance" between staff and inmates. The majority of forceful sexual assault was inmate on inmate (Robertson, 2010).

Inmate medical care is also covered by the concept of deliberate indifference. F. Cohen (2008) writes,

> Our jails and prisons have increasingly become the de facto clinical depositories for hundreds of thousands of inmates who are very sick and who require all manner of specialty medical, dental, and mental health care. Prisons are not only the new mental asylums; they are the community hospitals and emergency wards for certain segments of the poor. (p. 5)

Fourteenth Amendment: Contains the due process clause, which declares that no state shall deprive any person of life, liberty, or property without due process of law.

The medical needs of inmates in today's prisons are as well addressed as those of the average free person of roughly similar class background presenting with similar health problems. Indeed, inmates are the only group of people in the United States with a constitutional right to medical care. According to a Bureau of Justice Statistics report on inmate mortality in state prisons, prisoners between 15 and 64 years of age had a mortality rate 19% lower than that of the U.S. general population (Mumola, 2007). The majority of the difference was attributable to African American male inmates under 45, who had a mortality rate 57% lower than the rate of black males of similar age in the general population. Of course, not all of this difference is attributable to the medical care inmates receive, and no one claims that such care is better than—or even equal to—the average level of medical care available to most people on the outside. The lower mortality rate is most likely due to the fact that incarceration lowers the probability of being murdered, being exposed to drugs, having access to alcohol and tobacco, and other risks to a person's health and safety that those who pursue a criminal lifestyle face every day on the outside.

ETHICAL ISSUE 18.2

What Would You Do?

You are a district judge. Two male inmates claiming to be in love have filed a suit in your court demanding to be allowed to marry and be housed in the same cell. They also claim that prison authorities have purposely housed them in separate units so that they have no contact with each other. You know that the Prison Rape Elimination Act of 2003 (PREA) has been a potent tool for the selective sanctioning of inmates for any sexual expression at all. The state claims that prison officials must limit sexual interactions among inmates because of their potential liability regarding allegations of prison rape under PREA. The state also claims that such a thing is unprecedented and could lead to all kinds of unrest in the prison. The inmates claim that they are genuinely in love, that heterosexual inmates may marry, and that to deny their request is discriminatory and a violation of their human rights of sexual expression. How will you rule, and why?

FOURTEENTH AMENDMENT

The **Fourteenth Amendment** is a long one, with five sections; we cite only the first section here:

> All persons born or naturalized in the United States, and subject to the jurisdiction thereof, are citizens of the United States

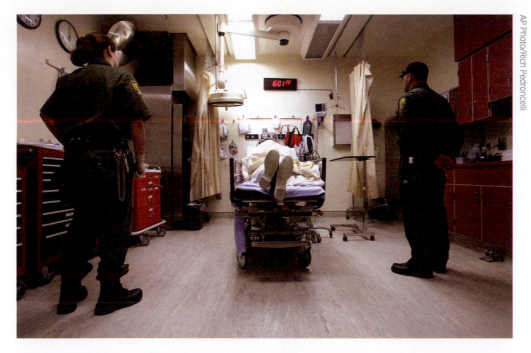

PHOTO 18.4: Correctional officers stand watch over an inmate receiving treatment in the emergency room at California State Prison, Corcoran, in Corcoran, California. What challenges does this situation present for correctional officers?

and of the State wherein they reside. No state shall make or enforce any law which shall abridge the privileges or immunities of citizens of the United States; nor shall any State deprive any person of life, liberty, or property, without due process of law; nor deny to any person within its jurisdiction the equal protection of the laws.

This is the due process clause of the Fourteenth Amendment and is the legal basis for granting limited procedural rights to individuals under correctional supervision. The due process clause was first applied to inmates facing disciplinary action for infractions of prison rules in *Wolff v. McDonnell* (1974). In *Wolff*, the Supreme Court declared that while inmates are not entitled to the same due process rights as accused but unconvicted people on the outside, they are entitled to some. These rights are (1) to receive written notice of an alleged infraction, (2) to be given sufficient time (usually 24 hours) to prepare a defense, (3) to have time to produce evidence and witnesses on their behalf, (4) to have the assistance of nonlegal counsel, and (5) to have a written statement outlining the disciplinary committee's findings.

In *Sandin v. Connor* (1995), the Supreme Court clarified and trimmed back inmate rights. The Court declared that the aforementioned due process rights are only triggered by any disciplinary action that may result in the loss of good time, which amounts to an extension of an inmate's sentence. Conner had been given 30 days of punitive segregation for making foul and abusive comments to an officer while being subjected to a strip search. The Court ruled that due process rights are not triggered by actions that result in temporary placement in a disciplinary-segregation unit, which does not amount to an extension of one's sentence. The Court also concluded that disciplinary segregation is not an atypical hardship relative to the ordinary hardships of imprisonment.

POLICY AND RESEARCH

Solitary Confinement, Mental Health, and the Eighth Amendment

Solitary confinement has been increasingly used in U.S. prisons as a way to punish and control difficult or dangerous prisoners. Thousands of prisoners spend weeks, months, or years locked up for 23 to 24 hours a day in small cells with extensive surveillance and security controls and may have only three to five hours a week of recreation, which they spend isolated in caged enclosures. It is typically used for especially difficult and dangerous criminals who pose substantial risks to the safety and security of correctional officers and other prisoners, but sometimes, it is used as a form of protective custody.

For instance, according to an exposé in *The Atlantic* (Cohen, 2012), bank robber Jack Powers witnessed three inmates kill another in a federal prison in Atlanta and was transferred to a segregated unit for his safety. Powers testified against these three in federal court and became the object of death threats. Powers was then transferred to a prison in Pennsylvania and put in protective custody, but the death threats continued. Because of these threats, he developed insomnia and anxiety attacks and was diagnosed with post-traumatic stress disorder. Instead of being treated, Powers was again transferred to another prison, from which he escaped upon being told he would be placed in the general population instead of the witness protection program. He was soon recaptured and transferred to the supermax prison in Colorado. In response, Powers mutilated himself by biting off his pinkie finger, amputating his earlobes, cutting his Achilles tendon and skin from his face, and slicing off his scrotum, and he tried to commit suicide. Prison officials told him that he could not get medication for his mental problems, as rules stated that no psychotropic medication was allowed in that unit.

Federal policy prohibits inmates with mental illnesses from being transferred to supermax prisons, but they are transferred there anyway. In many cases, as with Powers, inmates do not have mental-health problems until they are imprisoned in one. As a federal judge remarked in *Ruiz v. Johnson* (2001), "[Solitary confinement] units are virtual incubators of psychoses—seeding illness in otherwise healthy inmates and exacerbating illness in those already suffering from mental infirmities." One study (Andersen et al., 2000) found that 28% of inmates in solitary confinement developed some form of psychopathology, versus 15% in the general prison population. This occurs because "the stress, lack of meaningful social contact, and unstructured days can exacerbate symptoms of illness or provoke recurrence" (Metzner &

Fellner, 2010, p. 105). Powers's case is an admittedly rare one, but it certainly violates the deliberate-indifference rule we discussed in *Estelle v. Gamble*.

Solitary confinement has been called "cruel, inhuman or degrading treatment or punishment" in international law, and some argue that it is one of the "cruel and unusual punishments" prohibited by the Eighth Amendment of the U.S. Constitution, although it has proved difficult to argue in U.S. courts. However, California has severely restricted its use of solitary confinement in response to a lawsuit filed in 2012 on behalf of a group of Pelican Bay inmates who spent more than a decade in isolation. Justice Anthony Kennedy is said to have opined in 2015 that it is time for the court to take a look at the widespread use of solitary confinement because of the "human toll wrought by extended terms of isolation" (Barnes, 2015, n.p.). What the most influential justice on the Supreme Court is apparently looking for someone is sure to provide in the near future.

DISCUSSION QUESTIONS

1. Do you think the safety reasons cited for putting someone in solitary confinement are justified given the damage it can do to a person?

2. Discuss options for both isolating prisoners *and* maintaining their mental health.

3. Is solitary confinement "cruel and unusual" punishment?

References

Andersen, H., Sestoft, D., Lillebæk, T., Gabrielsen, G., Hemmingsen, R., & Kramp, P. (2000). A longitudinal study of prisoners on remand: Psychiatric prevalence, incidence and psychopathology in solitary vs. non-solitary confinement. *Acta Psychiatrica Scandinavica, 102*, 19–25.

Barnes, R. (2015, August 10). If Kennedy is looking for a solitary-confinement case, an inmate has one. *Washington Post*. Retrieved from https://www.washingtonpost.com/politics/courts_law/if-kennedy-is-looking-for-a-solitary-confinement-case-an-inmate-has-one/2015/08/09/b59a6444-3e0a-11e5-b3ac-8a79bc44e5e2_story.html

Cohen, A. (2012, June 18). An American gulag: Descending into madness at supermax. *The Atlantic*. Retrieved from http://www.theatlantic.com/national/archive/2012/06/an-american-gulag-descending-into-madness-at-supermax/258323

Metzner, J., & Fellner, J. (2010). Solitary confinement in U.S. prisons: A challenge for medical ethics. *Journal of the American Academy of Psychiatry and the Law, 38*, 104–108.

Ruiz v. Johnson, 154 F.Supp.2d 975 (S.D.Tex. 2001).

••• THE CIVIL COMMITMENT OF SEX OFFENDERS

The idea that people who engage in socially disapproved behavior are sick and require treatment is seen as particularly applicable to sex offenders. In 1997, the Supreme Court upheld Kansas's Sexually Violent Predator Act (SVPA), which allows the state to keep sex offenders in custody under civil-commitment laws *after* they have served their full prison terms if they demonstrate "mental abnormality" or are said to have a "personality disorder" (*Kansas v. Hendricks*, 1997). The federal government and many other states have since passed similar involuntary-confinement laws for sex offenders. Prior to *Hendricks*, civil commitments were limited to individuals suffering from mental illness, but seemingly for the express purpose of covering sex offenders, states have loosened the mental-illness criterion in favor of the mental-abnormality criterion (R. Alexander, 2004). The term *mental abnormality* can, of course, be used to cover almost anything society may disapprove of and serves as a justification for imprisonment in ways "reminiscent of Soviet policies that institutionalized dissidents" (Grinfeld, 2005, p. 2). There is no doubt that Leroy Hendricks was a repeat predatory pedophile and a thoroughly nasty piece of work, but while many applaud his incapacitation, what concerns civil libertarians is that the *Hendricks* decision created a special category of individuals defined as "abnormal" who may be punished indefinitely for what they *might do* if released.

Hendricks appealed his confinement on double-jeopardy (no person can be prosecuted twice for the same offense) and ex post facto (a person cannot be punished for acts that were not crimes at the time he or she committed them) grounds. The Supreme Court ruled that Hendricks's confinement was not double jeopardy because the commitment proceedings of the SVPA under which he was confined were civil rather than criminal and thus did not constitute a second prosecution. Likewise, Hendricks's ex post facto claim was rejected because the ex post facto clause of the U.S. Constitution relates only to criminal statutes. The Court declared that because Hendricks was committed under a civil act, his commitment did not constitute punishment. The majority of Supreme Court justices seem to have believed that putting a different name on state confinement against the will of the confined changes how that person experiences it.

CRITICISMS OF CIVIL COMMITMENT

In his analysis of civil commitment of sex offenders, R. Alexander (2004) lists a number of ways in which he believes the Supreme Court erred in its rulings in *Hendricks* and subsequent cases dealing with the same issue. The gist of most of these criticisms is that the ruling offends (R. Alexander's) ideas of social justice and does not accomplish any of the goals of state confinement (deterrence and rehabilitation) other than retribution and incapacitation. Farkas and Stichman (2002) also argue that what they call the "culture of fear" generated by atypically brutal sex offenses has resulted in laws that are constitutionally questionable and that have negative consequences for the treatment of sex offenders, the criminal justice system, and society in general. The popularity of the laws with the general public and the extremely negative view of sex offenders most people hold makes it unlikely that these laws will be changed in the near future. It should be noted that only between 1% and 2% of sex offenders are confined under civil-commitment orders (R. Alexander, 2004).

••• CURTAILING PRISONER PETITIONS

According to Federman (2004), two congressional acts signed into law in 1996—the Prison Litigation Reform Act (PLRA) and the Antiterrorism and Effective Death

Journal Article 18.1: The United States Supreme Court and the Civil Commitment of Sex Offenders

PHOTO 18.5: The exterior of the Civil Commitment Unit for Sexual Offenders (CCUSO), part of the Cherokee Mental Health Institute in Cherokee, Iowa. Only 1% to 2% of sex offenders are ever civilly committed.

Audio 18.2: Supreme Court Rules on Two Prisoner Rights Cases

Penalty Act (AEDPA)—have severely curtailed prisoner access to the courts. Both acts were passed, in part, to reduce the thousands of lawsuits filed by inmates that clog the federal courts. In the year of the passage of these acts, inmates filed 68,235 civil rights lawsuits in the federal courts, compared with less than 2,000 in the early 1960s (Alvarado, 2009). By 2000, the number of such lawsuits dropped to 24,519 (Seiter, 2005), a 64% decrease from the 1996 figure. Despite claims that these acts are "silencing the cells" (Vogel, 2004), the number of lawsuits filed is still more than 12 times what it was in the 1960s. Figure 18.1 is from a U.S. District Courts report (USDC, 2013) comparing all kinds of prisoner petitions to federal courts with other types of cases. In 2012, there were 54,300 prisoner petitions, indicating that they are climbing dramatically again to over double what they were in 2000, but they are still fewer than in 1996.

The primary intention of the PLRA was to free prisons and jails from federal court supervision, as well as to limit prisoners' access to the federal courts. Both intentions have largely succeeded. Among the requirements of the PLRA is one that state inmates cannot bring a Section 1983 (civil rights) lawsuit in federal court unless they first exhaust all available administrative remedies, such as filing a written grievance with the warden. The PLRA also states that inmates claiming to be unable to afford the required filing fee for the lawsuit may still have to pay a partial fee, which will be collected whenever money appears in their inmate accounts. This provision may limit the airing of genuine grievances in federal court because of financial difficulties.

The issues raised by the passage of the PLRA reached the Supreme Court in *Jones v. Bock* (2007). The specific issue in *Jones v. Bock* (2007) was whether the PLRA requires inmates bringing a federal civil rights suit to show they have exhausted all administrative remedies before suing or does it require the defense to prove that administrative remedies were not exhausted. In a unanimous opinion written by Chief Justice John Roberts, the Court ruled that the exhaustion of administrative remedies was not required by the PLRA and that prisoners could bring civil rights lawsuits without the need to demonstrate that they have exhausted all administrative remedies. The opinion did not ignore the flood of frivolous suits but intimated that this concern was secondary to the genuine complaints prisoners may have. In *Jones v. Bock* (2007), Justice Roberts wrote,

> Prisoner litigation continues to "account for an outsized share of filings" in federal district courts. In 2005, nearly 10 percent of all civil cases filed in federal courts nationwide were prisoner complaints challenging prison conditions or claiming civil rights violations. Most of these cases have no merit; many are frivolous. Our legal system, however, remains committed to guaranteeing that prisoner claims of illegal conduct by their custodians are fairly handled according to law. The challenge lies in ensuring that the flood of nonmeritorious claims does not submerge and effectively preclude consideration of the allegations with merit.

As the name implies, the AEDPA is mostly about antiterrorism and the death penalty rather than an act specifically designed to limit habeas corpus proceedings. It was

| **FIGURE** *18.1* | Comparison of Prisoner Petitions Filed in U.S. District Courts and Other Civil Cases, 2010–2014 |

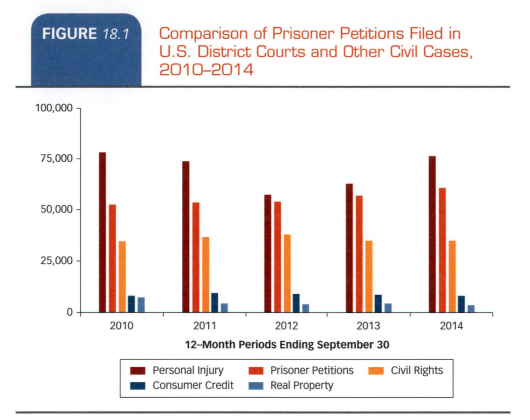

12–Month Periods Ending September 30

- ■ Personal Injury
- ■ Prisoner Petitions
- ■ Civil Rights
- ■ Consumer Credit
- ■ Real Property

Source: U.S. District Courts, Judicial Business 2014 (2014). Civil Filings. http://www.uscourts.gov/statistics-reports/us-district-courts-judicial-business-2014

passed in response to the bombing of the Murrah Federal Building in Oklahoma City, with the reform of habeas corpus law being a rider to it. The AEDPA does not eliminate inmates' rights to habeas corpus, but it does restrict its availability (Alvarado, 2009). It does so by limiting successive petitions and judicial review of evidence and may now apply only to inmates who have sought but have been denied state court remedies available to them. The AEDPA thus takes habeas corpus partially back along the road to again becoming the preconviction remedy against unlawful imprisonment that it was initially.

A review of Supreme Court decisions on habeas corpus since the AEDPA found that they have upheld the reforms largely as intended by Congress (Scheidegger, 2006). Although civil rights groups, such as the American Civil Liberties Union, tend to decry both statutes, the Court's attitude toward them is probably a good thing for all involved for a number of reasons. First, it frees up the federal courts to deal with pressing inmate issues that are really repugnant to the Constitution, as well as the numerous other matters it must deal with. Second, we all know that crying wolf too often leads to the dismissal of genuine claims, and if the situation continued as it was before the 1996 reforms, the solution may just have been the return to a completely hands-off policy. Third, it saves the taxpayer literally millions of dollars in frivolous legal exercises whose benefits were only to relieve the boredom of mischievous inmates. (Again, this does not mean that there are no substantively meaningful claims filed.) Many states, aware that the courts could swing back to more active involvement and of the high cost of defending lawsuits, have established internal mechanisms to more effectively deal with inmate concerns, such as outside mediators and the creation of ombudsmen. Although PLRA and AEDPA have limited inmate access to the courts, then, in a roundabout way, they have given inmates more immediate and local ways to make their grievances known.

Prior to AEDPA's passage, there was no statute of limitations on filings and no limit to their number (Orye, 2002). There was no requirement that separate claims be consolidated into one appeal so that one minor issue could be broken down into several even smaller issues and filed at different times. AEDPA imposed a number of limitations on the practically unlimited access to habeas corpus petitions. It imposed a strict one-year limitation on them, maintained that a petitioner could no longer file successive petitions unless a federal court of appeals approved, and stated that habeas relief is available only if a state court's ruling was deemed contrary to or unreasonably applied established federal law. Under AEDPA, then, defendants now are supposed to have one shot at habeas corpus, and all relevant appeal issues must be consolidated in that one petition.

With the passage of AEDPA, with its one-year statute of limitation, consolidation of issues, and promise of expedited federal review, death penalty proponents celebrated the end of interminable delays of execution. But as Figure 18.2 shows, AEDPA had more bark than bite because rather than decrease, the average time from sentencing to execution increased by 5 years between the date of its passage in 1996 (130 months) and 2012 (190 months).

The problem seems to have been that AEDPA's statutory language has led to numerous interpretive splits in different federal appeals courts (Blume, 2006). Also, the U.S. Supreme Court ruled in *Horn v. Banks* (2002) that the act is not retroactive, so the hundreds of pre-AEDPA cases can still proceed as before. More importantly, the act was not automatically applied to the states. In order for a state to opt into AEDPA's promises, it requires that they establish certain mechanisms and adhere to strict standards and procedures that, in effect, shift the financial burden from the federal government to the states. The major stumbling block is the provision that states must provide fully competent and adequately compensated counsel in order to avail themselves of AEDPA's reforms; no state has done so thus far (Spohn & Hemmens, 2012). The state of

FIGURE *18.2*   Average Time Between Sentencing and Execution, in Months

Source: Death Penalty Information Center. http://www.deathpenaltyinfo.org/time-death-row

Texas tried to opt in but failed to do so when the Fifth Circuit ruled that it had failed to meet the requirement to provide AEDPA-defined competent attorneys for defendants (Kannenberg, 2009).

••• LEGAL ISSUES IN PROBATION AND PAROLE

The prisoners' rights period also extended rights to offenders under community supervision. Probation and parole are statutory privileges granted by the state in lieu of imprisonment (in the first case) or further imprisonment (in the second case). Because of their conditional-privilege status, it was long thought that the state did not have to provide probationers and parolees any procedural due process rights either in the granting or revoking of either status. Today, probationers and parolees are granted some due process rights, although, like inmates, there are restrictions on them that are not applicable to citizens not under correctional supervision.

DUE PROCESS RIGHTS

The first important case in this area was *Mempa v. Rhay* (1967). Mempa was a probationer who committed a burglary, which he admitted, four months after he was placed on probation. His probation was revoked without a proper hearing or the assistance of legal counsel; he was sent to prison. The issue before the Supreme Court was whether probationers have a right to counsel at a deferred-sentencing (probation revocation) hearing. The Court ruled that under the Sixth and Fourteenth Amendments, they do because Mempa was being sentenced, and the fact that sentencing took place subsequent to a probation placement does not alter the fact that sentencing is a "critical stage" in a criminal case. The Court further stated that probationers facing revocation should have the opportunity to challenge evidence by cross-examining state witnesses (typically, only the probation officer), present exculpatory witnesses, and testify themselves.

A further advance in granting due process rights to offenders on conditional-liberty status came in *Morrissey v. Brewer* (1972). Morrissey was a parolee who was arrested by his parole officer for a number of technical violations and returned to prison without a hearing. Morrissey's petition to the Supreme Court claimed that because he received no hearing prior to revocation, he was denied his rights under the due process clause of the Fourteenth Amendment. The Court agreed that when a **liberty interest** is involved, certain processes are necessary. (A *liberty interest* refers to government-imposed changes in someone's legal status that interfere with his or her constitutionally guaranteed rights to be free of such interference). The ruling by the Court in *Morrissey* noted that parole revocation does not call for all of the rights due to a defendant who is not yet convicted but that there are certain protections under the Fourteenth Amendment that they are entitled to. These rights were laid out by the Court as follows:

a. Written notice of the claimed violations of parole.

b. Disclosure to the parolee of evidence against him.

c. Opportunity to be heard in person and to present witnesses and documentary evidence.

d. The right to confront and cross-examine adverse witnesses (unless the hearing officer specifically finds good cause for not allowing confrontation).

Liberty interest:
Refers to an interest in freedom from governmental deprivation of liberty without due process.

e. A "neutral and detached" hearing body such as a traditional parole board, members of which need not be judicial officers or lawyers.

f. A written statement by the fact finders as to the evidence relied on and reasons for revoking parole. (p. 485)

CONSTITUTIONAL RIGHTS

While individuals are on probation or parole, they have limited constitutional rights, and their probation or parole officers have broader powers to intrude into their lives than police officers. Because probationers and parolees waive their Fourth Amendment search or seizure rights, probation and parole officers may conduct searches at any time without a warrant and without the probable cause needed by police officers. Evidence seized by probation and parole officers without a warrant can be used in probation or parole revocation hearings but not as trial evidence in a new case (*Pennsylvania Board of Probation and Parole v. Scott*, 1998). The Court ruled that to exclude evidence from a parole hearing would hamper the state's ability to assure the parolee's compliance with conditions of release and would yield the parolee free of consequences for noncompliance. This "special needs" (of law enforcement) exception to the Fourth Amendment has been extended to the police under certain circumstances. The Supreme Court has held that if a probation order is written in such a way that provides for submission to a search "by a probation officer or any other law enforcement officer," then the police gain the same rights to conduct searches based on less than probable cause as probation and parole officers (*United States v. Knights*, 2001).

HUMAN RIGHTS

A major human rights issue has emerged with the reliance, in many states, on private probation services in misdemeanor cases. Private probation companies offer cash-strapped counties free misdemeanor probation services in return for the right to collect fees (typically 30%) from their probationers and for courts making probationers' freedom contingent on paying them. The fee collected from probationers' court costs, fines, and restitution constitute the revenue and profits of such companies. As fines and restitution have increasingly replaced jail sentences to limit jail overcrowding, and pay-as-you-go probation has been increasingly used by the criminal justice system to defray costs, misdemeanants and some felons have become serious debtors (Beckett & Murakawa, 2012). Private misdemeanor probation officers have become glorified debt collectors under this system, threatening jail if debts are not paid and actually following through with their threats since their salaries depend on collection fees.

This offender-funded system of supervision sounds like a good idea until it is realized that many thousands of offenders, some with very minor offenses and who are poor, accrue debts of thousands of dollars and are incarcerated for nonpayment. Such people are locked into a cycle of debt and incarceration, which signals a return to debtor's prisons. This is happening despite the fact that the Supreme Court outlawed the practice in *Bearden v. Georgia* (1983), unless the defendant willfully refuses to *pay* and has the funds to do so. Courts have circumvented this ruling by the use of civil-contempt (of court) charges for failure to pay their financial obligations. This only results in the incarceration of indigent offenders and is an affront to justice because it essentially results in a two-tiered system of justice.

SUMMARY

- The only way we can be reasonably assured that justice resides within a legal system is to determine the extent to which it adheres to the rule of law. That is, a nation must recognize the supremacy of certain fundamental values and principles that have been committed to writing, and there must be a system of procedures to hold the government to these principles and values.

- The courts have moved through three general periods with respect to inmates' rights: the hands-off period, a short period of extending many rights to prisoners, and the current retreat to a limited hands-off policy.

- During the hands-off period, prisoners were considered slaves of the state and had no rights at all. During the period of extending prisoners' rights, the federal courts extended a number of First, Fourth, Eighth, and Fourteenth Amendment rights to them, although these rights were obviously not as extensive as they would be outside of prison walls. (However, inmates are the only group of Americans with a constitutional right to medical treatment.)

- Because these rights were granted, the federal courts became clogged with Section 1983 suits, in which inmates challenged the conditions of their confinement, the great majority of which were demonstrably frivolous.

- A major source of concern for civil rights activists is the civil commitment of some sex offenders after they have served their prison sentences. These offenders are liable to be locked up because of something they might do rather than something they have done.

- The U.S. Congress passed the PLRA in 1996, limiting prisoner access to federal courts and loosening the grip of the courts on state correctional systems because of these excessive suits. Congress also passed the AEDPA in the same year, with a rider limiting inmates' habeas corpus rights. Prisoners' petitions to the federal courts dropped substantially for the first few years after the passage of the PLRA and AEDPA, but they are now climbing back up.

- Since the 1960s, the courts also have been active in providing rights to offenders under community supervision. The Supreme Court has ruled that probationers have a right to counsel at a deferred-sentencing hearing and that probationers and parolees have minimal due process rights (a fair hearing to establish cause) at revocation hearings. The Court has also extended the greater search powers of probation and parole officers to police officers under certain circumstances.

KEY TERMS

Bill of Rights 439

Civil-death statutes 437

Civil rights claim 440

Deference period 440

Eighth Amendment 445

First Amendment 441

Fourteenth Amendment 446

Fourth Amendment 442

Habeas corpus 439

Hands-off doctrine 437

Liberty interest 453

Rule of law 436

Section 1983 suits 440

DISCUSSION QUESTIONS

1. What were the two main reasons or justifications behind the hands-off doctrine?

2. Why does the concept of habeas corpus have such a revered place in common law?

3. In what way did the Court in *Jones v. Cunningham* (1963) go beyond the original meaning of habeas corpus?

4. Do you think that the majority of male-inmate complaints about female officers frisk searching

them or viewing their nakedness are genuine indications of outrage?

5. What do you think of laws permitting the civil commitment of some sex offenders? Are there any potential dangers for widespread abuse in the practice?

6. What sort of latitude should the law permit prisoners to file lawsuits without any obvious merit?

USEFUL INTERNET SITES

Please note that the sites listed can be accessed at edge.sagepub.com/stohrcorrections.

American University Law Review: www.wcl.american .edu/pub/journals/lawrev/aulrhome.htm

This site has some full-text articles available free of charge.

Cardozo Law Review: www.cardozolawreview.com

This site provides full-text articles free of charge.

Findlaw: www.findlaw.com

This is one of the best student-friendly legal sites, but it tends toward legalese.

Law Guru: www.lawguru.com

This is perhaps the best site because of its links to other search engines.

Nolo's Plain English Law Dictionary: www.nolo.com/ dictionary/worldindex.cfm

Supreme Court of the United States: www .supremecourt.gov

This site provides up-to-date access to Court decisions and many other things relevant to the Court. It is well worth a visit.

$SAGE edge™

Sharpen your skills with SAGE edge at **edge.sagepub.com/stohrcorrections**. SAGE edge for Students provides a personalized approach to help you accomplish your coursework goals in an easy-to-use learning environment. You'll find action plans, mobile-friendly eFlashcards, and quizzes as well as video, web, and resources and links to SAGE journal articles to support and expand on the concepts presented in this chapter.

19 The Death Penalty

TEST YOUR KNOWLEDGE

Test your present knowledge of the death penalty by answering the following questions, true or false. Check your answers on page 539 after reading the chapter.

1. Most Americans support the death penalty.

2. The United States is the only democratic country that currently uses the death penalty.

3. A white murderer is proportionately more likely than a black or Hispanic murderer to be sentenced to death and to be executed.

4. The gas chamber is still the favorite method of execution today.

5. Nearly all academics who study the death penalty believe that it has no deterrent effect.

6. The death penalty is cheaper than life in prison without the possibility of parole.

7. Women who commit heinous murders are far less likely to receive the death penalty than men who commit such acts.

8. In the United States, it is permissible to execute a person with a history of mental illness but not one with a mental disability (i.e., low IQ).

LEARNING OBJECTIVES

- Describe the impact of public opinion on the retention or abolition of the death penalty

- Explain the trends in the administration of the death penalty

- Identify the issues in major Supreme Court death penalty cases

- Analyze and discuss the financial cost–benefit ratio of the death penalty

- Evaluate the difficulty in determining whether the death penalty is a deterrent

- Articulate the arguments relating to racial disparity and the death penalty

- Identify the differences in sentencing between men and women when it comes to the death penalty

- Discuss some of the issues around mental illness and mental disability and the death penalty

- Explain the meaning of the innocence revolution and the issues surrounding the use of genetic and neuroimaging technology for determining exoneration and mitigation

A VERY UNUSUAL, **VERY EXPENSIVE SERIAL KILLER**

Charles Chi-Tat Ng is unique in a number of respects. He is the only known Asian American serial killer of the 20th century; he was a partner with Leonard Lake in one of the few documented serial-killing teams; he precipitated a legal wrangle between the United States and Canada over the status of the death penalty; and his trial was the costliest state criminal trial in American history, at almost $11 million.

Ng was born to wealthy parents in 1960 in Hong Kong. Ng was a troubled teen who was expelled for a variety of reasons from several schools, and when he was
arrested at the age of 15, his father shipped him off to a boarding school in England. He did not last long there, being expelled for stealing and returned to Hong Kong. Ng moved to the United States at age 18 to attend university but dropped out after being involved in a hit-and-run. He then joined the U.S. Marines, but shortly thereafter, he was caught stealing machine guns and attempted desertion and served 3 years in prison. Upon his release in 1982, Ng teamed up with a fellow ex-Marine named Leonard Lake and began a campaign of kidnapping, rape, torture, and murder. The pair is suspected of killing between 11 and 25 people.

Their orgy of murder ceased when Ng's compulsive stealing got him arrested for shoplifting in San Francisco in 1985, which eventually led to the arrest of Lake (who committed suicide). After Lake's arrest, the police went to the ranch shared by Lake and Ng and found the grisly evidence of their murders. Meanwhile, Ng ran off to Canada, where his stealing once again led to his downfall. He was arrested in Calgary for shoplifting and wounding a security guard and was sentenced to prison. While in Canadian custody, California embarked on a legal battle with Canada to get Ng extradited to the United States. Ng argued that it would be in breach of his human rights to send him back to face the death penalty. Ng finally lost the battle, and in 1991, he was shipped back to the United States. He was convicted in 1999 of the murders of six

men, three women, and two infants and sentenced to death. As of 2016, he is still on San Quentin's death row.

Ng's is a "classic" death penalty case. His murders (as many as 25) were horribly cruel, heartless, and remorseless. His guilt was never in doubt, and he never attempted to deny it. He was arrested in 1991 and convicted in 1999, so why is he still alive after California paid close to $11 million to see him executed? Many believe that we should not execute him or anyone else, regardless of the heinousness of their crimes; others believe that execution is the only solution to such evil but may object to the death penalty for financial reasons. These are some of the things to think about as you read this chapter.

••• THE DEATH PENALTY AND PUBLIC OPINION

Journal Article 19.1:
A Critique of
Contemporary
Death Penalty
Abolitionism

The most controversial issue in corrections is the penalty of death. Given the emotional and philosophical issues surrounding the death penalty and particularly its finality, it is understandable that it has been subjected to intense legal and ethical scrutiny. This has not always been the case, however. Throughout much of human history, the death penalty has been considered a legitimate, appropriate, and necessary form of punishment. As indicated in Figure 19.1, a clear majority of the American public still favors its retention. However, if life without parole (LWOP) is provided as an alternative to a death sentence, the percentage favoring the death penalty falls to about 50% (J. M. Jones, 2012).

Web 19.1:
Death Penalty
Information
Center

Note from Figure 19.1, illustrating trends in public opinion from 1937 to 2015, that in 1966, there were actually more people against the death penalty (47%) than for it (42%). ("No opinion" answers account for why the percentages in the figure never add up to 100%.) Note also that support for the death penalty was the greatest in the 1980s and 1990s, with 1994 marking the highest level of support (80%) in the Gallup poll's history. Why these large fluctuations? The most reasonable answer is that public opinion is swayed substantially by the crime rate—as crime goes up, so does support for the death penalty. According to Uniform Crime Report (UCR) data, the violent-crime rate in 1994 was 713.6 per 100,000 of the population, which is 3.25 times higher than the 1966 violent-crime rate of 220 per 100,000 (FBI, 2013a).

We also see from the bottom part of Figure 19.1 that opinions vary considerably across race, sex, political party, and ideology. The person most likely to support the death penalty is a white conservative male who votes Republican, and the least likely to support it is a black liberal female who votes Democrat. However, all categories are more in favor of it than opposed to it, except for those who identify themselves as ideologically liberal.

Public support for the death penalty is a major factor in its retention in the United States. It influences lawmakers, prosecutors, and judges, who fear electoral retaliation if they fail to show that they are "tough on crime." For example, former California Supreme Court chief justice Rose Bird, former justice Reynoso, and former justice Groin were all given their marching orders by the electorate, which felt frustrated over the Bird Court's reversal of over 90% of capital cases (Traut & Emmert, 1998). Public support for capital punishment in California was notably strong in 1986 (83% favored) when the three justices were up for reelection.

| **FIGURE** *19.1* | Gallup Poll on Public Attitudes About the Death Penalty, 1937–2015 |

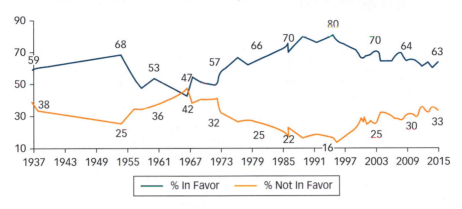

Are You in Favor of the Death Penalty for a Person Convicted of Murder?

Public opinion doubtless contributes to the number of states that have retained the death penalty, since legislators are more influenced by those currents than judges are. As seen in Figure 19.2, 30 states, the federal government, and the U.S. military retain the death penalty while 20 states and the District of Columbia have abolished it. (Delaware was the 20th state to abolish it, having done so in August 2016.) Executions are down 75% since 1996, and only 9 states executed anyone in 2012 (Death Penalty Information Center [DPIC], 2013). The fact remains, however, that among the world's democracies, only the United States, Japan, and South Korea retain the death penalty.

Figure 19.3 is a graph of the annual number of executions in the United States since the mid-1970s, when states were coming to terms with the Supreme Court's *Furman v. Georgia* decision, which precipitated a brief moratorium on the death penalty from 1972 to 1976. As of September 2016, 1,437 executions have taken place in the United States over the last 40 years.

••• METHODS OF EXECUTION USED IN THE UNITED STATES

AP Video 19.1: Electric Chair

The United States has historically used a variety of methods of execution. Table 19.1 lists methods used in the 20th century, the number of people executed by each method since 1976, and the jurisdictions authorizing each method. A short description of each method follows.

Hanging. The most common form of execution has been hanging. Although hanging seems fairly simple and "low tech," a number of factors have to be considered to assure a relatively painless death. The condemned person's height and weight have to be measured, the rope lubricated, and the noose placed around the neck with the knot behind the left ear. If all is done correctly, the drop should cause a rapid dislocation of the neck; if all is not done correctly, the condemned may suffer slow asphyxiation.

Electrocution. The electric chair was introduced in the late 19th century as a more humane method of execution than hanging. A person undergoing execution by this method is strapped to the chair with belts across the chest, groin, legs, and arms. A

Hanging: A method of execution in which the condemned was hung, causing either the neck to break or death by asphyxiation.

Electrocution: A person undergoing execution is strapped to the chair, and electrodes are attached to the person's body. The person is then subjected to a 15- to 30-second jolt of between 500 and 2,450 volts of electricity.

FIGURE *19.2* States With and Without the Death Penalty, as of August 2016

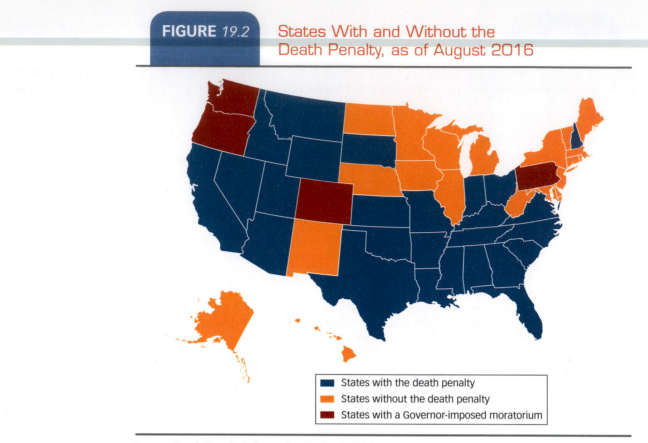

- ■ States with the death penalty
- ■ States without the death penalty
- ■ States with a Governor-imposed moratorium

Source: Death Penalty Information Center (2016c).

FIGURE *19.3* Number of Executions in the United States From 1976 to August 2016

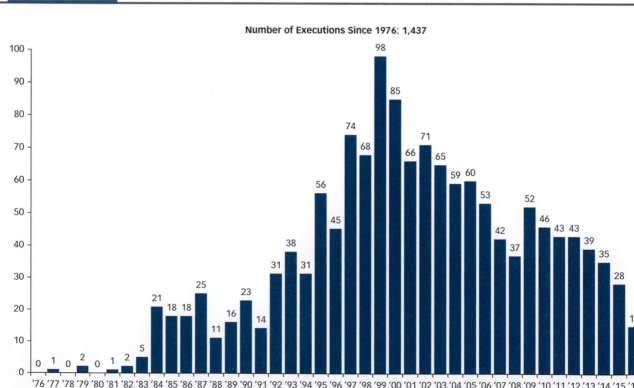

Number of Executions Since 1976: 1,437

Source: Death Penalty Information Center (2016a).

TABLE 19.1	Methods of Execution in the United States, by State, as of August 2016	
METHOD	**NUMBER OF EXECUTIONS SINCE 1976**	**JURISDICTIONS AUTHORIZING THE METHOD**
Lethal Injection	1,262 Executed	Alabama, Arizona, Arkansas, California, Colorado, Delaware, Florida, Georgia, Idaho, Indiana, Kansas, Kentucky, Louisiana, Mississippi, Missouri, Montana, Nebraska*, Nevada, New Hampshire, New Mexico*, North Carolina, Ohio, Oklahoma, Oregon, Pennsylvania, South Carolina, South Dakota, Tennessee, Texas, Utah, Virginia, Washington, Wyoming, U.S. Military, U.S. Government (New Mexico abolished the death penalty in 2009 and Nebraska in 2015. However, their laws were not retroactive, leaving 2 and 10 people, respectively, on death row.)
Electrocution	158 Executed	Alabama, Arkansas, Florida, Kentucky, Oklahoma, South Carolina, Tennessee, Virginia (All have lethal injection as the primary method.)
Gas Chamber	11 Executed	Arizona, California, Missouri, Wyoming, Oklahoma (All have lethal injection as the primary method.)
Hanging	3 Executed	New Hampshire, Washington (Both have lethal injection as the primary method.)
Firing Squad	3 Executed	Oklahoma, Utah (Both have lethal injection as the primary method. Utah has authorized the firing squad if lethal-injection drugs are unavailable. Oklahoma offers firing squad only if lethal injection and electrocution are found unconstitutional.)

Source: Adapted from Death Penalty Information Center (2016b).

moistened sponge is placed on the person's shaved scalp, and an electrode skullcap is attached over it. The executioner then delivers a 15- or 30-second jolt (depending on a state's protocol) of between 500 and 2,450 volts, after which the current is turned off to allow a physician to determine if the person is dead. If the person is not, a further jolt is administered.

Gas Chamber. To execute by this method, the condemned person is placed in an airtight chamber and strapped to a chair, below which is a bucket containing sulfuric acid. Sodium cyanide is then released into the bucket, causing a chemical reaction that releases hydrogen cyanide gas. Once the prisoner breathes the gas, he or she dies shortly thereafter because this method shuts off oxygen to the brain.

Firing Squad. For a firing-squad execution, the prisoner has a hood pulled over his head, and he is tied to a chair surrounded by sandbags. Five correctional officers, one of whom is issued a blank round, fire simultaneously at the inmate, thus causing death.

Lethal Injection. As we see from Table 19.1, lethal injection is the preferred method of execution in all states, even if other methods are available as options. The condemned person is strapped to a gurney, and two needles are inserted into the veins in the arms. These needles are connected to intravenous drips, one of which contains sodium thiopental, which puts the condemned person to sleep. The next drip is then released, containing drugs that paralyze the muscular system and stop the person's breathing, followed by a drip of potassium chloride that stops the heart.

This method of execution has resulted in legal challenges. In a 7–2 vote in *Baze v. Rees* (2008), the Supreme Court ruled that the three-drug combination used by

AP Video 19.2: US Execution

Audio 19.1: Death Penalty Expert on Why Lethal Injection Is So Problematic

Gas chamber: The use of cyanide gas to execute someone placed in an airtight chamber and strapped to a chair.

Firing squad: A method of execution by which the condemned was strapped and shot by a firing squad.

Lethal injection: Using this method, the condemned person is administered drugs that paralyze the muscular system and stop the person's breathing, followed by another drug that stops the heart.

Video 19.1:
Inside a Death
Chamber

Kentucky to execute prisoners does not carry a risk of substantial pain so great as to violate the Constitution's ban on cruel and unusual punishment. Chief Justice John G. Roberts wrote, "Simply because an execution method may result in pain, either by accident or as an inescapable consequence of death, does not establish the sort of 'objectively intolerable risk of harm' that qualifies as cruel and unusual" (p. 11). Because of several botched executions in which the condemned inmate experienced pain, the constitutionality of the method has wound its way through the courts again. In a narrow 5–4 decision, in 2015, the Court again upheld its constitutionality in *Glossip v. Gross* (2015).

••• CHALLENGES TO THE DEATH PENALTY

LEGAL CHALLENGES

Audio 19.2:
California's
Death Penalty
Declared
Unconstitutional

There have been a number of legal challenges to the death penalty revolving around the Eighth Amendment's prohibition of cruel and unusual punishment. These were typically about the constitutionality of the method of execution, not the penalty per se. The first case to successfully challenge the penalty itself was *Furman v. Georgia* (1972). William Henry Furman had shot and killed a homeowner during the course of a burglary and was sentenced to death. Furman challenged the constitutionality of his sentence, and the Supreme Court, in a 5–4 vote, agreed that he had been unconstitutionally sentenced. The Court ruled that the death penalty per se was not unconstitutional, but rather, the arbitrary way in which it was imposed was unconstitutional. The Court argued that because the death penalty is so infrequently imposed, it serves no useful purpose, and that when it is imposed, judges and juries have unbridled discretion in making life-or-death decisions. Furman's sentence was commuted to life imprisonment, but he was paroled in 1984. He is currently serving 20 years in prison for a 2004 burglary.

Because of the Supreme Court's decision, states began the process of changing their sentencing procedures. Some states introduced bifurcated (two-step) hearings, the first to determine guilt (the trial) and the second to impose the sentence after hearing aggravating circumstances (circumstances that increase the heinousness of the offense) and mitigating circumstances (circumstances that decrease culpability) to determine if death is warranted. Other states removed sentencing discretion (since this seemed to be the Supreme Court's problem with it) and made the death penalty mandatory for some murders.

The Supreme Court decided against mandatory death sentences in *Woodson v. North Carolina* (1976). In this case, the Court rejected the North Carolina statute that mandated that all persons convicted of first-degree murder should receive the death penalty as excessive and unduly rigid. James Woodson was involved in an armed robbery in which a convenience store cashier was killed and a customer seriously wounded. Woodson was released from prison in 1993 and has not been rearrested since.

PHOTO 19.1: The electric chair—nicknamed "old sparky"—was once considered a humane alternative to hanging.

Georgia revised its statute and opted for the bifurcated hearing. Using this process, Troy Gregg was sentenced to death for two counts of murder and two counts of armed robbery. In *Gregg v. Georgia* (1976), the Supreme Court upheld the constitutionality of the bifurcated hearing and thus of Gregg's death sentence. Gregg escaped from prison the day before his execution, but ironically, he was beaten to death in a bar fight that same night.

In *Coker v. Georgia* (1977), the Supreme Court ruled that the death penalty for rape was unconstitutional. Ehrlich Coker had escaped from prison, where he was serving time for murder, rape, and kidnapping, and promptly proceeded to commit another rape and kidnapping. Nevertheless, the Court struck down the Georgia statute authorizing death for rape under certain circumstances as "grossly disproportionate" and thus repugnant to the Eighth Amendment. Coker is currently serving multiple life sentences in Georgia.

Other legal challenges to the death penalty have to do with issues such as racial discrimination; the execution of juveniles, the mentally disabled, and the mentally ill; and the method of execution. These are addressed later in the chapter or were discussed in the chapter on juvenile corrections.

DOES THE DEATH PENALTY DETER?

The death penalty is unique in that it is the only punishment required to demonstrate its deterrent effect to validate its constitutionality. We take it for granted that penalties applied to other crimes have a general deterrent effect, if not necessarily the desired specific effect. We have seen that the major argument for punishing wrongdoers is to deter a specific wrongdoer from repeating the act and to prevent potential wrongdoers from committing a similar act. If murderers are executed, it is obvious that they will not be able to harm anyone else, so specific deterrence is not an issue; rather, the issue is about general deterrence. It is also obvious that the threat of the death penalty fails to deter every time a murder is committed, and we can easily document the number of these failures. On the other hand, it is just as evident that we cannot count the times the death penalty threat may have succeeded since we cannot count nonevents. That is, we cannot know how many (if any) people who might otherwise have committed murder did not do so for fear of losing their own lives. The question thus becomes, Will the presence of the death penalty deter some unknown number of individuals from committing murder? The question does not apply to all murders; it applies only to the heinous kinds of murder for which the death penalty is an option.

The deterrence argument generates an enormous amount of heat by those who state "conclusively" (mostly economists) that it deters and those who state just as "conclusively" that it does not (mostly criminologists and sociologists). Radelet and Lacock (2009) polled 77 leading criminologists, asking them if they believed that the death penalty is a deterrent to further murder; 88.2% agreed or strongly agreed that it was not a deterrent, 6% replied that they were "not sure," and the remainder believed that it was a deterrent. We are not aware of any surveys of economists on this issue, but according to Shepherd (2005), while "all modern studies that use panel data [comprehensive data from all 50 states and/or across time periods] find a deterrent effect . . . in contrast to economics studies, most of the sociological studies find no deterrence" (pp. 214–218).

Bushway and Reuter (2008) tell us, "Economists and criminologists have actively butted heads over the topic of deterrence almost since economists began studying the topic [and] have clashed heatedly over empirical research on the death penalty since the 1970s" (pp. 390–391). The different disciplinary ideologies, training, and theoretical assumptions play a huge part in the argument. Economists assume a human nature that is rational and self-serving (the view of the classical scholars discussed in Chapter 1); that is, humans respond to incentives and disincentives to maximize their pleasure and to minimize their pain. The deterrent effect of punishment is thus almost taken for granted by economists. On the other hand, most criminologists are sociologically trained (Cooper, Walsh, & Ellis, 2010) and may thus tend to be either agnostic about human nature or deny that such a thing exists.

Some criminologists and sociologists argue that capital punishment has a **brutalizing effect,** rather than a deterrent effect. That is, executions are perceived by some as saying that it is acceptable to kill people who have offended us and that a segment of those who perceive it this way will act on that perception; thus, executions increase the number of homicides. Once again, economists disagree: "The brutalization idea is not one that economists have given much credence" (Cameron, 1994, p. 206). Most (81.2%) of the anti–death penalty criminologists surveyed by Radelet and Lacock (2009) joined economists on this issue, either disagreeing or strongly disagreeing that the death penalty has a brutalizing effect.

Joanna Shepherd (2005) found evidence for both deterrent and brutalizing effects of capital punishment, depending on the number of executions. Shepherd's model is based on 3,054 counties in states with capital punishment and covered the years 1977 through 1996. She found a threshold effect whereby states with a deterrent effect (five states) had an average of 32 executions over the time period; states with no effect (25 states) had an average of 6.7 executions, and states with a brutalization effect (6 states) had an average of 8.6 executions. These effects differed across time

Brutalizing effect: The assumption that rather than deterring homicides, they actually increase following executions.

PHOTO 19.2: View of the execution chamber in a Santa Fe prison. Like the electric chair, the gas chamber is considered an outdated form of execution and is rarely, if ever, used in modern times.

periods, but there was an overall deterrent effect of 4.5 fewer murders per execution in her study.

These contradictory opinions and research findings are confusing to those who want definitive yes-or-no answer to their questions. It is difficult to tease any deterrent effect out of the death penalty for a number of reasons. First, it is extremely rare; only about 2% to 6% (depending on jurisdiction) of murders are tried as capital cases (Berk, Li, & Hickman, 2005). Second, of that small percentage, only 15% of people sentenced to death since the death penalty was reinstated in 1976 have actually been executed (Nagin & Pepper, 2012). If a person is sentenced to death, the time lapse between conviction and execution has dropped from an average of 14.4 months in the 1950s to an average of 14.5 years in 2010 (Snell, 2011). As we have seen, the deterrent effect of punishment depends on its certainty, swiftness, and severity. While the death penalty is certainly severe, it is far from being certain or swift. Third, there are so many other variables to consider for inclusion in statistical models, and the inclusion or exclusion of any one may completely change the results (Nagin & Pepper, 2012).

These difficulties led the National Academy of Sciences to convene a subcommittee (The Committee on Deterrence and the Death Penalty [CDDP]) of criminologists, sociologists, economists, and statisticians to try to reach a conclusion. The CDDP examined the results of all credible death penalty studies up to 2011 and concluded that the evidence is ambiguous. It examines every possible facet of death penalty studies, both their strengths and inevitable weaknesses, and provides sound mathematical and logical reasons why both the existing deterrence and brutalization literature is deficient in enabling us to reach firm conclusions one way or the other. The committee's conclusion reads as follows:

> The committee concludes that research to date on the effect of capital punishment on homicide is not informative about whether capital punishment decreases, increases, or has no effect on homicide rates. Therefore, the committee recommends that these studies not be used to inform deliberations requiring judgments about the effect of the death penalty on homicide. Consequently, claims that research demonstrates that capital punishment decreases or increases the homicide rate by a specified amount or has no effect on the homicide rate should not influence policy judgments about capital punishment. (As cited in Nagin & Pepper, 2012, p. 102).

Two statisticians came to similar conclusions using data from 102 deterrence studies in the United States from 1975 to 2011 and demonstrated "how easy it is to derive contradictory results by employing alternative specifications. Thus, our results reinforce the claim that the empirical evidence presented to date is by far too fragile in order to base political decisions on it" (Gerritzen & Kirchgässner, 2013, p. 1). They further concluded that ideology (pro– or anti–death penalty bias) may account for most contradictory findings: "If rather different results can be obtained under reasonable assumptions, researchers will consider those outcomes as being reliable which correspond to their pre-conceptions" (p, 24). With the death penalty being such an emotional issue about which many people have strong views, it may be wise to heed Scheidegger (2012): "Many academics who do research on the death penalty reliably produce results that favor one side, raising a suspicion of partisan bias" (p. 161).

FINANCIAL COSTS AND THE DEATH PENALTY

One of the arguments we frequently hear made by laypersons goes something like this: "Why should the taxpayer board and feed these thugs for life? Just execute them, and

Web 19.2:
Costs of the
Death Penalty

be done with it." However, the reality is that the cost of a capital case, from arrest to execution, far exceeds the cost of pursuing a LWOP sentence in the same case, even if the inmate spends 50 years in prison. For instance, the **Death Penalty Information Center** (DPIC, 2012) cites a 2011 California study stating that if the sentences of all prisoners on California's death row were commuted to life without parole, there would be a savings of $170 million per year. The DPIC also refers to a Nevada study showing that a capital-murder case costs Clark County from $170,000 to $212,000 per case more than the cost of a murder case where the death penalty is not pursued. The reason for all of this extra cost is the extensive investigations, expert witnesses, jury costs, deputy costs, and huge attorney fees for seemingly endless appeals.

The American Civil Liberties Union ([ACLU] 2012) also provides some shocking information about the financial costs of pursuing the death penalty in California. The ACLU reports that there was a $1.1 million difference between the least expensive death penalty prosecution and trial (*People v. Saurez*), which cost $1.8 million, and most expensive non–death penalty murder prosecution and trial (*People v. Franklin*), which cost $661,000. The ACLU also reports that the death penalty prosecution and trial of Charles Ng (featured in this chapter's opening vignette) cost an astounding $10.9 million, but Ng is still on death row in California and is unlikely to be executed.

When all appeals are finally exhausted, the average death row inmate has already spent about 15 years on death row, and many have died of other causes. According to the California Department of Corrections (CDC), of the hundreds of people on death row since 1978 in that state, only 13 (9 were multiple murderers) were actually executed (Tempest, 2005). This is a very small "return" for the multiple millions spent to get them to death row.

So why do death penalty states continue to invest in such a poor proposition? Professor Frank Zimring's answer to this question is,

> What we are paying for at such great cost is essentially our own ambivalence about capital punishment. We try to maintain the apparatus of state killing and another apparatus that almost guarantees that it won't happen. The public pays for both sides. (as cited in Tempest, 2005, p. B1)

The money spent on pursuing something we do not perhaps want would be better spent on other criminal justice practices designed to protect the public from the predations of criminals. Think of how many police officers, for example, California could hire with the $170 million it spends pursuing a goal it knows will be thwarted in all but the tiniest fraction of instances.

On July 23, 2014, federal judge Cormac Carney struck down the death sentence of Ernest Jones for raping and killing his girlfriend's mother in 1995 as unconstitutional (*Jones v. Chappell*, 2014). In doing so, he vacated the death sentences of 747 other death row inmates awaiting execution. Judge Carney stated in his opinion that

> inordinate and unpredictable delay has resulted in a death penalty system in which very few of the hundreds of individuals sentenced to death have been, or even will be, executed by the State. It has resulted in a system in which arbitrary factors, rather than legitimate ones determine whether an individual will actually be executed. And it has resulted in a system that serves no penological purpose. (n.p.)

Death Penalty Information Center: Major (partisan) source of information on the death penalty in the United States.

In effect, Judge Carney ruled that the delays caused by the system for the benefit of defendants create uncertainty in their minds as to when (or whether) they will actually be executed. The assertion was that systemic delay creates an uncertainty that constitutes cruel and unusual punishment. Furthermore, even if a person is executed, it will be so long after the crime that it serves neither retributive nor deterrent purposes. Carney's ruling is not the last word; the California attorney general filed an appeal with the U.S. Ninth Circuit Court of Appeals on December 1, 2014. We will not know the result of this case until at least 2017—three to four more years of expensive litigation.

••• RACIAL DISPARITY IN DEATH SENTENCES

A major concern among criminologists is whether the death penalty is applied in a racially discriminatory fashion. There is no doubt that African Americans have historically been convicted of capital crimes and executed in greater numbers than whites. Robert Bohm (2012) provides numerous statistics to demonstrate this. Here is a sample:

- In 1856, Virginia slaves could be convicted of 66 crimes carrying the death penalty while only murder carried the death penalty for whites.

- The attempted rape of a white woman was a capital crime for blacks until the mid-20th century in seven southern states.

- Although composing about 11% of the population, 50% of all people executed in the United States from 1800 to 2002 have been African American.

- Between 1930 and 1980, 53% of persons executed were black.

- A 1990 U.S. General Accounting Office report looking at 28 studies stated that 75% of them found that black defendants were more likely than white defendants to receive the death penalty.

This issue has been a major one since the Supreme Court addressed it in *McCleskey v. Kemp* (1987). Warren McCleskey was an African American parolee who had been sentenced to three life sentences for multiple armed robberies in 1970 but was released seven years later. In 1978, he shot and killed a white police officer in the course of a robbery and was subsequently sentenced to death. In challenging his sentence, McCleskey's attorneys offered as evidence a statistical study purporting to show that racial disparity existed in death penalty cases in Georgia (where the crime occurred). The data indicated that defendants who killed white victims were more likely to be sentenced to death than defendants who murdered black victims. In ruling against McCleskey's claim, the Court ruled that statistical risk represents averages and does not establish that a specific individual's death sentence violates the Eighth Amendment. In other words, a study of past cases indicating average outcomes does not constitute evidence that McCleskey himself was denied due process. He was executed in 1991, 23 years after his crime.

Figure 19.4, from the DPIC (2015), shows that black defendants are executed disproportionately to their percentage of the population. African Americans have been between 11% and 13% of the U. S. population between 1976 and 2015 but have constituted 35% of the executions. Likewise, blacks compose 42% of current U.S. death row inmates. Thus, blacks are overrepresented in proportion to their numbers in the population by roughly 3 to 1 in terms of both executions and as death row residents.

Of course, claims of disproportionality cannot be validly evaluated by comparing percentages of each race executed or on death row with their proportion of the general population. Rather, they should be evaluated by comparing each race's proportion of *murders* with its proportion executed or on death row. In 2013, 52.2% of individuals arrested for murder in the United States were African American and 45.3% were white (FBI, 2014). Because the FBI places Hispanics and non-Hispanic whites into a single "white" category (93% of Hispanics/Latinos are defined as white), we cannot make direct black/white comparisons between UCR and DPIC statistics. However, Steffensmeier, Feldmeyer, Harris, and Ulmer (2011, p. 209) tell us that when Hispanics/Latinos are taken out of the white category, the black homicide rate is 12.7 times greater than the white rate. A comparison of homicide with execution and death row data thus leads to the conclusion that "although they are overrepresented among death row populations and executions relative to their share of the U.S. population, blacks are underrepresented based on their arrests and convictions for murder" (M. Robinson, 2008, p. 191).

There seems to be an emerging trend for whites to be disproportionately more likely to both receive a death sentence and to be executed compared with the number of death-eligible homicides they commit. An early post-*Furman* study (Kleck, 1981) found that from 1930 onward, in the northern states, whites were more likely to receive the death penalty, and the discrimination evidenced against blacks in death penalty cases in earlier years in the South disappeared in later years. Greenfeld and Hinners (1985) looked at 1,405 prisoners under sentence of death and found that 15.8 per 1,000 white murderers were sentenced to death versus 11.6 per 1,000 black murderers. A large study by Gross and Mauro (1989) looked at death sentences in over 14,000 cases and found that whites received a death sentence in 26.5% of the cases involving felony circumstances (murder in the commission of another felony, such as rape or robbery) and in 1.4% of the cases with nonfelony circumstances. On the other hand, 17.2% of blacks convicted in felony circumstances and 0.4% in nonfelony circumstances received a death sentence (calculated by McAdams [1998] from Gross and Mauro's data). A U.S. Department of Justice (2001) study of federal death-eligible cases reached a similar conclusion:

FIGURE *19.4*   Race of Defendants on Death Row, 1976–2015 (*left*) and Race of Murderers Executed, 1976–2015 (*right*)

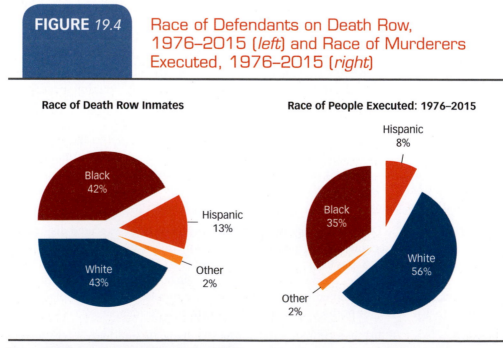

Source: Death Penalty Information Center (2015).

> United States Attorneys recommended the death penalty in smaller proportions of cases involving Black or Hispanic defendants than in those involving White defendants; the Attorney General's capital case review committee likewise recommended the death penalty in smaller proportions of involving Black or Hispanic defendants. . . . In the cases considered by the Attorney General, the Attorney General decided to seek the death penalty for 38% of the White defendants, 25% of the Black defendants, and 20% of the Hispanic defendants. (n.p.)

Blume, Eisenberg, and Wells (2004) looked at data from the 31 states that sentenced 10 or more individuals to death from 1977 through 1999 (5,953 death sentences) and compared the proportion of blacks convicted of murder in each state with the proportion of black inmates on death row. In California, Nevada, and Utah, the percentages of murders committed by blacks were 33.8%, 30.2%, 8.6%, respectively. The percentages of blacks on death row in these states were 35.3%, 33.1%, and 10.5%. African Americans were thus overrepresented by narrow margins in these three states but were substantially underrepresented in the 28 others. They were most underrepresented in Tennessee, Mississippi, and Missouri. The percentages of murders committed by African Americans in those states were 60.4%, 77.7%, and 62.6%, respectively; the percentages of blacks on death row in these states were 33.3%, 59.0%, and 44.1%, respectively.

THE ISSUE OF VICTIM'S RACE

With white defendants being sentenced to death and executed more often than black defendants, the race issue with regard to the death penalty has largely become *victim centered*—that is, the focus has moved from bias against black *defendants* to bias against black *victims*. To address this bias issue, we first have to realize that only a very small fraction of murders are committed in a fashion that makes perpetrators eligible for the death penalty. For a murder to be eligible for the death penalty, it must satisfy a number of elements, including such things as being premeditated and purposeful; being particularly brutal; involving multiple victims; being committed during the commission of some other felony, such as robbery or rape; or involving the killing of a law enforcement officer in the commission of his or her duties. A prior homicide conviction is also highly relevant.

Almost all studies show that before controlling for aggravating and mitigating factors, killers of whites (regardless of the race of the killer) are more likely to receive the death penalty than killers of blacks. To assess the issue of victim race in federal cases, the National Institute of Justice commissioned three studies by three independent teams. In a 209-page report examining these findings, Klein, Berk, and Hickman (2006) show that without controlling for case characteristics, the death penalty is more likely when victims are white. However, racial disparities disappeared in all three studies when adjustments were made for the heinousness of the crime. In other words, after controlling for all aggravating and mitigating factors that influence sentencing, there was no evidence of a race effect, regardless of whether they were examining just the race of the victim, the race of the offender, or the interaction between victim's and defendant's race.

The case characteristics that account for the *white-victim effect* were analyzed from the data used in *McCleskey v. Kemp* (1987) by statistician Joseph Katz (2005). Katz found 141 cases that involved a white victim and a black perpetrator (W/B) among the 1,082-case homicide defendant sample. In 67.1% of W/B cases, the victim was killed in the course of a robbery, compared with 7.4% in black-victim cases, and 70.6% of the time, the victim was a stranger, compared with 9.6% of black-victim cases. Katz (2005) concluded that "white victim homicides show a greater percentage of mutilations, execution style murders, tortures, and beaten victims, features which generally aggravate homicide and increase the likelihood of a death sentence" (p. 405).

IN FOCUS 19.1

Karl Marx on Capital Punishment and Brutalization

Most contemporary criminologists may not put much stock in the brutalization effect hypothesis, but one of the founders of modern sociology, Karl Marx, did. Karl Marx earned his keep for a while as a journalist. He wrote the article below for the New-York Daily Tribune, *February 17–18, 1853.*

It has often been remarked that in this country a public execution is generally followed closely by instances of death by hanging, either suicidal or accidental, in consequence of the powerful effect which the execution of a noted criminal produces upon a morbid and unmatured mind.

Of the several cases which are alleged by The Times in illustration of this remark, one is that of a lunatic at Sheffield, who, after talking with other lunatics respecting the execution of Barbour, put an end to his existence by hanging himself. Another case is that of a boy of 14 years, who also hung himself.

The doctrine to which the enumeration of these facts was intended to give its support, is one which no reasonable man would be likely to guess, it being no less than a direct apotheosis of the hangman, while capital punishment is extolled as the ultima ratio of society. This is done in a leading article of the "leading journal." The Morning Advertiser, in some very bitter but just strictures on the hanging predilections and bloody logic of The Times, has the following interesting data on 43 days of the year 1849:

EXECUTIONS OF MURDERS AND SUICIDES	
Millan	March 20
Hannah Sandles	March 22
M.G. Newton	March 22
Pulley	March 26
J.G. Gleeson—4 murders at Liverpool	March 27
Smith	March 27
Murder and suicide at Leicester	April 2
Howe	March 31
Poisoning at Bath	April 7
W. Bailey	April 8

EXECUTIONS OF MURDERS AND SUICIDES	
Landick	April 9
J. Ward murders his mother	April 13
Sarah Thomas	April 13
Yardley	April 14
Doxey, parricide	April 14
J. Bailey kills his two children and himself	April 17
J. Griffiths	April 18
Charles Overton	April 18
J. Rush	April 21
Daniel Holmsden	May 2

This table, as The Times concedes, shows not only suicides, but also murders of the most atrocious kind, following closely upon the execution of criminals. It is astonishing that the article in question does not even produce a single argument or pretext for indulging in the savage theory therein propounded; and it would be very difficult, if not altogether impossible, to establish any principle upon which the justice or expediency of capital punishment could be founded, in a society glorying in its civilization. Punishment in general has been defended as a means either of ameliorating or intimidating. Now what right have you to punish me for the amelioration or intimidation of others? And besides, there is history—there is such a thing as statistics—which prove with the most complete evidence that since Cain the world has neither been intimidated nor ameliorated by punishment. Quite the contrary. From the point of view of abstract right, there is only one theory of punishment which recognizes human dignity in the abstract, and that is the theory of Kant, especially in the more rigid formula given to it by Hegel. Hegel says,

> Punishment is the right of the criminal. It is an act of his own will. The violation of right has been proclaimed by the criminal as his own right. His crime is the negation of right. Punishment is the negation of this negation, and consequently an affirmation of right, solicited and forced upon the criminal by himself.

Source: Marx, K. (1853, February 17–18). Capital punishment.—Mr. Cobden's pamphlet.—Regulations of the Bank of England. *New-York Daily Tribune*. Retrieved from https://www.marxists.org/archive/marx/works/subject/newspapers/new-york-tribune.htm

Just as there are contradictory findings about the deterrence issue among different groups of scholars, there are also contradictions on this issue. For instance, Paternoster and Brame (2003) looked at 1,130 death-eligible homicide cases in Maryland and found no race-of-defendant bias but significant race-of-victim effects. In cases in which the offender was black and the victim was white, they found that defendants were about 3.5 times more likely than any other offender/victim pairing to receive a death sentence. Berk et al. (2005) looked at *the exact same data* and arrived at the opposite conclusion: "When race surfaces, cases with a black defendant and white victim or 'other' racial combinations are *less* likely to have death sentences imposed" (p. 381).

Sharma, Scheb, Houston, and Wagers (2013) looked at all first-degree murder convictions in Tennessee from 1976 to 2007. Prosecutors sought the death penalty for 76% of white and 62.6% of black defendants, and 37.3% of white defendants for whom the death penalty was sought received it, versus 23.6% of black defendants. Prosecutors sought the death penalty in 64% of the cases where the victim was white and in 33% of the cases where the victim was black. The researchers found that the killing of a law enforcement officer, prior violent offenses, and evidentiary (scientific proof, a confession, and strong eyewitness testimony) variables were the strongest predictors of receiving a death sentence. The victim's race did not play any significant part, but the victim's sex (female) did. The racial makeup of the crime (black offender/white victim; white offender/white victim, etc.) had no significant independent effect, but the race of the defendant did, with whites being 2.26 times more likely to receive the death penalty than blacks over the 30-year period.

Another study used a cutting-edge statistical method called *propensity score matching* (PSM) to examine all 1,356 death-eligible cases prosecuted in North Carolina from 1977 to 2009 (Jennings, Richards, Smith, Bjerregaard, & Fogel, 2014). PSM allows for a statistical approximation of an experimental design by removing systematic differences between cases prior to comparing the outcome of interest: death versus LWOP. The authors found that neither race of victim nor the racial makeup of offender/victim dyads had any independent effect on whether or not a defendant received the death penalty and concluded that "the 'White victim effect' on capital punishment decision-making is better considered a 'case effect' rather than a 'race effect'" (Jennings et al., 2014, p. 384). Cases are unique, and their numerous case characteristics (aggravating and mitigating circumstances) and varying evidentiary quality have to be considered.

Another study of 1,163 capital cases (Bjerregaard, Smith, Cochran, & Fogel, 2015) found that blacks who killed whites in *high-severity circumstances* (multiple aggravating "heinous, atrocious, and cruel" factors) had an increased probability of a death sentence, but blacks who killed whites at lower levels of severity (such as a shooting death in the process of a robbery) had decreased probabilities of receiving the death penalty. In low-severity cases, a black defendant who killed a white victim had almost half the odds of receiving a death sentence than a black defendant who killed a black victim or a white defendant who killed either a white or black victim. The average number of aggravating factors in black-defendant, white-victim cases (23.4% of the cases) was 2.20 while in white-defendant, black-victim cases (3.6% of the cases), it was 1.47 factors. The average number of aggravating factors in black/black cases (30.9% of cases) was 1.96, and for white/white cases (42.1% of cases), it was 1.84. This supports Judge Paul Cassell's (2008) contention that "black-defendant-kills-white-victim cases more often involve the murder of a law enforcement officer, kidnapping and rape, mutilation, execution-style killing, and torture—all quintessential aggravating factors—than do other combinations" (pp. 23–24).

THE DEATH PENALTY AND SOCIAL CLASS

Social class is another area of concern in capital-punishment discourse, but much less research has been done in this area compared with race. Systematic data on the social class of defendants are not available, although race and class are closely correlated. We do know, however, that the vast majority of people in our overflowing prisons come from poor backgrounds, so it is not too surprising that this is also true of people on death row. Upper- and middle-class people rarely commit murder in the commission of a robbery—or under any other circumstance for that matter. However, the legal "dream team" put together for the defense of O. J. Simpson for his murder trial speaks volumes about the power of great wealth to wheedle out of a murder conviction. Of course, middle-class people accused of murder could not afford anything like the cost of Simpson's team.

Nevertheless, the focus of the class issue is the quality of defense counsel. Asserting that the death penalty is applied in an economically discriminatory way, J. Johnson and Johnson (2001) write that "our failure as a society to ensure some semblance of economic equality in our harshest criminal punishment constitutes a kind of procedural cruelty that is inconsistent with the Eighth Amendment to our Constitution" (p. 517). On the other hand, Marquis (2005) notes that while prior to the 1963 decision in *Gideon v. Wainwright*, appointed counsel was often inadequate, after that decision, the notion that public defenders fight against "prosecutors with limitless resources" became an urban legend. He states,

> The *Chicago Tribune* . . . grudgingly admitted that the Cook County Public Defender's Office provided excellent representation for its indigent clients. . . . Many giant silk-stocking law firms in large cities across America not only provide pro-bono [free] counsel in capital cases, but also offer partnerships to lawyers whose sole job is to promote indigent capital defense. (p. 507)

Kent Scheidegger (2005) agrees with Marquis and claims that

> it has also been shown that lawyers appointed to represent the indigent get the same results on average as retained counsel. For example, Scott Peterson, with the lawyer to the stars, sits on death row, while the public defender got a life sentence for the penniless Unabomber. The mitigating circumstance of Theodore Kaczynski's mental illness made the difference, not the lawyers. (p. 801)

To the extent that wealth plays a part over and above case characteristics, however, it makes sense to take steps to nullify the wealth advantage. In a code law system, such as the one the French have (see Chapter 20), judges call expert witnesses paid for by the state to give evidence in search of the truth, not to support one side or the other. This not only neutralizes the advantages of wealth but also provides expert evidence in a truly neutral fashion (Walsh & Hemmens, 2014, p. 388). Perhaps the United States could adopt such a sensible strategy.

••• WOMEN AND THE DEATH PENALTY

Women, as well as men, commit murder, but women have constituted only about 2% of persons executed in the United States since its inception (M. Robinson, 2008). The first woman executed in the American colonies was Jane Champion, who was executed in the Virginia colony in 1632 for murdering her illegitimate infant. The first woman to be executed in the United States by the federal government was Mary Surratt, convicted as a conspirator in the assassination of President Abraham Lincoln. She was hanged in July 1865 (Hatch & Walsh, 2016). The first woman executed since the reinstatement of the death penalty in 1976 was Velma Barfield, a drug addict who murdered her lover with rat poison in North Carolina in 1984. She killed him because she was afraid that he would find out she was forging his checks to pay for her addiction.

Barfield confessed to three previous murders and was suspected in another, as well as being suspected of arson and insurance fraud. She was 45 at the time of the crime for which she was convicted and 52 when executed in 1984. Kelly Renee Gissendaner, age 47, convicted of orchestrating the murder of her husband in 1997, was the last woman to be executed in the United States. She was executed in Georgia on September 30, 2015 (see Photo 19.3).

As of January 2016, there were 55 women on death row, or 1.87% of the total death row population of 2,943 persons, and women have accounted for only 16 (0.9%) persons (12 white, 4 black) actually executed since 1976 (DPIC, 2016d). According to the U.S. Census, women constituted 53% of the U.S. population in 2012, which means they have been and are massively underrepresented as persons executed or on death row.

PHOTO 19.3: Kelly Renee Gissendaner, the only woman on Georgia's death row, looks through the slot in her cell at Metro State Prison in Atlanta. After several denied appeals, including several from the U.S. Supreme Court, Georgia executed its only female death row inmate on Wednesday, September 30, 2015.

Is this indicative of pro-female bias? It would be if females committed approximately the same number of death-eligible homicides as males, but they consistently commit only about 10% of all homicides each year. Many of these homicides are committed against spouses and lovers in self-defense situations, and only rarely do we find women committing the heinous kinds of murders that draw down the death penalty (Walsh, 2011). However, Bohm (2003) estimates that 4% to 6% of women murderers would receive death sentences "if women and men were treated equally [and if] no factor other than the offense was considered" (p. 211).

THE CHIVALRY HYPOTHESIS

The most obvious extralegal factor that leads to reluctance to impose the death penalty on women vis-à-vis men is the chivalrous or paternalistic attitudes about women that tend to prevail in our society (Reza, 2005). Reza (2005) cites the example of a petition to the governor of California signed by male inmates of San Quentin prison in 1941 to prevent the execution of Juanita Spinelli, a career criminal, ex-wrestler, and knife thrower who murdered a 19-year-old gang member she feared would inform on her. Such an execution, they wrote, would be "a blot on the reputation of the state and repulsive to the people of California because of *her sex and her status as a mother*" (p. 183; emphasis added).

Such chivalry is still in evidence today. The pending 1998 execution of Karla Faye Tucker—a rock groupie, prostitute, and drug abuser convicted in 1984 of the pickax murder of a man and a woman when she was 23—produced a spate of protests even from pro–death penalty sources. Colonel Oliver North exclaimed in opposition, "I don't think chivalry can ever be misplaced," and TV personality Geraldo Rivera said, "Please don't let this happen. This is—it's very unseemly. Texas manhood, macho swagger. . . . What, are ya' going to kill a lady? Oh jeez. Why?" (cited in M. Robinson, 2008, p. 205). Then there is the case of Susan Smith, who, in 1994, strapped her two young sons, ages 3 years and 14 months, into their car seats and rolled the car into a lake, drowning them both. Smith was attempting to reunite with her lover, who objected to the presence of her children. Smith was sentenced to life rather than death for her cold-blooded killings because, according to Reza (2005), she was viewed by the jury as a jilted victim "and loving mother with severe emotional issues" (p. 188).

THE EVIL-WOMAN HYPOTHESIS

But chivalry does not always prevail because, as we have seen, 15 women have been executed since 1976. To account for these, we have the "evil woman" counterpart to the chivalry hypothesis. Both Tucker and Smith were fairly good-looking young women who came across to TV audiences as matching the stereotype of femininity and "sweetness," despite having committed heinous acts. The *evil-woman hypothesis* avers that females who defy traditional gender roles by not enacting a feminine identity invite the wrath of the male-dominated criminal justice system (Reza, 2005). Such women tend to be unattractive and "unladylike" in their general demeanor and very much out of their proscribed gender roles by acting "manly" and being "man hating." Three women executed since 1976—Wanda Jean Allen, Aileen Wuornos, and Lisa Coleman—fit this description and were lesbians. Ethel Spinelli, for whose life her fellow male inmates begged earnestly, deviated from gender role expectations in many ways. Clinton Duffy, warden of the prison housing Spinelli, called her the "coldest, hardest character, male or female" and added that she was "a hag, evil as a witch, horrible to look at" (as cited in Shatz & Shatz, 2011, p. 2).

If female murderers, on the whole, are treated more leniently on the basis of their sex, then men are being discriminated against in a system that claims fairness and neutrality. Victor Streib (2003), a strong opponent of the death penalty, warns that if women want to be treated as men's equals, then if men are eligible for the death penalty, women should be, too: "Otherwise, women are lumped with juveniles and the mentally retarded as not fully responsible human beings" (p. 322). Similarly, Elizabeth Reza (2005) opines,

> When women commit similar [death-eligible] crimes, we should not withhold capital punishment simply because the murderer is a mother, sister, or wife. . . . The American judicial system must equalize the capital punishment system so that all, regardless of gender, are punished in a manner society and the legal system has deemed appropriate to impose on those who callously take the lives of others. (p. 211)

For those who believe in the death penalty, the only answer to the sentencing-equity issue is to execute more women convicted of death-eligible murders until they attain parity with men convicted of similar crimes who are executed or to reduce the number of men executed. For those who oppose the death penalty, the only answer to the issue is to execute no one.

●●● THE DEATH PENALTY AND MENTAL DISABILITY AND MENTAL ILLNESS

Mental illness and mental disability are two different things that impact the possibility of a death sentence differently. The legal issues the courts have to resolve pertaining to mental deficiency and illness with respect to the death penalty have been these: (a) Is this person competent to stand trial? (b) Did this person, at the time of the crime, have the requisite ability to form *mens rea* (guilty mind)? (c) Does the person's mental condition warrant a more lenient sentence than would normally attach to this crime? (Dillard, 2012).

POLICY AND RESEARCH

The Issue of Innocence

Policies governing under what circumstances it is legally permissible to take the life of another human being are formulated with the utmost care and consideration. Policies regarding the death penalty in the United States are set by state and federal legislative acts guided by the U.S. Constitution. These acts define the crimes eligible for the death penalty and under what circumstances. The execution of an innocent person is the ultimate injustice, but research on innocence is limited because there is no foolproof way of determining if a convicted person is actually innocent. The Death Penalty Information Center (n.d.) compiles a list of people convicted of a capital crime and later exonerated. Although acquittals, dropped charges, and pardons do not constitute incontrovertible proof of innocence, the vast majority of exonerees were probably innocent.

Using DPIC data, Gross, O'Brien, Hu, and Kennedy (2014) estimated that 4.1% (about 1 in 25) of the 7,482 people sentenced to death in the United States from 1973 through 2004 were likely innocent. Only 1.6% of those sentenced to death were actually exonerated, but the researchers included those who were executed (12.6%), were removed from death row but were not exonerated (35.8%), or died of natural causes while on death row (4%). The reason that the actual 1.6% became 4.1%, according to the researchers, is that those removed from death row (by execution, death by other means, or sentences commuted to life in prison) no longer receive the intense scrutiny of those under threat of death. Some of these "removals" are people who pleaded guilty to avoid the death penalty and may be innocent, but they rarely attract a rigorous reexamination of their cases. In other words, if those inmates taken off death row by means other than execution were all to have been placed and left there, then based on extrapolation from the 1.6% exoneration rate, there would have been a 4.1% exoneration rate. If a person is actually innocent, then that person's chance of being exonerated is less likely than if is he or she remained there!

Hatch and Walsh (2016) list their "big six" causes of wrongful convictions, beginning with

(1) *eyewitness identification*. People tend to trust eyewitness evidence, but it is the most unreliable form of evidence. (A witness may not be telling the truth, his or her perception or memory may not be accurate, or his or her recollection may have been influenced by outside suggestion.)

AP Photo/Charlie Riedel

PHOTO 19.4: Former death-row inmate Reginald Griffin went free in October 2013 after a small-town prosecutor declined to refile murder charges in connection with a 1983 prison stabbing for which he spent nearly three decades behind bars.

(2) *False confessions* are also a major cause of wrongful convictions. For a variety of reasons, such as mental illness, some people volunteer a confession to gain some form of notoriety. Hatch and Walsh (2016) say that voluntary confessions are discovered in 27% of DNA exoneration cases. Other confessions are prompted by stressful police interrogations, in which a person may seek short-term relief by confessing.

(3) *Bad science*—the use of improper or invalidated forensic science—is another cause, and it has been a contributing factor in about 50% of DNA wrongful-conviction cases (Hatch & Walsh, 2016). This "bad science" is really *poorly used* or *insufficiently validated science* rather than bad per se, and it includes things such as fingerprint evidence, hair comparison and analysis, arson analysis, and other forensic practices.

(4) *Snitch testimony* is false testimony by informants serving time or awaiting sentencing who conjure up stories to support a prosecutor's theory in exchange for some consideration, such as a reduction in their own sentences or even charge dismissal—"If you can't do the time, just drop a dime."

(5) *Ineffective defense counsel* is simply poor legal representation. One study of death penalty appeals over a 23-year period concluded that ineffective defense attorneys were the "biggest contributing factor to the erroneous

(Continued)

(Continued)

conviction or death sentence of criminal defendants in capital cases" (Gould, Carrano, Leo, & Young, 2012, p. 20).

(6) *Prosecutorial misconduct* typically involves the withholding of exculpatory evidence (evidence favorable to the accused), awareness of witness perjury, and the improper use of evidence. In a study of Ohio death penalty cases, it was discovered that 14 of 48 capital cases involved ethical violations by prosecutors (Johns, 2005).

DISCUSSION QUESTIONS

1. If you favor the death penalty, does the evidence of actual and possible innocence make you question your opinion?

2. If you were actually innocent of a heinous murder, but the prosecution had a very good case against you, and your lawyer said you were almost certain to be found guilty, would you plead guilty to avoid the death penalty and thereby receive less scrutiny of your case in the future?

3. Do you think it possible that Gross and his colleagues "twisted" the statistics a bit to make the 1.6% who were actually exonerated into the 4.1% they reported?

References

Death Penalty Information Center. (n.d.). Cases of innocence 1973–present. Retrieved from http://www.deathpenaltyinfo.org/cases-innocence-1973-present

Hatch, V., & Walsh, A. (2016). *Capital punishment: The theory and practice of the ultimate penalty*. New York: Oxford University Press.

Gould, J. B., Carrano, J., Leo, R., & Young, J. (2012). *Predicting erroneous convictions: A social science approach to miscarriages of justice*. Retrieved from http://nij.gov/topics/courts/sentencing/wrongful-convictions/predicting-preventing.htm

Gross, S., O'Brien, B., Hu, C., & Kennedy, E. (2014). Rate of false conviction of criminal defendants who are sentenced to death. *Proceedings of the National Academy of Sciences, 111*, 7230–7235.

Johns, M. Z. (2005). Reconsidering absolute prosecutorial immunity. *Brigham Young University Law Review*, 53–149.

The cases of two bizarre serial killers are particularly interesting in this regard. These two killers—one a white man, Gary Heidnik, and the other a black man, Harrison Graham—kidnapped, raped, and tortured women in Philadelphia and were arrested five months apart in 1987. Heidnik killed two women, and Graham killed seven. Heidnik had an extensive history of mental illness (schizophrenia) and Graham suffered from mild mental disability (Branson, 2013).

Despite having killed five fewer women than Graham, Heidnik was sentenced to death and executed in 1999. Graham was given six death sentences, but they were not to be carried out until his seventh sentence—life without possibility of parole—was completed. This guaranteed that he will never be executed. The states are constitutionally forbidden to execute the mental disabled (but not the mentally ill) today, but this was not the case at the time Graham's trial and conviction. So what is the difference between these two conditions that make one eligible for the death penalty and not the other?

MENTAL DISABILITY

Mental disability is

a lifelong condition of impaired or incomplete mental development. According to the most widely used definition, it is characterized by three criteria: significantly subaverage intellectual functioning; concurrent and related limitations in two or more adaptive skill areas; and manifestation before age 18. (Mandery, 2005, p. 352)

A subaverage level of intellectual functioning is defined as an IQ of 70 or below, a score that puts an individual at the bottom 2% of the general population. An 18-year-old with an IQ of 70, for instance, is functioning at the mental level of a child 12 to 13 years old. This does not mean that the mentally disabled cannot be held responsible for their actions; it only means that they should be held to a lower level of culpability than persons operating at higher intellectual levels.

In 1979, paroled rapist Johnny Penry was sentenced to death for a brutal rape and murder in Texas. Penry appealed to the Supreme Court on Eighth Amendment grounds that it is cruel and unusual to execute a mentally disabled person. Penry claimed that the jury was not instructed that it could consider his low IQ (between 50 and 63) as mitigating evidence against imposing the death penalty. The Supreme Court held in *Penry v. Lynaugh* (1989) that the jury should have been instructed it could consider "mental retardation" a mitigating factor when deciding Penry's sentence, but imposition of the death penalty on a mentally disabled defendant is not, per se, a violation of the Eighth Amendment. However, in 2008, Penry's sentence was commuted to life imprisonment in light of *Atkins v. Virginia* (2002).

In *Atkins v. Virginia* (2002), the Court overruled itself with regard to executing the mentally disabled. The Court concluded that there was a national consensus (public opinion again) against executing the mentally disabled and that since they are less capable of evaluating the consequences of their crimes, they are less culpable than the average offender. The Court also noted that mentally disabled individuals are more prone to confess crimes that they did not commit and therefore more prone to wrongful execution. Six of the justices concluded that the overwhelming disapproval of the world community must be considered a relevant factor in the Court's deliberations regarding the constitutionality of imposing capital punishment on the mentally disabled.

ETHICAL ISSUE 19.1

What Would You Do?

You are an assistant prosecutor who favors the death penalty. You have been assigned the case of a John Franks, who has admitted molesting and killing at least five girls, ranging in age between 4 and 12. The community is outraged and demands the death penalty. The problem is that Franks's IQ, averaged over three tests while in school, is 68, and it is constitutionally impermissible to execute anyone with an IQ lower than 70. You could argue that IQ scores are subject to a 5-point margin of error, and so, John's "true" IQ could be 73. (It could also just as easily be 63.) Will you seek the death penalty for Franks's heinous crimes, in accordance with your beliefs and with public demand based on this flimsy point, or select a non–death penalty option? What are the ethical issues involved?

MENTAL ILLNESS

It is constitutionally impermissible to execute the mentally disabled but permissible to execute the mentally ill because mental disability is permanent and unalterable, but mental illness is not (in many cases). Mental disability cannot be faked because there is a long history documenting each case from early childhood, but mental illness can be contrived. By adhering to a correctly prescribed medical regimen, most mentally ill individuals can be restored to sanity and lead meaningful lives.

In English common law and under the U.S. Constitution, the execution of the "presently insane" is not permitted; as Sir William Blackstone wrote, "Madness alone punishes the madman" (in Dillard, 2012, p. 461). Note that the operative phrase is "presently insane," not "insane at the time of the crime." Before the advent of antipsychotic medication, if a person was insane "at the time of the crime," that person would also have been insane "presently" as well because there was no acceptable method of restoring a person to sanity. Now that we have a number of effective antipsychotic medications, convicted

ETHICAL ISSUE 19.2 ?

What Would You Do?

You are a prison physician with no strong beliefs for or against the death penalty. Justin Williams, who is on death row in your prison, is a schizophrenic on medication. You have to declare Justin sane enough to be executed, and although you now believe that he is, you start feeling like a farmer fattening up his turkeys for the Thanksgiving slaughter. You can do your legal and medical duty and continue to medicate Justin, you can lie to prison officials about his insanity, or you can slowly reduce his medication until his insanity again becomes apparent to everyone, and thus, you have no need to lie. Which option do you think is the ethical one, if any?

murderers can be rendered "fit" for execution, and new Eighth Amendment and due process issues have arisen.

Although not a death penalty case, the Supreme Court ruled in *Jackson v. Indiana* (1972) that it is constitutionally impermissible to hold a defendant in custody indefinitely based on his or her incompetence to stand trial. It also ruled that he or she must either be civilly committed (committed by a noncriminal court) or released from criminal detention. This decision forced the states to undertake efforts to restore competency at a time when effective psychotropic drugs were becoming available.

The restoration of sanity was an issue in *Ford v. Wainwright* (1986). Career criminal Alvin Ford had been sentenced to death for the cold-blooded execution of a wounded police officer responding to a robbery being committed by Ford. There were no competency issues raised during Ford's trial, but he later claimed to have descended into insanity while on death row. Although prosecutors viewed Ford's claim of insanity to be a convenient ploy used just as his appeals were running out, three of four psychiatrists who examined him concluded that he was psychotic (Mello, 2007). In *Ford*, the U.S. Supreme Court held that the Eighth Amendment prohibits execution of the insane. The Court also ruled that Ford would still have to prove he was mentally ill (insanity is an affirmative defense in which the burden of proof lies with the defendant) (Mello, 2007). Ford died in 1991 of natural causes, 28 years after his crime.

In *Ford*, the Court ruled that society's retributive goals are only served if persons are aware of the punishment they are about to suffer and why they will suffer it. In *Panetti v. Quarterman* (2007), the Supreme Court was again confronted with the issue of the execution of the mentally ill. Panetti, who killed his mother-in-law and father-in-law in 1992, had a long history of mental illness, for which he was taking medication. Despite his undisputed mental illness and claim of mental incompetence, he was found competent to stand trial and to waive legal counsel. (He defended himself.) While the Court recognized that the Eighth Amendment forbids the execution of the insane, it declined to overturn Panetti's death sentence or to offer guidance for setting up standards for determining mental competence beyond what it called the *rational-understanding test*. This test goes beyond the *mere-awareness standard* for sanity set in *Ford*. *Rational understanding* essentially means that the condemned must have a sane, logical, and coherent grasp of why he or she is being executed in order to show the requisite competence to be executed (Sewell, 2010). The difference between the two standards is that while one might be fully aware that one is going to be executed (*mere awareness*), he or she might lack a *rational understanding* of why. For instance, such a person may believe that he or she is being executed because of religious or political views rather than because of a heinous murder. As of January 2016, Panetti is still on death row in Texas.

The law on competency and execution is still murky and in need of further clarification, but at present, it boils down to the fact that condemned individuals can be executed as long as they are mentally coherent enough to know they are about to die and to rationally understand the reason why. If someone is deemed currently incompetent to be executed, that person can be rendered competent with medication. The issue then becomes whether the state can forcibly administer antipsychotic drugs to insane inmates facing execution. Neither *Ford* nor *Panetti* touched on this issue, although in *Washington v. Harper* (1990), the Supreme Court ruled that in a prison environment, an inmate may be involuntarily medicated "if the inmate is dangerous to himself or others, and the treatment is in the inmate's medical interest" (Sewell, 2010, p. 1292). To the extent that medication is voluntary, the insane on death row are confronted with a horrible choice: madness or execution. To the extent that it is not voluntary, prison physicians are presented with an ethical dilemma, in that if they medicate someone "in the inmate's medical interests," they are simultaneously rendering the person "sane enough" for execution.

••• THE INNOCENCE REVOLUTION

The huge advances made by the genomic and brain sciences over the past three decades have revolutionized death penalty discourse in the United States. Abolitionist arguments used to center on such things as legalities, morality, fairness, financial cost, and deterrence issues. While these arguments are still forcefully made, the new and more powerful issue that now dominates abolitionist arguments is innocence. These arguments appear to have penetrated and influenced public opinion far more than other arguments because guilt and innocence have substance and are far more easily grasped than legal, statistical, and philosophical arguments. As Lawrence Marshall (2004) states,

> Unlike other challenges to the fairness of capital proceedings, which have failed to stimulate widespread public outrage, evidence of the system's propensity to factual error has the power to open closed minds and trigger reexamination of the costs and benefits of capital punishment. (p. 597)

Feature Video 19.1: False Conviction

Video 19.2: 2015 Was a Historic Year for the Death Penalty in America

Indeed, evidence of possible actual innocence was central in the decision not to reinstate the death penalty in New York in 2004, the repeal of the death penalty in New Mexico in 2009, and Governor George Ryan's clearing of Illinois's death row shortly before leaving office in 2003 (Aronson & Cole, 2009).

The Innocence Project is an organization founded 1992 by lawyers Barry Scheck and Peter Neufeld and has taken advantage of modern science to provide scientific and legal expertise for cases (most such cases are sexual-assault cases) in which false convictions may have occurred. The innocence movement received a large boost when President George W. Bush signed the Justice for All Act into law in 2004. This act includes a subsection called the Innocence Protection Act, granting federal inmates the right to petition a federal court for DNA testing to support a claim of innocence. The act provides for funding to encourage states to take measures to preserve organic evidence and to make DNA testing available to convicts claiming innocence. The law also requires states that are provided funding to certify the existence of government experts to monitor crime laboratories where allegations of misconduct and/or negligence have been made. The Innocence Project's website provides a list of all DNA exonerations in the United States; it included 344 cases as of August 2016, 20 of which were death penalty cases (Innocence Project, 2016). In 43% of DNA exoneration cases, the actual perpetrator was identified by DNA; thus, this technology has been used to convict the guilty, as well as to exonerate the innocent.

SOME CONCERNS WITH DNA TECHNOLOGY

A problem confronting death penalty opponents is that despite all of the celebrations surrounding the DNA exonerations of numerous inmates (death row and otherwise), it may breathe new life into arguments supporting the death penalty. That is, if the fear of executing an innocent person is a major argument against the use of the death penalty and if the "certainty of DNA" is the tool that prevents it, pro–death penalty advocates can now rely on that same "certainty" and say that we have removed the major obstacle (the possibility of executing the innocent) and can move forward with a more just death penalty. Thus, touting DNA as some sort of truth device is a double-edged sword—if it can be used to exonerate the innocent with apparent certainty, it can be used to condemn the guilty with the same apparent certainty. This kind of "certainty" can provide what advocates of the death penalty might describe as a "foolproof" death penalty. This, of course, upsets those who oppose the death penalty on moral grounds, regardless of certainty of guilt.

As wonderful as modern genetic and neuroscience technology is, the evidence supplied by it should not be accepted uncritically. There is an old saying that "statistics don't lie, but liars lie with statistics." Similarly, we can say that DNA doesn't lie, but people can (wittingly or unwittingly) lie with DNA. DNA samples must be meticulously handled so as not to become contaminated, and there are sometimes problems interpreting lab results, as well as problems beyond technical difficulties involving human errors, incompetence, and outright fraud (Hatch & Walsh, 2016).

A number of police labs have been accused and found guilty of falsifying and fabricating DNA. Others have been shown to be incompetent in their use of the technology and/or in interpreting results and to have cross-contaminated and mislabeled sample DNA (Aronson & Cole, 2009). Many of these things are to be expected when dealing with complicated technical matters, and human beings are expected to make errors, take shortcuts, and even fudge the data to conform to the desired conclusion. In a police lab, the "desired conclusion" is of course a match between the evidence DNA and the accused's DNA. Even without a biasing context, experts come to different conclusions. For instance, Dror and Hampikian (2011) presented *mixed-DNA evidence* (DNA from two or more sources) from a sexual assault case to 17 different DNA analysts, omitting the biasing contextual criminal case information. Dror and Hampikian (2011) found that only one of the 17 reached the same conclusion ("defendant cannot be excluded") as the original analysts in the criminal case while 12 concluded "exclude," and 4 concluded "inconclusive." Out-and-out fraud is a rarity, but the fact that it happens and the fact that experts often disagree in their interpretations of DNA evidence should be enough to stop us from thinking about DNA as the "holy grail" of guilt and innocence. However, the consequences of disregarding DNA evidence of someone's innocence are too far-reaching to doubt it, although a healthy skepticism in terms of it supplying the sole evidence of someone's guilt is a good thing.

▶ Feature Video 19.2: Awareness

Neuroimaging is typically used as evidence for mitigating punishment rather than exoneration. The workhorse of neuroimaging is **functional magnetic resonance imaging (fMRI)**. fMRI scans compare blood flow in the brain as it uses the oxygen to energize itself. Data from fMRI testing are based on aggregating these responses from a number of individuals. Because fMRI results emerge from data averaged over a group of subjects, they are problematic when applied to specific individuals. As O. Jones and Shen (2012) put it,

Functional magnetic resonance imaging (fMRI): The fMRI is the workhorse of neuroimaging used to assess the functioning of a person's brain while engaged in some task.

> Just because a particular pattern of neural activity is associated, on average at the group level, with impaired decision-making, it does not necessarily follow that a defendant before the court whose brain scans produce the same neural patterns necessarily has a cognitive deficit. (p. 356)

PERSPECTIVE FROM A PRACTITIONER

Ginny Hatch, Investigator for Idaho Innocence Project

Position: Investigator with the Federal Defender's Office, volunteer investigator with the Innocence Project, and adjunct professor of criminal justice at Boise State University

Location: Boise, Idaho

Education: MA in criminal justice, Boise State University

What are you primary duties and responsibilities?

I investigate claims of innocence and wrongful-conviction cases.

Please describe a typical workday.

When you work for the Innocence Project, there are no "typical days." Each day is different and presents new challenges. This type of work is unique because I investigate cases that have already been investigated and processed through the criminal justice system. The Innocence Project typically takes cases during the postconviction phase(s), after most or all of the appeals have been exhausted. This can be particularly frustrating because I am not in control of what has happened in the past, and oftentimes, the previous professionals presiding over the case (prosecution and/or defense) are responsible for the errors that have led to the wrongful conviction.

In the early phases of investigation, I spend quite a bit of time reading and abstracting important documents associated with the case (trial transcripts, appellate briefs and decisions, discovery, etc.). If my investigation leads me to believe that someone is truly innocent, I must try to figure out how the conviction resulted. In doing so, I spend a lot of time rereading the case file. After I have a working knowledge of a case, I look for any discrepancies among or between witnesses. If inconsistencies are found, they are followed up on accordingly. I often interview witnesses that testified during trial, as well as witnesses that have not yet been interviewed by the original investigators. Witnesses sometimes change their testimony, and they do so for a variety of reasons. It is my job to listen to their story and document it. Sometimes, I learn of things that are helpful to my case and sometimes not, but at the end of the day, I am only interested in the truth.

There are many factors that lead to wrongful convictions, including problems with eyewitness identification, false confessions, government misconduct, bad science, snitches or informants, and bad lawyers. Luckily, there is an abundance of academic literature on these issues to aid investigators and legal professionals in wrongful-conviction cases. This research helps me to understand how an innocent person can be convicted of a crime that he or she did not commit. We often enlist the help of expert witnesses to explain to the court what went wrong in a particular case. After all of the investigative work is completed, what really matters is the battle that takes place in the courtroom—where justice is meted out! If I have learned nothing else from working with the Innocence Project, it is that our justice system is not infallible, and we must always fight injustice of any measure.

What would be your advice to someone either wishing to study or now studying criminal justice to become a practitioner in this career field?

The Innocence Project work requires profound dedication, a passion for justice, and an inordinate amount of patience. The job is complex and can almost always be described as an uphill battle. It is extremely difficult to prove a person's innocence after he or she has been found guilty in our criminal justice system. In doing so, you are essentially admitting that our justice system makes mistakes, and no one likes to think that innocent people may be incarcerated.

I strongly recommend that students who are interested in working as an investigator complete an internship for the organization or agency of interest to them. Most agencies are looking for experience in their field, so every bit helps. It is beneficial to have a bachelor's degree in criminal justice, but this is certainly not required. The type of educational background needed for an investigator position really depends on the type of agency one wishes to work for.

PHOTO 19.5: Neuroscience techniques are sometimes used in death penalty cases to show that the offender's brain is somehow faulty, which supposedly reduces responsibility. The usual tactic is to show psychopathy because the psychopath's brain shows clear indications of the condition.

SOME CONCERNS WITH NEUROIMAGING TECHNOLOGY

The neuroimaging evidence relating to which parts of the brain are activated under what conditions and what parts are responsible for which behaviors is both consistent and strong. But we must understand that neuroimages are maps of the terrain, not the terrain itself, and are generated mathematically (not direct pictures as in an X-ray) from numerous signals coming from the fMRI machine. They are indirect rather than direct evidence of increased neural activity because they are based on a statistical aggregate forming a correlation between a particular trait, behavior, or brain process and neurological responses in a particular area. A correlation is a trend in a given direction, and that correlational trend in brain scans is not entirely true of all brains tested and certainly not in terms of the wide variations in strength of brain responses of different people to identical stimuli.

Even given this, it is a big jump from talking about "impaired judgment" inferred from mistakes subjects make on tasks they are asked to perform in the laboratory and a brutal murder performed in the real world. Just how impaired is the defendant's brain compared with the average level of those subjects said to be impaired, and how many of these subjects similarly impaired have committed murder?

Another matter is that imaging of defendants' brains is typically performed many years after the crime was committed. Today's brain is not yesterday's brain, and the images jurors may see in court may be vastly different from what they may have seen at the time of the crime for which the defendant is seeking mitigation. Scans of a killer's brain taken 5, 10, or 15 years after a murder may show that the person is a psychopath, but they tell us nothing about his state of mind when he committed his murder, nor do they show that he was incapable of controlling his behavior. Neuroimaging is vitally important in medicine and neuroscience research, but it cannot read minds, particularly mind states that occurred years prior to the scanning. Scanning tells us the probable state of the subject's mind at the time of the scan; it cannot settle matters of legal responsibility.

SUMMARY

- The majority of Americans support capital punishment, but their opinions fluctuate with the crime rate and with the availability of LWOP.

- Because the United States stands almost alone among democracies in retaining the death penalty, the issue has generated much debate and numerous court cases questioning its constitutionality.

- A variety of methods of execution have been used in the United States, but lethal injection is used almost exclusively today in all states with the death penalty.

- The death penalty is often defended for its deterrent effect, but there is heated disagreement about whether it deters. A committee of experts who examined all death penalty studies up to 2011 concluded that we do not really know whether or not it is a deterrent.

- Seeking the death penalty for a murderer is immensely more costly than seeking LWOP, and even those given the death penalty are rarely executed.

- Historically, African Americans have been executed disproportionately not only to their numbers in the population but also disproportionately to their number of murderers. However, today black murderers are proportionately less likely to be sentenced to death and to be executed than white murderers.

- The debate has now swung away from discrimination against black defendants to discrimination against black victims because killers (regardless of their race) of whites are more likely to receive the death penalty than killers of blacks. However, once aggravating and mitigating circumstances are taken into account, there is disagreement over whether this bias is still in evidence.

- Women have constituted only 2% of persons executed in the nation's history. They commit far fewer death-eligible murders than men, but it is estimated that if they were treated the same as men, they would have constituted between 4% and 6% of those executed in the United States.

- The chivalry hypothesis has been advanced to explain why we execute fewer death-eligible female murderers versus death-eligible male murderers, and the evil-woman hypothesis has been advanced for females who are executed.

- It is constitutionally impermissible to execute the mentally disabled (defined as an IQ less than or equal to 70) in the United States, but it is permissible to execute the mentally ill. The reasoning is that mental disability cannot be changed or faked, whereas mental illness can. It is impermissible to execute the "presently" mentally ill, but they can be restored to sanity with drugs and then executed.

- Advances in the genomic and brain sciences have led to an innocence revolution in death penalty discourse. DNA testing has resulted in many wrongly convicted persons being freed and the guilty being convicted. DNA is not a panacea for death penalty opponents, however, as death penalty advocates now say that with this advance, we can go forth with an "error-free" death penalty.

KEY TERMS

Brutalizing effect 466

Death Penalty Information Center 468

Electrocution 461

Firing squad 463

Functional magnetic resonance imaging (fMRI) 482

Gas chamber 463

Hanging 461

Lethal injection 463

DISCUSSION QUESTIONS

1. Why do you think that the United States retains the death penalty when almost all other democracies eliminated it long ago? Should we eliminate it? Why, or why not?

2. Argue your case for whether the death penalty does or does not deter.

3. If you are for capital punishment on the grounds of just deserts, do you think it is justified in financial terms? Why, or why not?

4. What do you think accounts for the fact that prosecutors today seek the death penalty proportionately more often for whites than for minorities—a reversal of past practices?

5. Regardless of your stance on capital punishment, should women be treated the same as men if they commit the same crime? Why, or why not?

6. Describe the reasoning behind the fact that the mentally ill may be executed but the mentally disabled may not.

7. If DNA evidence helps to reduce the possibility of executing an innocent person, can we also say that it has thereby presented us with an "error-free" death penalty?

USEFUL INTERNET SITES

Please note the sites listed can be accessed at edge .sagepub.com/stohrcorrections.

Coalition to Abolish the Death Penalty: www.ncadp.org

As the name implies, this website consists of a variety of arguments meant to convince people that the death penalty is a bad thing.

Death Penalty Information Center: www .deathpenaltyinfo.org

A partisan organization which is a font of information about the death penalty.

Pro Death Penalty group: www.prodeathpenalty.com

As the name implies, this website consists of a variety of arguments meant to convince people that the death penalty is a good thing.

$SAGE edge™

Sharpen your skills with SAGE edge at **edge.sagepub.com/stohrcorrections**. SAGE edge for Students provides a personalized approach to help you accomplish your coursework goals in an easy-to-use learning environment. You'll find action plans, mobile-friendly eFlashcards, and quizzes as well as video, web, and resources and links to SAGE journal articles to support and expand on the concepts presented in this chapter.

Eric Risberg/ASSOCIATED PRESS

Comparative Corrections

Punishment in Other Countries

TEST YOUR KNOWLEDGE

Test your present knowledge of correctional institutions in other countries by answering the following questions as true or false. Check your answers on page 540 after reading the chapter.

1. American style common law is the most popular legal system worldwide.

2. The United Kingdom has a single criminal justice system.

3. British probation officers today are mostly trained in social work.

4. In the French inquisitorial system of criminal justice, an arrested person is presumed guilty until proven innocent.

5. Chinese criminals released from prison have a recidivism rate about 8 times lower than American parolees.

6. The death penalty can be imposed for more than 50 different crimes in China.

7. The Saudi Arabian criminal justice system has few procedural rules, and judges make decisions based on their own interpretation of the facts and principles of Islamic law.

8. Under Saudi law, the death penalty can be imposed for acts not even recognized as crimes in Western countries.

LEARNING OBJECTIVES

- Discuss why a comparative perspective is important

- Describe the important differences between the various legal systems in terms of how they impact correctional systems

- Explain the reasons for the radical shift in U.K. and French corrections policies since the 1990s

- Explain the basic difference between Anglo-American common law and the code systems of France, China, and Saudi Arabia

- Identify the role that the combination of Confucianism and communism plays in informing China's correctional policies

- Explain the central role of Islam in the correctional practices of Saudi Arabia

- Analyze whether the United States is hard or soft on crime

THE DEBATE OVER CORPORAL PUNISHMENT

In September of 1993, Michael Peter Fay, an 18-year-old American living in Singapore, went on a 10-day rampage of vandalism during which he damaged cars with hot tar, paint remover, and a hatchet. Fay pled guilty to two (out of 53) counts and was sentenced to a fine, jail time, and six lashes of a rattan cane. Many Americans applauded Singapore, believing that this tiny country could teach us a thing or two about dealing with obnoxious and destructive teenagers. Others were appalled at what they considered barbaric treatment and thanked God that we do not whip our miscreants in this country anymore. Whatever anyone's opinions may have been on the matter, if they had one, they were in thinking about comparative corrections.

Although caning is a common penalty in Singapore for a number of offenses, because an American was involved,

it became a hot political issue in the United States. Twenty-four U.S. senators signed a letter condemning the sentence and appealing for clemency. Singaporeans resented such interference, pointing out that Singapore was a safe and orderly society while the United States was mired in crime. Many other commentators, in both the U.S. and Singapore, pointed to differences in correctional penalties as a key reason for differences in crime rates between the two countries. Although both countries are common-law countries, Singapore values the crime control model over the due process model, and its defenders point out that America pays the price for its liberal attitudes on crime and general mayhem.

Would the United States be a safer and more civic-minded country if it adopted a Singaporean attitude toward crime and punishment? Perhaps, but are we

*willing to go that far? If so, how about going further
and cutting off the hands of thieves, whipping
consumers of alcohol, and executing adulterers,
as is done in some Islamic countries that are even
safer (at least in terms of common street crime) than
Singapore? How about the opposite extreme? The
rambunctious chef Gordon Ramsay of TV fame recently
expressed his astonishment upon discovering that*

*inmates in British prisons were given five meal choices
every night and constant access to television, video
games, and gym facilities—a lifestyle that many poorer,
law-abiding Brits could not afford. Is this excessive
mollycoddling or good rehabilitative practice? These
are some of the things to think about when we read
about other correctional systems and ask, Why don't
we do that?*

••• THE IMPORTANCE OF COMPARATIVE CORRECTIONS

AP Video 20.1:
UN Death
Penalty

Journal Article
20.1:
Legal Systems
and Variance in
the Design of
Commitments to
the International
Court of Justice

Web 20.1:
International
Court of Justice

All societies develop rules for ensuring peace, order, predictability, and cultural survival and provide sanctions for those who do not follow them. These rules and the sanctions suffered by those accused and convicted of breaking them may differ significantly from society to society because they reflect a particular culture's history and its present social, political, and economic practices, philosophies, and ideals. This chapter briefly introduces you to correctional practices utilized in four societies other than the United States.

There are many advantages to studying a familiar subject from a different vantage point. Some wise person one once said that if you only know your own culture you don't know your own culture. How true that is. After all, we cannot know what *up*, *tall*, and *no* mean without knowing what *down*, *short*, and *yes* mean. Of course, other countries' correctional systems have many things in common with ours—they all have jails and prisons—but their goals and practices may depart significantly from ours. Knowledge of systems other than our own provides us with a new understanding and appreciation of our own and will better equip us to identify both the strengths and weaknesses of the American system.

We begin with a look at the United Kingdom (U.K.), a country with which the United States shares the heritage of law, language, and culture. Both the U.S. and the U.K. share the common-law system that evolved in England over many centuries. The other countries that we will look at all have legal traditions that differ substantially from the Anglo-American common-law tradition. We first look at France, which has a civil-law tradition, because modern civil (or code) law began under Napoleon in 1804. Civil law is by far the most popular system of law in the world today, with 48% of the world's nations using this system (Walsh & Hemmens, 2016). China was chosen because, with the collapse of the Soviet Union, it is the largest socialist legal system in the world, and Saudi Arabia was chosen to illustrate the Islamic legal tradition because the Koran (Islam's holy book) functions as the Saudi Arabian constitution (Walsh & Hemmens, 2016). The French, Chinese, and Saudi legal traditions are all code systems, which are systems that come "ready-made" rather than systems that have evolved slowly, as does the common law. Judges in code countries cannot "make law" by precedent, as they can in common-law countries. Rather, as a general rule, they are supposed to act uniformly in accordance with the criminal code, and consequently, there is generally much less judicial oversight of the correctional systems in those countries.

A useful method of viewing the different correctional systems in terms of something already familiar to you is to place them on the due process–crime control continuum. Remember, both models are ideal types that do not exist anywhere in their pure form. In a pure due process model, justice would be lost in a maze of legal ritualism; in a pure crime control model, there would be no procedural rights afforded the accused at all. Figure 20.1 places the countries to be discussed on a due process–crime control continuum according to the degree to which they emphasize one model or the other. Terrill

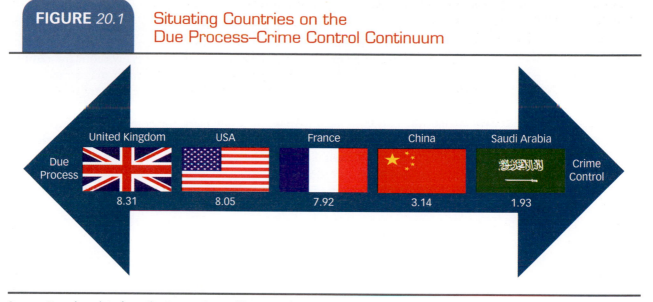

FIGURE 20.1   Situating Countries on the Due Process–Crime Control Continuum

Source: Based on data from the Economist Intelligence Unit (2016).

(2013) notes that the U.S., the U.K., and France "vacillate between the two models, but they are more sensitive to due process issues [while China and Saudi Arabia] favor the crime control model and often show little regard for the due process model" (p. 15).

 Web 20.2: International Crimes Database

One way of attempting to operationalize or measure the degree to which a society has a due process versus a crime control model is the degree to which a country respects the ideals of democracy. Although the United Kingdom has the highest democracy score, the United States is arguably the closest to a pure due process model of criminal law, and Saudi Arabia is the closest to a pure crime control model. The numbers beneath the respective flags represent each county's democracy score on a scale of 1 to 10, according to the Economist Intelligence Unit (2016). This score is based on 63 different factors, such as public political participation and respect for civil rights, and their scores support our placement of countries on the figure. On a world scale, the United Kingdom does not occupy the top spot, nor does Saudi Arabia occupy the bottom place. Norway had the highest democracy score (9.80), and North Korea had the lowest (1.08). In our estimation, the French system probably represents the "right" balance between the rights of the accused (due process) and the protection of society (crime control); others may disagree.

●●● THE UNITED KINGDOM AND THE COMMON-LAW SYSTEM

The U.K. is a constitutional monarchy ruled by a democratically elected parliament. Although it is a unitary rather than a federal state, it consists of three countries (England, Scotland, and Wales, plus Northern Ireland) and has three separate criminal justice systems (England and Wales, Scotland, and Northern Ireland) that differ in a number of ways. We concentrate only on England and Wales, the largest of the three. It is primarily a due process system but not to the extent that the United States is. For instance, it has never embraced anything like the exclusionary rule, believing that evidence is evidence and that other remedies for police misconduct are available. In 2004, the correctional systems of England and Wales were placed under a single umbrella in the form of the **National Offender Management Service (NOMS)**. NOMS now combines what were formerly the National Probation Service and Her Majesty's Prison Service.

National Offender Management Service (NOMS): New name for the service combining the National Probation Service and Her Majesty's Prison Service.

SENTENCING IN ENGLAND AND WALES

Video 20.1:
Tougher
Penalties
Proposed for
Carrying a Knife

The U.K. eliminated the felony-versus-misdemeanor distinction between crimes in 1966 and now uses the indictable-versus-summary distinction. A *summary offense* is a minor criminal offense that can be proceeded against summarily (swiftly) without the right to a formal indictment or trial by jury. Summary offenses are heard in magistrate courts by magistrates, who are lay volunteers. Although magistrates receive training for the job, they typically have no formal legal training, such as a law degree. They sit in panels of three and are assisted in legal matters by a law clerk (or court legal advisor), who is a trained lawyer. Fines are the most common sentence in magistrate court, with the maximum being £5,000 (about $6,600 in late 2016) for each offense. For more serious offenses, magistrates can order community sentences with any number of ancillary sentences, such as treatment and restitution. Magistrates can also impose custodial sentences of 6 months or less (Walsh & Hemmens, 2016).

An *indictable offense* is a more serious crime (like an American felony) and requires a trial by a judge and jury in Crown court (analogous to an American district court). Sentences for indictable offenses vary from straight probation to life in prison. (There is no death penalty in the U.K.) At the termination of a trial (or plea bargain) for an indictable offense, the defendant is referred to probation authorities for a presentence report. As a member of the European Union (EU) at present, the U.K. is bound by the EU Charter of Fundamental Rights, which demands "proportionality" in criminal sentencing (Albers et al., 2013), although this will change when it formally leaves the EU ("Brexit"). However, national governments retain a margin of discretion in such matters.

There are four types of sentence in England and Wales: discharge, fines, probation, and prison. A convicted person may be discharged conditionally or absolutely for minor offenses if the court decides not to impose any punishment. Prison sentences for serious offenses are of a fixed term, from 1 year to life. Sentences are more predictable in England and Wales than in the United States because they are all based on mandatory sentencing guidelines. The courts in England and Wales use a grid-based guideline much like those in fashion in the United States, although, as noted previously, U.S. guidelines are advisory rather than mandatory. In the British case, Parliament has mandated that the "courts 'must follow' definitive guidelines rather than merely 'have regard to' them" (J. V. Roberts, 2011, p. 1).

COMMUNITY CORRECTIONS IN ENGLAND AND WALES

Britain is the European home of probation. As we saw in Chapter 8, it began with Matthew Davenport Hill in 1841, which, coincidentally, is the same year that John Augustus launched probation in Boston. It began as a "soul-saving" temperance effort, and until the 1990s, it remained oriented toward rehabilitation. The probation service in England and Wales has also undergone some wide-reaching changes in response to crime levels in the 1990s. Prior to that decade, all probation officers held social-work qualifications. With the consolidation of the probation service and the prison service under NOMS, probation officers became "offender managers," and the social-work aspect of the job was de-emphasized. As G. Robinson and McNeill (2010) put it, "Probation officers in England and Wales . . . are no longer trained as social workers, and the context in which they work is no longer that of a social work agency, but rather a 'law enforcement agency'" (p. 744).

The probation service now seeks to hire ex-military personnel, which says a lot about the new emphasis. Of course, these probation officers–cum–offender managers still offer the same programs and services, but they deliver them in a more no-nonsense "pull up your socks, man" attitude than was heretofore the case. For instance, favored counseling theories are now much more of the directive and confrontational type, such as cognitive behavioral therapy, as noted in a U.K. Ministry of Justice (2014) publication: "There is growing international evidence that the type of cognitive-behavioural techniques that NOMS accredited programmes apply are the most effective in reducing offending

Getty Images News David Goddard

PHOTO 20.1: A high Victorian wall surrounds Dorchester Prison in Dorset, England. The prison was closed in 2013 because of overcrowding and lax control (25% of random drug tests on inmates were positive).

behavior" (para. 3). G. Robinson and McNeill (2010) quote a NOMS official in 1999 regarding its new correctional policy framework:

> We have put the focus firmly on outcomes—reducing reoffending and improving public protection. Success will be measured in those terms. The achievement of this common aim . . . must be first consideration for everyone engaged in delivering correctional policy, and not an afterthought. (p. 750)

British crime rates have fallen dramatically since the implementation of changes in correctional strategies. Whether there is a cause–effect relationship here is anyone's guess, but the British criminal justice system continues to make some very radical changes. In February of 2015, the U.K. government outsourced many of its probation services to private-sector companies (contracted out on a payment-by-result basis) and to voluntary organizations. Low-risk offenders are now supervised by 21 private community rehabilitation companies (CRCs) formed by former probation staff. The government also established the National Probation Service (NPS) for high-risk offenders. Existing staff have been split between CRCs and the NPS, with many teams now operating alongside each other (Rutter, 2015). Some may call this innovative and progressive; others may call it regressive and more concerned with cost cutting than with public protection and offender rehabilitation (A. Travis, 2013). Preliminary assessments reveal a chaotic system and demoralized staff, but because this is a major reorganization, this was expected, and many kinks need ironing out (Rutter, 2015).

PRISONS IN ENGLAND AND WALES

Prisons in England and Wales are categorized according to the level of security. Category A prisons are maximum-security prisons that house highly dangerous offenders, Category B prisons are medium-security prisons, Category C houses minimum-security prisoners who can't be trusted in open conditions but who are unlikely to try to escape, and Category D prisons are open and allow prisoners a lot of freedom, including working in

ETHICAL ISSUE 20.1 ?

What Would You Do?

You are a retired person in England who believes that as an early probation volunteer, it is your Christian duty to help others who are less fortunate. Since the country has moved to basically a two-tiered probation system, with the hard-core offenders being supervised by professional POs and lesser offenders being outsourced to private commercial companies and charities, you join your local church charity and are assigned a small caseload of 15 probationers. These charities involved in probation reforms potentially face a conflict of interest, as offenders involved in their program risk jail if they do not cooperate with needed treatment. Short-sentence offenders are compelled to abide by rules set up by the criminal justice system and are sent to prison if they do not.

You are aware that you are dealing with vulnerable and troubled people who are not very good at meeting obligations, and you believe that this is setting up people to fail. You are not involved in sending people back to prison, but you are involved with people who do. You see your responsibility as offering something voluntary for people to engage with, but you know that your charitable organization has to rely on government grants to offer the services it does. You become quite sympathetic to the plight of one of your charges named "Joe," who has no immediate family and who has little prospect of gainful employment due to his lack of education, low IQ, and, to put it bluntly, laziness. Now, Joe is a thoroughly likeable chap who likes to banter with you over a pint at the local pub (he doesn't have an alcohol problem), but he does not take your advice regarding treatment. You know you should report this, both for "Joe's sake" and because your charity may be in danger of losing its grant if Joe is arrested for another crime. Do you report Joe or leave him be and hope for the best?

the local community. There are also special prisons for the mentally ill and remand centers (analogous to American jails) for prisoners serving short sentences or for individuals awaiting trial or other court hearings.

As was the case in the United States in the 1990s, rising crime rates in the U.K. led to sustained public calls to "get tough on crime." Also, as in the United States, the U.K. government substantially increased the number of convicted offenders it sent to prison. As seen in the top half of Figure 20.2 from the U.K. Ministry of Justice, the prison population almost doubled from 1993 to 2012. Note that *recalls* refers to parole violators returned to prison, and *noncriminal* refers people such as illegal immigrants and asylum seekers awaiting resolution of their cases. The bottom half of Figure 20.2, from the British Crime Survey (analogous to the U.S. National Crime Victimization Survey), shows that, in common with the United States, crime rates fell (note that the large peaks in the early 1990s are almost identical with U.S. peaks) as rates of imprisonment rose (Burn-Murdoch & Chalabi, 2013).

As with any other country experiencing a rapid increase in its prison population and increased sentence lengths, overcrowding has become a major problem in prisons in England and Wales. Over the past 15 years, many older prisons have been closed down, and new ones have been built (U.K. Ministry of Justice, 2013). Despite such overcrowding, U.K. prisons do not appear to suffer one of the major problems seen in U.S. prisons: a prison gang culture and the violence that accompanies such a culture. However, there are occasional clashes that have flowed from the streets into the prisons (Phillips, 2012). Muslims and blacks do tend to cluster together in their separate groups. According to Phillips (2012), this represents more a racial, ethnic, or religious identity issue rather than an organizational gang structure defined by a criminal identity.

The main complaint about British prisons appears to be that they are expensive "bed and breakfasts" paid for by the taxpayer and "enjoyed" by those who have preyed on them. According to an ABC News report,

> Criminals are enjoying such a life of luxury in British jails that they are refusing to try to escape, a senior prison union official said. . . . Dangerous prisoners enjoy satellite television, free telephone calls and breakfast in bed in the country's "cushy" jails, Prison Officers' Association General Secretary Glyn Travis added. (Hough, 2008, n.p.)

Prisoners may or may not experience these prisons as "cushy," but the alleged "cushiness" of the prisons does very little to prevent recidivism, which is at about the same level as it is in the United States; that is, about two thirds of parolees recidivate within 3 years of release from prison (U.K. Ministry of Justice, 2010).

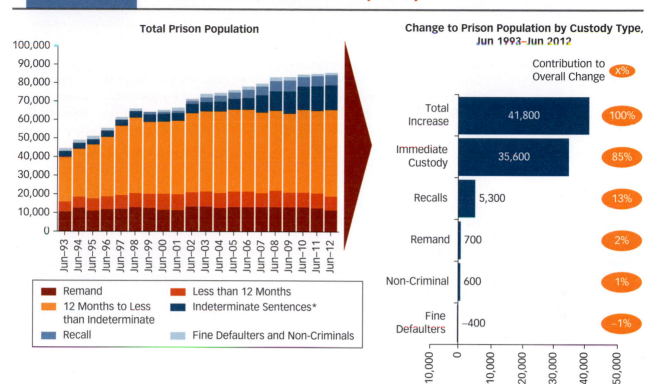

FIGURE *20.2* Increase in Prison Population in England and Wales, 1993–2012, by Custody and Type (*above*) and Trends in Violent Crime, 1981–2006 (*below*)

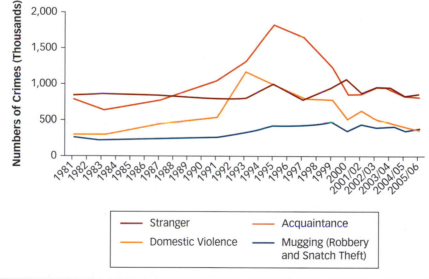

Sources: *Top*: UK Ministry of Justice (2013), public sector information licensed under the Open Government Licence v3.0; *bottom*: Jansson (2006), Office for National Statistics licensed under the Open Government Licence v3.0, http://www.nationalarchives.gov.uk/doc/open-government-licence/version/3/

In response to public outcry about stories of "prison luxury," the U.K. Ministry of Justice presented a series of proposals in a 2010 document outlining strategies designed to break the destructive cycle of crime and prison by ensuring that prisons become places of hard work and ones in which rehabilitation is to be opened up to innovative programs from the private and charitable sectors, which are paid according to the results they achieve. These proposals include the following:

- Making offenders work hard through the discipline of regular working hours in prison, more demanding tasks in the community, and greater use of tough curfew requirements

- Increasing reparations to victims through greater use of restorative justice, implementing the Prisoners' Earnings Act (PEA), and by passing other reforms to make offenders directly compensate victims of crime (The PEA requires prisoners making more than £80 a month—about $106—to use part of it to pay for their keep and to compensate victims.)

- Rehabilitating offenders by getting them off of drugs and benefits and into honest work

- Introducing payment-by-results so that independent providers will be rewarded for reducing reoffending— this will be paid for by the savings that this will generate within the criminal justice system

- Simplifying the sentencing framework to make it more comprehensible to the public, enhancing judicial discretion, and reforming the indeterminate sentence of Imprisonment for Public Protection (IPP) (*Note:* The IPP was abolished in 2013.)

- Improving youth justice to prevent and tackle offending by young people and to stop them from becoming the career criminals of tomorrow

- Working with communities to reduce crime, with local people playing a more central role in criminal justice— moving the focus from the center to local areas

- Creating more opportunities for other providers to deliver services and increasing transparency so that local communities are better able to hold services to account (U.K. Ministry of Justice, 2010, pp. 10–12)

As is the case in the United States, the courts in England and Wales are inundated with inmate complaints about things both serious and frivolous. Three examples from 2011, provided by Engelman (2012), supply us with the flavor of these complaints. (1) A prisoner who wanted a face-to-face interview with a reporter from the BBC was refused but successfully challenged that refusal on the grounds that it interfered with the right to freedom of expression. (2) A prisoner successfully challenged a decision that refused him an oral hearing in relation to his recategorization. (3) A claim that a pat-down search of a male inmate by a female prison officer was discriminatory and in breach of human rights was denied by the court.

The overarching institution looking after prisoners' rights in the U.K. (as well as all countries in the European Union) is the European Court of Human Rights. There are three national institutions in the U.K. overseeing prisoners' rights: (1) a prison inspectorate, (2) a prisons and probation ombudsman (IPO), and (3) local independent monitoring boards (IMB) (Owers, 2006). The prison inspectorate employs staff responsible for inspecting all prisons and jails in the country and monitoring compliance with mandated rules regarding prison conditions and prisoner treatment. IPOs deal with specific prisoner complaints after internal complaint procedures are exhausted, and IMBs are groups of volunteer citizens appointed by the government to monitor the jails and prisons in their areas.

••• FRANCE AND THE CIVIL-LAW SYSTEM

France is a unitary democratic country that has a civil-law tradition. The law in France is the *Code Civil des Français*. Consistent with its communitarian values, the French system operates more in line with the crime control model, emphasizing the rights of the victimized community (Reichel, 2005). Its legal system is inquisitorial rather than the common law's adversarial system. The term *inquisitorial* conjures up images of torture,

PERSPECTIVE FROM A PRACTITIONER

Cyndi Banks, Comparative Criminal Justice Scholar

Name: Dr. Cyndi Banks

Position: Chair and professor, Department of Criminology and Criminal Justice

Location: Northern Arizona University

Education: BA and MA in criminology, Simon Fraser University (Canada), PhD in criminology, University of Cambridge (U.K.)

As a criminologist who has worked in many justice systems, including corrections, in Bangladesh, Papua New Guinea, Iraq and Kurdistan, South Sudan, and Myanmar, I have seen and experienced how prisons and juvenile institutions are organized and operated in the developing world. As a scholar and researcher in Canada and the United States, I have studied women in prison and discussed ethical issues arising in corrections in the developed world. Through my engagement with corrections in different societies, I have gained an understanding of differences and commonalities in various correctional systems and why comparative corrections is useful.

Comparative criminal justice typically examines how various countries have organized their justice systems, including corrections. However, distinct policies, operations, and facilities in corrections have received little attention. Comparative texts typically include sections on the history of corrections and corrections policy (usually in the West), international standards for prisoners, prisoners' rights, and private prisons. The field of corrections is often conflated with punishment and criminal justice policy, especially the issue of penal policy convergence among Western nations.

Comparative criminologists have pointed out that differing conceptions in legal systems raise the question whether the comparative approach really compares like with like or whether it simply assumes system and conceptual universality. Concepts like the treatment of offenders are

culturally determined, and understanding them requires a contextual approach that investigates the social, economic, and cultural framework; how elements of justice systems actually function; and how they are impacted by social change. This suggests that the best comparative work will be interdisciplinary in nature. It is contended then that comparative studies are quite superficial; for example, in corrections much attention is paid to ranking rates of incarceration per unit of population, but the specific structural and cultural context is often ignored. Thus, comparative-corrections studies often fail to engage in questions of explanation or interpretation.

Through viewing commonalities and differences in different correctional systems, suggestions can be made as to how our own system can be improved. An international perspective provides insights into the U.S. system and challenges assumptions and the status quo—for example, that the United States has the world's best correctional system. Comparison thus enables a greater understanding of one's own system's virtues and defects. Comparing systems can then generate ideas for the improvement of existing systems, substitute a global perspective for a local one, and enhance and facilitate international cooperation in corrections.

Of late, increased interest in global criminal justice issues has encouraged criminologists to look beyond Western models in order to understand worldwide changes. In order to fully capture these changes, we ought to be not only comparative but also international. It is now common for rule-of-law and justice system improvement projects in developing nations to include a component for the review and development of the correctional system and of correctional practices in that nation. This indicates the need for a global approach to the study of corrections that explicitly acknowledges the diversity of country conditions.

and the notion that the accused is assumed guilty unless he or she can prove otherwise, all of which is untrue. Rather, it is a system of extensive investigation, interviews, and interrogations to ensure that an innocent person is not subjected to trial (Fairchild & Dammer, 2001). The inquisitorial focus is on truth and not so much on procedure, so many of the procedural protections afforded suspects in common-law countries either do not exist or exist in modified form.

This does not mean that the system ignores individual rights; the French provided attorneys for indigent defendants more than 50 years before the United States did. The French system protects the accused from adverse publicity by not releasing their names or other information pertaining to the case to the press unless or until the investigation leaves authorities with little doubt that they have a strong case against them. These and other such protections have led more than one comparative legal scholar to voice the opinion that civil law is more protective of the innocent and that common law is more protective of the guilty (Fairchild & Dammer, 2001; Maechling, 1993).

This suggests that civil-law procedure is more likely to arrive at the truth and serve the purpose of justice than is common-law procedure. It is for this reason that we opined earlier that the French system represents the "right" balance between protecting the rights of the accused and protecting the rights and concerns of the community.

Truth seeking is accomplished by active judicial supervision of evidence gathering and active participation in the investigation of the suspect and the crime. In our adversarial system, outcomes often rest on the relative skills of attorneys, and defendants able to bear the costs of good attorneys and related investigatory costs (expert witnesses and the like) have a significant advantage over less wealthy defendants. Such inequalities are much less relevant in a judge-controlled inquisitorial system, in which judges call expert witnesses on behalf of both sides. *All* relevant evidence as to the guilt or innocence of the accused is considered, including his or her character and hearsay evidence, and nothing is automatically excluded because of so-called technicalities. The only exception to this is when evidence or confessions are obtained via physical or legal threats (Reichel, 2005).

SENTENCING IN FRANCE

Video 20.2:
France Hands
Carlos the Jackal
Another Life
Prison Term

According to the official French government website (Service Public Française, 2015), offenses in France are divided into *crimes*, *délits*, and *contraventions*, which, with some exceptions, are analogous to felonies, misdemeanors, and infractions, respectively, in American law. *Crimes* are the most serious offenses. They are tried in assize courts with judges and juries and are punishable by 15 to 30 years in prison or, in exceptional cases, life in prison. (As in the U.K., there is no death penalty in France.) Examples of crimes are murder and rape. A *délit* is an offense punishable by imprisonment, ranging from 2 months to 10 years, and is tried in a correctional court. Although *délits* are classified as second-tier crimes, they are very serious offenses such as robbery, aggravated assault, and sexual assault. *Délits* can become crimes with aggravating circumstances. *Contraventions* are minor offenses tried in police courts and punishable only by fines up to 3,000 euros (about $3,400 in late 2016).

Because the termination of a French trial results simultaneously in a verdict and a sentence, a PSI is not necessary. All of the information typically included in a PSI is already known to the sentencing panel. Sentencing panels are juries that have heard the case and are typically composed of three professional judges and nine laypersons. Such juries or panels are only used when the penalty for the crime for which the defendant is being tried is 10 years or more (Service Public Française, 2015). PSIs are not necessary because the investigatory process in France is more thorough than in the Anglo-American common-law tradition. And because a French trial is more a review of the facts than a fact-finding process, much more is known about the character of the defendant and all of the relevant personal information regarding his or her background (Walsh & Hemmens, 2016). There are also no sentencing guidelines other than the statutory penalties attached to the crimes, leaving judges with excessive discretion that can lead to serious inequalities in sentencing (Padfield, 2011).

COMMUNITY CORRECTIONS IN FRANCE

In common with almost all Western nations, the French experienced large increases in crime from the late 1960s to the mid-1990s. This led to an increased concern with crime and public safety, as evidenced by the 1999 consolidation of institutional and community correctional systems under the umbrella of the *Services Penitentiaires d'Insertion et de Probation* (SPIPS—Prison and Probation Services), as was done in England and Wales (Herzog-Evans, 2011a). As in the U.K., this change was justified in terms of maintaining offender supervision from prison to release in the community and consolidating correctional administration under one roof.

Probation was not introduced into the French criminal justice system until 1946. Initially, probation services were limited to released prisoners (parolees) and were not extended to offenders on suspended sentences until 1958 (Herzog-Evans, 2011a). In the early years of probation in France, probation services were social-work oriented, with an emphasis on working with offenders' families. After consolidation and in common with England and Wales, the social-work emphasis was abandoned, and probation decrees have "systematically deleted the term 'social worker' from all the rules appertaining to probation within the Criminal Code" (Herzog-Evans, 2011a, p. 347).

Martine Herzog-Evans has few positive things to say about the French probation service. As is the case in the U.S. and the U.K., large caseloads are largely to blame for what she sees as low officer morale and a general sense of ineffectiveness. A problem not encountered in the U.S. and the U.K., however, is the apparent sense of indifference and semi-disengagement that Hertzog-Evans (2011b) documents. She says that the French have never developed a research tradition analogous to the West's "What Works?" tradition to provide them with practical guidelines and tools. Neither do French probation officers have training in risk and needs assessment. Reasons Herzog-Evans (2011a) gives for this include French culture's preference for poetic and philosophical, as opposed to scientific, thinking and its general Anglophobia, along with a protective attitude toward the French language "that leads to a refusal to read, quote, or work in English" (p. 349).

In another research article on offender desistence, Herzog-Evans (2011b) writes that "French probation services have a good idea what it takes to desist, but have neither the capacity nor the will to effectively help offenders do so" (p. 29). Interviews of a variety of judges, probation officials, and line officers across France showed an overall cynicism about probationers and rehabilitation. They see probationers (and the term includes what we would call parolees in the U.S.) as individuals from dysfunctional single-parent families and as unintelligent and lazy people who will not change unless they want to. Herzog-Evans (2011b) concludes that French probation officers want to help their charges desist from crime, but they mostly wait for offenders "to make the turning point decision to change; only then did they seem to believe they may be successful in working with them" (p. 42).

PRISONS IN FRANCE

There are four main types of prisons in France. The most secure is the *maison centrale* (central house), which is the equivalent to the British Category A prison. The next is the *centre de detention* (detention center), housing both medium- and minimum-risk offenders. The *centre de semi-liberte* (semirelease center) and *centre pour peines amenagees* (temporary detention centers) enable prisoners to maintain their employment outside of the facility and are analogous to American work release centers. Finally, there is the *masison d'arret*, which is the equivalent of an American jail or British remand center.

Kazemian and Andersson (2012) give French prisons a glowing report. They note that the inmate-to-staff ratio in a *maison centrale* can be as low as one to one and note that correctional officers complete 8 months of full-time training for their jobs, compared with an American average of 8 weeks. It was also noted that in some detention centers in which long-term prisoners not considered dangerous are held, meaningful work is sometimes available, for which the inmate can earn up to €1,000 (about $1,120 in late 2016) per month. The most progressive practice noted by Kazemian and Andersson (2012) is the use of *unites de vie familiale* (family life units). These units are small apartments within

PHOTO 20.2: French gendarme stand in front of the entrance of the Fleury-Merogis prison near Paris on April 27, 2016, after the arrival of a police convoy believed to be carrying Salah Abdeslam, possibly the sole survivor among a group of Islamist militants who killed 130 people in Paris in November.

the correctional facility where inmates (especially long-term inmates) can spend up to 72 hours with spouses and children in private. This allows married inmates to remain connected with their families and is designed to make the transition back into society easier.

In stark contrast to Kazemian and Andersson's (2012) glowing evaluation of French prison practices, we have the following from the European human rights commissioner, reported in *The Economist*:

> For years outsiders have pointed fingers at the deteriorating state of France's 194 prisons. In a 2006 report the Council of Europe's human-rights commissioner, Alvaro Gil-Robles, said that "some things I saw during my visit were deeply distressing and shocking." He pointed to chronic overcrowding, unsanitary cells, dirty lavatories, broken showers and mattresses on the ground. He described conditions in two prisons, La Santé in Paris and Les Baumettes in Marseilles, as "on the borderline of human dignity." ("French Prisons," 2009, n.p.)

Kazemian and Andersson also report no overcrowding conditions in French prisons, but the human rights commissioner noted that the number of inmates has jumped by 30% since 2000 to over 63,000, against a stated prison capacity of 51,000. In 2013, French prisons were suffering a crisis in overcrowding and, in 2010, recorded 15.5 suicides per 10,000 inmates, the highest in Western Europe (Hamel, 2013). Much of the increase in the French prison population has come from a tough-on-crime movement similar to that in the United States and the United Kingdom ("French Prisons," 2009).

There is an absence of a body of French prison law built on a series of cases comparable to the U.S. cases outlined in Chapter 18 (Mansuy, 2005). The French have a distrust of judicial review, viewing it as an inherently antidemocratic intrusion into the business of an elected legislature (Walsh & Hemmens, 2016). Until 2008, there was a very limited form of judicial review in France exercised by the *Conseil Constitutionnel*. This body is, strictly speaking, an advisory council rather than a court. It does not hear appeals from lower courts; rather, the Conseil reviews *proposed* legislation for its constitutionality and then only on referral from the president and other high-ranking government officials. Once a law is passed, it can only be rescinded by legislative action, not by any court.

However, in 2008, the *Conseil d'État* (council of the state), the legal advisor to the executive branch of the French government and the supreme court for matters of administrative justice, ruled the end of the "no-rights" era (similar to the American hands-off period), signaling a greater legal concern for prisoners' rights (Chantraine, 2010). The proposal opens the possibility of constitutional review of a law or practice after it is in place, which also opens up the possibility of a set of judicial precedents on issues such as prisoners' rights. In the first case heard by the Conseil Constitutionnel on prisoners' rights, it ruled a law regarding pretrial detainment was unconstitutional (Creelman, 2010).

Being part of the EU, the French prison system is held to the same standards we mentioned when discussing the British system. The French organization charged with monitoring French jails and prisons is the *Observatoire International des Prisons* (OIP). The OIP informs us that, also in common with the British, the French have a prison-overcrowding problem due to tough-on-crime policies. Despite the same level of judicial oversight as prisons have in the United States, the French judiciary appears to have a concern for prisoners' rights that is difficult for the average American to comprehend. Indicative of this, a recent court decision ruled that an inmate fired from her prison job had been subject to unfair dismissal and awarded her a compensation package that included a paid holiday entitlement, back pay, and €3000 ($4050) in punitive damages (Myles, 2013). French law provides for an hourly rate for prison work of between 20% and 45% of the minimum wage.

●●● CHINA AND THE SOCIALIST-LAW SYSTEM

China is an authoritarian socialist state governed by a single political party: the Communist Party of China. China operates under socialist law, a system that originated in 1917 with the Russian Revolution and the establishment of the Union of Soviet Socialist Republics (USSR) in 1922. After the collapse of the USSR, Russia and its former Eastern European satellites abandoned socialist law for civil-law systems, but variants of it remain in North Korea, Vietnam, and Cuba, as well as in China. Socialist law, in general, operates as a low-tolerance crime control model. The socialist attitude toward crime is exemplified by Marxist statistician Karl Pearson's forthright statement (as cited in Walsh, 2009):

AP Video 20.2: China Human Rights

> The legislation or measures of police, to be taken against the immoral and antisocial minority, will form the political realization of Socialism. Socialists have to inculcate that spirit which would give offenders against the State short shrift and the nearest lamp-post. Every citizen must learn to say with Louis XIV, *L'etat c'est moi!* ["I am the state!"]. (pp. 244–245)

This illiberal position stems from the socialist idea that individual rights and procedural protections against state power are meaningful only if the state and the individual are distinct entities at odds with one another. In a socialist society, the state and the laws that support it are supposed to "wither away," and whatever would be construed as the "state" thereafter would become one with and inseparable from the individual, which is what is meant by the French phrase, *"L'etat c'est moi"* ("I am the state"). Thus, offenders would not be in need of procedural protections and would simply be led to "the nearest lamp-post" and executed.

The Chinese criminal justice system has both inquisitorial and adversarial aspects, but its emphasis is squarely on the inquisitorial process. Until recently, the Chinese system did not operate under the presumption of innocence, and the burden of proof rested squarely on the accused. Under codes enacted in 1996, there is an assumption of innocence, but

China still stresses confession, contrition, and eventual reintegration of the defendant back into the community (Liu, Zhao, Xiong, & Gong, 2012). Chinese police place such emphasis on confession that they do not allow defendants to know what evidence is to be presented against them because such disclosure would taint the voluntary nature of a confession. If defendants were to confess guilt being aware of the evidence against them (as in an American plea bargain negotiation), they would merely be acknowledging the obvious, and remorse would be hard to gauge (Reichel, 2005).

SENTENCING IN CHINA

Audio 20.1:
China Sentences
Professor
Accused of
Separatist
Activities

Upon conviction in China, the person may be sentenced to death, life imprisonment, fixed-term imprisonment, criminal detention, public surveillance, or probation. The sentence may also be supplemented by fines, confiscation of property, and deprivation of political rights (Shaw, 2010). As opposed to many Western nations, where about of 70% of offenders are on probation or parole, in China, about 82% of offenders are incarcerated (Liu et al., 2012). Penal sanctions in China are characterized by the use of "reeducation" and forced-labor camps, with the stated function of resocializing inmates to rid them of "politically incorrect" thoughts and behaviors.

Until relatively recently, there was a lack of transparency in the sentencing process. There was no body of law outlining defendants' rights, and judges had virtually unlimited discretion (Chen, 2010). As in France, when a defendant is found guilty, he or she is simultaneously sentenced as part of the same process, without the aid of a presentence investigation. As Chen (2010) puts it, "Judges rarely discuss ways to individuate punishment for a particular defendant, so sentencing usually takes place in a vacuum without meaningful input from prosecutor, defendant, or defense lawyer" (p. 214). The Chinese devised experimental sentencing guidelines in 2008, and in 2010, the courts adopted them on a trial basis for 15 criminal offenses. According to an article the *South China Morning Post*, the guidelines "appear to be producing greater consistency in major cities and towns, although the position in the provinces and outlying areas is less clear" ("New Legal Guidelines," 2013, n.p.).

To understand Chinese punishment practices, we need to understand China's history of Confucianism, as well as the influences of socialist law in China. Confucius (551–479 BC) was a moral philosopher who taught that self-refinement leads to a harmonious society. Confucianism stresses the cultivation of morality through respect for elders, strong family ties, and strict adherence to the golden rule. Confucianism has a quasi-religious quality that has greatly influenced Chinese culture and has provided a social code that has been taught in homes and schools for centuries (Yun, 2008). The impact of Confucianism over the centuries is part of the reason that China is a highly collectivist or communitarian country, whereas countries such as the United States and the U.K. are individualist countries. Collectivism and individualism are reflected in the correctional policies of countries characterized by one or the other philosophy. Xin Ren (1997) informs us that when comparing the Western and Chinese systems of social control,

> the most important distinction, perhaps, is the efforts of the Chinese state to control both the behavior and the minds of the people. Social conformity in the Chinese vocabulary is not limited to behavioral conformity with the rule of law but always moralistically identifies with the officially endorsed beliefs of social standards and behavioral norms. (p. 6)

CHINESE COMMUNITY CORRECTIONS

China did not have anything that Westerners would recognize as a community corrections system until 2003, and these programs still lack designated state funding, relying instead on local community contributions (Jaing et al., 2014). China's official criminal justice policy is "Integration of Leniency and Rigidity" (Liu et al., 2012). China's promiscuous use of the death penalty (discussed later) and its low rate of use of community

PHOTO 20.3: A guard walks outside the main entrance to the number one Detention Center during a government guided tour in Beijing. The facility, which has capacity for 1,000 inmates, was opened to the foreign media as Beijing prepared for the 18th Congress of the Communist Party of China.

corrections point to the rigidity of its application of sanctions, but where is the leniency? Putting aside the point that leniency is open to wide interpretation, leniency is considered to reside in probation and public surveillance.

Probation is only granted to first-time minor offenders in China. The Chinese Criminal Code states that

> probation may be granted to a criminal sentenced to criminal detention or to fixed-term imprisonment of not more than three years if, according to the circumstances of his crime and his demonstration of repentance, imposing probation will not result in further harm to society. (in Tursun, 2010, p. 288)

Probation is typically granted for juvenile delinquency, dereliction of duty, and crimes of negligence; it cannot be applied to recidivists for any crime and is only granted in about 15% of cases (Liu et al., 2012). Chinese probation is viewed by many observers as the application of reintegrative shaming, whereby deviant acts are condemned (shaming) while leaving the door open to reacceptance into society upon payment of one's debt to it (Deng, Zhang, & Cordilia, 1998).

Probation is not strictly a formal legal sanction, as it is in the United States and other Western countries; it is more an informal means of social control, although the offender is placed under the supervision of a probation officer (Tursun, 2010). Because of China's Confucian heritage, there has been a long tradition of informal social control via sanctioning mechanisms available to **people's mediation committees** that are organized in work and neighborhood groups (Fairchild & Dammer, 2001). Every adult in China belongs to one or more of these groups, and thus, strong pressures toward conformity exist everywhere. Criminal behavior on the part of anyone in the community is seen as a bad reflection on the whole community and is intolerable to mediation committees.

Public surveillance is a sanction similar to probation but further requires that offenders be deprived of the freedom of speech, assembly, association, and demonstration "without

People's mediation committees: An informal Chinese social-control mechanism using the power of the community to sanction bad behavior.

Public surveillance: A form of sanction used in China. It is similar to probation but further requires that offenders be deprived of the freedom of speech, assembly, association, and demonstration without the approval of the authorities.

the approval of the organ executing public surveillance" (Tursun, 2010, p. 290). As Shaw (2010) describes surveillance of parolees, "In local communities, individual administration of justice stations work with street, village, and other satellite government offices, keeping an inescapable net of surveillance, education, assistance, discipline, and control over former inmates" (p. 65). If a person under public surveillance is deemed to be acting in a manner inconsistent with socialist principles, he or she is reported to the police and may then likely be imprisoned. The level of supervision and assistance afforded Chinese parolees is in stark contrast to the minimal supervision and assistance provided by correctional services in Western nations. This has to be viewed in light of Western individualism and its concomitant concerns for privacy and individual rights. China doubtless has lower crime rates than most Western societies, but it is bought at prices Western nations are not willing to pay.

Parole officially exists in Chinese law for offenders who have completed at least one half of their sentences but not in quite the same sense as it exists in the United States. Each year, only a few dozen are released from prison before the termination of their sentences and then mostly for medical reasons. According to Jaing et al. (2014), an average of just under 2% of criminals were paroled between 2008 and 2010. Offenders convicted of murder, rape, robbery, kidnapping, arson, drug dealing, organized violence, or those sentenced to more than 10 years are not eligible for parole (most of these offenders would have been executed), which leave very few offenders eligible for parole. In medical parole cases, offenders are considered on probation and can be returned if or when their medical condition is resolved. For instance, in 1984, a 21-year-old youth was sentenced to death for stealing a cap and public brawling, but later resentenced to life. He was medically paroled with a form of tuberculosis, and fully recovered. In 2004, the police turned up on his doorstep and took him back into custody to serve the remainder of his sentence although he never stopped reporting to his probation officer and complied with all parole conditions ("Case for Freeing," 2011).

CHINESE PRISONS

Confucius taught that people are born good and if they commit evil acts they can redeem themselves by showing genuine remorse (hence the emphasis on confessions and the practice of withholding evidence of a suspect's guilt from him or her) and then go about rehabilitating themselves through hard labor and self-contemplation. Thus, Deng et al. (1998) inform us that: "According to official correctional policy, Chinese prisons are conceived of as places to reeducate and reform people" (p. 284). The belief that the mind can be exercised by labor leads naturally to a situation where "all convicts of life or fixed-term imprisonment are required to work, making labor the bulk of the daily routine" (Shaw, 2010, p. 62). Denyer and Wan (2013) tell of the harsh conditions inmates face in these camps such as sleep deprivation, freezing temperatures, beatings, poor food, and fast pace and long days in prison fields and factories (prisons are designed to be self-financed). Prison conditions are "harsh and degrading;" human rights abuses include extrajudicial killings, torture and coerced confessions of prisoners, and the use of forced prison labor. According to Death Penalty Worldwide (2014),

> Death row prisoners are shackled and handcuffed while they await appeal, sometimes even during interviews with their attorneys, despite the international prohibition on leg-irons and chains…[and] are kept shackled and chained 24 hours a day, including during meals, visits to the toilet, and at all other times.
>
> The UN Special Rapporteur on Torture has observed that the continuous restraint of all death row prisoners by shackling and chaining amounts to infliction of additional punishment (beyond the death penalty) without justification, thus constituting torture. (n.p.)

How well does "reform through labor" work in terms of preventing recidivism in China? A large national study that followed 159,177 released prisoners over a three-year period found a recidivism rate (defined a new arrest for a punishable crime within three years after release) of 8.2% (Deng et al., 1998). This is very low compared with estimates of around 67% after three years for American parolees (M. Robinson, 2005). It is worth recalling here that the father of parole, Alexander Maconochie (see Chapter 12), also advocated honest labor as a way to "teach virtue," and that he claimed a 2.2% recidivism rate.

If we compare who is imprisoned in China with who is imprisoned in the United States, this dramatic difference in recidivism rates may be understandable. Given China's high rate of executions and low levels of tolerance for deviance, perhaps its prisoners are far less criminally involved than is the typical U.S. prisoner. On the other hand, Shaw (2010) cites an official Chinese document claiming 600 on-duty deaths of prison police (correctional officers) between 1994 and 2008. Asking various individuals in China to comment on the report, Shaw received a variety of replies ranging from it reflecting poorly on reform-through-labor programs to cynical dismissals as propaganda designed to cover up something else.

THE DEATH PENALTY IN CHINA

One of the reasons we see few chronic criminals in China is China's frequent use of the death penalty, a penalty that is particularly likely to be imposed on recidivists. China is the world's leader in the number of executions each year. The death penalty may be applied for 55 different offenses (down from 68 prior to 2011), including murder, rape, economic crimes committed by high-level officials, counterrevolutionary offenses, and hooliganism, which includes such offenses such as physical and sexual assault and indecent exposure (Liu et al., 2012). According to the Chinese human rights organization, Dui Hua (2013), there were at least 5,000 executions in China in 2009, but because the actual number is a state secret, it could be many more. The 5,000 figure is still 96 times more executions than occurred in the United States (52) in the same year (Stohr & Walsh, 2012).

Adjusting for population size, the Chinese rate of execution per 100,000 citizens is about 30 times greater than in the United States. Amnesty International (2012) writes that

> thousands of people were executed in China in 2011, more than the rest of the world put together. Figures on the death penalty are a state secret. Amnesty International has stopped publishing figures it collects from public sources in China as these are likely to grossly underestimate the true number. (n.p.)

There are two types of death sentence: immediate and delayed. A delayed sentence is a two-year suspension of sentence during which defendants must show that they are reformed. If a person is considered rehabilitated, the sentence is usually changed to a long period of incarceration; if not, he or she is executed. An immediate sentence is carried out within seven days of imposition of the penalty. Such a sentence is imposed when, in the court's opinion, the defendant is beyond rehabilitation. Execution was traditionally carried out by a single shot at the base of the skull but more recently by lethal injection (Dui Hua, 2013). The Chinese government claims that this switch in execution methods was motivated by humanitarian concerns. Others claim the motivation was economic. Because of the highly profitable organs-for-transplant industry in China, many bodily organs are "harvested" from executed inmates. According to the Death Penalty Worldwide (2014),

> China profits from its executions—65% of organ transplants originating from China are harvested from executed prisoners. Human rights organization Dui Hua speculates that the shift from firing squad execution to lethal injection may have been motivated by the ability to better preserve criminals' organs through lethal injection.

Elsewhere, the organization states,

> The cost of a single dose of lethal injection is cheaper. . . . Scholars point to this factor, profit, ease of secrecy, and reduction of family complaints (due to massive disfiguration caused by shots to the back of the condemned's head) as factors motivating the switchover to lethal injection, which has progressed at a slow pace. (n.p.)

••• SAUDI ARABIA AND THE ISLAMIC-LAW SYSTEM

Saudi Arabia is an authoritarian absolute monarchy that follows Islamic law, which originates in the Muslim holy book the Qur'an (Koran). In Saudi Arabia, the Qur'an functions as a constitution, and what emerges from the Qur'an and scholarly commentaries on it is called **shari'a**, "the path to follow." Shari'a law is extremely strict and rigid and informs all aspects of Saudi correctional practice, practices that make China's benign by comparison. Saudi law is a hybrid of the inquisitorial and adversarial systems, with strong emphasis on the former. Although the system contains very few procedural rules, suspects have the right to confront their accusers and are assumed innocent until proven guilty. Criminal court proceedings in Saudi Arabia are very informal. The judge (or *khadi*) makes decisions based entirely on his own interpretation of the facts and the testimony before him (it is always a *him*) and on the principles of Islamic justice as he sees them, being neither bound by precedent or by the decisions of higher courts. Thus, the Saudi legal system is not truly a code system in the sense that the French system is. Judges in civil-law systems are bound to strictly adhere to the code. Nor is it analogous to judicial law in common-law systems. The khadi's ruling is not bound by precedent from any other court, not even by his own prior rulings (Walsh & Hemmens, 2016).

In our discussion of Saudi Arabia, we cannot follow our system of discussing institutional corrections, followed by community corrections, because scholarly works on Saudi prisons do not exist, and there is no community correctional system there, as Westerners understand it, because there is no provision for such systems under shari'a. The U.K.-based organization Amnesty International is the primary source of much of our knowledge about Saudi prisons and the treatment of inmates. Based on the stories of former inmates, Amnesty International often reports arbitrary arrests, torture, and inhumane conditions inside Saudi prisons (Alahmed, 2013). The Saudi government provides information about its prison system that speaks broadly of rehabilitation and the humane conditions that exist inside it (Ministry of Interior, Kingdom of Saudi Arabia, 2011), but everything human rights groups tell us belies these self-serving government claims. Death Penalty Worldwide (2011) writes,

> The U.S. Department of State reports that in general, prison conditions in Saudi Arabia are below international standards, with particularly poor conditions prevalent in women's prisons. Overcrowding is a problem, with domestic human rights organizations reporting overcrowding so severe as to require prisoners to sleep in shifts. Inmates have died of tuberculosis and suffered from preventable infectious diseases. (n.p.)

Shari'a: Literally means "the path to follow." Shari'a law is extremely strict and rigid and informs all aspects of Saudi life, including its correctional practices.

Prison sentences are not the normal recourse in the country because of the extensive use of corporal punishment in Saudi Arabia. However, individuals are imprisoned awaiting trial, and many people are held for years for such offenses as mocking Islam, making politically incorrect statements, drug usage, suspicion of homosexuality, and any number of other offenses. As we see from Figure 20.3, despite its widespread use of corporal punishment, Saudi Arabia has a rate of imprisonment higher than China, France, and the U.K.

PHOTO 20.4: Dira Square in Riyadh, the capital city of Saudi Arabia, is the site of public amputations and beheadings. It has been macabrely nicknamed "Chop-Chop Square" by foreign residents.

SAUDI PUNISHMENTS

Unlike other legal systems that categorize the seriousness of crimes and the punishments they entail by the severity of the damage they cause to the victim and/or to society, Islamic law characterizes offenses by the types of punishment they engender. If a punishment is prescribed by the Qur'an, it tends to be more severe than if it is not, regardless of the seriousness of the crime as Westerners might view it. The following is part of a publication called *Information Pack for British Prisoners in Saudi Arabia* that the British embassy in Saudi Arabia issues to British nationals arrested there. It is a publication informing prisoners what the British government can and cannot do for them and how to apply for a transfer to a British prison. The cited part deals with the punishment individuals may expect if convicted:

> Criminal law punishments in Saudi Arabia include public beheading, stoning, amputation and lashing. . . . The Saudi courts impose a number of severe physical punishments. The death penalty can be imposed for a wide range of offences including murder, rape, armed robbery, repeated drug use, apostasy, adultery, witchcraft and sorcery and can be carried out by beheading with a sword, stoning or firing squad, followed by crucifixion. (British Foreign Office, 2015, p. 11)

Punishment for so-called *huddud* crimes are specified by the Qur'an and cannot be changed by mere mortals. *Huddud* crimes are the most serious crimes in Islamic law. These crimes and their penalties (in parentheses) are adultery (death); fornication (whipping—80 lashes); false accusation of any of the foregoing crimes (whipping—100 lashes); alcohol consumption (whipping—varies; death is possible after a third offense); apostasy—conversion from Islam to some other faith (death); theft (amputation of hand); and robbery (amputation of alternate-side hand and foot).

Audio 20.2: Saudi Arabia Executes Dozens, Exacerbating Sectarian Tensions

ETHICAL ISSUE 20.2   ?

What Would You Do?

You are a high-ranking diplomat at the U.S. Embassy in Saudi Arabia and also gay. You receive a call from a worker at a U.S. company operating in Saudi Arabia who informs you that a fellow American worker, Jack, was arrested by the Saudi religious police for using Twitter on three occasions to arrange dates with other men. Depending on the judge and on the moral climate of the moment, Jack can be sentenced to anything ranging from 80 lashes to the death penalty. The caller asks you to intercede on Jack's behalf. It is the duty of the embassy to offer aid and comfort to U.S. citizens arrested in foreign lands, and you are a strong advocate of gay rights, although you know there are no such rights in Saudi Arabia.

You confer with the ambassador, no friend of gays himself, who tells you that people in a foreign land have an obligation to know and abide by its rules, and that it's a matter of the old saying, "When in Rome, do as the Romans do." However, you consider all possible punishments that Jack may face barbaric and contact Saudi authorities. You are told that the punishment would be "minor" (80 lashes) because Jack was caught simply soliciting gay sex rather than engaging in it, but you continue to object, antagonizing the Saudis. Do you risk an incident between the United States and Saudi Arabia by publicizing Jack's plight (and jeopardize your own career, given the ambassador's attitude), or do you leave Jack to his fate?

Interestingly, murder, the most serious crime in all non-Islamic countries, is not considered a *huddud* crime because it is not recorded in the Qur'an as such. It is a *quesas* crime, which means "equal harm" or "retaliation" and, in principle, means an eye for an eye and a tooth for a tooth. *Quesas* crimes are crimes against individuals rather than against God. Thus, although death is prescribed for murder (equal harm), the crime may be forgiven in exchange for *diyya* ("blood money") paid to the victim's survivors. The *diyya* for killing a Muslim male is 300,000 riyals (about $80,000) for accidental deaths and 400,000 riyals ($106,600) for purposeful murder. Consistent with the Islamic principle that a woman is worth only one half of a man, the *diyya* for killing a Muslim woman is one half that of a man. The *diyya* for killing non-Muslims depends on the victim's religion ("Saudi Arabia Triples Blood Money," 2011).

A particularly gruesome example of blood money is that of a prominent Saudi cleric, Fayhan al-Ghamdi, who confessed to brutally raping and torturing his 5-year-old daughter to death. He was arrested in November 2012 and was set for release from prison in February 2013, upon paying the equivalent of $50,000 in blood money to the girl's mother (al-Ghamdi's ex-wife). Upon releasing al-Ghamdi, the judge reportedly said, "Blood money and the time the defendant had served in prison since Lama's [his daughter and victim] death suffices as punishment" (Hall, 2013, n.p.). However, because of the general public outrage over his light sentence for such a heinous crime, the Saudi royal court intervened to block his release, and he was retained in prison for further consideration of his sentence. Under Saudi law, a father cannot be executed for murdering his children (Hall, 2013). In October 2013, al-Ghamdi was resentenced to 8 years imprisonment and 800 lashes (Toumi, 2013).

The least serious crimes under Islamic law are called *ta'azir* (discretionary or "deterrence") crimes, which include consumption of pork, bribery, provocative dress, wifely disobedience, and traffic offenses. (Women are never guilty of traffic offenses in Saudi Arabia because women are not allowed to drive.) However, some *ta'azir* crimes are very serious, and many even carry the death penalty. This strange situation, whereby something as innocuous as consuming pork and drug trafficking are thrown into a single category, exists in order for the state or individual judges to get the sentence they desire for the defendant, which is not possible with *huddud* or *quesas* crimes. Punishments for *huddud* crimes are prescribed by the Qur'an and thus inviolable, and we have seen that the death sentence for a *quesas* murder depends on the discretion of a victim's family, which may "pardon" the offender for blood money. Some *ta'azir* crimes, such as sorcery, heresy, or "spying for infidels," carry the death penalty, as does drug smuggling and terrorism. Because there is little uniformity in Islamic law, judges even have discretion to ignore the *huddud/ta'azir* distinction in order to impose a harsher sentence. Peiffer (2005) points to one case of robbery, for which amputation is prescribed as a *huddud* punishment, but the judge sentenced two people to death by treating the robbery as a *ta'azir* crime, even though no one was hurt, and the money was returned.

Saudi Arabia shares China's voracious appetite for the death penalty. Saudi Arabia "officially" executed 82 people (it is suspected that there are many secret executions also) in 2012—a rate of 3.15 per million inhabitants (Amnesty International, 2013a). To put this in perspective, the United States executed 43 people in 2012—a rate of 0.139 per million. Thus, Saudi Arabia's rate of execution is at least 23 times higher than the U.S. rate. Even this high rate may be a gross underestimate because Alahmed (2013) reports that

> hundreds of people are executed in Saudi Arabia every year—because some executions are carried out in secret, no one knows the real numbers. In 2007, the newspaper *Arab News* reported that 400 people remained on death row in the province of Makka alone. There are 12 other regions in the kingdom, so the total number of people awaiting execution could easily reach several thousand. (n.p.)

After a sentence is passed by the *Musta'galah* (ordinary courts) for *ta'azir* crimes or *Kubra* (high courts) for *huddud or quesas* crimes, the appeals process may come into play. A major function of appeals courts in other legal traditions is to try to ensure uniformity of the law, but because legal uniformity is not a concern in the Islamic tradition, in Saudi Arabia, these courts exist only to hear appeals against sentences imposed by lower courts. Such appeals, heard by panels of three to five judges, are particularly likely to occur for sentences of death, stoning, or amputation (Walsh & Hemmens, 2016). These appeals courts exist only to determine if verdicts have been rendered in conformity with shari'a, and because shari'a is based on the word of God as written in the Qur'an, the final word as to correct interpretation rests in the hands of religious authorities rather than secular judges.

POLICY AND RESEARCH

Is the United States Hard or Soft on Crime?

Correctional policy is broadly made by national governments. In the United States, it is made by a variety of federal and state statutes, in accordance with the U.S. Constitution. In the U.K. and France, correctional policy is made by their respective parliaments, and its legality is determined by the U.K. Supreme Court or the French Conseil Constitutionnel, respectively.

From a Western perspective, Chinese and Saudi policy seem to be based on whim. In China, all policy is subservient to the Communist Party and in Saudi Arabia to each individual judge's interpretation the Qur'an. If we define hardness or softness in terms of incarceration rates, Figure 20.3 conveys the impression that United States is tough on crime. The closest any Western nation comes to the U.S. rate is England and Wales, with a rate almost 5 times lower. If we define hardness or softness in terms of alternative punishments or the conditions of confinement, then the United States is "soft" on crime relative to many countries. Although China is shown as having an incarceration rate more than 6 times

lower than the U.S. rate, its execution rate is at least 25 times higher. Punishment in Saudi Arabia includes barbaric corporal punishments for offenses considered relatively minor—or not offenses at all—in the West.

If we look for "softness" in criminal sanctions, we should look no further than the Scandinavian countries. Tapio Lappi-Seppälä (2009) reports that the most severe sentence in Denmark, Finland, and Sweden is a life sentence, which means, in practice, a prison term of around 15 years. Norway has abolished life sentences and replaced them with a 21-year maximum term. The maximum term of imprisonment for a single offense (including murder) in Denmark is 16 years. In Finland, it's 12 years, and in Sweden, it's 10 years. Anders Breivik, convicted of killing 77 people in a bombing and shooting attack in July 2011, was sentenced to 21 years in prison, which is the maximum available and which amounts to fewer than four months per victim (Lewis & Lyall, 2012). We can image the outrage that such a sentence would generate in the United States.

(Continued)

(Continued)

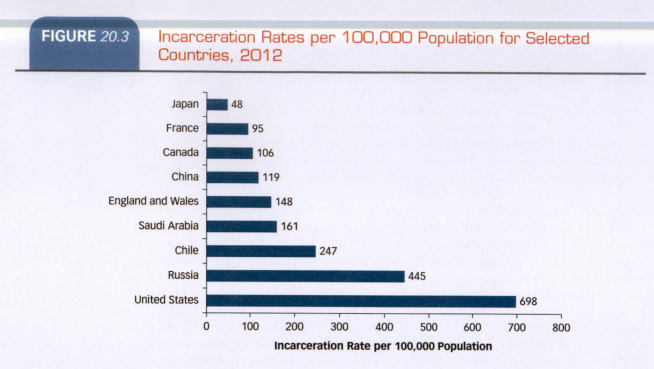

FIGURE *20.3*   Incarceration Rates per 100,000 Population for Selected Countries, 2012

Source: Constructed from figures provided by Walmsley (2015). World Prison Population List.

The issue of whether the United States is soft or hard on crime thus depends on how we conceptualize and measure the concepts of hardness and softness and with which countries we compare ourselves. Compared with countries that share our democratic ideals, we are tough on crime; compared with countries most distant from Anglo-American ideals, we are soft, and for that, we should be grateful.

DISCUSSION QUESTIONS

1. What is your personal opinion about the hardness or softness of the U.S. criminal justice system?

2. Should the United States move more toward the average sentences for burglars, or is our sentencing too lenient?

3. Do you think American public opinion would tolerate the 21-year prison sentence that Breivik received for killing 77 people more than the swift execution of murderers (assuming an American-style trial and conviction) practiced in China?

References

Lappi-Seppälä, T. (2009). Imprisonment and penal policy in Finland. *Scandinavian Studies in Law*, *54*, 333–380. Retrieved from http://www.scandinavianlaw.se/pdf/54-17.pdf

Lewis, M., & Lyall, S. (2012, August 24). Norway mass killer gets the maximum: 21 years. *New York Times*. Retrieved from http://www.nytimes.com/2012/08/25/world/europe/anders-behring-breivik-murder-trial.html

SUMMARY

- The importance of exposure to other systems of corrections (or anything else for that matter) is that it helps us to better understand our own. We looked at countries that represent the four legal traditions in the world today: the United Kingdom (common law), France (civil law), China (socialist law), and Saudi Arabia (Islamic law).

- The United Kingdom is a democratic country operating with a common-law system. It experienced a high rate of criminal activity in the early 1990s and responded by imposing more and longer prison sentences. As in the United States, this response was followed by a sharp drop in crime rates. As part of its "get-tough" policy, the U.K. has consolidated prison and probation and parole services and no longer requires its POs to have social-work credentials. The U.K. prison system receives a lot of criticism in Britain for the alleged "cushiness" of its prisons and the ineffectiveness of probation services.

- France is a democratic country that operates under a civil-law system that balances the rights of the accused with the rights of the community. It also experienced rising crime rates in the 1990s and responded similarly to the U.S. and U.K. by instituting tougher policies, such as combining prison and probation services and eliminating the social-work emphasis in probation. American researchers have positive things to say about French prisons, but European researchers are less than happy with them.

- China is a single-party authoritarian country that operates with a socialist-law system, which is clearly crime control oriented. China's long history of conforming to Confucian teachings, coupled with communism's desire to eliminate individualism, makes it a very collectivist or communitarian society, with strong pressures for conformity. Individuals who breach those pressures are subjected to harsh punishments, including the death penalty and long periods in prison with hard labor. The goal of Chinese corrections is rehabilitation through hard labor and thought control. China is, by far, the world's leader in the number of people it executes.

- Saudi Arabia is an authoritarian absolute monarchy with a criminal justice system based on Islamic law. It is very much a crime control–oriented society that applies medieval punishments to criminals for crimes not considered as such by Westerners, such as religious conversion from Islam, sorcery, adultery, and consuming alcohol. Most of what we know about Saudi prisons comes from ex-inmates, and there is no such thing as a probation service. Punishments typically involve lashing, amputation of limbs, or beheading for so-called *huddud* crimes. "Lesser" crimes (even murder) can be forgiven with the payment of blood money.

KEY TERMS

National Offender Management Services (NOMS) 491

People's mediation committees 503

Public surveillance 503

Shari'a 506

DISCUSSION QUESTIONS

1. Why is a comparative perspective useful?

2. Do you believe that the U.K.'s greater use of imprisonment is responsible for a large part of its recent reduction in crime rates, or is something else at work?

3. Keeping in mind that both the U.K. and France are unitary countries rather than federated states, as in the United States, is their consolidation of prison and probation and parole under one administrative roof a good idea? Why, or why not?

4. Both the U.K. and France have turned away from their former social-work orientation to probation and toward a more law enforcement orientation; is this a good or bad idea?

5. Do you think something like the Chinese people's mediation committees could work in the United States?

6. Saudi Arabia has a very low rate of common street crime. A conviction for robbery carries a sentence of having alternate-side amputations of a hand and a foot. Would you agree to the implementation for American armed robbers if it meant reducing robbery and the trauma and threat of death that comes with it by 90%?

USEFUL INTERNET SITES

Please note the sites listed can be accessed at edge.sagepub.com/stohrcorrections.

U.K. Ministry of Justice: www.justice.gov.uk

This is the official website of the government of the U.K. providing information of all aspects of the British criminal justice system.

The French Legal System: www.justice.gouv.fr/art_pix/french_legal_system.pdf

This is the English version of the official website of the government of the France providing information of all aspects of the French criminal justice system.

U.K. Crown Prosecution Service: www.cps.gov.uk/about/cjs.html

This website from The British Crown Prosecution Service provides much information about all aspects of the U.K. criminal justice system.

Facts and Details—Justice System in China: factsanddetails.com/china/cat8/sub50/item299.html

An excellent nonpartisan view of the Chinese criminal justice system.

Amnesty International—Annual Report on Saudi Arabia, 2015/2016: https://www.amnesty.org/en/countries/middle-east-and-north-africa/saudi-arabia/report-saudi-arabia

Because Chinese and Saudi official government documents are highly suspect, the Amnesty International website is the best source of information on these countries.

⑤SAGE edge™

Sharpen your skills with SAGE edge at **edge.sagepub.com/stohrcorrections**. SAGE edge for Students provides a personalized approach to help you accomplish your coursework goals in an easy-to-use learning environment. You'll find action plans, mobile-friendly eFlashcards, and quizzes as well as video, web, and resources and links to SAGE journal articles to support and expand on the concepts presented in this chapter.

Corrections in the 21st Century

TEST YOUR KNOWLEDGE

Test your present knowledge about the likely future of corrections in this country by addressing the following questions. Check your answers on page 540 after reading the chapter.

1. Based on the chapters you have already read in this book, what do you think are likely to be trends in corrections in the next several years?

2. Decarceration is likely related to state budgets. (True or false)

3. Privatization of corrections leads to greater professionalism of staff. (True or false)

4. Privatization of corrections leads to more safety and security for inmates, staff, and communities. (True or false)

5. Correctional work is fully professionalized. (True or false)

6. Resource use and waste production by correctional institutions should be a serious concern for communities. (True or false)

LEARNING OBJECTIVES

1. Identify the connection between punitive policies and the overuse of corrections

2. Describe what decarceration is and what is causing it

3. Understand why we might be entering an age of penal help and exiting a period of penal harm

4. Evaluate the value of relationships and innovation in corrections

5. Discuss the potential problems with privatization

CAN WE CURE CRIMINALITY?

Alex DeLarge is the product of a society in which no one takes personal responsibility for his or her actions and a culture that panders to our basest human instincts. He is the leader of a gang that is into what they call "ultraviolence," with strong sexual undertones. Alex engages in all kinds of crime, especially sadomasochistic rape. Betrayed by his associates, he was eventually caught by police after raping and murdering a woman. Two years into his sentence for murder, Alex volunteered as a test subject for an experimental treatment based on aversion therapy. Alex was given drugs and forced to watch violent images while becoming nauseated by the drugs. After two weeks of "therapy," Alex became incapable of fighting back against a man who attacked him. The mere thought of violence and sex now made him retch violently. He was then released from prison as "successfully cured" in order to reduce the financial burden of imprisonment. Only when he finally freely chooses to desist from crime does he do so.

Some of you may recognize that this is the storyline of the dystopian futuristic novel A Clockwork Orange.

The book is about efforts to "cure" criminality and its ultimate failure, since Alex reverted to his former self after the "cure" wore off. Another book (this time based on a futuristic utopian society) called Walden Two *contains a similar theme. One of the characters in the book explains the goal of such a society: "You see, we want to do something—we want to find out what's the matter with people, why they can't live together without fighting all the time. We want to find out what people really want, what they need in order to be happy, and how they can get it without stealing it from somebody else" (Skinner, 1948/2005, p. 4). Efforts to "do something" this time were based on the principles of behaviorist psychology, principally on positive reinforcement, instead of aversion therapy.*

Both books resonate with the perpetual problem of corrections: effectively identifying and treating the sources of criminality. We still need to "allot a portion of ground for a prison," as Nathaniel Hawthorne predicted in the opening vignette in Chapter 1. The financial cost of prisons is prohibitive, but we will always need them, barring some "miracle cure" awaiting us in the distant future. The great physicist Niels Bohr once said, "Prediction is very difficult, especially about the future," so we do not speculate about that here. And as Bill Clinton said in his successful campaign for the presidency, "It's the economy, stupid." Economic considerations will always drive corrections policy, as they always have. We enact mandatory sentencing laws that imprison people who perhaps should not

have been when state budgets allow and then release prisoners early who should not have been when state coffers are low. This generates public anger as their tormentors are released, and thus, renewed calls to "get tough" are generated, and the whole process recycles. Perhaps legalizing drugs and saving the prisons for folks like Alex is the only solution at present. These are some of the things to think about as you read this last chapter.

●●● INTRODUCTION: LEARNING FROM THE PAST SO THAT WE HAVE HOPE FOR THE FUTURE

Video 21.1: The Future of Corrections

Americans have a tendency to revisit old themes, efforts, and programming every generation or so, even when such endeavors were clear failures and rejected by generations past. Perhaps it is because we are a relatively new nation and are seemingly remade as new generations of immigrants flood our shores, bringing their histories and cultures that do not include memories of past reform efforts made in this country. Perhaps we keep retrying old endeavors because of the media influence that reduces very complex problems to a brief and simplistic message, and as a consequence, we do not understand that despite the fancy packaging and marketing, we have been there and done that before. Or maybe it is hand-in-glove collusion by the media and politicians in this reductionism of complex topics and collective memory loss.

Whatever the reason, we do not seem to learn much from the experience of those who have come before us, at least as that is related to correctional practice. Or more accurately, we certainly could learn more from our past than we have! It is an oft-cited truism, courtesy of the philosopher Santayana, and as already mentioned in this book, that those who do not know their history are doomed to repeat it. This adage bears repeating, as it clearly applies here, regarding correctional programs, operations, and practices.

In this chapter, we try to prognosticate about what we expect to happen in the world of corrections in the not-too-distant future. Not surprisingly, some of our best estimates in that regard are based on our recent past. So for instance, if decarceration is a recent trend, we would have to expect it might be a continuing trend. Therefore, we will explore some of these current and, we expect, future trends in corrections—some that have been mentioned before in this book and are only highlighted again here and others that are brand new.

●●● PUNITIVE POLICIES YIELD OVERUSE OF CORRECTIONS

To illustrate this point about the importance of history, all we need to do is consider the efforts of the last two decades that are declining in popularity—namely, the drug war, mandatory sentencing, supermax prisons, and the abandonment of treatment programming. Spurred by punitive sentiments that swept the political, social, and economic systems, the statutes, declarations, and practices that derived from these efforts profoundly changed corrections as Americans experienced it (Cullen, Jonson, & Stohr, 2014; Whitman, 2003).

First, they vastly increased the use of all forms of corrections in this country. Our imprisonment rate (just for prisons, not including jails) was stabilized at about 125 persons per

100,000 residents for 50 years (1920 to 1970) until the drug war, mandatory sentences, and other punitive policies increased it (Ruddell, 2004). At the end of 2009, this number had risen to 502 persons per 100,000 residents, or over 4 times the imprisonment rate of that 50-year period. In raw numbers, the offenders sentenced to prison increased by over 500%, from 319,598 in 1980 to 1,613,740 in 2009 (West, Sabol, & Greenman, 2010, p. 1). Notably, the number of people held in prison had decreased by 2013 to 1,574,700, but this still yielded a roughly 492% increase from 1980 to 2013 (Carson, 2014, p. 2).

A comparable steady and swift increase in the use of jails has occurred since punitive policies have been put in place: In 1986, the incarceration rate for jails in the United States was 108 persons per 100,000 residents, and by 2009, it was 250, or almost a 250% increase in the use of jails in more recent years, though it had decreased to 234 by 2014 (Minton, 2010, p. 4, Minton & Zeng, 2015, p. 1). Put another way, the number of persons incarcerated in America's jails more than quadrupled, or increased by 405%, from 183,988 in 1980 to 744,600 in 2014 (Minton & Zeng, 2015, p. 2).

Similarly astounding increases can be found in the use of probation and parole because of punitive practices. From 1980 to 2009, the number of people on probation more than tripled, with an increase of 376% (1,118,097 in 1980 to 4,203,967 in 2009) (Glaze, Bonczar, & Zhang, 2010, p. 2), though it decreases to 345% when the 1980 and 2014 figures for probation (3,864,100) are compared (Kaeble, Maruschak, & Bonczar, 2015, p. 2). Likewise, the number of persons on parole almost quadrupled during this time period (from 220,438 in 1980 to 856,900 in 2014), as most people in prisons and jails do eventually return to their communities (Bonczar, Kaeble, & Maruschak, 2016, p. 2). In sum, what all of these numbers and Figure 21.1 indicate is that because of punitive policies, the use of corrections—prisons, jails, and community corrections—has increased by almost unimaginable numbers from a generation ago, and though it is no longer increasing as much, it is not decreasing by much yet either.

FIGURE *21.1*   Total Adult Correctional Population, 1980–2014

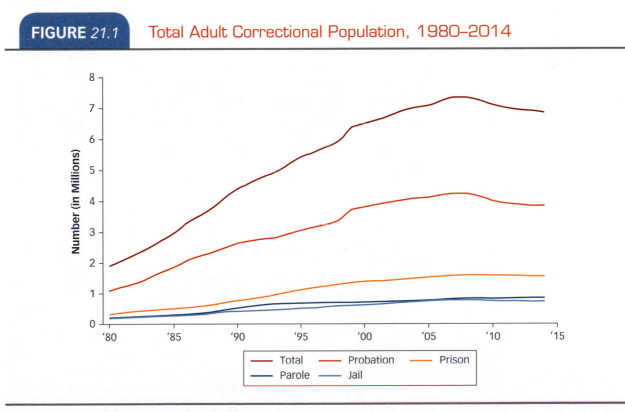

Source: Kaeble, Glaze, Tsoutis, and Minton (2016).

FIGURE *21.2* Violent and Property Victimization, 1993–2014

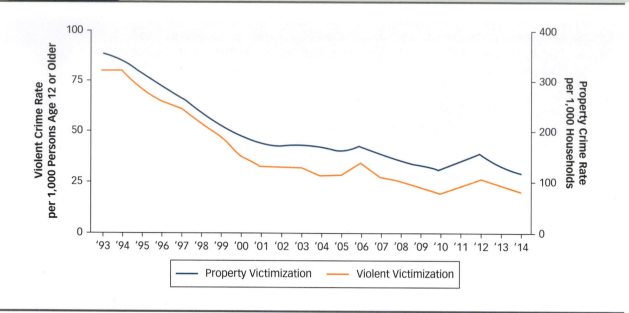

Source: Truman and Langton (2015, p. 1).

Yet, as best we can tell (and as was mentioned in Chapter 1), we do not have proportionately more crime these days than at any other period in our history (see Figure 21.2). In fact, based on victimization and police reports, it appears that by 2014, we had the lowest rate of victimization since the National Crime Victimization Survey began in 1973. As indicated in Figures 21.1 and 21.2, crime, even violent crime, has been decreasing at the same time as use of corrections has been increasing.

In addition, our use of corrections is not in sync with what other countries are doing. We have similar crime rates (Farrington, Langan, & Tonry, 2004), yet our incarceration rate (by 2012) was more than 14 times that of Japan; 5 to 7 times that of France, Canada, China, and England and Wales; and 3 to 4 times that of Saudi Arabia and Chile (Walmsley, 2013). Russia is the only other developed nation that gets close to our incarceration rate, and the United States still outpaces that nation, with 1.5 times their incarceration rate.

Second, interestingly enough, these punitive policies have not had the effect of increasing sentencing length. The average sentence to prison in state courts in 1992 was 6.5 years, as compared with 5.5 years in 2009 (Bonczar, 2011, p. 1). It is not clear why sentencing length has decreased at the same time that more punitive policies are in effect. It is possible that decreased sentence length might be one of those unintended consequences of the overuse of incarceration. The capacity of prisons and jails, along with probation and parole caseloads, has been vastly increased over the last 20 years, but it may not have increased enough to accommodate the numbers of processed felons in the courts. What this means is that courts are forced to adjust their sentences to the lower relative capacity of prisons, and parole boards are pressured to release inmates as prisons and jails fill up.

Third, punitive policies, as was discussed in other chapters, have led to an explosion in the number of women and minority group members who are incarcerated or under some form of correctional supervision (Bureau of Justice Statistics, 2006; Carson, 2015; Irwin, 2005; Pollock, 2004). Until the current version of the drug war was resurrected—yes, there were others in American history (Abadinsky, 1993)—the proportion of women to men and racial and ethnic minorities to whites in prisons, in jails, and on parole and probation was somewhat stable (Bureau of Justice Statistics, 2006).

PHOTO 21.1: The number of persons incarcerated in America's jails more than quadrupled, or increased by 405%, from 183,988 in 1980 to 744,600 in 2014.

Fourth, such policies have favored the use of more isolation, "punishment," and warehousing to deal with both bulging correctional populations and recalcitrant inmates. The number of supermax facilities has exploded, as has the number of supermax inmates, as management of the number of inmates turned to favoring punishment and warehousing over treatment (Irwin, 2005).

As a result of such policies, a fifth outcome has been the abandonment of a core principle of some correctional institutions and practices (e.g., probation, parole, minimum-security institutions, and work releases)—namely, treatment—based on insufficient evidence. Some correctional programs and institutions were formulated on the premise that treatment is a major goal of corrections. Though the public has continued to believe this (Applegate, Cullen, & Fisher, 2001), for all intents and purposes, real efforts at treatment—beyond basic Alcoholics Anonymous, Narcotics Anonymous, religious groups, and GED programs—in prisons, jails, and community corrections received little funding and virtually disappeared for 20 years in many places (from the mid-1970s to the mid-1990s).

Though some of these endeavors and efforts, such as the drug war and mandatory sentencing, continue and even grow in some communities, for the most part, scholars and some policy makers have deemed the former a failure and the latter a spectacular waste of money. Furthermore, though the number of supermaxes has grown in the recent past, there is not nearly the hype about their promise for eliciting inmate reform. Finally, all indications are that the belief in and embrace of treatment programming, albeit programs that can demonstrate their worth, is on the upswing, both in correctional institutions and in communities. Although all of these changes in attitudes and perceptions are positive, it is frustrating to realize that we knew—or should have known from our own past—that drug wars, mandatory sentencing, isolation, and pure punishment in the form of warehousing are not likely to reduce crime in this country, let alone reform those under correctional control. The long and the short of it is that we should have known better because it had all been done before.

••• DECARCERATION

 Web 21.1: Using the Federal Budget to Fuel Decarceration

As indicated in the foregoing, the numbers of persons incarcerated in jails and prisons and supervised in community corrections has been declining recently. By 2014, we had seen seven years of declines of about 1.0% per year, with many of the declines being in probation populations, but for five of those years, there were either decreases in incarceration at the state or federal level or only relatively small increases (Kaeble, Glaze, Tsoutis, & Minton, 2016, p. 2). These declines were generally at the state level, but there have been recent decreases at the federal level. In most states, by 2014, a greater proportion of their correctional population was on community supervision than had been true previously. As indicated by the data contained in Figure 21.3, from 2000 to 2014, there was a decline in the number of people on probation and decreases in the numbers of people in jails and prisons, though the steepest decline was in probation populations (Kaeble et al., 2016). But these decreases in correctional populations came in the second half of that time period (from 2007 to 2014), as from 2000 to 2007, there were just increases. Parole populations have been the exception to these decreases in correctional populations; they only increased from 2000 to 2014. These more recent decreases (and increases in parole) have not been uniform across the states or by region (Glaze & Herberman, 2013). In only three northeastern states—New York, New Jersey, and Maryland—were these declines a discernable trend over the last decade, though in Illinois, Michigan, Delaware, and Texas, the 2009 declines were preceded by anemic growth rates earlier in the decade (West et al., 2010). Nor have all states experienced such declines. The difference about the time period we are in, however, is that for the first time in a long time, we are seeing some steady, if not dramatic, declines in the use of corrections.

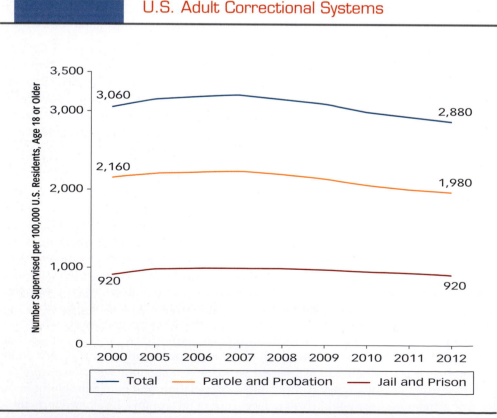

FIGURE 21.3 Rate of Persons Supervised by U.S. Adult Correctional Systems

Source: Kaeble et al. (2016, p. 2).

EXPLANATIONS FOR THE DECLINE IN THE USE OF CORRECTIONS

What might these declines in the use of corrections be attributed to? Is it possible that declining crime, particularly violent crime, has actually begun to affect the use of prisons in some states? Is it possible that enforcement of the drug war has waned as states have legalized medical marijuana—four states (Alaska, Colorado, Oregon, and Washington State) and the District of Columbia had legalized recreational marijuana by August 2016—and the drug hype tied to criminality (e.g., the hysteria over crack mothers producing crack babies) has receded in the minds of the public, politicians, and criminal justice practitioners? Is it possible, in the case of the northeastern states, that declines are tied to reduced state populations, particularly of young people, who are most engaged in street crimes? Could it be that the reduced use of incarceration for some of these states is a consequence of the recession that hit the United States in 2007 and the consequent declining tax revenues and increasing debts faced by states and localities that can no longer afford the bill for spiraling imprisonment?

We think it is possible that all of these scenarios have some value in explaining the decreased use of incarceration in some states in the last few years and for a few states for the last several years. We know that overall, the number of admissions and parole violators returned to state prisons declined in 2010, signaling a change in the number of people before the courts, a change in sentencing by court actors, a change in parole agents' behavior, or some combination of these (West et al., 2010).

We also know that about 60% of inmates in state prisons these days are violent offenders, perhaps signaling greater attention to them rather than to drug offenders (West et al., 2010, p. 7). Finally, we know that despite their greater contribution to the composition of prisons, these violent offenders were actually "doing" less time. In 2000, the mean length of stay for violent offenders was 46 months, but by 2008, this mean had declined to 44 months—a seemingly small effect, but when multiplied by hundreds of thousands of people, this lower mean can have a huge impact on some prison systems (West et al., 2010, p. 8). Reduced length of stay may be related to the effect of declining state revenues on state prisons.

THE RECESSION, COST CUTTING, AND THE DECREASED USE OF CORRECTIONS

In 2009, the Pew Center on the States published a report subtitled *The Long Reach of American Corrections* in which the authors make the case that "more prison spending brings lower public safety returns" (Saylor & Iwaszko, 2009, p. 17). They argue that over the last 20 years, we have incarcerated too many first-time and nonviolent offenders who never needed to be incarcerated. Doing so has cost us billions of dollars, with no collateral decrease in crime, as most of these people would either not reoffend or could have been handled in a much less expensive and intrusive way in the community. Moreover, the more we incarcerate, the less we achieve the ideal of incarcerating the serious repeat offenders (as there are far fewer of these); the more the lower-level offenders are "replaced," leading to greater involvement of more people in crime; and the less likely we are to deter current criminals, as the research does not show that longer sentences deter more effectively. Though Saylor and Iwaszko (2009) acknowledge that the huge incarceration increase was likely responsible for somewhere between 10% and 35% of the decrease in violent crime since the mid-1990s (depending on which researcher you listen to and which model and assumptions he or she adopts), the authors note that most of the drop in crime was likely attributable to factors outside of incarceration. It makes no sense financially, then, they argue, to continue to incarcerate low-level, aging, and less criminogenic offenders.

There are some recent examples from the news that indicate that some states and localities came to the same conclusion. Washington State, for instance, in April 2011, closed the 135-year-old McNeil Island Prison because of the need to cut that state's budget (the cut was projected to save the state $12.7 million) (Mulick, 2010, p. 1). Likewise, for the first time in state history, Oregon, in October 2010, closed a minimum-security facility for the same reason (the cut was projected to save the state $33.8 million) (Zaitz, 2010, p. 1). In both the Washington and Oregon instances, department of corrections officials claimed that none of the inmates would be released early because of the closures.

In another example from Washington State, this time involving a county jail and its finances (Thurston County), the county manager declined to open the newly built, $45-million facility, at least for a year, because the county could not afford to staff it or pay for its operation (Hulings, 2010, p. A4). In addition, the county manager noted that the new jail was not needed as much because of the declining jail population in the county, which happened after the jail's construction had begun.

These examples from Washington and Oregon came at a time when those states were still grappling with the Great Recession, but Texas closed three prisons between 2010 and 2014 and decided to invest some of the savings in treatment programming, both in prisons and in communities (Kruger, 2014, p. 1). Florida and New York were closing prisons in 2014 and 2015 and turning those vacant facilities into homeless shelters or reentry centers (Couch, 2015, p. 1). The rationale for these closures is not cost cutting to deal with the recession but just cost cutting in general and the belief that locking up low-level offenders does not result in less crime. Such a shift in perspective has led to changes in sentencing and, consequently, fewer inmates to fill prison beds in many states and localities.

And notably, as a phenomenon, this decreased use of incarceration appears to have some international legs. In Germany, the Netherlands, and Sweden, the number of inmates in prisons is decreasing. In Germany and the Netherlands, those decreases have been 20% and 36%, respectively (Zachariadis, 2013, p. 1). In Sweden, four prisons were closed in 2012, resulting in a 6% drop in inmates in 1 year alone. Instead of prison time, these countries are using fines or probation. When in prison, inmates have much more liberal visitation policies, have more freedom to move around within the prison, and are rarely sentenced to solitary confinement.

© iStockphoto.com/Jesse Karjalainen

PHOTO 21.2: An empty hallway in a prison cell block.

Moreover, in a report by the Sentencing Project (Porter, 2016, p. 1), the author revealed that in 2015, 30 states continued the trend of reforming sentencing policies and reducing the use of imprisonment. In the past, such policy changes have included medical-marijuana laws, reduced penalties for drug and property offenses, increased parole eligibility and reduced revocations, "ban the box" laws that delay questions regarding the criminal history of an applicant until he or she is interviewed, and modified policies regarding juveniles to reduce their incarceration and the severity of it (Porter, 2011, p. 3). Porter (2011) notes that developing alternatives to prison contributed to a 20% drop in incarceration from 1999 to 2009 in both New York and New Jersey. She argues that though several of these changes in state policies were done to reduce current and future budgets, they were also adopted because policy makers were no longer convinced of the efficacy of mass incarceration as a public-safety measure. In fact, in three states that cut their incarceration rate by more than the national average—New York and New Jersey (between 2009 and 2012) again but also California (between 2006 and 2012)—their violent-crime rate dropped by more than the national average (Mauer, 2014, p. 2).

Will decarceration continue? That is anybody's guess, but a betting man or woman might increase his or her odds by considering the recent attempts to reduce correctional populations at the local, state, and federal levels and then note the national mood, which has turned against the overuse of corrections. Another indication of the national mood is the consideration, at the time of this writing in August 2016, of a bill called the Sentencing Reform and Corrections Act of 2015 (S. 2123) by the U.S. Senate. The effect of this bill, should it become law, would be to retroactively reduce harsh drug sentences at the federal level. The effect on corrections would be to accelerate the reduction in correctional populations at the federal level. Should this happen, maybe then we really could talk about mass *de*carceration, at least at the federal level.

IMPLICATIONS OF DECARCERATION AND THE NEED FOR A PLAN OF ACTION

Should these early indications of decarceration turn into a flood of releases—dare we say *mass decarceration*—there will be many positive outcomes, such as less incarceration of low-level offenders, resulting in a greater sense of justice for community members; less incarceration of minority men and women, also resulting in a greater sense of justice for all; fewer tax dollars being devoted to incarcerating people; a reduction in the growth of the corrections–industrial complex, at least at the institution level (see a discussion of the complex later in this chapter); and more opportunities for people to age out of crime and contribute in a meaningful way to their communities. However, there are likely some negative outcomes that will result from decarceration, such as greater unemployment, more low-level crime, and increased use of drugs and alcohol by ex-inmates, which could occur if policy makers and correctional officials do not plan appropriately. There are also likely to be those working in corrections who oppose the closure of correctional institutions and programming, as it will threaten their livelihoods (Garland et al., 2014). Clearly, money will be saved through decarceration, but some of these monies will likely be needed to fund reentry programs in corrections and work and training programs for the decarcerated in communities, along with the expansion of drug and alcohol treatment in communities so that decarcerated people have the opportunity to rebuild their lives.

PENAL HELP VERSUS PENAL HARM

Another explanation for the decreased use of incarceration may be the increased use of treatment programming that addresses the appropriate risk, needs, and responsivity levels and types of offenders. As indicated in other chapters, there is a well-established science behind some of the best-formulated and best-implemented programs. There is evidence that these programs may be effectuating a decrease in criminal engagement, further convincing correctional managers that expenditures on programming may be a better bet for reducing crime and costs than the building of more institutions.

Some scholars have argued that this move to treatment over punishment may portend a move away from the **penal harm** movement of the last several decades to an age of reform embodied by the term **penal help** (Stohr, Jonson, & Cullen, 2014). The reform of state laws to liberalize marijuana use, the repeal of harsh sentences, and the reduction in the use of incarceration and correctional supervision generally, coupled with the increase in the use of rehabilitation, restorative justice, and reentry programming, all signal a sea change in the nature of the justice system and in corrections in particular. Taken together, they indicate that there has been a societal shift toward penal help over penal harm (Mauer, 2014; Pollock, Hogan, Lambert, Ross, & Sundt, 2012; Stohr et al., 2014; Tucker, 2014).

••• PROFESSIONALIZATION AND INNOVATION

As we look to the future, there are a number of problems, in addition to the amount of incarceration, that should preoccupy those of us concerned about correctional practice. One issue that affects almost all areas of practice is that of professionalism. As indicated in other chapters in this book, the effort to professionalize corrections has not yet yielded consistent fruit around the country. Some correctional institutions and programs have moved to enforce professional standards for their new hires, such as required college-level educational background, sufficient training, and pay that is commensurate with job requirements. However, most correctional organizations, perhaps primarily because of a lack of resources, have failed to move in a similar direction.

Yet hiring and keeping a professional staff is key to moving correctional institutions into the 21st century; it is key to the appropriate delivery of those treatment programs that are now valued in this age of penal help. When the correctional practitioner does not have the kind of education that acquaints him or her with the history, background, concepts, and research regarding corrections, then the correctional organization is simply ill prepared to meet the challenges it faces. Moreover, when turnover is high because training and pay are insufficient, the organization becomes less stable and less equipped to problem solve regarding pressing concerns. Therefore, if we ever hope to move beyond the past and failed correctional endeavors and perspectives, the ranks of correctional practitioners need to be professionalized.

CORRECTIONS IS A RELATIONSHIP BUSINESS

The correctional experience for clients, offenders, or inmates and staff and the success of treatment and probation and parole programming all hinge on the relationships among the people in these organizations. It is often said that the greatest expense for any public-service organization is its staff. A collateral expense for correctional institutions and programs is the care of their inmates and/or clients. Notably, these expenses wax and wane, to some degree, based on the relationships among the actors. If those relationships are characterized by respect and concern among staff and respect and care (coupled with a healthy degree of control) between staff and clients or offenders, then there are less likely to be costly lawsuits, staff turnover, riots, and just general stress that produces discord in the workplace.

In his groundbreaking work on less explored and identified types of intelligence—emotional and social—Goleman (1995; 2006, p. 4) argues that scientific research on the brain indicates we are "wired to connect" to others, which means that every time we engage with other human beings, we affect and are affected by their thoughts and, consequently, their behavior. Those relationships that are the most prolonged and intense in our lifetimes are most likely to affect us, not just socially or emotionally but biologically.

Penal harm:
Movement in corrections based on retribution in sentencing and the infliction of greater harm while inmates are under correctional supervision.

Penal help:
Movement that includes the reform of state laws to liberalize marijuana use, the repeal of harsh sentences, and the reduction in the use of incarceration and correctional supervision generally, coupled with the increase in the use of rehabilitation, restorative justice, and reentry programming.

Photo by Benj Drummond and Sara Joy Steele

PHOTO 21.3: Inmate Liz Louie feeds a Taylor's checkerspot honey water from a Q-tip. Doing "green" work in a correctional setting has benefits for both inmates and correctional facilities.

To a surprising extent, then, our relationships mold not just our experience but also our biology. The brain-to-brain link allows our strongest relationships to shape us on matters as benign as whether we laugh at the same jokes or as profound as which genes are (or are not) activated in T cells, the immune system's foot soldiers in the constant battle against invading bacteria and viruses (Goleman, 2006, p. 5).

Goleman (2006) identifies a "double-edged sword" in relationships, in that those that are positive are healthful, but those that are negative can lead to stress, fear, frustration, anger, and despair, all emotions that can manifest themselves in physical ailments (p. 5). Of course, correctional environments are chock-full of stressed, fearful, frustrated, angry, and despairing people, and we are not just referring to the inmates here! So this means that unless correctional environments can foster some positive relationships between and among staff and clients or inmates, all will suffer psychologically and physically.

Recognition of the need to provide opportunities for inmates to "maturely cope" while under correctional supervision (as discussed in Chapter 9) would appear to be an acknowledgment that something positive can come out of the decent incapacitation of offenders. Moves to democratize workplaces and give people a voice and choice in their work (as discussed in Chapter 14) may serve to reduce some of the negative emotions associated with working in corrections. More recent attempts to "treat" rather than just "warehouse" inmates in institutions and offenders on probation and parole, or efforts at penal help, also represent a move to more positive relationships and so a better future for corrections. As indicated by the findings from the research presented in the preceding chapters on these matters, there is reason to believe that some treatment and supervision tactics can work to help offenders as they endeavor to deal with their substance and other abuse issues.

Video 21.2:
Sustainable
Practices Lab
Gives Back to
Community

GREEN PRISONS AND JAILS

An emerging issue in corrections is the idea of reducing the environmental impact of jails and prisons by reducing the consumption of resources and creating a healthier living spaces for inmates. Prisons and jails have been characterized as "environmental hogs" (Stohr & Wozniak, 2014). They are often huge buildings or sets of buildings with outsized electrical needs because of their 24/7 lighting and security systems. Their inmates

Video 21.3:
Sustainability in
Prisons

produce tons of waste in concentrated areas and, in turn, consume food, clothing, and numerous other products at levels that sometimes rival small cities. In recognition of these realities and, at times, in the name of cost cutting, some prisons and jails have turned to solar panels to supplement their energy sources and composting and gardening to increase soil health, reduce waste, and improve the diets of their inmates. Some prisons in Washington State have even begun programs that benefit other species (e.g., the Taylor's Checkerspot Butterfly Rearing Program at the Mission Creek Corrections Center, see http://sustainabilityinprisons.org/what-we-do/science/taylors-checkerspot-butterfly-program-2). It is thought that these **green prisons and jails** are likely to yield a number of benefits in the form of reduced costs, waste, and energy consumption and the improvement of the overall environment for the humans incarcerated in prisons and other species as well. An ancillary benefit may be the preparation of inmates for jobs in emerging green industries (Stohr & Wozniak, 2014).

••• PRIVATIZATION

THE PROFIT MOTIVE IN CORRECTIONS

Audio 21.1:
Why For-Profit
Prisons House
More Inmates of
Color

Video 21.4:
The Future of
Corrections

Privatization in corrections is not a new phenomenon. As was discussed in the first chapters of this book, transportation and the convict lease system were both based on privatization. The privatization of parts of prison operations (e.g., health care, food service, or work programs) continues in many public prisons. Since the 1980s, however, the number of completely private prisons has grown at both the state and federal level. Several of those prisons have experienced problems with escapes, violence, staff turnover, inexperienced staff and deficient staff training, and brutality and abuse by staff, along with inadequate physical facilities (Camp & Gaes, 2002).

In her 1973 book, *Kind and Usual Punishment: The Prison Business*, Jessica Mitford details the misuse of public monies for prisons; instead of improving the diets and opportunities of inmates after the Attica riot (causes of the riot), for instance, millions of dollars were used by prison officials in New York to purchase riot gear and technology, as well as to hire more staff. Her argument is that closed-off institutions, like prisons and jails, with their relatively powerless inmates, are particularly susceptible to graft and corruption of both the legal and the illegal sort. She notes that state legislatures are particularly susceptible to contributions by private entities that want to do business with corrections.

Green prisons and jails: Correctional facilities that seek to reduce waste and energy consumption and focus on providing a more healthful environment for their staff and inmates.

Privatization: Privatization in corrections occurs when services or whole correctional institutions are provided or operated by private businesses or corporations.

Corrections–industrial complex: The collusion among politicians, business, and criminal justice officials to make money for themselves and their organizations from correctional services, construction, and operations.

Forms of corruption and abuse of monies, of the illegal sort, are easy to spot, though not always stopped. Mitford (1973) complains, "Convicts will tell you about profitable deals made with local merchants for supplies in which the warden pockets a handsome rakeoff, unexplained shortages in the canteens, the disappearance of large quantities of food from the kitchen" (p. 172). It is the legally sanctioned graft in corrections, however, whereby money from state legislatures is intended for one type of purchase but is diverted to another—such as the hiring of more administrators rather than the provision of adequate food—that fascinated her and caused her to characterize the operation of public-sector corrections in this country in the 1970s as a "business." She charges that correctional institutions, in many states, were out to make a profit for administrators and their supporters (among vendors and state legislatures), not to attend to their core mission of holding people decently and securely while assisting them in their reform.

Over 40 years later, if anything, the operation of corrections in the United States has become even more businesslike, in the worst way, with some commentators characterizing the system as the **corrections–industrial complex** (Welch, 2005). In his last speech, President Eisenhower warned the nation about the development of the *military–industrial complex*, or the collusion among politicians, defense contractors, and leaders in the military regarding the value of war and military spending as a money-making and

PHOTO 21.4: A for-profit prison, operated by Corrections Corporation of America, houses men awaiting trial on immigration matters.

power-generating enterprise for all three (Mills, 1956). Similarly, Welch argues that corrections has become such an enterprise for state legislatures, governors, and city and town leaders (politicians), who receive contributions from prison and jail contractors, vendors, and private-prison corporations (businesses) and directors and secretaries of corrections, wardens, sheriffs, and probation and parole managers (criminal justice officials), who participate in contracting with businesses. The criminal justice officials contract with the private-sector businesses, not necessarily because they provide better services or even less expensive services than the public sector but because they are pressured to do so by the politicians who appoint or select and fund them, or they receive kickbacks themselves in terms of remuneration or jobs when they leave public service for the private sector.

IDAHO'S OWN PRIVATE PRISON

One of the largest private-prison corporations, the Corrections Corporation of America (CCA), with earnings of $1.7 billion in 2012, was voluntarily removed as the operator of a private medium-security prison that it had been operating near Boise, Idaho, since the 1990s (Boone, 2013a). The CCA made $29 million from this Idaho contract alone (Boone, 2013b). The CCA stands accused of defrauding taxpayers by severely understaffing positions that they were paid for and was under investigation by the Federal Bureau of Investigation for this and the level of violence at the prison. As a result, inmates claimed they are less safe. Counselors and case managers were used to fill security positions, thus making it difficult for them to help inmates with programming or reentry planning. The Idaho Department of Corrections reportedly knew of this understaffing for years because their own auditors reported on it. There were lawsuits from inmates claiming understaffing and excessive violence as a result. In fact, the Idaho Department of Corrections auditor found that the CCA prison had nearly 3 times the number of inmate-on-inmate assaults as other publicly operated prisons in the state. As a result of an inmate lawsuit regarding the staffing and violence brought by the ACLU, the CCA settled and promised more staff, and they reported that the mandatory staff positions were filled, but it turns out they were falsifying those documents, and those staff positions were vacant. The only way this problem came to light was that an Associated Press request for staffing

Audio 21.2: Who Benefits When a Private Prison Comes to Town?

AP Video 21.1: Idaho Prison Abuse

Career Video 21.1: Case Manager

POLICY AND RESEARCH

Privatization and the Walnut Grove Correctional Facility

The perfect example of how this kind of collusion among politicians, business, and criminal justice officials in this corrections–industrial complex can lead to gross injustices can be found in a small Mississippi town. One hour's drive east of Jackson, Mississippi, is the Walnut Grove Correctional Facility for boys and young men (they incarcerate up to age 22 to increase the number and, thus, the profit the private corporation can make) in the town of Walnut Grove. It is the largest juvenile prison in the country, housing 1,200 juveniles and young men. The state of Mississippi pays the private corporation GEO Group to operate the prison, which they do for a profit. Before August of 2010, the prison was operated by another private-prison corporation, Cornell Companies. (August was when GEO Group bought Cornell Companies and so acquired the contract to operate the Walnut Grove facility.)

In a two-part investigation of the Walnut Grove facility by National Public Radio (NPR), Burnett (2011) found that violence is set up and encouraged by the correctional officers. They also found that sexual abuse of the young male inmates by female officers is rife. In 2011, the prison was under investigation by the U.S. Department of Justice and was being sued on behalf of 13 inmates by the Southern Poverty Law Center (SPLC) and the American Civil Liberties Union (ACLU).

> "When we began investigating conditions inside this facility and seeing how these kids were living with the beat downs and the sexual abuse and violence and corruption, it became a no-brainer. It became something we had to do," said Sheila Bedi, the lead attorney on the case and deputy legal director for the SPLC. (Burnett, 2011, p. 1)

According to Burnett (2011), the crux of the problem at Walnut Grove is the correctional officers. There are too few of them, there is little supervision of them, some are gang members themselves, and others are inclined to abuse the inmates, either physically or sexually. The national average of officers to inmates for juveniles is 1 to 10, but the 2009 audit at Walnut Grove determined that the ratio was only 1 to 60 there. As staff are the most expensive item for any correctional entity to fund, cutting staff and their salaries is one way to assure profits for a money-making enterprise like this prison (the GEO Group is traded on the New York Stock Exchange and made $1 billion in 2010) (Burnett, 2011, p. 1). According to the audit done in 2009, "There were three inmate injuries a day. In the first six months of 2010 there was more than one fight a day, an assault on staff at least every other day and nine attempted suicides" (Burnett, 2011, p. 1).

NPR found, after a review of public records, that the warden and deputy wardens at Walnut Grove were receiving supplemental checks from the federal government for administering educational grants for the juveniles, in the amount of $2,500 to $5,000, when they were already paid by GEO (Burnett, 2011, p. 1). The town of Walnut Grove also "makes money" out of the existence and growth of the prison: The mayor of Walnut Grove claims that it funds the local police department. "'It's been a sweet deal for Walnut Grove,' Sims [the mayor] said. Indeed, every month, the prison pays the town $15,000 in lieu of taxes—which comprises nearly 15 percent of its annual budget" (Burnett, 2011, p. 1). In addition, a vending company owned by the mayor has 18 machines inside the prison. Moreover, the correctional authority that sends the Walnut Grove prison its grant money is given $4,500 per month by GEO. Left unexplored in the investigation is the question of why the Mississippi state legislature and governor's office authorized the private operation of Walnut Grove in the first place.

DISCUSSION QUESTIONS

1. Why do you think the Mississippi state legislature and governor's office authorized the private operation of Walnut Grove?

2. If you were governor of Mississippi, what would you do to reduce corruption and the abuse of office in such prisons as Walnut Grove?

and payroll information from CCA spurred them to confess the truth to the Idaho Department of Corrections. On Friday, January 3, 2014, Idaho governor Butch Otter, a big fan of prison privatization, someone who once suggested that more private-prison operators should be able to operate in Idaho, ended the contract with CCA, saying, "We had better hopes for outcomes in privatization" (Russell, 2014, p. B1). In May 2016, a federal appellate court upheld a contempt-of-court ruling against CCA, which means the company will have to pay "higher-than-normal" attorneys' fees to the American Civil Liberties Union for its defense of inmates who brought suit because of the falsified staffing reports by CCA (Boone, 2016, p. 3A).

THE EXTENT OF PRIVATIZATION AND ITS PROBLEMS

In a related report by an NPR reporter, it was noted that 8% of all inmates in prisons are held in private prisons, and in federal prisons, that proportion rises to 16% (Shahani, 2011, p. 1). As the recession deepened and as state budgets tightened from 2009 through 2011, the projection was for the use of private prisons to grow and for private corporations to diversify into the "alternatives-to-corrections" market. Though private prisons do not cost less to operate—in fact, they might be more expensive when all costs are accounted for, such as lawsuits and monitoring and assistance from publicly funded police and fire departments—they are easier and faster to build, as they do not require the authorization of bonds from state legislatures (Camp & Gaes, 2002; General Accounting Office, 1996).

In a study of private prisons at the state and federal level by Camp and Gaes (2002), the researchers, who were employees of the Federal Bureau of Prisons at the time, found that "the private sector experienced significant problems with staff turnover, escapes and drug use" (p. 427). For instance, in 1999, security-facility private prisons experienced 18 escapes, whereas, out of all of the Bureau of Prison facilities, a system that was larger than all of the private secure prisons combined, there was only one escape that year (p. 433). The researchers concluded, "The failures that produce escapes or illegal drug use can result from problems in policy and procedures, in technology, and in staff capabilities" (p. 445). As the two recent examples of private-prison failures provided in this chapter—the Walnut Grove Facility in Mississippi and the CCA prison in Idaho—would indicate, when profit competes with professional staffing and just operation of prisons and jails, profit considerations often win out, with dire consequences for inmates and staff in such facilities.

In a surprising reversal of a 30-year trend toward greater privatization of corrections and in recognition of the recent history of abuses and scandals involving private prisons, the Department of Justice released a statement in summer 2016 indicating that the federal government will begin the process of ending the use of private prisons, claiming they are both "less safe and effective" than public prisons (Zapotosky & Harlan, 2016, p. 1). However, the decision to use private prisons at the state level is not affected by this decision; it will only affect the federal use of private prisons.

ETHICAL ISSUE 21.1

What Would You Do?

You are an auditor for a state public-prison system, and it is your job to make sure that all of the prisons in that system, both public and private, are using state funds appropriately and operating as they should be. Your office has filed more than one negative audit report in your state on a private prison that appears to have an abnormally low staff-to-inmate ratio. In those reports, you have noted that this understaffing has likely contributed to the high number of inmate-on-inmate and inmate-on-staff assaults and the relatively high number of medical- and psychiatric-related complaints filed by inmates at this prison. Unfortunately, despite your arguments that the problems in your reports should be attended to, your supervisors have paid them little mind, as the political atmosphere in the state is very pro-privatization. You know that a lawsuit has been filed by staff at the prison alleging that the understaffing endangers both them and inmates, and the staff attorneys have contacted you, though they are unaware of the content of your audit reports. Should you talk to them? If so, what will you tell them? What do you think are the likely outcomes of your action?

AP Video 21.2: Stanford Latest

Journal Article 21.1: Prison Privatization

••• CONCLUDING THOUGHTS

Web 21.2:
A World Without
Prisons

It is a stunning realization that much of the future looks like the past, but it is true, in a way. Current trends in corrections mimic those themes we laid out in the early chapters of this book. However, as has been demonstrated by the research presented throughout this book, there is also great progress in refining how we handle correctional practice and programming.

There is little doubt that most correctional experiences for clients or inmates are not tinged with violence or brutality. The vast majority of correctional staff, whether in communities or institutions, act professionally, whether the attributes of their work fit that designation or not. Basic health care, clean housing, and nutritious food are provided to most incarcerated persons in the United States. Probation and parole officers do provide referrals to their clients, when time permits, and programs are available. Despite crowded caseloads, these officers usually make every effort to carefully watch the most dangerous of their charges. Jails, though often overcrowded or, at least, overused, are generally helpful at ensuring the safety of suicide-prone or mentally disturbed inmates or people detoxing from drug- or alcohol-induced highs. Jails may not represent the best places for such people, but they are usually safer than the streets and do provide a minimum of much-needed services for them. There is much more programming for those incarcerated in prisons and even jails and available to probationers and parolees than there was even 15 years ago, an indication that we have entered an age of penal help. In short, though we tend to repeat our past mistakes, there has been some learning from them as well, as that is manifested in improved correctional practice.

SUMMARY

- The current decarceration trend in some states and now at the federal level is also hopeful, in that prisons can then be reserved for the truly violent and serious offenders, with the effects of increasing public safety; reducing minority community disruption; making the system fairer and more just, as the punishments fit the crime; increasing the likelihood of successful reentry by offenders; and reducing the monetary costs of corrections for the public.

- A key component of this movement toward greater justice, if there is one, is the progress made in providing worthwhile treatment and programming— what might be termed the penal-help movement in corrections. Should correctional managers and policy makers continue to support and increase funding for such initiatives, we may witness a true age of reform in this generation.

- Other trends that might catch fire in the near future are a greater understanding of emotional intelligence as it influences corrections, more green initiatives in corrections as cost-cutting and environment-saving efforts, and a continued push to professionalize.

- Another currently popular movement— privatization—should give us pause, however. As a number of studies and infamous examples indicate, private prisons tend to have more problems in the decent incarceration of inmates and the level of professionalism of their staff. For these reasons and given the susceptibility of these institutions (and state legislatures and all political entities) to corruption and profiteering, privatization of whole institutions should be reconsidered.

- As the political winds shift away from purely punishment-oriented corrections, it will be interesting to see how correctional organizations, programs, and their actors will adjust in terms of privatization, professionalism, and decarceration.

KEY TERMS

Corrections–industrial complex 526

Green prisons and jails 526

Penal harm 524

Penal help 524

Privatization 526

DISCUSSION QUESTIONS

1. Discuss the evidence that indicates our correctional practices do not fit the amount of crime in the United States. Note how we compare with other countries in terms of the use of incarceration.

2. Review the attributes of a professional and why and how the presence of those characteristics would serve to "improve" correctional operation.

3. What problems do "get-tough" policies create for correctional operations? What benefits, if any, do they provide?

4. What is the connection between biology and environment in correctional operation? How do positive and negative environments affect the "biology" of those who work in corrections and those who are clients and inmates within and outside of them?

5. What are the indicators that a penal-help perspective may come to guide corrections in the future? What are the indicators that a penal-harm perspective is very much alive in present-day corrections?

6. Why do you think that private prisons have more problems with the operation of their facilities in terms of both inmate and staff management? Would you argue that we, as a country, should continue to authorize the construction and operation of private prisons and privatization in corrections? Why, or why not?

7. In your opinion, what current initiatives in corrections offer the most promise for the future? Support this opinion with research and readings provided in this chapter or in the rest of the text.

USEFUL INTERNET SITES

Please note that the sites listed can be accessed at edge.sagepub.com/stohrcorrections.

American Correctional Association: www.aca.org

The ACA is an organization that has, for 146 years, focused on professionalizing corrections in the United States. Their website and materials provide information on the latest training, research, and ideas in corrections.

American Jail Association: www.americanjail.org

The AJA is an organization that also focuses on professionalization in corrections but as it involves jails. Their website provides information about the latest training, trends, and research in jails.

American Probation and Parole Association: www.appa-net.org

The APPA is an organization that focuses on the professionalization of probation and parole or

community corrections. From their website, you can learn about the best research and training and the newest ideas about practices in community corrections.

Bureau of Justice Statistics: www.bjs.gov

The BJS provides an incredible wealth of information about all manner of criminal justice topics, including corrections. It is one of our go-to websites when we are investigating a correctional topic (or police or courts, etc.).

Vera Institute: www.vera.org

The Vera Institute has been behind some of the biggest criminal justice reforms of the last 40 years. Check out their website to learn what important reforms and issues are on the correctional horizon.

SAGE edge™

Sharpen your skills with SAGE edge at **edge.sagepub.com/stohrcorrections**. SAGE edge for Students provides a personalized approach to help you accomplish your coursework goals in an easy-to-use learning environment. You'll find action plans, mobile-friendly eFlashcards, and quizzes as well as video, web, and resources and links to SAGE journal articles to support and expand on the concepts presented in this chapter.

CHAPTER PRETEST ANSWERS

CHAPTER 1

1. True. We have seen that we justify punishment in terms of retribution, deterrence, incapacitation, rehabilitation, and reintegration.

2. False. The strongest deterrent against crime is the certainty of punishment.

3. False. While the severity of the crime is the most important consideration, the defendant's prior record and certain other consideration come into play.

4. True. The brain's pleasure centers light up when wrongdoers are punished, indicating that they have received a shot of rewarding dopamine.

5. True. Every legal system in the world assumes this.

6. True. Philosophies of punishment depend on concepts of human nature.

7. False. Specific deterrence rarely works, as recidivism rates aptly demonstrate.

8. True. The United States incarcerates people at a higher rate than any other country in the world.

CHAPTER 2

1. True. The themes include money; religion; labor; technology; architecture, as it is related to supervision; the intersection of class, race, age, and gender; and the overall movement toward greater humanity in the treatment of others in Westernized countries.

2. True. A victim with wealth and status could demand more punishment of the offender, and an offender with wealth and status was allowed to avoid the most severe punishments.

3. Jails. In one form or another, they exist once civilizations form.

4. True. The labor of galley slaves was no longer needed once sails were developed.

5. False. Transportation was a form of punishment and was used as a way of clearing urban streets of the poor and sending the convicted to the colonies for a period of involuntary servitude.

6. John Howard was known as an ex-sheriff who tried to reform gaols by ending the fee system in jails, calling for the separation of inmates by age and gender and arguing that inmates needed decent accommodations (food, water, clothing, and shelter) and something to do while incarcerated in gaols (jails).

7. False. The panopticon, which was developed by Bentham, combined what was then known about architecture to improve supervision.

8. True. He believed that minor offenses, in particular, should not be punished harshly. He substituted fines and jail time for corporal punishment.

CHAPTER 3

1. The main difference between the Pennsylvania and New York models for prisons was that in Pennsylvania inmates were required to be "silent and separate" from other inmates at all times, and in New York, inmates were required to be "silent and congregate," in that they could work together and do other activities together, but they must be silent. The New York model was mostly adopted in the United States because it allowed inmates to work together, and they were able to make more and thus offset the cost of incarceration more than inmates under the Pennsylvania model, who were laboring alone in their cells.

2. True. First built and operated as a jail, a section of the Walnut Street Jail in Philadelphia, Pennsylvania, was remodeled with individual cells for inmates, where they could do penance, and separated by gender and offense.

3. False. The Auburn Prison, whose cornerstone was laid in 1816 and which is still in operation today, was part of the New York system of "congregate but silent" prisons. Inmates worked together but were housed separately and were to maintain silence no matter whether together or apart.

4. True. This was done because some inmates were psychologically harmed by the complete separation and because inmates could produce more when they worked together.

5. False. Charles Dickens thought that keeping inmates completely separate from others created "morally unhealthy and diseased" human beings.

6. True. Because inmates could be together for work and sometimes for worship, though they had to be silent, it was difficult to always control them. Therefore, Auburn staff used the lash frequently, along with solitary confinement and marching in lockstep.

7. False. Dorothea Dix favored Eastern State Penitentiary (or the Pennsylvania system) over the New York system because of the separation that prevented contamination in the former type of prison. However, she found both types of prisons and most prisons to be understaffed and overcrowded, with inept leadership that turned over too quickly. She particularly disliked the overly harsh discipline (too much use of the lash) at the Auburn and Sing Sing prisons and the overly long sentences for relatively minor offenses that she observed in communities.

8. False. The 1870 Prison Congress was held because the promise of the early prison reformers had not been realized, and as a consequence, attendees of this congress called for another round of reform.

9. True. Inmates were rewarded with "marks" for good behavior, which entitled them to other privileges.

10. True. Correctional institutions are supposed to "correct" and therefore include some programming geared toward achieving that goal.

CHAPTER 4

1. False.

2. Deontological ethical systems are concerned with whether the act itself is good, and teleological ethical systems are focused on the consequences of the act.

3. True.

4. True.

5. True.

6. True. Noble-cause corruption is concerned with the end (serving the noble cause) over the means to get there. Correctional organizations tend to employ persons who are moved by the plight of the victims ("the smell of the victim's blood") and by the need to act to make the world right ("running to the tower").

7. False. Official deviance is unethical or illegal acts that are done to benefit the organization or organizational members, not the person committing the act.

8. True. The isolated, secretive nature of much of the work with clients who are powerless and workers who have a great deal of discretion makes correctional work more susceptible to ethical violations.

CHAPTER 5

1. False. Basic principles of justice mandate that the criminal justice system punish only similarly situated offenders (equals) with the same punishment.

2. False. Other things include prior record, gang affiliation, and treatment considerations.

3. True. Three-strikes laws are laws that do allow states to imprison a person who has been convicted of a third felony for life.

4. False. He or she may be sentenced to serve concurrent sentences.

5. False. Victims or survivors can have input into sentencing decisions in all 50 states, if they wish, in the form of a victim impact statement.

6. False. Judges receive guidance or advice in the form of PSIs written by probation officers and in the form of sentencing guidelines.

7. False. Most studies find that once legally relevant variables are taken into account, it is rarely found that minorities are subjected to discriminatory sentencing.

8. True. Separate courts do exist for criminals with special problems such as drug addiction.

9. False. Some states do, and some states do not.

CHAPTER 6

1. False. Most adult jails are operated by counties, though a few states and the federal government administer them as well.

2. True. Most jails for juveniles are referred to as detention centers, and some adult jails are called this, too.

3. False. About 60% of inmates in adult jails have not been convicted of a crime.

4. True. The drug war has netted more women and minority group members because the war has focused on low-level offenders (not the drug kingpins) and because it has focused on impoverished areas of cities that are disproportionately occupied by minorities.

5. True. Jails hold more of the mentally ill than other social institutions in this country because the mental-health hospitals have steadily decreased their populations over the last 40 years, leaving no place else for the police to take people.

6. False. Incarcerated women tend to have more medical problems than incarcerated men.

7. True. Female staff are more likely to be the perpetrators of sexual victimization of male inmates than are male staff. Notably, there are about 10 times more male inmates in jails than there are females, making it more likely that female staff will supervise male inmates than that male staff will supervise females.

CHAPTER 7

1. False. Problem-solving courts are designed to keep offenders in the community while addressing the problem(s) that may have led to their criminal behavior.

2. True. Problem-solving courts are treatment oriented and consist of a team of cooperative professionals (judges, attorneys, probation officers, and mental-health professionals).

3. False. Reduction in recidivism rates in all types of problem-solving courts tend to be greater than in traditional probation and treatment programs.

4. This depends on what we mean by *like*. No one likes others supervising and monitoring his or her life, but compared with traditional probation or parole, problem-solving court offenders do better and feel like the treatment team cares about them. Those who successfully complete programs are typically very positive about the experience.

5. True. Better-than-average treatment outcomes are perhaps primarily due to the informality and less adversarial methods mental-health courts display when compared with traditional criminal courts.

6. True. Most people arrested in major cities have one or more of the problems that are addressed in problem-solving courts, especially drug or alcohol problems, and many also have mental-health problems.

7. True and False. There are no "homeless courts" designed specifically to deal with this problem, but it is a major issue dealt with in all problem-solving courts.

8. False. Although problem-solving courts are more expensive than traditional probation or parole (about twice as high), this is offset by lower costs of further crime and victimization. One study of problem-solving courts in 29 jurisdictions found that problem-solving courts saved the taxpayer $5,680 per participant compared with control probationers.

9. False. Problem-solving courts for juveniles exist all across the United States.

CHAPTER 8

1. True. Probation did start in the 1800s in both the United States and the United Kingdom and was run by volunteers.

2. False. Most members of the public consider it "soft on crime" and "getting away with it."

3. False. Parole occurs after a period in prison and is a function of the executive branch of government; probation is in lieu of prison and is a function of the judicial branch.

4. True. As many as 90% of cases are granted probation as the result of plea bargaining.

5. True. Law enforcement–type officers achieve better results than social-work-type officers, but both do less well than "hybrid" officers, who know when to act like a cop and when to act like a counselor.

6. True. Work release programs perform both functions; they satisfy a punitive urge and control offenders' lives more strictly but allow them to maintain their employment, which is good both for the offender and the community.

7. False. Most hardened criminals would rather serve time in prison than almost any form of community supervision other than straight probation.

8. False. With the odd exception, boot camps have proven ineffective in rehabilitating criminals of any age.

CHAPTER 9

1. True. Despite some real reductions in incarceration at the state and local levels over the last few years, the United States still has the highest incarceration rate in the world.

2. False. Though large by comparison to minimum-security prisons, about three fifths of all inmates are held in medium- and minimum-security prisons, with medium-security prisons holding more inmates overall than maximum- and minimum-security prisons.

3. In medium-security prisons, the exterior security can be as tight as it is for supermax and maximum-security prisons, but internally, the inmate has many more opportunities to attend school, treatment, and church programming and to work in any number of capacities. There is also greater diversity in rooming options, from dormitories to single cells, with the more preferred single or double cells used as a carrot to entice better behavior. Visiting and contact with the outside world are less restricted. Some medium-security inmates may even be allowed to leave the institution for work-related deliveries or on furloughs, though this is much more common in minimum-security prisons.

4. Importation occurs when inmates entering a prison import aspects of their own culture from the outside. Prisonization occurs when inmates adopt the inmate subculture of the institution.

5. Gangs are groups of people with similar interests who socialize together and who may engage in deviant or criminal activities; they are a common phenomenon in jails and prisons. They may serve to reinforce the prison subculture by providing for the needs of inmates and thereby reducing their deprivations and pains.

6. There is violence in prisons because incarcerated people are there unwillingly, forced to do things they normally would not do, with people they may not like, and most important of all, some of them are inclined to be violent.

7. True. Transgender inmates, particularly in men's prisons, are more likely to be sexually assaulted than any other group of inmates.

CHAPTER 10

1. False. In almost all cases, statistical data outperform the subjective judgment of mental-health professionals.

2. False. Predicting human behavior is more difficult than trying to predict almost anything else, even the weather.

3. True. This is because all that the authorities were concerned with was warehousing people and punishing them.

4. False. The primary purpose of assessing and classifying inmates is to determine custody level due to security and safety issues.

5. False. Since protection of the community is the primary duty of probation and parole, risk of reoffending is always the primary concern.

6. True. If probation and parole officers have a good idea of an offender's history, characteristics, and his or her risk and needs, they can plan their supervision time requirements accordingly.

7. False. Classification is useful for inmates as well because it places them in appropriate housing and gives prison officials an understanding of their treatment and programming needs.

CHAPTER 11

1. False. The more criminals we can rehabilitate, the more society is protected. Since almost all offenders eventually get out of prison, it is wise to see how we can prevent them from committing offenses that will put them back in.

2. False. The biggest budget outlay in corrections after salaries is for control and surveillance.

3. False. Many well-run programs expect to reduce recidivism by 10% to 20%, but many others find less recidivism reduction.

4. False. Actuarial data supply a better understanding of what does and does not work, averaged across all offenders. A person's experience is limited and subjective.

5. False. Correctional officials have been reluctant to use pharmaceutical treatment for addicts.

6. True. Contrary to many people's belief, sex offenders are less likely to reoffend than offenders in all offense categories other than murder.

7. True. In all major cities studied, well over 50% of arrestees test positive for some kind of illegal drug.

8. True. There are more mentally ill individuals in jails and prisons than in mental hospitals in the United States today.

CHAPTER 12

1. True. The philosophical basis for parole began in an Australian penal colony in the 1830s run by a British ex–naval officer named Alexander Maconochie.

2. False. Unlike probation, which is under court supervision, parole is an executive-branch function.

3. False. Many inmates are released on mandatory parole, determined by a mathematical formula rather than at the discretion of a parole board. Others prefer to remain in prison (to "max out") for their full sentence rather than be set free under the watchful eye of a parole officer.

4. True. It has been noted for as long as such statistics have been collected that at least 66% of parolees will reoffend within 3 years, and these are the just the ones the authorities know about.

5. True. The parolees most likely to recidivate are property offenders.

6. True or False. There is broad disagreement on this issue. Some believe that incarceration may lead to higher crime rates by weakening families and reducing supervision of children; others have shown that few inmates lived with their children prior to imprisonment. Furthermore, having such men in the house is a strong predictor of antisocial behavior by their children, and the harmful effects on children increase the longer they remain.

7. False. Parole success is determined differently in different states. Conservative states tend to hold parolees to higher standards, whereas liberal states allow them more leeway. Thus, a parolee in a conservative state may be sent back to prison after missing two appointments and testing positive for drugs once, whereas in a liberal state, he or she may have to be caught in something more serious to get sent back.

8. True and False. Sanctions such as halfway houses and electronic monitoring cut costs only if they are used appropriately, and they only increase offender surveillance relative to ordinary parole, not relative to prison. In other words, costs are reduced if electronic monitoring is not used as a "novelty" on offenders who don't really need it or on offenders who really should be behind bars rather than walking free.

CHAPTER 13

1. True. The bureaucratic structure of organizations tends to segregate tasks with specialists in the same tasks and makes the chain of command and decision making very clear.

2. False. By definition, closed institutions are not open to their external environments and so are less likely to be influenced by the changes and knowledge development that occurs there. These limitations make closed institutions less susceptible to innovations.

3. True. Because they hold inmates for at least a year and a day and oftentimes much longer, they tend to become more self-sufficient and become the "homes" of inmates and, to some extent, staff. All aspects of life happen under their roofs, and they are more removed from the larger community than jails are.

4. True. Organizations have a formal side because they are typically created by law (this is true of public correctional organizations) and have a mission and rules and procedures that guide them. When organizational actors are acting in their public role, their memorandums and e-mails are used to establish what decisions were made and why they were made. (This is why e-mails are often subpoenaed by courts.) However, people have a hard time always acting in their official or formal capacity and will react to people informally on a human level by telling jokes and stories and making recommendations that do not always conform to the formal rules and requirements for the organization.

5. True.

6. True.

7. True.

8. False.

9. False.

CHAPTER 14

1. True. Calling a correctional officer a "guard" can be perceived as demeaning the role and thus as an insult.

2. The five attributes of a profession are (1) prior educational attainment involving college,

(2) formal training on the job or just prior to the start of the job, (3) pay and benefits that are commensurate with the work, (4) the ability to exercise discretion, and (5) work that is guided by a code of ethics.

3. Generally speaking, police jobs pay the most, then probation and parole officer jobs, and then correctional-officer jobs.

4. Generally speaking, probation and parole officer jobs often require a bachelor's degree; policing jobs usually require some college, if not an associate's or bachelor's degree; and correctional-officer jobs rarely require a bachelor's degree or even some college.

5. False. Most depictions of corrections on television and in the movies show a distorted of view of what corrections is and what correctional staff in institutions and communities do.

6. True.

7. Stress for correctional staff comes from many sources: shift and evening work that interferes with sleep and family relationships; a working environment with people who are experiencing a negative time in their lives; lack of power, control, and voice in their work; low pay and training; a hack rather than a human-service role; and competitive and nonsupportive coworkers.

8. True.

CHAPTER 15

1. True.

2. False. In the early prisons, women were an afterthought, as these prisons were not built for them. Therefore, they were often placed in attics or out-of-the-way places. They were not separated like the men, as there wasn't room to do so. They tended to be preyed on by male staff and inmates before they were guarded by female matrons.

3. True. Race shaped the incarceration of men and women in Southern and Northeastern prisons before and after the Civil War because it determined where, how, and whether certain racial groups were incarcerated.

4. True.

5. False.

6. True. Women offenders are sometimes treated as double deviants because they are criminal deviants and because they are gender deviants (in that they do not conform to traditional gender expectations).

7. True. Feminists have advocated for equal treatment and gender-specific programming in corrections.

8. True.

9. False.

CHAPTER 16

1. True.

2. True.

3. Nine teenage black boys riding a train in 1931 were accused of raping two white girls. They were tried several times, most were found guilty by all-white juries of rape, sometimes without assistance of counsel, and their convictions kept getting overturned. At least one of the white women recanted and said the rapes were a fabrication. Four of the youths did prison time. This case is emblematic of how African Americans were handled by the criminal justice system in the first half of the 20th century because it demonstrates how racism permeated every part of the system from police, to prosecutor, to judge, to jury, to corrections.

4. As Bill Quigley writes, facts that indicate that racism still exists in the criminal justice system include how the war on drugs has been prosecuted, DWB, more arrests of minority group members for drug offenses, longer waits for trial while incarcerated for accused minority group members, underfunded defense attorneys who serve disproportionately minority group members, minority group member exclusion from jury service, the rarity of trials, longer sentences for minority group members, disproportionately more of the longest sentences for minority group members, and disproportionate incarceration of minority group adults and youth.

5. False. Some estimates put the number at 20,000.

6. False. Chinese and Japanese immigration was opposed in law and in practice, particularly after the railroads were built.

7. In 1942, Japanese Americans were interned in reaction to Pearl Harbor and the fear that they might conspire to help the Japanese government win the war. German Americans were not interned, though Germany had started the war, and German Americans were widely dispersed across several states. One explanation for the differential treatment is racial discrimination.

8. True. One basic connection between class, race/ethnicity, and crime is that most people who commit street crimes are poor, and a disproportionate number of minority group members are poor.

9. True.

10. False.

11. False.

CHAPTER 17

1. True. Juveniles do commit a disproportionate number of criminal acts. This has been found to be true at all times and in all historical periods.

2. True. Juvenile antisocial behavior is normal in that most adolescents engage in it. Adolescence is a period in time when the juvenile brain and body are undergoing profound changes. These changes are conducive to risky behaviors, including antisocial behaviors.

3. False. Special juvenile courts began in Cook County, Illinois.

4. True. The ultimate source of responsibility for a juvenile's behavior is the state. This is the principle of *parens patriae*.

5. True. Juveniles can be tried in adult courts and sent to adult prison. This is rare, however, and is typically confined to particularly heinous crimes or to serious repeat offenders.

6. False. Only relatively recently have they been afforded almost all the same legal rights as adults.

7. False. The Supreme Court has ruled that a juvenile can only be given an LWOP sentence for homicide. The Court has also ruled that LWOP sentences should not be mandatory and that judges must assess a juvenile's potential for rehabilitation and how his or her age might have influenced the perpetration of the criminal act.

8. False. It was permissible in the United States to execute those who committed murder while they were juveniles until 2005.

CHAPTER 18

1. True. This was known as the hands-off period, in which the courts did not interfere with the prisons because prisons were the business of the executive branch.

2. False. There are limits on it based on security concerns of the prison.

3. False. The vast majority of lawsuits filed by inmates are frivolous complaints.

4. True. Their prison cells are not "homes" and are therefore not afforded the same legal protection.

5. True. This is due mostly to the increased longevity of African Americans in prison because they are removed from violent neighborhoods and also from drugs, alcohol, and tobacco. Prison inmates are also the only Americans guaranteed medical attention. The quality of that attention may not be as great as the average person receives, but many inmates would not get any on the outside.

6. True. See number 5.

7. True. Involuntarily commitment to mental institutions is accomplished by civil law. Although rarely practiced against sex offenders (about 1%), they are the only group of offenders subjected to involuntary commitment based on their crime as opposed to being based on mental illness.

8. True, particularly in terms of search and seizure by a probation or parole officer and sometimes by any other law enforcement officer.

CHAPTER 19

1. True. Most Americans support the death penalty. However, if the LWOP alternative is offered, the percentage favoring death falls below 50%.

2. False. Japan and South Korea also retain the death penalty.

3. True. A white murderer is both absolutely and proportionately more likely than a black or

Hispanic murderer to be sentenced to death and to be executed.

4. False. Lethal injection is used almost exclusively today.

5. False. Academics are split on the issue: Economists tend to think it deters while sociologists and criminologists do not. A special task force on the issue that reviewed every major study done on the topic found that the evidence is inconclusive.

6. False. The death penalty is far more expensive than life in prison. This is mostly due to the legal costs involved in seeking the death penalty.

7. True. Women are much less likely than men to be sentenced to death for committing a similar crime.

8. True. It is permissible to execute a person with a history of mental illness but not one with a mental disability (IQ of 70 or below).

CHAPTER 20

1. False. The most popular legal system worldwide is the civil (or code) system.

2. False. The United Kingdom has three different (although almost identical) systems: England and Wales, Scotland, and Northern Ireland.

3. False. Although they used to be trained as social workers, they are now considered offender managers with a law enforcement emphasis.

4. False. The inquisitorial system relies more on truth seeking, but the state must prove its case beyond a reasonable doubt. There is a different set of procedural principles that protect the accused person's rights. Evidence and confessions are only excluded when obtained via physical or legal threats.

5. True. The Chinese recidivism rate is about 8% after 3 years, as opposed to the American

rate of about 67%. This may be due to the extremely harsh conditions in Chinese prisons and/or the fact that many Chinese are sentenced to prison for relatively minor offenses and are thus not as criminally involved as American criminals.

6. True. The death penalty can be imposed for 55 different crimes in China, ranging from murder and rape to "economic crimes" and "counterrevolutionary" crimes.

7. True. Saudi judges make decisions based on their own interpretation of the facts and principles of Islamic law.

8. True. Offenses that potentially carry a death sentence include religious conversion from Islam, homosexuality, adultery, witchcraft, and sorcery.

CHAPTER 21

1. Likely trends for the short-term future include continued decarceration, a focus on penal help over penal harm, a continued push toward professionalism for staff, greater understanding of emotions as they influence correctional operations, and the increased "greening" of correctional institutions.

2. True.

3. False.

4. False.

5. False.

6. True. Prisons and jails have been characterized as "environmental hogs" (Stohr & Wozniak, 2013). They are often huge buildings or sets of buildings with outsized electrical needs because of their 24/7 lighting and security systems. Their inmates produce tons of waste in concentrated areas and, in turn, consume food, clothing, and numerous other products at levels that sometimes rival small cities.

GLOSSARY

Abu Ghraib: A military prison in Iraq where untrained "correctional officers" subjected prisoners to torture.

Actuarial data: Data relating to what has actually occurred and been recorded over many thousands of cases. Evidence-based treatment modalities are based on actuarial data.

Actuarial method: A method of making predictions about people based on the behavior patterns of people similarly situated, averaged over many thousands of cases.

Addiction: A psychobiological illness characterized by intense craving for a particular substance.

Adult Internal Management System (AIMS): A prison classification instrument that is designed to create a profile of an inmate's likely behavior in a correctional setting. It establishes five groups based on the behavioral characteristics of inmates—Groups I and II ("heavy"), Group III ("moderate"), and Groups IV and V ("light").

Age–crime curve: The age–crime curve is formed from the statistical count of the number of known crimes committed in a population over a given period, mapped according to age. The curve reflects a sharp increase in offending beginning in early adolescence, a peak in mid-adolescence, and then a steep decline in early adulthood, followed by a steadier decline thereafter. The peak may be higher or lower at different periods, and the peak age may vary by a year or two at different times or in different places, but the peak remains.

Amicus curiae briefs: "Friend of the court" briefs presented to the court, arguing in support of one side or the other, by interested parties not directly involved with the case.

Anger management programs: Programs that consist of a number of techniques by which someone with problems controlling anger can learn the causes and consequences of anger in order to reduce the degree of anger and avoid anger-inducing triggers.

Assessment: The process of making a judgment about something or someone based on certain criteria.

Attica Prison Riot (1971): The riot began with a spontaneous act of violence by one inmate against an officer who had tried to break up a fight. The violence quickly spread because inmates were frustrated and angry about the overcrowded conditions, lack of programming, and other conditions of confinement. There were charges of racism by the mostly African American inmates regarding their treatment by the mostly white staff. As negotiations broke down, the prison was stormed by the state police and by correctional staff. As a consequence, 10 hostages and 29 inmates were dead or dying when the prison was secured, and another 80 inmates had gunshot wounds. It was the bloodiest prison riot in American history.

Balanced approach: A three-pronged goal of the juvenile justice system: (1) to protect the community, (2) to hold delinquent youths accountable, and (3) to provide treatment and positive role models.

Big House prisons: According to Irwin (2005), these are fortress stone or concrete prisons, usually maximum security, whose attributes include "isolation, routine, and monotony" (p. 32). Strict security and rule enforcement, at least formally, and a regimented schedule are other hallmarks of such facilities.

Bill of Rights: The first 10 Amendments to the U.S. Constitution.

Bridewells: Workhouses established in every English county in the 16th century. They were constructed to hold and whip or otherwise punish "beggars, prostitutes, and nightwalkers" and later were places of detention; their use began in London in 1553.

Brutalizing effect: The assumption that rather than deterring homicides, they actually increase following executions.

Bureau of Justice Assistance: A branch of the U.S. Department of Justice under whose umbrella problem-solving courts exist.

Bureaucracy: As defined by the German theorist and philosopher Max Weber (1946), it can be distilled down to these three elements of its structure: hierarchy, specialization, and rule of law.

Case Management Classification System: An assessment and classification instrument consisting of an interview schedule and risk and needs scales. The CMC system divides offenders into one of four supervision levels: selective intervention, environmental structure, casework control, and limit setting.

Chemical castration: A biomedical treatment for chronic sex offenders in which a synthetic hormone called Depo-Provera is administered. Depo-Provera works in males to reduce sexual thoughts, fantasies, and erections by drastically reducing the production of testosterone, the major male sex hormone.

Civil-death statutes: Statutes in former times mandating that convicted felons lose all citizenship rights.

Civil rights claim: A Section 1983 claim that a person has been deprived of some legally granted right.

Classical School: The Classical School of penology and criminology was a nonempirical mode of inquiry similar to the philosophy practiced by the classical Greek philosophers—that is, "armchair philosophy."

Classification: The process of sorting things into categories according to their shared qualities or characteristics to achieve some purpose.

Closed institutions: Closed institutions are separated from their outside environments and are unaffected by those environments, to some extent.

Coequal staffing: This practice involves the use of personnel processes that provide comparable pay and benefits for those who work in the jail to that of people who work on the streets as law enforcement in sheriff's departments.

Cognitive behavioral therapy (CBT): A counseling approach that tries to address dysfunctional cognition, emotions, and behaviors in a relatively short time through goal-oriented, systematic procedures using a mixture of operant psychology, cognitive theory, and social-modeling theory.

Community corrections: A branch of corrections defined as any activity performed by agents of the state to assist offenders in reestablishing functional law-abiding roles in the community while, at the same time, monitoring their behavior for criminal activity.

Community corrections acts: Legislation that provides state funds to local governments and community correctional agencies to develop alternative community sanctions in place of incarceration.

Community courts: Community courts seek to solve the problems of offenders using the court's leverage to ensure that they compensate the community for the damage they caused.

Community jails: These are jails organized so those inmates engaged in educational programs, drug or alcohol counseling, or mental-health programming in the community will seamlessly receive such services while incarcerated (primarily from community experts in those areas) and again as they transition out of the facility.

Community residential centers: Place where offenders (usually parolees) reside when correctional authorities deem them not yet ready to live completely free.

Community service order: Part of a disposition requiring probationers to work a certain number of hours doing tasks to help their communities.

Concurrent sentence: Two separate sentences are served at the same time.

Consecutive sentence: Two or more sentences that must be served sequentially.

Contract and lease systems: Systems devised to use inmates' labor. Inmate labor under Southern states' lease systems was leased by the prison to farmers or other contractors. Inmates under a contract system in Northern and Midwestern prisons worked in larger groups under private or public employers.

Contrast effect: The effect of punishment on future behavior depends on how much the punishment and the usual life experience of the person being punished differ or contrast.

Convict code: These are the informal rules that inmates live by vis-à-vis the institution and staff and include "1. Do not inform; 2. Do not openly interact or cooperate with the guards or the administration; 3. Do your own time" (Irwin, 2005, p. 33).

Correctional boot camps: Facilities modeled after military boot camps where young and nonviolent offenders are subjected to military-style discipline and physical and educational programs.

Correctional institutions: (This term originally applied only to prisons but now can refer to jails as well.) Correctional institutions (prisons) carefully classify inmates into treatment programs that address their needs and perceived deficiencies. They are also intended to be places where inmates can earn good time and eventual parole. Correctional institutions use the medical model to treat inmates who are believed to be "sick" and in need of a treatment regimen provided by the prison, which will address that sickness and hopefully "cure" the inmates so that they might become productive members of society.

Corrections: A generic term covering a wide variety of functions carried out by government (and increasingly private) agencies having to do with the punishment, treatment, supervision, and management of individuals who have been accused (in the case of some jail inmates) or convicted of criminal offenses.

Corrections–industrial complex: The collusion among politicians, business, and criminal justice officials to make money for themselves and their organizations from correctional services, construction, and operations.

Crime control model: A model of law that emphasizes community protection from criminals and stresses that civil liberties can only have real meaning in a safe, well-ordered society.

Criminogenic needs: Factors associated with recidivism that can be changed.

Custodial level: This refers to the prison housing area and degree of supervision the inmate receives, which can be minimum, medium, or maximum.

Death Penalty Information Center: Major (partisan) source of information on the death penalty in the United States.

Deference period: The period of time when there was a partial return to the hands-off approach. It refers to the courts' willingness to defer to the expertise and needs of the authorities.

Deferred adjudication: A decision made by certain criminal justice personnel to delay or defer formal court proceedings if a youth follows probation conditions.

Deinstitutionalization of the mentally ill: This happened in the United States as a result of the civil rights movement and the related effort to increase the rights of people involuntarily committed to mental hospitals.

Delinquents: Juveniles who commit acts that are criminal when committed by adults.

Deontological ethical systems: Systems concerned with whether the act itself is good.

Determinate sentence: A prison sentence of a fixed number of years that must be served rather than a range.

Deterrence: A philosophy of punishment aimed at the prevention of crime by the threat of punishment.

Discretion: The ability to make choices and to act or not act on them.

Discretionary parole: Parole granted at the discretion of a parole board for selected inmates who have earned it.

Discrimination: Occurs when a person or group is treated differently because of who they are (e.g., based on race, ethnicity, gender, age, disability, religion, nationality, sexual orientation or identity, or income) rather than their abilities or something they did.

Disparity: Occurs when one group is treated differently and unfairly by governmental actors, as compared with other groups.

Domestic-violence courts: Special problem-solving courts meant to deal with the most prevalent form of violence: domestic violence.

Double deviants: Double deviants are women and girls who are deviant because they engage in crime and because they have violated societal gender role expectations.

Driving while black or brown (DWB): Refers to the practice of police focusing law enforcement attention on black- or brown-skinned drivers.

Drug court: A problem-solving court that specializes in the supervision and treatment of substance-abusing offenders.

Due process model: A model of law that stresses the accused's rights to a fair trial more than the rights of the community.

Egoism: Under this framework, the needs of self are most important. Acting to satisfy one's own wants and needs under this framework is acting ethically.

Eighth Amendment: Constitutional amendment that forbids cruel and unusual punishment.

Electrocution: The electric chair was introduced as a more humane method of execution than hanging. A person undergoing execution is strapped to the chair, and electrodes are attached to the person's body. The person is then subjected to a 15- to 30-second jolt of between 500 and 2,450 volts of electricity.

Electronic monitoring (EM): A system by which offenders under house arrest can be monitored for compliance using computerized technology such as an electronic device worn around the offender's ankle.

Elmira Reformatory: It was founded in 1876 in New York as a model prison in response to calls for the reform of prisons from an earlier era. The inmates were to be younger men. It would encompass all of the rehabilitation focus and graduated reward system (termed the marks system) that reformers were agitating for. The lash was not to be used. Elmira was supposed to hire an educated and trained staff and maintain uncrowded facilities (Orland, 1975). The operation of Elmira led to the creation of good time, the indeterminate sentence (defined in Chapter 5), a focus on programming to address inmate deficiencies, and the promotion of probation and parole. Ultimately, in practice, it was not the model reformers had hoped it would be.

Enlightenment: Period in history in which a major shift in the way people began to view the world and their place in it occurred, moving from a supernaturalistic to a naturalistic and rational worldview.

Ethical formalism: "What is good is that which conforms to the categorical imperative" (Pollock, 1998, p. 48).

Ethics: Refers to right or wrong behavior on the job.

Ethics of care: A framework centered on good acts. It is a deontological perspective. Those who subscribe to this framework believe that "what is good is that which meets the needs of those concerned" (Pollock, 1998, p. 48).

Ethics of virtue: An ethical system that defines *good* as the middle ground between two positions and focuses on the practice of virtuous acts in order to determine who is a good person.

Ethnicity: Refers to the differences between groups of people based on culture. An ethnic group will often have a distinct language, as well as particular values, religion, history, and traditions. Ethnic groups may be made up of several races and have a diverse national heritage.

Evidence-based practice (EBP): EBP means that in order to reduce recidivism, corrections must implement practices that have consistently been shown to be effective.

Fair Sentencing Act of 2010: The act mandated that the amount of crack cocaine subject to the 5-year minimum sentence be increased from 5 grams to 28 grams, thus reducing the 100-to-1 ratio to an 18-to-1 ratio. (Twenty-eight grams of crack gets as much time as 500 grams of powder cocaine.)

Firing squad: A method of execution by which the condemned was strapped and shot by a firing squad.

First Amendment: Guarantees freedom of religion, speech, press, and assembly.

Flatter and fatter organizations: Organizations in which power and responsibility are distributed across positions rather than increasing as one progresses up a hierarchy.

Formal organization: The public face of the organization, which includes its mission statement; what's on its official website; its rules and procedures; its training manual, curriculum, and memorandums by its leaders (either in hard-copy or e-mail form); or anything officially sanctioned by its leaders.

Fourteenth Amendment: Contains the due process clause, which declares that no state shall deprive any person of life, liberty, or property without due process of law.

Fourth Amendment: Guarantees the right to be free from unreasonable searches and seizures.

Functional magnetic resonance imaging (fMRI): The fMRI is the workhorse of neuroimaging, used to assess the functioning of a person's brain while engaged in some task.

Galley slavery: This was used as a sentence for crimes or as a means of removing the poor from streets. Galley slavery also served the twin purpose of providing the requisite labor—rowing—needed to propel ships for seafaring nations interested in engagement in trade and warfare. Used by the ancient Greeks and Romans and in the Middle Ages, it ended sometime in the 1700s.

Gangs (prison): Groups of people with similar interests who socialize together and support each other but who also engage in deviant or criminal activities. Prison gangs have a hierarchical organizational structure and a set and often strict code of conduct for members.

Gas chamber: The use of cyanide gas to execute someone placed in an airtight chamber and strapped to a chair.

Gender identity: The gender one identifies with, rather than the sex of one's genitalia when born.

General deterrence: The presumed preventive effect of the threat of punishment on the general population—that is, deterrence is aimed at *potential* offenders.

Global positioning system (GPS) monitoring: A system of probation and parole supervision whereby probationers or parolees are required to wear a tracking unit that can be monitored by satellites.

Great Law: William Penn's idea, based on Quaker principles, that de-emphasized the use of corporal and capital punishment for all crimes but the most serious.

Green prisons and jails: These prisons and jails attempt to reduce the environmental impact of their large facilities and improve the health and job prospects of their inmates through the use of renewable energy, composting and gardening, creating habitats for species, and more.

Habeas corpus: Latin term meaning, "You have the body." It is a court order requiring that an arrested person be brought before it to determine the legality of detention.

Habitual-offender statutes: Statutes mandating that offenders with a third felony conviction be sentenced to life imprisonment regardless of the nature of the third felony.

Hack: A correctional officer in a prison who is a violent, cynical, and alienated keeper of inmates.

Halfway houses: Transitional places of residence for correctional clients who are "halfway" between the constant supervision of prison and the much looser supervision in the community.

Hands-off doctrine: An early American court-articulated belief that the judiciary should not interfere with the management and administration of prisons.

Hanging: The most common form of execution in the United States, historically.

Hare's Psychopathy Checklist–Revised (PCL-R): Instrument used around the world to measure psychopathy.

Hedonism: A doctrine maintaining that all goals in life are means to the end of achieving pleasure and/or avoiding pain.

Hedonistic calculus: A method by which individuals are assumed to logically weigh the anticipated benefits of a given course of action against its possible costs.

Hostile environment: Occurs when the workplace is sexualized with jokes, pictures, or in other ways that are offensive to one gender.

House arrest: Programs that require offenders to remain in their homes except for approved periods to travel to work, school, or other approved destinations.

Houses of refuge: Part of the Jacksonian movement (named after President Andrew Jackson) of the early 1800s to use institutions as the solution for social problems. Their stated purpose was to remove impressionable youth, mainly boys but also girls, from the contamination that association with more hardened adult prisoners might bring.

Hulks: These were and are derelict naval vessels transformed into prisons and jails.

Human agency: The capacity of humans to make choices and their responsibility to make moral ones regardless of internal or external constraints on their ability to do so.

Human-relations theories of management: Posit that people are motivated to do their best work in organizations where the power is more distributed across positions; where management listens to workers who know their jobs; where people work in teams; where communication is open, and ideas are freely disseminated; where people are allowed to make mistakes, and their colleagues are encouraged to learn from them; and where clients are allowed to provide feedback that is relevant to the improvement of the services they receive.

Human service: Describes a correctional officer who provides "goods and services," serves as an "advocate" for inmates when appropriate, and assists them with their "adjustment" and through "helping networks" (Johnson, 2002, pp. 242–259).

Importation: This is what occurs when inmates bring aspects of the larger culture into the prison.

Incapacitation: A philosophy of punishment that refers to the inability of criminals to victimize people outside of prison walls while they are locked up.

Indeterminate sentence: A prison sentence consisting of a range of years to be determined by the convict's behavior, rather than one of a fixed number of years.

Informal organization: This is often hidden from the public, even clients, but known, at least in part, by its employees, and it includes how the organization really operates. It can be found in the stories and jokes told by employees about the work, the management, other employees, or clients and the unofficial orders and requests by supervisors that do not fit the official rules.

Intensive-supervision probation (ISP): Probation that involves more frequent surveillance of probationers and that is typically limited to more serious offenders, in the belief that there is a chance that they may be rehabilitated (or to save the costs of incarceration).

Intermediate sanctions: Refers to a number of innovative alternative sentences that may be imposed in place of the traditional prison-versus-probation dichotomy.

Irish system: A prison system used in the 19th century. This system involved four stages, beginning with a 9-month period of solitary confinement, the first 3 months with reduced rations and no work. This period of enforced idleness was presumed to make even the laziest of men yearn for some kind of activity.

Jails: These are local community institutions that hold people who are presumed innocent before trial; convicted people before they are sentenced; convicted minor offenders, who are sentenced for terms that are usually less than a year; juveniles (usually in their own jails, separated from adults, or before transport to juvenile facilities); women (usually separated from men and sometimes in their own jails); and people for the state or federal authorities. Depending on the particular jail population being served and the capacity of the given facility, they serve to incapacitate, deter, rehabilitate, punish, and reintegrate.

Jim Crow laws: Laws devised by Southern states following the Civil War, starting in the 1870s and lasting until 1965 and the civil rights movement, to prevent African Americans from fully participating in social, economic, and civic life. These laws restricted the rights and liberties of black citizens in employment, housing, education, travel, and voting. Voter disenfranchisement, or preventing African Americans from voting, was a key part of the Jim Crow laws.

Judicial reprieve: British and early American practice of delaying sentencing following a conviction; it could become permanent, depending on the offender's behavior.

Judicial waiver: Involves a juvenile-court judge deciding, after a "full inquiry," that the juvenile should be waived to the adult system.

Justice: A moral concept about just or fair treatment consisting of "treating equals equally and unequals unequally according to relevant differences."

Leadership: "An ongoing process of activity involving organizing, decision making, innovating, communicating, team building, culture creation and molding that is engaged in by workers and supervisors to achieve organizational goals" (Stohr & Collins, 2014, p. 184).

Learning organizations: These organizations emphasize the improvement of their employees through education and training, encourage risk taking, highlight their mistakes and learn from them, and invite outside assessment in order to continually better themselves.

Lethal injection: Lethal injection is the preferred method of execution in all states today. Using this method, the condemned person is administered drugs that paralyze the muscular system and stop the person's breathing, followed by another drug that stops the heart.

Level of Service/Case Management Inventory (LS/CMI): A fourth-generation assessment instrument used in probation and parole.

Liberal feminist: One who believes that the problem for girls and women involved in crime lies more with the social structure around them (e.g., poverty and lack of sufficient schooling or training, along with patriarchal beliefs) and that the solution lies in preparing them for an alternate existence so that they do not turn to crime.

Liberty interest: Refers to an interest in freedom from governmental deprivation of liberty without due process.

Life without parole (LWOP): A life sentence with the additional condition that the person never be allowed parole—*life* means *life* for those receiving an LWOP sentence.

Management: One or more persons who have official control of an organization and/or its operations.

Management by objections (MBO): A theory of management that emphasizes the joint creation of work objectives between management and employees as a way to motivate employees to achieve goals that matter to them.

Mandatory parole: Automatic parole after a set period of time for almost all inmates.

Mandatory sentence: A prison sentence imposed for crimes for which probation is not an option, where the minimum time to be served is set by law.

Marks system: A graduated reward system for prisons, developed by Maconochie, in which, if one behaves, it is possible to earn "marks" that, in turn, entitle one to privileges.

Maslow's hierarchy of needs: A concept developed by Maslow (1943, 1961), who argued that people are first motivated by lower-level needs, such as physiological (food, water, and sex) and security (physical safety, security, provision for old age, etc.) needs, and then by higher-level needs, such as love (the need to belong, the need to give and receive love, and the need to be accepted by associates), self-esteem (also known as self-respect—the need for achievement, recognition, importance, and confidence in the world and the desire for reputation or prestige), and self-actualization (the need to be creative, to fulfill one's potential, to become what one is meant or fitted to be).

Mature coping: This occurs in prisons when the inmate deals "with life's problems like a responsive and responsible human being, one who seeks autonomy without violating the rights of others, security without resort to deception or violence, and relatedness to others as the finest and fullest expression of human identity" (Johnson, 2002, p. 83).

Maximum-security prisons: Prisons where both external and internal security are high. Inmates are often locked up for all or a large part of the day, save for showering or recreation outside of their cell, and they are ideally in single cells, deprived of much contact with others. Programming is limited or nonexistent. Visits and contact with the outside are restricted. The exterior security consists of some combination of layers of razor wire, walls, lights, cameras, armed guards, and attack dogs on patrol. Inmates in maximum security tend to be those who have very serious offenses or those who have problems with adhering to the rules in prisons. Death rows, if a state has capital punishment, are usually located in maximum-security prisons.

Medical model: Rehabilitation model that assumes criminals are sick and need treatment.

Medium-security prisons: Prisons that hold a mix of people in terms of crime categories but who program well. Medium-security prisons have high external security, but inmates are able to move around more freely within the "walls." Some are built like a college campus, with several buildings devoted to distinct purposes.

Mental disorders: Clinically significant conditions characterized by alterations in thinking, mood, or behavior associated with personal distress or impaired functioning.

Mental-health court: A court modeled on drug courts and designed to deal with the special problems of offenders suffering from mental illness.

Minimum-security prisons: Prisons created for lower-level felony offenders and those who are "short timers," or people who are relatively close to a release date. Those sent here are not expected to be an escape or behavioral problem. The ability and willingness to work is often a prerequisite for classification to this type of facility.

Mortification: A process that occurs as inmates enter the prison, and they suffer from the loss of the many roles they occupied in the wider world (Goffman, 1961; Sykes, 1958). Instead, only the role of *inmate* is available, a role that is formally powerless and dependent.

Motivational interviewing: The objective of motivational interviewing is to increase offenders' motivation for positive behavioral change through the exploration and resolution of the ambivalence about changing assumed to exist in offenders.

Mount Pleasant Prison: The first prison constructed for women in the United States. Built in 1839 close to the Sing Sing (New York) prison for men, it was, in part, administered by it but had its own buildings, staff, and administrator.

National Institute of Corrections Model of Custody and Need: A custody and need instrument that identifies eight areas of assessment that provide for objective custodial placement.

National Offender Management Services (NOMS): NOMS refers to the correctional systems of England and Wales after the National Probation Service and Her Majesty's Prison Service were placed under a single umbrella.

National Probation Act of 1925: The act that initiated the legal use of probation in the United States.

Natural law: Adherents of the natural-law ethical framework believe that "what is good is that which is natural."

Needs principle: A principle that refers to an offender's prosocial needs, the lack of which puts him or her at risk for reoffending and suggests that these needs should receive attention in program targeting.

New-generation or podular direct-supervision jail: Jails that have two key components: a rounded, or "podular," architecture for living units and the direct, as opposed to indirect or intermittent, supervision of inmates by staff; in other words, staff are to be in the living units full time. Other important facets of these jails are the provision of more goods and services in the living unit (e.g., access to telephones, visiting booths, recreation, and library books) and more enriched leadership and communication roles for staff.

New Mexico Prison Riot (1980): This prison exploded in a riot over the conditions of confinement and crowding, which were at epidemic levels. Despite repeated warnings that a riot was going to occur, the administration and staff failed to adequately prepare. The state eventually retook the prison; however, over 3 days, 33 inmates were killed by other inmates. Numerous other inmates, along with staff hostages, were beaten or raped, and millions of dollars in damage was done (Useem, 1985; Useem & Kimball, 1989).

New York prison system: These prisons and those modeled after them included congregate-work and -eating arrangements but silent and separate housing. This mode of operation allowed prison managers to offset the cost of incarceration by allowing inmates to work together and hence produce more. When inmates were allowed out of their cells, they could also perform maintenance jobs and other tasks in the prison, such as cleaning and cooking, which also reduced the cost of incarcerating. The ball and chain, lockstep, and striped uniforms also originated in these prisons.

Newgate Prison in New York City: Built in 1797, the prison was operated based on Quaker ideals, so it focused on rehabilitation, religious redemption, and work programs to support prison upkeep and did not use corporal punishment. The builders of Newgate even constructed a prison hospital and school for the inmates. Because of crowding, single celling was not possible for most, and a number of outbreaks of violence erupted (such as a riot in 1802).

Newgate Prison in Simsbury, Connecticut: According to Phelps (1860/1996), this early colonial "prison" started as a copper mine, and during its 54 years of operation (from 1773 to 1827), some 800 inmates passed through its doors. The mine was originally worked in 1705, and one third of the taxes it paid to the town of Simsbury at that time were used to support Yale College (p. 15).

Noble cause: "A profound moral commitment to make the world a safer place to live. Put simply, it is getting bad guys off the street. Police believe they're on the side of angels and their purpose in life is getting rid of bad guys" (Crank & Caldero, 2000, p. 35).

Norfolk Island: An English penal colony, operated 1,000 miles off the Australian coast. It was established in 1788 as a place designated for prisoners from England and Australia and was regarded as a brutal and violent island prison, where inmates were poorly fed, clothed, and housed and were mistreated by staff and their fellow inmates. Alexander Maconochie, an ex–naval captain, asked to be transferred to Norfolk, usually an undesirable placement, so that he could put into practice some ideas he had about prison reform, which he successfully did, vastly improving conditions at the prison.

Offender needs: Refers to deficiencies in offenders' lives that hinder them from making a commitment to a prosocial pattern of behavior.

Offender risk: Refers to the probability that a given offender will reoffend and, thus, the threat he or she poses to the community.

Official deviance: This type of deviance is one in which someone violates the official rules of an organization in order to benefit the organization or its members. In some organizations, there may be negative consequences for those who refuse to engage in official deviance.

Open institutions: Those who are fully part of their communities, both dependent on and responsive to them, and who are affected by their outside environment, such as changes in laws, norms, and values in their communities.

Organizational culture: The values, beliefs, history, traditions, and language held and practiced in a given organization. (Note that this definition is the same as that of a *subculture*, with the exception that an organizational culture is organization-wide, rather than referring to just a group of people within a population, as is true with a subculture.)

Overcrowding: A phenomenon that occurs when the number of inmates exceeds the physical capacity (the beds and space) available.

Pains of imprisonment: Gresham Sykes (1958) described these perils as the "deprivation of liberty, the deprivation of goods and services, the deprivation of heterosexual relationships, the deprivation of autonomy, and the deprivation of security" (pp. 63–83).

Panopticon: An idea of Jeremy Bentham's that ingeniously melded the ideas of improved supervision with architecture (because of its rounded and open and unobstructed views), which would greatly enhance the supervision of inmates.

Parens patriae: A legal principle giving the state the right to intercede and act in the best interest of the child or any other legally incapacitated persons, such as the mentally ill.

Parole: The release of prisoners from prison before completing their full sentence.

Parole board: A panel of people presumably qualified to make judgments about the suitability of a prisoner to be released from prison after having served some specified time of his or her sentence.

Participatory management: Occurs when employees are allowed to have a say in what they do and how they do their work.

Patriarchy: Involves the attitudes, beliefs, and behaviors that value men and boys over women and girls (Daly & Chesney-Lind, 1988). Members of patriarchal societies tend to believe that men and boys are worth more than women and girls. They also believe that women and girls, as well as men and boys, should have certain restricted roles to play and that those of the former are less important than those of the latter. Therefore, education, work training that helps one make a living, and better pay are more important to secure for men and boys than for women and girls, who are best suited for more feminine and—by definition, in a patriarchal society—less worthy professions.

Penal harm: The penal-harm movement in corrections is based on retribution in sentencing and the infliction of greater harm while inmates are under correctional supervision.

Penal help: The penal-help movement includes the reform of state laws to liberalize marijuana use, the repeal of harsh sentences, and the reduction in the use of incarceration, coupled with the increase in the use of rehabilitation, restorative justice, and reentry programming. Taken together, they indicate that there has been a societal shift away from penal harm as a guiding principle of corrections.

Pennsylvania prison system: These prisons and those that were modeled after them emphasized silent and separate eating and working and living arrangements that isolated inmates in their cells, restricted their contact with others, and reinforced the need for penitence. When labor was allowed at all, it was a solitary affair in one's cell.

Penology: Refers to the study of the processes adopted and the institutions involved in the punishment and prevention of crime.

People's mediation committees: A system of informal social control practiced in China in which committees are organized in work and neighborhood groups, and they can apply sanctioning mechanisms to offenders in the community.

Plea bargain: Agreements between defendants and prosecutors in which defendants agree to plead guilty in exchange for certain concessions.

Positivists: Those who believe that human actions have causes and that these causes are to be found in the thoughts and experiences that typically precede those actions.

Power: The ability to "get people to do what they otherwise wouldn't" (Dahl, 1961).

Predisposition reports: A report done in juvenile courts that is analogous to a *presentence investigation report* in adult courts.

Presentence investigation report (PSI): Report written by the probation officer informing the judge of various aspects of the offense for which the defendant is being sentenced, as well as providing information about the defendant's background (educational, family, and employment history), character, and criminal history.

Principle of utility: A principle that posits that human action should be judged moral or immoral by its effects on the happiness of the community and that the proper function of the legislature is to make laws aimed at maximizing the pleasure and minimizing the pains of the population—"the greatest happiness for the greatest number."

Prison Rape Elimination Act of 2003: Act that mandated that the Bureau of Justice Statistics collect data on sexual assaults in adult and juvenile jails and prisons and that it identify facilities with high levels of victimization.

Prison subculture: This is the norms, values, beliefs, and even language of the prison.

Prisonization: The adoption of the inmate subculture by inmates.

Prisons: Correctional facilities that have a philosophy of penitence (hence, *penitentiary*) and that were created as a grand reform, as they represented, in theory at least, a major improvement over the brutality of punishment that characterized early Western, English, and American law and practice.

Privatization: Privatization in corrections occurs when services or whole correctional institutions are provided or operated by private businesses or corporations.

Probation: A sentence imposed on convicted offenders that allows them to remain in the community under the supervision of a probation officer, instead of being sent to prison.

Problem-solving courts: Problem-solving courts (sometimes called *specialty courts*) are courts of limited jurisdiction designed to help mostly nonviolent offenders with specific problems and needs that have not been adequately addressed in traditional criminal courts.

Profession: Regarding the positions of corrections officers and staff, a profession is distinguished by prior educational attainment involving college, formal training on the job or just prior to the start of the job, pay and benefits that are commensurate with the work, the ability to exercise discretion, and work that is guided by a code of ethics.

Professionalization: Professionalization in corrections includes the enforcement of professional standards for their new hires, such as a required college-level educational background, sufficient training, pay that is commensurate with job requirements, training that sufficiently prepares people for the job, and a code of ethics that drives the work practice.

Prosecutorial discretion: Allows prosecutors to file some cases in either adult or juvenile court.

Public surveillance: A sanction similar to probation, but in addition, it requires that offenders be deprived of the freedoms of speech, assembly, association, and demonstration without the approval of the organ executing public surveillance.

Punishment: The act of imposing some unwanted burden, such as fines, probation, imprisonment, or death, on convicted persons in recompense for their crimes.

Quid pro quo sexual harassment: Involves something for something, as in you give your boss sexual favors and he allows you to keep your job.

Race: Refers to the skin color and features of a group of people. It is based on biology.

Rationality: The state of having good sense and sound judgment based on the evidence before us.

Recidivism: Occurs when an ex-offender commits further crimes.

Reentry: The process of reintegrating offenders into the community after release from jail or prison. Part of that process is preparing offenders through the use of various programs targeting their risks and needs so that they will have a chance of remaining in the community.

Rehabilitation: A philosophy of punishment aimed at "curing" criminals of their antisocial behavior.

Reintegration: A philosophy of punishment that aims to use the time criminals are under correctional supervision to prepare them to reenter the free community as well equipped to do so as possible.

Religious perspective: People who employ a religious perspective to guide their decisions believe that "what is good is that which conforms to God's will" (Pollock, 1998, p. 48).

Residential substance abuse treatment (RSAT): These RSATs typically last 6 to 12 months and are composed of inmates in need of substance abuse treatment and whose parole dates are set to coincide with the end of the program. RSAT inmates are separated from the negativity and violence of the rest of the prison and are provided with extensive cognitive behavioral counseling and attend Alcoholics Anonymous (AA) and Narcotics Anonymous (NA) meetings, as well as many other kinds of rehabilitative classes.

Responsivity principle: A principle maintaining that if offenders are to respond to treatment in meaningful and lasting ways, counselors must be aware of their different developmental stages, learning styles, and need to be treated with respect and dignity.

Restitutive justice: A philosophy of punishment driven by simple deterrence and a need to repair the wrongs done.

Restorative justice: A system of justice that gives approximately equal weight to community protection, offender accountability, and the offender. It is oriented toward repairing the harm caused by the crime and involves face-to-face confrontation between victim and perpetrator in the hope of arriving at a mutually agreeable solution.

Retribution: A philosophy of punishment that demands that criminals' punishments match the degree of harm they have inflicted on their victims—that is, what they justly deserve.

Retributive justice: A philosophy of punishment driven by a passion for revenge.

Risk principle: A principle that refers to an offender's probability of reoffending and maintains that those with the highest risk should be targeted for the most intense treatment.

Risk, needs, and responsivity (RNR) model: A treatment correctional model that maintains that offenders and the community are better served if offenders' risks for reoffending and their needs (their deficiencies, such as lack of job skills) are addressed in a way that matches their developmental stage.

Role: What a person does on the job every day.

Rule of law: The principle that the law, not people, governs and that no one is above the law.

Scientific management: A traditional theory of management developed by Taylor (1911), whose management determines, through observation, who is the "first-rate" worker who does the work in the "one best way"—meaning the person who does the most the fastest, also known as the most efficient worker (Taylor, 1911). Such a worker, for Taylor, is motivated by money and so will do his or her work best when he or she is paid by the product produced, or by *piece rate*.

Section 1983 suits: A mechanism for state prison inmates to sue state officials in federal court regarding their confinement and their conditions of confinement. Section 1983 is part of the Civil Rights Act of 1871, which was initially enacted to protect Southern blacks from state officials and the Ku Klux Klan.

Selective incapacitation: Refers to a punishment strategy that largely reserves prison for a distinct group of offenders composed primarily of violent repeat offenders.

Sentence: A punitive penalty ordered by the court after a defendant has been convicted of a crime either by a jury, a judge, or in a plea bargain.

Sentencing disparity: Wide variation in sentences received by different offenders that may be legitimate or discriminatory.

Sentencing guidelines: Scales for numerically computing sentences that offenders should receive based on the crime they committed and on their criminal records.

Shari'a: Literally, "the path to follow." Shari'a law is practiced in Islamic countries and is extremely strict and rigid and informs all aspects of life. Punishments under this system are extremely harsh and often applied to acts that are not crimes in Western societies.

Shock probation: A type of sentence aimed at shocking offenders into going straight by exposing them to the reality of prison life for a short period, followed by probation.

Specific deterrence: The supposed effect of punishment on the future behavior of persons who experience the punishment.

Split sentences: Sentences that require convicted persons to serve brief periods of confinement in a county jail prior to probation placement.

Stanford Prison Experiment: A 1971 experiment conducted at Stanford University, which utilized volunteer students divided into officers and inmates in a makeshift "prison" (Haney et al., 1981). In the end, about a third of the "officers" engaged in the abuse of "inmates," and other "officers" stood by while it was going on. The experiment was stopped after a few days and is often referenced as an example of how correctional work and the subcultures that develop as part of the job can foster corrupt behavior by officers.

Stateville Prison: Built in Illinois as a panopticon in 1925 in reaction to the deplorable conditions of the old Joliet, Illinois, prison built in 1860.

Status offenders: Juveniles who commit certain actions that are legal for adults but not for children, such as smoking and not obeying parents.

Status offenses: Offenses that apply only to juveniles, such as disobeying parents or smoking.

Statutory exclusion: These are waivers in cases in which state legislatures have statutorily excluded certain serious offenses from the juvenile courts for juveniles over a certain age, which varies from state to state.

Street-level bureaucrat: The position of workers at the entry level of criminal justice, who often have too much work, too few resources, and some discretion.

Subculture: A subset of a larger culture with its own norms, values, beliefs, traditions, and history.

Supermax prisons: High-security prisons, both internally and externally, that hold those who are violent or disruptive in other prisons in the state or federal system. Inmates are confined to their windowless cells 24 hours a day, except for showers three times a week (where they are restrained) and solitary exercise time a couple of times a week; they eat in their cells. Visiting and programming are very limited.

Teleological ethical systems: Systems focused on the consequences of the act.

Theory X: A theory advanced by McGregor (1957), based on previous work by Frederick Taylor and Max Weber, that proposes that workers are lazy and unintelligent and need to be motivated by strong leaders and the prospect of improved earnings.

Theory Y: This theory is distinct from Theory X in that it supposes that people are motivated to work, want a voice in the workplace, and hope to do interesting things and accomplish important goals. Therefore, management should focus on creating an environment that allows workers to meet these needs.

Theory Z: This theory, proposed by Ouchi (1981), combines Theory X and Theory Y while emphasizing the importance that the larger environment has on an organization and its workers.

Therapeutic communities (TCs): Residential communities providing dynamic "mutual self-help" environments and offering long-term opportunities for attitude and behavioral change and learning constructive prosocial ways of coping with life.

Total institution: "A place of residence and work where a large number of like-situated individuals, cut off from the wider society for an appreciable period of time, together lead an enclosed, formally administered round of life" (Goffman, 1961, p. 6).

Total quality management (TQM): This theory builds on Theory Z, emphasizing the value of worker-created

goals while maintaining a belief certain aspects of traditional management, like rewards and oversight.

Transportation: A sentence whereby the convicted person would be sent to another country, via a ship whose captain owned the right to sell the convict's labor for a period of time. The captain would, in turn, sell the convicted person's labor to others in the new land. It was in use for roughly 350 years by English or European countries, from 1607 to 1953.

Truth-in-sentencing laws: Laws that require there to be a truthful, realistic connection between the sentences imposed on offenders and the time they actually serve.

Unconditional release: A type of release from prison for inmates who have completed their entire sentences. They are therefore released unconditionally—with no parole.

United States Sentencing Commission: A commission charged with creating mandatory sentencing guidelines to control judicial discretion.

Utilitarianism: "What is determined by how many people were helped by the greatest number" (Pollock, 1998, p. 48).

Veterans court: A problem-solving court that is a hybrid of drug and mental-health courts. These courts deal with veterans of the U.S. military.

Victim impact statement: A statement made by persons directly affected by a crime (or victims' survivors in the case of murder) to inform the court of the personal and emotional harm they have suffered as a result of the defendant's actions and, in some states, to make a sentencing recommendation.

Victim–offender reconciliation programs (VORPs): Programs designed to bring offenders and their victims together in an attempt to reconcile ("make right") the wrongs offenders have caused, an integral component of the restorative justice philosophy.

Waiver: Refers to a process by which a juvenile offender is "waived" (transferred) to an adult court because he or she has committed a particularly serious crime or is habitually delinquent.

Walnut Street Jail: Originally constructed in 1773 in Philadelphia, Pennsylvania, it operated as a typical local jail of the time: holding pretrial detainees and minor offenders; failing to separate by gender, age, or offense; using the fee system, which penalized the poor and led to the near starvation of some; and offering better accommodations—and even access to liquor and sex—to those who could pay for it.

Warehouse prison: Large prisons, of any security level but more likely a supermaximum- or maximum-security prison, where inmates' lives and movement are severely restricted and rule bound. There is no pretense of rehabilitation in warehouse prisons; punishment, incapacitation, and deterrence are the only justifications for such places. The more hardened and dangerous prisoners are supposed to be sent there, and their severe punishment is to serve as a deterrent to others in lower-security prisons.

Work release programs: Programs designed to control offenders in a secure environment while, at the same time, allowing them to maintain employment.

REFERENCES

CASES CITED

Atkins v. Virginia, 536 U.S. 304 (2002).

Arizona v. United States, 567 U.S. ___ (2012).

Baze v. Rees, 553 U.S. 35 (2008).

Bearden v. Georgia, 461 U.S. 660 (1983).

Bell v. Wolfish, 441 U.S. 520 (1979).

Bordenkircher v. Hayes, 434 U.S. 357 (1978).

Breed v. Jones, 421 U.S. 517 (1975).

Coffin v. Reichard, 143 F.2d 443 (6th Cir. 1944).

Coker v. Georgia, 433 U.S. 584 (1977).

Cooper v. Pate, 378 U.S. 546 (1964).

Eddings v. Oklahoma, 445 U.S. 104 (1982).

Estelle v. Gamble, 429 U.S. 97 (1976).

Ex parte Crouse, 4 Whart. 9 (Pa. 1838).

Ex parte Hull, 312 U.S. 546 (1941).

Ex parte United States, 242 U.S. 27 (1916).

Ford v. Wainwright, 477 U.S. 399 (1986).

Furman v. Georgia, 408 U.S. 238 (1972).

Gagnon v. Scarpelli, 411 U.S. 778 (1973).

Glossip v. Gross 576 U.S. ___ (2015).

Graham v. Florida, 560 U.S. ___ (2010).

Gregg v. Georgia, 428 U.S. 153 (1976).

Holt v. Sarver, 309 F. Supp. 362 (1969).

Horn v. Banks, 536 U.S. 266, 272 (2002).

Hudson v. McMillian, 503 U.S. 1 (1992).

Hudson v. Palmer, 468 US 517 (1984).

In re Gault, 387 U.S. 1 (1967).

In re Winship, 397 U.S. 358 (1970).

Jackson v. Indiana, 406 U.S. 715 (1972).

Jones v. Bock, 549 U.S. 199 (2007).

Jones v. Chappell, 31 F. Supp. 3d 1050 (2014).

Jones v. Cunningham, 371 U.S. 236 (1963).

Jordan v. Gardner, 986 F.2d 1521 (9th Cir. 1993).

Kansas v. Hendricks, 521 U.S. 346 (1997).

Kent v. United States. 383 U.S. 541 (1966).

Lafler v. Cooper, 566 U.S. ___ (2012).

McCleskey v. Kemp, 481 U.S. 279 (1987).

McKeiver v. Pennsylvania, 402 U.S. 528 (1971).

Mempa v. Rhay, 389 U.S. 128 (1967).

Miller v. Alabama, 567 U.S. ___ (2012).

Morris v. Travisono, 310 F. Supp. 857 at 965 (1970).

Morrissey v. Brewer, 408 U.S. 471 (1972).

Panetti v. Quarterman, 551 U.S. 930 (2007).

Pennsylvania Board of Probation and Parole v. Scott, 524 U.S. 357 (1998).

Penry v. Lynaugh, 492 U.S. 302 (1989).

Pervear v. Massachusetts, 72 U.S. 475 (1866).

Powell v. Alabama, 287 U.S. 45 (1932).

Pulido v. State of California et al. (Marin Co. Sup. Ct. 1994).

Payne v. Tennessee, 501 U.S. 808 (1991).

Roper v. Simmons, 112 S.W. 3rd 397 (2005).

Ruffin v. Commonwealth, 62 Va. 790, 796 (1871).

Rummel v. Estelle, 445 U.S. 263, (1980).

Salazar et al. v. City of Espanola et al. (2004).

Sandin v. Conner, 515 U.S. 472 (1995).

Schall v. Martin, 104 U.S. 2403 (1984).

Smith v. Mosley, 532 F.3d 1270 (11th Cir. 2008).

Thompson v. Oklahoma, 487 U.S. (1988).

Turner v. Safley, 482 U.S. 78 (1987).

United States v. Booker, 543 U.S. 220 (2005).

United States v. Knights, 534 U.S. 112 (2001).

Washington v. Harper, 494 U.S. 210 (1990).

Wilson v. Seiter, 501 U.S 294 (1991).

Wolff v. McDonnell, 418 U.S. 539 (1974).

Woodson v. North Carolina, 428 U.S. 280 (1976).

WORKS CITED

$15.5 million settlement for mentally ill jail detainee held in solitary confinement. (2014). *Prison Legal News*, 25(4), 20. Retrieved from https://www.prisonlegalnews.org/news/2014/apr/15/155-million-settlement-for-mentally-ill-jail-detainee-held-in-solitary-confinement

Abadinsky, H. (1993). *Drug abuse: An introduction*. Chicago: Nelson-Hall.

Abadinsky, H. (2009). *Probation and parole: Theory and practice*. Upper Saddle River, NJ: Prentice Hall.

Alahmed, A. (2013, March 15). The execution of the Saudi seven. *Foreign Policy*. Retrieved from http://www.foreignpolicy.com/articles/2013/03/15/The_execution_of_the_Saudi_Seven

Alarid, L. (2000). Along racial and gender lines: Jail subcultures in the midst of racial disproportionality. *Corrections Management Quarterly*, 4, 8–19.

Albany County Judicial Center. (n.d.). The drug court process. Retrieved from http://albanycountyda.com/Bureaus/RevJohnUMillerOR/CommunityProsecution/drugcourtprocess.aspx

Albers, P., Beauvais, P., Bonert, J., Bose, M., Langbroek, P., Renier, A., et al. (2013). *Toward a common evaluation framework to assess mutual trust in the field of judicial cooperation in criminal matters*. Available at http://www.government.nl/documents-and-publications/reports/2013/09/27/.htm

Alcock, J. (1998). *Animal behavior: An evolutionary approach* (6th ed.). Sunderland, MA: Sinauer Associates.

Alexander, M. (2010). *The new Jim Crow: Mass incarceration in the age of colorblindness*. New York: New Press.

Alexander, R. (2004). The United States Supreme Court and the civil commitment of sex offenders. *Prison Journal, 84*, 361–378.

Alm, S. (2013). A new continuum for court supervision. *Oregon Law Review, 91*, 1180–1190.

Almquist, L., & Dodd, E. (2009). *Mental health courts: A guide to research-informed policy and practice*. New York: Council of State Governments Justice Center.

Alosi, T. (Writer & Director). (2008). *Eastern State: Living behind the walls* [Documentary film]. Folsom, CA: Dark Hollow Films.

Alvarado, J. (2009). Keeping jailers from keeping the keys to the courthouse: The Prison Litigation Reform Act's exhaustion requirement and Section 5 of the Fourteenth Amendment. *Seattle Journal for Social Justice, 8*, 323–365.

American Civil Liberties Union. (2012). Frequently asked questions about the cost of California's Death penalty. Retrieved from https://www.aclunc.org/blog/frequently-asked-questions-about-costs-californias-death-penalty

American Civil Liberties Union. (2015). Women in prison: An overview. Retrieved from https://www.aclu.org/words-prison-did-you-know

American Correctional Association. (1983). *The American prison: From the beginning . . . A pictorial history*. Lanham, MD: Author.

American Correctional Association. (2013). *Declaration of principles*. Retrieved from http://www.aca.org/ACA_Prod_IMIS/ACA_Member/About_Us/Declaration_of_Principles/ACA_Member/AboutUs/Dec.aspx?hkey=a975cbd5-9788-4705-9b39-fcb6ddc048e0

Amnesty International. (2004). *Abuse of women in custody: Sexual misconduct and shackling of pregnant women: A state-by-state survey of policies and practices in the United States*. New York: Author.

Amnesty International. (2012, March 26). Death penalty 2011: Alarming levels of executions in the few countries that kill. Retrieved from http://www.amnestyusa.org/news/news-item/death-penalty-2011-alarming-levels-of-executions-in-the-few-countries-that-kill

Andrews, D., & Bonta, J. (2007). *The psychology of criminal conduct* (5th ed.). Cincinnati, OH: Anderson.

Andrews, D. A., Bonta, J., & Wormith, J. S. (2006). The recent past and near future of risk and/or needs assessment. *Crime & Delinquency, 52*, 7–27.

Andrews, D. A., & Dowden, C. (2007). The Risk-Need-Responsivity model of assessment and human service in prevention and corrections: Crime-prevention jurisprudence. *Canadian Journal of Criminology and Criminal Justice, 49*(4), 439–464.

Antonio, M. E., Young, J. L., & Wingeard, L. M. (2009). When actions and attitude count most: Assessing perceived level of responsibility and support for inmate treatment and rehabilitation programs among correctional employees. *Prison Journal, 89*(4), 363–382.

Applegate, B. K., Cullen, F. T., & Fisher, B. S. (2001). Public support for correctional treatment: The continuing appeal of the rehabilitative ideal. In E. J. Latessa, A. Holsinger, J. W. Marquart, & J. R. Sorensen (Eds.), *Correctional contexts: Contemporary and classical readings* (2nd ed., pp. 506–519). Los Angeles, CA: Roxbury.

Applegate, B. K., & Paoline, E. A., III. (2007). Jail officers' perceptions of the work environment in traditional versus new generation facilities. *American Journal of Criminal Justice, 31*, 64–80.

Applegate, B. K., & Sitren, A. H. (2008). The jail and the community: Comparing jails in rural and urban contexts. *Prison Journal, 88*(2), 252–269.

Archibold, R. C. (2010, April 23). Arizona enacts stringent law on immigration. *New York Times*. Retrieved from http://www.nytimes.com/2010/04/24/us/politics/24immig.html

Aronson, J., & Cole, S. (2009). Science and the death penalty: DNA, innocence, and the debate over capital punishment in the United States. *Law & Social Inquiry, 34*, 603–633.

Aspinwall, L., Brown T, & Tabery, J. (2012). The double-edged sword: Does biomechanism increase or decrease judges' sentencing of psychopaths? *Science, 337*, 846–849.

Austin, J., & Irwin, J. (2001). *It's about time: America's imprisonment binge*. Belmont, CA: Wadsworth.

Austin, J., & McGinnis, K. (2004). *Classification of high-risk and special management prisoners: A national assessment of current practices*. Washington, DC: U.S. Department of Justice.

Awes, A. (Producer & Director), & Awes, M. (Producer). (2010). *Who really discovered America?* [Documentary]. Minneapolis: Committee Films.

Balazs, G. (2006). The workaday world of a juvenile probation officer. In A. Walsh (Ed.), *Correctional assessment, casework & counseling* (4th ed., pp. 414–416). Alexandria, VA: American Correctional Association.

Bard, S. (1997, July 31). Idaho inmates tell of assault in Texas: Nurses, who prisoners say fondled them, have been arrested and fired. *Idaho Statesman*, p. B1.

Barker, V. (2006). The politics of punishing: Building a state governance theory of American imprisonment variation. *Punishment & Society, 8*, 5–32.

Barlow, L. W., Hight, S., & Hight, M. (2006). Jails and their communities: Piedmont regional jail as a community model. *American Jails, 20*(5), 38–45.

Bartol, C. (2002). *Criminal behavior: A psychosocial approach*. Upper Saddle River, NJ: Prentice Hall.

Bartollas, C. (2004). *Becoming a model warden: Striving for excellence*. Alexandria, VA: American Correctional Association.

Bartollas, C., & Hahn, L. D. (1999). *Policing in America*. Needham Heights, MA: Allyn and Bacon.

Barton, A. (1999). Breaking the crime/drugs cycle: The birth of a new approach? *Howard Journal of Criminal Justice, 38*(2), 144–157.

Bass, E., & Golding, H. (2012). *The Veterans Health Administration's treatment of PTSD and traumatic brain injury among recent combat veterans.* Washington, DC: Congressional Budget Office.

Baunach, P. J. (1992). Critical problems of women in prison. In I. L. Moyer (Ed.), *The changing role of women in the criminal justice system* (pp. 99–112). Prospect Heights, IL: Waveland Press.

Bazelon Center for Mental Health Law. (2008). *Individuals with mental illness in jail and prison.* Retrieved from www.bazelon.org

Bazemore, G. (2000). What's "new" about the balanced approach? In P. Kratkoski (Ed.), *Correctional counseling and treatment* (pp. 1–22). Prospect Heights, IL: Waveland Press.

Beare, M. E., & Hogg, C. (2013). Listening in . . . to gang culture. *Canadian Journal of Criminology & Criminal Justice, 55*(3), 421–452.

Beaumont, G., & de Tocqueville, A. (1964). *On the penitentiary system in the United States and its application in France.* Carbondale: Southern Illinois University Press. (Original work published 1833.)

Beccaria, C. (1963). *On crimes and punishment* (H. Paulucci, Trans.). Indianapolis, IN: BobbsMerrill. (Original work published 1764.)

Beck, A. J., Berzofsky, M., Caspar, R., & Krebs, C. (2013). *Sexual victimization in prisons and jails reported by inmates, 2011–2012.* Washington, DC: Bureau of Justice Statistics. Retrieved from http://www.bjs.gov/content/pub/ascii/svpjri1112.txt

Beck, A. J., & Harrison, P. M. (2001). *Prisoners in 2000.* Washington, DC: Bureau of Justice Statistics. Retrieved from http://www.bjs.gov/content/pub/pdf/p00.pdf

Beck, A. J., & Harrison, P. M. (2007). *Sexual violence reported by correctional authorities, 2006.* Washington, DC: Bureau of Justice Statistics.

Beck, A. J., Harrison, P. M., & Adams, D. B. (2007). *Sexual violence reported by correctional authorities, 2006.* Washington, DC: Bureau of Justice Statistics. Retrieved from http://www.bjs.gov/content/pub/pdf/svrca06.pdf

Beck, A. J., & Rantala, R. R. (2014). *Sexual victimization reported by adult correctional authorities, 2009–11.* Washington, DC: Bureau of Justice Statistics. Retrieved from http://www.bjs.gov/content/pub/pdf/svraca0911.pdf

Beck, A. J., Rantala, R. R., & Rexroat, J. (2014, January 23). Allegations of sexual victimization in prisons and jails rose from 2009 to 2011: Substantiated incidents remained stable [Press release]. Washington, DC: Bureau of Justice Statistics. Retrieved from http://www.bjs.gov/content/pub/press/svraca0911pr.cfm

Becker, G. (1997). The economics of crime. In M. Fisch (Ed.), *Criminology 97/98* (pp. 15–20). Guilford, CT: Duskin.

Beckett, K., & Murakawa, N. (2012). Mapping the shadow carceral state: Toward an institutionally capacious approach to punishment. *Theoretical Criminology, 16*, 221–244.

Beckett, K., Nyrop, K., Pfingst, L., & Bowen, M. (2005). Drug use, drug possession arrests, and the question of race: Lessons from Seattle. *Social Problems, 52*, 419–441.

Belbot, B., & Hemmens, C. (2010). *The legal rights of the convicted.* El Paso, TX: LFB Scholarly Publishing.

Belknap, J. (2001). *The invisible woman: Gender, crime, and justice* (2nd ed.). Belmont, CA: Wadsworth.

Bench, L., & Allen, T. (2003). Investigating the stigma of prison classification: An experimental design. *Prison Journal, 83*, 367–382.

Bennett, K. (1995). Constitutional issues in cross-gender searches and visual observation of nude inmates by opposite-sex officers: A battle between and within the sexes. *Prison Journal, 75*, 90–112.

Bentham, J. (1948). *A fragment on government and an introduction to the principles of morals and legislation* (W. Harrison, Ed.). Oxford, UK: Basil Blackwell. (Original work published 1789.)

Bentham, J. (1969). *Panopticon papers: A Bentham reader* (M. P. Mack, Ed.). New York: Pegasus. (Original work published 1789.)

Bentham, J. (2003). *The rationale of punishment.* London: Robert Heward. (Original work published 1811.)

Bergner, D. (1998). *God of the rodeo: The quest for redemption in Louisiana's Angola Prison.* New York: Ballantine Books.

Berk, R., Li, A., & Hickman, L. (2005). Statistical difficulties in determining the role of race in capital cases: A re-analysis of data from the state of Maryland. *Journal of Quantitative Criminology, 21*, 365–390.

Best, B., Wodahl, E., & Holmes, M. (2014). Waiving away the chance of freedom: Exploring why prisoners decide against applying for parole. *International Journal of Offender Therapy and Comparative Criminology, 58*, 320–347.

Binder, A., Geis, G., & Bruce, D. (2001). *Juvenile delinquency: Historical, cultural, and legal perspectives.* Cincinnati, OH: Anderson.

Bissonnette, G. (2006). "Consulting" the federal sentencing guidelines after *Booker. UCLA Law Review, 54*, 1497–1547.

Bjerregaard, B. E., Smith, M. D., Cochran, J. K., & Fogel, S. J. (2015). A further examination of the liberation hypothesis in capital murder trials. *Crime & Delinquency.* doi:10.1177/0011128715574454

Black, M., & Smith, R. (2003). *Electronic monitoring in the criminal justice system* (Trends and Issues in Crime and Criminal Justice No. 254). Canberra: Australian Institute of Criminology.

Blackburn, A. G., Mullings, J. L., & Marquart, J. W. (2008). Sexual assault in prison and beyond: Toward an understanding of lifetime sexual assault among incarcerated women. *Prison Journal, 88*(3), 351–377.

Blalock, H. M. (1967). *Toward a theory of minority group relations.* New York: Wiley.

Bland, A. (2014, July 26). Tulsa County Drug Court a lifesaver, new graduate says. *Tulsa World.* Retrieved from http://www.tulsaworld.com/news/courts/tulsa-county-drug-court-a-life-saver-new-graduate-says/article_12fb55b9-c13f-53e8-a78e-5e654ea461f7.html

Blau, P. M., & Scott, W. R. (2001). The concept of the formal organization. In J. M. Shafritz & S. J. Ott (Eds.), *Classics of organization theory* (pp. 206–210). Fort Worth, TX: Harcourt College Publishers. (Original work published 1962.)

Bleckman, E., & Vryan, K. (2000). Prosocial family therapy: A manualized preventive intervention for juveniles. *Aggression and Violent Behavior, 5*, 343–378.

Blonigen, D. (2010). Explaining the relationship between age and crime: Contributions from the developmental literature on personality. *Clinical Psychology Review, 30*, 89–100.

Bloom, B., Owen, B., & Covington, S. (2003). *Gender responsive strategies: Research, practice, and guiding principles for women offenders*. Washington, DC: National Institute of Corrections.

Blue, E. (2012). *Doing time in the Depression: Everyday life in Texas and California prisons*. New York: New York University Press.

Blume, J. (2006). AEDPA: The "hype" and the "bite." *Cornell Law Review, 91*, 259–302.

Blume, J., Eisenberg, T., & Wells, M. (2004). Explaining death row's population and racial composition. *Journal of Empirical Legal Studies, 1*, 165–207.

Bohm, R. M. (2003). *Deathquest: An introduction to the theory and practice of capital punishment in the United States* (2nd ed.). Cincinnati, OH: Anderson.

Bohm, R. M. (2012). *Deathquest: An introduction to the theory and practice of capital punishment in the United States* (4th ed.). Boston: Anderson Publishing.

Bohm, R., & Haley, K. (2007). *Introduction to criminal justice*. New York: McGraw-Hill.

Bonczar, T. P. (2008). *Characteristics of state parole supervising agencies, 2006*. Washington, DC: Bureau of Justice Statistics. Retrieved from http://www.bjs.gov/content/pub/pdf/cspsa06.pdf

Bonczar, T. P. (2011). *State prison admissions, 2009: Sentence length, by offense and admission type*. Washington, DC: Bureau of Justice Statistics. Retrieved from http://www.bjs.gov/index.cfm?ty=pbdetail&iid=2056

Bonta, J., Wallace-Capretta, S., & Rooney, J. (2000). Can electronic monitoring make a difference? *Crime and Delinquency, 46*, 61–75.

Bookman, C. R., Lightfoot, C. A., & Scott, D. L. (2005). Pathways for change: An offender reintegration collaboration. *American Jails, 19*, 9–14.

Boone, R. (2013a, October 23). Staffing issues known for years at private prison. *Spokesman-Review*, 3A.

Boone, R. (2013b, October 29). Justice Dept. won't prosecute Idaho prison guards. *Spokesman-Review*, 5A.

Boone, R. (2016, May 24). Fed. Court upholds contempt ruling against prison company. *Moscow-Pullman Daily News*, 3A.

Bottcher, J., & Ezell, M. (2005). Examining the effectiveness of bootcamps: A randomized experiment with a long-term follow up. *Journal of Research in Crime and Delinquency, 42*, 309–332.

Branson, A. (2013). African American serial killers: Over-represented yet underacknowledged. *Howard Journal of Criminal Justice, 52*, 1–18.

Braswell, M. C., McCarthy, B. R., & McCarthy, B. J. (1991). *Justice, crime and ethics*. Cincinnati, OH: Anderson Publishing.

Breiding, M. J., Chen, J., & Black, M. C. (2014). *Intimate partner violence in the United States—2010*. Atlanta, GA: National Center for Injury Prevention and Control, Centers for Disease Control and Prevention. Retrieved from https://www.cdc.gov/violenceprevention/pdf/cdc_nisvs_ipv_report_2013_v17_single_a.pdf

British Foreign Office. (2015). *Information pack for British prisoners in Saudi Arabia*. Retrieved from https://www.gov.uk/government/uploads/system/uploads/attachment_data/file/452341/Saudi_Arabia_Prisoner_Pack_2015_final_July_2015.pdf

Britton, D. M. (2003). *At work in the iron cage: The prison as a gendered organization*. New York: New York University Press.

Bronson, J., Carson, E. A., Noonan, M., & Berzofsky, M. (2015). *Veterans in prison and jail, 2011–12*. Washington, DC: Bureau of Justice Statistics. Retrieved from http://www.bjs.gov/content/pub/pdf/vpj1112.pdf

Broussard, D., Leichliter, J. S., Evans, A., Kee, R., Vallury, V., & McFarlane, M. M. (2002). Screening adolescents in a juvenile detention center for gonorrhea and chlamydia: Prevalence and reinfection rates. *Prison Journal, 82*, 8–18.

Brown, M. (2006). Gender, ethnicity, and offending over the life course: Women's pathways to prison in the aloha state. *Critical Criminology, 14*, 137–158.

Bureau of Indian Affairs. (2014). Indian entities recognized and eligible to receive services from the United States Bureau of Indian Affairs. *Federal Register, 80*(9), 1942–1943.

Bureau of Justice Assistance. (2008). *Mental health courts: A primer for policymakers and practitioners*. New York, NY: Author.

Bureau of Justice Assistance. (2014). What are problem solving courts? Retrieved from https://www.bja.gov/evaluation/program-adjudication/problem-solving-courts.htm

Bureau of Justice Statistics. (2000). *Correctional populations in the United States, 1997*. Washington, DC: Author. Retrieved from http://www.bjs.gov/content/pub/pdf/cpus97.pdf

Bureau of Justice Statistics. (2001). *Probation and parole in the United States, 2000*. Washington, DC: Author. Retrieved from http://www.bjs.gov/content/pub/pdf/ppus00.pdf

Bureau of Justice Statistics. (2006). *Prevalence of imprisonment in the United States*. Washington, DC: Author. Retrieved from http://www.ojp.usdoj.gov/bjs

Bureau of Justice Statistics. (2007). *Prison and jail inmates at midyear series, 1998–2006*. Washington, DC: Author. Retrieved from http://www.bjs.gov

Bureau of Justice Statistics. (2008). *Jail statistics: Summary of findings*. Washington, DC: Author. Retrieved from http://www.bjs.gov

Bureau of Justice Statistics. (2011). *Expenditures/employment*. Washington, DC: Author. Retrieved from www.bjs.gov

Bureau of Justice Statistics. (2014). *PREA data collection activities, 2014*. Washington, DC: Author. Retrieved from http://www.bjs.gov/content/pub/pdf/pdca14.pdf

Bureau of Labor Statistics (2014). Probation officers and correctional treatment specialists. Retrieved from http://www.bls.gov/oes/current/oes211092.htm

Bureau of Labor Statistics. (2016a). *Labor force statistics from the Current Population Survey: Table 11*. Washington, DC: Author. Retrieved from http://www.bls.gov/cps/cpsaat11.pdf

Bureau of Labor Statistics. (2016b). Occupational employment and wages, May 2015: 33-3012 correctional officers and jailers. Last updated March 30, 2016. Retrieved from http://www.bls.gov/oes/current/oes333012.htm

Burke, B., Arkowitz, H., & Menchola, M. (2003). The efficacy of motivational interviewing: A meta-analysis. *Journal of Consulting and Clinical Psychology, 71*, 843–861.

Burn-Murdoch, J., & Chalabi, M. (2013, January 24). Crime statistics for England & Wales: What's happening to each offence? *The Guardian*. Retrieved from http://www.guardian.co.uk/news/datablog/2011/jul/14/crime-statistics-england-wales

Burnett, J. (2011). Town relies on troubled youth prison for profits. National Public Radio. Retrieved from http://www.npr.org/2011/03/25/134850972/town-relies-on-troubled-youth-prison-for-profits

Burns, H. (1975). *Corrections: Organization and administration*. St. Paul, MN: West Publishing.

Burrell, W. (2006). *APPA caseload standards for probation and parole*. Lexington, KY: American Probation and Parole Association. Available at www.colorado.gov

Bushway, S., & Reuter, P. (2008). Economists' contribution to the study of crime and the criminal justice system. *Crime and Justice, 37*, 389–451.

Butterworth, B. (1995, May 25). News release. Retrieved from http://myfloridalegal.com

Byrne, J. M., & Hummer, D. (2008). The nature and extent of prison violence. In J. M. Byrne, D. Hummer, & F. S. Taxman (Eds.), *The culture of prison violence*. Boston: Pearson.

Byrne, J. M., Hummer, D., & Stowell, J. (2008). Prison violence, prison culture, and offender change: New directions for research, theory, policy, and practice. In M. Byrne, D. Hummer, & F. S. Taxman (Eds.), *The culture of prison violence* (pp. 202–219). Boston: Pearson.

Bynum, J., & Thompson, W. (1999). *Juvenile delinquency: A sociological approach*. Boston: Allyn & Bacon.

Cahalan, M. W. (1986). *Historical corrections statistics in the United States, 1850–1984*. Washington, DC: Bureau of Justice Statistics.

Caldwell, H. (2011). Coercive plea bargaining: The unrecognized scourge of the justice system. *Catholic University Law Review, 61*, 63–96.

Call, J. (2011). *The Supreme Court and prisoners' rights*. In E. Latessa & A. Holsinger (Eds.), *Correctional contexts* (pp. 155–169). New York: Oxford University Press.

Cameron, S. (1994). A review of the econometric evidence on the effects of capital punishment. *Journal of Socio-Economics, 23*, 197–214.

Camp, S. D., & Gaes, G. G. (2002). Growth and quality of U.S. private prisons: Evidence from a national survey. *Criminology & Public Policy, 1*(3), 427–450.

Camp, S. D., Steiger, T. L., Wright, K. N., Saylor, W. G., & Gilman, E. (2013). Affirmative action and the "level playing field": Comparing perceptions of own and minority job advancement opportunities. In M. K. Stohr, T. Walsh, & C. Hemmens (Eds.), *Corrections: A text/reader* (2nd ed., pp. 360–373). Thousand Oaks, CA: Sage.

Carrigan, W. D., & Webb, C. (2015, February 20). When Americans lynched Mexicans. *New York Times*, p. A23.

Carroll, L. (1974). *Hacks, blacks and cons: Race relations in a maximum security prison*. Lexington, MA: Lexington Books.

Carroll, L. (1982). Race, ethnicity and the social order of the prison. In R. Johnson & H. Toch (Eds.), *The pains of imprisonment* (pp. 181–203). Beverly Hills, CA: Sage.

Carson, E. A. (2014). *Prisoners in 2013*. Washington, DC: Bureau of Justice Statistics. Retrieved from http://www.bjs.gov/content/pub/pdf/p13.pdf

Carson, E. A. (2015). *Prisoners in 2014*. Washington, DC: Bureau of Justice Statistics. Retrieved from http://www.bjs.gov/content/pub/pdf/p14.pdf

Carson, E. A., & Golinelli, D. (2013). *Prisoners in 2012: Trends in admissions and releases, 1991-2012*. Washington, DC: Bureau of Justice Statistics. Retrieved from http://www.bjs.gov/index.cfm?ty=pbdetail&iid=4842

Carter, K. (2006). Restorative justice and the balanced approach. In A. Walsh (Ed.), *Correctional assessment, casework, and counseling* (4th ed., pp. 8–11). Lanham, MD: American Correctional Association.

Carter, M., & Morris, L. (2002). *Managing sex offenders in the community*. Washington, DC: Center for Sex Offender Management.

Cartwright, T. (2011). "To care for him who shall have borne the battle": The recent development of veterans treatment courts in America. *Stanford Law and Policy Review, 221*, 295–316.

The case for freeing the "last hooligan." (2011, January 20). *South China Morning Post*. Retrieved from http://www.scmp.com/article/736208/case-freeing-last-hooligan

Casey, P., Warren, R., & Elek, J. (2011). *Using offender risk and needs assessment information at sentencing: Guidance for courts from a national working group*. Washington, DC: National Center for State Courts.

Caspi, A., & Moffitt, T. (1995). The continuity of maladaptive behavior: From description to understanding in the study of antisocial behavior. In D. Ciccheti & D. Cohen (Eds.), *Manual of developmental psychology* (pp. 472–511). New York: Wiley.

Cassell, P. (2008). In defense of the death penalty. *Journal of the Institute for the Advancement of Criminal Justice, 15,* 14–28.

Center for Community Corrections. (1997). *Community corrections: A call for punishments that make sense.* Washington, DC: U.S. Department of Justice.

Champion, D. (2005). *Probation, parole, and community corrections* (5th ed.). Upper Saddle River, NJ: Prentice Hall.

Chantraine, G. (2010). French prisons of yesteryear and today: Two conflicting modernities—A socio-historical view. *Punishment & Society, 12,* 27–46.

Chappell, C. A. (2004). Post-secondary correctional education and recidivism: A meta-analysis of research conducted 1990–1999. *Journal of Correctional Education, 55,* 148–69.

Chen, X. (2010). The Chinese sentencing guideline: A primary analysis. *Federal Sentencing Reporter, 22,* 213–216.

Chesney-Lind, M., & Irwin, K. (2006). Still "the best place to conquer girls": Girls and the juvenile justice system. In A. V. Merlo & J. M. Pollock (Eds.), *Women, law, and social control* (pp. 271–291). Boston: Pearson.

Chesney-Lind, M., & Shelden, R. G. (1998). *Girls, delinquency, and juvenile justice* (2nd ed.). Belmont, CA: West/Wadsworth Company.

Cissner, A., Labriola, M., & Rempel, M. (2013). *Testing the effects of New York's domestic violence courts.* New York: Center for Court Innovation.

CivilWarHome.com. (2002). Civil War prisons and prisoners. Retrieved from http://www.civilwarhome.com/prisonsandprisoners.html

Clark, J. (1991). Correctional health care issues in the nineties: Forecast and recommendations. *American Jails Magazine, 5,* 22–23.

Clark, M. (2005). Motivational interviewing for probation staff: Increasing the readiness to change. *Federal Probation, 69,* 22–28.

Clarke, R., & Cornish, D. (2001). Rational choice. In R. Paternoster & R. Bachman (Eds.), *Explaining criminals and crime: Essays in contemporary criminological theory* (pp. 23–42). Los Angeles, CA: Roxbury.

Clayton, S. L. (Ed.). (2003). Correctional officer education and training. *Corrections Compendium, 28*(2), 11–22.

Clear, T., Cole, G., & Reisig, M. D. (2011). *American corrections* (9th ed.). Belmont, CA: Wadsworth.

Clear, T., Rose, D., & Ryder, J. (2001). Incarceration and the community: The problem of removing and returning offenders. *Crime & Delinquency, 47,* 335–351.

Clement, M. (1993). Parenting in prison: A national survey of programs for incarcerated women. *Journal of Offender Rehabilitation, 19,* 89–100.

Clemmer, D. (2001). The prison community. In E. J. Latessa, A. Holsinger, J. W. Marquart, & J. R. Sorensen (Eds.), *Correctional contexts: Contemporary and classical readings* (2nd ed., pp. 83–87). Los Angeles, CA: Roxbury.

Coates, R. (1990). Victim–offender reconciliation programs in North America. In B. Galaway & J. Hudson (Eds.), *Criminal justice, restitution, and reconciliation* (pp. 177–182). Monsey, NY: Criminal Justice Press.

Cohen, A. (2013, June 9). One of the darkest periods in the history of American prisons. *Atlantic Monthly,* 1–8.

Cohen, F. (2008). Correctional health care: A retrospective. *Correctional Law Reporter, 20,* 5–12.

Cohen, T., & Kyckelhahn, T. (2010). *Felony defendants in large urban counties, 2006.* Washington, DC: U.S. Department of Justice.

Colbert, D. (Ed.). (1997). *Eyewitness to America: 500 years of America in the words of those who saw it happen.* New York: Pantheon Books.

Collins, R. (2004). Onset and desistence in criminal careers: Neurobiology and the age–crime relationship. *Journal of Offender Rehabilitation, 39,* 1–19.

Comack, E. (2006). Coping, resisting, and surviving: Connecting women's law violations to their history of abuse. In L. F. Alarid & P. Cromwell (Eds.), *In her own words* (pp. 33–44). Los Angeles, CA: Roxbury.

Conly, C. (1998). *The Women's Prison Association: Supporting women offenders and their families.* Washington, DC: National Institute of Justice.

Conover, T. (2001). *Newjack: Guarding Sing Sing.* New York: Vintage Books.

Cooper, A. (2011, February). Throwing away the key: Michelle Alexander on how prisons have become the new Jim Crow. *The Sun, 422,* 4–12.

Cooper, J., Walsh, A., & Ellis, L. (2010). Is criminology ripe for a paradigm shift? Evidence from a survey of American criminologists. *Journal of Criminal Justice Education, 21,* 332–347.

Cornelius, G. F. (2007). *The American jail: The cornerstone of modern corrections.* Upper Saddle River, NJ: Pearson/Prentice Hall.

Couch, R. (2015, February 5). Some states are closing prisons and turning them into homeless shelters, reentry centers. *Huffington Post.* Retrieved from http://www.huffingtonpost.com/2015/02/05/closing-state-prisons_n_6614220.html

Council of State Governments Justice Center. (2013). *The impact of probation and parole populations on arrest in four California cities.* New York: Author. Retrieved from https://csgjusticecenter.org/law-enforcement/publications/the-impact-of-probation-and-parole-populations-on-arrest-in-four-california-cities

Council of State Governments Justice Center. (2014). Mental health. Retrieved from http://csgjusticecenter.org/mental-health

Council of State Governments Justice Center. (2015, May 28). Launch of national initiative offers counties research-based support to address growing mental health crisis in jails. Retrieved from http://csgjusticecenter.org/mental-health/posts/launch-of-national-initiative-offers-counties-research-based-support-to-address-growing-mental-health-crisis-in-jails

Cowburn, M. (1998). A man's world: Gender issues in working with male sex offenders in prison. *Howard Journal of Criminal Justice, 37,* 234–251.

Cox, N. R., & Osterhoff, W. E. (1991). Managing the crisis in local corrections: A public–private partnership approach. In J. Thompson & G. L. Mays (Eds.), *American jails: Public policy issues* (pp. 227–239). Chicago: Nelson-Hall.

Crabbe, J. (2002). Genetic contributions to addiction. *Annual Review of Psychology, 53*, 435–462.

Craig, S. C. (2009). A historical review of mother and child programs for incarcerated women. *Prison Journal, 89*(1), 35S–53S.

Crank, J. P., & Caldero, M. A. (2000). *Police ethics: The corruption of noble cause.* Cincinnati, OH: Anderson Publishing.

Crank, J. P., & Caldero, M. A. (2011). *Police ethics: The corruption of noble cause* (3rd ed.). Cincinnati, OH: Anderson Publishing.

Creelman, A. (2010, October). US-style judicial review for France? *Primerus.* Retrieved from http://www.primerus.com/files/US-style%20Judicial%20Review%20for%20France%282%29.pdf

Crewe, B., Warr, J., Bennett, P., & Smith, A. (2014). The emotional geography of prison life. *Theoretical Criminology, 18*(1), 56–74.

Crime and Justice Institute at Community Resources for Justice. (2009). *Implementing evidence-based policy and practice in community corrections* (2nd ed.). Washington, DC: National Institute of Corrections. Retrieved from http://static.nicic.gov/Library/024107.pdf

Crouch, B. (1993). Is incarceration really worse? Analysis of offenders' preferences for prison over probation. *Justice Quarterly, 10*, 67–88.

Cullen, F. T. (1994). Social support as an organizing concept for criminology: Presidential address to the Academy of Criminal Justice Sciences. *Justice Quarterly, 11*(4), 527–559.

Cullen, F. T., & Jonson, C. L. (2012). *Correctional theory: Context and consequences.* Thousand Oaks, CA: Sage.

Cullen, F. T., Jonson, C. L., & Stohr, M. K. (2014). *The American prison: Imagining a different future.* Thousand Oaks, CA: Sage.

Cullen, F., & Gendreau, P. (2001). Assessing correctional rehabilitation: Policy, practice, and prospects. In *Criminal Justice 2000* (Vol. 3, pp. 109–175). Washington, DC: National Institute of Justice.

Culley, R. (2012). "The judge didn't sentence me to be raped": *Tracy Neal v. Michigan Department of Corrections*: A 15-year battle against the sexual abuse of women inmates in Michigan. *Women & Criminal Justice, 22*(3), 206–225.

Curran, D. J., & Renzetti, C. M. (2001). *Theories of crime.* Boston, MA: Allyn & Bacon.

Currie, E. (1999). Reflections on crime and criminology at the millennium. *Western Criminology Review, 2*(1). Retrieved from http://www.westerncriminology.org/documents/WCR/v02n1/currie/currie.html

Dahl, R. (1961). *Who governs? Democracy and power in an American city.* New Haven, CT: Yale University Press.

Daly, K., & Chesney-Lind, M. (1988). Feminism and criminology. *Justice Quarterly, 5*, 497–535.

Damrosch, L. (2010). *Discovery of America.* New York: Farrar, Straus and Giroux.

Davidson, J. (2015, September 1). Too many inmates, too few correctional officers: A lethal recipe in federal prisons. *Washington Post.* Retrieved from https://www.washingtonpost.com/news/federal-eye/wp/2015/09/01/too-many-inmates-too-few-correctional-officers-a-lethal-recipe-in-federal-prisons

Davis, K. C. (2008). *America's hidden history: Untold tales of the first Pilgrims, fighting women, and forgotten founders who shaped a nation.* New York: HarperCollins.

Davis, L., Bozick, R., Steele, J., Saunders, J., & Miles, J. (2013). *Evaluating the effectiveness of correctional education: A meta-analysis of programs that provide education to incarcerated adults.* Santa Monica, CA: RAND Corporation.

Davis, W. N. (2003, February). Special problems for specialty courts. *ABA Journal, 89*, 32–37.

Deane, E. (Producer & Director), & Bosch, A. (Producer & Director). (2000). *American Experience: The Rockefellers* [Documentary]. Boston: WGBH Educational Foundation. Retrieved from http://www.pbs.org/wgbh/americanexperience/films/rockefellers

Death Penalty Information Center. (2012). Financial costs. Retrieved from http://www.deathpenaltyinfo.org/costs-death-penalty

Death Penalty Information Center. (2013). Methods of execution. Retrieved from http://www.deathpenaltyinfo.org/methods-execution

Death Penalty Information Center. (2015). Fact sheet. Retrieved from http://www.deathpenaltyinfo.org/documents/FactSheet.pdf

Death Penalty Information Center. (2016a). Executions by year. Last updated July 16, 2016. Retrieved from http://www.deathpenaltyinfo.org/executions-year

Death Penalty Information Center. (2016b). Methods of execution. Retrieved September 6, 2016, from http://www.deathpenaltyinfo.org/methods-execution

Death Penalty Information Center. (2016c). States with and without the death penalty. Last updated August 18, 2016. Retrieved from http://www.deathpenaltyinfo.org/states-and-without-death-penalty

Death Penalty Information Center. (2016d). Women on death row. Retrieved September 7, 2016, from http://www.deathpenaltyinfo.org/women-and-death-penalty

Death Penalty Information Center. (n.d.). Time on death row. Retrieved from http://www.deathpenaltyinfo.org/time-death-row

Death Penalty Worldwide. (2014). Death penalty database: China. Last updated April 10, 2014. Retrieved from http://www.deathpenaltyworldwide.org/country-search-post.cfm?country=China

DeFina, R., & Arvanites, T. (2002). The weak effect of imprisonment on crime: 1971–1998. *Social Science Quarterly, 83*, 635–653.

De La Torre, M. (2013). Buried voices: Mexican migrants' views on the question of illegality. *Contemporary Justice Review, 16*(2), 264–279.

DeHart, D. D. (2008). Pathways to prison: Impact of victimization in the lives of incarcerated women. *Violence Against Women, 14*(12), 1362–1381.

Del Carmen, R., Parker, V., & Reddington, F. (1998). *Briefs of leading cases in juvenile justice.* Cincinnati, OH: Anderson.

Delany, P., Fletcher, B., & Shields, J. (2003). Reorganizing care for the substance using offender—the case for collaboration. *Federal Probation, 67*, 64–69.

DeLisi, M. (2005). *Career criminals in society.* Thousand Oaks, CA: Sage.

Economist Intelligence Unit. (2016). Democracy index 2015: Democracy in an age of anxiety. Retrieved from http://www.eiu.com/public/topical_report.aspx?campaignid=DemocracyIndex2015

Deng, X., Zhang, L., & Cordilia, A. (1998). Social control and recidivism in China. *Journal of Contemporary Criminal Justice, 14*, 281–295.

Denyer, S., & Wan, W. (2013, November 15). In reform package, China relaxes one-child policy, abolishes prison labor camps. *Washington Post.* Retrieved from http://www.washingtonpost.com/world/asia_pacific/china-relaxes-one-child-policy-abolishes-prison-labor-camps/2013/11/15/a3f3f476-4df7-11e3-be6b-d3d28122e6d4_story.html

Department of the Treasury. (2010). *Significant problems still exist with Internal Revenue Service efforts to identify prisoner tax refund fraud.* Washington, DC: Author. Retrieved from https://www.treasury.gov/tigta/audit-reports/2011reports/201140009fr.pdf

de Quervain, D., Fischbacher, U., Valerie, T., Schellhammer, M., Schnyder, U., Buch, A., & Fehr, E. (2004). The neural basis of altruistic punishment. *Science, 305*, 1254–1259.

Diamond, J. (1997). *Guns, germs, and steel: The fates of human societies.* New York: Norton & Company.

Diaz-Duran, C. (2010, December 30). The Scott sisters' life sentence for $11. *Daily Beast.* Retrieved from http://www.thedailybeast.com/articles/2010/12/31/haley-barbour-pardons-the-scott-sisters-life-sentence.html

Dickens, C. (1842). Chapter 7. In *American notes.* Retrieved from http://www.online-literature.com/dickens/americannotes/8

Dietz, E., O'Connell, D., & Scarpitti, F. (2003). Therapeutic communities and prison management: An examination of the effects of operating an in-prison therapeutic community on levels of institutional disorder. *International Journal of Offender Therapy and Comparative Criminology, 47*, 210–223.

DiIulio, J. J., & Piehl, A. (1991, Fall). Does prison pay? The stormy national debate over the cost-effectiveness of imprisonment. *Brookings Review*, 28–35.

Dillard, A. (2012). Madness alone punishes the madman: The search for moral dignity in the court's competency doctrine as applied to capital cases. *Tennessee Law Review, 79*, 461–514.

Dilworth, D. (1995). Prisoners' lawsuits burden federal civil courts. *Trial, 31*, 98–100.

Director addresses changes within BOP. (2006, March). *Third Branch, 38.* Retrieved from http://www.uscourts.gov/news/TheThird Branch/06-03-01/Director_Addresses_Change_Within_BOP.aspx

Ditton, P., & Wilson, D. (1999). *Truth in sentencing in state prisons.* Washington, DC: Bureau of Justice Statistics.

Dix, D. (1967). *Remarks on prisons and prison discipline in the United States.* Montclair, NJ: Patterson Smith. (Original work published 1843.)

Dodgson, K., Goodwin, P., Howard, P., Llewellyn-Thomas, S., Mortimer, E., Russell, N., et al. (2001). *Electronic monitoring of released prisoners: An evaluation of the home detention curfew scheme.* London: Home Office Research.

Dowden, C., & Tellier, C. (2004). Predicting work-related stress in correctional officers: A meta-analysis. *Journal of Criminal Justice, 32*(1), 31–47.

Dror, I., & Hampikian, G. (2011). Subjectivity and bias in forensic mixture interpretation. *Science and Justice, 51*, 204–208.

Drucker, P. F. (1954). *The practice of management.* New York, NY: Harper & Row.

Drug Policy Alliance. (2011, March 22). Drug courts are not the answer: Toward a health-centered approach to drug use. Retrieved from http://www.drugpolicy.org/drugcourts

Dui Hua. (2013). Criminal justice. Retrieved from http://duihua.org/wp/?page_id=136

Duran, J. (1996). Anne Viscountess Conway: A seventeenth-century rationalist. In L. L. McAlister (Ed.), *Hypatia's daughters: Fifteen hundred years of women philosophers* (pp. 92–108). Bloomington: Indiana University Press.

Duran, L., Plotkin, M., Potter, M., & Rosen, H. (2013). *Integrated reentry and employment strategies: Reducing recidivism and promoting job readiness.* New York: Council of State Governments Justice Center.

Durant, W., & Durant, A. (1967). *Rousseau and revolution.* New York: Simon & Schuster.

Durkheim, E. (1964). *The division of labor in society.* New York: Free Press. (Original work published 1893.)

Durnescu, I. (2008). An exploration of the purposes and outcomes of probation in European jurisdictions. *Probation Journal, 55*, 273–281.

Durose, M., Cooper, A., & Snyder, H. (2014). *Recidivism of prisoners released in 30 states in 2005: Patterns for 2005 to 2010.* Washington, DC: Bureau of Justice Statistics.

Durose, M. R., Farole, D. J., & Rosenmerkel, S. P. (2010). *Felony sentences in state courts, 2006.* Washington, DC: Bureau of Justice Statistics.

Duwe, G. (2014). An outcome evaluation of a prison work release program estimating its effects on recidivism, employment, and cost avoidance. *Criminal Justice Policy Review*. doi:10.1177/0887403414524590

Dworkin, A. (1993). Against the male flood: Censorship, pornography, and equality. In P. Smith (Ed.), *Feminist jurisprudence* (pp. 449–465). New York: Oxford University Press.

Ellis, A. (1989). The history of cognition in psychotherapy. In A. Freeman, K. Simon, L. Beutler, & H. Arkowitz (Eds.), *Comprehensive handbook of cognitive therapy* (pp. 5–19). New York: Plenum.

Ellis, L. (2003). Genes, criminality, and the evolutionary neuroandrogenic theory. In A. Walsh & L. Ellis (Eds.), *Biosocial criminology: Challenging environmentalism's supremacy* (pp. 13–34). Hauppauge, NY: Nova Science.

Ellis, T., Lewis, C., & Sato, M. (2011). The Japanese probation service: A third sector template? *Probation Journal, 58*, 333–344.

Ellis, L., & Walsh, A. (2000). *Criminology: A global perspective*. Boston: Allyn & Bacon.

Engelman, P. (2012, March). Judicial review and prison law. *Inside Time*. Retrieved from http://www.insidetime.org/articleview.asp?a=1170

Equal Justice Initiative. (2015). *Lynching in America: Confronting the legacy of racial terror*. Retrieved from http://www.eji.org/lynchinginamerica

Espinosa, P. (Senior Producer), Komatsu, S. (Series Producer), & Martin, G. (Director). (1998). *The U.S.–Mexican War (1846–1848)*. Dallas: KERA Unlimited; Mexico City: Once TV.

Ewing, C., & Dudzik, K. (2014, March 5). Nushawn Williams to remain confined. WGRZ. Retrieved from http://www.wgrz.com/story/news/local/2014/03/05/nushawn-williams-to-remain-confined/6089649

Fairchild, E., & Dammer, D. (2001). *Comparative criminal justice systems*. Belmont, CA: Wadsworth.

Farabee, D., Pendergast, M., & Anglin, M. (1998). The effectiveness of coerced treatment for drug abusing offenders. *Federal Probation, 109*, 3–10.

Farkas, M. A. (1999). Inmate supervisory style: Does gender make a difference? *Women & Criminal Justice, 10*, 25–45.

Farkas, M. A. (2000). A typology of correctional officers. *International Journal of Offender Therapy and Comparative Criminology, 44*, 431–449.

Farkas, M. A. (2001). Correctional officers: What factors influence work attitudes? *Correctional Management Quarterly, 5*(2), 20–26.

Farkas, M. A., & Rand, K. R. L. (1999). Sex matters: A gender-specific standard for cross-gender searches of inmates. *Women & Criminal Justice, 10*(3), 31–56.

Farkas, M., & Stichman, S. (2002). Can treatment, punishment, incapacitation, and public safety be reconciled? *Criminal Justice Review, 27*, 256–283.

Farrington, D. P., Langan, P. A., & Tonry, M. (2004). *Cross-national studies in crime and justice*. Washington, DC: Bureau of Justice Statistics. Retrieved from http://www.bjs.gov/content/pub/pdf/cnscj.pdf

Federal Bureau of Investigation. (2013a). *Crime in the United States, 2012: Uniform crime reports*. Washington, DC: U.S. Government Printing Office.

Federal Bureau of Investigation. (2013b). *Today's FBI: Facts and figures, 2013–2014*. Washington, DC: U.S. Government Printing Office.

Federal Bureau of Investigation. (2014). *Uniform crime reports: Crime in the United States 2012*. Washington, DC: U.S. Government Printing Office. Retrieved from http://www.fbi.gov/about-us/cjis/ucr/crime-in-the-u.s/2012/crime-in-the-u.s.-2012/persons-arrested/persons-arrested

Federal Bureau of Investigation. (2015). *Crime in the United States 2014*. Retrieved from https://ucr.fbi.gov/crime-in-the-u.s/2014/crime-in-the-u.s.-2014

Federman, C. (2004). Who has the body? The paths to habeas corpus reform. *Prison Journal, 84*, 317–339.

Feeley, M. M. (1991). The privatization of prisons in historical perspective. *Criminal Justice Research Bulletin, 6*(2), 1–10.

Fehr, E., & Gachter, S. (2002). Altruistic punishment in humans. *Nature, 415*, 137–140.

Ferri, E. (1917). *Criminal sociology*. Boston: Little, Brown. (Original work published 1897.)

Figlio, R. M., Tracy, P. E., & Wolfgang, M. E. (1990). *Delinquency in a birth cohort II: Philadelphia, 1958–1986*. Ann Arbor, MI: Inter-university Consortium for Political and Social Research.

Fink, S. L., Jenks, R. S., & Willits, R. D. (1983). *Designing and managing organizations*. Homewood, IL: Richard D. Irwin.

Finn, P., & Kuck, S. (2005). *Stress among probation and parole officers and what can be done about it*. Washington, DC: Department of Justice.

Finney, C., Stergiopoulos, E., Hensel, J., Bonato, S., & Dewa, C. S. (2013). Organizational stressors associated with job stress and burnout in correctional officers: A systematic review. *BMC Public Health, 13*. Retrieved from http://www.biomedcentral.com/1471-2458/13/82

Firestone, J. M., & Harris, R. J. (1994). Sexual harassment in the military: Environmental and individual contexts. *Armed Forces and Society, 21*, 25–43.

Firestone, J. M., & Harris, R. J. (1999). Changes in patterns of sexual harassment in the U.S. military: A comparison of the 1988 and 1995 DOD surveys. *Armed Forces and Society, 25*, 613–632.

Fishbein, D. (2003). Neuropsychological and emotional regulatory processes in antisocial behavior. In A. Walsh & L. Ellis (Eds.), *Biosocial criminology: Challenging environmentalism's supremacy* (pp. 185–208). Hauppauge, NY: Nova Science.

Fisher, W., Roy-Bujnowski, K., Grudzinskas, A., Clayfield, J., Banks, S., & Wolff, N. (2006). Patterns and prevalence of arrest in a statewide cohort of mental care consumers. *Psychiatric Services, 57*, 1623–1628.

Flavin, J., & Desautels, A. (2006). Feminism and crime. In C. M. Renzetti, L. Goodstein, & S. L. Miller (Eds.),

Rethinking gender, crime, and justice (pp. 11–28). Los Angeles, CA: Roxbury.

Fleisher, M. (1995). *Beggars and thieves: Lives of urban street criminals*. Madison: University of Wisconsin Press.

Fleisher, M. S., & Krienert, J. L. (2009). *The myth of prison rape: Sexual culture in American prisons*. Lanham, MD: Rowman & Littlefield.

Flores, A. R., Herman, J. L., Gates, G. J., & Brown, T. N. T. (2016). *How many adults identify as transgender in the United States?* Retrieved from http://williamsinstitute.law.ucla.edu/wp-content/uploads/How-Many-Adults-Identify-as-Transgender-in-the-United-States.pdf

Florida Department of Corrections. (2014). Major prison gangs. Retrieved from http://www.dc.state.fl.us/pub/gangs/prison.html

Foster, B. (2006). *Corrections: The fundamentals*. Upper Saddle River, NJ: Prentice Hall.

Foucault, M. (1979). *Discipline and punish: The birth of the prison*. New York: Vintage.

Frankel, L. (1996). Damaris Cudworth Masham: A seventeenth-century feminist philosopher. In L. L. McAlister (Ed.), *Hypatia's daughters: Fifteen hundred years of women philosophers* (pp. 128–138). Bloomington: Indiana University Press.

French prisons: Still miserable. (2009, May 14). *The Economist*. Retrieved from http://www.economist.com/node/13653923

Freudenberg, N. (2006). Coming home from jail: A review of health and social problems facing U.S. jail populations and of opportunities for reentry interventions. *American Jails, 20*, 9–24.

Gainsborough, J. (2002). *Mentally ill offenders in the criminal justice system: An analysis and prescription*. Washington, DC: Sentencing Project.

Gard, R. (2007). The first probation officers in England and Wales. *British Journal of Criminology, 47*, 1–17.

Gardner, L. (1996, March 1). Lessons from abroad [Online]. *Policy Review*. Retrieved from http://www.hoover.org/research/lessons-abroad-0

Garland, B., & Frankel, M. (2006). Considering convergence: A policy dialogue about behavioral genetics, neuroscience, and law. *Law and Contemporary Problems, 69*, 101–113.

Garland, B., Hogan, N., Wodahl, E., Hass, A., Stohr, M. K., & Lambert, E. (2014). Decarceration and its possible effects on inmates, staff, and communities. *Punishment and Society, 16*(4), 448–473.

Garland, D. (1990). *Punishment and modern society: A study in social theory*. Chicago, IL: University of Chicago Press.

Garner, B. R., Knight, K., & Simpson, D. D. (2007). Burnout among corrections-based drug treatment staff: Impact of individual and organizational factors. *International Journal of Offender Therapy and Comparative Criminology, 51*(5), 510–522.

Garofalo, R. (1968). *Criminology*. Montclair, NJ: Patterson Smith. (Original work published 1885.)

Gendreu, P., Goggin, C., Cullen, F., & Andrews, D. (2000). The effects of community sanctions and incarceration on recidivism. *Forum on Corrections Research, 12*, 10–13.

Gendreau, P., & Ross, R. R. (1987). Revivification of rehabilitation: Evidence from the 1980s. *Justice Quarterly, 4*, 349–407.

General Accounting Office. (1996). *Private and public prisons: Studies comparing operational costs and/or quality of service*. Washington, DC: Author.

George, T. (2012). *Domestic violence sentencing conditions and recidivism*. Olympia, WA: Washington State Center for Court Research, Administrative Office of the Courts.

Gerritzen, B. C., & Kirchgässner, G. (2013). *Facts or ideology: What determines the results of econometric estimates of the deterrence effect of death penalty? A meta-analysis*. Zurich, Switzerland: Center for Reasarch in Economics, Management and the Arts.

Gettinger, S. H. (1984). *New generation jails: An innovative approach to an age-old problem*. Washington, DC: National Institute of Corrections.

Giallombardo, R. (1966). *Society of women: A study of a women's prison*. New York: Wiley.

Gibbs, A., & King, D. (2003). The electronic ball and chain? The operation and impact of home detention with electronic monitoring in New Zealand. *Australian and New Zealand Journal of Criminology, 36*, 1–17.

Gilliard, D. K., & Beck, A. J. (1997). *Prison and inmates at midyear 1996*. Washington, DC: U.S. Department of Justice, Office of Justice Programs. Retrieved from http://www.ojp.usdoj.gov/bjs/pub/pdf/mhppji.pdf

Gilligan, C. (1982). *In a different voice: Psychological theory and women's development*. Cambridge, MA: Harvard University Press.

Glaze, L. E., & Bonczar, T. P. (2011). *Probation and parole in the United States, 2010*. Washington, DC: U.S. Department of Justice. Retrieved from http://www.bjs.gov/content/pub/pdf/ppus10.pdf

Glaze, L. E., Bonczar, T. P., & Zhang, F. (2010). *Probation and parole in the United States, 2009*. Washington, DC: Bureau of Justice Statistics. Retrieved from http://www.bjs.gov/content/pub/pdf/ppus09.pdf

Glaze, L. E., & Herberman, E. (2013). *Correctional populations in the United States, 2012*. Washington, DC: Bureau of Justice Statistics. Retrieved from www.bjs.gov/content/pub/pdf/cpus12.pdf

Glaze, L. E., & Kaeble, D. (2014). *Correctional populations in the United States, 2013*. Washington, DC: Bureau of Justice Statistics. Retrieved from http://www.bjs.gov/content/pub/pdf/cpus13.pdf

Glaze, L. E., & Palla, S. (2005). *Probation and parole in the United States, 2004*. Washington, DC: Bureau of Justice Statistics. Retrieved from http://www.bjs.gov/content/pub/pdf/ppus04.pdf

Glenn, S. (2010, October 7). Board suspends license of former McNeil Island nurse. *News Tribune* (Tacoma, WA), A4.

Goff, L., of Chieveley. (1997). The future of the common law. *International and Comparative Law Quarterly, 46*, 745–760.

Goffman, E. (1961). *Asylums: Essays on the social situation of mental patients and other inmates.* Garden City, NY: Anchor Books.

Goldfarb, R. (1975). *Jails: The ultimate ghetto.* Garden City, NY: Anchor Press.

Goleman, D. (1995). *Emotional intelligence.* New York: Bantam Books.

Goleman, D. (2006). *Social intelligence: The new science of human relationships.* New York: Bantam Books.

Gonnerman, J. (2001, September 4). Remembering Attica. *Village Voice.* Retrieved from http://www.villagevoice.com/news/remembering-attica-6414847

Goodale, G., Callahan, L., & Steadman, H. (2013). Law & psychiatry: What can we say about mental health courts today? *Psychiatric Services, 64*, 298–300.

Goodstein, L. (2006). Introduction: Gender, crime, and criminal justice. In C. M. Renzetti, L. Goodstein, & S. L. Miller (Eds.), *Rethinking gender, crime, and justice* (pp. 1–10). Los Angeles, CA: Roxbury.

Gordon, G. J., & Milakovich, M. E. (1998). *Public administration in America* (5th ed.). New York, NY: St. Martin's Press.

Gordon, J., Proulx, B., & Grant, P. (2013). Trepidation among the "keepers": Gendered perceptions of fear and risk of victimization among corrections officers. *American Journal of Criminal Justice, 38*(2), 245–265.

Gottfredson, M., & Hirschi, T. (1990). *A general theory of crime.* Stanford, CA: Stanford University Press.

Gottfredson, S., & Moriarty, L. (2006). Statistical risk assessment: Old problems and new applications. *Crime and Delinquency, 52*, 178–200.

Gray, T., Mays, G. L., & Stohr, M. K. (1995). Inmate needs and programming in exclusively women's jails. *Prison Journal, 75*(2), 186–202.

Greenfeld, L., & Hinners, D. (1985). *Capital punishment, 1984.* Washington, DC: U.S. Department of Justice.

Grinfeld, M. (2005). Sexual predator ruling raises ethical moral dilemmas. *Psychiatric Times, 16*, 1–4.

Gross, S., & Mauro, R. (1989). *Death and discrimination: Racial disparities in capital sentencing.* Boston: Northeastern University Press.

Grusec, J., & Hastings, P. (2007). *Handbook of socialization: Theory and research.* New York: Guilford Press.

Guerino, P., Harrison, P. M., & Sabol, W. J. (2012). *Prisoners in 2010.* Washington, DC: Bureau of Justice Statistics. Retrieved from http://www.bjs.gov/content/pub/pdf/p10.pdf

Hall, J. (2013, February 4). Saudi royal family intervenes over preacher released despite raping and killing daughter. *The Independent* (UK). Retrieved from http://www.independent.co.uk/news/world/middle-east/saudi-royal-family-intervenes-over-preacher-released-despite-raping-and-killing-daughter-8491812.html

Hamada, J. N. (2015). At peace with dementia. *American Jails, 29*(2), 34–36.

Hamel, M. (2013, June 14). Les misérables: French prisons bursting at the seams. *International Business Times.* Retrieved from http://www.ibtimes.com/les-miserables-french-prisons-bursting-seams-1306761

Hamilton, Z., Kigerl, A., & Hays, Z. (2015). Removing release impediments and reducing correctional costs: Evaluation of Washington State's housing voucher program. *Justice Quarterly, 32*(2), 255–287. doi: 10.1080/07418825.2012.761720

Haney, C., Banks, C., & Zimbardo, P. (1981). Interpersonal dynamics in a simulated prison. In R. R. Ross (Ed.), *Prison guard/correctional officer* (pp. 137–168). Toronto, Canada: Butterworth.

Hanson, K., & Bussière, M. (1998). Predicting relapse: A meta-analysis of sexual offenders recidivism studies. *Journal of Consulting and Clinical Psychology, 66*, 348–362.

Hardyman, P. L., Austin, J., Alexander, J., Johnson, K. D., & Tulloch, O. C. (2002). *Internal prison classification systems: Case studies in their development and implementation.* Washington, DC: National Institute of Correction.

Hardyman, P., Austin, J., & Peyton, J. (2004). *Prisoner intake systems: Assessing needs and classifying prisoners.* Washington, DC: National Institute of Justice.

Hare, R. (1996). Psychopathy and antisocial personality disorder: A case of diagnostic confusion. *Psychiatric Times, 13*, 1–8.

Hare, R. (2003). *Manual for the Hare Psychopathy Checklist–Revised* (2nd ed.). Toronto, Canada: Multi-Health Systems.

Harrington, P. E. (2002). Advice to women beginning a career in policing. *Women & Criminal Justice, 9*, 1–21.

Harris, G., Skilling, T., & Rice, M. (2001). The construct of psychopathy. In M. Tonry (Ed.), *Crime and justice: A review of research* (pp. 197–264). Chicago, IL: University of Chicago Press.

Harris, J. (1973). *Crisis in corrections: The prison problem.* New York: McGraw-Hill.

Hassine, V. (1996). *Life without parole: Living in prison today.* Los Angeles, CA: Roxbury.

Hassine, V. (2009). *Life without parole: Living in prison today* (4th ed.). New York, NY: Oxford University Press.

Hatch, V., & Walsh, A. (2016). *Capital punishment: Theory and practice of the ultimate penalty.* New York, NY: Oxford University Press.

Havercamp, R., Mayer, M., & Levy, R. (2004). Electronic monitoring in Europe. *European Journal of Crime, Criminal Law, and Criminal Justice, 12*, 36–45.

Hawkes, M. Q. (1998). Edna Mahan: Sustaining the reformatory tradition. *Women & Criminal Justice, 9*, 1–21.

Hawkins, H. C. (2005). Race and sentencing outcomes in Michigan. *Journal of Ethnicity in Criminal Justice, 3*(1/2), 91–109.

Hawthorne, N. (2003). *The scarlet letter*. New York: Barnes & Noble Classics. (Original work published 1850.)

Hayes, L. M. (2010). *National study of jail suicide: 20 years later*. Washington, DC: National Center on Institutions and Alternatives. Retrieved from http://static.nicic.gov/Library/024308.pdf

Hefferman, E. (1972). *Making it in prison: The square, the cool, and the life*. New York, NY: Wiley.

Heil, G., Bennis, W. & Stephens, D. C. (2000). *Douglas McGregor revisited: Managing the human side of enterprise*. New York, NY: Wiley.

Hemmens, C., & Atherton, E. (1999). *Use of force: Current practice and policy*. Lanham, MD: American Correctional Association.

Hemmens, C., & Marquart, J. W. (2000). Race, age, and inmate perceptions of inmate–staff relations. *Journal of Criminal Justice, 28*, 297–312.

Hemmens, C., Steiner, B., & Mueller, D. (2003). *Significant cases in juvenile justice*. Los Angeles, CA: Roxbury

Hemmens, C., Stohr, M. K., Schoeler, M., & Miller, B. (2002). One step up, two steps back: The progression of perceptions of women's work in prisons and jails. *Journal of Criminal Justice, 30*, 473–489.

Henriques, Z. W. (1996). Imprisoned mothers and their children: Separation-reunion syndrome dual impact. *Women & Criminal Justice, 8*(1), 77–95.

Henriques, Z. W., & Gilbert, E. (2003). Sexual abuse and sexual assault of women in prison. In R. Muraskin (Ed.), *It's a crime: Women and justice* (pp. 258–272). Upper Saddle River, NJ: Prentice Hall.

Herberman, E. J., & Bonczar, T. P. (2015). *Probation and parole in the United States, 2013*. Washington, DC: Bureau of Justice Statistics. Retrieved from http://www.bjs.gov/content/pub/pdf/ppus13.pdf

Hersh, S. M. (2004, May 10). Torture at Abu Ghraib. *New Yorker*. Retrieved from http://www.newyorker.com/magazine/2004/05/10/torture-at-abu-ghraib

Herzog-Evans, M. (2011a). Probation in France: Some things old, some things new, some things borrowed and often blue. *Probation Journal, 58*, 345–354.

Herzog-Evans, M. (2011b). Desisting in France: What probation officers know and do. A first approach. *European Journal of Probation, 3*(2), 29–46.

Hindman, J., & Peters, J. (2001). Polygraph testing leads to better understanding adult and juvenile sex offenders. *Federal Probation, 65*, 1–15.

Hirsch, A. J. (1992). *The rise of the penitentiary*. New Haven, CT: Yale University Press.

Hirschi, T. (1969). *The causes of delinquency*. Berkeley: University of California Press.

Hirschi, T., & Gottfredson, M. (1983). Age and the explanation of crime. *American Journal of Sociology, 89*, 552–584.

Hochstetler, A., DeLisi, M., & Pratt, T. C. (2010). Social support and feelings of hostility among released inmates. *Crime & Delinquency, 56*(4), 588–607.

Hockenberry, S. (2013). *Juveniles in residential placement, 2010*. Washington, DC: Office of Juvenile Justice and Delinquency Prevention. Retrieved from http://www.ojjdp.gov/pubs/241060.pdf

Hockenberry, S., & Puzzanchera, C. (2015). *Juvenile court statistics 2013*. Pittsburgh, PA: National Center for Juvenile Justice. Retrieved from http://www.ojjdp.gov/ojstatbb/njcda/pdf/jcs2013.pdf

Hogan, N. L., Lambert, E. G., Hepburn, J. R., Burton, V. S., & Cullen, F. T. (2004). Is there a difference? Exploring male and female correctional officers' definition of and response to conflict situations. *Women & Criminal Justice, 15*(3/4), 143–165.

Holcomb, I. (2008). *The carrying of firearms by probation officers*. Paper presented at the annual meeting of the American Criminal Justice Society, Cincinnati, OH.

Hough, A. (2008). UK jails too cushy for criminals? ABC News. Retrieved from http://abcnews.go.com/International/story?id=4724366&page=1#.UWhW11eRcg8

Houser, K. A., & Welsch, W. (2014). Examining the association between co-occurring disorders and seriousness of misconduct by female prison inmates. *Criminal Justice & Behavior, 41*(5), 650–666.

Houston, C. (2014). How feminist theory became (criminal) law: Tracing the path to mandatory criminal intervention in domestic violence cases. *Michigan Journal of Gender & Law, 21*, 217–311.

Howard, J. (2000). *The state of prisons in England and Wales, with preliminary observations, and an account of some foreign prisons*. London: Routledge/Thoemmes Press. (Original work published 1775.)

Hubbard, D. J., Travis, L. F., III, & Latessa, E. J. (2001). *Case classification in community corrections: A national survey of the state of the art*. Washington, DC: National Institute of Justice.

Hughes, K. A. (2006). *Justice expenditure and employment in the United States, 2003*. Washington, DC: Bureau of Justice Statistics. Retrieved from http://www.bjs.gov/content/pub/pdf/jeeus03.pdf

Hughes, R. (1987). *The fatal shore*. New York: Vintage Books.

Hughes, T., Wilson, D., & Beck, A. (2001). *Trends in state parole, 1990–2000*. Washington, DC: Bureau of Justice Statistics.

Hulings, N. (2010, October 5). Jail ready but still too costly. *News Tribune* (Tacoma, WA), A4.

Ignatieff, M. (1978). *A just measure of pain: The penitentiary in the industrial revolution, 1750–1850*. New York, NY: Columbia University Press.

Impey, E., & Parnell, G. (2011). *The Tower of London: The official illustrated history*. London, UK: Merrell Publishers.

Inciardi, J. A. (2007). *Criminal justice* (8th ed.). Boston, MA: McGraw-Hill.

Inciardi, J., Martin, S., & Butzin, C. (2004). Five-year outcomes of therapeutic community treatment of drug-involved offenders after release from prison. *Crime & Delinquency, 50*, 88–111.

Inderbitzin, M. (2006). Guardians of the state's problem children: An ethnographic study of staff members in a juvenile correctional facility. *Prison Journal, 86*(4), 431–451.

Innocence Project. (2016). DNA exonerations in the United States. Retrieved September 7, 2016, from http://www.innocenceproject.org/dna-exonerations-in-the-united-states

Ireland, C., & Berg, B. (2006). Women in parole: Gendered adaptations of female parole agents in California. *Women & Criminal Justice, 18*(1/2), 131–150.

Irwin, J. (1985). *The jail: Managing the underclass in American society.* Berkeley: University of California Press.

Irwin, J. (2005). *The warehouse prison: Disposal of the new dangerous class.* Los Angeles, CA: Roxbury.

Jacobs, B., & Wright, R. (1999). Stick-up, street culture, and offender motivation. *Criminology, 37*, 149–173.

Jacobs, J. B. (1977). *Stateville: The penitentiary in mass society.* Chicago: University of Chicago Press.

Jaffee, S., Moffitt, T., Caspi, A., & Taylor, A. (2003). Life with (or without) father: The benefits of living with two biological parents depend on the father's antisocial behavior. *Child Development, 74*, 109–126.

James, D. J., & Glaze, L. E. (2006). *Mental health problems of prison and jail inmates.* Washington, DC: U.S. Department of Justice, Office of Justice Programs.

Jansson, K. (2006). *British Crime Survey—Measuring crime for 25 years.* Retrieved from http://webarchive.nationalarchives.gov.uk/20110218135832/rds.homeoffice.gov.uk/rds/pdfs07/bcs25.pdf

Jay Farbstein & Associates. (1989). *A comparison of "direct" and "indirect" supervision correctional facilities* (with R. Wener). Washington, DC: National Institute of Corrections.

Jennings, W., Richards, T., Smith, M., Bjerregaard, B., & Fogel, S. (2014). A critical examination of the "white victim effect" and death penalty decision-making from a propensity score matching approach: The North Carolina experience. *Journal of Criminal Justice, 42*, 384–398.

Jiang, S., Xiang, D., Chen, Q., Huang, C., Yang, S., Zhang, D., et al. (2014). Community corrections in China: Development and challenges. *Prison Journal, 94*(1), 75–96.

Johnson, J., & Johnson, C. (2001). Poverty and the death penalty. *Journal of Economic Issues, 35*, 517–523.

Johnson, R. (2002). *Hard time: Understanding and reforming the prison* (3rd ed.). Belmont, CA: Wadsworth/Thomson Learning.

Johnson, R., & Raphael, S. (2012). How much crime reduction does the marginal prisoner buy? *Journal of Law and Economics, 55*, 275–310.

Johnston, N. (2009). Evolving function: Early use of imprisonment as punishment. *Prison Journal, 89*(1), 10S–34S.

Johnston, N. (2010). Early Philadelphia prisons: Amour, alcohol, and other forbidden pleasures. *Prison Journal, 90*(1), 4–11.

Jolliffe, D., & Farrington, D. (2009). *Effectiveness of interventions with adult male violent offenders.* Stockholm: Swedish Council for Crime Prevention.

Jones, J. C. (2016, January 23–24). Early Chinese contributions to Whitman County overlooked as unfair competition. *Moscow-Pullman Daily News*, 3D.

Jones, J. M. (2014, October 23). Americans' support for death penalty stable. Gallup. Retrieved from http://www.gallup.com/poll/178790/americans-support-death-penalty-stable.aspx

Jones, O., & Shen, F. (2012). Law and neuroscience in the United States. In T. Spranger (Ed.), *International neurolaw: A comparative analysis* (pp. 349–380). Berlin: Springer-Verlag.

Jones, S. R. (2013). *Strategies for success: A proactive response to public safety realignment.* Retrieved from https://www.sacsheriff.com/Pages/Organization/Documents/Strategies%20for%20Success%20web.pdf

Joseph, J., & Taylor, D. (Eds.). (2003). *With justice for all: Minorities and women in criminal justice.* Upper Saddle River, NJ: Prentice Hall.

Junger-Tas, J. (1996). Delinquency similar in Western countries. *Overcrowded Times, 7*, 10–13.

Jurik, N. C. (1985a). Individual and organizational determinants of correctional officer attitudes toward inmates. *Criminology, 23*, 523–539.

Jurik, N. C. (1985b). An officer and a lady: Organizational barriers to women working as correctional officers in men's prisons. *Social Problems, 33*, 375–388.

Jurik, N. C. (1988). Striking a balance: Female correctional officers, gender-role stereotypes, and male prisons. *Sociological Inquiry, 58*, 291–305.

Jurik, N. C., & Halemba, G. J. (1984). Gender, working conditions, and the job satisfaction of women in a nontraditional occupation: Female correctional officers in a men's prison. *Sociological Quarterly, 25*, 551–566.

Jury awards $14 million in historic SPLC case. (2015). *SPLC Report, 45*(1), 1–8.

Kaeble, D., Glaze, L., Tsoutis, A., & Minton, T. (2016). *Correctional populations in the United States, 2014.* Washington, DC: Bureau of Justice Statistics. Retrieved from http://www.bjs.gov/content/pub/pdf/cpus14.pdf

Kaeble, D., Maruschak, L. M., & Bonczar, T. P. (2015). *Probation and parole in the United States, 2014.* Washington, DC: Bureau of Justice Statistics. Retrieved from http://www.bjs.gov/content/pub/pdf/ppus14.pdf

Kannenberg, C. (2009). Wading through the morass of modern federal habeas review of state capital prisoners' claims. *Quinnipac Law Review, 28*, 107–82.

Kansal, T. (2005). *Racial disparity in sentencing: A review of the literature.* Washington, DC: Sentencing Project. Retrieved from https://www.opensocietyfoundations.org/sites/default/files/disparity.pdf

Karberg, J. C., & James, D. J. (2005). *Substance dependence, abuse, and treatment of jail inmates, 2002*. Washington, DC: Bureau of Justice Statistics. Retrieved from http://www.bjs.gov/content/pub/pdf/sdatji02.pdf

Katz, J. (2005). *Warren McClesky v. Ralph Kemp*: Is the death penalty in Georgia racially biased? In E. Mandery (Ed.), *Capital punishment in America: A balanced examination* (pp. 400–407). Sudbury, MA: Jones & Bartlett. Retrieved from http://www.ourpaws.info/cramer/death/katz.htm

Kauffman, K. (1988). *Prison officers and their world*. Cambridge, MA: Harvard University Press.

Kazemian, L., & Andersson, C. (2012). *The French prison system: Comparative insights for policy and practice in New York and the United States*. New York: Research and Evaluation Center, John Jay College of Criminal Justice, City University of New York.

Keil, T. J., & Vito, G. F. (2009). Lynching and the death penalty in Kentucky, 1866–1934. *Journal of Ethnicity in Criminal Justice, 7*, 53–68.

Keilitz, S. (2004). *Specialization of domestic violence case management in the courts: A national survey*. Washington, DC: National Institute of Justice.

Keiser, G. (2003). *Topics in community corrections: Offender assessment*. Washington, DC: National Institute of Corrections.

Kerle, K. (1991). Introduction. In J. Thompson & G. L. Mays (Eds.), *American jails: Public policy issues* (pp. 1–3). Chicago, IL: Nelson-Hall.

Kerle, K. (2003). *Exploring jail operations*. Hagerstown, MD: American Jail Association.

Kerle, K. E. (2011). *Exploring jail operations* [Unpublished manuscript].

Kiehl, K. (2006). A cognitive neuroscience perspective on psychopathy: Evidence for paralimbic system dysfunction. *Psychiatry Research, 142*, 107–128.

Kilmer, B., & Sussell, J. (2014). *Does San Francisco's Community Justice Center reduce criminal recidivism?* Santa Monica, CA: RAND Corporation.

Kim, A.-S., DeValve, M., DeValve, E. Q., & Jonson, W. W. (2003). Female wardens: Results from a national survey of state correctional executives. *Prison Journal, 83*, 406–425.

Kim, B., Benekos, P. J., & Merlo, A. V. (2016). Sex offender recidivism revisited: Review of recent meta-analyses on the effects of sex offender treatment. *Trauma, Violence, & Abuse, 17*(1), 105–117.

King, K., Steiner, B., & Breach, S. R. (2008). Violence in the supermax: A self-fulfilling prophecy. *Prison Journal, 88*(1), 144–168.

Kirkham, C. (2013, October 22). Private prison empire rises despite startling record of juvenile abuse. *Huffington Post*.

Kirshon, J. (2010, September 13). Attica prison riot ends in bloodshed. Retrieved from http://www.examiner.com

Kitano, H. H. L. (1997). *Race relations* (5th ed.). Upper Saddle River, NJ: Prentice Hall.

Kitchen supervisor gets prison time for sexually abusing two prisoners. (2014). *Prison Legal News, 25*(4), 20. Retrieved from https://www.prisonlegalnews.org/news/2014/apr/15/kitchen-supervisor-gets-prison-time-for-sexually-abusing-two-prisoners

Kleber, H. (2003). Pharmacological treatments for heroin and cocaine dependence. *American Journal on Addictions, 12*, S5–S18.

Kleck, G. (1981). Racial discrimination in criminal sentencing: A critical evaluation of the evidence with additional evidence on the death penalty. *American Sociological Review, 46*, 783–805.

Klein, S., Berk, R., & Hickman, L. (2006). *Race and the decision to seek the death penalty in federal cases*. Santa Monica, CA: RAND Corporation.

Klingele, C. (2013). Rethinking the use of community supervision. *Journal of Criminal Law and Criminology, 103*, 1015–1070.

Klofas, J. M. (1991). Disaggregating jail use: Variety and change in local corrections over a ten-year period. In J. Thompson & G. L. Mays (Eds.), *American jails: Public policy issues* (pp. 40–58). Chicago: Nelson-Hall.

Klofas, J., Stojkovic, S., & Kalinich, D. (1990). *Criminal justice organizations: Administration and management*. Pacific Grove, CA: Brooks/Cole.

Kluger, J. (2007). The paradox of supermax. *Time, 169*(6), 52–53.

Kramer, J., & Ulmer, J. (2009). *Sentencing guidelines: Lessons from Pennsylvania*. Boulder, CO: Lynne Rienner.

Kruger, D. (2014, December 1). Why Texas is closing prisons in favour of rehab. *BBC Magazine*. Retrieved from http://www.bbc.com/news/world-us-canada-30275026

Kruk, E. (2012). Arguments for an equal parental responsibility presumption in contested child custody. *American Journal of Family Therapy, 40*, 33–55.

Kyckelhahn, T. (2014). *State corrections expenditures, FY 1982–2010*. Washington, DC: Bureau of Justice Statistics. Retrieved from http://www.bjs.gov/content/pub/pdf/scefy8210.pdf

Labriola, M., Bradley, S., O'Sullivan, C. S., Rempel, M., & Moore, S. (2010). *A national portrait of domestic violence courts*. Washington, DC: Center for Court Innovation.

Lambert, E. G., Hogan, N. L., & Tucker, K. A. (2009). Problems at work: Exploring the correlates of role stress among correctional staff. *Prison Journal, 89*(4), 460–481.

Langan, P. A., & Farrington, D. (1998). *Crime and justice in the United States and England and Wales, 1981–1996*. Washington, DC: Bureau of Justice Statistics.

Langan, P. A., Greenfield, L. A., Smith, S. K., Durose, M. R., & Levin, D. J. (2001). *Contacts between police and the public: Findings from the 1999 national survey*. Washington, DC: Bureau of Justice Statistics. Retrieved from http://www.bjs.gov/content/pub/pdf/cpp99.pdf

Langan, P. A., & Levin, D. (2002). *Recidivism of prisoners released in 1994*. Washington, DC: Bureau of Justice Statistics.

Langan, P. A., Schmitt, E., & Durose, M. (2003). *Recidivism of sex offenders released from prison in 1994*. Washington, DC: Bureau of Justice Statistics.

Latessa, E. J., & Lowenkamp, C. (2005, 4th Quarter). What are criminogenic needs and why are they important? *Ohio Judicial Conference*, 15–16.

Latessa, W., Cullen, F., & Gendreau, P. (2002). Beyond correctional quackery—Professionalism and the possibility of effective treatment. *Federal Probation*, 66, 43–50.

Latimer, J., Dowden, C., & Muise, D. (2005). The effectiveness of restorative justice practices. *Prison Journal*, 85, 127–144.

Laudano, J. (2013). *The high cost of corrections in America*. Retrieved from http://www.pewstates.org/research/data-visualizations/the-high-cost-of-corrections-in-america-85899397897

La Vigne, N. G., Debus-Sherrill, S., Brazzell, D., & Downey, P. M. (2011). *Preventing violence and sexual assault in jails: A situational crime prevention approach*. Washington, DC: Justice Policy Center, Urban Institute. Retrieved from http://www.prearesourcecenter.org/sites/default/files/library/situationalpreventionof sexualassault.pdf

Lawes, L. E. (1932). *Twenty thousand years in Sing Sing*. New York: Long & Smith.

Lawrence, R., & Mahan, S. (1998). Women corrections officers in men's prisons: Acceptance and perceived job performance. *Women & Criminal Justice*, 9(3), 63–86.

Lee, C., Rottman, D., Swaner, R., Lambson, S., Rempel, M., & Curtis, R. (2013). *A Community court grows in Brooklyn: A comprehensive evaluation of the Red Hook Community Justice Center*. Williamsburg, VA: National Center for State Courts.

Lee, E., & Martinez, J. (1998). *How it works: A summary of case flow and interventions at the Midtown Community Court*. Washington, DC: Bureau of Justice Assistance.

Lee, J. A., & Visano, L. A. (1994). Official deviance in the legal system. In S. Stojokovic, J. Klofas, & D. Kalinich (Eds.), *The administration and management of criminal justice organizations: A book of readings* (pp. 202–231). Prospect Heights, IL: Waveland Press.

Leshner, A. (1998). Addiction is a brain disease—and it matters. *National Institute of Justice Journal*, 237, 2–6.

Library of Congress. (2010). *Old jail, State Route 6A and Old Jail Lane, Barnstable, Barnstable County, MA*. Retrieved from http://www.loc.gov/pictures/search

Lieb, S., Fallon, S. J., Friedman, S. R., Thompson, D. R., Gates, G. J., Liberti, T. M., et al. (2011). Statewide estimation of racial/ethnic populations of men who have sex with men in the U.S. *Public Health Reports*, 126, 60–72.

Leip, L. A., & Stinchcomb, J. B. (2013). Should I stay or should I go? Job satisfaction and turnover intent of jail staff throughout the United States. *Criminal Justice Review*, 38(2), 226–241.

Light, M. T., Lopez, M. H., & Gonzalez-Barrera, A. (2014, March 18). The rise of federal immigration crimes: Unlawful reentry drives growth. Washington, DC: Pew Research Center. Retrieved from http://www.pewhispanic.org/2014/03/18/the-rise-of-federal-immigration-crimes

Lightfoot, C., Zupan, L. L., & Stohr, M. K. (1991). Jails and the community: Modeling the future in local detention facilities. *American Jails*, 5, 50–52.

Lin, N. (1986). Conceptualizing social support. In N. Lin, A. Dean, & W. Edsel (Eds.), *Social support, life events, and depression* (pp. 17–30). Orlando, FL: Academic Press.

Linden, D. (2006). How psychotherapy changes the brain—The contribution of functional neuroimaging. *Molecular Psychiatry*, 11, 528–538.

Lipsey, M., & Cullen, F. (2007). The effectiveness of correctional rehabilitation: A review of systematic reviews. *Annual Review of Law and Social Science*, 3, 297–320.

Lipsky, M. (1980). *Street-level bureaucracy: Dilemmas of the individual in public services*. New York, NY: Russell Sage.

Litt, M., & Mallon, S. (2003). The design of social support networks for offenders in outpatient drug treatment. *Federal Probation*, 67, 15–22.

Liu, J., Zhao, R., Xiong, H., & Gong, J. (2012). Chinese legal traditions: Punitiveness versus mercy. *Asian Pacific Journal of Police & Criminal Justice*, 9, 17–33.

Livsey, S. (2012). *Juvenile delinquency probation caseload, 2009*. Washington, DC: Office of Juvenile Justice and Delinquency Prevention. Retrieved from http://www.ojjdp.gov/pubs/239082.pdf

Logan, C., & Gaes, G. (1993). Meta-analysis and the rehabilitation of punishment. *Justice Quarterly*, 10, 245–263.

Lombardo, L. X. (1982). *Guards imprisoned*. Cincinnati, OH: Anderson.

Lombardo, L. X. (2001). Guards imprisoned: Correctional officers at work. In E. J. Latessa, A. Holsinger, J. W. Marquart, & J. R. Sorensen (Eds.), *Correctional contexts: Contemporary and classical readings* (2nd ed., pp. 153–167). Los Angeles, CA: Roxbury.

Loper, A. B., & Tuerk, E. H. (2006). Parenting programs for incarcerated parents: Current research and future directions. *Criminal Justice Policy Review*, 14(4), 407–427.

Lowenkamp, C. T., Flores, A. W., Holsinger, A. M., Makarios, M. D., & Latessa, E. J. (2010). Intensive supervision programs: Does program philosophy and the principles of effective intervention matter? *Journal of Criminal Justice*, 38, 368–375.

Lowenkamp, C., & Latessa, E. (2002). *Evaluation of Ohio's community-based corrections facilities and halfway house programs: Final report*. Cincinnati, OH: University of Cincinnati, Center for Criminal Justice Research.

Lowenkamp, C., & Latessa, E. (2004). Understanding the risk principle: How and why correctional interventions can harm low-risk offenders. In D. Faust (Ed.), *Assessment issues for managers* (pp. 3–7). Washington, DC: National Institute of Corrections.

Lubitz, R., & Ross, T. (2001, June). Sentencing guidelines: Reflections on the future. *Sentencing & Corrections: Issues for the 21st Century, No. 10*. Washington, DC: National Institute of Justice.

Lundman, R. J. (2010). Are police-reported driving while Black data a valid indicator of the race and ethnicity of the traffic law violators police stop? A negative answer with minor qualifications. *Journal of Criminal Justice, 38*(1), 77–87.

Lurigio, A. (2000). Persons with serious mental illness in the criminal justice system: Background, prevalence, and principles of care. *Criminal Justice Policy Review, 11,* 312–328.

Lurigio, A., & Loose, P. (2008). The disproportionate incarceration of African Americans for drug offenses: The national and Illinois perspective. *Journal of Ethnicity in Criminal Justice, 6*(3), 223–247.

Lutze, F. (2014). *Professional lives of community corrections officers: The invisible side of reentry.* Thousand Oaks, CA: Sage.

Lutze, F. E., & Murphy, D. W. (1999). Ultra-masculine prison environments and inmates' adjustment: It's time to move beyond the "boys will be boys" paradigm. *Justice Quarterly, 16,* 709–734.

Lutze, F. E., Rosky, J., & Hamilton, Z. (2013). Homelessness and reentry: A multistate outcome evaluation of Washington State's reentry housing program for high risk offenders. *Criminal Justice & Behavior, 20*(10), 1–21.

Macher, A. M. (2007). Issues in correctional HIV care: Neurological manifestations of patients with primary HIV infection. *American Jails, 21,* 49–55.

MacKenzie, D. L., & Brame, R. (2001). Community supervision, prosocial activities, and recidivism. *Justice Quarterly, 18,* 429–448.

Mackin, J., Lucas, L., & Lambarth, C. (2010). *Baltimore County Juvenile Drug Court outcome and cost evaluation.* Baltimore, MD: NPC Research.

Maeching, C. (1993). The adversarial system should be replaced. In M. D. Biskup (Ed.), *Criminal justice: Opposing viewpoints* (pp. 35–42). San Diego, CA: Greenhaven.

Maletzky, B., & Field, G. (2003). The biological treatment of dangerous sexual offenders: A review and preliminary report of the Oregon pilot Depo-Provera program. *Aggression and Violent Behavior, 8,* 391–412.

Mallicoat, S. L. (2011). *Women and crime: A text/reader.* Thousand Oaks, CA: Sage.

Mandery, E. (2005). *Capital punishment in America: A balanced examination.* Sudbury, MA: Jones & Bartlett.

Mann, C. C. (2006). *1491: New revelations of the Americas before Columbus.* New York, NY: Vintage Books.

Mansuy, I. (2005). The principle of legality and the execution of sentences in France and Germany: Law = rights? *Champ Penal/Penal Field, 2,* 1–14.

Marion, N. (2002). Effectiveness of community-based programs: A case study. *Prison Journal, 82,* 478–497.

Marquart, J. W., Barnhill, M. B., & Balshaw-Biddle, K. (2001). Fatal attraction: An analysis of employee boundary violations in a southern prison system, 1995–1998. *Justice Quarterly, 18,* 877–910.

Marquis, J. (2005). The myth of innocence. *Journal of Criminal Law and Criminology, 95,* 501–522.

Marsh, R., & Walsh, A. (1995). Physiological and psychosocial assessment and treatment of sex offenders: A comprehensive victim-oriented program. *Journal of Offender Rehabilitation, 22,* 77–96.

Marshall, L. (2004). The innocence revolution and the death penalty. *Ohio State Journal of Criminal Law, 1,* 573–584.

Martin, G. (2005). *Juvenile justice: Process and systems.* Thousand Oaks, CA: Sage.

Martin, S., & Jurik, N. (1996). *Doing justice, doing gender.* Thousand Oaks, CA: Sage.

Martinez, D. J. (2004). Hispanics incarcerated in state correctional facilities: Variations in inmate characteristics across Hispanic subgroups. *Journal of Ethnicity in Criminal Justice, 2*(1–2), 119–131.

Martinson, R. (1974). What works? Questions and answers about prison perform. *Public Interest, 35,* 22–54.

Maruschak, L. M. (2006). *Medical problems of jail inmates.* Washington, DC: Bureau of Justice Statistics. Retrieved from http://www.bjs.gov/content/pub/pdf/mpji.pdf

Maruschak, L. M. (2008). *Medical problems of prisoners.* Washington, DC: Bureau of Justice Statistics.

Maruschak, L. M. (2015). *Medical problems of state and federal prisoners and jail inmates, 2011–12.* Washington, DC: Bureau of Justice Statistics. Retrieved from bjs.gov/content/pub/pdf/mspfpji1112.pdf

Maruschak, L., & Bonczar, T. (2013). *Probation and parole in the United States, 2012.* Washington, DC: Bureau of Justice Statistics.

Maschke, K. J. (1996). Gender in the prison setting: The privacy–equal employment dilemma. *Women & Criminal Justice, 7,* 23–42.

Maslow, A. H. (1998). *Maslow on management.* New York, NY: Wiley. (Original work published 1961.)

Maslow, A. H. (2001). A theory of human motivation. In J. M. Shafritz & J. S. Ott (Eds.), *Classics of organization theory* (pp. 152–157). Fort Worth, TX: Harcourt College Publishers. (Original work published 1943.)

Mason, K. (2016, May 4). Guest post: Justice Dept. agency to alter its terminology for released convicts, to ease reentry. *Washington Post.* Retrieved from https://www.washingtonpost.com/news/true-crime/wp/2016/05/04/guest-post-justice-dept-to-alter-its-terminology-for-released-convicts-to-ease-reentry

Mathias, R. (1995). Correctional treatment helps offenders stay drug and arrest free. *NIDA Notes, 10*(4). Retrieved from http://archives.drugbuse.gov/NIDA_Notes/NNVol10N4/Prison.html

Mattick, H. W. (1974). The contemporary jails of the United States: An unknown and neglected area of justice. In D. Glaser (Ed.), *Handbook of criminology.* Chicago, IL: Rand McNally.

Mauer, M. (2014). Fewer prisoners, less crime: A tale of three states. Retrieved on February 10, 2016 from http://www.sentencingproject.org/template/page.cfm?id=156

Mauer, M., King, R., & Young, M. (2004). *The meaning of "life": Long prison sentences in context.* Washington, DC: Sentencing Project.

Mawby, R. (2001). *Burglary.* Colompton, Devon, UK: Willan Publishing.

May, D. C., Applegate, B. K., Ruddell, R., & Wood, P. B. (2014). Going to jail sucks (and it doesn't matter who you ask). *American Journal of Criminal Justice, 39,* 250–266.

May, D., Wood, P., Mooney, J., & Minor, K. (2005). Predicting offender-generated exchange rates: Implications for a theory of sentence severity. *Crime & Delinquency, 51,* 373–399.

McAlinden, A. M. (2011). "Transforming justice": Challenges for restorative justice in an era of punishment-based corrections. *Contemporary Justice Review, 14,* 383–406.

McAuliffe, K. (2010). Are we still evolving? In J. Groopman (Ed.), *The best science writing of 2010* (pp. 218–231). New York, NY: HarperCollins.

McDermott, P. A., Alterman, A. I., Cacciola, J. S., Rutherford, M. J., Newman, J. P., & Mulholland, E. M. (2000). Generality of Psychopathy Checklist–Revised factors over prisoners and substance-dependent patients. *Journal of Consulting and Clinical Psychology, 68*(1), 181–186.

McGregor, D. (2001). The human side of enterprise. In J. M. Shafritz and S. J. Ott (Eds.), *Classics of organization theory* (5th ed.). Fort Worth, TX: Harcourt College Publishers. (Original work published 1957.)

McLean, R. L., Robarge, J., & Sherman, S. G. (2006). Release from jail: Moment of crisis or window of opportunity for female detainees? *Journal of Urban Health, 83,* 382–393.

McLeod, J. (2003). *An introduction to counseling.* Buckingham, UK: Open University Press.

McNeese, T. (2010). Inmate rights: Getting the courts to listen. In A. Walsh & M. Stohr, *Correctional assessment, casework and counseling* (5th ed., pp. 321–323). Alexandria, VA: American Correctional Association.

McNiel, D. E., Binder, R. L., & Robinson, J. C. (2005, July). Incarceration associated with homelessness, mental disorder, and co-occurring substance abuse. *Psychiatric Services, 56,* 840–846.

McShane, M., & Williams, F. (1996). *Encyclopedia of American prisons.* New York, NY: Taylor & Francis.

Meade, B., & Steiner, B. (2013). The effects of exposure to violence on inmate maladjustment. *Criminal justice and behavior, 40*(11), 1228–1249.

Mears, D. P. (2008). An assessment of supermax prisons using an evaluation research framework. *Prison Journal, 88*(1), 43–68.

Mears, D. P. (2013). Supermax prisons: The policy and the evidence. *Criminology & Public Policy, 12*(4), 681–719.

Mears, D. P., Stewart, E. A., Siennick, S. E., & Simons, R. L. (2013). The code of the street and inmate violence: Investigating the salience of imported belief systems. *Criminology, 51*(3), 695–728.

Mello, M. (2007). Executing the mentally ill: When is someone sane enough to die? *Criminal Justice, 22,* 30–41.

Menard, S., Mihalic, S., & Huizinga, D. (2001). Drugs and crime revisited. *Justice Quarterly, 18,* 269–299.

Menninger, K. (1968). *The crime of punishment.* New York, NY: Penguin Books.

Mercier, M. (2010). *Japanese Americans in the Columbia River Basin.* Columbia River Basin Ethnic History Project. Retrieved from http://archive.vancouver.wsu.edu/crbeha/projteam

Meredith, C., & Paquette, C. (2001). *Summary report on victim impact statement focus groups.* Ottawa, Canada: Policy Centre for Victim Issues, Department of Justice.

Merlo, A. V., & Benekos, P. J. (2000). *What's wrong with the criminal justice system?* Cincinnati, OH: Anderson.

Michigan Supreme Court. (2013). Mental health courts see recidivism drop, outcomes improve for mentally ill [Press release]. Retrieved from http://courts.mi.gov/News-Events/press_releases/Documents/Mental-Health-Courts-Survey-PR3.pdf

Miller, W., & Rollnick, S. (2002). *Motivational interviewing: Preparing people for change.* New York, NY: Guilford.

Mills, C. W. (1956). *The power elite.* New York, NY: Oxford University Press.

Ministry of Interior, Kingdom of Saudi Arabia (2011). *Prisons: Rehabilitation.* Retrieved from http://www.moi.gov.sa/wps/portal/prisons/!ut/p/b1/pZDLDo1wEEU

Minnesota Department of Corrections. (2009). *Review of guidelines for revocation of parole and supervised release.* Retrieved from http://www.doc.state.mn.us/publications/legislativereports/documents/ReviewofGuidelinesforParole-releaseRevocation2009Report_002.pdf

Minton, T. D. (2010). *Jail inmates at midyear 2009—Statistical tables.* Washington, DC: Bureau of Justice Statistics. Retrieved from http://bjs.ojp.usdoj.gov/index.cfm?ty=pbdetail&iid=2195

Minton, T. D. (2014). *Jails in Indian Country, 2013.* Washington, DC: Bureau of Justice Statistics. Retrieved from http://www.bjs.gov/index.cfm?ty=pbdetail&iid=5070

Minton, T. D. (2015). *Jails in Indian Country, 2014.* Washington, DC: Bureau of Justice Statistics. Retrieved from http://www.bjs.gov/content/pub/pdf/jic14.pdf

Minton, T. D., & Golinelli, F. (2014). *Jail inmates at midyear 2013—Statistical tables.* Washington, DC: Bureau of Justice Statistics. Retrieved from http://www.bjs.gov/content/pub/pdf/jim13st.pdf

Minton, T. D., & Zeng, Z. (2015). *Jail inmates at midyear 2014.* Washington, DC: Bureau of Justice Statistics. Retrieved from http://www.bjs.gov/index.cfm?ty=pbdetail&iid=5299

Mitchell, O., Wilson, D., Eggers, A., & MacKenzie, D. (2012). Assessing the effectiveness of drug courts on recidivism: A meta-analytic review of traditional and non-traditional drug courts. *Journal of Criminal Justice, 40,* 60–71.

Mitford, J. (1973). *Kind and usual punishment: The prison business.* New York, NY: Knopf.

Moe, A. M., & Ferraro, K. J. (2003). Malign neglect or benign respect: Women's health care in a carceral setting. *Women & Criminal Justice, 14*(4), 53–80.

Moffitt, T. (1993). Adolescent-limited and life-course-persistent antisocial behavior: A developmental taxonomy. *Psychological Review, 100*, 674–701.

Moffitt, T. (2005). The new look of behavioral genetics in developmental psychopathology: Gene–environment interplay in antisocial behavior. *Psychological Bulletin, 131*, 533–554.

Moffitt, T., & Walsh, A. (2003). The adolescence-limited/life-course persistent theory of antisocial behavior: What have we learned? In A. Walsh & L. Ellis (Eds.), *Biosocial criminology: Challenging environmentalism's supremacy* (pp. 125–144). Hauppauge, NY: Nova Science.

Moore, N., May, D., & Wood, P. (2008). Offenders, judges, and officers rate the relative severity of alternative sanctions compared to prison. *Probation and Parole: Current Issues, 1*, 49–70.

Morash, M. (2006). *Understanding gender, crime, and justice*. Thousand Oaks, CA: Sage.

Morash, M., Haarr, R., & Rucker, L. (1994). A comparison of programming for women and men in U.S. prisons in the 1980s. *Crime & Delinquency, 40*, 197–221.

Morgan, K. (2013). Issues in female inmate health: Results from a southeastern state. *Women & Criminal Justice, 23*(2), 121–142.

Morris, N. (2002). *Maconochie's gentlemen: The story of Norfolk Island and the roots of modern prison reform*. New York: Oxford University Press.

Motivans, M. (2015). *Federal justice statistics, 2012—Statistical tables*. Washington, DC: Bureau of Justice Statistics. Retrieved from http://www.bjs.gov/content/pub/pdf/fjs12st.pdf

Lennon, T. (Series Producer), Angier, J. (Producer), Tsui, M. L. (Producer), & Cheng, S. (Producer). (2003). *Becoming American: The Chinese experience*. New York: Public Affairs Television and Thomas Lennon Films.

Moynihan, J. M. (2002, July/August). What to do with historic jails. *American Jails*, 14–16.

Mueller, C. W., De Coster, S., & Estes, S. (2001). Sexual harassment in the workplace. *Work and Occupations, 28*, 411–446.

Mulick, S. (2010, November 20). Budget ax falls on McNeil. *News Tribune* (Tacoma, WA), 1.

Mumola, C. J. (2000). *Incarcerated parents and their children*. Washington, DC: Bureau of Justice Statistics.

Mumola, C. J. (2005). *Suicide and homicide in state prisons and local jails*. Washington, DC: Bureau of Justice Statistics. Retrieved from http://www.bjs.gov/content/pub/pdf/shsplj.pdf

Mumola, C. J. (2007). *Medical causes of death in state prisons, 2001–2004*. Washington, DC: Bureau of Justice Statistics.

Muraskin, R. (2003). Disparate treatment in correctional facilities. In Muraskin (Ed.), *It's a crime: Women and justice* (3rd ed., pp. 220–231). Upper Saddle River, NJ: Prentice Hall.

Mustaine, E., & Tewksbury, R. (2004). Alcohol and violence. In S. T. Holmes & R. M. Holmes (Eds.), *Violence: A contemporary reader* (pp. 9–25). Upper Saddle River, NJ: Prentice Hall.

Myles, R. (2013). Landmark case establishes workers' rights for prisoners in France. *Digital Journal*. Retrieved from http://digitaljournal.com/article/343132#ixzz2otpG27aG

Naday, A., Freilich, J. D., & Mellow, J. (2008). The elusive data on supermax confinement. *Prison Journal, 88*(1), 69–93.

Nagel, W. G. (1973). *The new red barn: A critical look at the modern American prison*. New York, NY: Walker & Company.

Nagin, D. (1998). Criminal deterrence research at the onset of the twenty-first century. In M. Tonry (Ed.), *Crime and justice: A review of research* (Vol. 23, pp. 1–42). Chicago, IL: University of Chicago Press.

Nagin, D. S., Cullen, E. T., & Jonson, C. L. (2009). Imprisonment and reoffending. In M. Tonry (Ed.), *Crime and justice: A review of research* (Vol. 38, pp. 115–200). Chicago, IL: University of Chicago Press.

Nagin, D., & Land, K. (1993). Age, criminal careers, and population heterogeneity: Specification and estimation of a nonparametric, mixed poison model. *Criminology, 31*, 327–362.

Nagin, D., & Pepper, J. (Eds.). (2012). *Deterrence and the death penalty*. Washington, DC: Committee on Law and Justice, National Academies Press.

National Center on Addiction and Substance Abuse. (2010). *Behind bars II: Substance abuse and America's prison population*. New York, NY: Author. Retrieved from http://www.centeronaddiction.org/addiction-research/reports/substance-abuse-prison-system-2010

National Center for State Courts. (2008). *State sentencing guidelines*. Williamsburg, VA: Author.

National Conference of State Legislatures. (2012). U.S. Supreme Court rules on Arizona's immigration enforcement law. Retrieved from http://www.ncsl.org/research/immigration/us-supreme-court-rules-on-arizona-immigration-laws.aspx

National Institute of Corrections. (2008). *Today's jails: Are you looking for a way to coordinate jail and community health services?* Washington, DC: National Institute of Corrections, Jails Division. Retrieved from http://nicic.org/JailsDivision

National Institute of Corrections. (n.d.). The principles of effective interventions. Retrieved from http://nicic.gov/ThePrinciplesofEffectiveInterventions

National Institute of Justice. (2011). *Electronic monitoring reduces recidivism*. Washington, DC: U.S. Department of Justice.

National Institute of Justice. (2012). "Swift and certain" sanctions in probation are highly effective: Evaluation of the HOPE Program. Retrieved from http://www.nij.gov/topics/corrections/community/drug-offenders/pages/hawaii-hope.aspx

National Institute of Justice. (2014). Drug courts. Retrieved from http://www.nij.gov/topics/courts/drug-courts/Pages/welcome.aspx

National Institute of Justice. (2015a). Delaware KEY/Crest substance abuse programs. Retrieved from https://www.crimesolutions.gov/ProgramDetails.aspx?ID=55

National Institute of Justice. (2015b). Juvenile proportion of arrests by offense, 2014. *OJJDP Statistical Briefing Book*. Retrieved from http://www.ojjdp.gov/ojstatbb/crime/qa05102.asp?qaDate=2014

National Institute on Drug Abuse. (2006). *Principles of drug abuse treatment for criminal justice populations: A research-based guide*. Washington, DC: National Institutes of Health and U.S. Department of Health and Human Services. Retrieved from www.drugabuse.gov/PODAT_CJ

Nellis, A. (2010). Throwing away the key: The extension of life without parole sentences in the United States. *Federal Sentencing Reporter*, 23, 27–32.

Nelson, W. R., & Davis, R. M. (1995). Podular direct supervision: The first twenty years. *American Jails*, 9, 11–22.

Nettler, G. (1984). *Explaining crime* (3rd ed.). New York: McGraw-Hill.

New Jersey Judiciary. (n.d.). New Jersey drug court program: Testimonials. Retrieved from http://www.judiciary.state.nj.us/drugcourt/testimonials.htm

New legal guidelines show China is getting tough on child sex abuse. (2013, December 3). *South China Morning Post*. Retrieved from http://www.scmp.com/comment/insight-opinion/article/1371941/new-legal-guidelines-show-china-getting-tough-child-sex

Ney, B. (2014). 10 facts about women in jails. *American Jails Magazine*, 27(6), 8–10.

Noonan, M. E., & Ginder, S. (2013). *Mortality in local jails and state prisons, 2000–2001: Statistical tables*. Washington, DC: Bureau of Justice Statistics. Retrieved from http://www.bjs.gov/content/pub/pdf/mljsp0011.pdf

Noonan, M., Rohloff, H., & Ginder, S. (2015). *Mortality in local jails and state prisons, 2000–2013: Statistical tables*. Washington, DC: Bureau of Justice Statistics.

O'Connell, D., Visher, C., Martin, S., Parker, L., & Brent, J. (2011). Decide your time: Testing deterrence theory's certainty and celerity effects on substance-using probationers. *Journal of Criminal Justice*, 39, 261–267.

O'Connor, M. L. (2001). Noble corruption—Police perjury—What should we do? In R. Muraskin & M. Muraskin (Eds.), *Morality and the law* (pp. 91–106). Upper Saddle River, NJ: Prentice-Hall.

O'Donohue, W., Downs, K., & Yeater, E. (1998). Sexual harassment: A review of the literature. *Aggression and Behavior*, 3, 111–128.

Office of National Drug Control Policy. (2014). *ADAM II 2013 annual report*. Washington, DC: Executive Office of the President. Retrieved from https://www.whitehouse.gov/sites/default/files/ondcp/policy-and-research/adam_ii_2013_annual_report.pdf

O'Keefe, M. L. (2008). Administrative segregation from within: A corrections perspective. *Prison Journal*, 88(1), 123–143.

Olivero, J. M., & Roberts, J. B. (1987). Marion Federal Penitentiary and the 22-month lockdown: The crisis continues. *Crime and Social Justice*, 27–28, 234–253.

Olson, S., & Dzur, A. (2004). Revisiting informal justice: Restorative justice and democratic professionalism. *Law and Society Review*, 38, 139–176.

Orange County. (n.d.). Volunteer Probation Officer Program (VPO). Retrieved from http://ocgov.com/gov/probation/employment/volunteer/vpo

Orland, L. (1975). *Prisons: Houses of darkness*. New York: Free Press.

Orland, L. (1995). Prisons as punishment: An historical overview. In K. C. Haas & G. P. Alpert (Eds.), *The dilemmas of corrections: Contemporary readings* (3rd ed.). Prospect Heights, IL: Waveland Press.

Orye, B. R., III. (2002). Failure of words: Habeas corpus reform, the Antiterrorism and Effective Death Penalty Act, and when a judgment of conviction becomes final for the purposes of 28 U.S.C. 2255(1). *William & Mary Law Review*, 44(1), 441–485.

Osher, F. C. (2007). Short-term strategies to improve reentry of jail populations: Expanding and implementing the APIC model. *American Jails*, 20, 9–18.

Oshinsky, D. M. (1996). *Worse than slavery: Parchman Farm and the ordeal of Jim Crow justice*. New York: Free Press.

Ostermann, M. (2011). Parole? Nope, not for me: Voluntarily maxing out of prison. *Crime & Delinquency*, 57, 686–708.

O'Sullivan, S. (2006). Representations of prison in nineties Hollywood cinema: From *Con Air* to *The Shawshank Redemption*. In R. Tewksbury (Ed.), *Behind bars: Readings on prison culture* (pp. 483–498). Upper Saddle River, NJ: Pearson/Prentice Hall.

Ouchi, W. G. (1981). *Theory Z: How American business can meet the Japanese challenge*. Reading, MA: Addison-Wesley.

Owen, B. (1998). *In the mix: Struggle and survival in a women's prison*. Albany: State University of New York Press.

Owen, B. (2005). Afterword: The case of the women. In J. Irwin (Ed.), *The warehouse prison: Disposal of the new dangerous class* (pp. 261–289). Los Angeles, CA: Roxbury.

Owen, B. (2006). The contexts of women's imprisonment. In A. V. Merlo & J. M. Pollock (Eds.), *Women, law, and social control* (pp. 251–270). Boston, MA: Pearson.

Owen, B., & Bloom, B. (1995). Profiling women prisoners: Findings from national surveys and a California sample. *Prison Journal*, 75, 165–185.

Owens, E. G. (2009). More time, less crime? Estimating the incapacitive effect of sentence enhancements. *Journal of Law and Economics*, 52, 551–579.

Owers, A. (2006). The protection of prisoners' rights in England and Wales. *European Journal of Criminal Justice Policy Research*, 12, 85–91.

Packer, H. (1997). Two models of the criminal process. In S. Wasserman & C. Snyder (Eds.), *A criminal procedure anthology* (pp. 3–9). Cincinnati, OH: Anderson. (Original work published 1964.)

Padfield, N. (2011). An entente cordiale in sentencing? *Criminal Law and Justice Weekly, 175,* 238–292.

Paoline, E. A., III, Lambert, E. G., & Hogan, N. L. (2006). A calm and happy keeper of the keys: The impact of ACA views, relations with coworkers, and policy views on the job stress and job satisfaction of correctional staff. *Prison Journal, 86*(2), 182–205.

Paparozzi, M., & Gendreau, P. (2005). An intensive supervision program that worked: Service delivery, professional orientation, and organizational supportiveness. *Prison Journal, 85,* 445–466.

Paparozzi, M., & Guy, R. (2009). The giant that never woke: Parole authorities as the lynchpin to evidence-based practices and prisoner reentry. *Journal of Contemporary Criminal Justice, 25,* 397–411.

Pastore, A. L., & Maguire, K. (Eds.). (2000). *Sourcebook of criminal justice statistics—1999.* Washington, DC: Bureau of Justice Statistics. Retrieved from https://www.hsdl.org/?view&did=711188

Pastore, A. L., & Maguire, K. (Eds.) (2005). *Sourcebook of criminal justice statistics—2003.* Washington, DC: Bureau of Justice Statistics. Retrieved from https://www.ncjrs.gov/pdffiles1/Digitization/208756NCJRS.pdf

Paternoster, R. (2010). How much do we really know about criminal deterrence? *Journal of Criminal Law and Criminology, 100,* 765–823.

Paternoster, R., & Brame, R. (2003). *An empirical analysis of Maryland's death sentence system with respect to the influence of race and legal jurisdiction: Final report.* College Park: University of Maryland.

Paternoster, R., & Deise, J. (2011). A heavy thumb on the scale: The effect of victim impact evidence on capital decision making. *Criminology, 49,* 129–161.

Payne, B., DeMichele, M., & Button, D. (2008). Understanding the electronic monitoring of sex offenders. *Corrections Compendium, 33,* 1–5.

Payne, B., & Gainey, R. (2004). The electronic monitoring of offenders released from jail or prison: Safety, control, and comparisons to the incarceration experience. *Prison Journal, 84,* 413–435.

Pearson, J. (2015, April 4–5). Study: NYC health workers' ethics are compromised in jails. *Moscow-Pullman Daily News,* 5B.

Pearson, F., Lipton, D., Cleland, C., & Yee, D. (2002). The effects of behavioral/cognitive behavioral programs on recidivism. *Crime & Delinquency, 48,* 438–452.

Peiffer, E. (2005). The death penalty in traditional Islamic law as interpreted in Saudi Arabia and Nigeria. *William and Mary Journal of Women and the Law, 11,* 507–539.

Penn, W. (1981). *The papers of William Penn, Volume One, 1644–1679* (M. M. Dunn & R. S. Dunn, Eds.).

Philadelphia: University of Pennsylvania Press. (Original work written circa 1679.)

Perroncello, P. (2002). Direct supervision: A 2001 odyssey. *American Jails, 15,* 25–32.

Perry, S. W. (2004). *American Indians and crime.* Washington, DC: Bureau of Justice Statistics. Retrieved from https://www.justice.gov/sites/default/files/otj/docs/american_indians_and_crime.pdf

Perry, S. (2008). *Justice expenditure and employment extracts, 2006.* Washington, DC: Bureau of Justice Statistics. Retrieved from http://www.bjs.gov/index.cfm?ty=pbdetail&iid=1022

Petersilia, J. (1998). Probation in the United States, Part 1. *Perspectives, 22,* 30–41.

Petersilia, J. (2000). Parole and prisoner reentry in the United States. *Perspectives, 24,* 32–46.

Petersilia, J. (2001). Prisoner reentry: Public safety and reintegration challenges. *Prison Journal, 81,* 360–375.

Petersilia, J. (2004). What works in prison reentry? Reviewing and questioning the evidence. *Federal Probation, 68,* 1–8.

Pew Charitable Trusts. (2015, November 18). Prison time surges for federal inmates. Retrieved from http://www.pewtrusts.org/en/research-and-analysis/issue-briefs/2015/11/prison-time-surges-for-federal-inmates

Pew Research Center. (2014, April 2). America's new drug policy landscape. Retrieved from http://www.people-press.org/2014/04/02/americas-new-drug-policy-landscape/

Phelps, R. (1996). *Newgate of Connecticut: Its origin and early history.* Camden, ME: Picton Press. (Original work published 1860.)

Phillips, C. (2012). "It ain't nothing like America with the Bloods and the Crips": Gang narratives inside two English prisons. *Punishment & Society, 14,* 51–68.

Piquero, A., & Blumstein, A. (2007). Does incapacitation reduce crime? *Journal of Quantitative Criminology, 23,* 267–285.

Pitts, L. (2010, November 21). Sisters may be guilty; state of Mississippi assuredly is. *Tacoma News Tribune,* B6.

Pizarro, J. M., & Narag, R. E. (2008). Supermax prisons: What we know, what we do not know, and where we are going. *Prison Journal, 88*(1), 23–42.

Plato. (2008). *Laws* (B. Jowett, Trans.). New York, NY: Cosimo.

Pogrebin, M. R., & Poole, E. D. (1997). The sexualized work environment: A look at women jail officers. *Prison Journal, 77,* 41–57.

Polcin, D. (2009). Community living settings for adults recovering from substance abuse. *Journal of Groups in Addiction and Recovery, 4,* 7–22.

Pollock, J. M. (1994). *Ethics in crime and justice: Dilemmas and decisions* (2nd ed.). Belmont, CA: Wadsworth.

Pollock, J. M. (1998). *Ethics in crime and justice: Dilemmas and decisions* (3rd ed.). Belmont, CA: West/Wadsworth.

Pollock, J. (2002a). Parenting programs in women's prisons. *Women & Criminal Justice, 14*(1), 131–154.

Pollock, J. (2002b). *Women, prison & crime* (2nd ed.). Belmont, CA: Wadsworth Thomson Learning.

Pollock, J. M. (2004). *Prisons and prison life: Costs and consequences.* Los Angeles, LA: Roxbury.

Pollock, J. M. (2010). *Ethics in crime and justice: Dilemmas and decisions* (7th ed.). Belmont, CA: Wadsworth Thomson Learning.

Pollock, J. M. (2014). *Women's crimes, criminology and corrections.* Long Grove, IL: Waveland Press.

Pollock, J. M., Hogan, N. L., Lambert, E. G., Ross, J. I., & Sundt, J. L. (2012). A utopian prison: Contradiction in terms? *Journal of Contemporary Criminal Justice, 28,* 60–76.

Porter, N. D. (2011). *The state of sentencing 2010: Developments in policy and practice.* Washington, DC: Sentencing Project. Retrieved from http://www.sentencingproject.org/publications/the-state-of-sentencing-2010-developments-in-policy-and-practice

Porter, N. D. (2016). *The state of sentencing 2015: Developments in policy and practice.* Washington, DC: Sentencing Project. Retrieved from http://sentencingproject.org/wp-content/uploads/2016/02/State-of-Sentencing-2015.pdf

Porto, P., Oliveira, L., Mari, J., Volchan, E., Figueira, I., & Ventura, P. (2009). Does cognitive behavioral therapy change the brain? A systematic review of neuroimaging in anxiety disorders. *Journal of Neuropsychiatry and Clinical Neurosciences, 21,* 114–125.

Powell, K. (2006). How does the teenage brain work? *Nature, 442,* 865–867.

Pryor, J., &. Stoller, L. M. (1994). Sexual cognition processes in men high in the likelihood to sexually harass. *Personality and Social Psychology Bulletin, 20,* 163–169.

Przybylski, R. (2015, July). *Recidivism of adult sexual offenders* [Sex Offender Management Assessment and Planning Initiative Research Brief]. Retrieved from http://www.smart.gov/pdfs/RecidivismofAdultSexualOffenders.pdf

Pugh, R. B. (1968). *Imprisonment in medieval England.* Cambridge, UK: Cambridge University Press.

Puzzanchera, C., & Kang, W. (2007). *Juvenile court statistics databook.* Retrieved from http://www.ojjdp.gov/ojstatbb/ezajcs/asp/process.asp

Quinsey, V. (2002). Evolutionary theory and criminal behavior. *Legal and Criminological Psychology, 7,* 1–14.

Radelet, M., & Lacock, T. (2009). Do executions lower homicide rates? The views of leading criminologists. *Journal of Criminal Law and Criminology, 99,* 489–508.

Radzinowicz, L., & King, J. (1979). *The growth of crime: The international experience.* Middlesex, UK: Penguin Books.

Rafter, N. H. (1985). *Partial justice: Women in state prisons, 1800–1935.* Boston, MA: Northeastern University Press.

Rafter, N. H. (2009). "Much and unfortunately neglected": Women in early and mid-nineteenth-century prisons. In M. K. Stohr, A. Walsh, & C. Hemmens (Eds.), *Corrections: A text/reader.* Thousand Oaks, CA: Sage.

Reaves, B. A. (2009). *State and local law enforcement training academies, 2006.* Washington, DC: Bureau of Justice Statistics. Retrieved from http://www.bjs.gov/index.cfm?ty=pbdetail&iid=1207

Reichel, P. L. (2005). *Comparative criminal justice systems: A topical approach* (4th ed.). Upper Saddle River, NJ: Prentice Hall.

Reid, S. (2006). *Criminal justice* (7th ed.). Cincinnati, OH: Atomic Dog Publishers.

Reilly, R. J. (2014, February 12). DOJ threatens to withhold grants from states that aren't protecting prisoners from rape. *Huffington Post.* Retrieved from http://www.huffingtonpost.com/2014/02/12/doj-prison-rape_n_4775411.html

Reisig, M. (1998). Rates of disorder in higher-custody state prisons: A comparative analysis of managerial practices. *Crime & Delinquency, 44,* 229–244.

Reisig, M. D., Holtfreter, K., & Morash, M. (2002). Social capital among women offenders: Examining the distribution of social networks and resources. *Journal of Contemporary Criminal Justice, 18*(2), 167–187.

Rembert, D. A., & Henderson, H. (2014). Correctional officer excessive use of force: Civil liability under section 1983. *Prison Journal, 94*(2), 198–219.

Ren, X. (1997). *Tradition of the law and law of the tradition.* Westport, CT: Greenwood.

Rengert, G., & Wasilchick, J. (2001). *Suburban burglary: A tale of two suburbs.* Springfield, IL: Charles C Thomas.

Rennison, C. (2003). *Intimate partner violence, 1993–2003.* Washington, DC: Bureau of Justice Statistics.

Restak, R. (2001). *The secret life of the brain.* New York, NY: Dana Press and Joseph Henry Press.

Reutter, D. M. (2007). Arizona jail sex results in charges for guards, prisoner. *Prison Legal News, 18*(12), 31.

Reynolds, M. O. (1998, August). *Does punishment deter?* [Policy Backgrounders No. 148]. Retrieved from http://www.ncpa.org/pub/bg148

Reynolds, R. (2009). Equal justice under law: Post-Booker, should federal judges be able to depart from the federal sentencing guidelines to remedy disparity between codefendants' sentencing? *Columbia Law Review, 109,* 538–570.

Reza, E. (2005). Gender bias in North Carolina's death penalty. *Duke Journal of Gender Law & Policy, 12,* 179–214.

Rice, S. K., Reitzel, J. D., & Piquero, A. R. (2005). Shades of brown: Perceptions of racial profiling and the intra-ethnic differential. *Journal of Ethnicity in Criminal Justice, 3*(1–2), 47–70.

Richards, S. C. (2008). USP Marion: The first federal supermax. *Prison Journal, 88*(1), 6–22.

Richmond, K. M. (2014). The impact of federal prison industries employment on the recidivism outcomes of female inmates. *Justice Quarterly, 31*(4), 719–745.

Rideau, W. (2010). *In the place of justice: A story of punishment and deliverance*. New York, NY: Knopf.

Rigby, M. (2007). Dallas, Texas, jail pays $950,000 for neglecting mentally ill prisoners. *Prison Legal News*, 18(12), 22.

Roberts, J. V. (2011). Sentencing guidelines and judicial discretion: Evolution of the duty of courts to comply in England and Wales. *British Journal of Criminology, 51*, 997–1013.

Roberts, J. W. (1997). *Reform and retribution: An illustrated history of American prisons*. Lanham, MD: American Correctional Association.

Robertson, J. (2010). Recent legal developments: Correctional case law, 2009. *Criminal Justice Review, 35*, 260–272.

Robertson, J. E. (2014, April/May). The one million: Reimagining the jails as the institution that says "yes" to the mentally ill. *Correctional Law Reporter*, 87–89.

Robinson, G., & McNeill, F. (2010). Probation in the United Kingdom. In M. Hertzog-Evans (Ed.), *Transnational criminology* (Vol. 3, pp. 741–762). Nijmegen, Holland: Wolf Legal.

Robinson, M. (2005). *Justice blind: Ideals and realities of American criminal justice*. Upper Saddle River, NJ: Prentice Hall.

Robinson, M. (2008). *Death nation: The experts explain American capital punishment*. Upper Saddle River, NJ: Prentice Hall.

Rocheleau, A. M. (2013). An empirical exploration of the "pains of imprisonment" and the level of prison misconduct and violence. *Criminal Justice Review, 38*(3), 354–374.

Rodney, E., & Mupier, R. (1999). Behavioral differences between African American male adolescents with biological fathers and those without biological fathers in the home. *Journal of Black Studies, 30*, 45–61.

Rodriguez, N. (2007). Restorative justice at work: Examining the impact of restorative justice resolutions on juvenile recidivism. *Crime & Delinquency, 53*, 355–379.

Rohr, J. A. (1989). *Ethics for bureaucrats: An essay on law and values*. New York, NY: MarcelDekker.

Roman, J. (2013, September). Cost–benefit analysis of criminal justice reforms. *NIJ Journal*, 31–38. Retrieved from https://ncjrs.gov/pdffiles1/nij/241929.pdf

Rosenfeld, R. (2000). Patterns in adult homicide. In A. Blumstein & J. Wallman (Eds.), *The crime drop in America* (pp. 130–163). Cambridge, UK: Cambridge University Press.

Ross, J. L., & Richards, S. C. (2002). *Behind bars: Surviving prison*. Indianapolis, IN: Alpha Books.

Rossman, S., Willison, J., Mallik-Kane, K., Kim, K., & Sherrill, P. (2012). *Criminal justice interventions for offenders with mental illness: Evaluation of mental health courts in Bronx and Brooklyn, New York*. Washington, DC: Urban Institute.

Roth, M. (2006). *Prisons and prison systems: A global encyclopedia*. Westport, CT: Greenwood.

Rothman, D. J. (1980). *Conscience and convenience: The asylum and its alternatives in progressive America*. Glenview, IL: Scott Foresman.

Routh, D., Abess, G., Lee, J., Makin, D., Hemmens, C., & Stohr, M. K. (2014). *Transgender inmates in prisons: The policies and statutes* [Unpublished manuscript].

Ruddell, R. (2004). *America behind bars: Trends in imprisonment, 1950 to 2000*. New York: LFB Scholarly Publishing.

Ruddell, R., Decker, S., & Egley, A. (2006). Gang interventions in jails: A national analysis. *Criminal Justice Review, 31*(1), 33–46.

Ruddell, R., & Leyton-Brown, K. (2013). All in the family: The role of the sheriff's wife in 20th-century mom and pop jails. *Women & Criminal Justice, 23*, 267–285.

Russell, B. (2014, January 4). Idaho to take over operation of prison. *Spokesman-Review*, B1, B3.

Russell, R. T. (2009). Veterans treatment courts developing throughout the nation. In C. Flango, A. M. McDowell, C. F. Campbell, & N. B. Kauder (Eds.), *Future Trends in state courts 2009* (pp. 130–133). Williamsburg, VA: National Center for State Courts.

Rutter, T. (2015, April 9). Probation service split: "Staff are staring into the abyss." *The Guardian*. Retrieved from http://www.theguardian.com/public-leaders-network/2015/apr/09/probation-service-split-staff-demoralised-divided-private-services

Sabol, W. J., & Minton, T. D. (2008). *Jail inmates at midyear 2007*. Washington, DC: Bureau of Justice Statistics. Available at http://www.bjs.gov/content/pub/pdf/jim07.pdf

Samenow, S. (1999). *Before it's too late: Why some kids get into trouble and what parents can do about it*. New York, NY: Times Books.

Sampson, R., & Laub, J. (1999). Crime and deviance over the lifecourse: The salience of adult social bonds. In F. Scarpitti & A. Nielsen (Eds.), *Crime and criminals: Contemporary and classical readings in criminology* (pp. 238–246). Los Angeles, CA: Roxbury.

Santayana, G. (1905). *The life of reason: Reason in common sense*. New York, NY: Dover Publications.

Saudi Arabia triples blood money to SR300,000. (2011, September 11). Emirates News 24/7. Retrieved from http://www.emirates247.com/news/region/saudi-arabia-triples-blood-money-to-sr300-000-2011-09-11-1.417796

Saylor, W., & Iwaszko, A. (2009). *One in 31: The long reach of American corrections*. Washington, DC: Pew Charitable Trusts.

Schaffner, L. (2014). Out of sight, out of compliance: U.S. detained girls' health justice. *Criminal Justice Review, 17*(1), 63–86.

Scheidegger, K. (2005). Should states adopt moratoriums on executions? Con. *Congressional Quarterly Researcher, 15*(33). Retrieved from http://library.cqpress.com/cqresearcher/document.php?id=cqresrre2005092306

Scheidegger, K. (2006). Supreme Court decisions on habeas corpus. Retrieved from http://fedsoc.server326.com/Publications/practicegroupnewsletters/PG%20Links/habeas.htm

Scheidegger, K. (2012). Rebutting myths about race and the death penalty. *Ohio State Journal of Criminal Law*, *10*, 147–165.

Schmalleger, F. (2001). *Criminal justice today* (6th ed.). Upper Saddle River, NJ: Prentice Hall.

Schmitz, J., Stotts, A., Sayre, S., DeLaune, K., & Grabowski, J. (2004). Treatment of cocaine-alcohol dependence with naltrexone and relapse prevention therapy. *American Journal on Addictions*, *13*, 333–341.

Schofield, M. (1997, August 24). Tape puts for-profit prisons back in spotlight: Video shows guards abusing inmates—and jeopardizes system. *Idaho Statesman*, A1, A16.

Schwirtz, M. (2014a, March 25). U.S. charges correction officer in death of a mentally ill inmate at Rikers. *New York Times*, A21.

Schwirtz, M. (2014b, March 26). Complaint by fired correction officers adds details about death at Rikers. *New York Times*, A19.

Scroggins, J. R., & Malley, S. (2010). Reentry and the (unmet) needs of women. *Journal of Offender Rehabilitation*, *49*(2), 146–163.

Seabrook, N. (2014, August 24). What's really wrong with Rikers. *New York Times*.

Seiter, R. (2005). *Corrections: An introduction*. Upper Saddle River, NJ: Prentice Hall.

Seiter, R., & Kadela, K. (2003). Prisoner reentry: What works, what does not, and what is promising. *Crime & Delinquency*, *49*, 360–390.

Selling, D., Solimo, A., Lee, D., Horne, K., Panove, E., & Venters, H. (2014). Surveillance of suicidal and non-suicidal self-injury in the New York City jail system. *Journal of Correctional Health Care*, *20*(2), 163–167.

Sentencing Project. (2011). *Racial disparity*. Retrieved from http://www.sentencingproject.org

Sentencing Project. (2013). Fact sheet: Trends in U.S. corrections. Retrieved from http://sentencingproject.org/doc/publications/inc_Trends_in_Corrections_Fact_sheet.pdf

Serin, R., Gobeil, R., & Preston, D. (2009). Evaluation of the persistently violent offender program. *International Journal of Offender Therapy and Comparative Criminology*, *53*, 57–73.

Serrano, R. A. (2006, November 20). 9/11 prisoner abuse suit could be landmark. *Los Angeles Times*. Retrieved from http://articles.latimes.com/2006/nov/20/nation/na-jail20

Service Public Française. (2015). Quelles sont les différences entre une contravention, un délit et un crime? Direction de l'information légale et administrative (Premier ministre) et Ministère en charge de la justice. Last updated August 6, 2015. Retrieved from https://www.service-public.fr/particuliers/vosdroits/F1157

Severson, M. (2004). Mental health needs and mental health care in jails: The past, the present, and hope for the future. *American Jails*, *28*, 9–18.

Sevigny, E., Fuleihan, B., & Ferdik, F. (2013). Do drug courts reduce the use of incarceration?: A meta-analysis. *Journal of Criminal Justice*, *41*(6), 416–425.

Sewell, M. (2010). Pushing execution over the constitutional line: Forcible medication of condemned inmates and the Eighth and Fourteen Amendments. *Boston College Law Review*, *51*, 1279–1322.

Sexton, L., Jenness, V., & Sumner, J. M. (2010). Where the margins meet: A demographic assessment of transgender inmates in men's prisons. *Justice Quarterly*, *27*(6), 835–866.

Shahani, A. (2011, March 25). *What is GEO Group?* National Public Radio. Retrieved from http://www.npr.org/2011/03/25/134852256/what-is-geo-group

Sharma, H., Scheb, J., Houston, D., & Wagers, K. (2013). Race and the death penalty: An empirical assessment of first-degree murder convictions in Tennessee after *Gregg v. Georgia*. *Tennessee Journal of Race, Gender, & Social Justice*, *2*, 1–39.

Sharp, B. (2006). *Changing criminal thinking: A treatment program*. Alexandria, VA: American Correctional Association.

Sharp, P., & Hancock, B. (1995). *Juvenile delinquency: Historical, theoretical, and societal reactions to youth*. Englewood Cliffs, NJ: Prentice Hall.

Sharp, S. F., & Marcus-Mendoza, S. T. (2001). It's a family affair: Incarcerated women and their families. *Women & Criminal Justice*, *12*(4), 21–49.

Shatz, S. F., & Shatz, N. R. (2011). Chivalry is not dead: Murder, gender, and the death penalty [Unpublished paper]. Retrieved from http://works.bepress.com/steven_shatz/1

Shaw, V. (2010). Corrections and punishment in China: Information and analysis. *Journal of Contemporary Criminal Justice*, *26*, 53–71.

Shepherd, J. (2005). Deterrence versus brutalization: Capital punishment's differing impacts among states. *Michigan Law Review*, *104*, 203–256.

Sherman, L. (2005). The use and usefulness of criminology, 1751–2005: Enlightened justice and its failures. *Annals of the American Academy of Political and Social Science*, *600*, 115–135.

Shilton, M. K. (1992). *Community corrections acts for state and local partnerships*. Laural, MD: American Correctional Association.

Shilton, M. (2003). *Increasing public safety through halfway houses*. Center for Community Corrections.

Short, K. (2015). *The supplemental poverty measure: 2014*. Washington, DC: U.S. Census Bureau. Retrieved from https://www.census.gov/content/dam/Census/library/publications/2015/demo/p60-254.pdf

Sickmund, M., & Puzzanchera, C. (Eds.). (2014). *Juvenile offenders and victims: 2014 national report*. Pittsburgh, PA: National Center for Juvenile Justice.

Sickmund, M., & Wan, Y. (2003). *Census of juveniles in residential placement: 2003 databook*. Washington, DC: Office of Juvenile Justice and Delinquency Prevention.

Siegel, L. (2006). *Criminology*. Belmont, CA: Thomson/Wadsworth.

Simon, H., & Wetstein, S. (2016, March 11). *Request for an investigation into the use of solitary confinement in*

Florida's prisons [Press release]. Retrieved from https://aclufl.org/2016/03/11/civil-rights-groups-call-for-federal-investigation-into-solitary-confinement-abuse-in-florida-prisons

Simpson, S. S., Yahner, J. L., & Dugan, L. (2008). Understanding women's pathways to jail: Analysing the lives of incarcerated women. *Australian and New Zealand Journal of Criminology, 41*(1), 84–108.

Skeem, J., & Manchak, S. (2008). Back to the future: From Klockars' model of effective supervision to evidence-based practice in probation. *Journal of Offender Rehabilitation, 47*, 220–247.

Skinner, B. F. (2005). *Walden two*. Indianapolis, IN: Hackett Publishing. (Original work published 1948.)

Skolnick, J. (1993). Shut the door again on sociopaths [Editorial]. *Los Angeles Times*. Retrieved from http://articles.latimes.com/1993-12-16/local/me-2264_1_richard-allen-davis

Slate, R., & Vogel, R. (1997). Participative management and correctional personnel: A study of perceived atmosphere for participation in correctional decision-making and its impact on employee stress and thoughts about quitting. *Journal of Criminal Justice, 25*(5), 397–408.

Slate, R., Wells, T., & Wesley Johnson, W. (2003). Opening the manager's door: State probation officer stress and perceptions of participation in workplace decision-making. *Crime & Delinquency, 49*, 519–541.

Slate, R. N., & Wesley Johnson, W. (2008). *Criminalization of mental illness*. Durham, NC: Carolina Academic Press.

Smith, E. L., & Farole, D. J., Jr. (2009). Profile of intimate partner violence cases in large urban counties. Washington, DC: Bureau of Justice Statistics. Retrieved from http://www.bjs.gov/content/pub/pdf/pipvcluc.pdf

Smith, P., & Smith, W. A. (2005). Experiencing community through the eyes of young female offenders. *Journal of Contemporary Criminal Justice, 21*, 364–385.

Smykla, J., & Williams, J. (1996). Co-corrections in the United States of America, 1970–1990: Two decades of disadvantages for women prisoners. *Women & Criminal Justice, 8*, 61–76.

Snell, T. (2011). *Capital punishment, 2010: Statistical tables*. Washington, DC: Bureau of Justice Statistics.

Snyder, H., Espiritu, R., Huizinga, D., Loeber, R., & Petechuck, D. (2003, March). Prevalence and development of child delinquency. *Child Delinquency Bulletin Series*. Washington, DC: Office of Juvenile Justice and Delinquency Prevention. Retrieved from http://www.ncjrs.gov/pdffiles1/ojjdp/193411.pdf

Solomon, A., Dedel Johnson, K., Travis, J., & McBride, E. (2004). *From prison to work: The employment dimensions of prisoner reentry*. Washington, DC: Urban Institute, Justice Policy Center.

Solomon, A., Kachnowski, V., & Bhati, A. (2005). *Does parole work?* Washington, DC: Urban Institute.

Solomon, R. C. (1996). *A handbook for ethics*. Fort Worth, TX: Harcourt Brace College Publishers.

Sonfield, M. C. (2009). Entrepreneurship and prisoner re-entry: A role for collegiate schools of business. *Small Business Institute Journal, 4*, 66–82.

Spelman, W. (2000). The limited importance of prison expansion. In A. Blumstein & J. Wallman (Eds.), *The crime drop in America* (pp. 97–129). Cambridge, UK: Cambridge University Press.

Spjeldnes, S., Jung, H., & Yamatini, H. (2014). Gender differences in jail populations: Factors to consider in re-entry strategies. *Journal of Offender Rehabilitation, 53*, 75–94.

Spohn, C., & Hemmens, C. (2012). *Courts: A text/reader* (2nd ed.). Thousand Oaks, CA: Sage.

Springer, C. (1987). *Justice for juveniles*. Washington, DC: Office of Juvenile Justice and Delinquency Prevention.

Stannard, D. E. (1992). *American holocaust: Columbus and the conquest of the New World*. New York, NY: Oxford University Press.

Staton-Tindall, M., Garner, B. R., Morey, J. T., Leukefeld, C., Krietemeyer, J., Saum, C. A., et al. (2007). Gender differences in treatment engagement among a sample of incarcerated substance abusers. *Criminal Justice and Behavior, 34*(9), 1143–1156.

Steadman, H., Davidson, S., & Brown, C. (2001). Mental health courts: Their promise and unanswered questions. *Psychiatric Services, 52*, 457–458.

Steffensmeier, D., Feldmeyer, B., Harris, C., & Ulmer, J. (2011). Reassessing trends in black violent crime, 1980–2008: Sorting out the "Hispanic effect" in Uniform Crime Reports arrests, National Crime Victimization Survey offender estimates, and U.S. prisoner counts. *Criminology, 49*, 197–251.

Stein, M., Jang, K., Taylor, S., Vernon, P., & Livesley, W. J. (2002). Genetic and environmental influences on trauma exposure and posttraumatic stress disorder symptoms: A twin study. *American Journal of Psychiatry, 159*, 1675–1681.

Steiner, B., & Giacomazzi, A. (2007). Juvenile waiver, boot camp, and recidivism in a northwestern state. *Prison Journal, 87*, 227–240.

Stephan, J. J. (1987). *1984 census of state adult correctional facilities*. Washington, DC: Bureau of Justice Statistics. Retrieved from http://www.bjs.gov/content/pub/pdf/csacf84.pdf

Stephan, J. J. (1992). *Census of state and federal correctional facilities, 1990*. Washington, DC: Bureau of Justice Statistics. Retrieved from http://www.bjs.gov/content/pub/pdf/csfcf90.pdf

Stephan, J. J. (1997). *Census of state and federal correctional facilities, 1995*. Washington, DC: Bureau of Justice Statistics. Retrieved from http://www.bjs.gov/content/pub/pdf/Csfcf95.pdf

Stephan, J. J. (2008). *Census of state and federal correctional facilities, 2005*. Washington, DC: Bureau of Justice Statistics. Retrieved from http://www.bjs.gov/content/pub/pdf/csfcf05.pdf

Stephan, J. J., & Karberg, J. C. (2003). *The census of state and federal correctional facilities, 2000*. Washington, DC: Bureau of Justice Statistics. Retrieved from http://www.bjs.gov/content/pub/pdf/csfcf00.pdf

Stohr, M. K. (2006). Yes, I've paid the price, but look how much I gained! In C. M. Renzetti, L. Goodstein, & S. L. Miller (Eds.), *Rethinking gender, crime, and justice* (pp. 262–277). Los Angeles, CA: Roxbury.

Stohr, M. K. (2014). *The etiology and status of the war on transgender women in men's prisons* [Unpublished manuscript].

Stohr, M. K., & Collins, P. A. (2009). *Criminal justice management: Theory and practice in justice-centered organizations*. New York, NY: Oxford University Press.

Stohr, M. K., & Collins, P. A. (2014). *Criminal justice management: Theory and practice in justice-centered organizations* (2nd ed.). London, UK: Routledge.

Stohr, M. K., Hemmens, C., Collins, P. A., Innacchione, B., Hudson, M., & Johnson, H. (2012). Assessing the organizational culture in a jail setting. *Prison Journal*, 92(3), 358–387.

Stohr, M. K., Hemmens, C., Shapiro, B., Chambers, B., & Kelly, L. (2002). Comparing inmate perceptions of two residential substance abuse treatment programs. *International Journal of Offender Therapy and Comparative Criminology*, 46, 699–714.

Stohr, M. K., Jonson, C. L., & Cullen, F. T. (2014). Lessons learned: From penal harm to penal help. In F. T. Cullen, C. L. Jonson, & M. K. Stohr (Eds.), *The American prison: Imagining a different future* (pp. 257–268). Thousand Oaks, CA: Sage.

Stohr, M. K., Lovrich, N. P., & Mays, G. L. (1997). Service v. security focus in training assessments: Testing gender differences among women's jail correctional officers. *Women & Criminal Justice*, 9, 65–85.

Stohr, M. K., Lovrich, N. P., Menke, B. A., & Zupan, L. L. (1994). Staff management in correctional institutions: Comparing DiIulio's "control model" and "employee investment model" outcomes in five jails. *Justice Quarterly*, 11(3), 471–497.

Stohr, M. K., Lovrich, N. P., & Wilson, G. L. (1994). Staff stress in contemporary jails: Assessing problem severity and the payoff of progressive personnel practices. *Journal of Criminal Justice*, 22, 313–328.

Stohr, M. K., Lovrich, N. P., & Wood, M. (1996). Service v. security concerns in contemporary jails: Testing behavior differences in training topic assessments. *Journal of Criminal Justice*, 24, 437–448.

Stohr, M. K., & Mays, L. G. (1993). *Women's jails: An investigation of offenders, staff, administration and programming* (Final report for grant No. 92J04GHP5 awarded by the National Institute of Corrections, Jails Division). Retrieved from http://nicic.gov/Library/008747

Stohr, M. K., Mays, G. L., Beck, A. C., & Kelley, T. (1998). Sexual harassment in women's jails. *Journal of Contemporary Criminal Justice*, 14(24), 135–155.

Stohr, M., & Walsh, A. (2012). *Corrections: The essentials*. Thousand Oaks, CA: Sage.

Stohr, M. K., & Wozniak, J. (2014). The green prison. In F. T. Cullen, C. L. Jonson, M. K. & Stohr (Eds.) *The American prison: Imagining a different future* (pp. 193–212). Thousand Oaks, CA: Sage.

Streib, V. (2003). Executing women, juveniles, and the mentally retarded: Second class citizens in capital punishment. In J. Aker, R. Bohm, & C. Lanier (Eds.), *America's experiment with capital punishment: Reflections on the past, present, and future of the ultimate penal sanction* (2nd ed., pp. 301–323). Durham, NC: Carolina Academic Press.

Streib, V. (2003). *The juvenile death penalty today: Death sentences and executions for juvenile crimes, January 1, 1973–June 30, 2003*. Retrieved from http://www.law.onu.edu/faculty/streib

Sturgess, A., & Macher, A. (2005). Issues in correctional HIV care: Progressive disseminated histoplasmosis. *American Jails*, 19, 54–56.

Sundt, J. L., Castellano, T. C., & Briggs, C. S. (2008). The sociopolitical context of violence and its control: A case study of supermax and its effect in Illinois. *Prison Journal*, 88(1), 94–122.

Surratt, H. L. (2003). Parenting attitudes of drug-involved women inmates. *Prison Journal*, 83(2), 206–220.

Sweeten, G., & Apel, R. (2007). Incapacitation: Revisiting an old question with a new method and new data. *Journal of Quantitative Criminology*, 23, 303–326.

Sykes, G. M. (1958). *The society of captives: A study of a maximum security prison*. Princeton, NJ: Princeton University Press.

Sykes, G. M., & Messinger, S. (1960). The inmate social system. In R. Cloward & D. R. Dressey (Eds.), *Theoretical studies in social organization of the prison* (pp. 5–19). New York, NY: Social Science Research Council.

Talbot, T., Gilligan, L., Carter, M., & Matson, S. (2002). *An overview of sex offender management*. Washington, DC: Center for Sex Offender Management.

Tally, H. (2015). A constitutional level of healthcare. *American Jails*, 29(2), 15–19.

Tanielian, T., and L. H. Jaycox, eds. (2008). *Invisible wounds of war: Psychological and cognitive injuries, their consequences, and services to assist recovery*. Santa Monica, CA: RAND Corporation.

Tapia, M. (2014). Texas Latino gangs and large urban jails: Intergenerational conflicts and issues in management. *Journal of Crime and Justice*, 37(2), 256–274.

Tartaro, C. (2002). Examining implementation issues with new generation jails. *Criminal Justice Policy Review*, 13, 219–237.

Tartaro, C. (2006). Watered down: Partial implementation of the new generation jail philosophy. *Prison Journal*, 86, 284–300.

Tartaro, C., & Ruddell, R. (2006). Trouble in Mayberry: A national analysis of suicides and attempts in small jails. *American Journal of Criminal Justice*, 31, 81–101.

Tauber, J. (2009). The role of the judge in community court. Retrieved from http://www.reentrycourtsolutions.com/wp-content/uploads/2009/10/The-Role-of-the-Judge-in-Community-Court.pdf

Taylor, F. W. (1911). *The principles of scientific management.* Norcross, GA: Engineering and Management Press.

Taylor, R., Fritsch, E., & Caeti, T. (2007). *Juvenile justice: Policies, programs, and practices.* New York, NY: McGraw-Hill.

Tempest, R. (2005, March 6). Death row often means a long life. *Los Angeles Times*, B1.

Terrill, R. (2013). *World criminal justice systems.* Cincinnati, OH: Anderson.

Tewksbury, R., & Collins, S. C. (2006). Aggression levels among correctional officers: Reassessing sex differences. *Prison Journal*, 86(3), 327–343.

Tewksbury, R., & Potter, R. H. (2005). Transgender prisoners: A forgotten group. In S. Stojkovic (Ed.), *Managing special populations in jails and prisons* (pp. 15-1–15-14). New York, NY: Civic Research Institute.

Thigpen, M., Beauclair, T., Brown, R., & Guevara, M. (2012). *Motivational interviewing in corrections: A comprehensive guide to implementing MI in corrections.* Washington, DC: National Institute of Corrections.

Thompson, G. (1847). *Prison life and reflections: Or a narrative of the arrest, trial, conviction, imprisonment, treatment, observations, reflections, and deliverance of Work, Burr and Thompson, who suffered an unjust and cruel imprisonment in Missouri Penitentiary for attempting to aid some slaves to liberty.* Oberlin, OH: Oberlin Press.

Thompson, J. A., & Mays, G. L. (1991). Paying the piper but changing the tune: Policy changes and initiatives for the American jail. In J. A. Thompson & G. L. Mays (Eds.), *American jails: Public policy issues* (pp. 240–246). Chicago: Nelson-Hall.

de Tocqueville, A. (2004). *Tocqueville: Democracy in America* (A. Goldhammer, Trans.). New York, NY: Library of America. (Original work published 1835.)

Tolan, P., Gorman-Smith, D., & Henry, D. (2006). Family violence. *Annual Review of Psychology*, 57, 557–583.

Toobin, J. (2015, May 11). The Milwaukee experiment. *New Yorker*, 24–32.

Torrey, E., Zdanowicz, M., Kennard, A., Lamb, R., Eslinger, D., Biasotti, M., & et al. (2014). *The treatment of persons with mental illness in prisons and jails: A state survey.* Arlington, VA: Treatment Advocacy Center. Retrieved from http://tacreports.org/storage/documents/treatment-behind-bars/treatment-behind-bars.pdf

Toumi, H. (2013, October 8). Saudi Arabia preacher Fayhan Al Gamdi gets 8 years, 800 lashes for torturing daughter to death. *Gulf News*. Retrieved from http://gulfnews.com/news/gulf/saudi-arabia/saudi-arabia-preacher-fayhan-al-gamdi-gets-8-years-800-lashes-for-torturing-daughter-to-death-1.1240527

Traut, C., & Emmert, C. (1998). Expanding the integrated model of judicial decision making: The California justices and capital punishment. *Journal of Politics*, 60, 1166–1180.

Travis, A. (2013, January 8). Probation service "revolution" means wholesale privatization. *The Guardian.* Retrieved from http://www.guardian.co.uk/society/2013/jan/09/probation-service-private-firms-grayling

Travis, J. (2000, May). But they all come back: Rethinking prisoner reentry. *Sentencing & Corrections: Issues for the 21st Century*, 7, 1–11. Washington, DC: National Institute of Justice.

Travis, J. (2005). *But they all come back: Facing the challenges of prison reentry.* Washington, DC: Urban Institute.

Travis, J., & Lawrence, S. (2002). *Beyond the prison gates: The state of parole in America.* Washington, DC: Urban Institute, Justice Policy Center.

Travis, J., & Petersilia, J. (2001). Reentry reconsidered: A new look at an old question. *Crime & Delinquency*, 47, 291–313.

Truman, J. L., & Langton, L. (2015). *Criminal victimization, 2014.* Washington, DC: Bureau of Justice Statistics. Retrieved from http://www.bjs.gov/index.cfm?ty=pbdetail&iid=5366

Tucker, E. (2014, April 24). Longtime inmates to get clemency. *Moscow-Pullman Daily News*, 1.

Tucker, J. (2014, March 4). 5 Keys Charter School helps S.F inmates. *San Francisco Chronicle.* Retrieved from http://www.sfgate.com/bayarea/article/5-Keys-Charter-School-helps-S-F-inmates-4233314.php

Tursun, G. (2010). Exploration of probation in Chinese criminal law. *Federal Sentencing Reporter*, 22, 288–293.

UK Ministry of Justice (2010). *Breaking the cycle: Effective punishment, rehabilitation and sentencing of offenders.* Retrieved from https://www.gov.uk/government/uploads/system/uploads/attachment_data/file/185936/breaking-the-cycle.pdf

UK Ministry of Justice. (2013). *Story of the prison population: 1993–2012, England and Wales.* Retrieved from https://www.gov.uk/government/uploads/system/uploads/attachment_data/file/218185/story-prison-population.pdf

UK Ministry of Justice. (2014). Offender behaviour programmes (OBPs). Last updated July 9, 2014. Retrieved from https://www.justice.gov.uk/offenders/before-after-release/obp

Ulman, T., & Walker, N. (1980). "He takes some of my time; I take some of his": An analysis of judicial sentencing patterns in jury cases. *Law and Society Review*, 14, 323–339.

Umbreit, M. (1994). *Victim meets offender: The impact of restorative justice and mediation.* Monsey, NY: Criminal Justice Press.

U.S. Census Bureau. (2001). *Population estimates.* Retrieved from http://www.census.gov

U.S. Census Bureau. (2010a). *Census of governmental employment and payroll.* Retrieved from http://www.census.gov

U.S. Census Bureau. (2014a). Facts for features: Hispanic Heritage Month 2014: Sept. 15–Oct. 15. Retrieved from http://www.census.gov/newsroom/facts-for-features/2014/cb14-ff22.html

U.S. Census Bureau. (2014b). State and local government employment and payroll data. Retrieved from http://www.census.gov/govs/apes

U.S. Census Bureau, Population Division. (2016, June). Annual estimates of the resident population by sex, race, and Hispanic origin for the United States, states, and counties: April 1, 2010 to July 1, 2015. Retrieved from http://factfinder.census.gov/faces/tableservices/jsf/pages/productview.xhtml?src=bkmk

U.S. Courts. (2013, July 18). Supervision costs significantly less than incarceration in federal system. Retrieved from http://news.uscourts.gov/supervision-costs-significantly-less-incarceration-federal-system

U.S. Courts. (2015). US district courts—Judicial business 2015. Retrieved from http://www.uscourts.gov/statistics-reports/us-district-courts-judicial-business-2015

U.S. Department of Justice. (2001). *The federal death penalty system: Supplementary data, analysis and revised protocols for capital case review.* Washington, DC: Author. Retrieved from http://www.justice.gov/dag/pubdoc/deathpenaltystudy.htm

U.S. Department of Justice. (2015). Prison gangs. Last updated May 11, 2015. Retrieved from https://www.justice.gov/criminal-ocgs/gallery/prison-gangs

U.S. Department of Labor. (2010). *National Compensation Survey: Occupational earnings in the United States, 2009.* Washington, DC: Bureau of Labor Statistics. Retrieved from http://www.bls.gov/ncs/ncswage2009.htm

U.S. District Courts. (2013). *Civil cases filed, terminated, and pending fiscal years 2008–2012.* Retrieved from http://www.uscourts.gov/Statistics/JudicialBusiness/2012/us-district-courts.aspx

U.S. Marshals Service. (2012). Witness protection program. Retrieved from http://www.usmarshals.gov/duties/witsec.htm

U.S. Sentencing Commission. (2011, January 28). Analysis of the impact of amendment to the statutory penalties for crack cocaine offenses made by the Fair Sentencing Act of 2010 and corresponding proposed permanent guideline amendment if the guideline amendment were applied retroactively [Memorandum]. Retrieved from http://www.ussc.gov/sites/default/files/pdf/research/retroactivity-analyses/fair-sentencing-act/20110128_Crack_Retroactivity_Analysis.pdf

Useem, B. (1985). Disorganization and the New Mexico prison riot. *American Sociological Review, 50*(5), 677–688.

Useem, B., & Kimball, P. A. (1989). *States of siege: U.S. prison riots 1971–1986.* New York: Oxford University Press.

van den Haag, E. (2003). Justice, deterrence and the death penalty. In J. Aker, R. Bohm, & C. Lanier (Eds.), *America's experiment with capital punishment* (pp. 233–249). Durham, NC: Carolina Academic Press.

Van Tongeren, D. R., & Klebe, K. J. (2010). Reconceptualizing prison adjustment: A multidimensional approach exploring female offenders' adjustment to prison life. *Prison Journal, 90*(1), 48–68.

Van Voorhis, P., Braswell, M., & Lester, D. (2000). *Correctional counseling and rehabilitation.* Cincinnati, OH: Anderson.

Vanstone, M. (2000). Cognitive-behavioural work with offenders in the UK: A history of influential endeavour. *Howard Journal of Criminal Justice, 39,* 171–183.

Vanstone, M. (2004). Mission control: The origins of humanitarian service. *Probation Journal, 51,* 34–47.

Vanstone, M. (2008). The international origins and initial development of probation. *British Journal of Criminology, 48,* 735–755.

Vaske, J., Galyean, K., & Cullen, F. (2011). Toward a biosocial theory of offender rehabilitation: Why does cognitive-behavioral therapy work? *Journal of Criminal Justice, 39,* 90–102.

Vaughn, M. (2009). Substance abuse and crime: Biosocial foundations. In A. Walsh & K. M. Beaver (Eds.), *Biosocial criminology: New directions in theory and research* (pp. 176–189). New York, NY: Routledge.

Vaughn, M. S., & Carroll, L. (1998). Separate and unequal: Prison versus free-world medical care. *Justice Quarterly, 15,* 3–10.

Vaughn, M., & Del Carmen, R. (1995). Civil liability against prison officials for inmate-on-inmate assault: Where are we and where have we been? *Prison Journal, 75,* 69–89.

Vaughn, M. S., & Smith, L. G. (1999). Practicing penal harm medicine in the United States: Prisoners' voices from jail. *Justice Quarterly, 16,* 175–231.

Vermont Department of Corrections. (2010, November 23). *Graduated sanctions for technical violation of probation in lieu of court referral* (DOC Policy No. 347). Retrieved from http://www.doc.state.vt.us/about/policies/rpd/rules/rpd/correctional-services-301-550/335-350-district-offices-general/doc-policy-347-graduated-sanctions-for-technical-violations-of-probation-in-lieu-of-court-referral

Visher, C. A., Debus-Sherrill, S. A., & Yahner, J. (2011). Employment after prison: A longitudinal study of former prisoners. *Justice Quarterly, 28*(5), 698–718.

Vito, G., Allen, H., & Farmer, G. (1981). Shock probation in Ohio: A comparison of outcomes. *International Journal of Offender Therapy and Comparative Criminology, 25,* 70–76.

Vogel, R. (2004). Silencing the cells: Mass incarceration and legal repression in U.S. prisons. *Monthly Review, 56,* 1–8.

Volkow, N. (2010, October). Important treatment advances for addiction to heroin and other opiates. Retrieved from http://www.drugabuse.gov/about-nida/directors-page/messages-director/2010/10/important-treatment-advances-addiction-to-heroin-other-opiates

Vose, B., Cullen, F., & Smith, P. (2008). Empirical status of the Level of Service Inventory. *Federal Probation, 72,* 22–29.

Walker, E. (2002). Adolescent neurodevelopment and psychopathology. *Current Directions in Psychological Science, 11,* 24–28.

Walker, S. (2001). *Sense and nonsense about crime and drugs.* Belmont, CA: Wadsworth.

Walker, S., Spohn, C., & DeLone, M. (1996). *The color of justice: Race, ethnicity, and crime in America.* Belmont, CA: Wadsworth.

Walmsley, R. (2015). *World prison population list* (11th ed.). London, UK: International Centre for Prison Studies. Retrieved from http://www.prisonstudies.org/sites/default/files/resources/downloads/world_prison_population_list_11th_edition.pdf

Walsh, A. (1986). Placebo justice: Victim recommendations and offender sentences in sexual assault cases. *Journal of Criminal Law and Criminology, 77,* 1126–1141.

Walsh, A. (1990). Standing trial versus copping a plea: Is there a penalty? *Journal of Contemporary Criminal Justice, 6,* 226–236.

Walsh, A. (2006). Evolutionary psychology and criminal behavior. In J. Barkow (Ed.), *Missing the revolution: Darwinism for social scientists* (pp. 225–268). New York, NY: Oxford University Press.

Walsh, A. (2009). *Biology and criminology: The biosocial synthesis.* New York, NY: Routledge.

Walsh, A. (2011). *Feminist criminology through a biosocial lens.* Durham, NC: Carolina Academic Press.

Walsh, A. (2014). *Criminological theory: Assessing philosophical assumptions.* Waltham, MA: Anderson.

Walsh, A. (2015). *Criminology: The essentials.* Thousand Oaks, CA: Sage.

Walsh, A., & Hemmens, C. (2014). *Law, justice, and society: A sociolegal approach* (3rd ed.). New York, NY: Oxford University Press.

Walsh, A., & Hemmens, C. (2016). *Law, justice, and society: A sociolegal introduction* (4th ed.). New York, NY: Oxford University Press.

Walsh, A., Johnson, H., & Bolen, J. (2012). Drugs, crime, and the epigenetics of hedonic allostasis. *Journal of Contemporary Criminal Justice, 28,* 314–328.

Walsh, A., & Stohr, M. (2010). *Correctional assessment, casework and counseling* (5th ed.). Alexandria, VA: American Correctional Association.

Walsh, A., & Wu, H.-H. (2008). Differentiating antisocial personality disorder, psychopathy, and sociopathy: Evolutionary, genetic, neurological, and sociological considerations. *Criminal Justice Studies, 21,* 135–152.

Walsh, A., & Yun, I. (2013). Schizophrenia: Causes, crime, and implications for criminology and criminal justice. *International Journal of Law, Crime and Justice, 41,* 188–202.

Walters, S., Clark, M., Gingerich, R., & Meltzer, M. (2007). *A guide for probation and parole: Motivating offenders to change.* Washington, DC: National Institute of Corrections.

Wang, X., Mears, D., Spohn, C., & Dario, L. (2013). Assessing the differential effects of race and ethnicity on sentence outcomes under different sentencing systems. *Crime & Delinquency, 59,* 87–114.

Ward, D., & Kassebaum, G. (2009). *Alcatraz: The gangster years.* Berkeley: University of California Press.

Ward, T., Melser, J., & Yates, P. (2007). Reconstructing the risk-need-responsivity model: A theoretical exploration and evaluation. *Aggression and Violent Behavior, 12,* 208–228.

Weber, M. (1946). Bureaucracy. In H. H. Gerth & C. W. Mills (Eds.), *From Max Weber: Essays in sociology.* New York, NY: Oxford University Press.

Wei, W. (1999). The Chinese American experience: 1857–1892. *Harper's Weekly.* Retrieved from http://www.Harpweek.com

Weibush, R., Baird, C., Krisberg, B., & Onek, D. (1994). *Risk assessment and classification for serious, violent, and chronic juvenile offenders.* San Francisco, CA: National Council on Crime and Delinquency.

Welch, M. (1996). *Corrections: A critical approach.* New York, NY: McGraw-Hill.

Welch, M. (2004). *Corrections: A critical approach* (2nd ed.). Boston, MA: McGraw-Hill.

Welch, M. (2005). *Ironies of imprisonment.* Thousand Oaks, CA: Sage.

Welsh, W. (1995). *Counties in court: Jail overcrowding and court-ordered reform.* Philadelphia, PA: Temple University Press.

Wener, R. (2005). The invention of direct supervision. *Corrections Compendium, 30*(4–7), 32–34.

Wener, R. (2006). Effectiveness of the direct supervision system of correctional design and management: A review of the literature. *Criminal Justice and Behavior, 33,* 392–410.

Wennerberg, I., & Pinto, S. (2009). Sixth European Electronic Monitoring Conference—Analysis of questionnaires. Retrieved from http://www.cepprobation.org/uploaded_files/EM2009%20Questionnaire%20summary.pdf

West, H. C. (2010). *Prison inmates at midyear 2009—Statistical tables.* Washington, DC: Bureau of Justice Statistics. Available at http://www.bjs.gov/content/pub/pdf/pim09st.pdf

West, H. C., Sabol, W. J., & Greenman, S. J. (2010). *Prisoners in 2009.* Washington, DC: Bureau of Justice Statistics. Available at http://www.bjs.gov/content/pub/pdf/p09.pdf

Western, B. (2003). *Incarceration, employment, and public policy.* Newark: New Jersey Institute for Social Justice.

Western, B. (2006). *Punishment and inequality in America.* New York, NY: Russell Sage.

White, A. (2004). *Substance use and the adolescent brain: An overview with the focus on alcohol.* Durham, NC: Duke University Medical Center.

White, M. D., Goldkamp, J. S., & Campbell, S. P. (2006). Co-occurring mental illness and substance abuse in the criminal justice system. *Prison Journal, 86*(3), 301–326.

Whitehead, J., & Lab, S. (1996). *Juvenile justice: An introduction.* Cincinnati, OH: Anderson.

Whitman, J. Q. (2003). *Harsh justice: Criminal punishment and the widening divide between America and Europe.* New York, NY: Oxford University Press.

Whittick, A. (1979). *Woman into citizen.* Santa Barbara, CA: ABC-Clio.

Wilson, D., Bouffard, L., & Mackenzie, D. (2005). A quantitative review of structured, group-oriented, cognitive-behavior programs for offenders. *Criminal Justice and Behavior, 32,* 172–204.

Wilson, D. B., MacKenzie, D. L., & Ngo, F. T. (2010). Effects of correctional boot-camps on offending. Crime Prevention Research Reviews No. 5. Washington, DC: U.S. Department of Justice, Office of Community Oriented Policing Services.

Wilson, J. Q. (1975). *Thinking about crime.* New York, NY: Vintage.

Wilson, S., & Lipsey, M. (2000). Wilderness challenge programs for delinquent youth: A meta-analysis of outcome evaluations. *Evaluation and Program Planning, 23,* 1–12.

Wimalawansa, S. (2013). Post-traumatic stress disorder: An under-diagnosed and under-treated entity. *Comprehensive Research Journal of Medicine and Medical Science, 1,* 1–12.

Winfree, L. T., & Wooldredge, J. D. (1991). Exploring suicides and deaths by natural causes in America's large jails: A panel study of institutional change, 1978 and 1983. In J. Thompson & G. L. Mays (Eds.), *American jails: Public policy issues* (pp. 63–78). Chicago, IL: Nelson-Hall.

Winter, M. M. (2003). County jail suicides in a Midwestern state: Moving beyond the use of profiles. *Prison Journal, 83,* 130–148.

Wodahl, E. J., Boman, J. H., & Garland, B. E. (2015). Responding to probation and parole violations: Are jail sanctions more effective than community-based graduated sanctions? *Journal of Criminal Justice, 43,* 242–250.

Wolff, N., Shi, J., & Blitz, C. L. (2008). Racial and ethnic disparities in types and sources of victimization inside prison. *Prison Journal, 88*(4), 451–472.

Wolfgang, M., Figlio, R., & Sellin, T. (1972). *Delinquency in a birth cohort.* Chicago, IL: University of Chicago Press.

Woo, Y., Stohr, M. K., Hemmens, C., Lutze, F. E., Hamilton, Z., & Yoon, O. K. (2014, February). *An empirical test of the social support paradigm on prisoner reentry.* Paper presentation at the annual meeting of the Academy of Criminal Justice Sciences, Philadelphia, PA.

Wood, P. B., & May, D. C. (2003). Research notes: Racial differences in perceptions of the severity of sanctions: A comparison of prison with alternatives. *Justice Quarterly, 20*(3), 605–632.

Wood, S., & Buttaro, A. (2013). Co-occurring severe mental illnesses and substance abuse disorders as predictors of state prison inmate assaults. *Crime & Delinquency, 59*(4), 510–535.

Wooldredge, J., & Steiner, B. (2014). A bi-level framework for understanding prisoner victimization. *Journal of Quantitative Criminology, 30*(1), 141–162.

Wright, E. M., Salisbury, E. J., & Van Voorhis, P. (2007). Predicting the prison misconducts of women offenders. *Journal of Contemporary Criminal Justice, 23*(4), 310–340.

Wright, R. (1999). The evidence in favor of prisons. In F. Scarpitti & A. Nielson (Eds.), *Crime and criminals: Contemporary and classic readings in criminology* (pp. 483–493). Los Angeles, CA: Roxbury.

Wright, R., & Decker, S. (1997). *Armed robbers in action.* Boston, MA: Northeastern University Press.

Wright, R., & Miller, M. (2002). The screening/bargaining tradeoff. *Stanford Law Review, 55,* 29–118.

Yates, H. M. (2002). Margaret Moore: African American feminist leader in corrections. *Women & Criminal Justice, 13,* 9–26.

Yochelson, S., & Samenow, S. (1976). *The criminal personality: A profile for change.* Livingston, NJ: Jason Aronson.

Young, V. D. (1994). Race and gender in the establishment of juvenile institutions: The case of the South. *Prison Journal, 74,* 244–265.

Young, V. D. (2001). All the women in the Maryland State Penitentiary: 1812–1869. *Prison Journal, 81*(1), 113–132.

Yun, I. (2008). Wengu Zhisxin: Review of the old and know the new. *Asian Pacific Journal of Police & Criminal Justice, 6,* 3–23.

Zachariadis, P. (2013). Some European prisons are shrinking and closing—What can America learn? *Takepart.* Retrieved from http://www.takepart.com/article/2013/11/14/some-european-prisons-are-shrinking-and-closing-what-can-america-learn

Zaitz, L. (2010, October 30). Budget crunch reaches prison. *The Oregonian,* 1.

Zapotosky, M., & Harlan, C. (2016, August 18). Justice Department says it will end use of private prisons. *Washington Post.* Retrieved from https://www.washingtonpost.com/news/post-nation/wp/2016/08/18/justice-department-says-it-will-end-use-of-private-prisons/?utm_term=.268cd0d2cfdc

Zedlewski, E. (1987). *Making confinement decisions.* Rockville, MD: National Institute of Justice.

Zimmer, L. (1986). *Women guarding men.* Chicago, IL: University of Chicago Press.

Zimmer, L. (1989). Solving women's employment problems in corrections: Shifting the burden to administrators. *Women & Criminal Justice, 1,* 55–79.

Zupan, L. L. (1991). *Jails: Reform and the new generation philosophy.* Cincinnati, OH: Anderson.

Zupan, L. L. (1992). The progress of women correctional officers in all-male prisons. In I. L. Moyer (Ed.), *The changing roles of women in the criminal justice system: Offenders, victims, and professionals* (2nd ed., pp. 323–343). Prospect Heights, IL: Waveland Press.

INDEX

ABOUT THE AUTHORS

Mary K. Stohr is a Professor in the Department of Criminal Justice and Criminology at Washington State University. She received a PhD (1990) in political science, with specializations in criminal justice and public administration, from Washington State University. Many moons ago, and before she earned her graduate degrees, she worked as a correctional officer and then as a counselor in an adult male prison in Washington State. Professor Stohr has published over 90 academic works in the areas of correctional organizations and operation, correctional personnel, inmate needs and assessment, program evaluation, gender, and victimization. Her books, with others, include *The American Prison* (with Cullen and Jonson); *Corrections: The Essentials* (with Walsh); *Correctional Assessment, Casework and Counseling* (with Walsh); *Corrections: A Text Reader* (with Walsh and Hemmens); *Criminal Justice Management: Theory and Practice in Justice Centered Organizations* (with Collins); and *The Prison Experience* (with Hemmens). She is the Executive Director of the Academy of Criminal Justice Sciences, received the Founders Award from ACJS in 2009, and is a Co-Founder of the Corrections Section of ACJS.

Anthony Walsh, Professor of Criminology at Boise State University, received his PhD from Bowling Green State University at the ripe old age of 43. He has field experience in law enforcement and corrections. He is the author of over 150 journal articles/book chapters and 34 books, including *Biology and Criminology* (Routledge, 2009), *Feminist Criminology Through a Biosocial Lens* (Carolina Academic Press, 2011), *Law, Justice, and Society* (with Craig Hemmens, Oxford University Press, 2011), *Correctional Assessment, Casework, and Counseling* (with Mary K. Stohr, American Correctional Association, 2011), *The Neurobiology of Criminal Behavior: Gene-Brain-Culture Interaction* (with Jon Bolen, Ashgate, 2012), *Corrections: The Essentials* (with Mary K. Stohr, SAGE, 2012), *The Science Wars: The Politics of Gender and Race* (Transaction, 2013), *Criminological Theory: Assessing Philosophical Assumptions* (Anderson/Elsevier, 2014), *Biosociology: Bridging the Biology-Sociology Divide* (Transaction, 2014), *and Criminology: The Essentials* (SAGE, 2015). His interests include the biosocial criminology, statistics, and criminal justice assessment and counseling.